THE HOUSE OF CROMWELL

For my mother, Joanna Malins, always

THE HOUSE OF CROMWELL

POWER, FAMILY AND THE MAKING OF MODERN BRITAIN

Miranda Malins

WILLIAM
COLLINS

William Collins
An imprint of HarperCollins*Publishers*
1 London Bridge Street
London SE1 9GF

WilliamCollinsBooks.com

HarperCollins*Publishers*
Macken House, 39/40 Mayor Street Upper,
Dublin 1, D01 C9W8, Ireland

First published in Great Britain in 2026 by William Collins

1

A catalogue record for this book is available from the British Library

ISBN 978-0-00-867131-0 (hardback)
ISBN 978-0-00-867132-7 (trade paperback)

Typeset in 11.5/14pt Kepler Std by Six Red Marbles UK, Thetford, Norfolk

Printed and bound in the UK
[using 100% renewable electricity at CPI Group (UK) Ltd]

MIX
Paper | Supporting responsible forestry
FSC® C013604
FSC
www.fsc.org

Mr Lely, I desire you would use all your skill to paint your picture truly like me, and not flatter me at all; but remark all these roughness, pimples, warts, and everything as you see me; otherwise I will never pay a farthing for it.

Oliver Cromwell's reported words on having his portrait painted, in Horace Walpole, *Anecdotes of Painting in England* (first edition, 1762)

AUTHOR'S NOTE

I have found so many fascinating Cromwells on my journey into the family, but there simply wasn't room for them all in this book. Neither did I wish to stray too far into genealogy. As a result, I have concentrated on key members of the family within its two primary branches, while mentioning some of the most interesting minor Cromwells along the way. For simplicity, I have named these branches the Launde Cromwells and the Hinchingbrooke Cromwells. The links between them all are set out in the following family trees. I hope to publish more stories of the more obscure Cromwells in due course. For similar reasons, I have attempted to mitigate the multitude of Cromwells with the same first names by using titles, jobs, maiden names or nicknames to distinguish them from one another. For instance, Oliver Cromwell's uncle of the same name is always referred to as Sir Oliver Cromwell even before he received his knighthood.

I set out to tell the biography of a dynasty over two centuries. Yet, the overwhelming fame of two of the Cromwells – Thomas and Oliver – presented a structural challenge. A conventional chronological narrative following each generation of the family would have been imbalanced and would not have allowed me to explore their shared family culture and common humanity, nor the wider meaning and resonance of the great events they shaped. I have therefore adopted a layered structure. The four parts of the book (Obscurity, Fame, Power and Infamy) retain a broad chronology charting the rise and fall of both Thomas and Oliver Cromwell and their immediate families in parallel. However, the real resonance of Thomas and Oliver's lives is best brought out by examining how their experiences echoed one another while setting both within their wider family context. The eleven chapters are themed to achieve this. Different characters come into the foreground at different times: in some sections Thomas and Oliver walk hand-in-hand; in others the focus is on one or the other, or another member of the family entirely. I hope readers will find that this has allowed me to explore memory, prize character and preserve the quirks of real life, while telling a coherent story.

Finally, dates have been modernised to reflect the new year beginning in January rather than in March as it was in the early modern period. For readability, I have also modernised spelling where appropriate.

CONTENTS

Part Three: Power

Part Four: Infamy

Tudor Britain Timeline

1485	Wars of the Roses ends with the Battle of Bosworth; Henry VII becomes king
1509	Accession of Henry VIII
1534	Act of Supremacy; England breaks with Rome
1536	Execution of Anne Boleyn
1536	Pilgrimage of Grace
1536–1541	Dissolution of the Monasteries

Stuart and Cromwellian Britain Timeline

1603	Accession of James I in England; Union of the Scottish and English Crowns
1625	Accession of Charles I
1629–1640	Personal Rule of Charles I
1640	Short and Long Parliaments
1642–1646	First Civil War
1643	Solemn League and Covenant between Parliament and the Scots
1653	**April:** Oliver Cromwell expels the Rump Parliament **July–December:** Nominated Assembly **December:** Oliver Cromwell becomes Lord Protector
1657	Oliver Cromwell re-invested as Lord Protector
1658–1659	Protectorate of Richard Cromwell
1660	Restoration of the monarchy; Charles II becomes king
1665–1667	Great Plague, Great Fire of London and Raid on the Medway

1536 & 1543	Acts of Union with Wales
1547–1553	Reign of Edward VI
1553–1558	Reign of Mary I
1558	Accession of Elizabeth I
1588	Spanish Armada defeated
1601	Essex Rebellion
1648	Second Civil War
1649	Trial and execution of Charles I; England declared a Commonwealth
1649–1650	Cromwellian conquest of Ireland
1650–1651	Cromwellian conquest of Scotland ends with Battle of Worcester
1683	Rye House Plot
1685	Accession of James II
1688–1689	Glorious Revolution; William and Mary crowned
1707	Acts of Union; creation of the Kingdom of Great Britain
1714	Death of Queen Anne; accession of the Hanoverian dynasty

Battle sites
Key towns
Cromwell houses
Other places of interest
0
40 miles
0
40 km
North Sea
Spey
Clyde
Dunbar, 1650
Tyne
Downpatrick
Dundrum Castle
Newburgh Priory
Marston Moor, 1644
Drogheda, 1649
Preston, 1648
Dublin
Throwley Old Hall
Trent
see inset above right
North Elmham
Great Yarmouth
Wexford, 1649
Severn
Naseby, 1645
Ouse
Helmingham Hall
Worcester, 1651
Edgehill, 1642
Standon
Colchester
Oxford
Felsted School
Cheshunt
Thames
see inset below right
Wolf Hall
Basing House
Leeds Castle
Ewhurst
Hursley
Lewes Priory
Dunkirk, 1658
Carisbrooke Castle

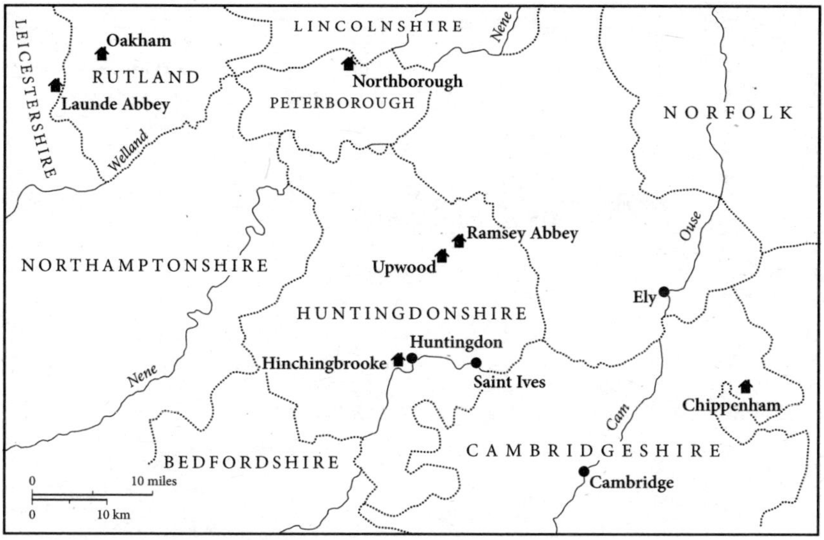
LINCOLNSHIRE
Nene
Oakham
LEICESTERSHIRE
RUTLAND
Northborough
Launde Abbey
PETERBOROUGH
NORFOLK
Welland
Ouse
Ramsey Abbey
Upwood
NORTHAMPTONSHIRE
Ely
HUNTINGDONSHIRE
Huntingdon
Hinchingbrooke
Saint Ives
Nene
Cam
Chippenham
CAMBRIDGESHIRE
BEDFORDSHIRE
Cambridge
0
10 miles
0
10 km

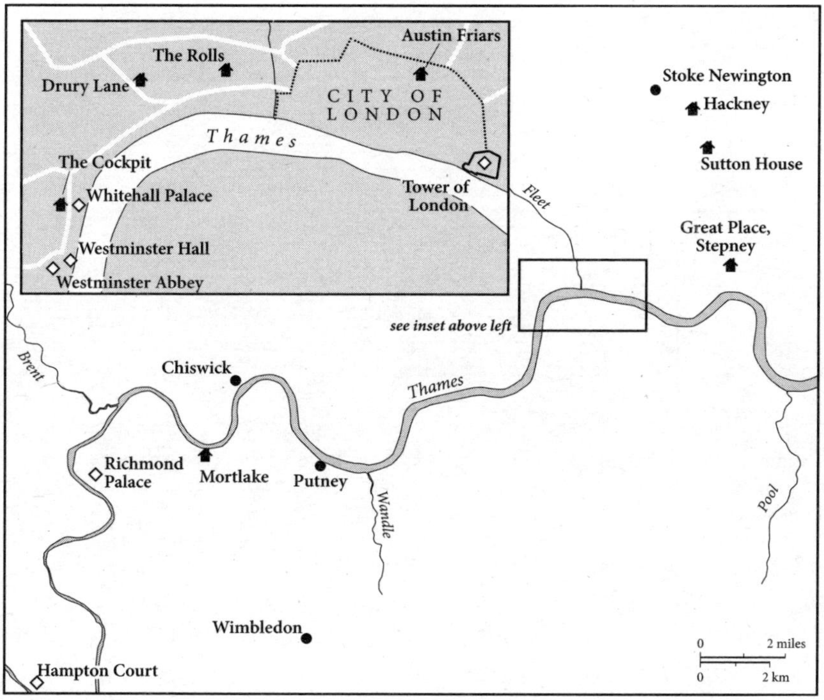
Austin Friars
The Rolls
Drury Lane
CITY OF LONDON
Thames
The Cockpit
Whitehall Palace
Tower of London
Westminster Hall
Westminster Abbey
Stoke Newington
Hackney
Sutton House
Fleet
Great Place, Stepney
see inset above left
Brent
Chiswick
Thames
Richmond Palace
Mortlake
Putney
Wandle
Pool
Wimbledon
Hampton Court
0
2 miles
0
2 km

Selected Family of Thomas Cromwelll

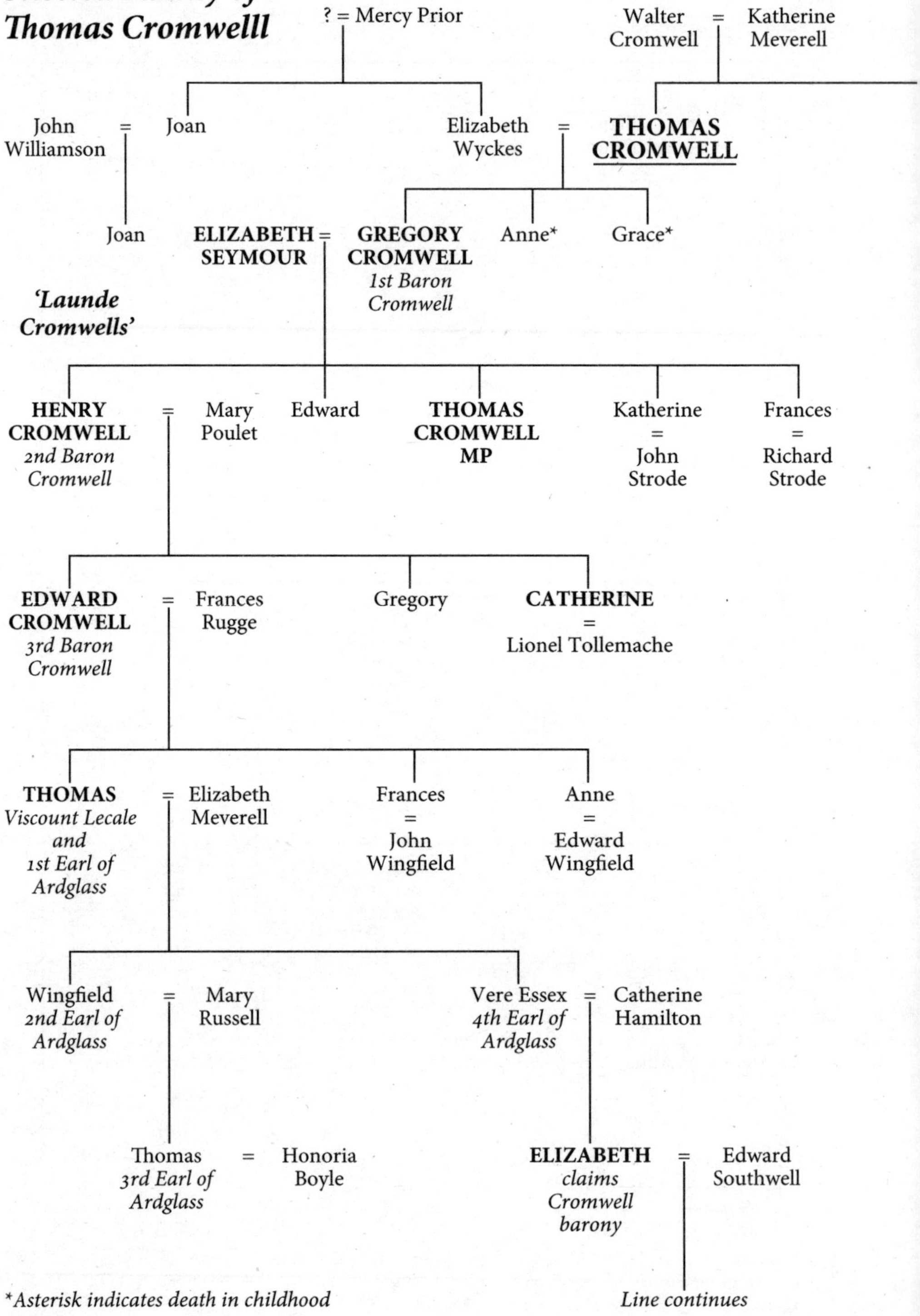

Asterisk indicates death in childhood

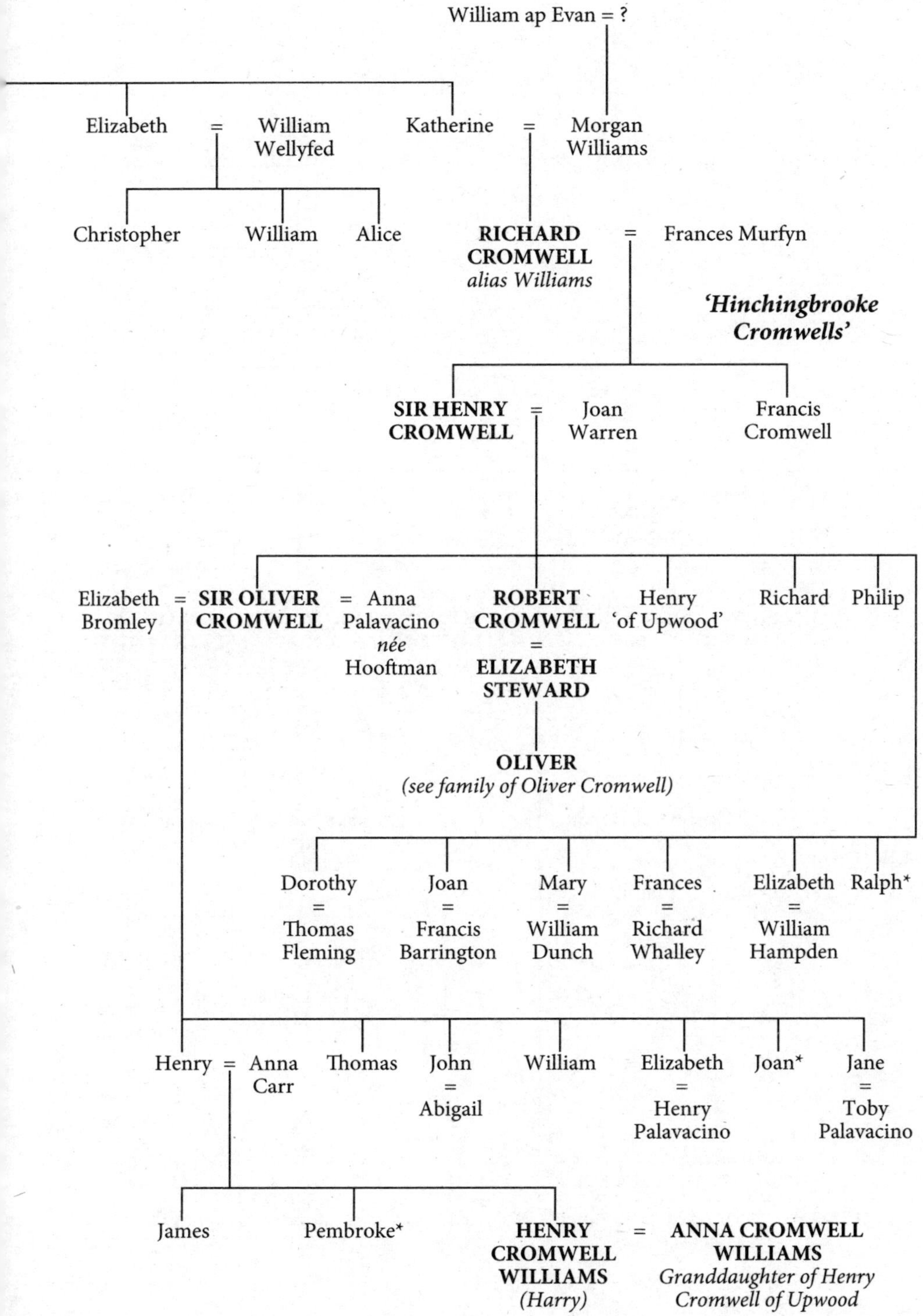

William ap Evan = ?
Elizabeth = William Wellyfed
Katherine = Morgan Williams
Christopher
William
Alice
RICHARD CROMWELL alias Williams = Frances Murfyn
'Hinchingbrooke Cromwells'
SIR HENRY CROMWELL = Joan Warren
Francis Cromwell
Elizabeth Bromley = SIR OLIVER CROMWELL = Anna Palavacino née Hooftman
ROBERT CROMWELL = ELIZABETH STEWARD
Henry 'of Upwood'
Richard
Philip
OLIVER
(see family of Oliver Cromwell)
Dorothy = Thomas Fleming
Joan = Francis Barrington
Mary = William Dunch
Frances = Richard Whalley
Elizabeth = William Hampden
Ralph*
Henry = Anna Carr
Thomas
John = Abigail
William
Elizabeth = Henry Palavacino
Joan*
Jane = Toby Palavacino
James
Pembroke*
HENRY CROMWELL WILLIAMS (Harry) = ANNA CROMWELL WILLIAMS
Granddaughter of Henry Cromwell of Upwood

Selected Family of Oliver Cromwell

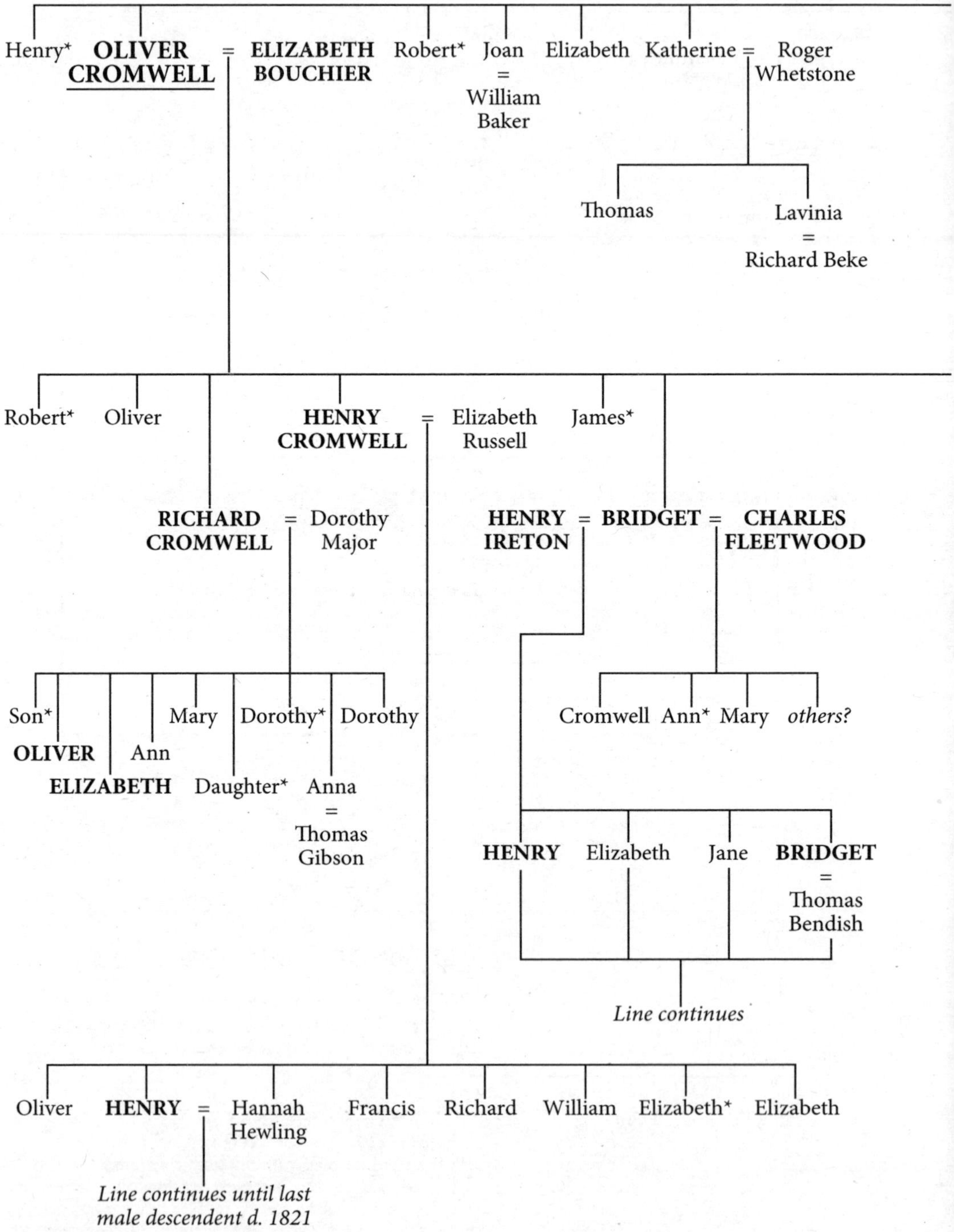

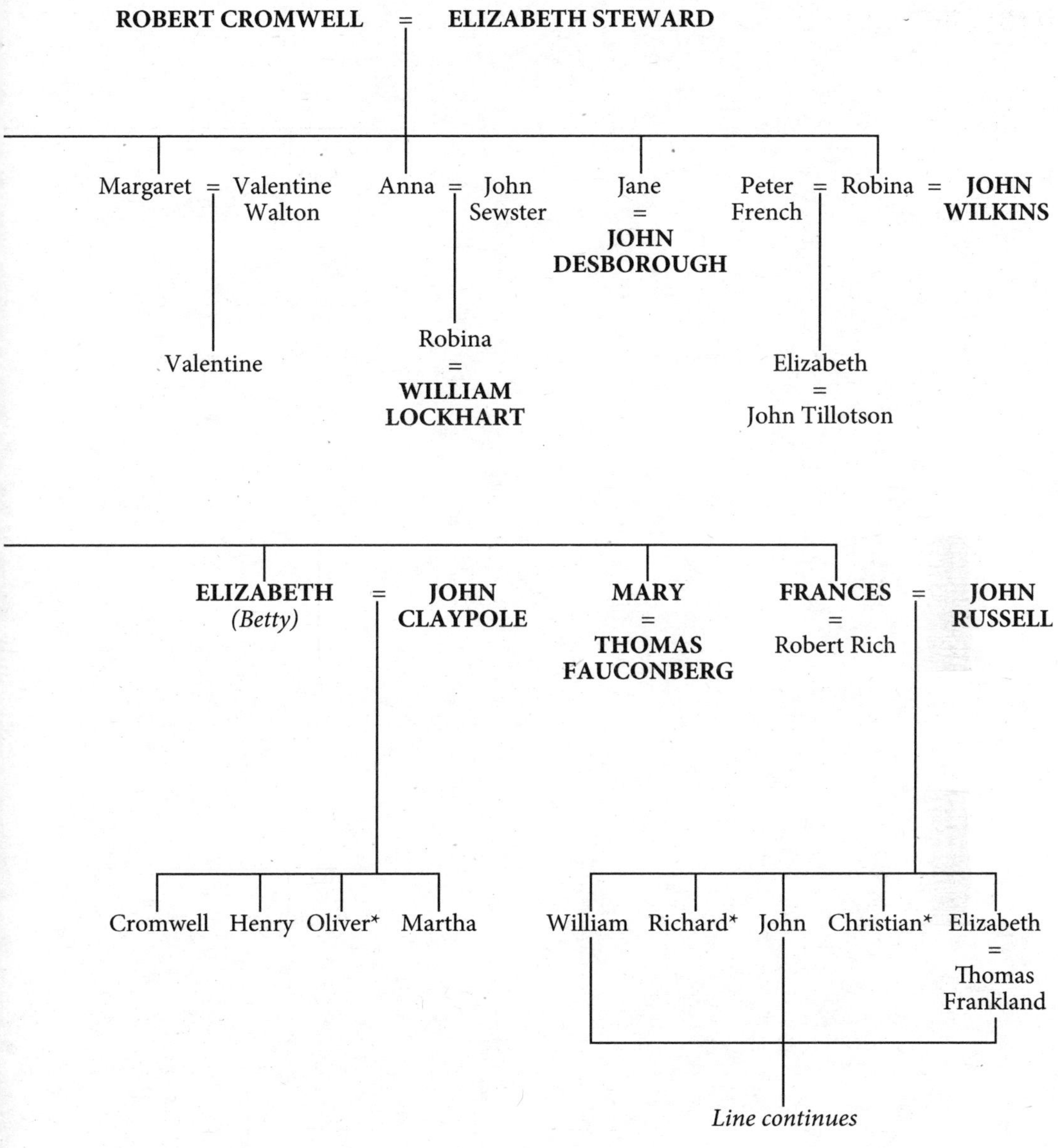

*Asterisk indicates death in childhood

PREFACE

St Mary's Church, Putney

If walls could truly speak, what would they say?

Step down into the cool quiet of St Mary's Church, the rushing River Thames close-by now scarcely audible above the passing buses, and listen. *For really I think that the poorest he that is in England hath a life to live, as the greatest he,* the carved walls declaim in eternal stone echo of Colonel Thomas Rainsborough: Leveller, Londoner, passionate liver of life. You hear the intake of hundreds of soldiers' breaths in reaction, the rustle of the secretary's papers, the scrape of leather on tile as the debate's chairman General Oliver Cromwell shifts in his seat, his head bowed beneath his broad hat.

But perhaps there is someone else listening in the shadows? Yes, a dark-haired boy has slipped into the church to escape his father and learn his letters. This is one of Rainsborough's 'poorest he's', you think. The boy – Thomas Cromwell, the priest tutor calls him – tips his head to the tower soaring above him, thinking of the life he has yet to live. The man – his great-great-great-nephew Oliver – now does the same, searching the word-filled air for God's voice.

Surely, he will show them both the way?

INTRODUCTION

As Thomas Cromwell, the brewer's son who had risen to become King Henry VIII's ablest and most powerful minister, climbed the scaffold to his death on a summer's day in 1540, he prepared himself to meet God. The Lord loomed large in Thomas's life and as he waited, hoping to ascend into his grace, he would have settled his account with his maker, revealing to him the truth of his heart: his denial of the trumped-up treason charges laid against him. One accusation – perhaps the most extraordinary – was that he had planned to marry Henry VIII's daughter Princess Mary and make himself king. Thomas might have laughed to himself at such a foolish notion, if his bravery allowed: the idea that an administrator and fixer like him, a soldier and pen-pusher, a man of his humble birth – a nobody from Putney – should wear the crown of England.

A little over a hundred years on, eight years after Henry VIII's successor monarch Charles I had been executed, Parliament begged another Cromwell – Thomas's descendant – to take the same crown for himself and his chosen heirs. Was this the Cromwells' revenge? A final proof that raw talent will out? And yet any satisfaction Thomas's ghost may have felt as he lingered around the Tudor Palace of Whitehall so familiar to him and over which the Cromwells now presided in splendour, would have been short-lived. Only a few years later, Lord Protector Oliver Cromwell, who had died peacefully in his bed as a king in all but name, was exhumed from his grand tomb in Westminster Abbey and hoisted onto a different scaffold where his rotting corpse was executed to satisfy the restored regime of Charles II who had regained his ancestors' throne.

Few names in British history have evoked more emotion over the centuries than that of Cromwell, thrust into the limelight by these two extraordinary, self-made men from the same family: Thomas, Henry VIII's right-hand man and architect of the Reformation; and Oliver, Parliament's hero of the civil wars of the 1640s who rose from tenant-farmer turned tax-collector and minor MP to become head of state and a global statesman. A century apart, the Cromwell family had produced two dazzling men who bestrode their times, their fates so intertwined with the famous dynasties of Tudor and Stuart that they became talismanic of each era. Through them the Cromwell family rose and fell from power twice, leaving its members to suffer ever since under the weight of their infamous name; a name that has held a unique power to unnerve the monarchs who followed them even into modern times.

Thomas and Oliver Cromwell were men who burst out of their ordinary backgrounds to stride the world stage and on into the history books. Every generation since has reinterpreted their lives in endless ink, creating the Cromwells to suit their own age. To their admirers they are saints: radicals, modernisers, men of devout conscience. To their detractors they are traitors: usurpers, manipulators and murderers. Together, they are either the despoilers of the true faith and destroyers of church buildings, or the fathers, respectively, of the Church of England and non-conformist traditions. The repressors who prevented radical progress or the reformers who advanced it. The inveterate enemies of the monarchy or its most powerful champions.

But how did this happen? Who were these Cromwells, who came from nothing and returned to nothing, but who changed Britain forever? How did they relate to each other and why should we care about that now? Traditionally, historians have not been interested in answering these questions. You will have to look hard to find scholars of either Thomas or Oliver speak of them in the same breath for more than a sentence or two.[1] Each is left to live separately in his own realm, four generations apart, the extraordinary echoes between them ignored. Yet Oliver himself was conscious of his heritage, keeping the family tree commissioned by his grandfather with him in the royal palaces and incorporating the Welsh insignia of his forebears in the Protectoral heraldry displayed from London to Edinburgh and Dublin. His contemporaries also explored the rich symbolism which linked Oliver back to Thomas, particularly in their comparable effects on Crown and church. Over time these lines blurred until the two Cromwells became muddled together as one person. This remains particularly prevalent in the destruction of buildings where the popularly imagined iconoclast Oliver often picks up the blame for damage caused over a century earlier during the dissolution of the monasteries under Thomas's guiding hand. The travel writer John Byng noticed this in the late eighteenth century, writing of visiting Wingfield Manor in Derbyshire. 'My guide . . . was puzzled, as all countrymen are, about the two Cromwells; the destroyer of monasteries and the destroyer of castles.'[2] Thus are the two infamous Cromwells forever linked in manuscript and myth.

The best way to detangle the Cromwells from these myths and retrieve them from emotive moral judgements is to examine them as a family and dynasty, before looking outwards from them to the turbulent times they inhabited and shaped. In other words, to see the Cromwells as they saw themselves and place them in the context they would recognise and which mattered to each of them beyond all others. Both Thomas and Oliver, like most of their contemporaries, believed in advancing their family along with themselves. Genealogy counted in early modern England, and not only to those of royal blood for whom a smooth succession to the throne could mean the difference between peace and civil war. For ordinary people too, people of strong faith and conscience who saw the world in terms both of the earthly and heavenly realms, the primary purpose of life was to leave one's children in a better position than they themselves were born into. Each generation of a family existed not in isolation but bound both to those who came before and those they hoped and planned would follow after.

Examining Thomas and Oliver in parallel, exploring how their lives and experiences echoed each other and how they were shaped by the same family culture, enables new interpretations. Recognising this personal context reframes the political Thomas, revealing the patriarch who invested in cultivating the wealth, status and security of his family as he climbed the shaky Tudor career ladder, unwittingly fuelling his enemies' jealousy and Henry VIII's paranoia, sowing the seeds of his destruction. Oliver also emerges in a new aspect, from the youth shaped by his complicated social inheritance to the ageing *de facto* king who moulded his family into a collective ruling enterprise that could carry his work forward after he returned to God. Moreover, the approach introduces a whole new cast of Cromwells, extraordinary and ordinary men and women living and labouring in their own spheres yet connected to the whole. Following their journeys we experience the dramatic years from the Wars of the Roses to the Hanoverian succession anew, equipped to see the impact this unique family had on the evolution of early modern Britain.

Thomas and Oliver Cromwell made their mark on the world, contributing, beyond the normal bounds of any one individual, to the evolution and indeed revolution of the English and then British state, church and culture. Their legacy can and has been interpreted in a galaxy of ways. Without Thomas at the helm, would there have been no English Reformation? For the reactionary Henry VIII was a fickle friend to the evangelical cause once the break from Rome had delivered Anne Boleyn to his bed and the wealth of the monasteries into his coffers. It was Thomas's vision and quiet commitment which smuggled a religious revolution onto the statute books under his king's nose. Likewise, without Oliver's Protectorate, would we have our constitutional monarchy today? An instinctive monarchist and reluctant regicide, it was Oliver's conservative rule which avoided anarchy and kept more radical, republican forces at bay. It was easier then for the monarchy to return in 1660 while memories of Oliver and the victorious parliamentary cause forced it to adapt and thus to survive.

Or, to swap them around in church and state: without Thomas, would there have been no 'Tudor revolution in government'? A bureaucratic overhaul which so centralised power and improved the efficiency of government process that, under the 'brief reign' of his reformist administration, 'Modern history, if it begins anywhere, begins, in England, with him.'[3] Without Oliver, meanwhile, would there have been a pluralist non-conformist church tradition in England? His tolerant Protectorate allowed the Civil Wars' proliferation of religious sects time to take root, seeding all the empire-building energy they would produce over the centuries to come; an empire he had shaped through his conquest and Parliamentary union with Scotland and Ireland and his forceful foreign policy. So much can the house of Cromwell claim: Thomas as the architect of a modern England, which, a century later, Oliver transformed into global Britain.

Part One: Obscurity

Thou didst begin with lesser Cares,
And private thoughts took up thy private Years:
Those Hands, which were ordain'd by Fates,
To change the World, and alter States,
Practis'd at first that vast Design
On meaner things with equal Mind.
That Soul, which should so many Scepters sway,
To whom so many Kingdoms should obey,
Learned first to rule in a Domestick way:
So Government it self, began
From Family, and single Man.

Three poems upon the death of His late Highnesse
Oliver Lord protector of England, Scotland,
and Ireland written by Mr Edm. Waller,
Mr Jo. Dryden, Mr Sprat of Oxford (1659)

One

Origins

Ghosts don't oppress the Cromwells. Walter does not rise by night, ale pot in hand, chisel in his belt, roistering by the wharves and showing his bruised knuckles to Putney. I don't have a history, only a past.

Hilary Mantel, The Mirror and the Light *(2020)*

King Oliver

The Stone of Scone can change a man's destiny. This plain block of sandstone, adorned only with a simple carved cross, holds the power to transport a mortal from earth to heaven. For weary Jacob using the stone as a pillow in the Holy Land, ascension came in a dream of angels climbing a ladder through the clouds. For the ancient kings of Ireland, Scotland and England, the stone, later enclosed in a Coronation Chair, enthroned them with sacred power as God's representative on earth. For the former fenland farmer Oliver Cromwell – hero of Parliament's victory over the last such king – a repose upon the stone one Friday afternoon in June 1657 elevated him from the already powerful Lord Protector into 'as great State as ever a King of England was'.[1]

The scene that took place in Westminster Hall on that cheerful summer's day is not recorded on any of the plaques recording the dramatic events that have occurred down the centuries under the hall's immense hammer-beamed roof. And yet it can claim to be every bit as momentous as the trial of King Charles I which took place there eight years before. Unlike the unfortunate Charles, Oliver was present on both occasions, but in startlingly different roles. At the King's trial he had brooded, black-hatted in the ranks of his fellow judges arranged on benches beneath the great window facing the small, solitary figure of the royal prisoner. Though his was an outwardly low profile in those grim proceedings, every one of the thousands of spectators present knew Oliver to be one of the key movers behind the scenes.

Eight years on, the court carpenters and clothiers had once again been called in to transform Westminster Hall from business hub of everyday legal and administrative affairs into a theatre of wonders. They built another raised platform beneath the great window and covered it with carpets. On the dais they hung gold-fringed, pink Genoese velvet and above it 'a prince-like canopy of state'. The Coronation Chair was placed in this sumptuous spot, moved to the Hall for the first and only time from Westminster Abbey where all previous coronations had taken place to symbolise the secular rather that sacred nature of this new investiture ceremony: man, not God, had chosen this monarch. In the air, great flags and standards captured from the royalist army swung from the rafters – a visual reminder of the new order of things and the violence that had brought them to pass.

Before the throne, a table displayed the ritual objects needed to confer the ultimate power upon Oliver: a robe of ermine-lined purple velvet, a gilt Bible, the sword of state and the solid gold royal sceptre. Banks of raised seating flanked the dais as church pews to an altar, with space allocated to all the most prominent members of civil society – the MPs, judges and City Aldermen – who would witness and so legitimise the extraordinary enthronement of one of their fellow commoners with no lineal claim upon the throne. More important still were the foreign ambassadors summoned to observe the scene and dispatch their impressions to their royal masters and governments across the sea. The French ambassador sat on the immediate right of the Coronation Chair, the ambassador from the United Provinces of the Netherlands on the left. The message was clear to all: the mighty Catholic and Protestant powers of Europe recognised the Cromwell dynasty as the newest member of their exclusive international club.

When Oliver Cromwell at last entered the Hall in the middle of the long summer afternoon with great pomp and spectacle, the audience would have seen a man at once ordinary and extraordinary, described by one of their number who knew him well: 'His body was well compact and strong, his stature under 6 foot (I believe about two inches) his head so shaped, as you might see it a storehouse and shop, both of a vast treasury of natural parts. His temper exceeding fiery, as I have known, but the flame of it kept down, for the most part, or soon allayed with those moral endowments he had. He was naturally compassionate towards objects in distress, even to an effeminate measure; though God had made him a heart, wherein was left little room for any fear, but what was due to himself, of which there was a large proportion, yet did he exceed in tenderness towards sufferers. A larger soul, I think, hath seldom dwelt in a house of clay.'[2]

Having arrived at the Palace of Westminster by river in the Lord Protector's liveried barge, Oliver had first formally assented to the new written constitution presented by Parliament, *The Humble Petition and Advice*, before MPs, officers of state, judges and his Council in the magnificent Painted Chamber. Then he processed into the Hall for his investiture accompanied by lavishly dressed courtiers, dignitaries and heralds led by the great Parliamentarian magnate, the Earl of Warwick, bearing the sword of state and the Lord Mayor of London the City sword. The service that followed was modelled on those of the Tudor and Stuart monarchs with a few subtle but significant differences. The Speaker of the House of Commons performed the rites usually administered by the Archbishop of Canterbury. There was no secret, mystical moment of divine ordination or anointment with holy oil. There were no bishops. There was no crown. King James I's famous warning 'no Bishop, no King' had been prophetic. These adaptations reflected the contradictions and innovations at the heart of the Protectorate which blended royal and republican elements in ever evolving recipes, in the search for a stable, lasting settlement palatable to all.

Oliver had refused the title of king but few at the time doubted that this was in effect what he had become, albeit in a new guise. When he swore his solemn oath to the nation to rule as 'Chief Magistrate' robed in his purple ermine-lined velvet, holding the sword and sceptre, the effervescent government newspaper *Mercurius Politicus* described him as 'standing thus adorned in princely state'. And the reception he received was in every way regal. In the magical moment when Oliver sat upon the Coronation Chair and above the Stone of Scone, a trumpet fanfare sounded three times and a herald proclaimed him 'Lord Protector of the Commonwealth of England, Scotland and Ireland, and the Dominions and Territories thereunto belonging, requiring all persons to yield him due obedience'. 'God save the Lord Protector!' the answering cry came from the assembled throng, accustomed as they had been for generations to shout 'God save the King!' as a reflexive response. And the acclamations continued outside in the June sunshine, where great crowds watched the Lord Protector pick up the train of his robe and climb into the magnificent state coach with his eldest son Richard and prominent councillors. Flanked by Oliver's personal protection force, the Life Guard, the Cromwells' gilded coach set off at the head of an enormous procession of dignitaries which wove its way through the teeming streets of a city in full festival mood, the air loud with the ringing of bells and crackling of bonfires as French wine flowed from the fountains.[3]

For the ancient City of London this was a timeless scene of public celebration which Dick Whittington would have recognised. And yet it was completely unprecedented. Though Oliver was in some ways following in the tradition of conquerors like William I or Henry VII, all such previous rulers who had disrupted reigning regimes by force of arms to launch new dynasties had done so with at least some underpinning claim based on personal royal lineage, however flimsy. William the Conqueror claimed to have been nominated by Edward the Confessor as his heir, with this sworn to by Harold Godwinson; Henry Tudor claimed descent from the Plantagenet king Edward III via his mother Margaret Beaufort, the great-granddaughter of Edward's son, John of Gaunt. Both arrived in England clutching their genealogical scrolls along with their swords: antiquaries and lawyers in their train as well as soldiers.

So powerful was this precedent, some contemporaries set about retrospectively fashioning an ancient royal pedigree for the new Lord Protector, scouring the archives for clues to the coming of this new conqueror. Oliver's distant cousin, the rehabilitated royalist conspirator and poet Edmund Waller, considered the 'only cure' for the nation's political woes was to invest 'so much power and clemency' in Oliver as 'One, whose extraction from an ancient line / Gives hope again that well-born men may shine'.[4] Outlandish origin myths circulated among the taverns and coffee houses tracing the Cromwells from all corners of the British Isles over which they now had dominion: Oliver was in fact a member of Charles I's own royal family of Stuart (formerly known as Stewart in Scotland) through his mother Elizabeth Steward who was descended from a Scottish prince shipwrecked off Norfolk in 1406;[5] Oliver was 'of lineal descent from the ancient Princes of Britain' (the conquering prince who, for one thousand years, had been prophesied to come out of Wales and heal a war-torn nation) and so heir to the legend of King Arthur;[6] Oliver's own name was a helpful anagram of 'Rule welcom Roy' or 'O welcom Reliver' in English and 'The Lyon so True' in Welsh.[7] A grail quest to find the source of the Cromwell dynasty had begun and it would take its crusaders to some unexpected places.

Crumwell

Oliver Cromwell's ancestors may in fact have come from Ireland. An entry for 1462 in the *Calendar of Ancient Records of Dublin* notes one 'Thomas Cromall', along with another man, being entrusted to build a clay wall to defend western Dublin in a garden near Crockers' Bar gate, keeping the garden itself until they had recovered their costs for work. Could this Thomas Cromall have been our Thomas's grandfather or another relation? It was twelve years later that Thomas's father Walter first appeared in the records of Wimbledon with no indication of where he had come from. This alone would not be sufficient to claim Thomas Cromwell's ancestors as Irish, but it triangulates with two independent contemporary sources. Writing of Thomas's attitude to Ireland in 1537, his contemporary, courtier George Paulet, repeated the story of a well-informed anonymous chronicler that Thomas 'was so affectionate unto the same land because his ancestors were born there'.[8]

Historians then as now had to content themselves with such scraps when seeking to piece together the origins of the Cromwell family. The Victorians used these morsels to cook up historical half-truths with all the energy of their industrious age. The Cromwells, they opined, hailed from the Nottinghamshire village of Norwell, two miles west of the village of Cromwell, and were lured to London on the promise of gold-paved streets.[9] Thomas's father Walter

Cromwell, another story ran, settled in Putney after serving Henry Tudor as a farrier in his conquering army.[10] There was a romantic symbolism to this tale linking the previous generation of Cromwells to the Tudors – a link we will see often over the course of this story – and in a way we can say that the two dynasties were born together. On 22 August 1485 Henry Tudor, an obscure Welshman with a tenuous Lancastrian claim to the throne, thundered to victory over the Yorkist king Richard III on Bosworth Field. It was this Henry, the ultimate victor of the Wars of the Roses, to whom the partly Welsh Oliver Cromwell – the cavalryman who emerged victorious from the next round of civil wars – would so often be compared. The infamous Richard III ended up dead and unceremoniously buried under what would become Leicester's most famous car park. Henry Tudor, by contrast, became King Henry VII, first of the mighty Tudor monarchs. When his own end came, peacefully after nearly 25 years' rule, Henry was entombed in the magnificent chapel he commissioned within Westminster Abbey – a resting place he would share for a brief time 150 years later with his conquering counterpart Oliver Cromwell.

In or around the same year of the Tudor accession, 1485, a boy named Thomas Cromwell was born 'of a simple Parentage, and a House obscure . . . at Putney or thereabout'.[11] His origins remain as vague today as they were to the Elizabethan martyrologist John Foxe, writing only two decades after Thomas's death. Yet a few things we do know. His father Walter Cromwell was a yeoman on the edge of respectability who ran a tavern and commercial brewery and farmed a good acreage of land in Putney, a village conveniently placed on the River Thames's approach into London. The brewery was likely sited on modern-day Brewhouse Lane, running down to the river just behind St Mary's Church. Later records show Walter moving to Wandsworth where he was granted the lease of a mill with additional lands in nearby Roehampton. These totalled 120 acres of largely wild, infertile lands on which he probably kept sheep.[12] Walter married well. His bride, possibly called Katherine, was of the minor-gentry Meverell family of Throwley Old Hall in Staffordshire. A local antiquary wrote of it in the sixteenth century as 'a very ancient house of gentlemen and of goodly living, equalling the best sort of gentlemen in the Shire'.[13] In his later career, Thomas maintained some contact with his maternal relations, engaging in the common currency of mutual favours, and indeed his great-great-grandson married into the same Meverell family.[14]

It was a modest start for a man who would one day govern England at his king's right hand, though perhaps not as bleak as popularly imagined by those who have made much of Walter's propensity to incur fines for watering down his ale, and occasional charges for drunkenness and assault. Here the records can mislead. The numerous entries in the local court rolls for Walter (and others) breaking the ale assize may in fact reflect the realities of how the licensing system operated.[15] The assault charges, likewise, are less damning on closer inspection. Both involved fights: in the first case, Walter and his adversary each drew blood and the latter was fined twice as much as Walter; in the second, Walter assaulted two 'servants' though only two small fines of six pence were applied. It is possible these incidents reflect nothing beyond the ordinary rough and tumble of Tudor working life.[16] Humbly born he may have been, a drinker and man of temper too, but Walter was evidently a substantial and successful businessman. He must have inspired a level of respect and trust in the area for he held a number of local offices over the years: deputy constable and constable of Putney and reeve and beadle of Wimbledon.

The Cromwell family also had useful social connections. The future Bishop of Ely, Nicholas West, was another local boy done good who would prove a friend and spiritual ally to Thomas in his later career, their relationship fortified by their shared Putney heritage. The Cromwells were known at Mortlake, the seat of the lord of the manor Archbishop of Canterbury William Warham, for whom Thomas's brother-in-law (or in some accounts uncle) was cook.[17] We know too of some relationship of dependence between Walter and Warham's nephew Anthony St Leger, who would go on to become Lord Deputy of Ireland, for he later wrote to Thomas 'But for the goodness that I found in your father and you, in my Lord Cardinal's days . . . I had been undone.'[18]

Nevertheless, when compared with the illustrious backgrounds of most of Thomas Cromwell's later colleagues at court, his opening hand in life was meagre. Tudor society was strictly hierarchical and there were few states more damaging or distrusted than to be a masterless man with no lord or local bigwig to serve. Young Thomas understood this instinctively and would seek and secure his own masters as soon as he was old enough to act independently. Once on the rise himself the tables turned and he would be inundated with requests from men begging for opportunities for them or their sons to enter his service: 'Next to God and my prince you have my heart . . .' one such wrote in 1532, 'for the love of God admit me to your service, not as a servant but as one of your dogs.'[19] But if Thomas's lowly start in life was a handicap it was also formative, not only for Thomas's character and career choices but for the mythology that formed around him and has endured to this day. His very name, though not that of an ancient noble house, carried its own strange, shape-shifting power.

Names in the sixteenth and seventeenth centuries were unstable: inconstant in spelling and pronunciation and often altered by occupation or interchanged with aliases. The Cromwell family sometimes used the common alias 'Smyth' which may explain why Thomas was often described by later writers as the son of a blacksmith. But one name exchange came to matter more than any other, so that it was in fact 'by the merest whisker' that England 'did not have a Lord Protector Williams'.[20] The marriages of Thomas Cromwell's two sisters provided him with the best prospects for building his kinship network and enhancing his social standing. Elizabeth married the aptly named cook to the Archbishop of Canterbury William Wellyfed while Katherine wed a Welsh gentleman named Morgan Williams. It was this latter union which was to become central to the onward success of the Cromwell family. In a move typical of the later Cromwells, Morgan's father William ap Evan – a renowned archer – had advanced his career through royal patronage, coming from Wales with his master Jasper Tudor to serve Tudor's nephew, the new king Henry VII as he established his ruling house. The Williams family which now joined to the Cromwells was a respectable, even genteel, one with a claim to ancient Welsh ancestry. Thomas Cromwell became very close to his in-laws, the Williams family, over the course of his life. One upwardly mobile member of the family, who became Lord Williams of Thame, would later host Thomas's son Gregory at his estate for a gentleman's summer camp. And when Thomas's brother-in-law Morgan Williams died in the 1520s, Thomas took his fatherless nephew, young Richard Williams, into his home and heart.

This Richard Williams became a second son to Thomas, and with a bright mind, soldier's skill and jouster's glamour, rose on the coat tails of his increasingly powerful uncle to a starring status at Henry VIII's court. In 1529, Richard changed his surname from Williams to that of his mother and his powerful uncle: Cromwell. It was this Richard Williams, now Cromwell, whose line would go on to produce Oliver Cromwell seventy years later. Oliver embraced this tangled history, giving the alias Williams on a land sale of 1627 and even on a contract with his in-laws at his marriage.[21] Indeed he made free with this family in-joke throughout his life, testifying to the matter being more of a quirk of ancestry than of any serious or legal import. As the caption below Oliver's own funeral effigy read 'Oliver Cromwell . . . born at Huntingdon, of the name of Williams, of Glamorgan, and by King Henry VIII changed into Cromwell.'[22] Whether it was the King's own suggestion or not, certainly, the two families merged to form one stronger dynastic entity. The Cromwells brought sturdy respected Englishness and Thomas's startling success at court. To this, the Williamses added an ancient, romantic Celtic heritage, traced back in a later pedigree of 1602 through a line of Welsh nobles to the Princes of Powys and a twelfth-century Norman knight.[23] In the mind of some later Cromwellian historians, Oliver's Welsh blood brought passion into his otherwise earthy East Anglian stock in the form of 'a fanaticism, a vision, a hidden fire, blazing out suddenly to consume all opponents'.[24]

Here pictures speak even louder than words. Just as Richard Williams was keen to take his uncle's name, Thomas used the opportunity to appropriate some of his Welsh glamour, referencing the lion rampant of Morgan Williams' heraldry in the three gold lions rampant on the coat of arms he was granted in the 1520s. Likewise, when, four generations later, the court heralds set about creating a new personal coat of arms for Lord Protector Oliver Cromwell, they chose his great-great-grandfather Morgan Williams' single silver lion on a black background. Powys, meanwhile – the princes of which Oliver counted among his ancestors – was at the centre of the Protectorate coat of arms. The lion which had flown in the service of one conquering Welsh king would now proclaim another. Oliver Cromwell was the new prince of the Welsh prophecies, born to take up the Tudor sword to overthrow the Scottish Stuart kings and restore England to its rightful rulers. Thus would the descendant of ancient British rulers return to claim his inheritance. Yet, as we shall see, what was done could be undone: Cromwells would become Williamses once again when their volatile fortunes changed.

Of their primary name, the look and sound of the word 'Cromwell' that has echoed down the centuries to modern ears is almost certainly wrong. Thomas signed his own name as 'Crumwell' and was addressed as such by English-speaking correspondents (he was 'Cremonello' or 'Cromuello' in Italy). Oliver too is likely to have pronounced his own name 'Crumwell' in the East Anglian dialect. Nevertheless, official documents during Thomas's life increasingly spelt his name with an 'o'; King Henry VIII himself favoured the 'o' while also abandoning the 'w' to write the name of his chief servant as the rather abrupt 'Cromell' – similar to the pronunciation 'Crummle' which Thomas's most recent biographer holds to.[25] This was changed even further at times when a 'b' appeared between the 'm' and the 'w', or the 'well' part was dropped entirely, particularly when the writer was summoning belittling imagery. As the rebels of the Pilgrimage of Grace liked to sing in threat to their sworn enemy Thomas Cromwell: 'we would crum him [and crum] him that he was never so Crumwed'.[26]

This very slipperiness imbued the earthy Cromwell name with layers of meaning. Anne Boleyn, in the hands of Hilary Mantel, always attacked her sometime ally, sometime enemy Thomas with a mocking French accent reflecting the time she spent at the French court. To her he is *Cremuel.* To Mantel's blustering, dangerous noble, the Duke of Norfolk meanwhile, he is *Crumb* – a term of faux familiarity designed in fact to remind the Duke's self-made rival that he is no more than dirt under the great magnate's boots. As the real apprentice cooks and pot-washers of the palace kitchens sang about Thomas Cromwell:

Much ill cometh of a small note,
As Crumwell set in a man's throat,
That shall put many others to pain, God wote;[27]

A brewer's son from Putney, Thomas was nothing and nobody, a crumb fallen from a nobleman's banquet table, beneath the contempt of the aristocrats of the court. And yet so powerful and dangerous that, like a crumb stuck in the throat, he could kill you. Later enhanced by Oliver's actions, the Cromwell name retained this aura of lurking menace into modern times, the British Government choosing 'Cromwell' as the codeword for imminent German invasion in 1940. Though whether 'Cromwell' represented the dark threat of dictatorship or the plucky resistance it would meet is unclear.

The popularity of the Tudor verse about the fatal crumb no doubt lay in its exquisite contradiction between the prima-facie unimportance of a common man and the unexpected power that can lie beneath an ordinary exterior. This conjures up much of the sixteenth and seventeenth centuries' obsession with class and fear of inversions of the natural order of society. Any whiff of labouring occupations was wielded as a strong weapon by a man's enemies. Thus Thomas's mentor Cardinal Wolsey was ridiculed as the son of a butcher and his friend and ally Archbishop Cranmer was attacked as an ostler (the man who looked after guests' horses at an inn). Thomas was frequently belittled by reference to his father Walter's occupations as a brewer (and possibly blacksmith or farrier) and was labelled a 'shearman' either thanks to his own time spent in the cloth trade or to his mother's possible second marriage to a cloth merchant. Even King Henry resorted to this name-calling when displeased with his chief minister, reducing his name to simply 'Thomas Cromwell, shearman' at the end of his life when he stripped him of his noble titles.

Obsession with Thomas's background characterised his enemies. Vainly, they sought explanations for his astonishing political rise which represented all that was unnatural and perverse to the nobles at Henry VIII's court. Eustace Chapuys, ambassador from the Holy Roman Empire, took great pains to describe the background of the King's right-hand man when he sketched his character for his Imperial master. Cromwell was 'the son of a poor farrier, who lived in a little village a league and a half from here, and is buried in the parish graveyard . . . Cromwell was ill behaved when young, and after an imprisonment was forced to leave the country'.[28] Like playground bullies confronted with a child they do not understand and suspect may be secretly superior to themselves, Thomas's rivals circled their subject pouncing on any sign of weakness. This, they found consistently in his family until, eventually, the sense that Thomas had overstepped his natural station in life became key to the constructed narrative which brought him down.

Rude beginnings

A century later, the hoppy whiff of the brewhouse attached itself with equal tenacity to Oliver, who was regularly stigmatised as hailing from a family of publicans thanks to his father's land including a brewhouse. Popular satires nicknamed him 'the Brewer', 'Nose', 'Ruby Nose' and 'Lord Copper Nose Cromwell', and gifted him a drunken adolescence as seemingly evidenced by his large (to the satirists red, bulbous) nose.[29] So in 1649, *A Curse against Parliament-Ale* contained 'A Hyme to Cromwell' whose 'hands are brew'd in Bloud', which opened with this verse, and whose last two lines became the repeated chorus:

> *SING old Noll the Brewer, sing old Noll the Brewer,*
> *With his Copper-face, and Ruby-Nose, now is Routed sure:*
> *Let Cromwels nose still reign, let Cromwels nose still reign,*
> *Tis no disgrace to his Copper-face, to Brew strong Ale again.*[30]

With Oliver's accession to power, the customary address of highness became 'high nose' while the poem 'The Protecting Brewer' squeezed every last drop of merriment from this concept, cataloguing the career of the 'Brewer': 'A Brewer may be as bold as Hector / When as he has drunk his cup of Nectar / And as a Brewer may be a Lord Protector / As nobody can deny.'[31] These slurs stuck to the Cromwell family as subsequent generations continued to seek either explanations for their strange rise or ammunition to explain it away. If these attacks heaped ridicule upon their subjects, they also imbued them with mystique. Thomas and Oliver Cromwell both leant into their backgrounds as a way of owning their stories and neutralising their opponents' ability to wield them against them. Thomas not only rode out the gossip about his humble origins, but contributed to it, turning an otherwise irredeemable social handicap to his own advantage. The few stories he told about his life only cultivated the alien aura around him. Famously, he boasted to his long-time friend and ally Archbishop Thomas Cranmer that he had been 'a ruffian ... in his young days'.[32] He also put it about that he had spent time in prison in his wayward youth and told the Imperial Ambassador that his mother had been 52 years old at his birth.[33] Thomas drew attention to his humble background with self-debasement and a frank and unembellished style of conversation which Henry VIII liked. The King enjoyed the way this unnerved the nobles around him and the living reminder of his own power provided by the brewer's son he had deigned to elevate.

From what we know of his playful sense of humour and conversational charm, Thomas may also have played up his past simply to unsettle his social superiors for his own amusement. He must have enjoyed taking the wind out of his detractors' sails by showing an unexpected pride in his low birth, most obviously, in choosing Wimbledon – the manor which included Putney – as the title for his barony in 1536. Thereafter, Thomas carried his brewhouse childhood around with him in his very name. Oliver shared his forebear's irreverent, inventive attitude to his own past, especially in sociable settings. At a party in Edinburgh in 1651, he entertained the Royalist Sir Walter Stewart with the story that his mother was also a Stewart (and thus related to both his companion and the Scottish royal house).[34] There is no other evidence that Oliver believed this, and it is most likely he was seeking to entertain and ingratiate himself with hosts he was trying to win over after his invasion of Scotland, which would have been firmly in character.

If Thomas could indulge the occasional frivolous boast among friends, he was also wise enough to know that pride came before a fall, and how much more precarious was the social climb for a self-made commoner like him. There were earlier, more prestigious but unrelated Cromwells from Nottinghamshire and Lincolnshire, yet Thomas reportedly refused to co-opt them into his pedigree, declaring that 'he would not wear another man's coat, for fear the owner thereof should pluck it off his ears'.[35] Thomas's words were prophetic – as much for Oliver and his heirs as for himself. When his enemies eventually succeeded in throwing him from the peak he had scaled, Thomas asserted his unshaken pride in having made himself from nothing. 'It is not unknown to many of you,' he addressed the crowd around his scaffold with piercing truth, 'that I have been a great traveller in this world, and being but of a base degree, was called to high estate.'[36] Oliver similarly trumpeted his modest origins when accounting for himself to posterity. He was, he told his Parliament as Lord Protector, nothing more exceptional than 'by birth a gentleman, living neither in any considerable height nor yet in obscurity'.[37] At the summit of his political power, Oliver owned up to his unremarkable lineage, even playing on his everyman qualities to present himself unthreateningly as the Biblical farmer-warrior Gideon sent to look after the people. As head of state, he was, in his own characterisation, nothing more than a 'good constable, to keep the peace of the parish'.[38] A king-conquering commoner raised to the status of a republican monarch, Oliver was alive to any charge of hypocrisy and went to great lengths to avoid it, even as far as rejecting the Crown – in spite of his better judgement – as the Army would account him a hypocrite were he to accept. He would not repeat the sin of the Biblical Achan whose greed brought God's punishment upon all the Israelites, but, like his hero Gideon, would refuse the Crown and return to his plough when the nation no longer needed him.

Far from provoking ridicule, for Thomas and Oliver's admirers, their rise from obscurity defined their greatness. Both the chroniclers John Foxe and Raphael Holinshed saw Thomas's life in these terms: Thomas had overcome his obscurity through 'the singular excellency of wisdom and dexterity of wit wrought in him by God' and, by his 'rude beginnings . . . we may see and learn that the excellency of noble virtues and heroical prowess . . . stand not only upon birth and blood' but are, as Psalm 113 tells us, as often bestowed by God upon those born in dunghills as in palaces.[39] For Oliver, as for Thomas before him, an obscure past coupled to a stratospheric career equalled a licence for myth-making. Future astrologers found his greatness predestined in the heavens on the night of his birth, 25 April 1599. That keenest of Stuart observers, John Aubrey, noted that Oliver had a rare birth sign – a *satellitium* with most of the known planets in the ascendant – which promised the baby would become 'more eminent in his life than ordinary'.[40] Later Cromwellian obsessives traded fabulous stories of Oliver's birth and childhood, often hingeing on the avoidance of premature death. The eighteenth-century antiquary Mark Noble, who did much to uncover the family history of the Cromwells, recorded a story handed down the generations: that once, when Oliver was at his uncle's house of Hinchingbrooke, a monkey snatched him from his cradle and carried him over the rooftop before deciding to return the 'fortune of England' safely.[41]

This wise primate was not the only being to intercede between young Oliver and death. A local curate was also fabled to have saved the boy Oliver from drowning in the River Ouse, a decision he later came to regret once the man Oliver had changed his world. Stories of miraculous brushes with death would dog the rest of Oliver's life.[42] Many poets celebrated Oliver's obscure upbringing as a positive virtue, while Andrew Marvell believed his hero's life was shaped by a heavenly force. 'So restless Cromwell could not cease / in the inglorious arts of peace, / But through advent'rous war / Urged his active star.'[43] Historians since have agreed with the assessment that 'no man who rises from a working farmer to head of state in twenty years is other than great'.[44] Or, as Oliver himself reportedly put it, 'No one rises so high as he who knows not whither he is going.'[45]

With adaptability and agility, a modest past could be a springboard. A man with little to inherit could travel lightly and become the vessel for others' hopes. Thus, down the generations of the Cromwell family, it was often those of the least means who flew highest while others with greater prospects were brought down by the weight of their inheritance. Yet every Cromwell instinctively tried to build a future for his children, for family mattered above all else. While there was a concept of the nuclear family of parents and children at this time, there was also a much larger definition of extended kin to whom one was related and with whom one was credited or indebted through constant personal services. Families were built sideways, not just downwards, and with a sense of the wider household which included servants and dependants. Thus we see Samuel Pepys opening his *Diary* with the balance sheet 'I lived in Axe-yard, having my wife and servant Jane, and no more family than us three.'[46] Power meant positions and people to fill them. So a nobleman brought his relations to court and placed them in key roles, running his covert network with ranks of overt liveried servants clad in his household uniform.

Thomas Cromwell's time was the final period of so-called 'bastard feudalism' where a nobleman retained trained bands of dependants on his land who bore his badge and answered his summons to war.[47] Indeed, important men were judged by the numbers they could personally raise and arm in their monarch's service. It was a sign of Thomas's growing status in the final years of his life that he could personally muster and equip a small army of troops; a fact that would later be used against him. For if a man's power rested on his private army, what if he used that army against his rivals or, worse still, his king? After all, this was a society still bleeding from the dynastic Wars of the Roses where the mere fact of possessing Plantagenet genes superior to the usurping *nouveau riche* Tudors could send you to the Tower.

No-one felt this more than a man who had to start his family from scratch, using all his wits to move up from the natural place in society that God had ordained for him. Especially a man who had seen how power operated when serving his apprenticeship on the battlefields and in the counting houses of the Italian banking dynasties. Whatever his devotion to the King's (and, often, the public) interest, for Thomas Cromwell the primal call of family was compulsively strong: 'place and family mattered profoundly to him and might outweigh religion'.[48] This echoed the driving obsession of his royal master's life to secure the Tudor line of succession whatever the human cost. This future was what Thomas worked for, so that as he climbed the ladder at court, acquiring positions, money, lands and titles, he took care to use these to build his powerbase and plant his family in an unassailable position in society. Nothing could be left to chance when the capricious king who had made him could unmake him in an instant.

Two

Inheritance

The abomination of religious persons throughout this realm, and a reformation to [be] devised therein.

Thomas Cromwell's Remembrances, February 1536

Reformation spoils

The 400-year-old Augustinian priory of Launde in Leicestershire held a special place in Thomas Cromwell's affections. He had lived nearby early in his career when he served his first English patron, Thomas Grey the 2nd Marquess of Dorset, at Bradgate Park, home now to the two-year-old future 'nine-day queen' Lady Jane Grey. In subsequent years, Thomas had visited Launde several times and bestowed on it a number of favours when he worked for Cardinal Wolsey. Monastic life fascinated Thomas, and when he stayed at Launde he would walk with the canons about their business. On one of these perambulations one winter's day, Thomas's companion fell flat on his back in the snow, a black beetle flailing on white. His friend reminded Thomas about this mishap years later, and Thomas may have thought of it again in October 1539 when he contemplated his retirement.[1] Now, approaching the summit of his career and considering where he would spend his twilight years, Thomas entered three simple words into his notebook in the list of those to receive the coming round of dissolved monastic properties: 'myself for Launde'.[2]

Over the previous decade, Thomas had presided over an astounding series of political and religious reforms amounting to no less than a revolution. Central to this had been the legislative programme decoupling England from the Catholic Church in Rome, a process which became known as the Reformation. A longstanding project dissolving monastic houses, first begun under Cardinal Wolsey, escalated in these years, flooding the property market with new land. This was a golden opportunity not only for the old nobility to pick up choice investments but for the new 'service aristocracy' of men who had risen through political office to create their own estates retrospectively.[3] Chief architect of the scheme, Thomas enriched himself and his family as much as anyone else, buying up sizeable monastic lands to augment his expanding property portfolio. This began in Rumney in Wales, close to the Williams family's heartlands, but had been concentrated mostly in London and the home counties of Sussex, Kent and Essex since. In 1535, Thomas's accounts show that these estates were yielding an income of £417 (around £130,000 today) though this may have been higher in actuality.[4] From 1536 onwards, the pace and scale of Thomas's accumulation rapidly increased, moving from the piecemeal acquisition of smaller land to much larger concentrated purchases and royal grants, some from the newly available monastic lands.

One hundred miles from London, peacefully nestled in a bowl of open land surrounded by rolling hills with rich woods and farmland, it is easy to see why numinous Launde promised Thomas the safe quietude he now wished for in his old age. Fittingly, it is today a Christian retreat owned by the diocese of Leicester, its own 'Launde Prayer' wishing that 'here may the weary find rest and the strong be renewed; here may we all find inspiration, and that peace which the world cannot give'. Yet Thomas never lived to enjoy his promised peace at Launde. Less than a year after he bought his retirement home, he was dead. 'But Cromwell (if we may believe some of our Authors) foresaw his fall two years before and therefore provided for his Family,' the seventeenth-century historian Lord Chirbury wrote.[5] In these final years, Thomas helped his son Gregory and nephew Richard establish themselves as wealthy landowners with sufficient security and wealth to sustain their descendants should the worst befall him. It was they who would continue his hopes and ambitions as his dynastic heirs, established as landed gentry on the back of the Reformation.

❦ ❦ ❦

Thomas Cromwell first began to help his nephew Richard put down roots in 1534 when he secured the hand of Frances, heiress to former Lord Mayor of London Thomas Murfyn, and set the young couple up with a household in Stepney. Widows and daughters of prosperous London merchants were highly sought after as spouses at the time and the Cromwell family would return again and again to source brides from this pool. Richard wanted a country powerbase and his eye settled on Huntingdonshire where he became High Sheriff in 1536 and a Justice of the Peace from 1538. It was now that his career really gathered steam. In 1539 the King appointed Richard a Gentleman of the Privy Chamber and he was elected MP for Huntingdonshire. All his plans fell into place when the King granted him the beautiful nunnery of Hinchingbrooke, just outside Huntingdon in Cambridgeshire. Sitting a little above the town with a fine vista over the Great Ouse river and surrounding meadows, and comprising a church, chapter house, cloister gardens, refectory, dormitory, kitchen and parlour, the nunnery was an attractive prospect. By the time of its suppression in 1536 its occupants numbered only around three nuns, meaning local opposition was limited.[6] Furthermore, the area was an enticing choice for a man on the make as it boasted few noble families for him to compete with. The industrious Richard immediately set about remodelling the buildings, moving into the Prioress's lodgings – now renamed Cromwell Tower – and building above and around the existing nunnery footprint to transform it into a splendid manor house. Thomas saw for himself how grandly Richard was settled when he visited in September 1539 on a pleasurable detour from the royal progress.[7]

Like his uncle, Richard had no qualms about desecrating holy property for profit. In the course of remodelling Hinchingbrooke nunnery, Richard's builders disturbed the lids of two stone coffins. Long assumed to contain the bones of nuns who subsequently haunted the house, testing has revealed them to be much older, possibly a prominent Anglo-Saxon couple. If so, Hinchingbrooke's history as a site of religious worship may pre-date the coming of William the Conqueror who its later nuns celebrated as their founder.[8] By 1540 Richard had also acquired the priories of Huntingdon and St Neots and a recently dissolved Cistercian abbey at Sawtry and the Benedictine abbey on the fenland isle of Ramsey, the King himself witnessing the grant at Westminster.[9] A convenient twelve miles north-east of

Hinchingbrooke, Ramsey was rich and prestigious, its abbot third in parliamentary precedence after only Glastonbury and St Albans. Yet, after a long campaign prising the Abbey from the hands of its 'conformable' abbot, the hard-nosed Richard plundered it as his own personal quarry.[10] Stones were taken for building walls, cottages and parish churches. Down came the gatehouse to be reassembled stone by stone at Hinchingbrooke at a new entry point chosen to offer a more imposing entrance directly facing the town of Huntingdon. The gatehouse still stands proudly on this site today, a pair of ethereal carved green men – possibly a Reformation substitute for former saints – standing sentinel above it, sacred stones repurposed for secular life.

The event that clinched Richard's rise was the lavish, week-long jousting tournament which opened on 1 May 1540 to celebrate the King's ill-fated marriage to Anne of Cleves. Even as the vultures circled for its orchestrator Thomas, Richard rode into the lists and the Tudor chroniclers' hall of fame. How it must have galled the nobles at court to see the Cromwells from Putney taking part in the ultimate chivalric ritual. For the Cromwells were out in full force and fashion on that spring day, enemies be damned: Richard appearing as a challenger, chosen by the King as one of his champions, with Gregory entering as a defender. Both were 'richly apparelled' with Richard and his horse clothed 'all in white velvet' while his arms hung with those of the other challengers on a pomegranate tree in front of a castle.[11] When Richard triumphed, the King congratulated him, reportedly saying: '"Formerly thou wast my Dick, but hereafter thou shalt be my diamond'" and 'thereupon dropped a diamond ring from his finger, which Sir Richard taking up, his majesty presented it to him, bidding him ever afterwards bear such a one in the fore gamb of the demy lion in his crest.'[12] Richard was then knighted and rewarded with an annual fee of 100 marks and yet more Reformation income: a house bought from the proceeds of the dissolution of the Friary of St Francis in Stamford.

This Camelot moment swiftly assumed pride of place in Cromwell family folklore. The King's diamond ring would indeed grace the Cromwell/Williams heraldry thereafter as he had instructed, held aloft in the claws of the family's signature rampant lion.[13] Richard knew the value of this moment in marketing his newly elevated family and it was probably he who commissioned the monumental murals of the May Day tournament across the walls of the family's parlour on the ground floor of their Tower lodgings at Hinchingbrooke.[14] Although this colourful scene would have no doubt delighted the boy Oliver Cromwell on his childhood visits to his family's ancestral home 60 years later, his elders would have seen a faint shadow of hubris beneath its glittering paint. For it was only weeks after that bright day that Thomas, the fount of their feast, had fallen. Richard's ascension to fame and fortune had slipped under the last inch of wire, with the mythology of his May Day heroics affording him vital armour against the disaster of his uncle's execution. Hinchingbrooke and Ramsey were safe for his heirs.

Gregory's protection in 1540 came in a different form: that of his glamorous and guileful wife, no less a figure than the late Queen Jane Seymour's sister, Elizabeth. While his son's joining the royal family had fatally enhanced Thomas's reputation for overweening ambition, as we will see, Gregory's bride was perhaps the greatest future-proofing gift Thomas gave his son. Her well-timed intercession on his behalf, and close relationship to the King, enabled Gregory to salvage some of his father's estates when the King made Gregory Baron Cromwell – a fresh, fourth iteration of the Cromwell barony with no specific lands attached and not the same title his father had held in Wimbledon. Gregory's rehabilitation provoked speculation: a merchant reported that the King had in fact conferred Thomas's 'title and many of his domains while he was yet in prison upon his son Gregory' as a ruse 'in order that he [Thomas] might the more readily confess his offences at execution'.[15] But Thomas had been cautious and often added Gregory to deeds as joint owner, or stipulated somewhere in the paperwork that his estates would pass to Gregory at his death. In the case of the sizeable manor of North Elmham in Norfolk which Thomas acquired in 1536, he made a feoffment two years later to Gregory and his wife Elizabeth to use during their lives and entailing the estate on their children – a decision which saved North Elmham for his descendants in the teeth of decades of legal challenge. The document itself reveals Thomas's attitude to the hierarchy of his dependants: for if Gregory were to have no sons, the remainder of the estate passed to his nephews and their sons – first Walter Williams alias Cromwell (Richard's brother) then William Wellyfed – before defaulting to 'Richard Williams alias Crumwell' and his heirs.[16] Thomas did the same with the lordship of Oakham in Rutland and

Gregory was allowed to keep both of these properties, given some new lands in Oakham and, most poignantly, granted the neighbouring, longed-for Launde.

These places formed the compass points for Gregory and his descendants. An ancient, royal lordship, Oakham was the title he and his heirs tended to use, styling themselves 'Baron Cromwell of Oakham'. While it was Launde which Gregory and Elizabeth, like Richard and Frances at Hinchingbrooke, hastily set about converting into a family home for their five children. Now a country house in a fashionable 'H' shape, Launde Priory was rebranded as Launde Abbey.

❦ ❦ ❦

Thomas was dead but he had used his Reformation spoils to found two branches of the Cromwell family which we will follow in this story: his son Gregory Cromwell's descendants in Leicestershire and Norfolk (for convenience the 'Launde Cromwells'); and his nephew Richard Cromwell alias Williams' descendants in Huntingdonshire (the 'Hinchingbrooke Cromwells'). For both sides, their inheritance from their infamous founder was a complex one, yet each continued to prosper and quietly celebrate their controversial heritage.

Gregory and Elizabeth lived quietly at Launde for the rest of Gregory's life. At his death, the formidable Elizabeth, after facing a hard few years, moved on and up to her third husband, John Paulet, future 2nd Marquess of Winchester, joining him at his palatial home of Basing House in Hampshire. As will happen again in this story, two houses joined by one marriage subsequently reinforced this with others as two of Elizabeth's sons from her first two marriages married their Paulet stepsisters.[17] The family continued to live at Launde but also spent time at the manor of North Elmham in Norfolk, perhaps suggesting tightening budgets. North Elmham was a fine and pleasant estate but had not been grand enough to tempt the Duke of Norfolk, who had once contemplated buying it from Thomas, until he visited and found its woodland and park 'not of the value he weened they had been'.[18]

Certainly the value of the Launde Cromwells' estates did not always translate into ready cash. Gregory's eldest son and heir Baron Henry Cromwell – apparently impoverished and politically irrelevant – sought to line his pockets through local schemes such as a proposal to build new breakwaters at Sheringham paid for by a grant from the Crown of certain farming fines.[19] In 1572 Baron Henry Cromwell was arrested for debt in a private lawsuit in the Court of Chancery. While Tudor gentlemen often found themselves pursued by their creditors, this must have been serious, for Baron Henry petitioned the House of Lords for release on the grounds of parliamentary privilege, slipping his hearing into the very end of Parliament's session. The peers agreed, ordering 'Lord Crumwell' be freed as his incarceration was 'derogatory and prejudicial' to that ancient privilege.[20] This was not the last time a Cromwell was arrested and examined by the great lords of the land, nor that the Cromwell name appeared in the defence of parliamentary privilege. As we will see, Baron Henry's younger brother Thomas – a new and presumably embarrassed MP in this same session of Parliament – would contribute to the strengthening of Parliament his grandfather and namesake had begun.

Gregory's son Baron Henry Cromwell's marriage to his stepsister Mary Paulet was evidently a happy one. Within months of his 'beloved' wife's death in her fifties Henry too died, his family fulfilling the wish of his will that he join her resting place 'by the tomb of my late father' under the marble at Launde. The will Baron Henry wrote in November 1592, soon after his wife's death, reveals a leisured life for Thomas's grandson at North Elmham surrounded by a close family to whom he bequeathed his treasures. Shrewdly Henry left his 'jewel of unicorn's horn set in gold' to 'my especiall and singular good Lord', Queen Elizabeth I's chief minister William Cecil, in recognition of their longstanding family friendship but, more importantly, to encourage Cecil 'to stand good Lord unto my children and name'. Little did he know how much Cecil and his son Robert Cecil would be tried in this matter by Baron Henry's own heir, Thomas's great-grandson Edward Cromwell.[21]

Besides the estate, Henry bequeathed Edward himself one specific object which was clearly of great significance to him: 'my basin and ewer of silver parcel gilt, which was my grandfathers'. Thomas Cromwell's own will of 1529 had left this same basin and ewer to Gregory and now, more than 70 years later, Gregory's son Henry passed the heirloom onto his own son Edward.[22] There are other signs that Thomas was not forgotten by his family who took pride in their

Cromwell name. Baron Henry's daughter, Edward's sister, the talented polymath Catherine, remained close to her parents after her marriage, probably returning to them to have her first baby.[23] Keen to honour her heritage, she decorated her new marital home of Helmingham Hall in Suffolk with murals of her shared family heraldry, the lion rampant of the Cromwells prominent besides the fret of her husband's Tollemache family in the centre of her designs, red 'Catherine' pears hanging from the tree bearing the arms a witty reference to her own name.[24] Similarly, the lavish monument that Catherine's son erected for his father and his three Tollemache forebears in Helmingham Church bears her Cromwell arms and in its affectionate lines of eulogising verse concludes:

Happy in Soul, in Body, Goods and Name,
Happy in Wedlock with a Noble Dame
Lord Cromwells Daughter Happy in his heir
Whose Spring of Virtues Sprouts so Young, so Fair.

As the century wore on Thomas Cromwell's direct descendants, the Launde Cromwells, seemed secure, living comfortably if always with one eye on their bottom line. Meanwhile, Thomas Cromwell's great-nieces and nephews, the Hinchingbrooke Cromwells, lived in splendour. At their deaths, Richard Cromwell alias Williams and his wife Frances left their two young sons a fortune in property which is likely to have generated an income of around £2,500 a year (around £600,000 today).[25] The elder son and heir, Henry – eventually Sir Henry – Cromwell, grew up to be the grandest figure in the locality for the rest of the sixteenth century and one of the wealthiest commoners in England. Sir Henry Cromwell was every inch the Elizabethan patriarch. His life's ambition was to build a wealthy and enduring local lordship from his courtier father's romantic, chivalric legacy. After studying at the University of Cambridge and Lincoln's Inn, Sir Henry lived at Hinchingbrooke and continued his father's transformation of the medieval nunnery into an Elizabethan mansion.[26] Like his father, he married the daughter of a Lord Mayor of London – Joan Warren. Again, like his father, he served as MP and sheriff for the region from his Hinchingbrooke base, cementing this hereditary position as leading local magnate. His tenants sometimes found him a hard landlord, yet it was his reputation for generosity that endured, his reported habit of throwing coins to the well-wishing multitude who lined the route of his annual summer progress from Hinchingbrooke to Ramsey earning him his nickname 'the Golden Knight'. Thus the Cromwell family's eighteenth-century chronicler Mark Noble praised him as 'a worthy gentleman, both in court and country, and universally esteemed'.[27]

Following his father Richard and great uncle Thomas Cromwell, Sir Henry was utterly loyal to the ultimate source of his station: the Crown. Accounted 'earnest in religion and fit to be trusted' in letters from the bishops to the Council, he acted as a conduit for the Queen's commands, sitting on local commissions, surveying church lands, contributing to county levies and musters and unsuccessfully hunting a wanted Jesuit.[28] He even penned his own 'Allegation of Services to the Queen' detailing the occasions he had been in Elizabeth I's presence, how he had served her as Sheriff of Huntingdonshire, and that he had travelled to France with the Queen's future lord chamberlain. Sir Henry dedicated a third of this account to his father Richard's glamorous military reputation, venerating the father he had lost as a boy and revealing his Cromwellian lineage as his most prized asset.[29]

Queen Elizabeth honoured this loyalty by staying at Hinchingbrooke in 1564. The Golden Knight spared no expense in hosting his Queen, including presenting a play by students from the nearby University of Cambridge.[30] Unfortunately the play backfired, angering the quick-tempered Queen with its anti-popery agitprop at a time when Elizabeth was trying to smooth relations with Catholic Spain. The scene is reminiscent of another badly received anti-Catholic farce; that of 'Cardinal Wolsey Going Down to Hell' that Elizabeth's grandfather Thomas Boleyn and great-uncle the Duke of Norfolk had performed before the much offended French ambassador in 1531.[31] Whether the Queen knew or thought of this parallel, as she looked around Cromwellian Hinchingbrooke with its Welsh Williams heraldry carved in the stonework and the fairytale moment her father gifted his diamond ring to the victorious jouster Richard Cromwell painted on the walls, she surely thought of Anne Boleyn – the mother she could not remember, whose execution her host's great uncle Thomas Cromwell had orchestrated. But the past was the past and the Tudors were pragmatists. Any unhappy thoughts about his uncle – or irritating student politics – did not prevent the Queen bestowing Sir Henry's knighthood upon him in thanks for her visit and visiting him again at Ramsey in 1578.[32]

Time and the Tudors had forgiven the Cromwells who continued their stunning social climb. Yet their inheritance from the seismic events of the 1530s was complicated. The Cromwells were still a young house and Sir Henry was sensitive to issues of precedence. He maintained a long and petty feud with his nearest regional rival centring on such weighty matters as who had put which name at the top of the new commission of the peace. Furthermore, along with their country estates, new secular landlords like the Cromwells acquired complex local relationships previously managed by the ousted religious houses. Family ambition mingled with the changing religious beliefs and social upheaval of the Reformation. Clashes between recent landowners' social ambitions and their tenants' traditional ways of life were common. For these new gentry families, land needed to be profitable and to offer the elite leisure activities to underpin their status and enable their Tudor state-building in miniature – their own contribution as representatives of an increasingly powerful Crown. In 1585, this impulse provoked a clash with a large group of Sir Henry's tenants over his hunting haven of 'Muchwood chase', which he had cleared from land they used and knew as 'Muchwood common'. The case went all the way to the Queen's court of Star Chamber which found largely in Sir Henry's favour even if he was denied an outright win.[33]

Sir Henry Cromwell may have bested his tenants over Muchwood, but within a few years other community tensions reached into the very heart of his home with tragic consequences. The late 1580s and 1590s were a feverish time in England. Protestant patriotism and anti-Catholic sentiment peaked following the Spanish Armada of 1588 and anxiety about the anticipated end of a century, a long reign and a domineering royal house abounded. It was in this uncertain climate that Sir Henry was dragged into a dispute between two of his tenants in the Ramsey Abbey estate of Warboys: his friends, the piously puritanical, wealthy and well-connected Throckmorton family and their neighbours, the poor, quarrelsome and disorderly Samuel family. In November 1589, the five Throckmorton daughters began to suffer regular fits, blaming them on their neighbour Alice

Samuel who they accused of being a witch, largely on the basis that she was poor, old, wore a black cap and liked to sit in the corner of the inglenook fireplace.

News of this phenomenon spread through the district and soon the local bigwigs waded in. Sir Henry's second wife, Lady Susan Cromwell, visited the Throckmortons and summoned Alice Samuel to explain herself. When she could not, Susan cut off a lock of Alice's hair, giving this and her headband to the children's mother to burn; a surefire way to counter Alice's witchcraft. Appalled, Alice protested, 'Why do you use me thus? I never did you any harm *as yet*.'[34] That night Lady Susan suffered a nightmare where she was tormented by a huge cat which threatened to pluck all the flesh from her body. So violently did she convulse in her sleep that she woke her daughter-in-law who was sharing her bed while her own husband was away. From that night onwards, Lady Susan grew strangely ill with terror and fits. She died in July 1592, seemingly frightened to death. A year later, Alice Samuel, her husband and daughter were tried and hanged for bewitching the Throckmorton girls and Lady Cromwell, causing her death. For his part, Sir Henry Cromwell was convinced that his wife had been murdered by witchcraft: a subject of growing interest in this time of religious insecurity and paranoia. Granted £40 (about £7,000 today) as landlord from the proceeds of the poor Samuels' forfeited estate, he used this to fund an annual sermon against 'the detestable practise, sin, and offense of witchcraft' in the Cromwell family church of All Saint's, Huntingdon where Lady Susan was buried.[35] Oliver Cromwell would have attended for the first 40 years of his life, regularly reminded of the story of his step-grandmother's strange death only seven years before his own birth.

Sir Henry Cromwell put these dark years behind him as the century turned. Now of 'great years and infirmities', he celebrated the new seventeenth century by commissioning a splendid pedigree of the Cromwell family, detailing in full their descent from the Princes of Powys.[36] On thick creamy vellum the eight-foot-long tree unfurls its blossom of brightly coloured shields and inked, linked names. The pride in the Cromwell lineage is unmistakeable and there, three quarters of the way down the scroll, is our Putney boy Thomas, noted with celebration not stigma as 'Thomas, Ld. Cromwell created Earl of Essex 31 of king H. 8'. From this alone – a document produced at such vast labour and expense – we can deduce that the Hinchingbrooke

Cromwells carried no shame for their disgraced forebear. The pedigree also speaks in its silence. Sir Henry did not include the late Lady Susan, perhaps to obliterate the stain of her murder. As his second wife – who had not borne him any children – Susan could be omitted easily from the family tree. But the pedigree also overlooked the living. There is no mention of Sir Henry's three-year-old grandson Oliver Cromwell, though someone, later on, has scribbled the name 'Oliver C' in pencil with an arrow to his proper place in the pedigree.[37]

As a child, Oliver was of no great importance to his family. His father Robert Cromwell was the second of Sir Henry's six sons and so not destined to inherit the estate. Sir Henry, furthermore, had many other claims on his attention as the pious patriarch had also fathered five legitimate and two illegitimate daughters. After Robert's childhood at Hinchingbrooke and spells at Queens' College Cambridge and Lincoln's Inn, Sir Henry set him up comfortably, if not grandly, as a gentleman in nearby Huntingdon.[38] The Elizabethan townhouse he now called home was itself built upon a medieval house of the Austin Friars – similar no doubt to the Austin Friars house Thomas Cromwell developed into his own primary residence in London in the 1530s. Robert Cromwell drew an income of around £300 per year from local rents and a share of tithes (the tax paid to support the clergy which since the Reformation had in some places been reassigned to local landowners). Robert's good name and father's influence secured him one term as MP for Huntingdon in 1597 and stints as a justice of the peace and high sheriff. He was, in short, a well-named and connected but modestly moneyed member of the lower gentry.

Robert Cromwell was a reasonable catch for Oliver's mother, Elizabeth Steward. Her long and extraordinary life had already seen its share of drama. Elizabeth's family were prosperous gentry from Norfolk, with some of her relatives' coats of arms claiming dubious kinship with the ancient Scottish royal house of Stewart. Ely – the remote 'island of eels' floating on a vast waterland far from civilisation – was her home. There Elizabeth's father Sir William Steward farmed lands around the ship-like cathedral, ground which emerged each spring enriched from the winter floods. Elizabeth had been married young to one William Lynne and blessed with a baby daughter, Katherine. Life was set fair. But in 1589 both had died and were buried in the cathedral, surrounded by the grand tombs of

Elizabeth's relations, the medieval wonder of the lantern-topped Octagon tower rising 142 feet above their resting place. The 24-year-old widow Elizabeth might have assumed she would join them there one day, but providence had lain another path before her. A year later she appears to have embarked on an aborted courtship with one William Beck. Beck called her his 'sweet Princess', but it was marriage to Robert Cromwell the following year which set Elizabeth's life on a royal course thanks to their sole surviving son who would transform her from Norfolk widow to the effective dowager queen of England.[39]

In the space of Sir Henry Cromwell's lifetime, the Cromwell family had risen from that of a 'base stock and house' to one considered an ancient and knightly family.[40] The old man who had been held in Thomas Cromwell's arms as a baby now held his grandson Oliver Cromwell in his. He was the one person who knew both. The Cromwells had flourished in the Tudor century: the message was there for all to see in ancestral scroll, painted plaster and carved stone. But there was rot beneath the gilt; a fragility evidenced in the very buildings of Hinchingbrooke itself where awkward joints reveal when money ran out for building projects. Thomas Cromwell's dissolution had gifted his descendants enormous wealth and grand estates, but it also bequeathed them enduring challenges. At Launde and Hinchingbrooke, debts mounted up and lives were gambled. Now the Cromwells found that service to a greedy Crown could impoverish as much as it could enrich. Reformation wealth had a blood price.

This was believed at the time, with one particular superstition derived from the Book of Exodus gaining currency as the century turned that the third generation of any family that had helped itself to former religious lands would fail.[41] 'We be taught by experience, how Almighty God never suffereth the third heir to enjoy his father's wrong possessions,' the Church *Homilies* pronounced.[42] Clergymen preached this dissolution curse from the pulpit, with one in 1612 stating: 'I am persuaded many a house of blood in England had stood at this hour, had not the forced springs of impropriations turned their foundation to a quagmire. In all your knowledge, think but on a church-robber's heir that ever thrived to the third generation.' Another in Cambridge the following year mused: 'If we should make a catalogue of all those courtiers and others who in the dissolution of the abbeys were much enriched by the spoil of the Church, how few of so great estates are not already ruinated? It is true that . . . it is a vain thing for men to think that their names, lands and houses shall continue for ever; but yet that in so short a space so great a change should be of so many families, so likely to have continued for longer space, must needs make men see . . . that the fact was displeasing unto almighty God.'[43]

Twenty miles away the Hinchingbrooke Cromwells had begun to feel the curse that by now already plagued the Launde Cromwells. For the next generation of the family – the third since Gregory and Richard had taken their monastic riches – would ruin it all.

Rebellious spirits

In February 1601 Robert Devereux, the glamorous and powerful Earl of Essex, hero of Cadiz and populariser of the spade beard, took his and his friends' lives in his hands. Queen Elizabeth I's former favourite had fallen low; returned from a failed campaign in Ireland prematurely, he met with the Queen's fury and her Council's hostility, none more inveterate against him than chief minister Sir Robert Cecil. Cornered, Essex gathered his circle of friends and supporters at his house on the Strand to plot a coup – the very house his son would later use to plan impeachment proceedings against Oliver Cromwell in December 1644. But such drastic action needed mood music, something to inspire and incite his men, and this being Shakespeare's London, Essex heeded Hamlet's advice that 'the play's the thing'. The Lord Chamberlain's men hastened to his summons and performed a play about King Richard II. Whether this was Shakespeare's own version or that of Sir John Hayward, the parallel of the weak sovereign thankfully deposed by a virtuous member of the nobility – who happened to be Essex's own ancestor – was plain for all to see. Even the old Queen got the point. 'I am Richard II,' she is recorded as saying in despair at the time, 'know ye not that?'[44]

The next day, Essex and his faithful acolytes rose in rebellion. Having escaped the envoys sent to stall them, Essex and his men marched through the City, shouting that there was a plot against him, that Cecil would betray England, and calling for its citizens to join them. But the grateful masses did not rally to their hero; the streets were silent. The Essex rebels retreated in shame and mounting fear to Essex House where Essex eventually gave himself up without a fight. The future looked bleak for the failed rebels: rising up against a Tudor monarch only tended to one outcome. Government loyalists swiftly rounded up the plotters, arresting the assorted band of brothers who had attached themselves to the rising Earl seeking favour and camaraderie. Among them was a familiar name. 'And although my house be an unfit place for keeping prisoners,' the Lord Chief Justice wrote to Cecil the following day, 'yet have I taken care for the custody of the Lord Cromwell, who most pitifully moveth his misery and protesteth ignorance of the attempt, and that he casually fell into the Earl of Essex's company, nor was any way partaker of any plot.'[45] This Cromwell was but the latest addition to the rogues' gallery processed in the past twenty-four hours, following Robert Catesby who, in four years' time, would mastermind the Gunpowder Plot.

The Lord Cromwell who kept such notorious company was Edward, third Baron Cromwell of the Launde Cromwells, son of Baron Henry Cromwell, grandson of Gregory and great-grandson of Thomas. A professional soldier, Edward Cromwell had fought his way through the Elizabethan military campaigns on land and sea that made a generation of heroes in the English imagination, including Sir Philip Sidney, Sir Walter Raleigh and Sir Francis Drake. His career took Edward to the United Provinces of the Netherlands to fight the Spanish where he injured his leg at Ghent and secured the patronage of the Queen's favourite, the Earl of Leicester. Sir Philip Sidney praised him as 'having here well deserved and very commendably behaved himself'. When the English followed the defeat of the Spanish Armada by sending their own in 1589, Edward Cromwell was on board, now 'Lieutenant of the Foot'. Two years later he popped up in Normandy where the English under the Earl of Essex's command aided the French King Henry IV in his unsuccessful attempt to take Rouen from the forces of the Catholic League.[46] He was among the lords who attended the King's 'princely' reception and garter ceremony at Elizabeth's court in 1596.[47]

Though Edward did his duty for Queen and country, this came at a cost. When home from campaign, he fell into scrapes, such as the brawl outside the Old Swan pub in London which landed him in house arrest in the City and saw him brought before the Privy Council for reprimand. He was overlooked for promotion, failing to secure a number of military posts he applied for such as Governor of the Dutch port of Brill and Lord Marshal of Ireland which he was expected to be given at the time.[48] Edward's father Baron Henry had struggled with debts and, on his death in 1592, left his son a legacy of long and expensive legal disputes, the worst of which was against All Souls College, Oxford over lands that had been granted to Thomas by Henry VIII. Living at the family estate at North Elmham, Edward resisted demands from the Privy Council for payment of the ship money tax (which would go on to play a crucial role in the build up to the first Civil War in 1642), 'reluctantly' paying up in 1596.

In 1598 Edward sold North Elmham to the Attorney-General Sir Edward Coke and wrote to Cecil asking him for help securing a place on the Earl of Essex's campaign in Ireland 'in order to re-advance the estate of his now decaying house'.[49] A year later he asked Cecil to grant his son's wardship to his wife in consideration of their poor estate.[50] These letters were among many applications Edward made to Cecil, surely prompted by the close relationship the Cecil and Cromwell families had enjoyed since Cecil's father had advanced in the service of Thomas Cromwell and his circle during the reign of Henry VIII. Yet Edward Cromwell hampered his chance of securing Cecil's favour by attaching himself to Essex, Cecil's great rival.[51]

Now however, for Edward Cromwell, Essex had transformed from luminary to liability. Charged with High Treason after Essex's rebellion and imprisoned in the Tower, Edward continued to protest his innocence while Essex and several of his other followers went to the block. His chances of survival looked bleak, as Cecil acknowledged in March: 'For the rest of the noblemen that are in the Tower, as Rutland, Sandes, Cromwell, Monteagle, excepting Sandes and Cromwell, I presume the other two shall have mercy, but Sandes and Cromwell are appointed to be tried to-morrow by the Peers at Westminster hall.'[52] Edward's second wife, Frances Rugge, pleaded leniency for her husband just as his grandmother, the stalwart Elizabeth Seymour, had done for his grandfather Gregory at Thomas's fall in 1540. Thus Edward opened his latest appeal to Cecil in August 1601: 'Since I have understood by my poor wife that you would see me, I have been emboldened to address you these few lines.' His desperation and self-reproach are clear. Writing to Coke he praised the Queen for her 'great favour and grace extended towards me in pardoning mine offences so rashly committed against her' but worried that the losses he had sustained through his 'late troubles' would continue as long as the Queen maintained her 'heavy countenance' towards him.[53] Of Cecil, he asked 'To whom shall I complain, whose crimes have deprived me of everything – friends, allies, means. Alas, I know not, if God, her Majesty and you shall forsake me. God, by her Majesty, hath heard my prayers, and I entreat you to read my petition and relieve my overthrown fortunes.'[54]

Eventually Edward's entreaties succeeded and he was released and pardoned. His life may have been spared but his reputation was destroyed and his future ruined. Fined £6,000, Edward was forced to mortgage his land to the Queen who never forgave him; as Edward pleaded with Cecil only a fortnight before her death in 1603 'I beseech you to further my better reconcilement to the favour of my most dread sovereign, who I grieve so unadvisedly to have offended.'[55] Nevertheless, Edward was given the honour of carrying one of the banner rolls at Elizabeth's funeral.[56] Elizabeth was succeeded by her closest relative, the Stuart King James VI of Scotland (who now became James I of England). An admirer of Essex, the new King James I appeared more sympathetic to Edward, swearing him to the privy council at his accession, but it was not enough to save Edward's estates. We learn as much from the king himself who remarked how 'I was daily troubled with the poor Lord Cromwell's begging leave to sell the last pieces of his land, who had valiantly served the State in the wars.'[57]

Impoverished, humiliated and 'utterly overthrown', in 1605 Edward sold his remaining English lands and exiled himself to Ireland.[58] This may have been a return to family roots or because Edward knew Ireland from his campaigns with Essex. There he managed to make something of his last years, salvaging a residue of royal trust to become Governor of Lecale. He built a house at Downpatrick where he died in 1607 and was buried in the nearby cathedral (though he had to wait a further 80 years for the family to afford a proper memorial). The future of Thomas Cromwell's direct line would be an Irish one, though memories of lost glories in England lingered and the Crown would continue to exert its pull. But Launde Abbey – dream of Edward's great-grandfather Thomas, burial place of his grandfather Gregory, his parents and his first wife, and primary seat of the

Cromwells – was long gone, lost by the third generation of dissolution profiteers in the high stakes game of royal service.

Bad bargains

Edward Cromwell's sister Catherine was made from entirely different mettle. Catherine loved to read widely: books on every possible subject from theology to fishing, heraldry to medicine, horticulture to lace-making. But reading alone did not satisfy her. Books were objects both of desire and of practical instruction to be collected, inscribed, collated and compared, copied, learned from and, ultimately, written. Both her Cromwell birth family and the Tollemache one she married into gave her unparalleled opportunities to indulge her passion, develop her remarkable talents and make a historic contribution to bibliography. When in 1580, aged twenty-three, Catherine travelled south from her family home at North Elmham in Norfolk to marry the 18-year-old Lionel Tollemache of Helmingham Hall in Suffolk, her luggage likely contained valuable medieval manuscripts acquired by her great-grandfather Thomas from the great monastic libraries he had plundered. These would form the heart of a renowned library still treasured by the Tollemaches in their moated manor – a Tudor glory reminiscent of Hampton Court with its blazing brickwork, white stone windows and forest of chimneys.

As they welcomed Catherine Cromwell to Helmingham, the Tollemaches could never have imagined the polymath who had joined their ranks, nor the impact she would have on their family and the whole community. She would have cut a striking figure at once: statuesque, with pale skin and cool, appraising grey eyes, her thick dark hair curled in a high crown around her head as the Queen's was. And like Elizabeth too, Catherine wore a large ruff, her dress thick and luxurious with balloon slashed sleeves above wide skirts, rows of pearls dangling down to her pointed waist, jewelled gloves encasing nimble fingers. She was a devotee of fashion, summoning up expensive clothes from her London tailor who sent updates on each season's trends along with the latest court gossip.[59] While Catherine looked the part of the grand lady she also acted as one, behaving with piety, charity and lavishing love and loyalty on her husband and the many children she bore: 'Happy in wedlock' as her husband's monument describes his relationship with his 'faithful wife'.

But Catherine brought more than these traditional attributes of a high-status wife to Helmingham. Alongside the trunk of her great-grandfather's books, she brought Thomas's inquiring scholarly mind, formidable energy, practical talents and zeal for improvement. The library Catherine collated at Helmingham included medieval treasures like an illuminated breviary and a manuscript of *The Canterbury Tales* with family scribbles in the margins.[60] She asserted her personal claim to many of these volumes, inscribing them with her own distinctive ex-libris wording in her clear, rounded hand: 'Catheren Tallemache ow[n]eth this boocke.' Her choices, such as the reformist thinker Amandus Polanus's *The Substance of Christian Religion*, reflected her interest in new ideas. Catherine's most prized book was a *Book of Secrets* which bound 38 medieval manuscripts together into a guide for household management – an early forerunner of Mrs Beeton.[61] This contained published works on angling, trees and wine, as well as instructions for making laces, planting and grafting, restoring a dovecote, making gummed wax, tempering and mixing colours and ink, carving and making sauces for meat and fish, alongside the correct dimensions of a man's shirt and what a good hawk should look like. Academic primers mixed with the domestic, with pages containing mathematical terms, multiplication tables, the Ten Commandments and The Conclusion of Ptolemy. Most intriguing of all were the lists of 'charms, prognostications and recipes' to help with such challenges as becoming invisible, mind-reading, carrying fire with bare hands, knowing which eggs will produce cocks and hens, putting enemies to flight, catching snakes and escaping from sharks.

Catherine also collected 42 of her own recipes in a cookbook, each set out neatly and methodically. Many were fruit-based, using the produce of the Hall's extensive gardens, but others required exotic ingredients like pearls and unicorn's horn.[62] Rather than basic recipes for family meals, they were magical guides to create the luxurious delicacies which would elevate an ordinary meal to an extravagant banquet. Pomanders, perfumes and washing balls also featured which would have helped mask the pungent smells of early modern life, scenting the Hall instead with the fragrance of flowers. All of this Catherine saw not as a careless distraction but as vital daily work and she altered the layout of the Hall to accommodate it, converting a bedroom between her own and the nursery into a study and work-room where she could perfect her recipes. Here she occupied herself not only with culinary and household innovations, but with medical work too.[63] An unassuming, unbound and unnamed volume in the library contains instructions for 17 treatments, four of which were written by Catherine herself.[64] Catherine used these and other remedies working as a physician, becoming indispensable to her community until her death, aged sixty-four, in 1621. So much is clear from her remarkable memorial tabled in Helmingham Church which records: 'While she lived, for her piety towards God, pity toward the poor, and charity in relieving (through her skill and singular experience in surgery) the sick and sore wounded, [she] was beloved and honoured of all, as now missed and lamented in her death.'

Such an end contrasted strongly with Catherine's disgraced brother Baron Edward Cromwell's shameful exile in Ireland. Where Catherine had enhanced their family, Edward had alienated them. His uncle Thomas – the younger son of Gregory Cromwell who became a successful MP – spent his retirement in the frustrated, fruitless management of his nephew's crumbling estate of North Elmham before its eventual sale. As he made clear in his will, his own property near King's Lynn was 'inspired by evil debtors, losses sustained by death of cattle and sheep, bad bargains and my neglecting of mine own business for the following of the business of my brother and nephew'.[65] Brother and sister illustrate a recurring feature of the Cromwell family: often the male heirs who had custody of the family's name and fortune disappointed expectations, while their sisters who married into other families made great successes of their lives. As the historian Bishop Gilbert Burnet observed of Oliver Cromwell's children in the late seventeenth century 'those who wore breeches deserved petticoats better; but if those in petticoats had been in breeches they would have held faster'.[66] Never was this more true than with Catherine Tollemache, of all the Cromwells the truest inheritor of her great-grandfather Thomas Cromwell's intellectual prowess.

Over at Hinchingbrooke, another male Cromwell heir disappointed his more impressive sisters. Sir Henry Cromwell's five (legitimate) daughters made excellent marriages, moulding families which would come to be of great benefit to their nephew Oliver Cromwell who relied on them for advice and advancement. But – like his cousin and counterpart at the helm of the Launde Cromwells – Sir Henry's eldest son and heir was a gambler. This was Sir Oliver Cromwell: uncle, godfather and namesake to the future Lord Protector Oliver. Captured twice in oils, Sir Oliver Cromwell commands attention. The young man, painted in around 1580, poses haughtily, svelte and sophisticated in sombre black velvet, his ruff and cuff brilliant white folded against his pale, smooth skin. The old man, recorded in 1647, is as sharp-eyed and long-nosed, though the fashion then clothed him in a glossy, gold doublet beneath a draped white collar and orange jewelled sash. Gazing on these, it is easy to believe the royalist historian, cleric Thomas Fuller, who recorded that Sir Oliver Cromwell was famous for four things: his hospitality and prodigality in entertaining; his honesty in selling lands excessively cheaply; his longevity; and his loyalty to the Stuarts.[67]

After the family's traditional education at Queens' College, Cambridge and Lincoln's Inn, Sir Oliver was a regular fixture at court in the last years of Elizabeth I's reign. There he enjoyed the social scene and patronised the arts with the composer and lutenist John Dowland dedicating his *Second Book of Songs* to him in 1600.[68] But Sir Oliver had the misfortune of having to wait a long time for his aged father to die and was, by the late 1590s, likely to have been already several thousand pounds in debt. Selling off some inherited lands from his mother's family bought him some time, but it was his second marriage after the death of his first wife that brought the windfall he hoped would sustain him however long his tenacious father clung on to life. Sir Oliver's bride was a prize that must have made him the envy of London: Lady Anne Palavacino, the young Dutch-born widow of one of the wealthiest financiers and diplomats of the Elizabethan era, the colourful Italian Sir Horatio Palavacino, who lived in the great house at nearby Babraham.

No less a figure than Sir Robert Cecil himself – he who poor Baron Edward Cromwell of Launde was even then petitioning to no avail – had brokered the match in his position as overseer of Sir Horatio's will, making the unctuous recommendation to the widowed Anne that 'Mr. Oliver Cromwell, hath disposed his heart to seek you and deserve you not only by true affection but by offer and performance of all such conditions as may be consonant to the will of the dead and the desire of those that live, whose chiefest care must appear in the hindering of all courses which may prove to the prejudice of his children whose memory and trust we cannot forget . . .'

Sir Oliver Cromwell, he concluded, was eminently suited to Anne in view of his 'expectations, sufficiency, carriage and reputation.'[69] Cecil's concern for the departed Horatio's children, and certainty that Sir Oliver Cromwell was the man to protect their interests, were to be horribly misplaced. As both men were no doubt aware, the greatest prize Anne brought into the Cromwell family was her claim to the famed Palavacino debt. This was a vast sum of around £29,000 owed to Palavacino by Queen Elizabeth I arising from his contribution to her backroom financing of the Dutch in their insurgent war against the French and Spanish. Anne's claim to this money had technically fallen away on her remarriage, but such a detail would not stand in the way of her new husband who set about strengthening her claim through an audacious series of inter-marriages. These were not uncommon in a marriage market populated by widows and widowers with unmarried offspring.[70] Yet Sir Oliver's scheme was brazen even by the standards of the day.[71] Horatio and Anne's two young teenage sons were married to Sir Oliver Cromwell's two daughters by his first marriage. Later on, the remaining child, a daughter, was wedded to Sir Oliver's heir. Hemmed in by all of these marriage binds, there was no way the Palavacino fortune could escape.

Yet these manoeuvres were not enough to save the Cromwells' estate. Not when career preferment rested on lavish royal entertaining. Conveniently located on the Great North Road, Hinchingbrooke hosted the new King James I for two nights on his grand journey south from Scotland to take his throne in April 1603. The timing could not have been better as Sir Oliver had just splashed out on the new Great Bow Window at Hinchingbrooke: a magnificent two-floored edifice, with stained-glass and stone-carved depictions of the Cromwell and Williams heraldry. The whole structure had been topped by the royal arms of Queen Elizabeth I – surely one of the last depictions of these in the old Queen's lifetime. It would have been a fitting venue for entertaining the royal party on the very day of Queen Elizabeth's funeral: a visual reminder of this historic transitional moment from the Tudor to the Stuart age.

Old Sir Henry Cromwell was still alive to welcome his new sovereign, but his son Sir Oliver was effectively in charge and he set the bar unfortunately high for hosting the royal party.[72] At Hinchingbrooke, 'his Majesty with all comers whatsoever had such entertainment as the like had not been seen in any place before, since his first setting out of Scotland', a point James himself reportedly made to his hosts at his departure. It was a veritable free for all. 'There was such plenty and variety of meats, such diversity of wines, and those not riffe-ruffe but ever the best of the kind, and the cellars open at any man's pleasure.' Rich and poor alike feasted at the Cromwells' expense. 'As this bounty was held back to none within the house, so for such poor people as would not press in, there were open beer-houses erected wherein there was no want of bread or beef for the comfort of the poorest creatures.'

To the King, Sir Oliver presented 'many rich and acceptable gifts, [such] as a very great and a very fair wrought standing cup of gold, goodly horses, fleet and deep-mouthed hounds, diverse hawks of excellent wing, and at the remove gave fifty pounds amongst his Majesty's Officers'. It was a splendid occasion for the whole district, with the top brass from Cambridge University attending 'all clad in scarlet gowns and corner-caps', performing an Oration and offering gifts to the King (without missing the opportunity to request his confirmation of their charter and privileges). Old Sir Henry had won a knighthood from Elizabeth for her visit, so his son Sir Oliver was rewarded with a post of Gentleman of the Privy Chamber and a knighthood of the Bath at James's coronation.[73] So enthralled was James I by Hinchingbrooke that he visited again many times during his reign, as did his second son, the future King Charles I, such that a tradition grew that the boy prince Charles once quarrelled with his future nemesis Oliver Cromwell when they played in the grounds of the house as boys, the latter giving the young prince a bloody nose. As Mark Noble observed with delicate understatement: 'This was looked upon as a bad presage for that king when the civil wars commenced.'[74]

Judging by the lavish provision Sir Oliver made for James's first visit, it is unsurprising that many years of royal trips to Hinchingbrooke took their toll on the Cromwell family finances which were already depleted by the time of Sir Henry Cromwell's death in 1604. Bad luck also played a part. Sir Oliver successfully threw his political lot in with King James's eldest son and heir Prince Henry, securing the post of Master of the Prince's Game in 1611. It was a wise move: the popular Henry was a true Renaissance prince, now forging his own path away from his father by aligning himself with militantly Protestant and anti-Spanish politics. The Cromwell family might have fitted in well in this future, yet it was snatched away the following year when the young Henry died suddenly of typhoid, shortly after a visit to Hinchingbrooke. Sir Oliver's relationship with Prince Henry had been the closest this generation of Cromwells came to power, but his premature death left Sir Oliver in the political wilderness (and young, shy Prince Charles now heir to the throne). Hinchingbrooke, meanwhile, continued to delight King James with its fine hunting and he furthered his own pleasure at his regular autumn visits by enhancing its facilities, appointing a Keeper of the Wardrobe there, paying for a new bridge for his own use, and sending advance requests for dead pheasants (killed from the outer woods with those in the park left for him to hunt).

These high-handed interventions gave the increasingly desperate Sir Oliver hope that the King might wish to purchase the impoverished estate for himself. Around January 1623 he wrote to James offering his house for which he asked no more 'to buy, than a penny for a pennyworth'. His creditors were pressing and his friends thought him out of favour, he added, reminding the king that he was old and had to 'sustain the children, now grown up, whom he had bred for his Majesty's service'. A year later he begged for an answer or at the very least 'some token of favour that he may not retire with obloquy in his old age'.[75] James's death in 1625 put paid to Sir Oliver's plans, though he was accorded the honour of bearing one of the heraldic banners at the king's funeral.[76] In June 1627 he was forced instead to sell the family's crown jewel, Hinchingbrooke, to the up and coming Montagu family: a family which would play its own significant role in the extraordinary political events of succeeding years. Even this did not save the Cromwell family's future as Sir Oliver had ensnared his brothers in his financial troubles and their sons and his own would struggle to free themselves from the burden. For now, he downsized to his summer estate of Ramsey Abbey where he would continue to make trouble for his long-suffering family.

All this was an inglorious diminution to the landed life the bold, dashing Sir Richard Cromwell had established at Hinchingbrooke for his uncle Thomas's great house almost ninety years earlier, such that historian Lawrence Stone branded the Cromwells with Sir Oliver at their head 'a family of wastrels', noting a contemporary's observation in 1602: 'There lives a houseful at Hinchingbrooke, like a kennel.'[77] The Cromwells might equally deserve the judgement Stone made of the poor Palavacinos in his observation that swift social mobility once enjoyed could be as easily reversed: 'The children of the *nouveaux riches* all too often adopted the prodigal habits of those whom their father had exploited, and sank down again without a trace in two generations.'[78] The reckless streak within the Cromwell family's steadfast conservatism had undermined its foundations. Oliver had been born in the twilight years of his family's grandeur at the end of the Elizabethan golden age. As he grew to maturity in the Jacobean 1610s, the family position he inherited was but a shadow at sunset.

Three

Home

Feather-footed through the plashy fen passes the questing vole.

Evelyn Waugh, Scoop *(1938)*

Private years

Nestled between Brunelleschi's monumental Santo Spirito church and the bustling riverbank, in a narrow street in the Oltrarno district of Florence a few blocks from Niccolo Machiavelli's house, stands a grand palazzo: four stories of grey stone and pale plaster, its roof of overhanging wooden rafters just touched by the late afternoon sun. Huge lantern-framed wooden doors set in elegant archways provide passage from the busy street to the cool quiet of a courtyard garden, the church bells echoing softly off the whitewashed walls. It was here in one of these doorways that in the early 1500s the powerful Frescobaldi family, patrons of the arts, bankers and vintners to the princes of Europe, found a waif and stray begging charity – a youth washed 750 miles across Christendom from the shores of the Thames to the banks of the Arno.

'Frescobaldo seeing him so ill accoutred and noting signs of gentle breeding in his countenance, was moved to pity, more by token that he knew him to be English; and accordingly he asked him what countryman he was. He answered that he was English and Frescobaldo asking him divers particulars concerning England, as one who was thoroughly conversant therewith, the young man very aptly satisfied him of the whole, saying, "I am called Thomas Cromwell and am the son of a poor cloth dresser"'.

The masterless Thomas Cromwell had found himself a master. If this account sounds like fiction, that's because it is. The story of Thomas Cromwell's apprenticeship with the Frescobaldis in Florence was penned by the contemporary Italian novelist Matteo Bandello whose account was then reproduced and legitimised by historian John Foxe.[1] Bandello may have written with a degree of romantic licence, but there is little reason to doubt that Thomas spent some years in Florence in the service of the Frescobaldi family. As a friend reminded Thomas in 1539, he had often heard Cromwell say of the Florentines that he had 'been conversant amongst them'.[2] Explaining his destitution to Francesco Frescobaldo, Bandello's dramatised Thomas claims he had escaped from the Battle of Garigliano where he carried a pike for an infantryman in the French army.[3] If he was with the French for their calamitous defeat by the Spanish sixty miles north of Naples in December 1503, Thomas might well have joined their miserable march to Milan, detaching himself midway through the journey at Florence.[4]

Why had the youthful Thomas boarded a ship from England in the first place? Bandello's soldier of fortune explains that he 'fled from my father'. Foxe, using Bandello, shifts his translation to 'strayed from my country'. Ambassador Eustace Chapuys, meanwhile, claimed that Thomas Cromwell left England after a spell in prison.[5] Any or all of these could be true. Certainly, he did not harbour sufficiently antagonistic feelings towards his parents to prevent him offering prayers for them in his later will. Perhaps the most convincing explanation is one offered elsewhere by Foxe writing of Thomas that 'a great delight came into his mind to stray into foreign countries, to see the world abroad and to learn experience'.[6] With no access to formal education it stands to reason that Thomas would have sought other opportunities to enrol his bright and agile mind in the school of life.

And for a talented youth with an eye for figures, a gift for languages and a hunger for beauty and learning, there could be no better city at the turn of the sixteenth century than Florence. Florence in these years was at the height of its power and in the white heat of the Renaissance. Within the last decade the Republic had ousted the powerful Medici family and lived through the reactionary religious rule of the monk Savonarola and his Bonfire of the Vanities. The

Frescobaldis' neighbour Machiavelli was an influential official in the government, now a diplomat following the rampaging Cesare Borgia who would inspire his great work of political philosophy, *The Prince*. Michelangelo was sculpting his David for the Palazzo della Repubblica and trading smaller art works with the Frescobaldis for wine. The Frescobaldis, meanwhile, had fingers in every continent-wide pie from banking and the prestigious wine and cloth trades to the covert alum smuggling which had circumvented the papal monopoly to fill King Henry VII's coffers. For an autodidact like Thomas Cromwell, working in the Frescobaldi palace in Florence offered a priceless education.

Thomas soaked it all up, transforming from a wastrel boy to a Renaissance man. He was well suited to the task being, in Bandello's words, 'a youth of exceeding high spirit, quick-witted and prompt of resolution, knowing excellent well to accommodate himself to the wishes of others, and could, whenas him seemed to the purpose, dissemble his passions better than any man in the world. Moreover, he endured all bodily fatigue with patience . . .' Such skills must have proved useful in the Frescobaldi clerks' office and beyond. It is possible Thomas travelled with his master on business, notably to Venice where he trained in accounting. New evidence also places him in Padua at some point during these years, where it is likely he frequented academic circles and attended lectures at the university.[7] When Thomas eventually left the Frescobaldis' service, with a handsome parting gift of 16 gold ducats and a strong horse, it was to pursue his fortune in the Low Countries, most likely with the Frescobaldis' contacts in the cloth business there.[8] Thus a friend, writing in 1535, reminded Thomas of their first meeting, proclaiming 'the good love and true heart that have held unto you since the Syngsson Mart (Whitsun fair) at Middelburg in anno 1512'.[9] Although he had left the family's service, Thomas retained his affectionate loyalty to the Frescobaldis for the rest of his life and would later help them when their situations reversed and he was able to alleviate their financial difficulty.[10]

We can deduce some of what Thomas learned in these years abroad from his later life. His correspondence evidences the many languages he mastered: Italian and French; Spanish, at least to read; an understanding of Latin; and, unusually, some Greek. Chapuys commented later that Thomas 'speaks well in his own language, and tolerably in Latin, French, and Italian'.[11] Such language learning armoured Thomas to stand toe to toe with his later court rivals whose traditional education had been vastly superior to his own. His enemy Stephen Gardiner, Bishop of Winchester, later commented acidly that Thomas was often 'very stout' towards him 'for that conceit he had, what so ever he talked with me, he knew ever as much as I, Greek or Latin and all'.[12] Later commentators continued to be impressed by his skill, the Elizabethan intellectual Gabriel Harvey seeing in his self-education 'a Roman disposition', placing him in illustrious company with the generals and statesmen Gaius Marius and Julius Caesar as being of 'Small Learning, but nobly minded, and Industrious, with sufficiency of common wit, utterance, and experience'.[13]

Thomas's correspondence also testifies to his intellectual interests, particularly in history, theology, law, trade, economics and political philosophy. Letters with his cosmopolitan friends criss-crossed the continent, sharing books, objects and nuggets of information to delight the curious. Writers, eager to impress him and perhaps secure his patronage, sent him political treatises and elaborate Latin panegyrics. Many of the most accomplished authors of the day found in him a close friend, active patron and intellectual sounding board: theorists like the humanist Sir Thomas Elyot, his maintained scholar Richard Morison, and the gifted poet and diplomat Sir Thomas Wyatt who would stand with Thomas at his end. They likely shared the reformist writer Thomas Starkey's experience of finding a complex question unlocked through discussion with Thomas Cromwell, who customarily 'touched the string and knot of the matter': so much so that Starkey declared he possessed a wisdom rarely found among scholars, let alone men of business.[14] Thomas often sent friends and contacts to hunt down specific books or make translations. The dissolution provided ample opportunity for this. When one contact was mining the monastic documents at Ramsey Abbey with Richard Cromwell, for instance, he found a charter of King Edgar which would not only delight Thomas but help substantiate his quest to justify breaking with Rome and establishing the Royal Supremacy of Henry VIII.[15] But all this lay ahead of the young traveller.

❦ ❦ ❦

When Thomas eventually returned to England at some point in the mid-teens of the century, he had money in his pocket and invaluable professional skills on his CV: military experience, clerical, banking and accounting training, knowledge of the cloth trade and a valuable continental contact book. He would draw on all of this to astonishing effect once in government and would retain a pride in his commercial background: it was no accident that Thomas had Hans Holbein paint him holding a pair of scissors to signify his membership of the Merchant Taylors' Company. For now, setting himself up as a lawyer and money lender was the obvious next step once he returned to London, and Thomas soon acquired a respectable private practice for himself, notwithstanding his lack of formal legal training, securing a profitable pipeline of work and eventually membership of Gray's Inn.

Above all it was Thomas's love and knowledge of all things Italian that was central to his identity and 'much of Cromwell's early career rested on his ability to be the best Italian in all England'.[16] He enjoyed exchanging Italian literature with his friends, one of whom joked that 'As you wished to make me a good Italian some time since, by promising to lend me the "Triumphs of Petrarch", I beg you to send it . . . and specially if you have it, the Cortigiano [Castiglione's *The Book of the Courtier*] in Italian.'[17] Years later the Venetian government instructed its ambassador to approach 'the Magnifico Cromwell' to help renew their import of English wool because they did 'not doubt that the secretary will easily procure what they wish'.[18] Yet this familiarity with Italian culture also exposed Thomas to suspicion: his enemy Cardinal Reginald Pole painted him as the evil English disciple of Machiavelli who followed the teachings of *The Prince* in his handling of Henry VIII.[19]

Thomas's adopted Italian identity influenced his choice of home in London. After a spell living in Fenchurch Street, in September 1522 he moved to the north-east of the City which surrounded Austin Friars.[20] Here he could further his cloth business and legal practice in the commercial heart of the City while living among the Italians who formed a large part of Austin Friars' 'alien' community. Indeed, the church was known as an inclusive place for outsiders otherwise precluded sacred spaces and it is perhaps no coincidence – but an eerie foreshadowing – that its churchyard boasted a disproportionate number of traitors executed at nearby Tower Hill, including Henry VII's nemesis, the pretender Perkin Warbeck. When Thomas moved to Austin Friars the latest of these, the Duke of Buckingham, was barely cold in his grave.[21]

Thomas's Italian knowledge and connections also proved key to some of his early briefs as he set himself up as a merchant and lawyer. In 1514 he seems to have travelled back to Italy as an agent in an ecclesiastical dispute, staying at the English Hospice in Rome, visiting again in 1518–19, this time to represent Our Lady's Guild of Boston, Lincolnshire, in their appeal to Pope Leo X to defend their sale of indulgences against competitors – an ironic endeavour for the man who would go on to mastermind England's Reformation. Thomas put the long, arduous journey to good use, continuing his self-education by reportedly learning Erasmus's Latin translation of the New Testament by heart. Once he arrived, the means he used to win the Pope to his client's cause was emblematic of his ingenuity and flair for the original: learning of the Pope's sweet tooth he ambushed him out hunting, offering him English jellies he claimed only English kings and princes ate, accompanied by delightful madrigal singing.[22]

Thomas's Italian expertise may also have contributed to the single greatest step in his career to date in around 1524: entering the service of the king's chief minister, Cardinal Thomas Wolsey. The son of a tavern keeper from Ipswich, Wolsey was a brilliant scholar who had shone at Oxford before entering Henry VII's court as a chaplain. His many precocious talents led to diplomatic appointments and Wolsey swiftly made himself indispensable to Henry VIII when he came to the throne in 1509, handling much of the young king's workload, particularly foreign policy. By the time Thomas entered Wolsey's service, he had spent a year or so working for Thomas Grey, 2nd Marquess of Dorset – possibly through the introduction of his brother-in-law Morgan Williams. This too provided valuable career experience, with Thomas's remit likely to include close secretarial work on the Marquess's correspondence that would bring him into the heart of a powerful household.

Now approaching forty, the formidably useful Thomas Cromwell was an attractive addition to the Cardinal's payroll. The prompt for this was Wolsey's grand memorial project to commission a huge ornamental tomb for himself and establish a pair of Cardinal Colleges in his home town of Ipswich and former university of Oxford. Thus would the great man leave behind him a lasting legacy: places where future generations of scholars could access an education as he had done and pray for his immortal soul. A scheme on this scale needed considerable capital and this was to be provided through the closure of 29 small religious houses. This was not, as sometimes assumed, the first wave of monastic dissolution in service to the Reformation but a traditional means the Crown had previously used to fund new institutions and one endorsed by both the King and the Pope.

With his legal experience, Thomas Cromwell was well equipped to complete the complicated task of travelling the country overseeing this vast asset transfer. This he did with his customary energy and diligence for the next five years, building up an extensive knowledge of England's monastic community and establishing a wide network of friends and contacts across the increasingly splintering religious spectrum. His actions in closing some religious communities invoked local anger but, perhaps more surprisingly, his choices to reprieve or grant favours to others like Launde earned him their inhabitants' gratitude and friendship. But it was in the matter of Wolsey's elaborate tomb that Thomas's Italian know-how came into its own and the reason for his employment over any of the many other available London lawyers becomes clear. The tomb had been placed in the hands of a Florentine sculptor with fellow Italians handling the gilt work and involved in the financing. Thomas was ideally placed to move the project along.

Thomas Cromwell took the first step to establish his own family when he returned to London from Italy. At some point, probably in the late 1510s, he married Elizabeth Wyckes, who he probably met through local business connections.[23] Elizabeth may have been born into the Wyckes family, though the evidence for this is slim: a letter from one Harry Wyckes to Thomas referring to 'my sister and your good bedfellow' could have indicated Elizabeth was Harry's sister-in-law or stepsister as well as a blood sister.[24] She may instead have been born Elizabeth Prior as her mother was known as Mistress Mercy Prior, but this may indicate that Mercy had remarried by this time and that Prior was the name of Elizabeth's stepfather. Perhaps Elizabeth's maiden name was something else entirely.[25]

We glimpse the nature of Thomas and Elizabeth's marriage in autumn 1525 when Thomas sent his wife the carcass of a roe deer he had slain while indulging in some recreation on a business trip to Kent. Elizabeth was no doubt touched at his gesture for, not only was this privately sourced venison a luxury for her larder, but the gift was also a love token. Available only from royal or private deer parks, venison was a highly prized present among the Tudor elite and one with romantic overtones, hunting being an allegory for the courtly chase of a lover.[26] Thomas's future employer Henry VIII himself would later use the same gift in this way, sending a deer carcass to Anne Boleyn during their courtship with the felicitation 'And to cause you yet oftener to remember me, I send you by the bearer of this a buck, killed late last night by my own hand, hoping that when you eat of it you may think of the hunter.'[27]

Thomas Cromwell's missive was rather more business-like, opening 'Elizabeth I commend me unto you and have sent you by this bearer a fat doe.' Yet his affection for the addressee whom he described as 'my well beloved wife Elizabeth' is clear. Not only was Elizabeth the object of his love and generosity, she was also the recipient of his trust and his partner in business. For the letter asked her to deliver half of the doe to a useful contact, to pass a message to another friend, to send news back to Thomas via the deer delivery man and, lastly, 'to send me word in writing who hath resorted unto you since my departure from you to speak with me'. Elizabeth, it seems, was an educated woman entrusted with her husband's confidences and deemed capable of managing his affairs while he was away.[28]

As the sole surviving exchange between Thomas and Elizabeth Cromwell, this short letter is required to do some heavy lifting, standing in for all our lost knowledge of their relationship. All we can know is that the Cromwell marriage appeared happy and fruitful, with the couple having three children within a few years: a son, Gregory, and two daughters, Anne and Grace. Thomas was a generous father devoted to his children's welfare. The will he drafted in 1529 specified sums for both his daughters' and son's education when they came of age or married.[29] Thomas took meticulous care, even when consumed by affairs of state, to ensure his only son Gregory enjoyed the educational opportunities he never had; not for Gregory the 'knowledge gathered by painful travail' of his father.[30] His education was the best that money could buy (and a rich contact book could supply).

For the most upwardly mobile Tudor gentlemen of considerable means, this took the form of private tuition and placements in socially superior households. Young boys from wealthy families were often placed in the care of distinguished career women and it is telling that Thomas chose his good friend, the formidable administrator Margaret Vernon, Prioress of the Benedictine nunnery at Little Marlow, to oversee Gregory's early education under a succession of tutors. Her letters to Thomas reveal an intimate friendship and respectful working collaboration through both their careers. 'She relied on him, she asked him for favors, but she also paid him and socialized with him, suggesting a relationship of some complexity.'[31] Margaret was not afraid to cross swords with Thomas when she disagreed with him, most notably over Thomas's decision in 1528 to transfer Gregory to Cambridge.

Her letter of complaint also reveals the misdating of Gregory's birth which has persisted down the centuries up until only the last few years. Previously, historians had assumed Gregory was born in 1516 and branded him a dunce for his childish scrawl and perceived lack of academic prowess when it had been assumed he was a teenager. But Margaret berated Thomas for moving Gregory when he had promised her the care of him until he was twelve. This, and other evidence from Thomas's archive, suggests a birth year of at least 1519 and more likely 1520 for Gregory, meaning the hand of the teenager was in fact the hand of a much younger boy.[32] In fact, while initially described by his tutors as 'rather slow, but diligent', after a few months Thomas received word that 'Little Gregory is becoming great in letters'.[33] Yet if Gregory was not the idiot of historical assumption, neither did he show the astonishing intellectual prowess of his father.

Thomas's primary home of Austin Friars was the heart of his family life. The building complex of Austin Friars was a several-acre site probably dating from the 1260s, its church a landmark of the north side of the City, being 'a large Church, having a most fine spired steeple, small, high, and straight'.[34] As the church stood long before Thomas Cromwell found a home in its precinct, so it lived for centuries after him, surviving the dissolution by transforming into a 'Dutch Church' gifted to religious refugees from the Germanic portions of the Holy Roman Empire by King Edward VI. And so it might stand still if not for another German visitor – this time a parachute mine which destroyed it in October 1940. The Friary leased tenements and parcels of its land to the public and it was one of these, sited on Throgmorton Street on the south-west side of Austin Friars Church and close to the Friary gatehouse, that Thomas leased. Thomas invested heavily in his home and neighbourhood, swiftly joining the Broad Street wardmote, a community group concerned with local safety and sanitation, and getting involved in local justice.[35] Over the next 20 years he would transform his Austin Friars home, pushing back neighbours' fences and gobbling up their properties, even moving one out of the way on rollers.[36] This quadrupled its size, making Austin Friars one of the very grandest private homes in London, in keeping with his exalted status: a 'fair' house 'very large and spacious, built in the place of old and small Tenements by Thomas Cromwell'.

For his first decade there, though, the house remained the same size, with fourteen rooms in three wings over three floors, a cellar and large attic. Recent research on the building together with the contemporary inventory of its contents has reconstructed its layout, with the main reception rooms on the ground floor facing the churchyard.[37] Chief of these was the parlour, decorated with red and green hangings, carpets on the floor and in the great glass window, carved and gilt wainscotting, a screen and wooden painted panels, including one of Cardinal Wolsey's coat of arms. A 'cloth stained with the images of a man and a woman, lovers' hung alongside traditional religious images to reflect Thomas's cultured tastes to his guests. Furnished with a long table and seats and 'a pair of playing tables of wood and bone', this room would have been the venue for intimate meals, after-dinner games and entertainments.

These were a regular feature of life at Austin Friars whose open, social nature reflected that of its master, who his neighbour and regular guest Eustace Chapuys described as 'hospitable, liberal both with his property and with gracious words'.[38] Day to day the house welcomed Thomas's expanding circle of business colleagues and public intellectuals becoming in effect a salon with dinner-time 'an occasion for learned discourse', usually along reformist lines. So a conservative lawyer later thanked Thomas for invitations to his 'board, divers dinners and suppers, where he heard such conversations as was the very cause of his conversion'.[39] In the years to come a veritable who's who of Tudor society would pass through Austin Friars' revolving doors for cosy dinners or lavish parties, including the King himself. Larger feasts and meals for the wider household probably took place in the hall next door to the parlour with its grand gallery and buttery for storing dinnerware and serving food. This too was decorated with hangings, carpets and cushions decorated with Tudor red roses, a Flanders mirror and paintings adorning the walls, including – intriguingly – one of the Holy Roman Emperor Charles V; a choice which no doubt pleased Chapuys as the Emperor's ambassador.

Thomas's time abroad had bequeathed him cosmopolitan tastes and a particular appreciation for Flanders craftsmanship.[40] Other specific objects with decorative details give touching glimpses of real lives lived: the painted image of a foal to hold a towel; the figure of a dragon and a leopard; a little bottle of rosewater. Thomas's love of travel, fine art and hard work emerge from two world maps and a tapestry depicting 'Occupation and Idleness'. It is in the inventory of the private chambers and bedrooms on the first and second floors that we catch the fleeting female presence so often elusive in other sources: 'a woman's "round" gown, furred with squirrel', 'a coif of Venice gold', '3 women's purses, of cloth of gold', 'needlework, wrought with an antelope'. Here too we find precious objects which would have delighted the three Cromwell children: ribbons, pearls and buttons, two coral beads, 'a relic closed in crystal, garnished with silver and gilt, like a fish', 'a silver gilt brooch of Gregory's'.

Rich clothes and jewels worn by the men and women of the family speak of fine living and Thomas's professional eye for tailoring. Gowns, frocks, doublets, nightgowns, coats and capes in myriad colours of velvet, damask and satin are lined with rabbit, lamb, squirrel, fox, sable and marten. Chests overflow with linen, handkerchiefs, purses, caps, hoods, gloves, jerkins and hose; knives, daggers and swords the finishing touches for a Tudor gentleman. More than any item, it is the Cromwells' large collection of rings that signals their comfortable wealth and status. Twenty-eight rings are itemised, mostly gold with engraved images or precious stones – rubies, diamonds, emeralds and jacinths – with three of them listed as being on Thomas's fingers on the June day in 1527 when the inventory was carried out.[41]

Thomas could afford all this thanks to the substantial income he drew from his commercial legal practice and work for Cardinal Wolsey. Generous hearted, he spread his success widely among his kin, sponsoring their education, finding them employment and often inviting them to make their home within his. Thomas's mother-in-law Mercy Prior lived with him in considerable comfort with a richly appointed chamber as a much loved and respected member of Thomas's inner circle, appearing frequently in the letters of his correspondents who send their good wishes or requests to her through him.[42] She was also a talented pharmacist with one friend asking Thomas 'to ask my mistress your mother for another plaster for my knee' and another crediting her next only to God as the reason for his good health. That Thomas's great friend and trusted man of business Stephen Vaughan could write to him that Mercy was 'after you my most singular friend' testifies to a sincere partnership and true friendship between son-in-law and mother-in-law.[43]

Housing a widowed mother or mother-in-law was not uncommon at the time, but the rarer aspect of life at Austin Friars was Thomas's close relationship with the families of his two sisters and sister-in-law. At one time or other, Thomas's sister-in-law Joan and her husband John Williamson and Thomas's own sister Elizabeth and her husband William Wellyfed lived at or close to Austin Friars, probably with their various children. John Williamson earned his keep in the early 1530s by serving Thomas as comptroller of his household, overseeing its provision and building works as well as various financial matters. So Thomas received a report in 1532 when he was away that 'Your household are well, including your mother-in-law, your brother-in-law and his wife, and your trusty servant Williamson, who takes great pains to accomplish your pleasure. Your brother-in-law also calls on the workfolks daily. The steward and the rest of your servants do their duties well.'[44]

Alongside adopting his late sister and brother-in-law Katherine and Morgan Williams' son Richard, Thomas also provided for his Wellyfed nephews and niece. He paid for the boys to be educated alongside Gregory at Cambridge, sending them presents and parcels of cloth for new warm clothes in the winter months, and visiting them when his punishing workload allowed.[45] This education led to careers in the church sponsored by the boys' mentor, Thomas's friend Rowland Lee who had by then become Bishop of Coventry and Lichfield.[46] The Wellyfeds' sense of obligation to their uncle ran deep, as William wrote to him when he was struggling at university apologising for wasting his time and money and explaining that he 'Never thinks about the kindness of his uncle Cromwell without blaming himself for not taking more pains to preserve his honour and fulfil his duty.'[47] Young Alice Wellyfed meanwhile was helped to a position in the household of the boys' tutor by her uncle, whose suggestion of the arrangement makes clear his sense of financial responsibility. 'Let me send my sister's daughter unto the gentlewoman your wife, to bring up,' he wrote in 1529, 'for which I well reckon myself much bound to you and her; and, besides the payment of her board, will so content her that I trust she will be well pleased.'[48] Thomas later arranged for Alice to marry his ward Thomas Rotherham.[49] Joan and John Williamson's single child Joan also benefited from her association with her uncle, growing up to marry well.[50] That all of these nephews and nieces were mentioned by name in Thomas's will, and bequeathed valuable items and sums of money, shows their importance in his life. Indeed, in his will Thomas explicitly defines 'my poor kinsfolk' as the children of his two sisters and sister-in-law.[51]

It was not only children related to him by blood who Thomas took under his wing. As he grew in Cardinal Wolsey's trust, Thomas found himself shepherding Wolsey's three illegitimate children, answering their regular pleas for advice and funds; something he continued to do even after Wolsey's death. He clearly suited this avuncular role which he assumed throughout the rest of his life for a multitude of young people from servants, clerks and family friends to distressed wives, widows and daughters and the King's own bastard Henry Fitzroy. Dearest of these to Thomas was Ralph Sadler who entered the Cromwell household a fair-haired, blue-eyed boy, possibly slight in stature given the later assessment of him that 'little was his body but great his soul'.[52]

Born in 1507, possibly in Warwickshire but now hailing from Hackney, Ralph probably came to Thomas's attention thanks to his father's service as steward to the Marquess of Dorset. He joined Thomas's household at some point probably in the 1510s and certainly by 1521. Quick to perceive Ralph's fierce intelligence, tact and loyalty, Thomas gave him the education at Austin Friars that he himself had received in the Frescobaldi palace in Florence. Over the following years he trained Ralph in Latin, Greek and French, finance, law and politics until at 19 he was ready to become Thomas's principal secretary and right arm, even trusted to be an executor of Thomas's will. Ralph knew his good fortune, years later describing his master as 'him that hath hitherto from the years of discretion nourished brought up and advanced him' (a fact also proclaimed proudly on his magnificent tomb).[53] But neither man could have foreseen the grand and powerful public lives ahead of them both, nor the mortal danger Ralph would face to repay his debt to the man who raised him. For the 1520s were private years with no thought or ambition for public office: quiet prosperity in his legal practice and the Cardinal's service might easily have been the summit of Thomas Cromwell's career.

Reading books and men

Oliver Cromwell too lived a private life into his early forties, with barely a look beyond the flat fenland horizon. Like Thomas, all of his energies as a young man were directed at building a life which could provide for a large household of dependants. The bricks and mortar for this were the same a century on: education, inheritance, income, investments, property, marriages and children. First came education, and in that the gentrified Oliver benefited from what Thomas had not – school. This was the free grammar school by the marketplace in Huntingdon, a few minutes' walk from Oliver's home. The school occupied a grand stone-arched building of one vaulted room, the last remains of a twelfth-century hospital for travellers and pilgrims, which today houses the Cromwell Museum.

Also the alma mater of Samuel Pepys, Huntingdon grammar school was presided over at the time by the Cambridge graduate and cleric Dr Thomas Beard, author of the 1587 bestseller, the well-named *The Theatre of God's Judgements*.[54] Its pages provide some insight into the man who dominated Oliver's early educational years, conjuring a world familiar to those acquainted with the adult Oliver's mental landscape: a world where God is thunderingly present and interventionist; where 'providences' reveal His motives; and rulers are subject to judgement in this world, not simply the next. Beard was clearly a close friend to the whole Cromwell family, not least to Oliver's uncle, the rakish Sir Oliver Cromwell of Hinchingbrooke, to whom Beard dedicated his next book.[55] Yet young Oliver himself had an uneasy relationship with his schoolmaster who was more of a 'greedy pluralist' hoovering up lucrative posts than a simple, devout puritan.[56] This came to a head in the 1630s when Oliver acted against Beard in local politics, falling out with the worthies of Huntingdon over various issues including an endowment which involved Beard's town lectureship.

Oliver went on to study at Cambridge University, enrolling at Sidney Sussex, a new college built on the site of a former Grey Friars monastery only three years older than Oliver himself. This may have been because Sidney Sussex's fees were cheaper, a key consideration for Oliver's father Robert who was much less wealthy than those in his older brother Sir Oliver's senior branch of the family. Nevertheless, Robert still had to stump up for the requisite gift of silverware to secure Oliver's place as a 'fellow commoner', effectively a gentleman student, rather than a 'sizar' like Pepys who received a meaner board and lodging, sometimes with financial assistance in return for service work.[57] Sidney Sussex's close association with the gold standard of Puritan colleges, Emmanuel, upon whose statutes its own were modelled, may also have added to its appeal for Robert, suggesting he leaned towards a Puritan outlook, though his son's own fervent Puritanism still lay ahead of him. At this point, the overwhelming majority of Puritans were committed supporters of the Church of England, though their place within it was coming under increasing pressure. In its evangelical independence, Sidney Sussex stood at the forefront of the university revolution Thomas Cromwell had started a century earlier. In the coming years it proved a headache to the traditional ceremonialist Archbishop of Canterbury William Laud whose 1636 report on the college noted 'They have no Consecrated Chapel; they read the Lessons after an order of their own & not as they are appointed in the calendar. And much like Emmanuel for the rest.'[58]

Oliver cultivated some friendships at Cambridge – with Henry Downhall, fellow of St John's, who Oliver later asked to be godfather to his third son, and probably others who would go on to fight or work alongside him in his later career.[59] For Oliver's greatest delight, in the words of his biographer Samuel Carrington, was in 'reading men rather than books' – a talent which, perhaps more than any other, propelled him to the highest office in the land.[60] His natural intelligence lay out in a world where he 'showed stronger evidence of thinking, ruminating and meditating than reading voraciously' in an unusual character which combined extreme physicality with spiritual questioning.[61] His worldly, pragmatic approach to problem-solving was a trait he shared with Thomas for all the latter's learning, and would at times pit both men against the donnish scholarship of some of their more extensively educated peers.

We know next to nothing of the content of the education Oliver received at school or Cambridge, beyond the assumption that it covered the standard humanist curriculum of Latin, Greek, mathematics and history which had developed from Thomas Cromwell's reforms. This was a sufficient, if not expansive, educational foundation for a member of the lesser gentry but far from adequate for a future head of state. As Lord Protector, Oliver bemoaned the paucity of his education, sharing his limitations openly in his customarily self-deprecating manner. Financial matters, he told his second Parliament in 1657, were 'exceedingly past my understanding (for I have as little skill in Arithmetic, as I have in the Law)'.[62] He complained to the Swedish ambassador that 'it was a matter of grief to him that he had been so ill-educated that he scarcely ventured to speak any other language than English'.[63] This accords with the somewhat scathing judgement of Gilbert Burnet, writing later, that Oliver had been handicapped by 'the roughness of his education and temper' which had left him with no foreign language besides 'a little Latin that stuck to him from his education, which he spoke very viciously and scantily'.[64] Oliver's geography was little better: the Brandenburg envoy, to whom Oliver admitted his lack of knowledge of the Baltic, helped him with a lecture and maps.

Later detractors latched onto this, circulating hostile stories of Oliver's student years to belittle and besmirch him as a rough-hewn philistine. Thus his most critical biographer, James Heath, asserted that during Oliver's time at university 'he was more famous for his exercises in the Fields than in the Schools'.[65] Oliver was certainly no natural scholar as Thomas had been, for all John Milton would later praise his 'native vastness of intellect'.[66] One searches in vain for evidence of his reading any books in particular beyond his beloved Bible and the Elizabethan hero Sir Walter Raleigh's *History of the World* which he once pressed upon his wayward son Richard, writing to advise him in 1650 to 'Recreate your self with Sir Walter Raleigh's history, it's a body of history, and will add much more to your understanding, then fragments of story.'[67] But Oliver did consider a passing acquaintance with other fields of study desirable, as he suggested to Richard's father-in-law who was mentoring the young man while he was 'in the dangerous time of his age', 'I would have him mind and understand business, read a little history, study the mathematics and cosmography, these are good with subordination to the things of God, better than idleness, or mere outward worldly contents, these fit for public services for which a man is born.'[68]

Oliver did not take his own advice; unlike Thomas, he was no autodidact. His was, however, an active, enquiring mind open to inspiration. Oliver found this as a young man, not only in Raleigh but in the great Queen Elizabeth I, whose reluctance to open 'windows into men's souls' he shared, and who he described to Parliament as 'Queen Elizabeth of famous memory, we need not be ashamed to say so'. [69] Further afield, Oliver was captivated by the European Protestant hero, the 'Lion of the North' King Gustavus Adolphus of Sweden. Later as Lord Protector, he recalled the 'glorious memory' of the great man, telling the Swedish ambassador that: 'being then a private person, he nevertheless had always followed his campaigns with the greatest pleasure, had many times thanked God, with tears of joy in his eyes, for His gracious mercies, and when the tidings came of his death, had so mourned it that he could scarcely believe that any Swede could mourn it more bitterly'.[70]

Perhaps another year or two studying at Cambridge would have given Oliver a greater aptitude for study, but it was not to be. After only a year there, in 1617 the 18-year-old Oliver put away childish things forever to enter into his new season. His father Robert Cromwell had died suddenly and Oliver was summoned home to step into his boots to care for his widowed mother and seven sisters, three older than him and four younger. His was a lonely duty – as the middle and only surviving brother of three – but Oliver had a devoted partner with whom to manage this entirely female household in his mother Elizabeth Cromwell, née Steward. Mother and son shared a deep bond, living together for all or nearly all of the rest of her long life. Years later, Oliver apologised for failing to deliver his son's long negotiated marriage deed in person to his new in-laws by explaining 'truly my aged mother is in such a condition of illness, that I could not leave her with satisfaction'.[71] Their devotion was increased by the early years they had to work closely together to steer the family ship, not least because Oliver's father Robert had made Elizabeth sole executrix of his will and left two thirds of his estate to her to provide for Oliver's sisters.

One sister, Margaret, had just made an advantageous marriage to local landowner and Oliver's childhood friend Valentine Walton, a ward of Oliver's uncle Sir Oliver of Hinchingbrooke. Oliver's other sisters – possibly Joan and certainly Elizabeth, Katherine, Anna, Jane and Robina – were still at home. Sister Elizabeth would never leave, remaining close to Oliver for the rest of her life and living out her final years after his death with Oliver's son Henry. A letter from Oliver to her in 1651 testifies to their warm relationship, with £20 enclosed 'as a small token of my love', and with Oliver signing himself 'your affectionate brother'.[72] Oliver's other sisters were also fond of him. His 'best beloved sister' Katherine once said of him 'I have a brother tenders me as dearly as a brother can do'. When living with him later in life, she was reportedly persuaded by a Royalist to carry a message to her brother in the next room. After she and Oliver spoke, she 'came back with tears in her eyes, saying that he was the dearest brother in the world, and she would never forgive herself if through her means any injury should befall him'.[73]

Katherine, Anna, Jane and Robina all married, two of them twice. Their early marriages, if a strain for Oliver to arrange, brought him an extended local network of gentry families he thereafter considered his kin and whom he would help to promote. His brothers-in-law fought alongside him in the Civil War, with Jane's husband John Desborough, from a minor gentry family of Eltisley in Cambridgeshire, rising to become a major-general and member of Oliver's Protectoral Council of State. For Oliver, his sisters, brothers-in-law, nieces and nephews were key figures in his life with many of the women and children living with him at various times of spinster- or widowhood, their fortunes hitched to his own. Like Thomas he had a talent for friendship and an indulgent spirit which delighted in gathering waifs and strays and providing for those to whom he felt some responsibility, particularly women in distress. This was a habit that stayed with him so that in 1651 he reportedly invited the family of his devoted, late French manservant to live with his own.[74]

The position young Oliver inherited in 1617 was financially precarious. With an income of probably only £100–£200 a year, a lean urban portfolio of business interests inherited from his father (chiefly the collection of tithes) and occasional election to minor local town offices, his was not a gentlemanly life of leisure. Later commentators would paint a picture of an uncouth, bumptious and town-dwelling Oliver cut adrift from his wealthier (and later royalist) country relations. The hostile James Heath told a scurrilous story of Oliver embarrassing his uncle Sir Oliver at his customary Christmas festivities at Hinchingbrooke by smearing excrement on himself and the capering Lord of Misrule who had him thrown in the pond. In so doing, Heath claimed, 'Oliver had run himself out of that little Patrimony he had, and brought his Mother to the same near ruin'.[75]

Yet this calculated smear upon Cromwell family dynamics rings hollow, particularly in the case of Oliver's aunts – Sir Henry Cromwell's five daughters – whose marriages into a social echelon higher than Oliver's sisters' husbands furthered his opportunities beyond the limits of Huntingdon. Many of these families produced future Parliamentarian leaders. Oliver would, in due course, find inspiration in his cousin, the ship money warrior and Parliamentarian grandee, John Hampden. Another cousin, Edward Whalley, would be a key ally throughout Oliver's career. So too Oliver's Cambridge contemporary, the lawyer Oliver St John, who twice married Oliver's cousins.[76] Oliver's aunt Joan – who in 1579 had married Sir Francis Barrington of Hatfield Broad Oak in Essex – was a particular pillar to her nephew and likely introduced him to the woman who above all others would undergird the life that awaited him, his wife Elizabeth Bourchier.

The Barringtons probably knew the wealthy Bourchier family from their shared social life in Essex where Elizabeth's grandfather, a fur and leather trading merchant, had used his London profits to buy up a country residence at Little Stambridge. Theirs was a not dissimilar story of rising gentility to that of the Cromwells, illustrated by the fact that Sir James Bourchier and Oliver's uncle Sir Oliver Cromwell were both knighted by King James I at his coronation. The successful, mercantile Bourchiers with their lucrative London connections were an appealing match for this scion of provincial Cromwells, just as the similar Murfyns, Warrens and Palavacinos had been for his Hinchingbrooke uncle, grandfather and great-grandfather. It was Sir James Bourchier and his wife Frances Crane who brought the latest in this line of London brides, their eldest daughter, 23-year-old Elizabeth, to marry the (just) 21-year-old Oliver at St Giles Cripplegate in the City of London on 22 August 1620.

Oliver's relative youth as a bridegroom may suggest a degree of ardour between the couple beyond that of a purely arranged match. This would not have been unlikely as, in these moderately Puritan circles, great care was usually taken in arranging marriages to ensure there was a compatibility and liking between the couple as a happy marriage was considered the foundation of a successful and godly life. Moreover, whatever its social benefits for him, the marriage cannot have arisen out of a pure and immediate financial need on Oliver's part as he does not seem to have received a dowry but rather himself settled a substantial marriage jointure on his wife. Returning to Huntingdon, his new bride would simply be one more woman to support in his large, female household. Her obvious contribution was what contemporary Puritan commentary and subsequent historians pruriently labelled the 'benefit of the bed', the proof of which was in her speedy and regular production of the couple's first seven children: Robert (1621), Oliver (1623), Bridget (1624), Richard (1626), Henry (1628), Elizabeth (1629) and James (1632). To this has traditionally been added her obvious abilities as a homemaker and helpmeet whose steady quietness in private enabled her husband's turbulent brilliance in public. Most writers have left their analysis of the woman who would go on to be England's *de facto* queen there, content to keep within the confines of what has been dubbed the 'dull Elizabeth school of thought'.[77]

There was, however, much more to Elizabeth Bourchier than this. The letters that survive between her and Oliver attest to their love: he wrote to her once with very little to say but explaining that he could not let the post go without sending something to her as 'I love to write to my dear who is very much in my heart'; Elizabeth in turn wrote 'Truly my life is but a half-life in your absence.'[78] The fact that as Lord and Lady Protectoress the couple broke with royal tradition to share rooms in the royal palaces speaks further of their closeness and determination to preserve the intimacy of their hitherto ordinary married life amid their monarchical transformation. Elizabeth even took her love for her husband beyond her own projected death, reportedly suggesting during his Protectorate that he should marry Queen Christina of Sweden if anything happened to her – a suitable bride for his new station.[79]

Beyond romantic love and affection, Elizabeth's surviving letter to Oliver when he was away on campaign reveals a strong woman, aware of her own mind and confident expressing this as an equal partner. Thus she chides Oliver for daring to criticise her for not writing often enough (itself betraying his fondness for her) when it is he who neglects to write to her, as she puts it 'when I have sent three for one: I cannot but think they are miscarried'.[80] The same letter contains pointed reminders of influential men within the Commonwealth Oliver should write to – men 'of whom I have often put you in mind'. In the second of the three surviving letters from Oliver to Elizabeth, written while he was in Scotland in 1651, he cautioned her against one colleague should he visit her often and commissioned her to instruct another on 'the Business of my Estate' on his behalf.[81] We glimpse Elizabeth's hand in family business again in one of Oliver's letters to the intermediary handling his son Richard's marriage, in which he reported his recent negotiation with the bride's father. Concerning some family lands in Cambridgeshire and Norfolk his counterparty was angling for, Oliver carefully avoided making any offer of these because 'I desired to be advised by my wife.'[82] Once Oliver's public profile and career grew, so too did Elizabeth's, transforming this genteel and capable housewife into a woman of national power and influence; so much so that she became a lightning rod for debate and satire, her very wifely qualities weaponised against her as the personification of a paradoxical regime which was too republican for Royalists and too royalist for republicans.

As parents, Oliver and Elizabeth raised a large, close-knit family. Their sons and daughters grew up to be strong personalities, forthright in their sometimes conflicting views, but always with a sense of shared belonging – their language of loving nicknames, gossip and in-jokes the timeless currency of ordinary siblings. Yet family life was tested almost from the outset. It was only seven years into Oliver and Elizabeth's marriage that Sir Oliver Cromwell sold the debt-ridden Hinchingbrooke. As his humiliated uncle removed the powerful Cromwell name and its patronage from Huntingdon, so Oliver struggled to maintain his own standing in the town, selling two pieces of land that year that had belonged to his family for three generations.[83] The new family now at Hinchingbrooke, the Montagus, initially accommodated him in their new fiefdom, allowing Oliver the junior seat of the two representing Huntingdon in the Parliament of 1628–9, perhaps as a sop to the departing Sir Oliver. This gave the impecunious, provincial Oliver his first taste of Westminster politics and brought him into the ambit of the coalition forming in opposition to royal policy – a group which included a number of his own relations through his aunts. Yet it was also a frustrating episode where Oliver achieved little beyond making one speech and sitting on a few committees before King Charles I's peremptory dissolution packed him back to hostile Huntingdon, his horizon shrinking once more.

There he picked a fight with the town leaders over the oligarchic powers vested in them by the new town charter from which he and his (to his mind) less self-interested and venal friends had been excluded. Hauled before the Privy Council in London to answer for his behaviour, Oliver found himself remanded in custody, before the investigator – none other than Hinchingbrooke's new owner Edward Montagu, Earl of Manchester – ruled that he make a public apology for his ungentlemanly behaviour in the marketplace, though he did find for Oliver on some of the substantive issues. Humiliated beyond repair, Oliver sold his family home and other properties in Huntingdon and moved his wife and children five miles east to the smaller settlement of St Ives. There he at least had the prospect of fellowship: Henry Downhall became vicar there later that same year and the lord of the manor from whom Oliver leased his land was Henry Lawrence, a man Oliver knew and respected who would become a staunch ally, eventually serving as President of his Council of State. It seems one at least of his sisters came with him, for Jane Cromwell appears in the manor records, but his mother possibly remained behind, living now as a tenant in the house she had previously owned and keeping an eye on the family's 17 remaining acres in the town.[84] If so, it would not be the last time her beloved son changed his living circumstances in a way she struggled with. For his dependent family, life with Oliver was to exist at the extremes.

Faith and suffering

Oliver Cromwell's time in St Ives transformed his life. For it was in this quiet corner of the fens that he heard the omniscient voice which would direct his future. He was not the first to find God here. In the early years of the first millennium a ploughman uncovered the bones of the Celtic Christian bishop and hermit Ivo. These were enshrined in Ramsey Abbey, where Ivo remained in peace until 1540 when

Thomas Cromwell's nephew Richard carried off its stones to remodel his nearby stately home of Hinchingbrooke. The town, which had been called Slepe, took the name of St Ives in his honour and retained a spirituality into Oliver's lifetime and beyond.[85]

The journey to spiritual awakening always requires hardship. To Oliver, travelling from the familiar security of Huntingdon to St Ives would have seemed like the experience of Christ entering the wilderness. And here Oliver would indeed be tested. The motto of the town he moved to in 1631 was *Sudore non Sopore*, namely 'By Sweat not Sleep': a word play marrying an exhortation to hard work with a call-back to the town's former name. It was an appropriate instruction for the downwardly mobile Cromwell sliding towards a life of toil. In Huntingdon, particularly while his uncle had remained the local bigwig, Oliver had still managed – just – to live as the Jacobean gentleman he had been raised. But those days were gone. In one of his earliest surviving letters, written in the year he moved to St Ives, his shifting status lurks between the lines. The letter concerns a stray hawk which had been found and traced back to Oliver as she was wearing a metal ring with his name. Hunting with a hawk was a popular pursuit for country gentlemen in the early decades of the seventeenth century, and one Oliver had clearly enjoyed in his youth when he flew his own, named birds. Yet now Oliver was forced to admit that the bird was not his but being flown by another 'poor man' of Huntingdon who 'made use of' his rings. Even were the bird his, Oliver could not collect it, 'being utterly destitute of a falconer at this present, and not having any man home I durst venture to carry a hawk of that kind so far'.[86]

Oliver no longer had the means for leisure activities or spare servants. Instead, he was now at the lowest ebb of his life, working as a tenant farmer, possibly keeping sheep. The house he likely rented, Slepe Hall, was probably fairly comfortable, the farming land about it rich in fenland nutrients. Yet his rank, as noted in occasional local records, had sunk from 'esquire' in Huntingdon to 'Mr' in St Ives, and life as a yeoman farmer in and out of trouble with the authorities was precarious.[87] This decline made Oliver vulnerable in his own time and since, as such fleeting appearances in official registers became an archival battleground where his shadowy early life could be easily manipulated. Two entries in the Huntingdon parish register in the 1620s, which purport to record his doing penance for unspecified bad behaviour, were likely inserted later to blacken his name.[88] The vestry minute book of St Ives Parish Church, meanwhile, contains two uncertain instances of his signature – one of which has been cut out entirely and may have been, like the other which survives, eighteenth-century additions.[89]

The pressures of Oliver's downward spiral took a heavy toll on his health. An observer later recalled seeing him in the 1630s with a red flannel around his neck, assuaging acute bronchitis.[90] It was now too, labouring in the marshy farmland, that he first caught the malaria which would plague him down the years, and ultimately cost him his life. Oliver was already struggling with his mental health in 1628 when, during his short time in London attending Parliament, he may have consulted an eminent physician who diagnosed 'Monsieur Cromwell' as *valde melancholicus*, namely very depressed.[91] Depression was a topic of growing interest and understanding at the time with Robert Burton's famous *Anatomy of Melancholy* published only seven years earlier. As the popular contemporary Christian comfort manual *The Sick Man's Salve* opined 'Inward trouble is the greatest grief in the world. Declare I pray you what it is, and we will do the best we can to quiet your mind.'[92] Oliver's own conception of his wellbeing echoed these words as he wrote in letters to his wife of the varying health of his 'inward' and 'outward' man.[93] These preoccupations produced moments of hypochondria and his doctor in Huntingdon recollected being 'called up to him at midnight, and such unseasonable hours, very many times, upon a strong fancy, which made him believe he was dying'.[94] Much of Oliver's later words and actions, and what we can glean of his character from how others observed him, suggest he had manic depressive tendencies. His weathervane moods, strong emotions and ready tears, mental and spiritual anguish and elation, propensity for pranks and high-jinks, periods of paralysing doubt and moments of sudden reckless action, extremely loving tenderness and shocking brutality all point in this direction. Certainly, throughout the rest of Oliver's life, ill health often accompanied political or spiritual crisis.

Oliver and Elizabeth's marriage too suffered during these lean years. It was dealt a dreadful blow in 1632 when they lost the seventh of their children, a boy James who died as a baby. It is probable that grief, depression and financial fears laid a cold blanket over their marriage bed for Elizabeth did not conceive again for the next five years. Yet if the loss of the infant James was a wound, the couple's next loss was a catastrophe. While living in St Ives, they sent their oldest sons 50 miles away to Felsted school in Essex. Oliver's angry departure from Huntingdon no doubt influenced the choice. Originally founded by Thomas Cromwell's protégé Richard Rich, Felsted still enjoyed the patronage of the wealthy, influential and Puritanical Rich family who were friends with Oliver's aunt's family, the Barringtons, in Essex. It was the Barringtons, indeed, who secured places for Oliver's sons at the school: in a letter to one of them in 1638 he wrote of the family 'I am much bound unto them for their love. I blesse the Lord for them, and that my son by their procurement is so well.'[95] There was a further inducement in the fact that Elizabeth's parents, Sir James and Lady Bourchier, lived in retirement from London a couple of miles from Felsted school at Grauntcourts Manor House on former monastic land leased from the Rich family. This meant the boys were able to live for free with their grandparents during term-time.

Their days were long and arduous: rising in the dark to traipse across the Essex fields in time for the twelve-hour school day which started at dawn. The whole school was taught in the long timber-vaulted room of the former guildhall above a covered arcade of shops, half of the boys facing the Deputy Headmaster at one end and half facing the Headmaster (who naturally had the one fireplace warming his back) at the other. The Headmaster, Puritan academic the Reverend Martin Holbeach, maintained the school's stellar reputation by forbidding the boys from speaking English and immersing them in a broad curriculum of Latin, Greek, some Hebrew, logic, maths, music and French described by their contemporary, the future Oxford mathematician and Commonwealth cryptographer John Wallis.[96]

Robert, the eldest and first to enrol at the school in 1634, would have been *in situ* to comfort his grandmother when his grandfather Sir James Bourchier died in 1635, his three brothers – Oliver, Richard and Henry – following him to Felsted over the next five years. But, unlike the others, Robert would never return home to his parents.[97] At the end of May 1639, just as the Essex fields warmed into early summer, 18-year-old Robert sickened suddenly and died. The sadness and shock this caused the small school and village community suffuses the vicar's entry in the Holy Cross Church Burial Register. In a few lines of Latin, he records the death of the son of the 'honourable'

Mr Oliver Cromwell and his wife Elizabeth on 31 May who was 'a young man of outstanding promise and exceptionally pious'.[98] His grave's exact location is lost but it was certainly within the church grounds which abut the school, possibly, tradition has it, in the south porch a mere few yards from the schoolroom.[99] Today it is a tranquil spot, which still echoes with the voices of Felsted pupils.

Having children at this time was a dangerous endeavour. Many women died in childbirth and child mortality was common. In the sixteenth century, Gregory's daughters Katherine and Frances died early in their marriages: Katherine in her late twenties after bearing six children and poor Frances at only eighteen during or soon after delivering her first child. Their niece, Gregory's talented granddaughter and mistress of Helmingham Hall, Catherine Tollemache, lost two of her nine children. In the royal family, the untimely death of a child could alter the course of national, not merely personal, life. Both the kings whose lives would intersect so momentously with those of the Cromwells should never have been king at all. Henry VIII only became heir to the throne on the sudden death of his older brother Prince Arthur, while it would have been King Henry IX on the throne a century later had Charles I's older brother, the famously talented and widely admired Prince Henry, not died as a youth. A spare was always needed to supplement an heir, as Henry VIII knew well. As it was with the houses of Tudor and Stuart, so it was for that of Cromwell: as Oliver had become the heir to his father when his older brother died, so now his second-born son, 16-year-old Oliver junior, was thrust into that prominent role upon the death of his brother and schoolfellow Robert.

The frequency of death in childhood has often led those comfortably safe in the era of modern medicine to assume that parents of earlier times did not grieve for their children as they would do now. But any cursory reading of contemporary accounts and literature soon dispels this myth. Shakespeare, as is well known, lost his young son Hamnet, inspiring his lines from *King John* where Constance, mourning her son, challenges those who taunt her for being 'as fond of grief as of your child':

Grief fills the room up of my absent child,
Lies in his bed, walks up and down with me,
Puts on his pretty looks, repeats his words,

Remembers me of all his gracious parts,
Stuffs out his vacant garments with his form.[100]

The diarist John Evelyn's despair at the many losses of his children packs a similarly powerful corrective. As he recorded in 1658 'died my dear son Richard to our inexpressible grief and affliction, five years and three days old only, but at that tender age a prodigy for wit and understanding; for beauty of body, a very angel; for endowment of mind, of incredible and rare hopes'. After four paragraphs describing his son's cherished life and desperate death, Evelyn concluded 'Here ends the joy of my life, and for which I go even mourning to the grave.'[101] We know that the sudden death of young Robert Cromwell on the cusp of manhood caused devastation to his parents. Oliver spoke of it on his own deathbed two decades later, recalling the impact of Robert's loss as 'a dagger to my heart'.[102] Given the wealth of traumatic memories he had amassed from the years of war that followed, the fact that he reached back to this early bereavement in his private years speaks to its profound effect upon him.

What those who recorded their grief tells us can help to interpret the silences others left behind. Thomas Cromwell bequeathed us no diary or many confessional letters, whether by his own design or that of those who destroyed his papers to protect him and his family from further royal wrath at his fall. By contrast to Oliver's more than 1000 letters, writings and speeches preserved (albeit by others, not as his own archive), most of what exists for Thomas is his 'in-tray'. Nevertheless, what scraps remain piece together to reveal a purgatorial period at a similar stage in his life to that his great-great-great-nephew would suffer. In late 1529, Thomas picked up a pen to amend his will. The document was only a few months old and it is likely that Thomas had it drawn up in the first place in response to a terrible change in his circumstances which brought him face to face with mortality. The will itself reveals what had happened, for in it Elizabeth Cromwell is described as his 'late Wife'.[103]

Elizabeth had died sometime in the second half of 1528 or early 1529, possibly of the deadly sweating sickness which regularly swept through towns into homes, beds and cradles. This killer was known and feared: Elizabeth and Thomas's son Gregory was even then hiding from it with his tutor and companions in the countryside near Cambridge. But Austin Friars, the bustling open-doored household in the heart of commercial London, could not escape. June 1528 sees the last mention of the living Elizabeth in a letter written to Thomas; a chatty letter from a friend which sent greetings to the couple and, poignantly, thanked Thomas for his good cheer when they last met.[104] Thereafter, the effect of his love for and loss of Elizabeth upon Thomas can only be glimpsed through omissions: in his unusual negligence of his business affairs in the dying months of 1528 as he left letters unanswered and payments unmade – as one historian recently put it 'Cromwell, a man who oozed self-control and order, was missing in action';[105] in the generous provision Thomas made for Elizabeth's mother, sister and her children in his will; and in his choice never to re-marry despite society's expectations that he should.

Friends certainly wrote to Thomas wishing him luck in his presumed search for a new wife.[106] As a wealthy widower, eligible ladies would have made themselves known to him, as his future daughter-in-law possibly intended to do when she applied to him for aid in 1537 upon her widowhood as a 'poor woman alone' seeking the 'favour' 'promised' to her when she was last at court by the man her late husband served second only to the King.[107] Once Thomas was a great man, other great men would have advertised the women of their households to him either for marriage – or in one invitation from the Duke of Norfolk, for recreation: 'If Cromwell will lodge at his house at York, he may be sure of a welcome,' the great magnate wrote to him in June 1537, continuing with a jibe at Thomas's friendship with his own wife, 'if you lust not to dally with his wife he hath a young woman with pretty proper tetins.'[108] Though it is unlikely Thomas availed himself of the amply bosomed woman at his rival's ready disposal, it may be that he sought comfort in at least one liaison after his wife's death. A 'mistress Jane' Cromwell, who is fleetingly present receiving a generous clothing allowance in Gregory's household in 1539, may have been Thomas's illegitimate daughter, probably born in the early 1530s.[109] Margaret Vernon asked to educate her, just as she had Gregory, writing cryptically to Thomas 'I hear there is a little gentlewoman with Master Sadler which I would very fain have the governance and bringing up: it were to my comfort now in mine age.'[110]

If Jane was his own, Thomas showed the same care and generosity to her that he bestowed upon all those he assumed responsibility for;

a sense of fatherly duty which trumped formal status. It may be that Jane afforded Thomas a partial reminder of the further losses he had endured in the raw months after Elizabeth's death, losses revealed once again in his will. Here two entries have been crossed out: those making provision for his little girls Anne and Grace. Both died, probably in late 1529 and possibly from the same sweating sickness that may have carried off their mother only months earlier. Life at Austin Friars shifted to adapt. Thomas amended his will and up stepped his redoubtable mother-in-law Mercy Prior to run his household in her daughter's stead, as past and future Cromwell grandmothers who outlived their daughters would do.[111] We catch glimpses of her efforts in Thomas's correspondence: as his brother-in-law John Williamson reported to him on 5 September 1529, 'Took Mr. Paulman half of the buck Cromwell sent home after his departure; his mother made the neighbours cheer with the rest . . . Cromwell's mother and household are well.'[112] Yet the cumulative grief at these cruel deaths for Thomas, his sole surviving child Gregory and the wider family and household must be imagined – Shakespeare's vacant garments, Evelyn's end of joy and Oliver Cromwell's dagger to his heart standing in for theirs in our minds as we contemplate the nuclear family suddenly and brutally reduced from five to two.

While we can understand the universality of grief and other suffering from our own lives, the contribution that faith made to how the Cromwells and their contemporaries came to terms with it is more temporally particular. Religious belief moulded souls and shaped careers in the sixteenth and seventeenth centuries, and for both Thomas and Oliver, their personal and evolving relationships with God steered their earthly lives and posthumous reputations. Returning to the snapshot of Thomas's life preserved in his will, we find a man of ostensibly traditional faith leaving money for 'a priest to sing for my soul' and bequests to 'the five Orders of Friars in London' for further prayers for his soul and various charitable acts.[113] His household inventory of 1527 too reveals a home filled with religious artwork and icons such as 'painted tables of our Lord, our Lady' and a 'gilt altar table of the Nativity of our Lord'.[114] An account of him whispering orthodox prayers at a key moment of trouble in 1530 further bolsters this picture of a man yet to discover an evangelical spirit. This was, after all, the man who secured the Boston Guild's right to sell indulgences from the Pope, now a trusted servant of the highest churchman in the land, the papal legate Cardinal Wolsey, and busy closing monasteries to finance his tomb. A man who, in a moment of intense frustration in 1530, had wished Martin Luther, fount of the Reformation and decrier of indulgences, had never been born.[115]

Yet such a picture may obscure more than it reveals. In due course Thomas would do more than any other to advance reform of the Church of England, risking the King's ire and likely hastening his own demise to do so. It may be that he found this cause in or after this period of personal devastation in his life, perhaps inspired by it. But it may instead be that evangelical faith already stirred within him. After all, he was famously supposed to have used his arduous journey to Rome in 1518–19 to memorise Erasmus's translation of the New Testament. Later Protestant chroniclers would see the seeds of his rejection of the papacy in his experience of the greedy Pope he so easily seduced. Thomas was involved in the English networks of early evangelicals of the 1520s, not least through his quiet appointment of Cambridge men of future Protestant leanings to the posts in Oxford's Cardinal College within his sphere of influence.[116] Viewed in this light, service to Cardinal Wolsey may have seemed the likeliest vehicle for effecting church reform by the back door, and it was to Wolsey, perhaps in an effort to please, that he had denied Luther.

The timing and extent of Thomas's conversion to the emerging Protestant movement forms a key pillar of the cases made by those who have sought to revere or revile him down the centuries, from the hero of Foxe's *Martyrs* sincerely motivated by religious reform to the villain of Robert Bolt's play *A Man for All Seasons* spurred on by Realpolitik, cruelty and greed. Taken at his own word, the private Thomas Cromwell of the 1520s had already embarked on a lifelong journey through his faith, wittingly or unwittingly. As he later told his great friend and closest political and spiritual collaborator Thomas Cranmer, at the time of his trip to Rome to lobby the Pope as a young man, he 'had yet no sound taste nor judgement of religion, but was wild and youthful, without sense or regard of God and his word'.[117]

This struggle from ignorance to knowledge was a central tenet of a Calvinist conversion narrative in which God revealed himself personally to the believer to show him the way to redemption in the manner of St Paul on the road to Damascus. 'O I lived in, and loved darkness, and hated the light,' Oliver Cromwell wrote to his cousin Elizabeth St John in 1638 in unconscious echo of his forebear in his earliest and most spiritually revealing letter recounting his own evangelical experience: 'I was a chief, the chief of sinners, this is true, I hated godliness yet God had mercy on me.'[118] Oliver had been raised a churchgoer within a family supportive of the Elizabethan religious settlement. Yet this was a broad church sheltering those with Puritan leanings at its most radical point, and the Cromwells may have tilted to this end of the Church of England's spectrum. The puritanical preamble to Oliver's grandfather Sir Henry Cromwell's will which prayed his descendants might 'so live in this world that in their life to come they may be accepted among the elect' suggests as much.[119] Now in the 1630s, Oliver must have expected his wider family to understand his new faith, otherwise he would not have shared his conversion story with his cousin – with a postscript, furthermore, indicating he expected her to circulate it among their friends and relations. Nevertheless, Oliver had travelled some distance from the religion of his youth as he looked back upon his younger self from the safe harbour of his new-found faith with impatience. His conversion shifted his place on the Protestant scale from cautious, conformist Puritanism to something more restless and radical. And it was this religious awakening yeoman Oliver found in his wilderness years. It lit a fire within him which fuelled the rest of his extraordinary life.

Debate rages around the obscured details of his conversion just as it does around his great-great-great-uncle's. For the Restoration writer James Heath, Oliver's conversion to Puritanism was an expediency having lost his wider family's patronage: it was but the 'appearance of such a Reformation' made 'not out of Seduction and Ignorance, but Sedition, and Malice, and Treasonable design'.[120] While to the mind of the Victorian historian Thomas Carlyle who considered Oliver a 'genuine king among men', he possessed a 'living God-inspired soul'.[121] The providentialist nature of Oliver's new beliefs pose their own problem with cynics arguing that justifying his actions by a personal interpretation of God's will gave Oliver a blank cheque to behave as it suited him: 'the Divine Right of Oliver' in other words.[122] Certainly belief in providence was 'extraordinarily elastic', with Puritans able to praise God for both sending them gifts in reward and challenges to overcome.[123] Yet a Machiavellian Oliver hiding behind false prophecies does not account for his anguished searching for Providential meaning at crucial moments of his life.

Oliver did experience a genuine religious turning point in this period, fed by his depression and nurtured in the fertile religious climate of St Ives. It can be no coincidence that the small town hosted a Puritan lecturer, Job Tookey, and was led by a Puritan landlord, Henry Lawrence. Indeed, Lawrence was one the trustees of the godly outpost of Connecticut and may have intended to emigrate there, having already lived abroad in Holland. Several contemporary sources claim Oliver considered the same. Edward Hyde, later Earl of Clarendon, records a story of Oliver whispering to another in Parliament in 1641 that if its complaints to the King were rejected, he 'would have sold all he had the following morning and never have seen England more'; 'So near was the poor kingdom to its deliverance,' the Royalist Hyde could not help but add.[124] Other sources even claim that Oliver boarded a boat to make the journey only to be fatefully stopped by no less a figure than the Archbishop of Canterbury William Laud, whose anti-Puritan church reforms Oliver and his parliamentary circle so vehemently opposed, paving the way to civil war.[125]

There are memories of Oliver attending church while living in St Ives but recent research has revealed evidence that he frequented and perhaps preached at an underground conventicle in the town.[126] Certainly no evidence after this point in the mid-1630s places him worshipping in church, except at some of the marriages of his daughters and listening to sermons in the royal chapels. Hereafter Oliver would converse with God in private through studying the Bible or at so-called 'gathered churches' of fellow Puritans convened in any place and without formal liturgy. Like Thomas, he harboured a dislike of clergymen. Where Thomas 'could not abide the snoffing pride of some prelates', Oliver considered that the Irish Catholic clergy certainly, and the Scottish Presbyterian clergy *possibly*, acted in a 'covenant' made 'with death and hell'.[127] Yet if this was the language of hate, Oliver's faith was primarily characterised by love – the love of Christ into which he was born again and thereafter armed against the vicissitudes of fortune. His deathbed conversation, where he relived the pain of his son Robert's death, shows how this operated. Sensing his own approaching end, he called for the Bible and asked for a portion of St Paul's Letter to the Philippians: 'I have learnt in whatsoever state I am, therewith to be content; I know both how to be abased, and I know how to abound: every where, and in all things, I am instructed, both to be full and to be hungry, both to abound and to suffer need. I can do all things through Christ that strengtheneth me.' This passage, he said 'did once save my life, when my eldest son died'.[128] As contemporary devotional manuals show, faith, particularly in predestination, could ease the pain of parental bereavement for those believing the death of their child was God's will.

Oliver was in need of such comfort after six years' seclusion in St Ives. But now family as well as faith would be his salvation. Oliver's maternal uncle Sir Thomas Steward, a prosperous landowner in the region, died in 1636 leaving him a substantial inheritance. This was a game changer for the struggling yeoman, so much so that some hostile writers later accused him of attempting to get his hands on the estate while his uncle still lived by declaring him insane. If Oliver had done such a thing, his uncle did not hold it against him, bequeathing him a reversion of leases from Ely Cathedral, some leasehold land, a role administering the lands and tithes of the parishes of Ely and a fine house in the centre of the town: all in all, an income (after discharging his uncle's debts) of around £300 a year.[129] Oliver did not forget his Steward relatives or their help and in subsequent years was able to help his family in return.[130]

Ely had been the fiefdom of Oliver's great-grandfather Richard Cromwell who, with Gregory, had together acquired the stewardship of the diocese.[131] Now, almost exactly a hundred years later, Oliver's family moved into the black and white timbered townhouse that still stands on the cathedral green and back into the ranks of the gentry. The effect of this relief from financial pressure is evident in the immediate marriage of Oliver's sixth sister, thirty-year-old Jane, to John Desborough which could now be afforded; and in the reinvigoration of Oliver and Elizabeth's marriage with the rapid conception of their last two children, Mary (1637) and Frances (1638). This pair of girls – their father's much indulged 'little wenches' – were destined for a very different upbringing from their older two sisters Bridget and Elizabeth.

Oliver was sustained by his closest relationships: a network of local friends and relatives to whom he would show a loyalty in friendship that he never bestowed upon those friends he made later in life.[132] Moreover, it was the women in his life – his mother, sisters, wife, daughters, daughters-in-law, wider relations and friends – who would inspire his greatest devotion and most revealing confidences. This makes sense for a man who, when not in the masculine environment of the Army but at home, lived exclusively with women, as an only surviving son whose own sons left home for school at a young age. His role as the fond patriarch would even influence how Oliver later saw his role as Lord Protector. Thomas too nurtured an instinct and insight into the female experience which may have come from his family life, cherishing his wife, mother-in-law, sisters and daughters and going to great lengths to help the many women who later applied to him for aid with their problems from the Duke of Norfolk's wife to Princess Mary. He had also built for himself a strong, loyal network of wider relations, friends, mentees and servants: the beginnings of a private household which, as he grew in office, would transform into a public hub of bureaucrats busy on State business.

If these years provided both men with future sources of private strength, they had also cost them dear. While Oliver's trajectory now was upwards, these years of stagnation had damaged his economic status, mental and physical health, and taken two of his children. Thomas's family too had endured the anguish of bereavement, a short twelve months at the end of the 1520s taking from them Elizabeth and her daughters, leaving one precious remaining child, Gregory, to whom his sole surviving parent would devote his life. And the decade had not finished with Thomas Cromwell. One further loss lurked around the corner: a personal and professional blow which would propel him to bold action. Yet both Cromwells had found a new faith to direct their actions and armour them for the tumultuous years ahead. 'It hath pleased his goodness to use me as an instrument, and to work somewhat by me,' Thomas wrote of God in 1538; an idea Oliver echoed in his own deathbed prayer in 1658 'Thou hast made me, though very unworthy, a mean instrument to do them [the people] some good, and Thee service.'[133] While both Thomas and Oliver would come to see themselves as instruments of God's will, other contemporaries believed them instruments of their own or others' greed. Few, though, denied the instrumental roles in the development of national life which now awaited them both. 'My body rests in hope,' Oliver wrote in that extraordinary letter to Elizabeth St John, 'and if here I may honour my God either by doing, or suffering I shall be most glad.'[134] There had been plenty of suffering, now was the time for doing.

Part Two: Fame

And, if we would speak true,
Much to the man is due,
Who from his private gardens where
He liv'd reserved and austere,
As if his highest plot
To plant the bergamot,
Could by industrious valour climb
To ruin the great work of time,
And cast the kingdom old
Into another mould.

Andrew Marvell, 'An Horatian Ode
upon Cromwell's Return from Ireland', 1649

Four

Emergence

That great God who is the searcher of my heart knows with what a sad sense I go upon this service, and with what a perfect hatred I detest this war without an enemy; . . . We are both upon the stage and must act such parts as are assigned us in this tragedy, let us do it in a way of honour, and without personal animosities.

Parliamentarian commander Sir William Waller to his friend, the Royalist commander Sir Ralph Hopton, on the eve of the battle they fought against each other, 16 June 1643

Make or mar

The Cromwells' story is about many things: the importance of family, the impact of religious faith, and the intersection of both in the development of the Church of England and the British monarchy. But more than anything else, it is about an institution – Parliament. It was in Parliament that Thomas and Oliver began their public careers, and through Parliament that they effected change, while questions about Parliament's rights and responsibilities, its purpose, power and potential would define their legacies. However, the two Cromwells' relationships with Parliament differed wildly. Thomas would become a master at managing Parliament, using it so effectively to the King's ends and his own that he empowered it for the centuries to come in the process. Oliver too would have a profound effect on Parliament, one still felt to this day where his statue stands in solemn guard outside the Palace of Westminster. Yet while Oliver rode to war in 1642 for 'the authority of the Parliament to maintain it in its rights', once he wielded his own executive power over a decade later he could not find a way to work smoothly with it.[1] Parliament would become both the repository of all his hopes and a source of bitter disappointment.

Thomas Cromwell first entered the House of Commons for its brief session in 1523. We know little of his time there: he may have delivered a speech against the King's proposed military action in France. Certainly it was a formative experience, prompting him to pen a witty account of the House to a friend detailing how he and others 'have endured a Parliament, which contained by the space of seventeen whole weeks, where we communed of war, peace, strife, contention, debate, murmur, grudge, riches, poverty, penury, truth, falsehood, justice, equity, deceit, oppression, magnanimity, activity, force . . . Howbeit, in conclusion, we have done as our predecessors have been wont to do, that is to say, as well as we might, and left where we began'.[2] Far from betraying the contempt for Parliament many historians have read into this, Thomas's irreverence is delivered with the fond frustration of a junior official who knows he could have organised things better than his superiors; a man of vision seeing opportunity squandered. The next time he sat in Parliament six years later, it would be Thomas himself who seized that opportunity. In the interim, Thomas's life had changed entirely. In 1523 he was working safely and quietly within the grandeur of Cardinal Wolsey's powerful operation, his wife and growing family healthy at home. In November 1529 he was a widower who had lost his daughters and was now implicated in the treacherous fall of his master: a seat in Parliament now was not a mere step up the social ladder but a means to salvation. At this point Henry VIII had been infatuated with Anne Boleyn for three years. Anne disliked Wolsey but Henry looked to him to solve the intractable problem of extricating him from his marriage to Katherine of Aragon so he could marry Anne – the King's 'Great Matter' as it became known. When Wolsey failed to do this, relations between king and Cardinal soured and Thomas found himself working as an emissary for his beleaguered patron. A further failure in his negotiations with the French saw Wolsey attainted and banished to Esher, his lavishly remodelled house at Westminster – later known as

Whitehall for its gleaming stone – seized for the Crown and destined to become a royal palace and home to the future Lord Protector Oliver Cromwell.

This was nothing short of a catastrophe for Thomas Cromwell: the double loss of the fall of the master he loved and the likely end of his own career. So Wolsey's servant George Cavendish found Thomas weeping in a window at Esher on All Hallows' Day 1529. 'It is my unhappy adventure', he explained, 'which am like to lose all that I have travailed for all the days of my life, for doing of my master true and diligent service'. Intriguingly, as he cried Thomas held a Latin primer and murmured 'Our Lady Matins' – in other words he was seeking comfort in traditional, not evangelical, faith. Yet more intriguing is how subsequent writers and editors approached this story, which appeared of such dramatic importance that the entire scene made its way into Shakespeare's *Henry VIII*.[3] Cavendish, when he recalled this event in his later biography of Wolsey, wrote that Thomas engaged in such prayer was 'a strange sight in him afore' i.e. that he had been previously evangelical but now veered back to the faith of his youth in a time of crisis. His Victorian editor Samuel Singer, however, struggled with this yo-yoing and changed the line to 'which had been since a very strange sight', securing Thomas's complete conversion safely after this event.[4] Yet when Cavendish's *Life of Wolsey* was republished in 1641, on the eve of the Civil War, the event vanished altogether. If a deliberate choice, it suggests that Thomas Cromwell's unblemished reputation as a Protestant reformer mattered in the highly charged context of the early 1640s.[5]

Without a great family to help him in his distress, Wolsey depended on the support of loyal servants like Thomas Cromwell and George Cavendish. Thomas needed to act boldly to salvage what he could of the situation. Aware he was 'in disdain with most men' for his master's sake, he told Cavendish of his resolution 'to ride to London, and so to the court, where I will either make or mar, or I come again'. Cavendish tells us the phrase 'make or mar' was a favourite of Thomas Cromwell's and it captures at once both his confident, can-do attitude and the inherent risk always attached to his public actions as a self-made man. His friends were well aware of the gamble he took in riding into the lists to defend his master rather than retiring quietly to his home and legal practice. On hearing nasty reports of Thomas, his close friend Stephen Vaughan wrote that he was anxious to hear how he was being treated after the 'sudden overthrow' of Wolsey which he had feared might happen, 'yet do I not doubt but your truth and wisdom shall deliver you from danger. You are more hated for your master's sake than for anything which I think you have wrongfully done against any man'.[6] Thomas knew he was backing the losing horse yet he placed his bet anyway. The wager was a seat in Parliament for Taunton in Somerset – hastily and complicatedly acquired for him by the redoubtable Ralph Sadler through a frenetic series of meetings with patrons at court. From here on the Commons benches, Thomas could speak for his master and hope to temper the prosecution coming his way. He was, as Wolsey himself wrote, 'my only aide in this mine intolerable anxiety and distress'.[7]

This Thomas did publicly, inveighing against the Articles brought against Wolsey 'so discreetly, with such witty persuasions and deep reasons, that the same bill could take there no effect' and privately, siphoning gifts and grants at Wolsey's disposal into the hands of his enemies at court.[8] He also laboured to salvage what he could of Wolsey's legacy project, his Cardinal colleges at Oxford and Ipswich and the monumental tomb, around which the vultures circled. Thomas's time in Parliament brought him other benefits such as a place on the committee addressing clerical excess and the opportunity to broaden his network. Yet saving Wolsey was his priority. This campaign brought Thomas to the attention of the King, whose reaction to this lowly man's loyalty to the disgraced Cardinal would make or mar Thomas's fortune.

The exact moment when Thomas caught the King's eye was likely in January 1530, for by February Thomas's friends were writing to congratulate him on reports they had heard that he was now serving the monarch. Wolsey's move to Richmond Palace and his pardon in February may too have reflected his protégé's newfound influence on the King.[9] The means by which Thomas entered the King's service is less certain. Foxe details how various courtiers recommended Henry overlook Thomas's apparently disreputable manhandling of the monasteries he closed for Wolsey to employ him as a man to take on his ultimate enemy, the Pope.[10] Pole, writing later in the full knowledge and hatred of the break with Rome Thomas masterminded, has him entice Henry with the promise to increase his power through creating the Royal Supremacy.[11] Cavendish however, who knew Thomas best, told a less dramatic tale of how 'his access to the king' enabled

Henry to see his merit.[12] Forty-five was an unusual age to enter royal service, a Putney brewhouse a still more unusual background. Yet Henry spotted Thomas's hungry potential and likely enjoyed the power trip of elevating another low-born fixer with a sharp mind and real-world skills to fill Wolsey's shoes and ruffle the feathers of the complacent nobles on his Council.

However it occurred, Thomas Cromwell was now the buffer between Wolsey and the King, given the delicate task of managing the Cardinal's colleges and tomb for the King who was busily asset-stripping them. Thomas did his best to shield Wolsey from Henry's renewed wrath and enjoin him to modest behaviour, but he could not save the Cardinal from his own folly. 'I entreat your Grace to be content, and let your Prince execute his pleasure,' he pleaded but his advice fell on deaf ears.[13] Now installed at York, Wolsey kept spending money, requesting further funds from the King and intriguing with foreign powers. Moreover, he began to mistrust that his former favourite was truly acting in his interests, asking Thomas to visit and blaming his ill health upon him.[14] Affection remained between them, nonetheless. 'My own loving Mr Crumwell,' Wolsey wrote to him in August 1530 asking him to remain his 'friend and comfort'.[15] In his last letter to Wolsey in October, Thomas wrote cheerfully of the future, recommending 'my scholars in Cambridge', likely his nephew Christopher Wellyfed and dependent Nicholas Sadler, to Wolsey's patronage. Mere days later Wolsey was under arrest and summoned back to London but, already ill, he died on the journey while at Leicester Abbey.

Service to Wolsey had elevated and enriched Thomas Cromwell yet it had also brought him into harm's way. In 1527, with Wolsey in France, Thomas had fought off an assassination attempt while house-sitting York Place.[16] But now in 1530, Wolsey's death brought an even greater moment of peril. Protection could only be found in the King's pleasure with him and his work and Chapuys records how Thomas secured this 'At the said Cardinal's fall he was the only person who acquitted himself well towards him; and on the Cardinal's death . . . [Cromwell] saw no other refuge or remedy than to resort to the King. He did so much by entreaties and gifts that he gained a royal audience, at which he must have promised to make him the richest king that England had ever seen – and spoke so well and eloquently that the King from that moment made him of his Council.'[17] Thomas had shown resolute loyalty to Wolsey and would remember those who had brought his master down; a stance Ralph Sadler emulated in turn at Thomas's fall, exacting his revenge on his patron's enemies in later years. For now, Thomas was a newly minted councillor in Henry's favour with a bright future before him, but only if he could please the King. As Sir Thomas More is supposed to have advised him after his own resignation as Chancellor in 1532, 'ever tell him [Henry] what he ought to do, but never what he is able to do . . . For if a Lion knew his own strength, hard were it for any man to rule him.'[18]

❦ ❦ ❦

As he began his royal service, it was evident to Thomas Cromwell that the best way to please the King was to help solve his Great Matter. With the Pope unwilling to sanction Henry's annulment, it looked increasingly that a solution would have to be found within the realm itself, requiring England to formally break away from the Church in Rome with the King Supreme Head of a national church – a monumental act which gladdened evangelicals and horrified traditionalists. Sure enough, Thomas soon began to make himself indispensable to his new master by designing the practical steps needed to achieve the King's abstract desires. For this he needed a secretariat and Thomas set about recruiting a personal, professionalised workforce of clerks, secretaries and accountants. A capacity for hard work was essential, for Thomas once told Chapuys that he had so much business to do 'he had scarcely time to take his daily meals'.[19] His chief secretary Ralph Sadler, whose timed and dated letters testify to his long hours, expressed a Cromwellian ethos when he explained 'I cannot endure the spending of that time in designing an action which might perform two; or that delay in performing two which might well perform twenty.'[20] Above all, Thomas valued character and was swift to spot potential. 'He preferred more men of worth and integrity, whether Lay or Clergy, in his time, than any other in great place and favour at court had done.'[21]

Based out of Austin Friars, with outposts at Thomas's other office spaces in London and with him at court, this body of bureaucrats grew over the course of the 1530s to resemble a burgeoning civil service of 400 men.[22] A role on Thomas's staff, decked out in his own grey livery 'with skirts large enough for their friends to sit upon them', was a coveted prize.[23] The brightest and best were funnelled into the king's personal service, providing him with a pipeline of talent, including the triumvirate of Thomas's leading protégés Ralph Sadler, Thomas Wriothesley and Richard Rich. It was from this office in the 'law parlour' at Austin Friars, that Thomas now marshalled supporters for the royal annulment, organised a literary campaign of persuasion and drafted a parliamentary programme. By late summer 1531 he was receiving formal written instructions from the King to be relayed to the Council and executed. By the end of the year he had become the King's parliamentary manager, the man to whom MPs had to apply for any leave of absence. It was reported that 'one Mr. Cromwell penned certain matters in the Parliament house, which no man gainsaid'.[24]

Thomas was also increasingly visible at court, appearing at King Henry's shoulder to feed him the right lines to say about his scandalous love life. When Henry foolishly answered the rumour he had slept with both Anne Boleyn's sister and mother by exclaiming 'Never with the mother', Thomas quickly interjected, 'Nor never with the sister neither.'[25] Thomas's position there was formalised with his first appointment in April 1532 as Master of the Jewel House – a lucrative if minor position from which Thomas characteristically squeezed every possible drop of power and influence. The role of Clerk of the Hanaper soon followed, giving him a post within the Chancery department. Neither of these jobs actually reflected the political power Thomas had begun to amass. He would have to wait longer for formal social elevation and job titles to catch up with his real work, not least because Anne Boleyn – long assumed to have been Thomas's ally by virtue of their shared reformist religion – was in fact wary of, if not hostile to, the man who had been protégé to Cardinal Wolsey, blaming him for failing to end Henry's marriage to Katherine of Aragon. Thomas's rapid rise was clear nonetheless. 'All my hope is in you,' one of Wolsey's illegitimate sons wrote to him in October 1532, 'You are now placed in that position which I and all your friends have long wished for and you have attained that dignity that you can serve them as you please.'[26]

Thomas soon set about displaying this new dignity, though he was always mindful to remain modest in his person and avoid Wolsey's flashy wealth and fateful pomp. It was the honour and enrichment of his family and household which he focused on. When the King granted a survivorship of the lordship of Rumney in Glamorgan in

May 1532, it was made out to 'Thos. Cromewell and Gregory, his only son'.[27] Assuming that Thomas had petitioned for this particular estate, it is striking not only that he ensured Gregory was named in the grant but that the location itself was Glamorgan from which his prized brother-in-law Morgan Williams had originated. The Williams family also featured in Thomas's new coat of arms as the likely inspiration for its three golden lions rampant, as did Wolsey, whose symbols of two choughs and a Tudor red rose Thomas appropriated. Thus Thomas honoured his beloved former master and kept him and his Williams family in-laws proudly at the heart of his public identity.[28]

This identity was given its most enduring expression in the portrait Thomas commissioned from the celebrated court painter Hans Holbein at about this time. Here he sits on a bench behind a table in a dark coat richly lined with fur, his pinched face beneath the black cap focused intently away from us, already contemplating his next item of business. Gazing on this we see the middle-aged Thomas Cromwell emerge from his shadowy past into the Tudor limelight. He brought his whole self to the sitting. His courtly self in the letter on the table addressed to him as Master of the Jewel House and in the green tablecloth referring to the royal household's financial managers the 'Board of Green Cloth', to whom he was at least adjacent if not a member. His commercial self in the scissors and possibly the expensive cloth wall hanging alluding to his mercantile career and membership of the Merchant Taylors' guild. And his private self in the jacinth ring on his finger, noted in the 1527 inventory as upon his person, and the bejewelled Book of Hours before him – possibly the book he clutched in the window at Esher as he wept for his Wolsey on All Hallows' Day 1529.[29] Holbein's masterful depiction of Thomas is unsparing, the true aspects of his severe and jowled countenance unflattered but presented 'warts and all' just as Oliver would insist upon when his time as a celebrity came.

Thomas brought this commanding presence into the January 1532 session of Parliament where he directed a campaign against the Church of England, striking a heavy blow with the 'Supplication of the Commons Against the Ordinaries' (i.e. bishops and senior clergy) in the spring. This attacked the church's courts and procedures, laying the foundation for the royal supremacy over the church which would follow over the next few years. Fierce wrangling resulted in the bishops assembled in their Convocation signing the so-called Submission of the Clergy and claimed the prestigious scalp of Lord Chancellor Sir Thomas More who resigned in protest. Thomas Cromwell was now the dominant force in Parliament as 'few would displease' him.[30] This status enabled Thomas to introduce the key piece of legislation that finally resolved the King's Great Matter in March 1533: the 'Act of Restraint of Appeals' which prevented any appeals on marital matters to Rome. While Thomas Cranmer, newly made Archbishop of Canterbury, was the public face of these dramatic events, it was Thomas Cromwell who oiled the cogs of the constitutional machine in the background. His was the overseeing hand that organised the extravagant royal trip to meet the French king at Calais in the autumn, during which it is possible that Anne Boleyn finally allowed Henry into her bed before they were privately married sometime after returning to England. By April 1533 Parliament had formally declared Henry's marriage to Katherine invalid and at the end of May, Anne was crowned Queen in considerable splendour.

Through his manoeuvrings, Thomas Cromwell had in fact achieved not one new marriage for the King but two. To win Anne Boleyn, Henry had entered a 'marriage of convenience' with Parliament that strengthened them both.[31] This long 'Reformation Parliament', as it became known, for the first time gained a say in religious matters as the King – via Thomas – used the Commons to drive through the legislation he needed to attack the church in the teeth of opposition from the bishops in the Lords. In the century that followed, Parliament guarded this new-gained territory jealously whenever Henry VIII's children and their Stuart heirs experimented with religious structures. Though Elizabeth I's broad and balanced church settlement was largely stable, when tensions between Puritan and Catholic minorities grew in the 1580s, relations between the Queen's government and Parliament felt the strain. In 1587, when Puritan MPs who argued for Parliament's right to legislate on religious matters were imprisoned by the government, it was none other than Thomas Cromwell's grandson, Gregory's third son Thomas Cromwell MP, who led their defence.

Born only months before his grandfather's execution, Thomas's family name and contact book had smoothed his entry into Parliament in the 1570s. His grandfather's protégés Ralph Sadler and

William Cecil helped him secure successive parliamentary seats. Indeed, it was probably for Cecil, elevated from the Commons to the upper house as Cecil in February 1571, that Thomas began to keep the detailed parliamentary diary for which he is known, repaying his patron with valuable information to help him manage Parliament.[32] It was Sir Thomas More who had first lobbied for parliamentary privilege and now, a half century later, Thomas Cromwell MP took up the argument, declaring that MPs had a right to 'the liberty of speech and of the body'. In 1587 he produced a 'significant paper' to this effect in defence of his Puritan colleagues' freedoms earning by this, and through the almost 100 committees he sat on during his long career, the assessment that he was: 'the model type of Parliamentarian, deeply versed in the history and procedure of the institution, though like all his generation . . . hopelessly, yet profitably lacking in historical perspective; eminently responsible, but fearless in defence of liberty; liberal, not to say radical, by instinct'.[33]

Under Elizabeth I, Thomas Cromwell MP contributed to a process begun by his grandfather under Henry VIII: that of developing Parliament's role in government by expanding its remit. Yet our original Thomas Cromwell did not strengthen Parliament to oppose the King. Rather he always saw Parliament as the junior partner in an indivisible and harmonious union with the monarch. A powerful, purposeful Parliament furthering its sovereign's policy agenda and providing the pre-eminent meeting point for the King and his subjects. Burdened with the contested legacy of the Reformation, there were periods of strain under Elizabeth and James I, but after each, collaboration was restored and the partnership held. It had worked for almost a century until it didn't. And that time came at the outset of Oliver Cromwell's political career under the reign of the second Stuart monarch, Charles I.

Roundheads and cavaliers

Like Thomas, Oliver sat in a first, brief Parliament many years before his full parliamentary career started in earnest. This was the short-lived, acrimonious Parliament of 1628–9 which an angry Charles I summarily dissolved. The new king had inherited huge problems from his father – bare coffers which rendered him dependent on the tax-raising of a self-confident Parliament, and three kingdoms each with their own political and religious characters. But where the astute James I had upheld a fragile balance between these by taking a backseat, his obdurate son took the opposite approach of imposing his vision of church and state on his subjects. This vision was of a European-style divinely ordained and interventionist monarchy supported by a deferential and hierarchical society. Charles's first steps in this direction met with fierce resistance in Parliament so the King decided to do away with Parliament altogether. For 11 years, from 1629 to 1640, he ruled alone with free rein to implement his contentious ideas.

Governing successfully without a troublesome Parliament meant finding alternative sources of revenue and Charles and his Privy Councillors dug up ancient and controversial fines, taxes and monopoly grants. 'Ship Money' – a levy to fund the navy extended from coastal areas to the whole country – was a particularly unpopular scheme, famously tested in the trial of Oliver Cromwell's cousin John Hampden who refused to pay. Charles's religious policy was even more provocative. Working with his Archbishop of Canterbury, William Laud, and others Charles reformed the Calvinist-leaning Elizabethan Church of England which his father had maintained by stripping out its more Puritan elements and taking it in an 'Arminian' or high church direction. This new Church of England was hierarchical, beautiful and ordered. Communion tables were moved to the east end and railed off from the congregation, churches were richly refurnished, sermons were sidelined by ceremony and sacrament. Moreover, the central tenet of Arminianism favoured the Catholic worldview that events were directed by human free will over the Protestant belief in God's determinism (the Calvinist belief in predestination). All this was compounded by the strong influence Charles's Catholic wife, the French princess Henrietta Maria, exerted upon him.

When the King attempted to impose his new Prayer Book on Scotland in 1637, a great swathe of the Scottish political nation took up arms in resistance. Their preferred Presbyterian form of the church, which had removed bishops altogether, was repelled by this seemingly papist liturgy. Instead, the protesters instituted a National Covenant: a Presbyterian manifesto agreed between the Scottish people and God. The king's army failed to defeat these Scottish 'Covenanters' in the field and the prospect of a long, expensive war forced Charles to call a Parliament in spring 1640 to raise the money he needed. He expected a pliant body united in defence of the Crown but instead found an indignant assembly steered by a powerful opposition group known as the 'Junto' who, sympathising with the Scots, saw their rebellion as a heaven-sent opportunity to pressure the King to dismantle the hated apparatus of his 'Personal Rule' in England. The Junto's brilliant political manager and elder statesman, Somerset-born lawyer John Pym, set the aggrieved tone from the outset, delivering a two-hour speech on the second day cataloguing the ills the Crown had imposed on the State since 1629. The first sitting of Parliament ended swiftly in stalemate but the Scottish army's triumphant march south to Newcastle, a petition from opposition peers to recall Parliament, and agitation on the streets of London compelled the King to call a new Parliament. This Parliament – the 'Long Parliament' – would change Britain (and the Cromwell family) forever.

Oliver Cromwell joined the Parliaments of 1640 as MP for Cambridge, possibly at the instigation of local Puritans and perhaps with some help from his Essex kinship network of Barringtons and Bourchiers who were connected to Robert Rich, the Earl of Warwick and benefactor of Felsted School.[34] He began with the disadvantage of being among the poorest members of the house despite his hasty sale of most of his recently inherited Ely assets to raise ready cash.[35] This occasioned sneering comment from his contemporaries. The Royalist Sir Philip Warwick remembered first seeing Oliver in the House 'ordinarily apparelled, for it was a plain cloth-suit which seemed to have been made by an ill country tailor; his linen was plain, and not very clean, and I remember a speck or two of blood upon his little band [at his throat] which was not much larger than his collar; his hat was without a hatband, his stature was of a good size, his sword stuck close to his side, his countenance swollen and reddish, his voice harsh and untenable'.[36]

Historians have followed suit, fitting this impression of an uncouth sloven to their accounts of a loner backbencher, socially marginalised and prone to impulsive gaffes. There is some truth in this: Oliver lacked a patron, spoke plainly with no hesitation in ruffling feathers and some of his interventions were counterproductive. Yet if Oliver was not a parliamentary leader at this point, neither was he a nobody.[37] His large and well-connected family provided him with at least 17 relatives in the Commons and probably more: there were at least 53 MPs related to Oliver across the various Parliaments of 1640–60, with 28 of these in the Long Parliament by the late 1640s.[38] This family network contained Oliver's cousins, John Hampden and Oliver St John, who acted as a gravitational force pulling Oliver into the orbit of their powerful Junto group. Hampden certainly valued him, describing Oliver in an opaque sporting analogy as 'one that would sit well at the mark'.[39] Of course, kinship was no guarantee of political affiliation and Oliver may not even have been aware that he was related to his most distant cousins. There were occasions too when Oliver acted independently and at variance with family members, but it is striking how often Oliver worked alongside his relations on shared causes.[40]

Family mattered to Oliver's early experience of Parliament in 1640–2 and clearly overlapped with the other two interwoven networks Oliver belonged to – the godly Puritans and the patriotic defenders of parliamentary privilege – which both sought interconnected reforms and restraints on the King's power to protect Protestantism and Parliament.[41] Energetic and dogged if something of a loose cannon, Oliver served these interests with vim, sitting on tens of committees, initiating motions, moving on business, sponsoring petitions, acting as a teller and as a go-between with the Junto's members in the House of Lords, the Earls of Warwick and Bedford and Viscount Saye and Sele. When he waded into debates Oliver often irritated, but he had a strangely compelling oratorical style – 'his eloquence full of fervour', as Sir Philip Warwick conceded, his rhetoric 'very much hearkened to'.[42] He was emotional in speech, often moved to tears and indignation, particularly on behalf of petitioners who had suffered punishment by judicial bodies wielding the royal prerogative during the 1630s.[43]

Initially drawn to parochial and pet causes like the rights of locals facing land enclosure and fen drainage – issues also dear to his forebear Thomas Cromwell's heart – Oliver increasingly concerned himself with the national issues occupying the Junto and his relatives within it. Chief among these was the need to empower Parliament against the Crown to ensure the forced dissolutions of 1629 and 1640, and the King's eleven-year Personal Rule between them, could not happen again. In November 1640, in the heady atmosphere of mounting rumour and military manoeuvres, the King's hated chief adviser,

Thomas Wentworth, Earl of Strafford was arrested. On Christmas Eve 1640 the Junto introduced a bill for annual Parliaments and six days later it was Oliver who moved the second reading of the bill. The bill was duly diluted to provide for a Parliament every three years and, after much agonising, accepted by the King.

Allied to this cause was the need to preserve the Protestant religion. While Puritans like Oliver had previously believed that the church only needed to be reformed sufficiently to allow Protestants to worship freely in their own ways (the doctrine of liberty of conscience), Charles and Laud's creation of an Arminian established church meant wholesale change was now needed. Oliver's voice joined those in the House attacking their excesses: working to abolish or at least disempower bishops, arguing against the Book of Common Prayer and in favour of a Protestation Oath to protect reformed Protestant religion from innovations. In December 1640 Laud himself was impeached and arrested. The twin issues of Parliament's rights and safeguarding the Protestant church had dovetailed. Only Parliament could now protect Protestantism from the Crown. Only Parliament could be the vehicle for further godly reformation. In this way, Oliver's new-found faith drove him into opposition to the King.

At this stage in early 1641, it appeared as if Crown and Parliament might yet find a consensus. But instead escalating events caused positions to harden and trust to fray as the year wore on. The Junto were outraged when Charles was implicated in a plot to seize the Tower of London and free Strafford. The King was then devastated by Strafford's trial and execution. John Pym drafted a grand 'Remonstrance' attacking the Personal Rule, and the King rode north once more to resume his campaign against the Scots. In this fevered atmosphere the question of who controlled the Army loomed large, particularly when violent rebellion broke out again in Ireland. Both King and Parliament agreed that an army should be raised to quash the rebels but neither trusted the other to lead it. Shocking reports of the massacre of Protestants reached London and Pym and his colleagues harnessed the full propaganda potential of this, terrifying London with talk of Catholic plots. It was the violence in Ireland, more than any other event, that alarmed Oliver, who saw in it not Irish resistance to oppressive English rule but a Catholic crusade in prelude to an invasion of England. Soon he was sitting on a Commission for Irish Affairs overseeing the reconquest of Ireland and recklessly investing an astonishing amount of his own funds to the venture – as much as Pym and twice as much as Oliver St John – probably a large part of what he had raised when he cashed in his Ely estates in 1640.[44]

Returned to London, Charles and Parliament negotiated and jockeyed for popular support over a febrile winter until the impatient king made a fateful misstep. On 4 January 1642, he arrived at the House of Commons with soldiers to arrest five members of the Junto, only to find 'all the birds have flown'.[45] The 1970 blockbuster film *Cromwell* has Oliver Cromwell as one of these five members; an inaccurate if understandable attempt to shoe-horn the as yet minor figure Oliver into this crucial staging post on the road to civil war. Yet one of the five members was in fact a Cromwell by blood: William Strode, Thomas Cromwell's great-great-grandson through Gregory's daughter Frances. Thus for the second time, one of the Launde Cromwells defended parliamentary privilege against the Crown's prerogative. Thwarted and humiliated, the King left London and military preparations began, with few members of Parliament so single-minded and active in this as Oliver Cromwell. It was on his motion that a committee was formed to put the country on a war footing. The Militia Ordinance it produced, and the Commissions of Array with which the King answered it, competed to take military control of the localities, arming the nations for civil war.[46]

The London presses, meanwhile, mobilised themselves for a war of words as each side justified its own case. The Crown occupied high constitutional ground, accepting that government was mixed between king, lords and commons but insisting that Charles maintain his right to veto legislation using his royal prerogative. Indeed this 'Negative Voice' was the defining feature of the monarch who ruled by divine right. In contrast, Parliamentarian authors argued that the most important principle was that inherited from the Romans that *Salus populi suprema lex est* ('the safety of the people is the supreme law'). If this was ever threatened in times of emergency, Parliament could act alone. At first Parliament asserted that it had the right to do so as the highest court, but soon the theorist Henry Parker developed the more radical explanation that Parliament could act in this way as it represented the people and it was the people (and not kings) who originally held supreme power. This theory of popular sovereignty and representative government would change the western world.[47]

The first Age of Journalism had begun and in it the hand of the past weighed heavily. Writers argued over its political legacy: where original power had come from before the first societies were formed, what lessons should be drawn from the Roman republic and whether the Norman Conquest of 1066 had been a legitimate way for the ancestor of the present King Charles to acquire power and impose an intolerable 'Norman Yoke' upon the people. Both sides presented themselves as the defenders of traditional government now threatened by dangerous innovation: where Royalists claimed to uphold centuries-old kingship against a radical Parliament, Parliamentarians rallied around the 'ancient constitution' which they argued was now threatened by a newly autocratic Crown. Religious history was every bit as contested and in many ways Oliver Cromwell's Long Parliament of 1640 was grappling with the legacy of Thomas Cromwell's Reformation Parliament of 1529–36; before itself, the longest sitting Parliament. For Oliver and the godly, the Reformation this Henrician Parliament had achieved had not gone far enough. The Pope may have been sent packing but the church that emerged through the Elizabethan compromise retained bishops and many Catholic rituals. Conversely, Charles I and Henrietta Maria increasingly believed that Henry VIII's attack on the church had been a sinful crime for which Charles was now called to account as Henry's monarchical heir. This notion increasingly appeared in print as writers applied the well-established superstition of the third generation since the dissolution paying for its crimes at the national level.

In these arguments, the familiar characters of the 1530s drama re-emerged in the 1640s pamphlet war, weaponised by both sides. The autocracy of Henry VIII's Reformation was compared with Charles I's Personal Rule. Parallels were drawn between the prelates Cardinal Wolsey and William Laud. The 1641 edition of Cavendish's *Life of Wolsey,* which pointedly omitted Thomas Cromwell's weeping lapse into traditional faith in the Esher window, attached another publication of the same year: *A True Description or rather A Parallel between Cardinal Wolsey Archbishop of York and William Laud Archbishop of Canterbury etc. Printed in the Yere 1641.*[48] As its later Victorian editor explained with no pretence at neutrality, 'the enemies of Archbishop Laud, particularly in the time of his troubles, were fond of comparing him with Cardinal Wolsey: and a garbled edition of this life was first printed in the year 1641 for the purpose of prejudicing that great prelate in the minds of the people, by insinuating a parallel between him and the cardinal'. The pamphlet offered a moral lesson, describing how 'The cardinal died at Leicester some say of a flux; Canterbury [i.e. Laud] remains still in the Tower, only sick of a fever. Vanitas vanitatum, omnia vanitas.'[49] Both men were also attacked for their low birth as 'the sons of mean and mechanic men, Wolsey of a butcher, Laud of a clothworker'.[50] Thomas Cromwell, no stranger to such snobbery, featured in these narratives, but his surname was given added piquancy in subsequent years once Oliver emerged onto the public stage; writers relishing the symmetry of the two key commoners of the same name who were implicated in their sovereigns' fates.

Such pamphlets reached not only the political elites in London, but ordinary people throughout the kingdoms. As the Long Parliament abolished the censorship of the Personal Rule there was an explosion of cheap print with readers increasingly hungry for political news. Changes in the printing process created professional journalists and the first weekly newspapers to cater to this new appetite. The output was extraordinary: the London bookseller George Thomason collected 24,000 pamphlets, manuscripts and newspapers between 1640 and 1663. A print revolution had begun which would reflect but also shape the political revolution to come. What people read and heard read aloud to them influenced the choices they now had to make about whether to support the King or Parliament. Political conviction and religious faith often determined decisions, but people were also motivated by more personal or even prosaic reasons from local affairs, social position and individual wealth to the influence of employers, patrons, family or friends. Individual temperament, ambition and risk appetite must have also factored.

It is hard to draw patterns from such individualistic choices, particularly given that the majority of English people retained key fundamentals in common. Very few people at this point conceived of any alternative system of government than monarchy: both sides entered the war in the expectation that Charles I would retain his throne. At this stage, with both king and Parliament promising a return to a rose-tinted past, continuity not change was the stated goal. Nevertheless, in the broadest terms, Royalists were often motivated by an immutable loyalty to the Crown and a conservative impulse to preserve the political, religious and social order, while many Parliamentarians were more flexible in their thinking and open to alternative structures. Landowning families like the Cromwells often divided along the lines of inheritance. Older sons with a vested interest in maintaining the status quo often fought for the king while younger sons, without estates to venture nor a promised inheritance with which to make their name and fortune, threw in their lot with Parliament. Some families even seem to have deliberately sent one son into each army as a way of hedging their bets. Such inter-family divisions within the elite belie the historic assumption that the nobility sided with the king, while the middle and lower classes largely fought for Parliament. In fact, both armies were fairly evenly mixed. What we can say for certain is that none of this was straightforward or set in stone. Though the war divided communities, individual social ties often remained. Choices of allegiance were thus complex and slippery, made in an ever-shifting context, and with a web of competing loyalties which saw many swap sides throughout the conflict. The need not only to make a near impossible choice once, but to continue to make such choices throughout the Civil War period has seen it aptly described as the Age of Conscience.[51]

The Cromwell family were the ultimate example of a network divided by the outbreak of the Civil War. The curious combination of disruptive radicalism and stolid traditionalism that ran through the lives of the Cromwells now fractured the family. Thomas Cromwell's direct descendants, the Launde Cromwells, generally sided with the king. The senior branch was now in Ireland following Gregory's disgraced grandson Baron Edward Cromwell's sale of his English estates in 1605 after his part in the Essex rebellion. Edward's only son Thomas, who had become the 4th Baron Cromwell on his father's death in 1607, was an adventurer in the mould of his father and great-grandfather and namesake: a 'noble gentleman', and 'true blade' as he described himself, keen to prove himself through derring-do.[52] Lineage mattered to this young Baron Thomas Cromwell and it is notable that it was around 1612 that a copy of Holbein's portrait of the original Thomas Cromwell was made 'for the then Lord Cromwell, Gregory's descendant, which that peer must have considered worth the expense'.[53] His own portrait marks him out as a Cromwell, though one leaning more to Oliver's side of the family with his long nose and hooded eyes. But if Baron Thomas Cromwell's features echo those of his distant cousin, his flamboyant appearance does not: long, thick, chestnut curls fall spaniel-like either side of an elaborate neck-tie bow, a breastplate gleaming between gold embroidered sleeves.

Baron Thomas Cromwell was eager to escape the shadow of his father's disgrace and reverse his family's fortunes through loyal service to the Crown. In the 1610s and 1620s, he served in the military in Ireland and at sea and moved in with his wife's Meverell family at Throwley Old Hall in Staffordshire. He gravitated to those close to the throne to advance his career: first the newly restored 3rd Earl of Essex, the young son of the traitorous Earl who his father had followed, and then the most dazzling royal favourite of them all, George Villiers, Duke of Buckingham, eventually receiving elevation to the Irish peerage as Viscount Lecale in November 1624.[54] The letters patent granting 'the honour of Viscount Lecale to Thomas Lord Cromwell & the heires male of his Body' still survives and is exquisitely illuminated with portraits of King James I and his family on one side and Baron Cromwell's coat of arms on the other.[55] The new Viscount Lecale was prickly about his status. His insistence within the navy that an Irish viscount trumped an English baron no doubt reflected his desire to feel his recently earned title as the Irish Viscount Lecale was a step up from his inherited title as the English Baron Cromwell.[56] His visit to the family's former seat at Oakham Castle in Rutland in 1631 may also have informed his insecurity. For Lecale, who would have had the lordship were it not for his father's firesale of the family estates, was forced to follow the historic custom that all visitors present a horseshoe to the lord in tribute.[57]

Viscount Lecale continued to cosy up to prominent royal servants to improve his fortunes right up to the outbreak of the Civil War. A cache of letters in the Earl of Strafford's archive reveals how Lecale courted Strafford's favour when he was Lord Deputy of Ireland. Lecale petitioned Strafford for appointment as Lord Marshal of Ireland which he believed he had some claim to through his father. While Strafford would not support this, he did put in a good word for Lecale at court and employed him as a gossipy go-between with key figures there, including Laud and Essex, causing one household expense account to record 'Wine and sugar when Lord Cromwell was here, 1s.'[58] Lecale emerges from these letters as a 'cavalier' in every meaning of the word, not only a supporter of the King but a ladies' man prone to flippancy. Thus the editor of the State Papers primly summarises one of his more salacious letters as containing 'various indecent allusions', while a correspondent recounted how the accidental drowning of a servant would have upset him if Lecale and others had not been drinking toasts to his master 'as if his man had never been drowned'.[59] Yet one topic about which Lecale was always serious was his declining means. Facing legal challenges from his neighbours in Downpatrick, in March 1639 he begged Strafford for help to escape 'the narrowness of my fortune'.[60] Strafford, of course, was soon in no position to help, but the outbreak of civil war within the three kingdoms offered the opportunity Lecale had been waiting for.

Viscount Lecale may have been the 'Captain Cromwell' recorded as commanding infantry in the Bishops' Wars between Charles I and the Scots in June 1639.[61] He complained of poor pay and promotion, 'But such is my zeal to the King's service and my obligations to the Lord Lieutenant, that I will go in any condition rather than stay.'[62] Certainly, he rallied to the government's taskforce in November 1641 when he hastened to quash the Irish Catholic rebels with 'other such noblemen and gentry as have commands there'.[63] His motives were likely as much personal as ideological, however, as the rebels had done much damage to his estates in Lecale. As one witness described: 'the Lord Cromwell had his town of Downpatrick, the shiretown and his house burned, his whole estate in Lecale to the value of 2600 li. per annum or thereabouts overrun and wasted his cattle and corn taken and burned'.[64] Lecale continued to serve the King as the Civil War in England broke out fully, commanding his cavalry troop in the East Ulster British Horse fighting initially against the Irish Confederate army, though he seems to have spent some of the war years in England.[65] During this time he may have encouraged his sons Wingfield and Vere Essex, now around 21 and 20 years old and fresh from their educations at Trinity College Dublin, to associate with the Royalist cause too.[66]

Where the Launde Cromwells were ardent Royalists in 1642, the Hinchingbrooke Cromwells were divided among themselves. Oliver Cromwell was first to declare, leaving Parliament around 10 August 1642 to ride to his constituency of Cambridge before the war had even officially started. In a characteristically reckless move, having picked up his brother-in-law Valentine Walton to act as his wingman, he seized the arms and ammunition at Cambridge castle on behalf of Parliament and intercepted the majority of the university's plate and money en route to fill the King's war chest. The real risk of arrest for treason should the rebellion have fizzled out did not deter the zealous Oliver. Within a few days of war formally breaking out, on 27 August, Oliver based himself at the Falcon Inn in Huntingdon marketplace to recruit about sixty horses.[67] With another of his brothers-in-law John Desborough as Quartermaster, they were soon on the road to join the main parliamentary force commanded by the Junto peer, the Earl of Essex.

Representing his father's younger branch of the Hinchingbrooke family, Oliver had staked his future on Parliament. He was not alone in his family on this side of the divide: the families his aunts and cousin had married into all supported Parliament and sent sons into its army, as did his younger uncle.[68] There may indeed have been more parliamentary supporters in their ranks than we know about.[69] But the most important members of the Hinchingbrooke Cromwells, Oliver's oldest uncle, head of the family Sir Oliver Cromwell, and his heirs, followed the family tradition of royal service to side with the King. This was a natural step for Sir Oliver who had been actively recruiting men into the King's forces to fight the Scots in recent years while his eldest son had been entrusted by the government to disarm Catholic recusants in the district.[70] Now in 1642, Sir Oliver's sons and grandson took up arms for the King, raising men and money locally as Huntingdon went 'wild'.[71] Soon Sir Oliver's eldest son was marching fifty armed soldiers through the town declaring themselves ready to escort the university's treasures safely to the King's headquarters.[72]

It was inevitable that Oliver Cromwell and his uncle Sir Oliver would clash: Huntingdonshire was not big enough for both of them. Soon Oliver visited his uncle in the great house of Ramsey – now the family seat since Hinchingbrooke had been sold to the Montagus. Nephew showed dutiful deference to uncle, removing his hat for the duration of his stay and asking his blessing as head of the Cromwell family. That Oliver did so despite Sir Oliver's sworn allegiance to the King's cause shows the power that family dynamics retained over political alliance in Oliver's mind. Oliver's uncle and godfather was, after all, heir to the Hinchingbrooke Cromwells, the glamorous courtier who had entertained both Queen Elizabeth and King James at his own table and let the boy Oliver play in his house. But social nicety would not get in the way of practical necessity in a time of war. Before he left, Oliver 'disarmed' and 'plundered' his patriarch, taking away all his weapons and plate for Parliament's war coffers.[73]

A few months later, Oliver visited again with a cavalry troop, and this time the gloves really came off. Oliver wrote ahead demanding a fine from his uncle, otherwise he would torch the town of Ramsey. Unable (or unwilling) to pay, Sir Oliver asked to meet his nephew for a parlay on the High Bridge in the town.[74] There they met – a local woman and fan of young Oliver offering him a cushion to sit on which he politely refused. Sir Oliver agreed to pay £1,000 and provide forty saddle horses to save the town while, on the banks of the river, Oliver's troopers staved off their boredom by 'riding through a fen-man's legs, who was mounted like the great Colossus at Rhodes, upon something very high, that served for pedestals'.[75] There was little doubt which Oliver Cromwell was now in command.

This must be the man

Few could have predicted the military career that lay ahead of Oliver Cromwell. Not only was he already 43 years old at the start of the war, but he had no military experience whatsoever: fields of crops not of battle had been his landscape. This was not uncommon among the soldiers hastily recruited to the two opposing armies as England had enjoyed several golden generations of peace. But a sizeable minority of men, and most of the highest ranks of officers on both sides, had seen some action in the recent war against the Scots or as volunteers in the Thirty Years War which had long been ravaging continental Europe. Where Thomas Cromwell had travelled widely and fought for European armies, Oliver had never left England nor picked up a weapon other than to hunt. He may have fought in the final stages of the first major battle of the Civil War at Edgehill on 23 October 1642 – the sources are conflicted. If he did, it was a baptism of fire as he experienced the shock of finding Parliament's cavalry routed by a thunderous charge in the modern Swedish style from the Royalist horse led by the King's nephew Prince Rupert of the Rhine. It was only the cavaliers' lack of discipline as they rode off in pursuit of the fleeing troops that enabled the Earl of Essex to launch a counter-attack that saved the day from one of absolute defeat to a draw.

It was clear that a large and competent cavalry was going to be crucial in the war and Oliver made it his mission over the next few years to recruit, train and position himself to lead such a force. Within a year of assembling his initial single troop of horses in Huntingdon in August 1642, Oliver had raised ten troops of around eighty men each to serve under his command. Promotion from captain to colonel accompanied this effort and in January 1643 he brought his men into the new Eastern Association army formed to protect the region from Royalist incursion. Oliver's relationship with his new regiment of horses was intimate and emotional: 'I have a lovely company,' he wrote to his cousin in September 1643.[76] This was hardly surprising given that it was stuffed with his own family. Oliver's oldest surviving son and namesake Oliver junior (now 20 years old), his nephew Valentine Walton, his brother-in-law John Desborough and his cousin Edward Whalley each commanded a troop. But Oliver also took an unusual interest in the calibre of men he recruited. These were to be godly men whose religious convictions were at least as important, if not more, than their social status. As he famously wrote in August 1643 'I had rather have a plain russet-coated captain, that knows what he fights for, and loves what he knows, than that which you call a gentleman and is nothing else. I honour a gentleman that is so indeed.'[77] It was these religious independents in the Army who would become Oliver's most important friends and allies as the war progressed and his relationship with former parliamentary colleagues deteriorated.

The welfare of his men exercised Oliver greatly and the constant quest for pay, provisions and equipment occupied much of his time and thoughts, sometimes reducing him to tears. 'I count not myself worthy to be employed by God,' he wrote to another cousin, 'but for my poor men, help them what you can, for they are faithful.'[78] His men returned his ardour, clearly inspired by his devotion, charisma and skilful communication both in rallying them and advocating on their behalf. It was thanks to their intervention that Oliver did not die in a skirmish at Winceby in October 1643 when his horse was killed under him and he was then knocked over again on foot, only escaping on a borrowed mount after his men had fought off his assailant. Less worthily, this camaraderie continued off the battlefield where Oliver and his troops rode roughshod over the region ostensibly in its defence. Royalists were rooted out, Cambridge was looted and old scores settled.

Oliver's military actions in 1643 were relatively minor, regional incidents, yet collectively they gave him the experience, growing reputation and blistering self-confidence that would drive him onto the national stage. They also introduced him to some of the key men who would shape his career. Two in particular: the swarthy Yorkshire gentleman Sir Thomas Fairfax who commanded Parliament's northern force with his father, and with whom Oliver would go on to form his most enduring and consequential military partnership; and the tall, dark-haired Henry Ireton, a young Puritan firebrand from Nottinghamshire, who would become not only his closest political ally but a member of his own immediate family. It was Ireton who Oliver installed as his deputy when he was rewarded for his local industriousness by being appointed Governor of the Isle of Ely. And it was at Ely that Ireton met Oliver's wife, mother and daughters. They were still living in the timber-framed house near the cathedral, now effectively a makeshift military headquarters as the home front became the front line.

Already Oliver's family were struggling with the costs of the war. With official funds promised but rarely materialising, Oliver often paid to clothe and equip his men himself despite rarely receiving his own pay. 'My estate is little,' he wrote in one of his many desperate letters. 'I tell you, the business of Ireland and England hath had of me in money between eleven and twelve hundred pounds, therefore my private can do little to help the public.'[79] Matters were so dire that on 3 July 1643 Oliver's mother sent a proudly worded request for the return of £50 of her own money to a cousin, writing 'I wish there might be care to spare some monies for my son who hath I fear been too long and much neglected.'[80] This short letter in a neat, sloping script reveals much, not only that the family's financial struggles were sufficient to overcome Elizabeth's evident pride in calling in this debt, but her fervent belief in her son and his cause. She wished 'the all mighty prosper the work and our precious friends engaged in his service against the antichristian and malicious enemies of his Church and people'. Oliver's family shared in his crusade, though this never eclipsed the need to maintain respectful affection between relations, particularly between women, and Elizabeth sent her 'loving respects' to her cousin's wife, mother and sister.

By the close of 1643, Oliver could reflect that he had got his war off to a good start. He commanded a regiment and, though his actions had been limited to Eastern England, his shrewd knack for self-promotion had won him a wider reputation, both positive and negative; as he rose in prominence, he acquired enemies on his own side as much as the other. The wider picture was more concerning. Parliament's military position was fragile after a series of defeats culminating in the fall of Bristol. They had also lost some key figures in the cause, including John Hampden from battle wounds in June and John Pym from cancer in December. Yet Pym had secured help just before his death, hammering out an alliance with the Scottish Covenanters. Ideologically in step with Parliament since their own troubles with Charles I in the late 1630s, the two had now signed a 'Solemn League and Covenant' under which the Scots provided an army in return for all citizens of England, Scotland and Ireland declaring to uphold the Presbyterian church of Scotland and reform the churches of England and Ireland along its lines. These 21,000 Scottish troops would transform the war, yet the carefully and ambiguously worded alliance in which England promised to reform itself along Presbyterian lines stored up future trouble.

For now, Oliver's fortunes continued to improve. Parliament rewarded him and his commander, his family's erstwhile rival from Huntingdon, Edward Montagu, the Earl of Manchester, while the Eastern Association was placed on a stronger footing. Oliver was promoted to Lieutenant General in January, second in command to Manchester and overall commander of the Eastern Association's cavalry. Just as important was his appointment in February 1644 to the Committee of Both Kingdoms – the executive body created to coordinate the war effort by Parliament and its new Scottish allies. It was now, as his later colleague Bulstrode Whitelocke noted, that Oliver 'began to appear in the world'.[81] Yet the war was about to extract terrible personal costs.

❦ ❦ ❦

On 2 July 1644 at Marston Moor, just outside York, five armies of almost 50,000 men clashed in one of the largest and most brutal battles ever fought on English soil. Parliament's Allied force of the Fairfaxes' Yorkshire army, the Eastern Association and the Earl of Leven's Scottish army inflicted a stunning defeat upon Prince Rupert and the Earl of Newcastle's Royalist forces. Oliver Cromwell, commanding the left wing of Parliament's combined cavalry, played a key role in the rout, breaking the opposing cavalry and pressuring the infantry; this was the battle that made his name. Afterwards he was elated, despite a bullet wound to his neck, his conviction that God had given them victory mingling with an unleashed blood-lust, writing 'we never charged but we routed the enemy, the wing which I commanded being our own horse, saving a few Scots in our rear, beat all the Prince's horse, God made them as stubble to our Swords'.[82] Victory was his but there had been a price. As Oliver's cavalry charged Rupert's artillery train, a cannon shot ripped into four horses, including that ridden by his young nephew, Valentine Walton, eldest surviving son of Oliver's sister Margaret and her husband and Oliver's great friend Valentine Walton.

The Waltons were stalwarts of the Cromwell family war effort: Valentine Walton senior had been the first to ride with Oliver to seize the Cambridge plate and now commanded the town of King's Lynn while his son, Valentine junior, led one of the troops in Oliver's regiment. It was to his brother-in-law, Valentine Walton senior, that a blood-stained Oliver sat down to write his account of the battle and break the news of the horrible death of Walton's son. This condolence letter is one of Oliver's most famous. 'There is your precious child,' one bereaved father wrote to another, 'full of glory, to know sin nor sorrow anymore.'[83] Yet again a keen-eyed God had plucked the best from among them to reclaim for himself. Oliver knew the comfort this belief brought from bitter experience and recommended to Walton the same Bible passage he leaned on in his grief. 'Sir you know my trials this way,' he reminded Walton. It was 'trials' plural, not only referring to the loss of his son James as a baby and Oliver's eldest son Robert as a teenager away at Felsted School, but to reflect yet another son seen into the ground. In a disturbing repeating pattern reminiscent of God's plague upon the first-born sons of Egypt, Oliver and Elizabeth's second son, 21-year-old Oliver junior – who had become the eldest surviving son and heir at Robert's sudden death five years before – had recently died of smallpox while garrisoned with Parliament's army at Newport Pagnell. 'Colonel Cromwell . . . hath lost his eldest son, who is dead of the smallpox at Newport,' reported the *Parliament Scout* newspaper adding, 'a civil young gentleman, and the joy of his father'.[84]

Both observations ring true, for young Oliver had commanded a troop in his father's regiment, fought in several skirmishes and acquired a reputation for disciplined godliness. A solitary letter of his survives from August 1643 giving a snapshot of the boy officer. In this, Oliver junior writes to the Steward of Norwich from his quarters at Peterborough to request he dispense aid and punishment to members of his troop. Thanking the city for supplying godly men to the Army, he complains that 'among honest men some knaves have been admitted into my troop'. Finding themselves unable to achieve their own 'base ends', these scoundrels had 'deserted the cause and me their captain' rendering them 'displeasers of my father, myself and the whole regiment'. Oliver asked such men to be made 'severe examples' of, imprisoned and punished as the Steward saw fit. Like his father, Oliver junior balanced strict discipline for the wayward with tender care for the loyal, requesting the Steward to return speedily 'all that had liberty from me to go to their friends' and that horses be found for those men recruited by the messenger and one particular soldier 'who was lately taken prisoner by the enemy and by that means destitute'.[85] Presented with such a chip off the old Cromwellian block, it is tempting to reflect on the strange fate that befell Oliver and Elizabeth's sons: the catastrophic loss of an older brother twice over now transforming the eighteen-year-old Richard, their third son, into his father's heir. At this point the teenage Richard could never have imagined that his eventual inheritance would be not a small collection of property in Ely but no less than the throne of England. Might a Robert or Oliver Cromwell II have made a better fist as Lord Protector after their father's death than 'Tumbledown Dick' managed?

In a horrible mirror image, both Oliver Cromwell and Valentine Walton had seen their eldest surviving sons and namesakes sacrificed on the altar of Parliament's 'Good Old Cause' within months. Oliver's 'odd and strained' signature on the warrant he signed delivering horses to his son's replacement as captain hints at a shaken father.[86] But once again his faith helped disarm his grief, enhanced now by his sense of the war's holy purpose. After such personal devastation, it was vital that the victory should not be wasted. Yet in a series of missteps and defeats during the autumn of 1644, the parliamentary army's senior aristocratic leadership squandered the miraculous achievement at Marston Moor. Oliver and his allies suspected them of nervousness at the prospect of an outright parliamentary victory – a nervousness confirmed by Oliver's commander the Earl of Manchester's famous wail that 'If we fight a hundred times and beat him [the King] ninety-nine he will be King still, but if he beats us but once, or the last time, we shall be hanged, we shall lose our estates, and our posterities undone.'[87] Manchester's estates included the former Cromwellian seat of Hinchingbrooke – a prize Oliver knew all too well how painful it was to lose. But for him, with no great estate to gamble but a heavy personal price already paid, only a decisive victory would do. Only then would Parliament be in a strong enough position to achieve its aims. As Oliver rebuked Manchester at his complaint, 'If this be so, why did we take up arms at first?'[88]

Taking their quarrel to Parliament in November 1644, Oliver inveighed against Manchester in the Commons while Manchester railed against Oliver in the Lords, both reaching for exaggeration if not outright falsehoods. To Oliver, Manchester was an incompetent leader who had sabotaged the war effort to enable a peace with the King on the basis of a Presbyterian church settlement. To Manchester, Oliver was a dangerous hothead, a religious and social radical prejudiced against their Presbyterian Scots allies, and a warlord who embezzled money and used threats to set himself up as 'Lord of the Fens'. Manchester even called into question Oliver's arrangement that £5 a week out of his army pay be paid by the treasurer of Ely directly to his wife Elizabeth 'to bear the extraordinary charges' she was incurring at home.[89]

Their dispute crystallised the position between the war and peace parties now gathering within the parliamentary coalition. Manchester had powerful support in the shape of the Army's commander-in-chief the Earl of Essex, sympathetic MPs like Denzil Holles and their Scottish friends who, in December, met at Essex's house to consider impeaching Oliver. Oliver meanwhile had his own allies including the former Junto members Lord Saye and Sele, Lord Wharton and Oliver St John, as well as fellow army leaders William 'the Conqueror' Waller and Henry Ireton. A deadlock loomed but Oliver, by now skilled in the art of politics, broke it on 9 December 1644 by agreeing to a kamikaze move: suggesting in the Commons that the dispute be resolved by a 'Self Denying Ordinance' preventing any member of Parliament from holding military command. This, at a stroke, would sweep away not only Manchester and Essex from their posts but Oliver himself too. Yet it would enable the refashioning of a systematically funded, professionally trained and equipped, single, united army under the new leadership of the apolitical, popular Sir Thomas Fairfax; a 'new modelled' army bred for the sole purpose of indisputably defeating the King in the field.

Oliver did not at the time foresee the eventual form the Ordinance would take after four months' wrangling in Parliament. Having led parallel lives as a politician and a soldier for nearly three years, he seemed to accept that his future would now follow a single track at Westminster where he busied himself on the committees recruiting and organising the New Model Army. Some bemoaned this waste, wishing Oliver's evident talent and industry could be applied in both spheres. The Ordinance 'will fetch that gallant man Cromwell from the Army, which will be a mighty loss to the kingdom', acknowledged his friend the Leveller leader John Lilburne, in print. But it was worth it, for 'if he come into the House of Commons . . . and do them ten times more service there, than he doth, or can do in the Army, what loss hath the Common-Wealth then? . . . O for self-denying Cromwell home again!'[90] Yet Oliver did not need to deny his services to the Army for long. Parliament found a loophole in spring 1645 by re-employing him in the Army on a series of temporary 40-day commissions, eventually according him the plum role of lieutenant-general of horse.

On receiving this last command in June, Oliver raced with 600–800 men to join the New Model Army at Naseby in Northamptonshire: his acclaimed arrival the last piece needed for the Army council to order it to march immediately upon the King's. As at Marston Moor, Oliver's stellar command of the cavalry on the right wing was central to an outright victory for the New Model, particularly when Henry Ireton's troopers on the left were routed. Ireton himself had his horse shot under him and was wounded in the face and thigh before being captured, though he escaped in the confusion of the battle. A comprehensive win for Parliament, Naseby brought outright victory over the King for the first time within grasp. The hour was at hand, and Oliver Cromwell was there to seize it. Destiny now called, as Andrew Marvell saw it:

> *That 'tis the most which we determine can,*
> *If these the times, then this must be the man.*[91]

Five

Victory

More threateneth them which enterprise difficult and urgent matters than those which only seeketh easy and light matters.

Stephen Vaughan to Thomas Cromwell, 3 February 1530

Saints and sinners

Thomas and Oliver Cromwell had both won fame and formative success through service to Parliament. But it was the nation's spiritual welfare which concerned them above all, and which each addressed from his growing platform. By 1534 Thomas felt emboldened to advance his own desire for evangelical reform on the coat-tails of the King's political break from Rome. The schism may not have been his idea, but he was the man who made it happen and the one now in a position to use it as a vehicle to achieve much more. The parliamentary Acts of Succession and Supremacy brought Henry's new autonomous England into being, flushing out its opponents in the process as much of Christendom watched in horror. The Pope excommunicated Henry and the Emperor Charles V warned of dire consequences if his aunt Katherine of Aragon and cousin Princess Mary were mistreated. At home there was great sympathy for the wronged Queen Katherine and widespread dislike for the usurping Anne Boleyn while leading opponents in the church and court like Bishop John Fisher and Sir Thomas More hovered on the edge of events, a hair's breadth from treason.

The embattled King and his chief minister embarked on a campaign of diplomacy and propaganda to shore up their fragile position. But an iron fist was needed inside the velvet glove if the new England was to endure, sending them down a dark path of brutal enforcement. Since the new Princess Elizabeth's birth in September 1533, the King's line of succession had to be safeguarded and the English people bullied into submission. This unedifying task fell on the stout shoulders of the only man it could: the King's new principal secretary, 'Lord Crumwell, the King's ear and mind, to whom he had entrusted the entire government of the kingdom'.[1]

All men now had to swear an oath to the lawfulness of the King's marriage to Anne Boleyn and the rightful succession of her children. Not to do so, or to speak against the new arrangement, was punishable under the draconian Treason Act. The King was determined to punish those who disobeyed him, his victims including the Carthusian monks of the Charterhouse, and most notoriously, the elderly Bishop Fisher and the former Chancellor and famous intellectual Sir Thomas More. This campaign of terror has long been laid at Thomas Cromwell's door, gaining its widest audience in Robert Bolt's play, and the later film, *A Man for All Seasons*, which pits a conniving Cromwell against a sainted More. Certainly, Thomas was as effective in this bloody work as in everything else he did and he cannot escape some culpability. Yet he saw to the prisoners' material comfort and went to great lengths to try and reconcile their positions with the King's, clearly hoping, particularly of More whom he much admired, that they would swear the oath and save themselves. In so doing he earned the gratitude of More's wife Alice who wrote to Thomas that she was 'most deeply bound . . . for your manifold goodnesses and loving favour, both before this time, and yet daily, now also showed towards my poor husband and me'.[2] More himself had sent many people to their deaths for not supporting the papacy, as Thomas pointed out to him, and this was but the same mechanism in reverse. But More was as immovable as Henry was implacable and Thomas could do nothing to mitigate either. The Thomas who emerges from his fatal battle of words with More is an exasperated and saddened one: the instrument but not the instigator of a brutal and inescapable policy that destroyed, in More, one of the leading lights of Christendom.

The newly tilled ground laid with blood, Thomas ascended to a unique and powerful new role as Henry's 'Vice-Gerent in Spirituals', effectively his deputy in religious matters. The whole of the new Church of England now lay at his feet, including the supervision of Oxford and Cambridge universities, the latter of which also elected him its Chancellor. The uneducated Putney ruffian had come far. Thomas lost no time in arranging a national visitation of churches and religious houses, his commissioners inspecting them and recording all their assets in their *Valor Ecclesiasticus*, a modern-day version of the Domesday Book. These commissioners earned a bad reputation as brutes, some of this opprobrium refracting back onto Thomas when it reached the ear of the King. The information they collected was, after all, political dynamite: amid some positive reports, sufficient apparent evidence of loose living and corruption to justify legislation to dissolve the lesser monasteries.

Through the pens of many – not least the approving Foxe – Thomas is widely held to be the author of what followed, the masterminding scourge of the monasteries. In fact, it is hard to know for certain the extent to which Thomas pre-planned this policy or whether he intended it to extend to all the larger monastic houses, which it did eighteen months later. The King had long had the monasteries in his sights and he and many in his Council were greedy for the Church's wealth. There are signs Thomas himself preferred a more limited and piecemeal approach: the slimming down and reforming of monasticism rather than its total destruction.[3] His *Injunctions* to the clergy which travelled with his commissioners stipulated reforms which would redirect monastic living along more evangelical lines.

Education lay at the heart of this project. Thomas had long wished to widen access to reformed learning: for children of the upper classes to be brought up 'in good literature' with other children schooled 'after their abilities, wits and aptness, in sciences and crafts' with the education of all 'to the great advancement of the common weal'.[4] In his *Injunctions*, Thomas went into meticulous detail on how children should be taught 'even from their infancy, their Paternoster, the Articles of our Faith, and the Ten Commandments in their mother tongue'. This was to be done by curates plainly reciting a clause daily, giving this out in writing, and showing children where to find it in printed books, instilling a lifelong thirst for learning.[5] Abbots were now to send one or two of their monks to university and pay for an expansion in schooling, funding exhibitions for students at grammar schools and the universities to the tune of one scholar per £100 of each cleric's annual income.[6] In this vision, many dissolved monasteries could become centres of new learning. A bill for the King to establish new bishoprics which he introduced in May 1539 envisaged transformed religious houses 'whereby God's word might be better set forth, children brought up in learning, clerks nourished in the universities, old servants decayed to have livings, almshouses for poor folk to be sustained in, readers of Hebrew, Greek and Latin to have good stipends, and daily alms to be administered'.[7]

All this echoed Thomas's programme of university reform once he became Chancellor of Cambridge University in 1535: a remarkable achievement for a man of no formal education. Thomas had already developed a network of reformist academic friends at Cambridge, many of whom he had earlier recruited to posts in Wolsey's Oxford college. From now on, he funnelled talent from both universities into the King's political causes, personally funding many scholars. He widened access to education and reformed the universities' curriculum, breaking the historic monopoly of medieval scholasticism (a system of theology and philosophy based on Aristotelian logic and the writings of the early Christian Fathers which emphasised tradition and dogma) to usher in new continental humanist and evangelical thinking. His injunctions to both Cambridge and Oxford universities removed canon law, allowed students to study the Bible privately for themselves and stipulated daily lectures (including two open to the public) not only in Latin but in Greek – the language of the New Testament. Humanities courses in logic, arithmetic, rhetoric, music and geography added to a holistic education. The universities officially welcomed the changes, though many dons resisted. Yet students were keener. From Cambridge Thomas heard that 'they say you have done more for the advancement of learning than ever Chancellor did'.[8]

Thomas had begun to transform university education, and also now took his first steps towards securing an officially sanctioned English translation of the Bible for ordinary people to access in their parish church. Yet the grand schemes he may have harboured for the dissolved religious houses faltered when faced with grubby reality. The monasteries, abbeys and friaries of England were parcelled out by the new Court of Augmentations helmed by Thomas's protégé

Richard Rich to be converted into fine houses for the wealthy, repurposed as community buildings or, in many cases, simply left to crumble, their carcasses littering the countryside as a constant reminder of a bygone life. By the zenith of the dissolution in 1538, friaries and nunneries, holy sites, shrines and images had been drawn into the line of fire. Even the most famous English shrine of all – St Thomas Becket's at Canterbury – was not safe despite Becket's role as the patron saint of all Tudor 'Thomases' including Thomas Cromwell. Thomas himself attracted the hatred of many in the monasteries he closed but also received gratitude and affection from those he helped to avoid or mitigate closure.

If not as violent a process as sometimes assumed – most monks surrendered for transfers or pensions – the dissolution was devastatingly destructive to the lives of those caught up in it and to the nation's cultural and physical landscape. About 50 years later, a man wrote down his uncle's memories of the dissolution of Roche Abbey: 'It would have pitied any heart to see what tearing up of lead there was, and plucking up of boards, and throwing down of the spars; and when the lead was torn off and cast down into the Church, and the tombs in the Church all broken . . . and all things of price either spoiled, carped away or defaced to the uttermost.'[9]

The author felt some complicity, having challenged his father who had himself suppressed his love of the monasteries to profit from their fire sale, concluding that men, through their sin, had become the instrument 'to punish themselves, and all their posterity from generation to generation!' Thus the family became the repository of these complicated feelings. This remained the case another half century on when the Civil Wars brought further iconoclasm as Puritans sought to finish what Thomas's Reformation had started. The London Puritan Nehemiah Wallington, offering an opposite perspective, kept some broken objects from the purge of the City churches 'to keep for a remembrance to show to the generation to come what God hath done for us, to give us such a Reformation that our forefathers never saw the like'.[10]

❦ ❦ ❦

The destructive events of the 1530s' dissolution of the monasteries had cast a long shadow in popular memory. A conversation about the Cromwell family in the 1620s (and later noted down in the 1650s) reveals a scurrilous tale heard from one of Henry VIII's courtiers about how Thomas Cromwell's nephew Richard acquired Hinchingbrooke nunnery – a 'most pleasant seat' he 'much thirsted after'. Taking matters into his own hands, the wicked Richard had ridden with this courtier and other young gentlemen 'to visit the nuns with a purpose to debauch them, and so render them odious to the intent [that] he might accomplish his ends' of acquiring the property. All did not go to plan, however. The men were 'repulsed in their enterprise with much scorn' by the plucky nuns, who behaved with 'exceeding modesty and gravity'. So Richard and his fellows used the other weapon so often wielded against women and 'gave it out, that they lived viciously, and were whores'. As a result, Richard got his hands on Hinchingbrooke while the courtier, alive years after Richard had died, told this tale 'with great reluctance and sorrow, apprehending his part to be very foul, which he much repented of'.[11]

This account of Richard's behaviour is hearsay, and we cannot know the full truth of its assertions. The Cromwell family was undoubtedly eager to acquire former religious estates, yet it is unlikely they resorted to such brutal tactics, given accounts of Hinchingbrooke's history suggest few nuns were left at this time. We can be certain, however, that the violence of the Reformation which bloodied the hands of gentry families across England caused some individuals and their descendants great guilt, bequeathing a bitterly contested legacy to the 1640s generation which struggled with 'the radioactive afterlife of England's unfinished Reformation'.[12] In the matter of religious change, the past and the present shared a charged relationship: to the scribe of the 1650s, the events of the 1530s felt closer and more relevant than we might assume. Contemporaries like the antiquarian William Dugdale – whose book contained the Cromwell family tale – even worried history was repeating itself with the iconoclasm of the Civil Wars damaging churches just as the dissolution of the monasteries had done. It was this fear that prompted Dugdale to record the antiquities of Warwickshire, condemning 'that barbarous generation' who had first attacked the church under Henry VIII, chief among them Thomas Cromwell 'so active an Instrument to accomplish the [monasteries'] ruin'.[13]

For Dugdale's generation, enough time had passed for the Reformation to move from personal memory to a neutral space where they could argue over what had actually happened. The 'Dissolution' of the monasteries itself was not yet seen as a distinct event and worthy of study, and it was only through the work of the Royalist historian Thomas Fuller in the 1650s that the concept of the events of the 1530s as a 'Reformation' was fully cemented.[14] Fuller's notion has endured, yet we can now see that there was not only one distinct and finite Reformation but at least two, the final phases of which lasted into Fuller's own lifetime; a second Reformation in continued dialogue with the first.[15] Consequently, interest in the events of the 1530s, and in Thomas Cromwell's role in them, grew in the 1640s. New editions of Tudor texts emphasised the revolutionary nature of the dissolution, introducing a new audience to Thomas as evil counsellor or reformist hero.[16]

Charles I himself took an interest in the topic, commissioning the historian Lord Herbert of Chirbury to write a history of the reign of Henry VIII which he oversaw.[17] A letter from an ill and flustered Chirbury to Secretary Coke of 1636 captures the importance of Thomas Cromwell to this endeavour as Chirbury asked for a copy of Sir Henry Spelman's *Cromwell's Life*, for his own history now required 'that he mention him with much particularity'.[18] Henry VIII remained a problematic figure for Royalists, many of whom – including Queen Henrietta Maria – now believed the Civil War to have been unjust punishment on Charles I for the sins of Henry's greedy Reformation. Their enemies, meanwhile, saw parallels between the two kings' tyrannical styles, likening Henry's Royal Supremacy to Charles's period of Personal Rule.[19]

For the King's opponents in Westminster, the upheaval of civil war produced an opportunity to enact religious reforms – if they could agree on them. The plan to dismantle and reform the Laudian church, which the King had theoretically agreed to in 1642, fell apart once he declared war. An altogether more radical proposal emerged from the Westminster Assembly of clergy, in large part designed to appeal to Parliament's new Scots allies in the war effort. This moved the Church of England towards Presbyterianism, with bishops ejected from the House of Lords and the Elizabethan Book of Common Prayer abandoned in favour of a simplified Directory of Public Worship. Christmas, and other festivals, fell victim to this new religious austerity, first downgraded as 'Christ-tide' (a seventeenth-century 'Winterval') and then abolished entirely by a victorious Parliament in June 1647. Puritans welcomed the removal of a wasteful, drunken, debauched and commercialised excuse for a knees-up with no justification in the Bible. Oliver Cromwell was likely of this view, though, contrary to popular belief, he never expressed an opinion on Christmas and took no part in the ban. The majority of the population, though, objected to losing their precious yuletide celebration, decrying its removal as top-down meddling of the worst sort. As one popular ballad bemoaned, 'Christmas was killed at Naseby fight.'[20]

As in the first Reformation, the fabric of church buildings was also targeted. Indeed, the Puritans of the 1640s took the violence of the dissolution up a notch shifting from iconoclasm to outright iconophobia.[21] The State itself sponsored this through Parliament's 1643–4 legislation for 'the utter demolition . . . of all Monuments of Superstition and Idolatry'. Cathedrals and royal chapels were stripped out while London crowds attacked churches and monuments like the Cheapside Cross. Most notoriously, Parliamentarian soldiers used the rampaging opportunities of their campaigns to desecrate churches and sacred sites; their efforts to erase ironically perpetuating local memory of their actions. While these are remembered widely in folklore, reliable contemporary accounts of these events are few and far between and myth and legend cloud the picture still further.

This is particularly clear in the case of Oliver Cromwell's involvement. He is popularly supposed to have defaced and defiled sites across the three kingdoms – indeed it can feel hard to find an extant church that does not claim that a callous Oliver stabled his horses in it. In most cases evidence of his personal involvement is sketchy; indeed, it is often impossible that he was present as it would have required him to be in multiple places at once. There is only one incidence of iconoclasm which we can confidently lay at his door: the spoliation of Peterborough Cathedral in April 1643. Witnessing his men ransacking the church, he is reported to have commented approvingly that they 'did God good action in that service', even joining in, climbing a ladder to pull down a crucifix high in the west window. His son Oliver's troops were also involved, though some tried to protect rather than obliterate. One man rescued the cathedral ledger book, writing in it 'I pray let this scripture book alone, for he hath paid me for it . . . By me Henry Topcliffe, soldier under Captain Cromwell, Colonel Cromwell's son.'[22]

Oliver also intervened in this raging culture war when it came to his hometown of Ely where he was Governor. There he famously interrupted a cathedral choir service demanding the choristers disperse – an incident taken by many as indisputable evidence of his menacing iconoclasm. Yet the particulars of the event reveal a subtler situation. He had previously written to the vicar, Reverend Hitch, advising him to stop holding choral services 'lest the soldiers should in any tumultuary or disorderly way attempt the Reformation of your Cathedral church'. This too has been seen in threatening terms, yet the tone is more of friendly warning to a man Oliver knew well and who probably later performed the marriage of his daughter Elizabeth; indeed, Oliver signs off 'your loving friend'. The letter was sent the day after some soldiers had unilaterally vandalised the cathedral and so represents Oliver's attempt to restore order and keep the peace.[23] Oliver's sympathy with his men's objection to the sung services did not spring from any Philistinism on his part but from the Puritan attitude that music in church was a distraction from the word of God. He was a great lover of music: as Lord Protector he saved the organs at Magdalen College Oxford and Exeter Cathedral, having them transported to London for his own secular enjoyment. The rest of his letter to the vicar conveys his desire for the spoken word to be prioritised over the sung, advising him to 'catechise and read, and expound the scriptures' and requesting more sermons.

Oliver's sympathies may have lain with the iconoclasts within the Army, but his reputation as their barbaric leader is largely constructed. This narrative has arisen in part from the tendency for every roundhead action of the Civil Wars to be retrospectively ascribed to the man who would eventually come to represent the entire cause. But much of it stems from centuries of local confusion between Oliver and Thomas Cromwell and their respective roles in damaging buildings through the 1530s' dissolution or the 1640s' iconoclasm or warfare. In a process recently dubbed 'mnemonic telescoping' and 'temporal compression', the century between the two men was collapsed by later generations who ascribed destruction which occurred under the early Cromwell to the later; the first Reformation muddled with the second.[24]

At the end of the seventeenth century, the name of Cromwell was said to be 'as fatal now to ministers [i.e. minsters] as once it had been to monasteries' while, a hundred years on, the travel writer John Byng noted at a ruined castle near Eynsham, that 'Whenever I enquire about ruins I always get the same answer, that it was some papish place, and destroyed by Oliver Cromwell, to whose share is laid even much more devastation than he really committed.'[25] At Farringdon church, a 'voluble clerk' told him 'all the old stories of O. Cromwell, of loss of brasses, and demolition of tombs'. Eventually Byng became exasperated by this, complaining of the monotony at every castle he visited 'to detail the demolitions, real or false, of O. Cromwell'.[26] Byng would have recognised the confusion in the local tradition at Husbands Boswell where a perpetually wet stain of communion wine or blood was spilled by a priest escaping 'Cromwell's men' – whether Thomas's commissioners or Oliver's soldiers is unclear. So too, the speech for the reopening of the restored Covington Church in the nineteenth century which recorded that many generations had believed the church once had a spire which was destroyed by Oliver's cannon. However, recent archaeology suggests there may well have been a spire, but the stones and masonry discovered date from three hundred years before the Civil Wars.[27]

It has been the work of centuries to conflate Thomas and Oliver to create a national bogeyman to soak up local traditions and explain moments of historic change. But the family link between them was spotted as soon as Oliver began to operate on the national stage in 1644. In a satirical pamphlet, the Royalist writer Peter Hausted mock-celebrated Oliver's reforming campaign by casting him as the heir to his 'grandparent' Thomas:

> *Arch Deacon Cromwells visitation*
> *Hath cleansed all (in whose pure veins doth run*
> *Th'reforming Bloud and vertues of his Grand*
> *Parent, that Man of Iron, whose tough Hand,*
> *Arm'd with his Fathers Hammer, at one Blow*
> *Made many a stately Abbey lie full low)*
> *Who in one godly March upon his way*
> *(Help'd by his Surrogate the good Lord Grey)*
> *Five Crosses kill'd, Five bookes of Common Prayers,*
> *Five Surplices, Five Fiddles, and Five Beares.*
> *Bless'd Reformation!*[28]

Thus Oliver, the military leader coming to be known as 'Ironsides', derived his strength and reforming zeal from his ancestor Thomas, the 'Man of Iron', who his father (the supposed blacksmith Walter) had armed for this work 'with his Father's Hammer'. Oliver was now an 'Arch Deacon' and his campaign a 'visitation' just as that sent out to all religious houses by Thomas, the Vice-Gerent, had been. Four years on, the connection was stronger still, with another Royalist cursing 'Oliver Cromwell a name that hath been ever ominous to the Church: for in Henry the eights days . . . a Cromwell was the hammer that beat down the monasteries' while now 'this Cromwell' was 'defacing, demolishing, and levelling Churches'. For Oliver's admirers, by contrast, his association with Thomas was a positive one. A decade later, John Milton wrote of Oliver's surname that it was 'a name distinguished of old in the State-administration of England when it was under good Kings, and distinguished still more in connexion with the first restoration or establishment among us of the Protestant Religion'.[29] From either viewpoint, history appeared to be repeating itself through the vehicle of the Cromwell family.

The Civil War finally came to an end in June 1646 when the King's wartime capital Oxford surrendered to a besieging Sir Thomas Fairfax. Charles himself had slipped out of the city in disguise at the outset of the siege, handing himself over to the Scots who he assumed would treat him more favourably than Parliament. Four years of violent conflict had shaken the nations with fragments of the past alongside those of the present now settling in new patterns with the New Model Army's completed victory. All minds now shifted to politics as winning the war gave way to securing the peace. In the tortuous months of negotiations which lay ahead, Charles must have contrasted the growth of Henry VIII's supremacy with his own receding power, especially with disputes over the nations' religious future so central to a settlement. Reflecting on this led him to swear an oath 'to restore to the church all lands and lay impropriations held by the Crown if he should ever be restored to his "just kingly rights"'.[30] Perhaps the dissolution could be undone after all? The four years of civil conflict had revealed a new Cromwell to take on the mantle of the first, just as it had forced the current king to atone for the actions of his predecessor. Where the partnership between Thomas Cromwell and Henry VIII was flourishing in 1535, in 1646 enemies Oliver Cromwell and Charles I were soon to meet for the first time to see if they could work together

St Mary's Church, Putney: Thomas Cromwell's parish church and the site of the 1647 Putney Debates chaired by Oliver Cromwell

Hans Holbein's 1532 portrait of Thomas Cromwell as a busy royal servant

A Holbein miniature of Gregory Cromwell likely painted as a pair with a miniature of his father Thomas, probably to commemorate Gregory's marriage in 1537

The title page of Thomas Cromwell's own hand-coloured presentation copy of the Great Bible he produced in 1539, with Thomas featured prominently on the right distributing the Bible to the laity, his family coat of arms at his feet. Both his portraits and arms were removed in later versions

A Holbein portrait long assumed to be of Katherine Howard but almost certainly of Elizabeth Seymour, sister of Queen Jane, who married Gregory Cromwell

Launde Abbey, Thomas Cromwell's planned retirement home where Gregory Cromwell lived with his family after his father's death

Gregory Cromwell's magnificent memorial in the Chapel of Launde Abbey

The polymath Catherine Tollemache, mistress of Helmingham Hall and great-granddaughter of Thomas Cromwell

Helmingham Hall in Suffolk, home of Thomas Cromwell's great-granddaughter Catherine Tollemache and later of her Royalist grand daughter-in-law Elizabeth (Bess) Murray who hosted meetings of the Sealed Knot

The Cromwell family seat of Hinchingbrooke House in Huntingdon. This bow window, added in 1602 and crowned with the arms of Elizabeth I, features Cromwell heraldry in the stonework

The Cromwells' rampant lion holding the diamond ring Henry VIII gave to Sir Richard Cromwell, carved into the bow window

Detail from the one visible panel of the mural depicting Sir Richard Cromwell's May Day joust and knighthood in the parlour of the Cromwell Tower, Hinchingbrooke House

The Cromwell family pedigree commissioned by Sir Henry Cromwell in 1602 which traced the family's lineage back to the Welsh Princes of Powys

Thomas Cromwell's coat of arms which paid tribute to Cardinal Wolsey and to his Williams in-laws

The Protectorate coat of arms modelled on Tudor predecessors, with the crowns and heraldic supporters symbolising monarchy, the Cromwells' rampant lion in the middle of the shield on top of the Commonwealth's arms, and Oliver's personal motto 'Peace is sought through war'

Sir Oliver Cromwell, courtier and Royalist head of the Hinchingbrooke Cromwells and uncle to Oliver Cromwell

Thomas Cromwell's great-great grandson, Thomas Cromwell, 4th Baron Cromwell, Viscount Lecale and 1st Earl of Ardglass, who fought for the King in the Civil Wars

The house Oliver Cromwell inherited in Ely where the family lived from 1636-1646, and which is now a museum

The churchyard of Holy Cross, Felsted with the old schoolroom on the left, where Oliver Cromwell's sons studied and his eldest, Robert, died in 1639. Both he and Oliver's son-in-law Robert Rich are buried somewhere here

Robert Walker's martial depiction of Oliver Cromwell became the template image of the Lord Protector which travelled across Europe constructively. But, as always, changes in the fortunes of the leading Cromwell men affected their families every bit as much as themselves. For both households, victory expanded their homes and horizons to bring new tests and temptations.

London calling

As Thomas Cromwell grew in stature in the King's service, so did his household. In October 1534, he added another plum job to his portfolio: the prestigious legal position of Master of the Rolls. The role came with a handsome manor house in Holborn, the chapel of which still exists today within the Maughan Library of King's College London. Thomas immediately set about transforming the Rolls house into his central office, moving many of his staff there from Austin Friars.[31] It became a hub of activity. Gregory's former supervisor and Thomas's friend, the prioress Margaret Vernon, complained to him that she was unable to get in to see him at the Rolls house: 'I have divers times been at the Rolls to have spoken with your mastership, but by reason of the great number of suitors, and also for lack of friendship with your mastership's house, I am kept back; so that I cannot come to your presence to solicit my cause . . .'[32] Thomas clearly relished this new prestigious headquarters, refusing to relinquish it when his tenure as Master of the Rolls ended in 1536.

Thomas now had two bases in central London: Austin Friars and the Rolls house. With much business now undertaken at the latter, he could continue to develop the former into a spacious family home and office befitting his status as the King's chief minister and earning the praise of Chapuys for being 'magnificent in his household and in building'.[33] While work on Austin Friars continued, Thomas also acquired two country houses within easy reach of London, at Hackney and Stepney, and another bolthole in Ewhurst, Surrey. Thomas needed space for his expanding household, places of quiet to enjoy his hobbies if ever his schedule permitted, assets to trade and, in one particularly dark future instance, secure and private prisons. Of these properties, he visited Stepney most often and Chapuys' report of visiting him at Stepney in September 1533 for a discreet conversation captures Thomas at his leisure: 'The day before yesterday I went to the country to find Cromwell, who had gone hawking, in order to talk with him and learn something.'[34] The house he leased at Stepney was a new-build aptly called Great Place, described in the 1790s as an 'ancient wooden mansion', beside St Dunstan's Church.[35] The Hackney property, meanwhile, was positively palatial, so much so that Thomas surrendered it to the King only a few years later at a politically opportune moment.

A flurry of letters from his overseer in summer 1535 detail the extensive renovations underway at all of the Cromwell properties. 'Your households at the Rolls, Friars Austins, Hackney, and Stepney, are in good health,' he begins on 11 August before detailing the works in progress: at Stepney, a grand staircase with a window built to link Thomas's private rooms with the gallery; at Hackney, a new tiled roof and chimneys, an enlarged kitchen, buttery, scullery raised a level, and his lodgings furnished with windows and hangings; at Ewhurst, the hall raised and rebuilt; and at Austin Friars, a new kitchen, scullery and offices with his own lodgings with chambers, gallery and staircase remodelled. Each site employed a large permanent workforce (74 men at Hackney and 67 at Ewhurst) in need of a constant supply of materials and pay.[36] By the time Thomas had finished with Austin Friars, not long before his death, it was one of the finest private residences in London: a three-storey house, timber-framed with a tiled roof and three distinctive double-height oriel windows facing the street, built around several courtyards with a large formal garden.

If all this seems profligate, Thomas put every corner of his property empire to good use. Most importantly, these were shrewd investments designed to provide a secure income to support his family and dependants in the decades to come, and to house them in the meantime. This was becoming ever more necessary as his family grew with two weddings by spring 1534: marriages for Thomas's beloved nephew Richard Cromwell and ward Ralph Sadler, both now in their mid-twenties. Richard had already made a quick and brilliant impression at court, being appointed to the Privy Council in 1531 and working for Bishop Stephen Gardiner. He was soon perceived as a man of influence and standing by his relatives. His cousin Christopher Wellyfed, already the beneficiary of a first-rate education paid for by uncle Thomas, noted Richard's standing with Gardiner as a potential help to his own church career.[37]

By late 1533, Richard had left Gardiner's service to work for his uncle, joining Ralph Sadler as joint chiefs of staff, trusted to act as their master's emissaries and handle his affairs. Thus we see one correspondent apologising for contacting Thomas about something as his other letters were 'in my packet to Mr. Ralph Sadler' and eminent figures at court recognising Ralph's status.[38] Richard likewise was probably the messenger Thomas described to Gardiner as 'my kinsman this bearer'.[39] In September 1533, one or other of Richard and Ralph held an item of no less importance than the King's signet ring, as one of the signet clerks addressed his letter asking for a warrant to be sealed 'To Mr. Richard Crumwell or Master Sadler, being at Hampton Court.'[40]

Though each a rising star at court, dependent on and closely associated with their successful uncle, Thomas allowed his two young men to marry for affection not advancement. Richard's marriage to wealthy Frances Murfyn seemed to achieve both. Ralph, meanwhile, chose entirely with his heart, falling in love with Ellen Barre, a widowed servant at Austin Friars. Ellen's low status did not prevent Thomas from welcoming her into his *de facto* family and helping the two young people to settle, first in his own houses, and then in the fine Sutton House at Hackney which Ralph built for himself and today belongs to the National Trust. Both couples would provide Thomas with much joy and godchildren akin to grandchildren.

Thomas's growing fortunes also enabled him to finance a princely education for Gregory, from which his own high status and dynastic ambitions now required more than academic prowess alone. It was essential his young heir be armed with the skills of a noble gentleman to prepare him for the social bearpit of court life. In Tudor times it was common for older children to be placed in other families of a higher status, creating an informal exchange programme operating across social networks which tied families together. Thus, where the young Ralph had been educated in Thomas's household, Gregory now spent holidays with his father's courtly contacts – extending even as far as his enemy the Duke of Norfolk's household – often escorted by Thomas's great friend, the tough but good-hearted Rowland Lee. Lee was dotingly fond of Gregory, even if New Year's Day 1533 saw him affectionately complain of his Cromwell, Wellyfed and Sadler charges ('your little men'), that he was 'among a houseful of children, God help'.[41]

Gregory continued his academic tuition and religious instruction throughout, bending his head over texts, attending lectures and mass.[42] But there was also time and opportunity now to play music, train with weapons and for outdoor pursuits: 'for his recreation he [Gregory] useth to hawk and hunt, and shot in his long bow, which frameth and succeedeth so well with him that he seemeth to be thereunto given by nature'.[43] Such was Gregory's natural inclination for sport, particularly in the summer months, the ever vigilant Thomas urged his tutor to restrict his recreation to improve his learning. This had the desired effect with Thomas reassured that 'if he continues in this way, this summer shall be consecrated to Apollo and the Muses, as was the last to the wild goddess Diana'.[44] It had taken great expense and effort but Gregory was slowly transforming into the accomplished young gallant who could make his father proud. Even Norfolk conceded as much, writing to Thomas when Gregory stayed with him in 1536 'your son is in good health here, sparing no horseflesh to run after the deer and hounds. I trust you will not be discontent that I now cause him to forbear his book. Be sure you shall have in him a wise, quick piece'. More importantly, perhaps, Gregory was growing up in ways which brought him closer to his father, sharing a reformist religious outlook and a reverential love. 'I desire your blessing,' Gregory wrote to Thomas aged eleven or twelve, 'which is more valuable than all earthly goods.'[45] Thomas returned this affection and theirs was now the central relationship in his life.

Beyond his family and household, Thomas's growing portfolio of properties also benefited his outward status and natural munificence. They facilitated the lavish entertaining that was expected of an official of his high standing, impressing Chapuys in the process. 'He lives splendidly,' the ambassador reported of Thomas, 'and [is] remarkably fond of pomp and ostentation in his household and in building.'[46] His large gardens and grounds enabled his important guests to relax over bowls, hawking or in the 'dicing house', his galleried halls accommodated a house orchestra and regular plays by 'My Lord Cromwell's players' and his revamped kitchen fed not only Thomas's family and 200 servants but also 200 poor at his gate twice a day.[47] His generosity endeared Thomas to the poor of London and he swiftly gained a reputation for his open house attitude, even when travelling. So a friend wrote to him while he was with the King in Calais in 1532 'Also of your housekeeping, it is showed me there is never an Englishman, the King's grace except, that doth keep and feast Englishmen and strangers as you do. I pray God to send you ten times as much as ye have to the maintenance thereof.'[48] Although it was customary for wealthy men to be generous hosts and provide local charity, the scale of Thomas's outreach suggests he had not forgotten what it was to be down and out. The King's principal secretary and chief minister had travelled a long way from his boyhood upriver, but life in Putney had left its mark.

Oliver Cromwell too had reached the time in life when his family and expenditure swelled as his children reached maturity. On a June day in 1646, at Holton Park, the fortified manor house serving as Sir Thomas Fairfax's headquarters for his siege of Oxford, military life paused so that the staff could celebrate a wedding. The timing was no coincidence. With the King secured and Oxford taken, war could at last give way to peace and personal lives begin once more. With Fairfax's own chaplain presiding, the bride and groom were married in the midst of the New Model war machine, doubtless to the delight of the General and his wife Anne and the other senior officers who attended. None was more delighted than Lieutenant-General Oliver Cromwell, for the bride was his eldest daughter, 21-year-old Bridget, and the groom his close friend and deputy, the 34-year-old Commissary-General Henry Ireton. The young couple, thrown into close proximity in wartime Ely, could now look forward to a peacetime marriage.

It was the Cromwell family's second wedding of the year. Back in Ely in January, Bridget's younger sister Elizabeth (or Betty) had married John, heir to the gentry Claypole family of Northborough, just north of Peterborough. The service had taken place in Holy Trinity, the old Lady Chapel within Ely Cathedral, overseen by the same Reverend Hitch who Oliver had warned not to hold choir services in the cathedral.[49] Betty and John's was likely a love match given that she was only 16 and John 22 when they married and that the wedding happened hastily when Oliver himself was away. Bridget and Henry meanwhile may have been a slower burn since their first meeting, likely in 1643. Certainly, their marriage settlement had been negotiated for some time, with Oliver signing the eventual agreement in April, assigning Henry the lease of a farm in Ely which would have been especially welcome to Ireton, a man of no great means himself.[50]

These conjectures are borne out by what we know of the young people's personalities. The surviving sources paint a consistent picture of two well-matched pairs. Ireton was pious and conscientious, famed (and criticised) for attempting to turn Ely into a new

Amsterdam – that is, a Puritan enclave – while he had been governor there. In combination, Ireton's questioning faith and quick mind forged a steely man whose stubborn self-confidence, even as an Oxford student, prompted him to challenge authority which he did not respect.[51] Bridget, meanwhile, held 'a great opinion' of her new husband, being herself every bit as godly and serious-minded as him, so much so she was the only member of the family to escape later criticism by the Puritan author Lucy Hutchinson who instead praised her 'piety and humility'.[52] Fashionable Betty, meanwhile, combined a less pronounced, more traditional faith with an eye for a good time which would see her romanticised by Royalist writers. As such she was, for now, well-suited to the country gentleman and Parliamentarian officer John Claypole whom Hutchinson branded with Betty's brother Henry Cromwell 'insolent fools' and 'ungodly cavaliers'.[53] Both the Ireton and Claypole couples would find themselves at the centre of national life, leaving contrasting marks on the revolutionary events to come.

Oliver's letters provide tantalising insight into his daughters' personalities and their marriages – or at least into his paternal perception of them. He was a father who constantly worried about his children's material, emotional and spiritual welfare, long into their adulthood: a puritanical helicopter parent. Writing to Bridget a few months after her wedding, he shared his worries about Betty before offering his own brand of marriage advice. Betty was 'exercised with some perplexed thoughts, she sees her own vanity, and carnal mind, bewailing it, she seeks after (as I hope also) that which will satisfy . . .' But there was help for the teenager as she strove to focus on her faith over superficial pleasures. We all seek the Lord as sinners, but we will find his grace: 'Happy seeker, happy finder.' Betty cannot have been wholly successful in her self-reformation, as her father worried at her lack of spirituality again in a letter to his wife four years later: once more 'poor Bettie' was 'couzened with worldly vanities and worldly company'. At least she had company in Claypole who Oliver also prayed and feared for in a 'vain world', wishing the Lord 'give them truth of heart to him'. The couple were, it seems, well-matched in 'pressing after full enjoyment' and Oliver loved them both. 'Truly they are dear to me: very dear' he wrote.[54] Oliver's attention was well-intentioned if, one suspects, somewhat suffocating. Yet it reflects the great love he felt for Betty – a devotion which would shape the end of his life.

The pious Bridget caused him altogether less concern, yet Oliver still felt moved to share his tips for marital bliss with his eldest daughter, now a new wife. These centred around allowing Christ to be the third member of her marriage to Ireton. 'Dear heart press on', he wrote, 'let not any thing cool thy affections after christ, I hope he will be an occasion to inflame them. That which is best worthy of love in thy husband, is that of the image of christ he bears, look on that, and love it best, and all the rest for that'. This was the Puritan attitude to marriage laid bare: a vision of shared faith and companionship within a happy relationship which would be the foundation of a successful and godly life. As one of Oliver's Hinchingbrooke cousins put it, love for a wife 'only because she is thy wife, and because she serveth and pleaseth thee after the flesh, for beauty, birth, riches and such life' is no true love in God's eyes, lacking 'the religious love that ought to be betwixt man and wife'.[55] This, it seems, was the kind of life partnership Oliver shared with his wife and which he wished his children to find. So he took great care in arranging his children's marriages to ensure a compatibility of personalities and outlooks and a liking that could mature into love between the couple, in each case prioritising this over a simple quest for the most prestigious match.

Oliver's evident affection for all of his sons and daughters-in-law demonstrates this: nothing less would do for his 'dear' and 'beloved' children. This may have been easier to achieve at this stage in the Cromwell family's life, however, when Bridget and Betty's suitors hailed from their father's circle of army colleagues and local gentry. When the time came 11 years later for their younger sisters Mary and Frances to marry, they were *de facto* princesses with the nobility of Europe at their feet. Their marriages were of national importance and much more vulnerable to their father's political imperative. Yet even then love would find a way.

Now, at the end of the Civil War in 1646, importing Henry Ireton into the Cromwell family as Bridget's husband had profound consequences for them all. Bridget found herself ensconced at the heart of the Army, living with Ireton at the Fairfaxes' quarters and taken under the wing of the commanding Lady Fairfax: 'my Service and dear affections to the general, and generaless,' Oliver wrote to his daughter there, 'I hear she is very kind to thee, it adds to all other obligations, my love to all.' A wife to one of the Army's senior leaders, Bridget also found herself sharing a status with her mother and the two of them would often be at public occasions from now on alongside their husbands. Ireton has been overshadowed by his famous father-in-law in the centuries since while Bridget has been ignored entirely. Yet they were the dynamic young power couple at the centre of the revolution. Even the satirical press judged them well matched in their prominence: 'And my Son (you all know) wants no Spirit (if he did, he should never have married my Daughter, that you may well think),' comments 'Lieut-Generall Crumwell' in a spoof of 1649.[56]

As Ireton's wife and Oliver's daughter, Bridget was uniquely placed to observe and coordinate their lives, even acting as their go-between and mediator. Oliver's letter to her in October 1646 opens with his explanation that he is writing to her and not to her husband partly because he is too busy and partly 'to avoid trouble, for one line of mine begets many of his which I doubt makes him sit up too late'. Ireton's famous workaholism was already a source of concern to his new father-in-law.[57] Through Bridget, Ireton and Oliver were now doubly bonded as close colleagues and effective father and son; a point frequently made in the press, particularly by their detractors, one of whom dubbed them 'King Cromwell and his son Prince Ireton'.[58] Their lives would be thereafter entwined, even beyond the grave.

Oliver's family now moved closer to the centre of the stage as they made plans for a life of peace. With the war ended, London politics became the focal point, and Oliver moved his family from their home in Ely down to the capital to be with him. With the promise at least of an income of £2,500 a year awarded to him for his military service by a grateful Parliament, he took a house in fashionable Drury Lane in Holborn, a comfortable walk from either Westminster or the City of London. This was a huge turning point in the lives of Elizabeth and her children: a change of lifestyle from the quiet backwater of Ely to the vast and teeming streets of London, opening the door to high fashion, an enhanced social and cultural life and political influence. Betty probably stayed behind with John Claypole at his home in Northborough, while Bridget and Henry Ireton would have lived at Drury Lane if not nearby. With their older sisters married and setting up their own households, there would have been much to delight Frances and Mary, now eight and nine, who would grow up as London ladies of leisure. The long and frequent stays of their cousins Robina and Lavinia and Oliver's widowed sister Katherine Whetstone would have added to the gaiety. With no expectation of further fighting, the Cromwells' oldest surviving son Richard entered Lincoln's Inn for a gentleman's legal training while his younger brother Henry probably lived at home with his sisters.[59] Oliver's unmarried sister Elizabeth seems to have stayed in Ely but his aged mother made the seventy-mile journey to remain by her son's side in this new chapter.

For all the Cromwells, Oliver's growing fame and their presence with him in London brought their lives into the public eye, exposing them both to sweet and savage comment in the flourishing, uncensored press. A satirical cookbook of 1664 which purported to contain Oliver's wife Elizabeth Cromwell's own recipes, skewered her household management at this time of transition with her 'arrival in town'. Mrs Cromwell, it claimed, had 'abandoned the dull country . . . partly to partake in the supreme fruition of the city's more elaborate and exquisite pleasures'. She and the other 'ladies of the cause' gorged themselves at the many 'thanksgiving dinners' thrown for their triumphant husbands and took 'immoderate bribes'. Meanwhile her own home became a Midas palace with only gold to eat, her own natural frugality allowing nothing but 'small beer and bread and butter' served when the Cromwells could not wangle an invitation out to a free meal. Elizabeth herself, the author complained, did not dress and behave as 'a woman of that state' ought, going about with only a 'horse boy' to wait on her, dressed 'like a baggage lady' who was 'out of her element, in her vicinity to the court and city'. Her daughters attracted the opposite criticism being 'otherwise vested and robed, and a constant expense . . . with each their maid and servant to attend them: and by their array and deportment, their quality might have been guessed at'.[60] The comedy is cruel and malicious but it unwittingly gives a sense of the contours of the Cromwells' new London life, and what an enormous change it was for them all.

Putney revisited

Oliver Cromwell's Drury Lane house swiftly became a place of business as well as a home as Oliver, his son-in-law Henry Ireton and their circle of political and military allies met there to discuss the grave state of affairs: veterans of both sides and their shattered communities needed support while a deeply divided Parliament confronted the existential question of what the new peaceful nations should look like now it had won the war. Over the last few years, Parliament had established sophisticated welfare processes funded by heavy taxation – specialist military hospitals like Ely House and the Savoy in London to treat the wounded, and a petition system to award benefits and pensions to injured servicemen and bereaved families. While some defeated Royalists received help, most were subjected to 'sequestration' – the confiscation of their estates which were only returned if they paid a fine, called 'compounding'. This was the punishment now facing the Royalist Cromwells of the Hinchingbrooke and Launde branches, with the last of the family's Reformation spoils now hanging in the balance.

Sir Oliver Cromwell and his son (the senior branch of Hinchingbrooke Cromwells now downsized to Ramsey and its satellite manor of Upwood) chose to compound to save their homes. They presented their petition shrewdly, emphasising their submission to Parliament but also stressing the real, lesser value of their sequestered estates, providing context which revealed their desperate plight. Sir Oliver (still officially noted as 'alias Williams') pleaded his advanced age which rendered him 'unapt for travel', engaging in some creative age inflation to claim in 1645 that he was 84 and, three years later as the appeal continued, that he was 90. His son, meanwhile, acknowledged that 'being much indebted, he went into the King's quarters and bore arms' but explained that he had been 'much wounded', suffered sickness as a result and was now in prison. His health must have been severe for he claimed his aged father was likely to outlive him. Sir Oliver recalled his nephew's armed visit at the outset of the war, claiming he was sequestered then 'for some opposition he should make against the Parliament's forces under the command of Lieut-General Cromwell at Ramsey'. But now Oliver would come to the aid of his Royalist family. The committee referred the Cromwells' appeal to Oliver himself who 'desired' first that his cousin's own assessment figures be used and then requested 'that his fine be remitted, and the sequestration discharged . . . and rents in arrears . . . be paid to him'. Consequently Ramsey was returned to Sir Oliver and Upwood to his son.[61]

Oliver's continued sense of loyalty and obligation to his family clearly transcended politics. More remarkably, he extended this familial sympathy to the Launde Cromwells with whom he otherwise had little to do. The head of this branch of the family – Thomas Cromwell's great-great-great grandson, the impecunious cavalier Viscount Lecale – had initially prospered in the war, receiving an Irish peerage as the 1st Earl of Ardglass from the King on 15 April 1645.[62] Finally Lecale had the status he had so long hoped for, but it had come too late. Now his English lands inherited from his father in Wiltshire, Leicestershire and Rutland were sequestered along with those he acquired through his wife in Staffordshire and Derbyshire. He soon petitioned the House of Lords and in 1646 appealed to the committee for compounding. For all his former bravado and zeal for the King's service, Lecale was quick to distance himself from the defeated monarch now in Parliament's custody, explaining to the Lords 'That he, not truly understanding the justness of the cause this state hath in handling till of late, did, through some plausible persuasions of His Majesty, continue with him; until, by true information of some friends, I found that His Majesty was not only misled, but his deafness to those he ought to hear best was like to increase.'

He was, Lecale assured the other Lords, 'ambitious to redeem himself in the good opinion of your Lordships, and also of the honourable House of Commons; and, secondly, to preserve his honour and reputation with those that stood for religion and the liberty of the subject . . . and resolved to become a new man, and to be faithful in the cause now depending here, either by oath or otherwise'. As ever, Lecale was at pains to plead 'my high poverty', asking that he be spared 'any chargeable prison, or other restraint . . . not being in any present capacity any ways able to subsist, having not had fifty pounds of his own estate these four years, either in England or Ireland'.[63] Perhaps there was an elderly lord listening who, sixty years earlier, had heard Lecale's grandfather Lord Henry Cromwell, the 2nd Baron and Gregory's son, petition the Lords for release from debtors' prison.

Lecale was fined £460 and retired from public life.[64] He may have lost his ultimate gamble, but the extent of his losses was mitigated by an unlikely champion. While the Committee was weighing Lecale's case, Oliver Cromwell wrote to one of its members to intervene on his distant relation's behalf. He goes into albeit muddled detail in support of Lecale's lesser valuation of his estates but the letter ends with the clearest statement of Oliver's loyalty to this beleaguered branch of his family: 'what favour you shall shew my Lord Cromwell herein you shall oblige your very loving friend Oliver Cromwell', and a postscript to hammer the point home, 'if it appear that there be such mistake as is here alleged let it be amended as is desired'. Two days later Lecale's fine was significantly reduced.[65] In one letter the space which had grown between Gregory and Richard's branches of the family over the course of the century collapses. Oliver not only knew of his relationship to Thomas Cromwell and his descendants, but he felt a powerful sense of kinship with them.

Now an influential public figure at the end of the Civil War, Oliver had larger matters to deal with besides helping the senior members of his own family mitigate their losses. Within his own side, MPs entertained conflicting visions of their ideal political and religious settlement. Generally speaking, 'Presbyterian' MPs (many of whom had been in the peace party which emerged in 1644) wanted to establish a national Presbyterian church and demobilise the increasingly radical army, dispatching a remaining core to fight the Royalists in Ireland. 'Independent' MPs, meanwhile, (many of whom had been in the opposing war party), sought religious toleration for congregations independent of a national church and allied themselves with the Army's interests. For it was within the Army that now the more radical, separatist tendencies in Puritanism had begun to gain expression, breaking away from the Presbyterian mainstream. The soldiers themselves looked for protection for their religious freedoms, indemnity for their actions in the war and backpay. Furthermore, any compromise that could be agreed upon had then to be negotiated with the defeated King who most people still thought was essential to peace. Initially, Parliament managed to coalesce around some stiff peace propositions to put to Charles, temporarily united by the publication of the King's damning private correspondence with the Irish and other foreign nations. Charles refused the deal, however, and as the months dragged on the mounting argument between the Presbyterians in Parliament and the Army with its Independent MP allies took centre stage.

As two of the few remaining officer MPs, Oliver and Ireton found themselves increasingly caught between Parliament and the Army and spent most of the coming months at Westminster working to prevent a permanent breach in the wartime coalition. In the early months of 1647, relations between them deteriorated further and in May Parliament dispatched Oliver and Ireton alongside two other officer-MPs Charles Fleetwood and Philip Skippon to the Army's headquarters in Saffron Walden, Essex, to offer reassurances in return for obedience. There they found an army far more angry and political than the one they had left the previous summer. Even now the alliance might have held, but once they reported their lack of progress back to Parliament, the MPs voted to disband the Army. Oliver's mediation had failed and there was no going back now. Spiralling events forced him to choose whether to side with the Parliament he revered or the comrades he loved. He chose the latter. Leaving London once more, this time in secretive haste, he returned to the Army to take his place at Fairfax's side.

Things were now moving quickly. In the same few days of early June 1647, a junior officer, Cornet Joyce, seized the King from the custody of Parliament (to whom the Scots had sold him) and delivered him to the Army: a brazen action Joyce later claimed Oliver had ordered him to take at a meeting in his Drury Lane home. However it began, the outcome was to bring Oliver Cromwell and Charles I together, probably for the first time. Now perhaps was the chance for the army leaders to agree a settlement directly with the King over the heads of the majority Presbyterian Parliament they no longer trusted. Keen to maximise their hand, and cognisant that the future they hoped for included a willing, if de-fanged, Charles on his throne, the generals treated their royal prisoner with courtesy. He was placed under the protection of Oliver's cousin Edward Whalley and Oliver himself was initially charmed by the King's natural grace and kissed his hand, though he did not kneel. As a devoted father, he was particularly moved to witness 'the tenderest sight' of the King's loving reunion with his children. Relating this he 'wept plentifully' saying: 'That never man was so abused as he in his sinister opinions of the King, who he thought was the uprightest and most conscientious of his three Kingdoms.'[66] To Oliver, being a good father outweighed all else in the measure of a man.

Encouraged, the army leaders drafted some political manifestos culminating in the blueprint for an agreement called the *Heads of the Proposals*. These were largely penned by Henry Ireton with help from an impressive young Yorkshire commander and budding theorist, John Lambert. The *Heads* offered the most generous terms Charles would receive: his restoration provided he accepted biennial Parliaments and franchise reform, parliamentary control over the military and key political appointments for ten years, a broad indemnity for most Royalists, and a national Church which retained bishops and the Book of Common Prayer but protected Independent Protestants' freedom to worship outside it. It ought to have been an attractive offer for the King, for the army leaders' approach was more cautious and nuanced than their Presbyterian rivals': under the *Heads* Parliaments would be more frequent and internally reformed, but not notably more powerful. Yet this was not how Charles saw it and he received the terms angrily. Before any progress could be made, however, events elsewhere shifted the landscape once again.

A London mob, incensed at what it saw as the Army tyrannising Parliament and supportive of the Presbyterian MPs, stormed the Lords and Commons and demanded the return of the King to the capital. The Independent MPs, including the Speaker, rushed out of London to the Army, throwing themselves upon Fairfax for protection. Emboldened by the air of legitimacy they brought with them and with an invitation from the borough of Southwark to return to restore order, Fairfax ordered the army to cross its own Rubicon and march upon London. The 15,000-strong army entered the city on 5 August 1647 to no resistance but the ringing of bells, restored the Speaker to his chair and received Parliament's thanks while the Presbyterian leadership quietly filtered away. As they paraded out again in triumph two days later, Oliver riding at the head of the cavalry, his wife Elizabeth rode with Lady Fairfax in her carriage: symbols of feminine civility in support of their all-conquering husbands. The Independent MPs had triumphed over their Presbyterian opponents with the help of the Army. But now the Army faced its own identity crisis, which took Oliver upriver to the birthplace of his family's fortunes.

The early seventeenth-century poem 'The Legend of Great Cromwell' imagines Thomas Cromwell speaking of his native village where, at his birth, 'Twice flow'd proud Thames':

Putney the Place made blessed by my Birth,
Whose meanest Cottage simply Me did shrowd,
To Me as dearest of the English Earth;

So of my bringing that poor Village proud,
Though in a time when never lesse the Dearth
Of happie Wits, yet Mine so well allow'd,
That with the best She boldly durst prefer
Me, that my breath acknowledged from Her.[67]

If Putney was indeed proud of her most famous son, the event that brought his great-great-great nephew Oliver Cromwell to her Thame-side streets in October 1647 would secure the village lasting fame. For it was here – now the Army's headquarters – that Oliver chaired a week of democratic debates in October 1647 which would reverberate down the ages.

Whether or not Oliver actually stayed in a house belonging to his ancestor Walter Cromwell as the Victorians romanticised, in St Mary's Church and the narrow lanes around it he shared the spaces of his forebears.[68] As the autumn leaves bronzed and browned, he was busy in his favourite role as conciliator, visiting his friend, the outspoken Leveller leader John Lilburne, and other prisoners in the Tower of London, speaking on the King's behalf in Parliament, and shuttling between the Army at Putney and Charles himself, now lodged in style in his former palace at Hampton Court, still under the guardianship of Oliver's cousin Whalley. The army leaders' meetings with the King to discuss the *Heads* had become so cordial that their wives were invited along, with Elizabeth and Bridget presented to the King by the hand of his chief courtier and feasted in the palace which would, unbeknown to them all, be their future home.

This cosy proximity to the King carried its own dangers. Where fighting for the King had diminished the Launde and Hinchingbrooke Cromwells, negotiating closely with him now jeopardised Oliver and Ireton's own positions. For they were told to their faces that their 'credits and reputation had been blasted' among the soldiers for treating with Charles.[69] At this time many expected Oliver and the other army leaders to sell them out by accepting rewards or money, titles or high office from the King in return for their support. The Army Council complained 'that Cromwell's and Ireton's door was open to us [the King's advisers] when it was shut to them'. Charles himself had even anticipated as much, sharing his astonishment that none of the army leaders asked anything for themselves in their negotiations. His conclusion that their altruism made it hard for him to trust them reveals as much about the King and his experience of power politics and courtly patronage as it does about the officers' country principles and straightforward scruples.[70]

Oliver himself feared nothing so much as to be judged a hypocrite, and he was troubled by one rumour in particular which reached back into his family's past. Namely, that a grateful Charles would buy Oliver and Ireton's cooperation by making Ireton Lord Lieutenant or Field-Marshal of Ireland and granting Oliver the now vacant Earldom of Essex; the title held at the brief summit of his life by his great-great-great-uncle Thomas, the bauble offered to him by Henry VIII as a poisoned chalice only weeks before sending him to the block on charges of over-weening ambition.[71] The gossip was baseless, yet it showed how Oliver's enemies could discredit him in the eyes of his men by linking him back to his infamous forebear. Such talk found a receptive audience within the rank and file who were now marshalled by 'agitators' aligned with the Leveller movement of London-based political radicals. It was in order to ameliorate this volatile atmosphere that the Army Council convened a debate with the agitator representatives of the soldiery and a few of their civilian supporters.

With Oliver presiding at the Putney Debates in lieu of an ill Fairfax, the Army Council planned to discuss the radicals' new manifesto, *The Case of the Army Truly Stated*, but in fact found themselves facing an even newer document: a revolutionary draft constitution called *The Agreement of the People* that proposed a kingless future, the people free from the 'Norman Yoke' of their monarchical overlords, with extensive rights guaranteed by a sovereign Parliament elected by a widened franchise. Such a revolution was too rich for the conservative Oliver's blood, but he did not dismiss it out of hand, rather sought to question its practicability. Ireton, meanwhile, took on the role of chief prosecutor, deploying his forensic legal skills to counter the agitators' arguments, passionately put by the eloquent Levellers Colonel Thomas Rainsborough, John Wildman and others. Both father and son-in-law worried that adopting the *Agreement* would force the Army to go back on the commitments it had made both to King and Parliament, undoing months of work. Yet the radicals were compelling and Oliver's distinct lack of interest in constitutional arrangements left some space for innovation: he was not 'wedded and glued to forms of government', he said, which were after all only 'dross and dung in comparison of Christ'.[72] Oliver sympathised with much of the Levellers' programme and was not against the idea of extending the franchise among property owners.

Gradually the *Agreement* gained ground and the Council agreed to pause its negotiations with the King, but then Oliver and Fairfax drew up the drawbridge: the leadership would continue to work with the radicals to find a moderate way forward, but the debates must end and the agitators disperse. Yet Oliver's contributions to the debates reveal how they had influenced his own developing views, crucially about the King. When he admitted that 'we all apprehend danger from the person of the king', we see the beginning of Oliver's mental separation of Charles himself from the institution of the monarchy. There could be 'no safety' with the King or the House of Lords 'having the least interest in the public affairs of the kingdom', he declared, but this did not mean that 'God will destroy these persons or that power', in other words monarchy itself.[73]

The stage was set for future showdowns, but once again the principal actors were on the move as the scenery changed. The King, alarmed at reports of the radical discussions downriver at Putney including a letter from Oliver himself, fled from Hampton Court on the night of 11 November and rode south, eventually finding himself at the coast where he threw himself upon the charity of the governor of the Isle of Wight. He had fled from the custody of one of Oliver's cousins to that of his good friend and later cousin by marriage, Colonel Robert Hammond. Although Hammond had fought for Parliament, his precise affiliation at this crucial moment was in question. As he was also the nephew of Charles's chaplain Henry Hammond, and a man who had voluntarily withdrawn from the centre of the Army at its politicisation, the King hoped the young officer would be sympathetic to him. Oliver, meanwhile, harboured his own hopes of his close friend and relative's continued loyalty to the Army. Over the next twelve months, poor Hammond, who considered his first duty to Parliament, found himself in the epicentre of the earthquake that pulled all three apart.

Already the tremors had begun. An Army rendezvous at Corkbush Field sparked a brief Leveller mutiny. A Narnia winter – the first without Christmas – brought riots to the streets of Canterbury on 25 December, while a popular ballad wailed: 'The world's turned upside-down, from bad to worse.'[74] As the year of negotiations neared its end in cold and dismal failure, the spectre of war loomed again. Oliver and Ireton met the prospect with hearts hardened against the King for good. His escape from custody, rumours of his secret negotiations with the Scots, and intercepted letters to the Queen in which he gleefully wrote of duping the army leaders, had convinced them of Charles's inherent untrustworthiness. They now accepted that this particular King would need to be removed, though neither yet knew how, when or what their role in this should be.[75]

With the new year, 1648, came clarity. It would be, for Oliver, 'the most memorable year . . . that ever this nation saw'.[76] The strained alliance between Parliament, its army and the Scottish Covenanters fractured as the Scots signed a secret treaty with the King by which they would invade England and restore him to power in return for his establishing Scottish Presbyterianism in England. This 'Engagement' was a bad deal for both Charles and the Scots, but its outcome was to transform the landscape for everyone. When it became known, Oliver argued in Parliament to support a Vote of No Addresses to the King and prepared to return to the battlefield for another civil war, this time with the Scottish army as enemies and not allies. First, he put his political and personal affairs in order. Oliver moved his family from Drury Lane to the more secure (and aptly named) King Street next to Whitehall and opened marriage negotiations for his son and heir Richard. With Parliament fulfilling its former promise to grant him the confiscated estate of a Royalist – with land in Gloucestershire, Hampshire, Monmouthshire and Glamorgan – he could leave his family content that they were well provided for. Oliver also set about building political bridges, throwing dinner parties for Presbyterians, Independents and radicals at home in King Street, one of which ended in a bout of Oliver's childish high jinks when he threw a cushion at the republican Edmund Ludlow's head.[77]

Soon he was off on campaign with more suitable opportunities to channel his rambunctious instincts. He took with him his youngest son, twenty-year-old Henry Cromwell, who was by now a captain in the millenarian Thomas Harrison's Horse regiment. The Second Civil War opened with Royalist uprisings in Wales, Kent and Essex. Oliver set off west, back to the Cromwells' ancestral homelands in Glamorgan, while Fairfax and Ireton rode east and John Lambert stalked the north, tracking the Scots as they readied their forces. Once he had subdued the Royalist Welsh, Oliver joined Lambert to tackle the greatest challenge, the Scottish-Royalist army. The fighting that took place over the spring and summer was altogether nastier and more ferocious than that of the first conflict. From Oliver and much of the Army's point of view, this reflected their anger that the Royalists they had already once defeated had broken their parole to return to the field (rejecting God's judgement upon them in the process), and also their resolve to resist invasion by a foreign power. This war was characterised by uprisings and brutal sieges, the last of which at Colchester saw the starving townsfolk reduced to eating dogs, cats and candle wax, and the royalist leaders executed at their eventual surrender. This was a marked deterioration from the civility of the 1646 siege of Oxford when food shortages in the town prompted Fairfax to send a luxury hamper inside to Charles I's second son, the Duke of York. Attitudes hardened as the bodies piled up with many soldiers now considering the King a traitor whose unprincipled double-dealing had caused an unnecessary, 'uncivil' war.

It was Oliver who, in his first action in overall command of an army, comprehensively defeated the Scottish-Royalist army at Preston in stunning fashion before marching on to Edinburgh as the feted guest of the newly installed pro-Parliamentarian government. Henry Cromwell, who probably fought at Preston fresh from a prominent role in a skirmish at Appleby earlier in the summer, was on hand to witness his father's triumph. Once again Parliament's army had vanquished the King and once again the victorious coalition would find negotiating the peace harder than winning the war. But now Oliver and his son-in-law Ireton were on the same page as their radicalised men, convinced not only that Charles I should be brought to trial but that the 'man of blood' who had made war on his people twice over deserved to die. For the first time, after more than a century of royal service, the Cromwells considered a future kingdom without its king.

Six

Fallout

Went you to conquer? and have so much lost
Yourself, that what in you was best and most,
Respective friendship, should so quickly die?

John Donne, 'H. W. in Hibernia Belligeranti', poem to Sir Henry Wotton fighting in Ireland (1599)

Men of blood

On 11 January 1536, Thomas Cromwell sent his trusty protégé Ralph Sadler to Greenwich Palace to give the King an ingenious gift – an elaborate lock which Henry liked 'marvellously well'.[1] Thomas would have been pleased to receive his master's hearty thanks for the present, though less so that it had not softened the King sufficiently to permit the elaborate obsequies Thomas had planned to dignify Katherine of Aragon in death. Three months later, he dispatched his other beloved boy, nephew Richard, to Greenwich bearing another offering for Henry. Not a lock this time but a key; the key to the King's happiness in the form of a confession from the young lutenist Mark Smeaton to an affair with Queen Anne Boleyn.[2] Within two days Anne was arrested and taken to the Tower of London, the Norman fortress and symbol of royal might neither she – nor, four years later, her prosecutor Thomas Cromwell – would ever leave.

Anne had been in trouble since the winter. She had displayed unbecoming glee at Katherine's death, celebrating openly with Henry, but hers was a pyrrhic victory. For Katherine's removal cleared the roadblock to England allying with her nephew, the Holy Roman Emperor Charles V of Spain, who was no longer bound to defend his aunt's honour. This shifted England away from Anne's preferred alliance with France. Furthermore, shortly after Katherine's death, Anne had miscarried following her shock at Henry suffering a near-fatal fall in the tiltyard. The King, it was reported, now hated the Queen as she had not provided him with an heir and it looked unlikely now that she would. Henry's passion for Anne had curdled, but fortunately for him there was a sweet and potentially fecund maid waiting in the wings upon whom he had now set his heart: Jane Seymour, from the ancient if lowly gentry family of Wolf Hall in Wiltshire, now making herself at home in Thomas's old rooms next to the King's at Whitehall which Henry had ordered he vacate for her. Taken together, these events created the conditions for the King to turn against his unpopular Queen, while rumours arriving from France of Anne's adultery offered him a possible route out of his marriage.

So Henry set his faithful servant Thomas Cromwell on Anne like a hound to the scent. Anne was a worthy quarry who many had chased before him with different motives. 'Whoso list to hunt I know where is a hind,' Thomas Wyatt had written probably in longing for Anne who was likely his lover before her marriage. Yet now Queen Anne belonged to the King and was – or should have been – out of bounds:

> *Who list her hunt, I put him out of doubt,*
> *As well as I may spend his time in vain.*
> *And graven with diamonds in letters plain*
> *There is written, her fair neck round about:*
> Noli me tangere, *for Caesar's I am,*
> *And wild for to hold, though I seem tame.*[3]

But now Caesar wanted others to touch his possession and his chief minister to bring him the evidence. This was nasty work, but Thomas was not unwilling to bring down the hind. Though Thomas had paved the way to Anne becoming Queen and they were both religious reformers, the two had never been allies, contrary to prevailing assumption over the years. They had different instincts on foreign policy and religious reform. Anne had recently objected to the closure of the monasteries, perceiving the project as a hostile takeover by an asset-hungry Crown and court. The Queen now had the scheme's chief architect in her sights, and the Imperial ambassador Chapuys offered Thomas the timely reminder that the previous year Anne had said she 'would like to see his head off his shoulders'.[4]

Thomas had ignored Anne's animus to further her cause when it was in the King's interest. But now that was no longer the case. The precise moment when Thomas 'had set himself to arrange the plot' of contriving Anne's fall may have come two weeks later when Henry publicly turned on Chapuys and denounced the Emperor.[5] There was no logic to Henry's sudden, peevish outburst but it threw the whole prospect of an Imperial alliance into doubt and a distraught Thomas took to his bed bemoaning 'who trusts in the word of princes, who say and unsay things, and promises himself anything from them, is not over wise, as he had found on Tuesday last'. Yet he soon rallied, resolving as he always did to make or mar. The game was not entirely lost, he comforted Chapuys, for he still hoped for success in their mutual plan to ally their masters and Chapuys, at least, now believed Thomas to be 'an honest man'.[6] Thomas could not control Henry but he could improve both his mood and the chances of an Imperial alliance at one stroke by removing the Queen.

Thomas set about his plan to bring Anne down with his customary brutal efficiency. His household and their new homes at Stepney and Hackney had starring roles in what unfolded. It was at Stepney that Thomas interrogated and perhaps tortured poor Mark Smeaton into his fatal confession of sleeping with the Queen. Hackney, meanwhile, was sacrificed to the cause. Thomas surrendered his remodelled stately home to the King probably as part of a strategy to buy Henry Percy's admission that he had been pre-contracted in marriage to Anne by returning his former home to him. Over the coming days many of Anne's other supposed lovers were arrested. Besides Smeaton, four gentlemen were tried, inevitably found guilty and executed: Henry Norris, William Brereton, Francis Weston and Anne's own brother, George Boleyn. None were likely guilty of the outlandish charges framed around them, but by now that hardly mattered. Last of all to the block at Tower Green came Anne herself who died with courageous dignity. Eleven days later Henry married Jane Seymour.

If the King was the original author of these judicial murders, Thomas was the mastermind of all. Only he could have secured the reprieve for his protégé Thomas Wyatt whose inevitable arrest he had mitigated in the first place by sending his own henchman, the ever-reliable nephew Richard, to intercept Wyatt and ensure he was treated well.[7] Wyatt would live to write another day, but the slaughter of his friends and childhood sweetheart left lifelong scars. 'The bell tower showed me such sight / That in my head sticks day and night,' he wrote of his incarceration. Worse still:

These bloody days have broken my heart.
My lust, my youth did them depart,
And blind desire of estate.
Who hastes to climb seeks to revert.
Of truth, circa Regna tonat *['Around the throne the thunder rolls'].*[8]

While Wyatt grieved, Thomas put out press releases. To Stephen Gardiner and Sir John Wallop in France, he wrote his official narrative that all his actions had been taken at the King's command. He put the same to Chapuys for his official dispatch to the Emperor.[9] Yet only days earlier Thomas had hinted at his own agency, reminding Chapuys of their conversation in February where, when discussing Anne's evolving position, Thomas had boasted that 'he hath done and would do marvels'. [10]

* * *

Anne Boleyn and her brother had been tried as peers in the King's Hall in the Tower of London, but the other condemned men were tried in Westminster Hall: their legal summons there from the Tower including the famous exhortation to 'bring up the bodies'. It was this same Westminster Hall, with its astonishing medieval hammer-beam roof, that housed an even more infamous trial a little over a century later. This time there were not many prisoners but one, not an ordinary man but a king. Charles I's position had deteriorated since his defeat in the Second Civil War in August 1648. Soon afterwards, King and Parliament began re-negotiating at Newport on the Isle of Wight. Prima facie the talks progressed well, with the gap between the parties narrowing even if a final settlement remained just out of reach. But two growing problems meant time was not on their side.

First, Charles was in fact conducting other secret negotiations and continuing to plot his escape from the Isle. Though he and Governor

Robert Hammond had initially got on well – with the two travelling around the island and playing bowls – their relationship had deteriorated as the months passed. Hammond received letters throughout the year claiming to reveal plots and conspiracies, the threat sufficient for Parliament to offer communication through cipher. Charles attempted to escape several times, only failing on 20 March because he became stuck climbing through his window, sending Hammond into a rare burst of anger, locking the gates, doubling the guards and banishing the King's servants.[11] The second threat to the Newport negotiations was that trust had once again broken down between the Army and Parliament. Over the autumn the regiments became increasingly agitated, issuing petitions and refusing orders while the mood darkened further when the Leveller leader Thomas Rainsborough was murdered. The movement culminated in the Army issuing a 'Remonstrance' in November which demanded that Parliament stop negotiations and that 'the King should be brought to Justice, as the Capital cause of all'. *Salus Populi Suprema Lex* it declared: the safety of the people is the supreme law.[12]

The Remonstrance was most likely drafted by Henry Ireton, now firmly in the driving seat of the Army as it sped towards its collision with Parliament. Bridget Cromwell's husband was, according to Lilburne, now the brains of the Army, its 'alpha and omega', and she was no doubt on hand to contribute to the many meetings of the army leaders which took place in his quarters.[13] Ireton had turned even further from the King over the course of the Second Civil War, frustrated no doubt at being forced back onto the field when he wanted to enjoy married life, traumatised by his role in the brutal siege of Colchester, and distraught at the death of his best friend from home, 31-year-old Colonel Francis Thornhaugh, at Preston. The smart and determined Ireton could now see only one route ahead for the King. The sequence of letters he and his father-in-law Oliver sent to Charles I's prisoner Robert Hammond document this evolution. On 9 July, Ireton was de-legitimising Parliament to Hammond, laying the intellectual groundwork for the army to move against it.[14] By November, with his Remonstrance Accepted by the Army Council, he was urging Hammond to support their efforts to stop the Treaty of Newport using the coercive language of mutual interest.[15] On 22 November, the gloves were off: Ireton appealed directly to Hammond's conscience to side with the Army, to whom he really owed allegiance, and not the

Parliament he wrongly cleaved to, in a letter packed with guilt and loyalty which contained the word 'trust' twelve times.[16]

Lilburne once described how the 'father and son' Oliver and Ireton liked to perform a good cop bad cop routine, appearing to diverge in negotiations as a coordinated move to divide their enemies.[17] At the time Ireton was badgering Hammond and plotting a coup against Parliament, Oliver was in fact 180 miles away taking an inordinately long time mopping up the Second Civil War's last gasp, the siege of Pontefract Castle. Yet Hammond's correspondence suggests father-in-law and son-in-law were acting with some coordination nonetheless. Three days after Ireton wrote to Hammond, Oliver did the same. Just as Ireton had, he appealed to Hammond's sense of loyalty and sought to persuade him that the Army's actions were providential. Only his tone differed: his was a fatherly voice, more subtle and affectionate than the younger Ireton's direct and threatening approach. 'Dear Robin' was, like Oliver's beloved but wayward daughter Betty Claypole, at risk of those pesky 'fleshly reasonings' – in other words human considerations over divine will. These had caused him to write to Oliver for advice in his troubles, putting to his close friend and mentor whether it was not right that he should serve Parliament. Oliver replied by dismissing Parliament as a mere 'human institution' and its Newport Treaty a 'ruining hypocritical agreement'. Hammond, he urged, should ask instead 'Whether this Army be not a lawful power, called by God to oppose and fight against the King upon some stated grounds; and being in power to such ends, may not oppose one name of authority.'[18]

This is one of the most famous letters Oliver ever wrote, preserving, as it seems to do within its lines, his acceptance that the King might need to be tried and Parliament countered by force if it got in the way of this, God's will.[19] Within the next few days Sir Thomas Fairfax sent men to fetch Charles I from the Isle of Wight in the teeth of Hammond's resistance and the Army set off from Windsor to Westminster to pressurise Parliament into accepting its Remonstrance. When it did not, Ireton and other leading officers met with their MP allies to decide on their response. Ireton wanted to dissolve Parliament and hold fresh elections – a step which would have given the next assembly greater legitimacy for what it would do with the King – but others favoured a purge and they carried the day. The next morning, 6 December, Colonel Thomas Pride stationed his troops at the doors of Parliament to block those MPs who had voted to continue negotiations with the King. Forty were arrested with sixty to seventy more kept out in the coming days. Parliament had been purged with only a rump remaining, which gave the reduced assembly its name, the Rump Parliament.[20] Despite a summons from Fairfax many days earlier, Oliver did not make it back to London until that evening. Commentators then and since have variously attributed his convenient absence while others did dirty work either to political guile or to the fact that he did not yet agree with Ireton that military force was necessary. Just as with Thomas Cromwell, questions over Oliver's culpability for the seismic events of his life shape our understanding of him even as he slips between the sources.

Oliver could not know of the plan for Pride's Purge as it was made on the hoof. Although he was swift to give it public approval, he may yet have harboured private doubts about the way forward: how to try the King and what the nation's future constitution should be. Over the coming weeks Oliver concentrated on the first of these questions and Ireton the second, falling naturally into their preferred roles. Ireton, the lawyer and constitutional theorist, chaired a month of debates at Whitehall every bit as important though less well known than those at Putney. Here the Army Council worked with the Levellers on a new watered-down *Agreement of the People.* The Levellers were less than happy with the draft, less so still when Parliament promptly ignored it. Meanwhile Oliver, the natural conciliator, tried to rebuild the coalition the purge had fractured. The King's trial – if it went ahead – must have the widest possible base of support. Over these darkest weeks of the year, Oliver worked to bring moderates back into the fold, securing the release of all but sixteen of the arrested MPs.[21] This work was deemed so crucial Oliver was allocated a bedroom in the palace itself rather than returning to his family at neighbouring King Street, receiving the lawyer Bulstrode Whitelocke while actually lying in one of the royal beds.[22] Oliver's conviction against Charles did not extend to an ideological desire to end the monarchy itself. With Whitelocke and others he discussed the possibility of a settlement by Parliament rather than the sword. He may too have returned to previous plans to persuade Charles to abdicate in favour of one of his sons, probably Henry Duke of Gloucester. If so, neither came to anything. Throughout these weeks, Oliver had wished decisions to be taken slowly and cautiously and by the broadest coalition. Momentum, however, was in one direction: towards the swift trial of the King.

On 20 January all eyes turned to Westminster Hall where the House of Commons had unilaterally established a High Court of Justice. Oliver – by now irrevocably persuaded of the 'cruel necessity' of the King's trial – took his place on the tiered benches within the ranks of the black-hatted commissioners chosen to judge their sovereign. Many summoned to this dark duty had not come, including the cautiously apolitical Fairfax himself, though his wife Lady Anne did and heckled the court. Oliver himself sat silently throughout but when it was time for the commissioners to withdraw to deliberate, his was one of the most commanding voices. The King, who Oliver had so admired when they met in the summer of 1647, sat alone on a red velvet chair in the middle of the vast hall facing his judges: a small if splendid figure in demure black with his Garter ribbon bright around his neck. Proceedings did not run smoothly. Charles decided his best defence lay in refusing to acknowledge the court's legitimacy and to enter a plea – a blow to any of the commissioners who still hoped to avoid regicide – with each subsequent stage held up by further delays. That he was eventually found guilty and sentenced to death was the most likely outcome, if not perhaps a foregone conclusion.[23]

The commissioners gathered in the Painted Chamber next door to sign the death warrant. King Henry III's medieval marvel had once been richly decorated with large wall paintings of Old Testament narratives and of virtues overcoming vices. But these had been whitewashed in the Reformation so offered no guidance for the troubled men in their fateful task. The atmosphere among them was charged: the King's death would be no happy victory but a sad failure and their own parts in it fraught with danger. Stories of what took place inside that room circulated later, several emerging in the show trials of the men themselves at the Restoration as many deflected the blame for their actions onto Oliver. Oliver's relation Richard Ingoldsby (Sir Oliver Cromwell's Parliamentarian grandson) later claimed that Oliver had actually held his hand forcing him to sign.[24] Another told of how Oliver and others had broken the tension by flicking ink at each other; something only too believable of the prankster Oliver's bouts of schoolboy behaviour. In the end, Oliver was the third of the 59 to sign their names on the warrant that would condemn the King (and for some of them in future years themselves) to death.

Charles I was executed on 30 January, wearing an extra shirt to prevent his shivering in the bitter cold. He died bravely to instant martyrdom and widespread shock. When his re-stitched corpse was buried quietly in St George's Chapel Windsor, it found itself next to that of Henry VIII: eternally mismatched bedfellows to rival those of Thomas Cromwell and Anne Boleyn, who still slumber near one another in the Tower of London's chapel of St Peter ad Vincula. A few years later, a satirical pamphlet *The Messenger* imagined the ghosts of kings Henry and Charles in conversation in the vault at Windsor, upbraiding each other and the infamous Cromwells in their lives for their fates. Henry did not at first recognise Charles as a fellow monarch: 'As though thou indeed hadst worn the kingly diadem? Why thou hast no head at all whereon to put it, Man.' But he soon confessed his crimes of the Reformation and the bloodshed it cost his successor whom he told had only inherited the crown as a Stuart because God had punished Henry by ending the Tudor line. Charles took up his own part of the national narrative with its common Cromwellian theme: 'Now a sect of independents hath broke out (God revenging so the sin of thy sacrilege) who regarding neither king nor bishops, first took off my spiritual head, then my own cut and severed from my shoulders; one Cromwell in thy time then lived (of thy cabinet and most secret councils) who persuaded thee (a king) to spoil the church; now another of that name (and not unlike him) forced the people to destroy their king.'[25]

Oliver had destroyed Charles I for the sins of Henry VIII and his own forebear Thomas. Recounting his view from the scaffold, Charles remembers: 'I beheld also (but with what sence of indignation?) his head covered, and eyes sternly fixed on me, Oliver Cromwell one of ordinary extraction and (abstracting from what fortune hath reared him to) much more despicable then the meanest of my nobles (how much short then of the majesty of a king) sitting umpire of my life and death.'[26] Just as with Thomas, Oliver's crime was twofold: not only his actions but his impudence in wielding political power when he was so humbly born. *The Messenger* was written in 1657 at the height of Oliver's power which explains the leading role he is given in the King's death. Generations of school children have been taught from this script, that Oliver Cromwell killed the King and took his place. Yet today we need suffer under no such polemical anachronism. Oliver did not single-handedly drive through these revolutionary events but was one significant figure within a small group with varying views who did. If any member of the Cromwell family occupied the driving seat of these events it was Oliver's son-in-law, Bridget's husband Henry Ireton, and even he did not get his own way in everything. As for Oliver, it has been put well before that he was 'at once a bitter opponent of Charles, a reluctant regicide, and a firm monarchist'.[27] His assumption of power, moreover, did not happen upon the King's execution but almost five years later. Charles meanwhile was the primary cause of the Second Civil War which claimed thousands of innocent lives, unnecessarily. His forebear Henry VIII desired the love and then death of Anne Boleyn and those others who needed to die to secure her fate, while his minister Thomas Cromwell happily fulfilled his wishes. All of them traded in blood.

❦ ❦ ❦

Many of the Cromwells' contemporaries in the 1530s and 1640s saw them, as the author of *The Messenger* did, as agents of demolition. Yet violent destruction was only one of their means and certainly not their whole ends. Where Thomas and Oliver resorted to pulling structures (or people) down, it was for the opportunity to build something better in their place: the clearing of a field before spring planting. 'My prayer,' Thomas wrote, 'is that God give me no longer life than I shall be glad to use mine office in edification and not in destruction.'[28] But what did each man wish to create? For Thomas, the brightest future for the 'common wealth' lay with a reformed church under the leadership of an empowered, imperial monarchy. Yet a century on, Oliver looked beyond that now corrupted, overstretched monarchy for an alternative commonwealth which would safeguard religious freedom. In the intervening years, much had changed to make this possible. The dominion of the English Crown had spread as successive monarchs subdued the North of England, incorporated Wales, conquered much of Ireland and united with the Scottish Crown in the person of a joint Stuart monarch. Meanwhile old assumptions about the nature of royal authority vied with new ideas about constitutional government. In many of these areas, it was Thomas himself who laid the groundwork for the developments that would take his nation and his family to unimaginable places.

In the weeks after Anne Boleyn's death, an extraordinary story circulated court that Thomas Cromwell was to marry the Princess Mary, only lately restored to the succession. They had become bound together in jeopardy while Mary refused to acknowledge her father's royal supremacy and Henry weighed her life in the balance, and that of Thomas if he failed to bring her around. Mary – like the later Charles I – refused to recognise the political dangers facing her. Yet, working with Chapuys, Thomas had engineered the young woman's capitulation, earning her eternal gratitude. 'How much I am bound unto you', Mary wrote to him, 'which hath . . . travailed, when I was almost drowned in folly, to recover me before I sunk and was utterly past recovery'.[29] Thomas arranged a private reconciliation between Mary and Henry at his vacated country house at Hackney and when he commissioned a commemorative medal for Mary and acted the courtly part of her 'Valentine', tongues began to wag. It was only gossip with no basis in fact. Yet time would tell how dangerous gossip could be when it circled the throne.

In the short term, however, orchestrating Anne Boleyn's fall and restoring Princess Mary to her father's good graces had earned Thomas substantial rewards. In July 1536, the King knighted his Lord Privy Seal, Thomas Cromwell, creating him Baron of Wimbledon. While Anne Boleyn had lived, Thomas had never been ennobled; his official social status always lagging behind his real power. But now, the tables had turned. Custody of the King's privy seal – lately in the hands of Anne's father Sir Thomas Boleyn – clinched Thomas's position as royal gatekeeper, even more with Ralph Sadler now placed in the King's privy chamber for optimal coordination. The Barony brought him extensive lands and properties of a new magnitude, chiefly the Archbishop of Canterbury's former riverside manor of Mortlake. But it was the geography of his new power and prestige that perhaps meant the most. The lordship of Wimbledon which Thomas chose included the hamlet of Putney where he had grown up a 'ruffian' with little to his name. Far from burying his humble origins now he topped the social ladder, Thomas shouted them from the rooftops for all to hear, disturbing the old nobility and traditionalist commoners alike. At once he set about provisioning and improving the already palatial Mortlake with his customary energy. Invoices came in for expensive new windows and huge quantities of fish for the same kitchen where it is likely his own brother-in-law William Wellyfed had once been the chief cook.[30]

It was now that Thomas also acquired the manors of Oakham in Rutland and North Elmham, provocatively sited in his rival the Duke of Norfolk's heartlands: two centres of local power which his descendants, the Launde Cromwells, would dominate. Thomas would have been gratified to know this, for he more than anyone else set the patterns of local government for the next 100 years, always moving towards greater political centralisation and administrative uniformity. These reforms not only strengthened the Crown but also county identity, empowering a rising gentry class to which his family belonged at the expense of the traditional landed nobility.[31] Thomas guided some of the key legislation for this through the Parliament of spring 1536, even as he gathered his dossier against Anne Boleyn. Acts abolished existing franchises and the medieval 'liberties' (independent territories governed by local lords), regulated land law and inheritance, and gave the Crown the right to appoint all Justices of the Peace, whose numbers and remit swelled. Poor relief was standardised in the first step towards full nationalisation, presented by the King himself at Thomas's suggestion as 'a common wealth to his subjects'. Later, his *Injunctions* regulated local communities by ordering every parish to maintain a register of baptisms, marriages and burials.[32]

This notion of a 'commonwealth' was dear to Thomas's heart. In 1523 he had noted how his first Parliament discussed 'how a commonwealth might be edified and also continued within our realm', and his nephew William Wellyfed junior later congratulated him on his political rise for earning 'the praise of the people at his having assumed a troublesome office from love to the commonwealth'.[33] Now agriculture, trade and industry, drainage and defence also felt his reformist hand. His bill to regulate the unpopular enclosure of public land for large scale sheep farming, for instance, was aimed at those men 'to whom God of his goodness hath disposed great plenty and abundance'.[34] Tackling their greed at the expense of the poor was, he told the King, 'the most noble, profitable and most beneficial thing that ever was done to the common wealth of this your realm'.[35] In many of these endeavours, Thomas ran up against strong vested interests and often his schemes came to little. Yet it is enough to read the index of failed bills to recognise the Cromwellian desire and the drive behind them to hunt for efficiency and equity in every corner of human endeavour from the washing of linen to the sale of hides, from the management of swans to the care of orphans.[36]

Beyond London, this comprehensive programme would be enforced by an army of lay volunteers, into which Thomas's own descendants would be recruited. This was easy to achieve in the Tudor heartlands of the southern lowlands of England but far trickier to implement in the remote borderlands of the North and Wales which required greater cultural imperialism. The Tudors were Welsh of course, and Thomas had land and friends there, like Gregory's guardian Bishop Rowland Lee, who could help him manage sweeping reorganisation. Nevertheless, the Act of Union with Wales, begun in 1536, was an ambitious project. Gradually over the next few years Wales was brought into full union with England, given English law and local government structures. The process was inevitably traumatic for the Welsh who suffered heavy-handed law enforcement and mourned the passing of their heritage. Yet they gained the same rights and privileges as Englishmen and the benefits of strengthened law and order.

Through their experience in Wales, Thomas Cromwell and Henry VIII acquired a taste for state-building which Henry's heirs would continue throughout the sixteenth century and beyond. Indeed Thomas and his King had 'tapped into cultural energies that would not dissipate fully until the twentieth century'.[37] Northern England, however, was if anything a tougher nut to crack. Thomas did not know the land or people well, nor have many friends there to keep him informed of events and carry out his wishes. But the people of the North knew him. They knew that he was the architect of the recent religious policies they hated: closing monasteries, issuing *Ten Articles* of reformist doctrine, ordering every parish church to provide copies of the Bible in both English and Latin and instructing the clergy that all adults and children should learn the *Articles*, Lord's Prayer and Ten Commandments in English. They knew too that he was but a mere brewer's son whom the King had ennobled to rule over them all as his Vice-Gerent, out of the natural order of things. When resentment erupted in rebellion in a 'Pilgrimage of Grace for the Commonwealth' in autumn 1536, it was Thomas who was the prime target, not Henry; it was his name which the pamphlets and petitions chewed on.[38] The popular pilgrim's hymn sang of 'Crim,

Crame and Riche' [Cromwell, Thomas Cranmer and Richard Rich] while the rebels concluded government policy was 'the deed of Crumwell'.[39] The common people in every town were instructed by them to 'rise on pain of death and make all lords and gentlemen swear . . . To put down the lord Cromwell, that heretic, and all his sect, the which made the King put down praying and fasting'.[40]

It was a 'queasy time' for Thomas, his family and household – his own servants at his property Legbourne Priory in Lincolnshire were rounded up and imprisoned by the rebels, narrowly avoiding a lynching, though rumours reached London that they had been killed.[41] Anyone aligned with Thomas or his interest was in danger: one of Thomas's associates in York was forced to tear down the Cromwell family arms from above his front door to avoid his house being torched.[42] As soon as the scale of the Pilgrimage of Grace became clear, the King ordered Thomas's nephew Richard Cromwell to gather a force of gentlemen and Richard then took weapons and ammunition from the Tower of London.[43] That done, Richard rode north with 100 men, most of them workers from Mortlake manor, while Thomas dispatched a second force of 200 men drawn from his London and regional servants, including one of his cooks.[44] Later, a rumour reached court that Richard had been accidentally killed by a murderer who was so enraged he had slain Richard and not his uncle that he vowed to imitate an ancient Roman story of mistaken murder and burn off his own hand for striking down the wrong victim.[45] These were dangerous times to be a Cromwell.

Richard himself appreciated the dangers, adding as a postscript to one of his reports to Thomas, 'I beg your Lordship to comfort my poor wife in my absence.' Yet he had a thirst for adventure and was fired up by anger at the rebels, writing of the 'arrant traitors' of Lincolnshire, wishing 'that the whole shire should be sacked up'.[46] Richard's competence earned him the respect of his colleagues who reported to Thomas that his nephew was 'forward, conformable, and very desirous to do the King service', with his company 'as well horsed and well ordered as any in this army'.[47] Richard's presence among them was doubly useful to Thomas and the King, for not only could he deploy his martial talents on the rebels, he could also keep watch on the other government commanders.[48] For the uprising had exposed (and in part sprung from) the deep fault lines at court which had been obscured while Anne Boleyn lived. Thomas's power was now clear to all and his opponents, no longer entangled in the complex web of allegiance that grew out of Henry's 'Great Matter', were freed to work against him. Thomas Howard, Duke of Norfolk delighted in his certainty the Pilgrimage of Grace would spell the 'ruin and destruction of his competitor and enemy, Cromwell, on whom he puts all the blame for these events, and whose head it's said the insurgents demand'.[49] Thomas's head was certainly at stake as his enemies circled, sensing a moment of weakness. Lord Thomas Darcy, one of the most prominent northern nobles who joined the Pilgrimage, vented himself on the subject when under examination:

'Cromwell it is thou that art the very original and chief causer of all this rebellion and mischief, and art likewise causer of the apprehension of us that be noble men and dost daily earnestly travail to bring us to our end and to strike off our heads, and I trust that or thou die, though thou wouldest procure all the noblemen's heads within the realm to be stricken off, yet shall there one head remain that shall strike off thy head.'[50]

Thomas's common birth threatened the nobility and appalled his own class in equal measure. Yet ultimately his fate rested in the hands of one man, the King. For one terrifying moment, it looked as if Henry might throw Thomas to the northern wolves in the service of peace. The rebel leader, Yorkshireman Robert Aske, had told the King to his face that he allowed himself 'to be governed by a tyrant named Cromwell', and in the truce negotiated by Norfolk, Henry did not defend his minister and promised all possible redress to the rebels.[51] But Henry liked no man telling him what to do and a spell at Richmond Palace close to Thomas's new home at Mortlake may have enabled Thomas to talk his head off the block. The King's next proclamation defended Thomas as one added into his Council as 'most meet for the same rooms'.[52] Henry meanwhile was soon saying 'he will not forego my lord of the Privy Seal for no man living', and Aske was to live no longer.[53] When fighting renewed in early 1537, Henry ordered him seized whereupon he was convicted of treason and hung from the walls of York. The Pilgrimage of Grace was over and, as long as he kept the King's good grace, Thomas was safe. 'It seems, Cromwell, that the country does not know thee as I know thee,' Henry is reported to have told his grateful minister after the crisis had passed, 'Whoever harms thee shall harm me.'[54]

❦ ❦ ❦

There had been much for a relieved Thomas to enjoy at home over the Christmas season of 1536–7 with Richard's safe return and Gregory's long-awaited homecoming from Norfolk. His accounts list payments for luxuries for Gregory, sweet treats, actors for plays and even money paid out by Richard for Thomas's part in a masque.[55] Greatest of all perhaps was the safe deliverance to Ellen and Ralph Sadler of a son they named Thomas; a birth of added poignancy as they had already lost a son. Thus in Ralph's letter to Thomas telling him of the birth and inviting him to the christening, he asked Thomas 'to vouchsafe once again to be gossip [godfather] unto so poor a man as I am, and that he may bear your name; trusting you shall have more rejoice of him then you had of the other, and yet there is no cause but of great rejoice in the other, for he died an innocent, and enjoyeth the joys of heaven.' Ralph would also 'be right glad to have Mr. Richard's wife . . . to be the godmother', but because of a superstitious belief 'amongst women' that a pregnant woman should not christen another man's child 'and therefore not knowing whether Mr. Richard's wife be with child or not' he had asked another.[56] Frances Cromwell may well have been with child for the future 'golden knight' and Oliver's grandfather, Sir Henry Cromwell, was born that same year.

For all Thomas's indulgence of his favourite protégé, he did not grant Ralph long to enjoy his son before sending him north to inform on the rumblings among the northern gentry. His own health faltered in these months, with a particular pain in one of his legs which caused him to summon doctors to examine him on several occasions and to purchase two footstools to elevate his leg.[57] Yet Thomas continued to press forward with his plans for effective local governance and full-throttled evangelical reform to the outermost corners of the realms. He reinvigorated the historic Council of the North to implement royal will on the chastened northerners and undercut Norfolk's powerbase. In doing so he employed a very Cromwellian form of social engineering, filling the ranks of the northern council with low-born men like himself, just as Oliver would go on to recruit his russet-coated captains in the face of his social superiors. Predictably the haughty Norfolk opposed this, complaining that 'the multitude of wild men upon the Borders cannot be restrained by such mean men, but that some man of great nobility should have the rule'. The Privy Council – itself placed on a more formal footing since the rebellion – responded robustly that the King had been 'worse served' on other occasions by arguments between local magnates and asked 'if he appoint the meanest man to rule there, is not his Grace's authority sufficient to make him respected?'[58] If Thomas was pleased the rest of the Privy Council supported him in slapping down Norfolk, he would have also appreciated that, in formalising its role, the rebellion had granted his fellow councillors the power to check his future actions. The process of extending royal control throughout the kingdom and integrating the Welsh and northern borderlands into a greater England was underway, if still precarious. Yet even greater challenges loomed beyond those blurry edges of the map: Scotland and Ireland.

Game of thrones

In March 1543 Ralph Sadler found himself heading north once more on a delicate diplomatic mission, this time to Scotland. It would prove useful to his trip that he was now well used to babies, with the Sadler nursery he left behind boasting two daughters and three sons. Now Ralph beheld a baby girl and, refuting rumours she was weak and frail, pronounced her 'as goodly a child as I have seen, of her age, and as like to live, with the grace of God'.[59] As he gazed on the infant, Ralph could not have imagined the extraordinary life that lay before her, nor his strange role in it. For this pretty little girl was not his own daughter but that ill-fated star of the next decades of Tudor history: Mary Queen of Scots.

Ralph had been sent to Edinburgh by Henry VIII to inspect his new great-niece and negotiate a marriage between the infant and his five-year-old son, Prince Edward. The two kingdoms had been at peace since May 1534 when Thomas Cromwell had been part of the team which negotiated a treaty between them. Events since then had strained relations, most recently the death of the baby Queen's father King James V of Scotland following a skirmish with the English at Solway Moss. Yet his death had also opened up an opportunity and under the new Treaty of Greenwich, this marriage would unite the two kingdoms in perpetual peace. Ralph was the natural choice for such a mission having undertaken three previous embassies for his sovereign north of the border, becoming the English court's resident expert on Scottish affairs in the process. Ralph's wife Ellen even featured in the King's plan which appointed the couple to watch over the upbringing of the young Queen, ensuring her suitability for the Prince. Ralph could not see his lowly wife – who had once been Thomas Cromwell's servant – comfortable in such an exalted role, however, thanking his sovereign 'that they are thought meet for a place of such trust' but politely refusing as 'his wife is most unmeet for the purpose, having never been brought up at Court, and she is great with child, so that he cannot convey her hither this summer, and in winter the journey is too long and foul for any woman'.[60]

Besides, this marriage was a tough sell to the 'proud, beggarly Scots', as Ralph later described them, with one of them putting it to him: if 'your lad were a lass and our lass were a lad, would you then . . . be content that our lad should marry your lass and so be King of England? I assure you . . . that our nation, being a stout nation, will never agree to have an Englishman to be King of Scotland'.[61] The political climate at Edinburgh was hostile to the English and relations deteriorated in the months after Ralph's visit to the infant Mary. With war brewing and several attempts made on his life, Ralph soon found himself on the run as an enemy agent. But King Henry was not about to let anything happen to his man and wrote to his intermediary the Earl of Angus demanding he use force to extricate Ralph from any danger and threatening to destroy Edinburgh if he was harmed.[62]

Ralph maintained his low opinion of the Scots, railing as he ran against 'the rage and beastliness of this nation, which God keep all honest men from!'[63] Yet he would remain deeply engaged in Scottish affairs for the rest of his life. Following the Treaty's failure, the English harried the Scots over the next eight or nine years in a campaign which later became known through the romantic language of Ralph's biographer and admirer Sir Walter Scott as the 'Rough Wooing'. After Henry VIII's death, his son Edward's uncle Edward Seymour, Duke of Somerset, the new Lord Protector ruling on behalf of the boy king, continued the aggressive policy of demanding the marriage alliance with Mary and an English reformation of the Scottish Church. Though a peace negotiator by instinct, Ralph was with Somerset when he invaded Scotland in September 1547, securing martial glory in the battle of Pinkie, his trophies from which would later decorate his grand tomb in St Mary's Church, Standon.

In 1560, the new Queen Elizabeth I answered appeals from Scottish Protestants to invade Scotland in their support and drive out the Catholic French who had been deeply involved in Scottish affairs during the regency of Mary's mother. These events secured Scotland's own Reformation and Ralph was once more on hand to negotiate another peace treaty. Eight years later, he came face to face with the now 25-year-old Mary Queen of Scots once more in very different circumstances. Mary had had a torrid few years: returned to a bloody power struggle in Scotland on the death of her husband, King Francis II of France, she married first the Anglo-Scottish Lord Darnley – by whom she had a son James, future King James VI of Scotland and James I of England – then, after his murder, the Earl of Bothwell. Facing more violence, she escaped to England and into the arms of Elizabeth's three commissioners, one of whom was Ralph.

The Catholic fugitive Queen was by blood-right next in line to the English throne upon the death of her cousin, the childless Elizabeth. This impossibility plunged Protestant England into a 20-year succession crisis. Ralph maintained ambivalent feelings towards Mary throughout, arguing in Parliament from the beginning that she could not be allowed to succeed to the throne yet feeling some sympathy and affinity for her personally. This was complicated further by the year from 1584 to 1585 he spent living with her as Elizabeth's 'special choice' for Mary's gaoler at Wingfield Manor and Tutbury Castle in Staffordshire. Ralph was generous in his reports of the unfortunate Queen and allowed her more freedom than others had done, taking her out hawking with him and earning a rebuke from Elizabeth's secretary Francis Walsingham in the process. Mary appreciated his treatment of her, thanking Queen Elizabeth 'for making so good a choice of a grave and ancient counsellor; well known to her'.[64]

Yet, at 77 years old now and susceptible to the cold, the elderly statesman found his charge a heavy one, writing in language strikingly similar to that in which Robert Hammond would describe his own unwanted guardianship of Mary's grandson King Charles I at Carisbrooke Castle in 1648: 'I long as much to be rid of this charge, whereof I trust God and her majesty will deliver me shortly.'[65] Queen Elizabeth, in her turn, expressed how much she valued Ralph and her awareness of his plight: 'as we nothing doubt but you will acquit your self with that care and circumspection that may answer the special trust and confidence we repose in you, so may you be well assured, that in regard as well of your loving service as of your great years, we will, for our part, have also a care to ease you of that charge as soon as conveniently may be'.[66]

Their year of convivial cohabitation did not prevent the aged Ralph rising slowly to his feet from the government's front bench in the House of Commons a year later to call for Mary's execution as the only answer to the continuing threat she posed to his Queen.[67] Her fate had been a long time coming when it was arranged stealthily by Elizabeth's Council in March 1587. Elizabeth was furious when she found out but that did not stop Ralph's friend and his old master's grandson, the diarist Thomas Cromwell MP, thanking the Queen in Parliament for doing justice upon her enemy.[68] Ralph was there at the trial and execution of the woman he had admired as a baby 44 years earlier. It was the last act of his more than half a century of public service, for he too was dead – in his case of old age – just six weeks later.

Over the preceding years, the prospect of Mary Queen of Scots inheriting the throne had prompted Elizabeth's chief minister, William Cecil, to rethink the entire project of Tudor monarchy. Hereditary monarchy had suffered blow after blow under the 'barren princes' of the Tudors since Henry VIII's death: a child king (Edward VI), a nine-day deviation from the succession (Lady Jane Grey), and then two queens (Mary I and Elizabeth I – one married to a foreign king, the other single).[69] These blows, and the religious upheavals that accompanied them, created the conditions for assertive counsellors and innovations in constitutional thought, such as Protector Somerset's pursuit of an Anglo-Scottish union. At two moments of particular crisis, in 1563 and 1584, Cecil planned for an interregnum if Elizabeth died with no heir. Rather than the crown instantly and automatically passing to her blood successor Mary Queen of Scots, the Privy Council would meet and govern until Parliament declared who should succeed. The English would no longer have a hereditary but an elective monarchy. These actions, among others, have been seen as evidence that England under Elizabeth was in reality a 'monarchical republic' peopled by 'citizens . . . concealed within subjects'.[70] Cecil's friend and colleague Sir Thomas Smith was simultaneously developing his own views with his famous treatise *De Republica Anglorum*. In this, despite allocating powerful rights to the monarch, he argued that Parliament was the most absolute power in England.[71]

To the Tudors the words 'republic' and 'commonwealth' were interchangeable, and the antecedents of Cecil and Smith's thinking can be traced in the humanist ideas which first emerged in England in Henry VIII's reign. Thomas More had dreamed of a perfect government in his *Utopia*, and Thomas Cromwell – far from supporting Tudor despotism as was long-assumed – had believed in the supremacy of the king in Parliament and applied his talents and patronage to furthering the 'common-wealth' through the writings and social policies of men like Thomas Starkey and Richard Morison.[72] These 'commonwealthsmen' – the young William Cecil among them – continued to work together after Thomas's death, coming closer to the crown once it was occupied by the young Protestant Edward VI. After Edward's early death they endured political exile for the five-year reign of the Catholic Queen Mary I, before returning to court once more under the Protestant Elizabeth I. By the end of the century humanist, civic and quasi-republican ideas were circulating among educated local elites busying themselves in public office as the Cromwells were doing in eastern England.

On Elizabeth's death in 1603, Mary Queen of Scots' son James VI of Scotland inherited her crown the old-fashioned way, by birthright. Though he was not appointed through the elective parliamentary process Cecil had toyed with, Cecil's son and successor Robert Cecil certainly helped James secure the throne after Elizabeth's unclear, deathbed nomination.[73] To some ardent monarchists like the government lawyer and philosopher Francis Bacon it was a relief to return to the *status quo ante* of an adult, male monarch whose new Stuart dynasty would endure forever.[74] The new King James I of England, an experienced monarch, author of his own robust handbooks on the divine right of kings, and with two sons already lined up to ensure the succession, seemed a safe pair of hands to take the now double monarchical project of England and Scotland forwards.[75] Yet the tentative republican ideas which had developed under the Tudors and influenced opposition to the succession of the Catholic Mary Queen of Scots continued to bubble away beneath the surface for the godly to use in times of need. They were there to hand when Parliament constructed its case for going to war against Mary's grandson Charles I in 1642 and again when he, like his grandmother, went to the block in 1649. Mary's name was even included in the opening speech at Charles's trial, given by the court President John Bradshaw, among the list of previous rulers who had needed to be forcibly removed.

Threatened by the thought of the King's eldest son, Charles Prince of Wales, declaring himself King Charles II, the House of Commons rushed to abolish the monarchy. No natural republican, Oliver Cromwell went along with this as expedient, though he actively argued against the accompanying abolition of the House of Lords. His political instinct, as ever, tended towards pragmatic conservation rather than ideological destruction. Plunged into a crisis of legitimacy, the new regime was cautious at first, its utterings defensive rather than triumphalist. But the publication of John Milton's strident defence of the regicide, *The Tenure of Kings and Magistrates*, in February 1649 boosted its marketing campaign with its insistence that the people always retain their sovereign right and power over government. Milton himself was inspired by Thomas Cromwell's intellectual heirs, the 'commonswealthsmen' of Edward VI's government, when 'the whole assembled authority of England' in the 'full vote of Parliament' set about 'the reformation of this land'.[76]

In March the Rump Parliament explained its workings: 'The Representatives of the People now Assembled in Parliament, have judged it necessary to change the Government of this Nation from the former Monarchy, (unto which by many injurious encroachments it had arrived) into a Republique, and not to have any more a King to tyrannize over them.' England was a 'Commonwealth and Free State by the supreme authority of this nation, the representatives of the people in Parliament, and that without King or House of Lords'.[77] New coins were struck in the Mint, as well as a new Great Seal with a picture of the House of Commons in session engraved on one side and a map of England, Wales and Ireland on the other. Ships were renamed, liveries and furnishings changed, and by January 1650, all adult men were required to swear an oath of engagement to the new Commonwealth, though this was diluted to appeal to a pragmatic, war-weary population, and some – like Sir Thomas Fairfax – were allowed not to swear; a concession unthinkable to Henry VIII in his dealings with Thomas More.

Not everyone was convinced. Royalists predictably rejected the Commonwealth by circling back to re-assert the divine right of kings, helpfully handed a public relations boost in the late King's own thoughts on his martyrdom in the bestselling pamphlet *Eikon Basilike*.[78] The Presbyterians who had been excluded at Pride's Purge argued that everything that had happened since had been imposed at the point of a sword and was illegal. The Levellers too agreed that the free-born English had entered a new enslavement under another arbitrary power – *England's New Chains Discovered* as the title of John Lilburne's latest tract put it.[79] Having pivoted now to rebuilding alliances with political moderates who had been outraged by the King's execution, the new executive Council of State took a hard line against the Levellers who they had been working with closely only weeks before. Lilburne was hauled before the Council, reporting later that he had heard Oliver tell the other members: 'I tell you, sir, you have no other way to deal with these men but to break them or they will break you.'[80] Break them he did when some Levellers within the Army mutinied at Burford in May and Oliver and Fairfax shot the ringleaders up against the church. The Levellers were broken as a political force just as Lilburne had predicted when he argued in the Whitehall Debates that the *Agreement of the People* must be enacted before the King was tried or else it would never happen.

If the regicide had splintered public opinion, so it disrupted Oliver's wider family network and social circle. A story later circulated that Oliver had been visited at home in King Street a few days before the King's execution by one of his royalist relatives pleading for Charles's life. The man existed – a Colonel John Cromwell who commanded an English regiment in the Netherlands and pops up in the State Papers of the 1640s – even if the visit was concocted.[81] And his supposed warning shows contemporary awareness of the measurable effect Oliver's public actions had upon his family. 'Cousin . . . tis in your own power not only to make yourself, but your Posterity, Family and Relations happy and honourable for ever, otherwise as they have changed their name before, from Williams to Cromwell, so now they must be forced to change it again, for this Fact will bring such an ignominy upon the whole generation of them, that no time will be able [to] wipe away.'[82] Oliver's own immediate family were certainly dealing with the shockwaves of the regicide. This was not a family in which Oliver's views as the patriarch were accepted unquestioningly and silently by the others. Oliver's older, widowed sister Katherine Whetstone expressed her outrage at the King's death freely in a letter shortly before visiting Oliver in London, writing 'I was very troubled at that stroke which took the head of this poor kingdom from us, and truly had I been able to have purchased his life, I am confident I could with all willingness have laid down mine.' 'They say I am a royalist', she admitted to her cousin, but 'the Lord make me what he will have me to be, for shall I submit to his will in all things, and let us strive to possess ourselves in patience as well in the public as in our more private affairs'.[83] Nonetheless, with radical Bridget and Henry Ireton also around the family dining table, conversation must have been frank.

Yet differences of opinion and strong female voices were accommodated within a loving and functional family. Katherine Whetstone's forthrightness tallies with what we know of Oliver's closeness and reliance upon the advice of his female relatives with whom his relationships were far more equal and progressive than previously assumed. Similarly, Katherine's passionate view did not prevent her later marrying one of Oliver's fellow regicides, the Welsh Parliamentarian John Jones. Henry Ireton, though like his father-in-law 'extremely well pleased' with how events were unfolding, was snubbed by the new regime, being excluded from the new Council of State without even a vote by a Parliament keen to distance itself from the Army, though Oliver and Fairfax had been accommodated.[84] Oliver was always the easier and more charming of their partnership, as we see in Whitelocke's tale of their contrasting reactions to being stopped at an army checkpoint one night and asked to prove their identity: Ireton was annoyed while Oliver laughed, praised the men's diligence and give them a tip.[85]

Oliver's children featured in the news when the hostile *Mercurius Elenticus* newspaper printed the unlikely rumour that the late King's captive daughter, Princess Elizabeth, was to be given to one of Oliver's sons as a wife – a faint echo of the rumour in 1536 that Princess Mary's hand was to be given to Thomas Cromwell. Oliver's supposed offer to apprentice the Duke of Gloucester as a shoemaker or brewer reveals the continued public fascination with Oliver's own humble (and widely assumed beer-making) background, as does the use of his alcoholic nickname 'Nose' in the vivid conclusion 'Nose went blowing out.'[86] In truth, one of Oliver Cromwell's boys was destined for the altar, though not with a royal bride. A year earlier, Oliver had spent a great deal of time and effort negotiating a marriage for his son Richard after he had reached his majority. He had found an enticing prospect for his third (and now eldest surviving) son and heir, Dorothy, daughter and heiress of Parliamentarian Richard Major of Hursley in Hampshire.

Richard was keen: Dorothy was a catch, potentially offering him the suitable life of a country squire of an estate which current archaeological work reveals was far larger and grander than previously thought. Oliver, as always, prioritised the prospective couple's feelings, writing that he would spare no effort to finalise the match 'if God please to dispose the young ones hearts thereunto'. But this did not stop him squabbling over the fine print of the marriage settlement, breaking off negotiations in spring 1648 and renewing them in spring 1649. As both Richard and Dorothy were their fathers' heirs, the marriage was consequential for both families, and Major – described by one of his tenants as 'thrifty even to miserliness' – drove a hard bargain.[87] Oliver, meanwhile, insisted that Hursley be settled upon Dorothy and her heirs and free of any charge to provide potential dowries for his two younger, unmarried daughters.[88] Yet, Oliver was inspired most of all by the personal qualities of the godly Major family, and hoped they would be an improving influence on Richard who he always felt needed it. 'I have delivered my son up to you, and I hope you will counsel him,' he wrote to Major a few months after Richard and Dorothy were finally married on 1 May 1649. 'He will need it, and indeed I believe he likes well what you say, and will be advised by you, I wish he may be serious, the times require it.'[89]

Oliver formed a strong attachment to Dorothy herself – her 'virtue and godliness' having 'so great a place in my heart' – treating 'Doll' with all the devotion he lavished on his own daughters, writing to her often and telling her 'I like to see anything from your hand, because indeed I stick not to say I do entirely love you.'[90] Oliver took his customary eager interest in the newlyweds' welfare, writing of the couple's happy honeymooning, even hinting at his hope Dorothy already had pregnancy cravings. 'I am very glad . . . that our children have so good leisure to make a journey to eat cherries, it's very excusable in my Daughter, I hope she may have a good pretence for it.'[91] He dispensed his usual brand of Puritan marriage advice, exhorting Richard and Dorothy to incorporate God in their mutual love, but this could be touchingly practical too, with one postscript adding 'I hear thou didest lately miscarry, prithee take heed of a coach by all means, borrow thy father's nag when thou intendest to go abroad.'[92] Dorothy inspired her husband's love as well as that of her new father, as Richard's own later letters demonstrate. But theirs would be a marriage tested beyond endurance by an unfathomable future. Separation and tragedy awaited the young cherry-picking couple on the other side of the throne itself.

For now, that empty throne at Whitehall still dictated events. In executing Charles I, the English had killed a British king.[93] Their unilateral decision did not end an English Civil War but prolonged several British Civil Wars – wars which, now set fully in their British and Irish context, have also come to be known as the Wars of the Three Kingdoms.[94] In 1649 Ireland, where even now Catholic rebels massed with royalist forces against England, had to be subdued. Scotland – ignored since the King's execution and abolition of the monarchy had dissolved the 1603 Union of Crowns – would be next, after it defiantly proclaimed and then crowned Charles II not simply King of Scotland but King of Great Britain. Only then could the fledgling, friendless English Commonwealth be secured. Oliver was the obvious man for the job. Having seen his heir securely married, he spent his last few weeks in London settling his affairs, feasting his friends and being painted by Robert Walker in the manner of an armoured viceroy of Ireland: a simple and steely iconography of power which would be endlessly repeated to enduring success. On a summer morning, to great cheers and trumpets, Oliver set off from King Street in a grand coach and six, the road west taking him towards the violent campaign which would come to define him.[95]

His active star

Dundrum Castle in Ireland sits sentinel on a wooded hill above a wide bay in the Irish Sea. If walls could talk, these stones would speak of conquest. Built upon the site of an elite early Christian settlement by the invading Normans in the twelfth century, the fortress controls access to the whole Lecale region of north-east Ireland, dominating the coastline and the inland passage from Drogheda to the south to Downpatrick to the north. In 1538 it was taken by the new Lord Deputy of Ireland, Leonard Grey, whom Thomas Cromwell had appointed the next conqueror to cross the sea from England, sword in hand.[96] This was part of Thomas's plan to roll back the dominance of the Anglo-Norman lords and strengthen the King's rule in Ireland by establishing local government with an Irish Parliament in the wake of recent rebellion. Falling to the Crown when England for the first time took control over the whole island of Ireland in 1603, Dundrum was bestowed on Thomas Cromwell's great-grandson Baron Edward Cromwell when he re-located to Ireland following the Essex rebellion. Edward's son, the Royalist Thomas, Viscount Lecale, later sold the castle and local tradition has it that it was then slighted by the next English conqueror to subdue the Irish; the invader who would come to eclipse all others in national memory.

When Oliver Cromwell arrived in Dublin on 15 August 1649, at the head of 3,000 parliamentary soldiers, he had reason to thank God for his safe deliverance. This was the first time Oliver had left his native island and the old landlubber had not found his sea legs on the two-day crossing being, in the words of the Army's fiery chaplain Hugh Peter, 'as sea sick as ever I saw a man in my life'.[97] Restored to terra firma – even more at home no doubt once into a saddle – he recovered quickly to enjoy a hero's welcome from the Protestant inhabitants of the area around Dublin (known as the Pale). With the great guns of the city booming in salute, Oliver stood, hat in hand, and addressed the swelling throngs with a 'most sweet and plausible speech'. These honeyed words promised truth and peace, happiness and tranquillity, if those assembled joined with him in his 'great work against the barbarous and bloodthirsty Irish'.[98] Contemplating Ireland, Thomas Cromwell had once questioned 'Whether it shall be expedient to begin a conquest or a reformation?'[99] Oliver Cromwell knew his answer.

The Ireland he found in summer 1649 was a chaotic and daunting prospect. Formally converted into a full kingdom annexed to the English Crown shortly after Thomas's death, Ireland had suffered under its neighbour's imperialism. Henry VIII's successor monarchs had continued his colonial project, experimenting with martial rule, 'composition' where local lords allowed English troops and their governors to occupy their land in return for tax breaks, and English plantations, straining local relationships and provoking regular rebellion. Under Elizabeth I, swathes of English adventurers crossed the Irish Sea in search of estates and advancement. The fissures between the ancient Gaelic territory in the west and the factional English region, and the fragile relationship of each to the Crown continued under the Stuarts and bloody conflict had raged across the island since the uprising of 1641 with catastrophic loss of life.

Now, most of the original Catholic Irish rebels, who had formalised their governance as a confederate association based in Kilkenny, had allied with Protestant and Catholic Royalists under the capable command of the Marquis of Ormond, though some minorities of

Protestants and Catholics held out to fight independently. Huge numbers of Scottish Presbyterians – haters of the Catholic Irish but no longer natural allies of the English – were also in Ulster, having been sent by the Scottish government to Ireland over the previous few years to fight the rebels. Meanwhile, the English Parliament retained a toehold in and around the traditional English government centre of Dublin, with some other scattered forces further north. The violence of Oliver's subsequent conquest is best understood within this confused ethnic and religious context and as the latest chapter in a centuries-old pattern of colonial English policy. Over the next nine months, he deployed his now well-honed military talents to take more than thirty fortified towns and castles. Most capitulated without a shot fired, but two that resisted were taken with such brutal force that the names Drogheda and Wexford have forever stained Oliver's reputation with blood.

When Oliver first drew up his 10,000-strong army before the medieval walls of the port of Drogheda 35 miles north of Dublin, he wrote to the English royalist governor demanding he surrender, explaining darkly 'if this be refused you will have no cause to blame me'.[100] In this he was strictly correct according to the contemporary conventions of warfare, which maintained that a garrison which refused to surrender and continued to fight could expect no mercy if it was then stormed. Yet the killing that followed was inordinate. The exact number of casualties, particular horrific stories of their murder, and Oliver's personal involvement in the atrocity have been hotly debated ever since. Oliver himself took responsibility for what happened, describing his instruction to his men: 'being in the heat of the action, I forbade them to spare any that were in arms in the town'. Certainly, they slaughtered the large garrison of several thousand troops but also probably a number of civilians. The governor was reputedly beaten to death with his own wooden leg.

Though this was not the wholesale massacre of the population which has been widely believed ever since, it was undoubtedly violence of a new order and sufficiently troubling to Oliver he afterwards felt the need to send detailed explanations to the Westminster government. He justified the brutality as revenge for the 'innocent blood' spilled in the Irish massacres of 1641, which had indeed been terrible with around 9,000–13,000 killed though fewer than the exaggerated numbers given at the time in the hysterical London press.[101] His treatment of Drogheda would also act as a deterrent to other towns contemplating resistance, he argued, 'to prevent the effusion of blood for the future'. Yet Oliver's confident reasoning does not hide the unease beneath it. These 'are the satisfactory grounds to such actions,' he wrote, 'which otherwise cannot but work remorse and regret'.[102] Such Cromwellian logic might have applied too at the siege of Wexford a month later, where at least 1,500 people in the town were killed, had not events there been even more confused. A turncoat from the garrison betrayed the castle, enabling Oliver's troops to storm that town while he was still officially negotiating terms for its surrender. The violence they unleashed was not therefore ordered by him, but equally he had not taken sufficient steps to prevent it. With the atrocity further from his own hands, Oliver ascribed it to God's 'unexpected providence'.[103]

This belief in divine judgement blended over these months with Oliver's nationalist contempt for the Irish and Protestant mistrust of Catholics to colour his natural ruthlessness with a distasteful fervour. 'I am persuaded,' he wrote after Drogheda, 'that this is a righteous judgement of God upon these barbarous wretches.'[104] This bigotry was not peculiar to him but rather represented mainstream English (and Scottish) views. Indeed, throughout the British Civil Wars until this point, armies had behaved most brutally where ethnic animosity or local tribalism played a part. It was the rumour that the women in the royalist baggage train at Naseby were Irish which inspired Parliamentarian troops to attack them. Likewise, in Scotland, the presence of Irish forces fighting with the royalist Highlanders encouraged greater violence between the already ferocious clans. But there was another ingredient in Oliver's toxic mix in 1649: a now inveterate hatred of royalism. There had already been an escalation of violence from the First to the Second Civil War and now, for a third time, the Royalists had ignored God's two previous judgements upon them to drag Oliver and his men onto the battlefield yet again. Thus English Royalists fighting in Ireland – such as the commander at Drogheda – often provoked the worst of Oliver's fury.

By the time Parliament summoned him home from Ireland the following spring, Oliver had destroyed Ormond's royalist alliance, though the final and devastating mopping up exercise he left for his subordinates would take another three years. In nine months, he had achieved the military objectives set for him by the Commonwealth government, but in the process, Oliver's brutality and unique charisma had established him as the greatest villain in Irish history. This persona would continue to grow in his absence as his name was attached to the future destructive actions of others which his conquest had made possible, and projected backwards to represent the whole pattern of England's colonialist actions in Ireland in the early modern period. At this point, though, Oliver himself envisaged a more conciliatory settlement for Ireland than that which Parliament eventually enacted in 1652–3 in the face of his opposition. The *Declaration of the Lord Lieutenant of Ireland* he published before he left vented fury at the Catholic clergy but suggested the general Catholic population should have liberty of conscience and not be forced to attend Protestant services. Those who had stayed out of the war should be protected, those who fought against Parliament should be treated as Royalists were in England with fines and confiscations with only their leaders subjected to the harshest punishment if Parliament wished to make examples of them. Oliver had come to Ireland to avenge the 1641 rebellion, he explained, not to destroy Irish Catholic lives and livelihoods or enrich English adventurers. This was not a blueprint for the mass executions, transportations and land transfer which followed and with which he would forever be associated.[105] Nevertheless it was Oliver's conquest which made these brutal policies possible.

Oliver sailed home in May 1650, his forensic attention now turned elsewhere. He would never return to Ireland yet, though his wife Elizabeth was waiting to greet him with the government representatives at Windsor, other members of the Cromwell family remained closely bound to Ireland's future. Oliver left behind him two Henrys close to his heart. His 21-year-old Henry Cromwell had crossed to Ireland over the winter in command of a new regiment. He may not have seen much of his father as Oliver was careful to place him in a separate force to his own, but Henry did see plenty of action, contributing to an important victory near Limerick in April and the following spring jointly leading military expeditions. This was a formative beginning to an Irish-focused career and a time to grow into his adult self with all the self-examination that involved. 'Your son, to my great rejoicing, it hath pleased God, I am persuaded, to begin a work of grace in his soul', a resident preacher wrote to Oliver, 'he hath had inward temptations in his soul, and many words of grace made very precious and comfortable to his soul, and . . . is much crying to God in secret, and very forward to propound doubts and cases of conscience, betwixt him and I'.[106] Oliver's son-in-law Henry Ireton, meanwhile, was at the apex of the Irish chapter of his own eventful life. Over the course of the previous year's campaign, Ireton had become Oliver's second-in-command and was rewarded with the Lord Presidency of Munster. When Oliver departed for England he left Ireton in charge of the Army as his lord deputy, a military and administrative mountain ahead of him.

Back in London, Oliver would have assured the family of the two Henrys' welfare, none more so than Bridget, now separated from her husband for the first time in their marriage and left to care for three young daughters. She would herself travel to Ireland to see him the following year, and again another year later in circumstances both very different and oddly similar: stony ground lay ahead for her. Oliver did not enjoy the comforts of home for long for within a month he was on the road again, this time heading north to Scotland. There the new King Charles II, denied his Irish army, had taken the Presbyterian Covenant his father never had in return for another Scottish invasion force. With Fairfax's flat refusal to lead the Army against his former allies despite Oliver's entreaties, Parliament promoted Oliver to overall command of its army for the first time. He was under no illusions about his or the Commonwealth's popularity among the populace at large, however. As he passed cheering crowds in the towns along their route, Oliver quipped in characteristic style to his relation Sir Henry Ingoldsby and his faithful deputy from the northern campaign of the Second Civil War, Yorkshireman John Lambert, that the masses would be as noisy to see them hang.[107]

Oliver's last visit to Scotland, after he had defeated the Scottish-Royalist army in the Second Civil War of 1648, had seen him welcomed by its new, sympathetic government. But the government's sympathy had since evaporated with the regicide, and it was now recruiting a force with which the newly crowned Charles II could invade England to regain his other throne. Dispatched by the Commonwealth government to cross England's northern border and head off this threat, Oliver faced a very different challenge to that he had lately faced in Ireland. Unlike the Catholic Irish, he saw the

Protestant Scots, his former allies, as a godly people deluded by their single-minded pursuit of Presbyterianism into supporting an ungodly cause. Oliver proceeded carefully. Alongside his military invasion, he ran a parallel propaganda campaign to win the Scots over which they in turn were only too willing to answer in print. 'I beseech you in the bowels of Christ, think it possible you may be mistaken,' he famously asked the Church leaders, who quickly fired back: 'would you have us to be sceptics in our religion?'[108] Returning to his favourite gastro-intestinal imagery, Oliver confided his concerns by letter to Ireton, who was better placed than anyone to understand his father-in-law's difficulty. 'We made great professions of love, knowing we were to deal with many who were godly, and pretended to be stumbled at our invasion; indeed our bowels were pierced again and again, the Lord helped us to sweet words, and in sincerity to meane them we were rejected again and again, yet still we begged to be believed that we loved them as our own souls, they often returned evil for good'.[109]

With stalemate, supply shortages and camp sickness, the outlook seemed bleak but then God revealed himself. On 3 September 1650, Oliver won a stunning and unexpected victory at the great battle of Dunbar. Amazed, Oliver unspooled his tumbling thoughts to three close family members, writing to his wife Elizabeth in London, son-in-law Ireton in Ireland and Richard's father-in-law Richard Major at Hursley. To all he expressed his awe at the providential victory God had granted them, but the remainder of the letters were bespoke, revealing the nature of these relationships. To Ireton, his devoted deputy and effective son, he painted the full background and events of Dunbar complete with statistics, and knitted him as a colleague into their shared endeavour: 'I know the acquainting you with this great handy work of the Lord would stir up your minds to praise and rejoicing, and not knowing but your condition may require mutual experiences for refreshment, and knowing also that the news we had of your successes was matter of help to our faith in our distress, and matter of praises also, I thought fit (thought in the midst of much business) to give you this account.'[110] Just as news of Ireton's victories in Ireland had inspired Oliver when at a low ebb in Scotland, so he hoped now to return the favour.

Richard Major, meanwhile, received Oliver's affectionate messages for Richard, Dorothy and their new baby, and angling for more grandchildren. Doll 'is too modest to tell me whether she breeds or no,' he wrote, 'I wish a blessing upon her and her husband the Lord make them fruitful in all that's good.' As ever, he could not resist a fond jibe at the young couple and their safe, comfortable life in Hampshire which so contrasted with his own hardship on campaign; a long-standing complaint which fitted well with his frustrations with Richard and desire to tease Dorothy about giving him grandchildren.[111] 'I know my Son is idle, but I had better thoughts of Doll,' he had written in his last letter to Major. 'If I had as good leisure as they, I should write sometimes, If my Daughter bee breeding I will excuse her, but not for her nursery, the Lord bless them.'[112] Letters from Oliver's loved ones were essential fuel for his soul while he travailed far from home. 'My love to the dear little ones . . . I thank them for their Letters: let me have them often,' he wrote of his youngest daughters later in the Scottish campaign.[113]

Now at Dunbar, his letter to his wife Elizabeth reflected on their separation. 'I have not leisure to write much, but I could chide thee that in many of thy letters thou writest to mee that I should not be unmindful of thee and thy little ones. Truly if I love you not too well I think I err not on the other hand much. Thou art dearer to me than any creature let that suffice.' To her, he revealed his innermost feelings, sparing any detail of the battle itself but explaining how his victory had strengthened his faltering self-belief even as he felt his physical self deteriorate. 'The Lord hath shown us an exceeding mercy, who can tell how great it is! My weak faith hath been upheld, I have been in my inward man marvellously supported, though I assure thee I grow an old man, and feel infirmities of age marvellously stealing upon me, would my corruptions did as fast decrease.'[114] Though renewed in confidence, the severe illness Oliver suffered in the early months of 1651 attests to the toll campaigning was taking on his health. Finally recovering in April, he updated Elizabeth on his well-being again, this time with reassurance. 'I praise the Lord I am increased in strength in my outward man . . . Pray for me; truly I do daily for thee, and the dear family: and God Almighty bless you all with his spiritual blessings.'[115]

While the miraculous victory at Dunbar was of course welcome, the logistics of its immediate aftermath were troubling, particularly the large number of Scottish soldiers wounded and the 8,000–10,000 unexpectedly taken prisoner. Oliver issued a proclamation allowing local people to remove wounded soldiers and care for them while he wrote to the government in Whitehall and Sir Arthur Haselrig, Governor of Newcastle, outlining the problem of avoiding either losing or starving the prisoners 'neither of which would we willingly incur'.[116] In the end he sent '5000 poor wretches of them' into England to be disposed of by the Council of State, predicting accurately that many would die en route. In 2013, two mass graves were discovered in the grounds of Durham Castle which likely contain Scottish prisoners from Dunbar.[117] The Council of State later ordered over 1,000 of the survivors to be transported to Virginia and New England. The English soldiers meanwhile were presented with commemorative medals.

Dunbar was not the end of the war, but it laid the groundwork for eventual victory. Oliver could now enter Edinburgh, and his large army could be supplied up the east coast over a long and cold winter. Still the Scots dug in behind Stirling and the English faced a hard grind over many months. Eventually Lambert broke the stalemate with a victory at Inverkeithing. The Scots could surrender, starve or take the greatest gamble of all and invade England. The young King Charles threw the dice and the Scots marched down the west coast, Lambert and Harrison's cavalry snapping at their heels. Oliver and the main army meanwhile raced to catch up with Charles leaving General George Monck behind to continue the campaign in Scotland. Reinforcements flocked to Oliver so that by the time he caught up with the King and his army at Worcester, the last hope of the royalist cause faced the largest army assembled in all the years of civil war. This was – finally – the end, or to Oliver, the 'Crowning mercy'. Oliver's huge, sprawling force operated with impeccable discipline and coordination to win the day: 3 September 1651, a year to the day since the battle of Dunbar.

On behalf of the Commonwealth, Oliver had managed a feat no monarch had achieved before him: incorporating Ireland and Scotland into an enlarged English state as Thomas Cromwell had done on a smaller scale with Wales. The islands of the British archipelago had been transformed in the century from Thomas to Oliver Cromwell, first by Tudor imperialism, then the Stuart Union of Crowns, and now by a conquering Commonwealth. Throughout, the relationships between the constituent parts of the British Isles had been as unstable as they were ambiguous and it would take much of the new Commonwealth's political will and financial resources to hold together its new militarised agglomerate in the coming years. But for now, the

England Thomas Cromwell had done so much to sculpt and strengthen dominated the Britain Oliver Cromwell had conquered.

In the days after Worcester, Charles II escaped to the continent, climbing the famous oak tree to evade capture on his way, while Oliver Cromwell rode home to London an all-conquering Caesar. At last, the battlefields of the Civil Wars lay behind him. But Oliver's fighting days were far from over. As Andrew Marvell's heroic poem on Oliver's return from Ireland captures with marvellous, pragmatic ambivalence, Oliver was an elemental force that could not be resisted, his very triumphs – though laid at the republic's feet as sacred offerings – a challenge to the nation's future:

And like the three-fork'd lightning, first
Breaking the clouds where it was nurst,
Did through his own side
His fiery way divide.[118]

Part Three: Power

First, Brutus entered in Anno Mundi 2781
Then the Scots, Picts, and Danes, Anno Christi
Then the Saxons, English &c. 450
Then the Danes 1013
Then the Normans 1066
Then the Scots 1602
And now his Highness the Lord Protector.

Thomas Pugh, British and Outlandish Prophesies *(1658)*

Seven

Survival

Farewell, a long farewell to all my greatness!
This is the state of man: today he puts forth
The tender leaves of hope; tomorrow blossoms,
And bears his blushing honours thick upon him;
The third day comes a frost, a killing frost,
And – then he thinks, good easy man, full surely
His greatness is a-ripening – nips his root,
And then he falls, as I do.

Cardinal Wolsey's farewell, in
William Shakespeare, *Henry VIII*

Shifting alliances

On 1 March 1538, a baby of the extended royal family was given a splendid christening. It was probably at Hampton Court Palace, beneath the star-sparkled ceiling of the chapel, that Thomas Cromwell's first grandchild – Gregory's son Henry Cromwell, named for his grandsire's sovereign master – was held at the font. Thomas bore the expense of his grandson's safe delivery and his nephew Richard its logistics, with the family accounts listing £44 15s for 'Lady Ughtred, by Mr Richard, for things she needed at her lying down'.[1] The use of Gregory's wife Elizabeth's title from her first husband Sir Anthony Ughtred is a reminder that she remained Gregory's social superior even after their marriage. For Gregory's wife was the widowed sister of Henry VIII's new queen Jane Seymour and, as such, the key to the Cromwells' new eminence. She was the reason her baby Henry Cromwell was also a Tudor, nephew by marriage to the King. Through her the Cromwells had breached the walls of the royal family itself. The point was underlined further by Princess Mary acting as godmother, paying money to the women who had delivered the baby and gifting the baby the customary christening cup.[2] It may have been to celebrate his grandson that Thomas commissioned a new table carved with the family coat of arms and organised his players and musicians to stage an elaborate masque at court before the King himself.[3]

The astonishing match Thomas Cromwell had secured for his only son began in the previous summer of 1537, with the dust settled from the Pilgrimage of Grace. The expensively educated and much cherished Gregory was now about seventeen, his features – the boyish version of his father's – captured probably at this point in charming miniature by Holbein. Thomas was aware of Elizabeth, Lady Ughtred for she had dangled herself before him when she asked for help at her widowhood a few years earlier. Now Elizabeth was a confident young woman several years Gregory's senior, and certainly aware of her new attraction since her sister's accession to the throne and recent pregnancy – as were her friends, one of whom wrote flirtatiously to her predicting 'that some Southern lord shall make you forget the North'.[4] A likely portrait of Elizabeth confirms her charms. This is the portrait of a richly dressed young woman by Hans Holbein, long assumed to be of Katherine Howard, but now thought to be of Elizabeth Seymour. The age and appearance of the sitter and the fact that two versions of it – that in the Toledo Museum of Art and the National Portrait Gallery – were preserved within a group of portraits of other Cromwells, one handed down within the Cromwell family itself (at one point mislabelled as 'Oliver Cromwell's Mother') and the other through a connection to it, leave little room for doubt.[5]

Thomas entered into negotiations for her hand with Elizabeth's brother Edward Seymour, Lord Beauchamp, and his accounts show much socialising and largesse between his own palatial home at Mortlake and the Seymours downriver at Twickenham in the warm summer months while the court was at Hampton Court. The household received a constant stream of luxuries from greyhounds, crossbows and rich clothes for the family and their servants, to venison, gooseberries, cherries, quinces, artichokes, ginger, nutmeg and even a porpoise centrepiece. Quinces were particularly prized at the time, yet hard to use, and Gregory's granddaughter Catherine Tollemache's books contain many recipes for preserving them.[6] For now, though, her grandfather Gregory was enjoying his last weeks of bachelorhood, staying for a time with his older cousin Richard in Stepney, and being fitted with new shirts, a 'cape of velvet trimmed with gold and two girdles' and a new sword and dagger. Thus adorned, he married his bride at Mortlake on 3 August 1537 with guests sending presents and Richard giving him fifty pounds as a wedding present from Thomas.[7]

On a personal level, the young couple were evidently happy as attested by Gregory signing a later letter to Elizabeth as 'your loving bedfellow' and the fact that Henry was born a mere seven months after their wedding.[8] Elizabeth's pre-emptive pregnancy may have been known among the family as her brother, writing to Thomas on 2 September, sent his 'commendations to his brother-in-law and sister' adding 'I pray God to send me by them shortly a nephew.'[9] His son in love, Thomas also enjoyed the addition to his family of a gracious and affectionate daughter-in-law. Later, Elizabeth wrote to him:

'In most humble wise, as your assured poor beadwoman, I cannot render unto your lordship the manifold thanks that I have cause, not only for your great pain taken to devise for my surety and health, but also for your liberal token to me, sent by your servant Wriotheseley; and farther, which doth comfort me most in the world, that find your lordship is contented with me, and that you will be my good lord and father the which, I trust, never to deserve other, but rather to give cause for the continuance of the same.'[10]

But Gregory and Elizabeth's marriage meant much more than happy affections. By their wedding Thomas had pulled off an audacious coup which at once transformed the youth Gregory into the King's brother-in-law and Thomas into his monarch's effective 'uncle'. Once Jane Seymour gave birth to Prince Edward on 12 October 1537, Gregory became uncle to the future king. The Cromwell and Seymour families were now united in close mutual interest, together forming a nexus of power which had the potential to achieve great strides for the Reformation, enduring from this reign into the next. Thomas proclaimed their union and its intentions by updating his coat of arms with the evangelical symbol of the pelican which also alluded to the bird wings of the Seymours' coat.[11] He needed a heraldic upgrade for the King had recognised their new kinship relationship by adding Thomas to the most ancient and revered Order of the Garter. The fact that Thomas replaced the executed Pilgrimage of Grace rebel Lord Darcy, who had ranted about the low-born Thomas cutting off the heads of the nobility, only added to his triumph. 'This Cromwell,' the *Spanish Chronicle* commented, now 'had more command even than the Cardinal had had, and the gentlemen [i.e. the council] obeyed him as if he were the King.'[12]

The formidable Cromwell–Seymour alliance seemed set to sweep all before it. But a cruel loss snatched away the families' shared joy only eight short weeks after Gregory's wedding. Twelve days after giving birth to Prince Edward, 28-year-old Jane Seymour died, possibly from post-birth complications or infection. King Henry was heartbroken and the Cromwell family wounded in ways which would only later become clear once the future had revealed itself. Now so closely connected to the Seymours, they were prominent at the Queen's funeral which Thomas organised. Both Gregory and Richard carried banners in the procession while their wives were among the chief mourners. All Thomas could do was press on with his grand plans for securing the family's future which were now, if anything, more urgent. These centred around Gregory and Elizabeth's installation among the leading families of Sussex at Lewes Priory. The move served a dual purpose: elevating the social status of the young couple by establishing them in a grand, landed estate; but also tempering the Duke of Norfolk's power and influence in Sussex while mollifying him by not placing Gregory at North Elmham in the Duke's own heartlands.[13]

Gregory and his new bride travelled down to Sussex shortly after little Henry Cromwell's christening. They found their new home a formidable prospect: a Norman priory which once housed fifty monks, lay incumbents and guests, with one of the largest monastic churches in England, rising in limestone on a ridge beside the town. The priory was now a building site overseen by trusty cousin Richard, with Thomas's Italian engineer Giovanni Portinari leading a demolition team now repurposing materials to build a grand manor house to be known as 'the Lord's Place', and preparing the extensive parkland for leisure pursuits, with huge numbers of falcons gathered for Gregory's sport.[14]

The young couple's arrival was much anticipated by the locals and they were welcomed into high society as Gregory took up his first public post as Justice of the Peace. He soon reported to his father that the house and its setting 'doth undoubtedly right much please and content both me and my wife, and is unto her so commodious that she thinketh herself to be here right well settled'. Listing the local grandees who had welcomed them 'both with their presences and also presents' and offered them 'right friendly' entertainment, Gregory asked Thomas to thank them for their 'kind gentlenesses', revealing the political significance that now accompanied his social life.[15]

But it soon became clear that young Gregory was not cut out for the highly visible place he now held at the top of society with his royal bride. Even as Portinari raised the couple's new mansion, an earthquake brought the cornerstone of the future Thomas had so recently built for his family crashing down. The facts are obscure, but it seems that in November or December 1538, the newlyweds' marital bliss at Lewes was marred by a sex scandal. A seething letter to Richard Cromwell from the Bishop of Chichester reveals that a 'young man' we can presume to be Gregory had 'scornfully refused' to undertake the penance agreed for him of praying for forgiveness in the cathedral and distributing bread to the poor. The crime which had attracted this penalty, Richard learned, 'touches the honesty of your friend' and so must have been out of the ordinary, suggesting some act of sexual immorality.[16]

It was in keeping with the relationship between the close Cromwell triumvirate of Thomas, Richard and Gregory that Richard should be the first approached to hold Gregory's feet to the fire, having the rank above him in the Cromwellian chain of command. Thomas had always entrusted his nephew Richard with responsibility for his younger cousin from the day-to-day oversight of his renovations at Lewes to the symbolism of giving him his father's wedding gift of money. The Bishop made clear that if matters deteriorated he would go over Richard's head not only to the King but, perhaps worse, to Gregory's father. Thomas must have heard the truth or at least enough of it to act. Perhaps it is to this moment we can pin Gregory's wife Elizabeth's undated letter to her father-in-law informing him that she would continue to stay with her brother despite Thomas's offer of her choice of his own houses.[17] Was Thomas trying to help heal a marital breach? If so, her final sentiments to Thomas assume a heightened significance:

'And where it hath pleased your lordship to give me leave, and also commandeth me, if I want, to send to you, and that I may be bold to open my heart, I ensure your lordship my heart hath been a great time in such trust; and now this letter from you, with that I find in it, doth me more pleasure than any earthly good, for my trust is now only in you.'[18]

Certainly, Thomas lost no time in removing Gregory and Elizabeth from Lewes which he had spent so much time and money shaping into their permanent seat. Happily, the similarly grand Leeds Castle in Kent came into the Lord Privy Seal's possession at New Year and he shuffled his deck to replant his beloved heirs there in March 1539, snapping up a further portfolio of local estates to pad it out. If Gregory had violated his marriage and forfeited his wife's trust, the damage done did not prevent their reconciliation. More children would follow, more fond words inked on paper, and a lasting memorial to their love in stone. 'I am, thanks be to God, in health, trusting shortly to hear from you like news,' Gregory wrote to his 'loving bedfellow' in December 1539 – a year after the scandal – 'as well of yourself as also my little boys, of whose increase and towardness be you assured I am not a little desirous to be advertised.'[19]

That summer, the younger Cromwells enjoyed happy scenes at Leeds Castle which must have resounded with the cries and chatter of small souls, as Thomas's brother-in-law and steward John Williamson reported to him from there: 'My lady, my cousin Henry, and my cousin Richard's son are in good health. My cousin Gregory's son has been sore sick, but is now well.'[20] Thomas provided for the many progeny Gregory, Richard and Ralph steadily produced, his accounts listing payment to a court launderer for cleaning 100 dozen 'bends and cloths [nappies] for my Lord's issue'.[21] Also at Leeds was Gregory's likely half-sister Jane, now around nine years old, and Thomas's account lists a large payment of £12 14s 6d for 'apparel for mistress Jane' to Gregory's wife Elizabeth.[22] Jane too, in time, would produce a daughter, Alice, though by then Thomas was no longer alive to enjoy and spoil his grandchildren.[23] For Thomas's ambitions for Gregory and his growing house had done irreparable damage to the Cromwell family.

❦ ❦ ❦

Thomas had a political blind spot where Gregory was concerned. Thus, only weeks after Gregory was relocated to Leeds Castle in Kent after the shadowy Lewes scandal, his father put him forward to sit as one of the two knights of the shire in the upcoming parliamentary session. Technically Gregory's seat at Leeds Castle qualified him for this, though at 19 he was two years shy of the standard age of 21 to enter Parliament. But between the speed of it, his youth, and his father's origins, it was a brazen move which was bound to antagonise the established elites. Either Thomas could not see this, or he judged it a price worth paying for his boy's future. This was after all a brave new world of his own making, with the new Parliament swiftly passing his 'Act for the Placing of the Lords in Parliament' (a new seating plan for the House of Lords) which upturned the apple cart in the face of the hereditary peerage. From then on, a man's office at court trumped his inherited rank. This not only catapulted the King's Vice-Gerent Thomas Lord Cromwell to the top but promised to do the same for any brilliant brewers' sons or butchers' boys who followed in his footsteps.

Into Parliament too went Thomas's other young men, his nephew and adopted son Richard and protégé Ralph Sadler. All three were now playing parts upon the public stage, caretakers of their *de facto* father's trust. Both Richard and Ralph now stood high at court, acting as emissaries for Thomas and as confidants and companions to the King in their own right. As Richard reported in one letter to his uncle, 'I have not myself spoken with the King, but he has declared his pleasure to Mr. Sadler, whereof ye shall be advertised by his letters. Today in riding I hope to commune with His Highness on your letters and other matters, and will send you his sayings therein.'[24] The up-and-coming generation of Cromwells were increasingly visible as they took their places in Thomas's newly made social order. The London muster of all military forces before the King in May 1539 showcased the new great house of Cromwell in glorious technicolour. Ralph himself led the 15,000–20,000 soldiers from close to Richard's home in Stepney through the City to where Henry waited at Whitehall. Gregory and Richard were prominent in the procession as captains, leading the Cromwells' personal force of 1,500 men equipped from Austin Friars' extensive armoury. As it was reported to Lord Lisle, the Lord Deputy of Calais: 'My Lord Privy Seal advanced the City as his cost with xvc [1,500] men, ready armed; and at the end of the last battle followed the Master of the Ordnance, Mr. Gregory, and Mr. Richard Cromwell, with divers other gentlemen accompanied a' horseback, well apparelled and richly beseen, which marched with them till the dissolution of their array.'

Thomas himself had been badly ill that spring with malaria and temporarily reoccupied his old lodgings in St James's Palace. It was from the park there that he watched the parade, his three heirs marching into the future before his eyes over the very ground where Oliver's family would later promenade in their finery. But jealousy encircled these Cromwells just as it would do their descendants. As Lord Lisle's informer ended his account, 'I think all such strangers as had the view of them did little thereat rejoice'; an observation sure to please Lisle who, like so many others, was even now shifting from being Thomas's ally to his opponent.[25] It was perhaps because he sensed this growing animus and his own vulnerability, that in the summer and autumn of 1538, Thomas went on the offensive against his enemies. As he pushed the dissolution to a crescendo, Thomas steered the King to punish those members of the old nobility who remained irreconcilable to his reformation and who Henry had always envied for their superior Plantagenet blood: chiefly the Pole, Montagu and Courtenay families.

These aristocrats had, for a short time, allied with Thomas to bring down their shared enemy Anne Boleyn. But without the hated Anne to unify them, cracks at court became chasms with Thomas's evangelical bloc (which included the Seymours) now in open conflict with its conservative rivals. Once more Thomas conjured a manufactured case to ensnare his opponents, now accused of plotting the death of the King and restoration of England to the papacy in what would become known with retrospective nominative determinism as the 'Exeter Conspiracy'. The King's nemesis Reginald (now Cardinal) Pole remained beyond his reach overseas, but his family and their network were not. A wave of arrests and interrogations was followed by the shocking executions of Henry Courtenay, Marquess of Exeter, Lord Montague of the Pole family, Sir Nicholas Carew and several of their supposed associates. Thomas contrived for Reginald Pole's mother, the 65-year-old Margaret Countess of Salisbury, to be condemned on attainder alone, and she was eventually executed in 1541. Thomas had bested some of his opponents but not all. Despite his efforts to draw the Duke of Norfolk into the conspiracy, Norfolk was impervious and their fractious relationship now more hostile than ever. The return of Norfolk's ally Bishop Stephen Gardiner from his embassy in France further strengthened the hand of the conservative faction at court who celebrated the execution of a prominent evangelical – a different John Lambert – while missing no chance to poison the King against his evangelical and overmighty chief minister.

The volatile Henry himself was increasingly open to such whisperings as storm clouds blocked Thomas from the light of the King's favour. Jane Seymour's death had started the clock on the search for a new wife and Thomas's initial forays into the minefield of the international royal marriage market had angered Henry into declaring that he was 'a good manager but not fit to intermeddle in the affairs of kings'.[26] The fallout had stemmed from the central conundrum of early modern foreign policy which would occupy Oliver Cromwell as much as it did Henry VIII: how best to balance the 'Two Crowns', the great continental powers of France and Spain. Thomas's preference for an alliance with the Spanish King Charles V (the Holy Roman Emperor) was well known, as was Norfolk's for alignment with the French King Francis I. This intersected uneasily with the other geopolitical avenue Thomas was keen to explore – an alliance with the Protestant Schmalkaldic League of cities within the Holy Roman Empire.

A marriage with one of the League's allies – the Duchy of Cleves – received the impetus it needed in early 1539 when the King of France and the Holy Roman Emperor signed an exclusive peace treaty, pushing England out into the cold. Henry, once more excommunicated by the Pope, needed new allies and Cleves, which brought with it close links to the powerful Schmalkaldic League, seemed a shrewd choice. For the evangelical Thomas, chief sponsor of the match, the new King Henry and Queen Anne would head the poster dynasty for the Protestant Reformation. This Reformation had seemed – until recently – to be taking great leaps forward; greatest of all the King's long-awaited authorisation for a 'Great Bible' in English which Thomas steered to publication in April 1539. His own central role in its genesis was immortalised in the Bible's original iconic frontispiece which shows Thomas on one side of the munificent Henry VIII distributing copies, the Cromwell coat of arms beside him. But the reactionary Henry was a fickle master, and even as Thomas nurtured his precious English Bible, the King pulled back from the reformist cause, strengthening the conservative faction at court at Thomas's expense. While Thomas had been incapacitated by his likely malaria in spring 1539, his enemies had seized upon his absence from court to steer Henry's religious policy back in their direction. Neither Thomas's constant letters of apology to the King nor his delegation to Ralph could prevent Norfolk introducing to Parliament six arguments for traditional religious practice which passed into law a month later as the Act of Six Articles – or, as evangelicals branded it, 'the bloody whip with six strings'.[27] The Cleves marriage might just give the recovered Thomas the boost he needed to repeal the Act.

Royal alliances were matters of statecraft, or so Thomas had told Cranmer in one of their rare fallings out when Cranmer had suggested the King be allowed to marry someone of his own choosing who took his 'fantasy and love'.[28] But it was a high-risk strategy. Henry had made it clear this was an alliance entirely of his Lord Privy Seal's making: all the blame, if it misfired, would fall on him. So Thomas marshalled his family behind the project. In December 1539, Gregory boarded a ship as part of the grand welcome delegation Henry sent to meet Anne as she journeyed across Europe to her new home. Gregory had never been to sea before, but he had the stomach for it. While all around him heaved up their guts, Gregory calmly watched the shoreline of France emerge from the blurred horizon, as the winter Channel gusts whipped the '100 banners of silk and gold' which decked the King's ships the *Lion* and the *Sweepstake*.[29] Geographically the land he eventually stepped onto was France, but the town he entered was a little piece of England: the bustling port of Calais, Henry VIII's precious toehold on the continent. Gregory was no penniless adventurer as his father had been when he stowed away to Europe as a teenager, but a royal emissary of love sporting 'three collars of cloth of gold and purple velvet and chains of gold'. Not for him the hand-to-mouth existence of a street boy turned mercenary but feasts, tournaments and parades.[30] Once Anne of Cleves had crossed over to England, Thomas placed his daughter-in-law, Gregory's pregnant wife Elizabeth Seymour, among Anne's ladies in waiting – a role which must have pained her remembering her late sister Queen Jane.

Richard and Ralph were part of the royal entourage which rode through Greenwich Park in full pageantry on 3 January 1540 to meet Anne on her approach to London, Thomas himself amid the other lords with the ambassadors of France and Spain immediately preceding the King.[31] In the train alongside Gregory rode Lionel Tollemache of Helmingham Hall, the grandfather of the Lionel who would marry Gregory's granddaughter Catherine.[32] Thomas controlled all the details of the day, according to one observer looking 'more like a post-runner than anything else, running up and down with his staff in his hand'.[33] Yet he could not control the one piece on the chessboard that mattered: the King. Henry's romantic sensibilities had taken over to disastrous effect. Emulating the chivalric knights of a bygone era, the overweight, middle-aged King had anticipated this formal meeting with Anne by riding down to Rochester on New Year's Day to woo her in disguise and 'to nourish love'. But instead of finding her a worthy object for his courtly love as imagined in Holbein's likeness, Henry took an instant dislike to Anne, complaining of her looks and even her smell. 'I like her not! I like her not!', he ranted, she was 'nothing so well as she was spoken of'.

The King demanded a 'remedy' but Thomas had none; there were no loopholes to wriggle out of the marriage. Railing at being 'not well handled', Henry married Anne at Greenwich a few days later, telling Thomas after the wedding night, 'I liked her before not well, but now, I like her much worse.'[34] Unable to consummate their union, Henry was humiliated and dangerous, more so now his eye had alighted on Norfolk's pretty young niece Katherine Howard. Where Thomas had once been tasked with the nigh impossible feat of marrying Henry to an Anne he loved, he must now – for the second time – perform the reverse trick of undoing a marriage to an Anne he despised. 'For God's sake,' the clear-eyed Thomas Wriothesley urged his master in what should have remained a private conversation when Thomas revealed the King's impotence to him, 'devise for the relief of the King; for if he remain in this grief and trouble, we shall all one day smart for it'.[35] Thomas's other protégé Richard Rich was also well placed to carefully note the Lord Privy Seal's increasingly unguarded outbursts as he edged around the boxing ring, fists aloft. 'If the King would turn from it, yet I would not turn,' Thomas reportedly shouted about the true Protestant faith hearing of evangelicals arrested while at home in Austin Friars, 'and if the King did turn, and all his people, I would fight in the field in mine own person, with my sword in my hand, against him and all others.'[36]

The time for fighting was almost at hand. Rumours circulated about the failure of the King's marriage, the blame laid at the Lord Privy Seal's door, and his enemies were soon whispering against him once more in Henry's ear. What they muttered to the King they had for some time been emboldened to speak plainly to Thomas's face. The previous summer, the King had ordered Cranmer to host a peace-keeping dinner party for his fractious councillors. The night descended into a shouting match between Thomas and Norfolk after Norfolk was provocatively rude about Cardinal Wolsey. Thomas retorted with rapier-like precision that the hypocritical Norfolk had planned to wait on Wolsey in Rome if he had become Pope, even recalling 'what number of florins he should have received'.[37] Norfolk probably never recovered from his fury while Thomas was now open in his contempt for Norfolk and the other nobles ranged against him. 'If the Lords would handle him so,' he reportedly raged, 'he would give them such a breakfast as never was made in England, and that the proudest of them should know.'[38] 'Cromwell is tottering,' Ambassador Marillac of France reported gleefully in April 1540 on the 'farce' playing out before his eyes, predicting that 'within few days there will be seen in this country a great change'.[39]

But if this was clear one day, it was not the next. Another reconciliatory dinner party, this time hosted by Thomas, seemed to clear the air between him and his nemesis, the Archbishop of Winchester, Stephen Gardiner. Meanwhile, Thomas still received marks of the King's favour as he pressed on with his business, pushing a large volume of legislation through Parliament in a successful session. Thomas also took practical steps to shore up his position at court while further securing the future of his dear young men. With the King's consent, he relinquished his office of Principal Secretary to a job-share between Ralph Sadler and Thomas Wriothesley who were both given knighthoods and would attend Council meetings. Although an outward surrender of position, placing his two trusty adherents as his eyes and ears in the King's intimate moments, within the Council and as go-betweens in the Lords and Commons, brought Thomas obvious advantages and he seemed to take pleasure in immediately addressing Ralph as 'Master Secretary' in his handover letters. Evidently Thomas trusted Ralph and Wriothesley to stay loyal to him through anything the future held, as he surely assumed all of his protégés would.

The pillar perished

A few weeks later, when Thomas Cromwell watched his nephew Richard riding in the May Day tournament in dazzling white velvet, he no doubt hoped he would keep his seat. Some weeks before the Earl of Essex had not been so lucky, suffering a fatal fall from his horse. Essex had no heir, so the earldom was vacant, but the King knew just who to give it to. On 17 April 1540, Henry VIII made his Putney ruffian handler Thomas Cromwell the 16th Earl of Essex and, a day later, placed him at the head of the royal household as Lord Great Chamberlain. So it was as Earl of Essex that Thomas watched Richard Cromwell triumph in the tournament to celebrate the King's marriage to Anne of Cleves, earning his legendary knighthood and diamond ring from the King on the spot.[40]

It may have been a bright spring day, but the court was clouded by Henry's dissatisfaction with his marriage which placed all his subjects' lives on a knife-edge. The last time this had happened, in the brooding weeks before Anne Boleyn's arrest four years earlier, Thomas had talked with Chapuys of Cardinal Wolsey, and the warning his life offered those who followed in royal service. Thinking of Wolsey – who Shakespeare in his play *Henry VIII* would later give great eloquence in understanding the mutability of life – Chapuys warned Thomas to take care not to provoke Anne Boleyn. But more important still was to please the King and find a way to give him what he wanted. Thomas received this advice in a philosophical mood, saying 'it was only now that he had known the frailty of human affairs, especially of those of the court, of which he had before his eyes several examples that might be called domestic, and he always laid his account that if fate fell upon him as upon his predecessors he would arm himself with patience, and leave the rest to God'.[41] That moment had now come.

On 10 June Thomas Cromwell, the blushing honour of the Earldom of Essex barely settled on his shoulders with the scattered spring blossom, was running late as he hurried from the House of Lords across the Westminster estate to the Privy Council chamber for a 3 pm meeting. He arrived into an ambush. Within a heartbeat he was arrested by the Captain of the Guard for treason and heresy, and his fellow councillors fell upon him in fury, Norfolk tearing off his collar of St George while his former ally William Fitzwilliam plucked the garter off his knee. In these first moments of dawning disaster, Thomas did not show the patience he envisaged but righteous fury at the injustice and indignity of the attack. 'Cromwell in a rage cast his bonnet on the ground, saying to the Duke of Norfolk and others of the Privy Council assembled there that this was the reward of his services, and that he appealed to their consciences as to whether he was a traitor . . .'[42] Thomas would have time in the coming weeks for reflection and resignation, but his first reaction was instinctive and emotional: that of a tracked animal at last trapped by its hunters. He was taken to the Tower of London by river, just as Anne Boleyn had been, and probably imprisoned in the rooms he had renovated for her coronation and in which she too spent her last days.

The blast area caught the rest of the Cromwell family quickly. Gregory was nearby in the House of Commons to hear the devastating news of his father's arrest. He was in immediate and terrible danger. Richard Cromwell too was frighteningly exposed. The two Secretaries Ralph Sadler and Thomas Wriothesley, meanwhile, were swiftly put to work on the paperwork of their patron's calamity: Wriothesley drafting statements from the Council, Ralph summarising and reading aloud reactions from Europe for the King, the words bitter in his mouth. A few miles away in the City, the household at Austin Friars learned of the catastrophe when the King's archers arrived to seize their master's goods. Thomas's mother-in-law Mercy Prior – still alive at the beginning of the year when Gregory sent her a gift – may have been *in situ* to watch.[43] Certainly a quorum of Williamsons, Wellyfeds and loyal servants would have been. With the traipsing boots, the world collapsed about their ears as men hunted out Thomas's treason, carting off books and papers as evidence, and seizing £7,000 (over £2 million today), 'silver plate, including crosses, chalices, and other spoils of the Church' as booty for the royal treasury.[44] When more of Thomas's goods were delivered to Hampton Court a few weeks later, the King commanded their distribution among other gentlemen, though his 'robes of the Garter of crimson and purple velvet' Henry kept for himself.[45]

The Cromwell family home and possessions were no longer private sanctuaries but items of public account to be weaponised against the man who built them. The considerable armoury which Thomas had contributed to the suppression of the Pilgrimage of Grace and at the

1539 City muster, and which in happier times he had showed off to Ambassador Marillac before boasting of this to the King, was now a sinister sign of his planned insurrection.[46] Letters with Lutheran lords and papers on the Cleves marriage showed his purported heresy and duplicity, enraging the King so much 'that he would no longer hear him spoken of, but rather desired to abolish all memory of him as the greatest wretch ever born in England'.[47] This Henry could do more easily because of Thomas's low origins. Thus the King 'proclaimed that none should call him lord Privy Seal or by any other title of estate, but only Thomas Cromwell, shearman (*tondeur de draps*), depriving him of all his privileges and prerogatives, and distributing his less valuable movables among his (Cromwell's) servants, who were enjoined no longer to wear their master's livery'.[48]

The trumped-up charges against Thomas similarly emphasised his 'very base and low degree', using this as the foundation for the outrage that such a man could plot to become more powerful than the King, plan to marry his daughter Mary and commit countless other high-handed crimes and acts of corruption.[49] The Cleves match was, of course, the proximate cause of Thomas's fall, exacerbated by his implied indiscretion about the King's virility. Inextricably bound up in the fiasco, Thomas was even made to keep working on unravelling the marriage from his cell in the Tower. But class anxiety and resentment also played a key role as Thomas and his family's growing power, status and wealth opened him up to the King's aggression, fanned by the indignant jealousy of the nobility, and especially Norfolk. Marillac captured this in his aside on Austin Friars' inventory, that all this was 'not of such value as people thought, although too much for a *compaignon de telle estoffe* (man of his sort)'.[50] Wolsey's fellow servant George Cavendish saw this all too clearly, writing of Thomas's first political emergence:

> *With royal eagles a kite may not fly;*
> *Although a jay may chatter in a golden cage,*
> *Yet will the eagles disdain his parentage.*[51]

The attainder itself decried Thomas for enriching himself and treating the nobility with disdain.[52] 'If his pride had not betrayed him, and he had kept friendly with the lords, he would not have come to the end he did,' the *Spanish Chronicle* concluded.[53] Later commentators agreed. 'Had he loved the nobility of his country as he seemed to love foreigners, belike he had yet been alive,' the novelist Bandello sighed.[54] For the Stuart historian Lord Chirbury, Thomas was 'odious by reason of his low birth to all the nobility';[55] while his contemporary Thomas Fuller agreed. 'This was the cause why he was envied of the nobility, being by birth so much beneath them and by preferment so high above most of them. Besides, many of his advancements were interpreted not so much as honours to him as injuries to others, as being either in use improper or in equity unfit or in right unjust or in conscience unlawful for him to accept.'[56]

Thomas had naturally collected enemies as he climbed the perilous ladder of Tudor court politics. But his ambitions for his family and household, most visibly marrying Gregory into the royal family, setting him up among the nobility and promoting him into Parliament, made it easier for his inveterate enemies to convince the King of his limitless ambition. He had simply grown too grand, with his hundreds of servants (many of whom he had placed in the King's service) and fine houses, the chief of which, Austin Friars, was now the largest private residence in London. Thus another charge levelled at him was the unlawful keeping of retainers – an accusation he was vulnerable to, given his open-handed charity taking on dependants. This prompted particular indignation in the hospitable, fatherly Thomas who asserted that he only cared for his friends' children 'to my great charge and for none evil'.[57] Henry himself must have privately accepted the innocence of Thomas's retinue for he was 'very kind' to the Cromwell servants at their master's fall, protecting their personal possessions and taking many of them into his and others' service 'to save them from want'.[58] He even showed some feeling towards Thomas himself, sending him money and inviting him to write to him; the only opportunity Thomas had to defend himself as the Act of Attainder mechanism – which he himself had wielded against his enemies – required no trial.

Those who had benefited from Thomas's care showed their true colours now in his hour of need. It seems likely loyal members of his household managed to burn some of his own letters and files before they were seized.[59] Gregory had no choice but to stay silent and out of sight, his honorific title of 'lord' swept away along with his future security as all his father's estates were forfeited. Although Richard and Ralph could not speak publicly in their beloved honorary father's defence, they likely did what they could for him behind the scenes as their future loyal actions suggest. John Foxe claimed that Ralph delivered a letter from Thomas to the King when no-one else would; a touching scene later dramatised in a play once attributed to Shakespeare.[60] Archbishop Cranmer was probably the only man who could speak for his friend and survive the King's ire, and he wrote a courageous letter in his defence much as he had done four years before for Anne Boleyn. 'If the noble princes of memory, King John, Henry II and Richard II had had such a Councillor about them, I suppose they should never have been so traitorously abandoned, and overthrown as those good princes were,' he said of Thomas. 'I loved him as my friend, for so I took him to be; but I chiefly loved him for the love which I thought I saw him bear ever towards your Grace.'[61]

Thomas Wyatt, obsessed with betrayal, had written of his own greatest moment of peril at his arrest in 1536 that, 'But they that some time liked my company / Like lice away from dead bodies they crawl.'[62] Now, like Wyatt's lice, Thomas's protégés Thomas Wriothesley and Richard Rich betrayed their master to testify against him with evidence drawn from their private conversations when his guard was dropped. Wriothesley now followed the advice he had once repeated to Thomas to 'spare no man when the time shall come, but be thine own friend and thine own executor'.[63] Wriothesley had enjoyed acting as a student at Cambridge and kept up his performance at court, joking with Wyatt that he 'played the honest man' with him but 'the jolly courtier' with everyone else.[64] In recent weeks, he had had need of his skill, having reverted to the service of his former employer Stephen Gardiner. The ambitious Richard Rich meanwhile gave false testimony against his mentor just as he had done at Thomas More's trial, earning him widespread and everlasting condemnation as 'the most wretched person in England'.[65] Thomas alluded to his former closeness to Rich and sense of betrayal when he denied speaking treasonous words to him, reminding Henry 'what Master Chancellor [Rich] hath been towards me god and he best knoweth, I willne can accuse him. What I have been towards him your Majesty right well knoweth I would to Christ I had obeyed your often most gracious grave councels and advertisements then it had not been with me as now it is'.[66]

Thomas's hopes of reprieve dimmed with the passing weeks, among his last words to Henry the devastating postscript to one letter,

'Most gracious prince: I cry for mercy, mercy, mercy!' which it was said poor Ralph was forced to read to the King three times.[67] As his end neared, all other concerns evaporated to leave the central mission of Thomas's life: the preservation of Gregory and his family. 'Sir upon my knees I most humbly beseech your gracious Majesty to be a good and gracious lord to my poor son, the good and virtuous lady his wife and their poor children,' he wrote to Henry.[68] The reference to his daughter-in-law Elizabeth was a deliberate reminder to the sentimental King that she was his adored late wife's sister. Perhaps now that the King had finally been freed from his marriage to Anne of Cleves and was planning his next to Katherine Howard, he would be in a more receptive mood. But no answering letter came. No sign of favour, no reprieve. All that remained to Thomas now was one final act to save his precious son and his heirs: to die in the right way.

Gregory was no doubt in his thoughts as Thomas walked to the scaffold on Tower Hill on 28 July 1540, the last day of his life. Perhaps he thought too of his latest grandchild, a third son born to Elizabeth probably only weeks earlier and named for him. Another Thomas Cromwell had come into the world to replace him before he left it. A Thomas Cromwell who would also sit in the House of Commons and take part in the great affairs of the realm. A thousand halberdiers escorted the prisoner, it was reported, 'as a revolt was feared; and if all those who formerly wore his livery and called themselves his servants had been there, they might easily have raised the city, so beloved was he by the common people'. But in the end, the Cromwellians attempted no last-ditch rescue of their founder. Thomas was, in any event, calm and accepting, having been 'very pensive' all the previous night.[69]

Thomas's last act was to give a masterful speech from the scaffold which safeguarded his family and appeased his King, even as it left his enemies empty-handed. He admitted his lowly origins and fatal pride, but in so doing reminded those listening of his astonishing rise and the injustice of being condemned now for his low birth. He acknowledged himself a sinner who had offended God and the King, but so could anyone else say of themselves. He accepted he was lawfully condemned but conceded no treasonous actions. He refuted the charge most dangerous to his family – that of heresy – by professing himself in irrefutable yet vague terms as dying 'in the Catholic faith'.

He asked the crowd to pray for the King and for Prince Edward who was, of course, not only the royal heir but his son's nephew and the hope for Cromwells and Cromwellians of the future. Thomas looked back on the great journey of his life as the end came into sight: 'And it is not unknown to many of you that I have been a great traveller in this world, and being but of a base degree, was called to high estate, and since the time I came thereunto, I have offended my prince, for the which I ask him hearty forgiveness, and beseech you all to pray to God with me, that he will forgive me.'[70]

The end came moments later. Accounts vary on the number of blows needed, but it was certainly a swifter death than it would have been had the King not granted a final mercy for Thomas Cromwell to be beheaded as a lord rather than hanged, drawn and quartered as the shearman he had reduced him to. But before Thomas placed his head under the axe, he enjoyed a final moment of friendship. His friend Thomas Morison had written to him years before that 'Friendship should be like a marriage, for better for worse, for richer, for poorer, till death depart. They cannot be separated whom true amity knitteth.'[71] And so it was now with Thomas Wyatt who stood beside his friend at the end, the friend who had shielded him at Anne Boleyn's fall and who he may in turn have unwittingly undermined through his ambassadorial work easing a Spanish alliance. Now Wyatt stood 'in such grief' that Thomas urged him 'do not weep, for if I were no more guilty than thou wert when they took thee, I should not be in this pass'. Instead he bade him, 'Oh, gentle Wyatt, good-bye, and pray to God for me.'[72] Shakespeare in his *Henry VIII* would later have Wolsey describe to Thomas Cromwell at his own fall how his strong shoulders had become 'These ruined pillars'.[73] Perhaps he had read Wyatt's lament for his own fallen hero, his 'assured loving friend', Wolsey's 'good Cromwell':

The piller perish'd is whereto I leant
The strongest stay of mine unquiet mind;
The like of it no man again can find,
From east to west still seeking though he went.[74]

Thomas's will of 1528–9 had been puritanical about his wishes for his body at his death, desiring 'His body to be buried where he shall die' and a funeral 'without any earthly pomp.'[75] A lack of interest in venerating their mortal remains would become a Cromwell family trait (fortunately in some cases). Thomas's grandson Thomas Cromwell MP, for instance, specified 'that no pomp or sumptuousnes be used in about or by reason of my burial, being not willing to have vanities continued for me after my death whereto I have been too much subject in my lifetime'.[76] Now the executed Thomas Cromwell would have his wish met, after a fashion: his remains were interred where he died – in the Chapel of St Peter ad Vincula within the Tower of London – but not before his head had suffered the traitors' indignity of a spell on a spike on London Bridge.

It was an extraordinary end to an extraordinary life and many, like Wyatt, wondered at the wheel of fortune that spun great men down from what he called the 'slipper top'.[77] That great political power was dangerous was well understood: 'The first place by the king is a slippery one' went a common motto, while a century later John Desborough would use the same language to warn Oliver Cromwell that 'high places are slippery, except God establish our goings'.[78] The Catholic monarchs of Europe celebrated the death of the King's Vice-Gerent Thomas Cromwell, while in England, 'Many lamented, but more rejoiced, and specially such, as either had been religious men, or favoured religious persons, for they banqueted, and triumphed together that night . . . Other who knew nothing but truth by him, both lamented him, and heartily prayed for him.'[79] It was said that the common population of London mourned him most as he had been a neighbour and champion for them.[80]

Faithful servants

None would feel Thomas's loss like his family. The courageous Richard mourned his uncle openly at court in defiance of the King's determination to banish all mention of his fallen minister – a fearless attitude reminiscent of Thomas's own fidelity to the memory of the fallen Cardinal Wolsey. Yet Henry tolerated this behaviour by one of his favourite, and most recent, knights. Richard perhaps felt emboldened by the continuation of signs of royal favour during his uncle's imprisonment, such as the grant in June of two licences to transfer his property. Yet it still paid to take precautions. The first licence Richard signed as 'Sir Richard Cromwell alias Williams', the second as 'Sir Richard Williams'.[81] This would not be the last time family members harnessed the fluidity of the Cromwell/Williams name at a time of crisis. It was also perhaps Richard, Gregory or another of their family who was sufficiently in the King's esteem to be given some expensive clothes on 21 July during Thomas's time in the Tower, alongside Ralph and other gentlemen of the court.[82]

Ralph, though personally bereft, had helped to distance himself from the fiasco of the Cleves marriage by performing his secretarial duties for the Privy Council during the annulment process.[83] At the end of this, Anne was pensioned off as the King's 'sister', her new house furnished with rich pickings from Austin Friars.[84] She would spend her remaining years in quiet safety surrounded by the treasures of the man who had arranged her disastrous marriage and paid for it with his life. By the autumn, it seemed that the Cromwells and their allies' moment of acute danger had passed as the King's anger softened. Thomas's friends and servants continued his work in their key positions, with others picking up the posts he had vacated. Ralph was given Thomas's position of Clerk of the Hanaper and granted the manor of Standon in Hertfordshire while the King re-appointed Richard as Sheriff of Cambridgeshire and Huntingdonshire.[85]

Henry meanwhile had satisfied his bloodlust with a further round of executions for heresy and treason, and had had time to watch his court bureaucracy flounder without his able chief minister at the helm. Having spent the summer reputedly exclaiming 'I have got Cromwell' whenever dealt a knave at cards, he now repented his death, being 'heard oftentimes to say, that now he lacked his Cromwell'.[86] Such repentance did not weigh on his own conscience, of course, for he had a Council to blame as 'upon light pretexts, by false accusations, they made him put to death the most faithful servant he ever had'.[87] Now, if any, was the time for the most vulnerable Cromwell to appeal for mercy and secure his future. Gregory and Elizabeth had been living at Leeds Castle, though Elizabeth may have spent time at court waiting on Katherine Howard, who Henry had married on the day of Thomas Cromwell's death. Yet they remained in danger, with a dark cloud hanging over them and their children. Thomas had done his best to shield them at his fall, and it was Elizabeth now who continued his campaign. She wrote the King a short, confident letter which recast the past. Writing as the King's 'bond woman', she thanked him for his 'mercy and infinite goodness, notwithstanding the heinous trespasses and most grievous offences of my father-in-law, yet so graciously to extend your benign pity towards my poor husband and me, as the extreme indigence and poverty wherewith my said father-in-law's most detestable offences hath oppressed us'.

It was, she hoped, a good moment now the King's 'high and weighty affairs' were 'partly overpast' to offer her 'most obedient suit' for him to extend his 'accustomed pity and gracious goodness towards my said poor husband and me'. Her brave signature as 'Elizabeth Cromwell' ended her plea.[88] It was the letter of a skilled politician and one her father-in-law would have admired and understood, for all her sentiments would have pained him. He could have been satisfied at least that Elizabeth Seymour was the greatest gift he could have given his son. For her petition worked and Gregory was soon afterwards made Baron Cromwell in his own right, entailed upon his male heirs. The great lords of the Privy Council witnessed the ennoblement of Thomas's line including the Duke of Norfolk.[89] Gregory already had the estates over which his father had wisely given him joint tenure – including Rhymney in Wales and the family's future homes of North Elmham and Oakham – but now he was granted back Thomas's beloved Launde, and it was here that he moved his family for the safety and quiet his father had looked forward to. The grant itself of 10 February 1541 still hangs in Launde today, a large parchment letter fixed with the King's 14 cm wide great seal showing the magisterial figure of Henry riding a warhorse with a greyhound at its feet.

Gregory and Elizabeth may have felt safe moving north to remote Leicestershire, but the Cromwellians at court were still in danger from the aftershocks of Thomas's fall. On 17 January 1541, an event stunned the court and sent ambassadors scribbling to their masters. Out of the blue Ralph Sadler and Thomas Wyatt were arrested and hauled from Hampton Court and 'with their hands bound, conducted by 24 archers to the Tower'.[90] This was yet another turn of the wheel of fortune or, as Marillac saw it, a destructive cycle of revenge: 'there could be no worse war than the English carry on against each other; for after Cromwell had brought down the greatest of the realm, from the Marquis to the Grand Esquire Caraud, now others have arisen who will never rest till they have done as much to all Cromwell's adherents, and God knows whether after them others will not recommence the feast'.

While the exact charges were cloaked in secrecy, Marillac did not doubt that this was a coup against the Cromwellians. Of Wyatt, he commented that it was the third time he had been imprisoned in the Tower 'and apparently it will be the last, for this must be some great matter and he has for enemies all who leagued against Cromwell, whose minion he was'. He noted further that Wriothesley 'who rose by Cromwell's means, is on the verge of descending more quickly than he came up, for he has already been examined upon some rather ticklish articles, and others are said to be by no means out of danger'.[91] For himself, Wyatt knew that his 'familiar friends [were] examined in hold and apart'.[92]

In the end, the well-schooled Ralph was able to talk himself out of the Tower within a few days with a testimony so convincing the King apparently began to question the case against Thomas Cromwell himself.[93] Perhaps Henry wanted to keep the balance between reformers and conservatives within his advisers. Perhaps he was right when he claimed to now know his 'good servants from his flatterers'.[94] Perhaps he simply did not want to lose another competent bureaucrat. Wriothesley, if he was ever in genuine danger, emerged stronger than ever as he increasingly eclipsed Ralph as the more prominent Secretary in closer proximity to the King, eventually becoming Lord Chancellor. Wyatt languished a further two months until the King pardoned him 'for his wit', possibly on the persuasion of his new Queen Katherine Howard who admired his poetry.[95] The eloquent courtier had survived once more against the odds, though his natural life did not have long to run and he died the following year. Gardiner and the other conservatives' purge of the Cromwellians had failed, but this was not the end of their long duel. Marillac's revenge cycle continued. It was the romantic Queen Katherine herself who provided Thomas's protégés with the next opportunity to eliminate his enemies when she embarked on an affair with the courtier Thomas Culpeper. Cranmer led the investigation against the young Katherine, but it was Ralph who deployed his master's meticulous methods to assemble the case against her. He hoped to do more, to draw Norfolk, Gardiner and their allies into the Queen's downfall, but he could not persuade the King who still needed his leading councillors as France and Scotland threatened war. So the ever-careful Ralph settled down to wait for a more propitious time to avenge his patron.[96]

The brewing conflicts with France and Scotland cast the leading Cromwells out of the realm. This was when Ralph was sent to Scotland to negotiate the marriage of Prince Edward and the baby Mary Queen of Scots. Though Ralph lost his Secretaryship during his travels, he was evidently so highly valued only three years after Thomas Cromwell's fall for Henry to threaten the Scots if they harmed him. Richard's skill in the tiltyard, meanwhile, was all too transferable to the battlefield and the King sent him first to campaign in the Netherlands where he garnered more honour by saving his commander from a bullet by leaping upon the shooter.[97] Gregory managed to obtain an exemption from serving in Henry's 1544 expedition to France, but Richard went.[98] Though in 'most health', the sensible soldier wrote a will before departing, perhaps motivated to expedience by the death of his wife Frances Murfyn and the prospect of leaving his two young boys orphaned. It was a prescient decision for Richard died, most likely from disease contracted on campaign, on 20 October 1544, just four years after his uncle. It was a sad end to what had become a gilded life in spite of Thomas's fall. Richard's will bequeathed Gregory a 'great horse' but this could hardly have made up for the loss of the *de facto* older brother he adored, and so relatively soon after his own father's death.

When he at last returned from Scotland, Ralph faced his own domestic troubles. His wife Ellen's first husband, long assumed to be dead, turned up very much alive, meaning that the Sadlers had been living together bigamously, their children born bastards. So scandalous was this, some later historians claimed the whole event had been invented as a slur against Ralph.[99] Devoted to his wife, Ralph 'took his matter very heavily'.[100] His ally Cranmer headed a clerical commission to look into it, but this found the original marriage lawful and so could suggest no remedy.[101] Ralph's only recourse now was to take the matter to Parliament and use his experience and high standing with Henry to obtain a private bill to ratify his marriage and legitimise his children. Parliament obliged, the Commons, convinced of Ellen's husband's 'evil behaviour' and Ralph's 'pure conscience', recording an unblemished account of the Sadlers' marriage: after her husband abandoned her and having been assured of his death and spent time in a nunnery, Ellen had entered '"the service" of one Mistress Prior, mother-in-law to the lord Cromwell, late earl of Essex'. There the honest and godly Ralph, fully aware of her circumstances, had courted her for a long time, and after their marriage she had 'lived as an honest wife to him, ordered his house wisely, and bore him nine children, seven of whom . . . are living'.[102] Thus were two of Thomas Cromwell's much-doted-on godchildren saved from ignominy by a powerful Parliament.

This was a torrid time for Ralph, but his political fortunes were improving. He had rejoiced when Henry married his final wife, the reformist Queen Katherine Parr in 1543, and delighted in Standon which he was transforming into the great house his family would live in for generations. Though the conservative faction had since been in the ascendancy at court, by 1546 the tide was once more against them.[103] In December, the Cromwellians struck against Thomas's enemies in a coup that saw Norfolk arrested, his son executed, and Gardiner demoted. When Henry VIII died just weeks later holding Cranmer's hand, it was clear that Thomas Cromwell's reformist friends and heirs would hold sway in the minority government of the boy prince, Jane Seymour's son and Gregory's nephew Edward VI. Ralph's ally and Gregory's brother-in-law, the new king's uncle Edward Seymour, would be particularly powerful, becoming Lord Protector to govern in the boy king's name as the Duke of Somerset. Ralph himself continued to sit on the Privy Council.

Edward VI only lived to reign for six years. Yet this was a vital time for both the Cromwells and England which saw the next steps of Thomas Cromwell's religious reformation taken by the men who had grown up in his orbit. Wriothesley lost his Lord Chancellorship then died in 1550, while Norfolk and Gardiner spent Edward's reign in the Tower, Ralph himself arresting Gardiner.[104] The ever-flexible Richard Rich meanwhile continued to climb, becoming Lord Chancellor himself in 1547. Edward's reign should have been a happier time for the Cromwells. Gregory had been living a quiet but not insignificant life with Elizabeth in the last years of Henry's reign, administering to the Launde estate and shire business while regularly attending the House of Lords. Here he was conscientious – present at 80 per cent of recorded sittings from 1542–3 – though not prominent, with no roles on any committees.[105] His public profile rose with the accession of his nephew Edward VI. Gregory's first duty, and one that must have carried with it many conflicting emotions, was to carry one corner of the canopy over Henry VIII's coffin at his funeral. After seeing off the king who had killed his father, he saw in the young king who would drive his father's reformation forward. The change in tone was exemplified by Edward VI making Gregory a knight of the Bath at his coronation and granting him a new estate in Rutland.

Yet the good times were not to last. The realm was unsettled by popular disturbances over agricultural policies, notably land enclosure. The largest of these, Kett's Rebellion, took place close to Gregory's estate of North Elmham, and in fact his local parish funded the rebels.[106] Further trouble arose in the person of Thomas Seymour, Gregory's wife Elizabeth's brother, who had once been patronised by Thomas Cromwell but had degenerated into an overambitious loose cannon in the mould of the later Earl of Essex, earning him execution in 1549. His brother, Lord Protector Edward Seymour, was then brought down by the powerful nobility alienated by his Cromwellian concern for social justice. And so the second of Elizabeth's brothers and King Edward's uncles followed their former ally Thomas Cromwell to the block at Tower Green. 'Ah, how unfortunate I have been to those of my blood, my mother I slew at my birth, and since have made away two of her brothers,' a seventeenth-century historian reported the young king saying regretfully.[107]

Elizabeth Seymour had lost two brothers in four years. But it was not her only bereavement in this dreadful time. Her husband Gregory was only around 30 years old when, in July 1551, he succumbed to the same sweating sickness that had claimed his mother and sisters all those years earlier. It was a tragic end for Thomas's beloved boy, only 11 years after his own death. Elizabeth was bereft, her situation all the more burdensome when, at her brother Somerset's execution the following year, the Council chose her as guardian to his four fatherless daughters whose mother had been imprisoned. To Launde in disgrace they came with 100 marks a year (each mark worth 13 shillings and four pence) granted by Parliament to Elizabeth to maintain them.[108] Taking on these girls alongside her many children so soon after Gregory's death placed considerable strain on Elizabeth's hitherto strong shoulders. Thus she wrote to the rising man and Cromwellian ally, privy councillor Sir William Cecil, 'the nearest friend I have in the world', to plead her case, much as she had to Henry VIII after Thomas's death. She had accepted her nieces out of duty, Elizabeth explained, yet she was in reality 'a lone woman' living in 'the poor house of Launde' with 'the weighty burden and care which nature bindeth me to be mindful of, as well for the bestowing of my own children, as also for such poor family as my late lord and husband hath left me unprovided for'. Furthermore, she lived far from any of her Seymour kin and was 'destitute of friendly advice and counsel', while her own nieces 'have not taken in such good part as my good meaning was, nor according to my expectation in them'.[109] Elizabeth hoped to relinquish the girls at the end of one year and got her wish when they were returned to their mother on her release from the Tower in 1553.

A few years later, Elizabeth transformed her fortunes with her third marriage, to John Paulet, future 2nd Marquess of Winchester, moving herself and her children to live with his family at the majestic Basing House in Hampshire – one of the grandest homes in England which would become the site of a dreadful siege during the Civil Wars. She took her memories of Launde Abbey with her but left something important behind. Gregory had been buried in the chapel, beneath its blue star-speckled ceiling reminiscent of Hampton Court, '[with a stand]ard, a banner of arms, and coat, helmet, sword, target, and sc[ochyons, and] harold' but Elizabeth had gone one step further to commemorate her second husband and their marriage.[110] She commissioned for him a magnificent stone memorial later considered 'One of the purest monuments of the early Renaissance in England, very grand and restrained'.[111] Large but graceful, with winged horses supporting the Cromwell coat of arms flanked by elegant pilasters decorated with trophies, and surmounted with a high pediment, it is an eternal resting place both Gregory's father and Cardinal Wolsey would have envied. The brief inscription about Gregory does not mention Thomas – still *persona non grata* in 1551 – yet in its celebration of Cromwell heraldry, it commemorates him with every carving. Elizabeth too lives on in the stone, her initials EC at the base of one pillar, GC at the other. Indeed, she may well have intended to share Gregory's tomb at her own death which would explain the empty plaque beneath his which might have been left for her own inscription. She never came back to rest with the husband she evidently loved but was interred in St Mary's Church Basing at her death in March 1568. Yet a part of him returned to her in her own memorial on the wall of the church vault which names her as 'D[omi]na Cromwell', still her highest title at her death.[112]

The Seymour brothers' executions and King Edward's own death aged 15 in 1553 brought to an end the apotheosis of the Seymours with the brief bounce it had brought for the Cromwells. The leader of Edward's Council, John Dudley, the Duke of Northumberland, attempted to save the Reformation from Edward's Catholic sister Mary by persuading Edward to nominate his Protestant cousin Jane Grey as his successor. Ralph Sadler was among those who supported him in this, signing the device which made Jane heir. But the attempt ended in bloody disaster. The Tollemaches – as clients of the Duke of Norfolk – picked the winning side, rallying to Mary at Framlingham Castle, from where she successfully overthrew Jane to claim the throne for herself. Ralph, meanwhile, was placed under house arrest. Though he sued out his pardon, Ralph lost some of his offices, and the next five years were a worrying time for Cromwellians like him with the re-emergence of the conservative faction under a Catholic queen. Gardiner was restored to his see and appointed Lord Chancellor while Norfolk was released and restored to his dukedom, though both died within the next two years. Richard Rich of course sailed on. Poor Cranmer went to the stake to face a more dreadful end even than his old friend Thomas Cromwell's had been. Young Thomas Wyatt, son of the poet father who had stood and wept by Thomas Cromwell's side at his death, met his own execution after rebelling against Mary's marriage to the Catholic King Philip II of Spain.

Thomas Cromwell's legacy – the people and the ideas he loved – were in great jeopardy, yet an ironic saviour would safeguard their future. On Mary's death in 1558, her younger sister, Anne Boleyn's daughter the Protestant Elizabeth I, came to the throne. Elizabeth's accession was a happy event for the Cromwellians and it was under her considered stewardship that Thomas's Reformation bedded irrevocably into England's foundations. Two of his beloved boys Gregory and Richard Cromwell did not live to see it, but the third did. Ralph, his master's political heir, was at last home and dry with the queen he loved – appointed to her new Privy Council among a slew of other reformist politicians who had served their apprenticeships in Thomas's circle, headed by his friend Sir William Cecil. Supremely talented but instinctively cautious, Ralph was the ultimate Cromwellian survivor who would live to serve his queen as a Privy Councillor, Chancellor of the Duchy of Lancaster and parliamentary statesman, and guard her enemies from Norfolk's son to Mary Queen of Scots. This earned him the admiration of the great Scottish novelist Sir

Walter Scott who wrote his memoir and cited him in his novel *Kenilworth* as evidence that talent can rise: 'What was Thomas Cromwell but a smith's son? and he died my lord – on a scaffold, doubtless, but that, too, was in character. And what was Ralph Sadler but the clerk of Cromwell?'[113] To a royalist clergyman writing in the turbulent 1660s, Ralph offered lessons in constancy and survival from a vanishing breed of gentlemen of an earlier, simpler age:

'He learned in king Henry the Eighth's time, as Cromwell's instrument, what he must advise (in point of religion) in Queen Elizabeth's time, as an eminent counsellor: His maxim being this, that zeal was the duty of a private breast, and moderation the interest of a public state . . . He saw the interest of this state altered six times, and died an honest man: the crown put upon four heads, yet he continued a faithful subject: religion changed, as to the public constitution of it, five times, yet he kept the faith.'[114]

When Thomas Cromwell was executed in 1540, the Cromwell family fell for the first time. Yet its survivors were able to haul themselves from the wreckage to rebuild their lives. Though the founder of their house had lost his earthly life and, perhaps worse in his eyes, his reputation, he had succeeded in what mattered more to him than anything else in this world or the next. He had armed his family against his own downfall and launched them upon the journey that, a century later, would bear them all the way to the throne which had taken his life.

Eight

Splendour

He seems a King by long succession born,
And yet the same to be a King does scorn.
Abroad a King he seems, and something more,
At Home a Subject on the equal Floor.

Andrew Marvell, 'The First Anniversary of the Government under O. C.' (1654)

Inglorious arts

When Henry VIII had taken the future Whitehall Palace from the fallen Cardinal Wolsey in 1530, he set Thomas Cromwell to upgrade its leisure facilities. Papers in or amended by his own hand list the workmen and supplies needed to enlarge the King's 'new manor besides Westminster'.[1] The area was fashioned into an entertainment complex with a tennis court, tiltyard, bowling greens and a cockpit with a village of lodgings and a garden clustered around it. Thomas would have known it down to the last stone and timber but could never have guessed its future occupants: first the bookies and gamblers at the Tudor cockfights, then the players and courtiers of the Stuart masques, and from February 1650 his own family. For a grateful Parliament rewarded Oliver Cromwell for his Irish campaign with 'the use of the lodgings called the Cockpit, the Spring Garden, and St. James's House, and the command of St. James's Park', adding lodgings at Hampton Court and further estates after his victory over the Scots.'[2]

Living now within the Whitehall estate, the Cromwell family enjoyed considerable comfort at the centre of the Commonwealth's humming social scene. Contrary to the popular imagining of a joyless, lacklustre society devoid of cavalier style and fun, the London elites were enjoying themselves under peacetime republican rule. Suppers and balls were all the rage and fashion resurged, the dowager countess of Devonshire reporting that 'the garb in the town is ladies all in scarlet, shining and glittering'.[3] This was the setting within which Oliver and Elizabeth began to be referred to as Lord and Lady Cromwell and their children spent pleasant days shopping at the Royal Exchange (just a five-minute walk from where Thomas and his Elizabeth had lived at Austin Friars) and strolling from the Cockpit garden into St James's Park. There had been much to occupy them while Oliver was away in Ireland and Scotland. The family had grown with the births of several grandchildren: three daughters for Bridget and Henry Ireton and a son – named Cromwell – to Elizabeth and John Claypole.

Meanwhile, the teenage Mary Cromwell entertained herself by matchmaking for her brother Henry, trying to contrive a marriage between him and one of her friends. This was not a success, primarily because Henry was in love with the royalist beauty Dorothy Osborne. As ever, Oliver would not countenance a marriage for one of his children without the prospect of love, commenting that 'If there be not freedom and cheerfulness . . . let this affair slide easily off.' He unscrambled Mary's mess when he finally returned home, though he was careful to do so in such a way as to 'save the labour of little Mall's fooling, least she incur the loss of a good friend'.[4] Henry did not secure the longed-for Dorothy Osborne in any event for she was holding out instead to marry the future diplomat and baronet William Temple. Yet Henry proved useful to Dorothy as a means to rouse Temple's jealousy ('if I cannot be yours', she told him, 'Henry Cromwell will be as acceptable to me as anyone else') and also as a procurer of Irish greyhounds.[5]

Bridget, meanwhile, wife of one of the Army's leading generals like her mother, engaged herself in the more serious business of political networking and patronage. In a mark of their prominence, both women now attracted literary dedications. The radical author and Fifth Monarchist prophetess Mary Cary honoured Bridget and her mother as two of the three dedicatees of her 1651 work defending the regicide, *The Little Horn's Doom and Downfall*, observing 'how that among the many pious, precious, prudent, and sage matrons, and holy women, with which this Common-wealth is adorned; as with so many precious jewels, and choice gems . . . God hath selected and chosen out your Ladiships, and placed you in some of the highest places of honour (according to your present capacities) in the three nations; wherein you have more than ordinary opportunities to honour him'.[6]

To Cary's mind, Bridget and Elizabeth were no mere spectators of the glories of the Commonwealth but active participants in it. Cary explains that she chose them 'being of your own sex' and seeing not only that they had been elevated by God but that He had 'fitted' them for such influence: 'the tendency of your aims, studies, and endeavours, (as it is well known) being to the exaltation (as far as lies in you) of that great King of Saints, the Lord Jesus'. God had not swollen their heads, however, but kept them 'in a sweet, meek, and humble frame, which crowns all the favours which he hath conferred upon you . . . that as transplendent stars you may shine gloriously'. Oliver's wife and daughter were not passive recipients of praise but assumed to be proactive patrons of considerable power, under whose 'favourable aspects' Cary would publish her Treatise 'to the world'. Others would follow her lead in the coming years.

Bridget had an unparalleled opportunity to shine gloriously when she travelled across to Ireland in January 1651 with her eldest daughter to be reunited with Henry Ireton.[7] There she found herself the *de facto* First Lady of Ireland, presiding over her husband the Lord Deputy's winter civil and military headquarters. This she did with suitable godliness possessing 'the poor of god's grace in her soul' and being 'a woman acquainted with temptations and breathing after Christ'. There she was reunited too with her brother Henry Cromwell who, was undertaking his own spiritual journey.[8] Bridget must have welcomed her brother's presence, particularly when her four-year-old daughter was for a brief time dangerously ill. If their positions were exulted and powerful, daily life for the Iretons was arduous, still more so for the Irish under their rule. Workaholic Ireton 'never regarded what clothes or food he used, what hour he went to rest or what horse he mounted' as he managed the inglorious aftermath of his father-in-law's conquest, attempting to govern the regions Oliver had subdued and secure the rest.[9] It was he who steered Oliver's policies for the long-term land settlement of Ireland in a more severe direction, developing the harsh qualifications which sorted huge swathes of the population into categories of people exempted from pardon.

Bridget returned to the family home in London when the campaigning season restarted in the spring of 1651. She may have intended to rejoin her husband in the winter, but she never had the chance. In late November, news arrived at the Cockpit that the 40-year-old Henry Ireton was dead. He had driven himself to death as he besieged Limerick: working all hours, hardly changing his clothes, riding through a snowstorm and catching a fever.[10] Bridget, 'swallowed up with sorrow', was left a widowed mother of three young girls and pregnant with their fourth child – a son she would name for his dead father.[11] Oliver had lost perhaps his closest friend and helpmeet and we can glimpse his despair in a letter he sent to his sister Elizabeth at Ely. 'What is of this world will be found transitory,' he wrote, 'a clear evidence whereof is my son Ireton's death.'[12] Ireton's death 'struck a great sadness into Cromwell', Bulstrode Whitelocke observed, for 'it was a great loss to him of so able and active, so faithful and near a relation and officer under him'. Thereafter, many wondered what course Oliver's role in public affairs might have taken had Ireton lived, for 'no man could prevail so much nor order him so far as Ireton could'.[13]

Henry Cromwell, who had been with Ireton when he died, was bereft of a brother-in-law, commander and role model, the 'mutual tender affection' between them and Henry's presence with Ireton 'in his last trial and conflict' broadcast to all in the published version of the sermon at Henry Ireton's funeral which was dedicated to Henry Cromwell.[14] For it was not only the family who mourned. The Ireton – Cromwell family were now national figures and Ireton – the leading force and principled intellectual of the revolution – was treated as an inaugural martyr in the young Commonwealth's pantheon of virtuous heroes. In stark contrast to the typical Puritan belief that the earthly body should not be venerated, Ireton's corpse was escorted back to London with ceremony, lay in state for six weeks at Somerset House and on 6 February 1651 was interred in the Henry VII chapel in Westminster Abbey after an elaborate funeral which royalist writers were quick to mock. Republicans too baulked at the ritual, with Edmund Ludlow, who had been with Ireton shortly before his death, commenting that if Ireton had foreseen these obsequies he 'would certainly have made it his desire that his body might have found a grave where his soul left it, so much did he despise these pompous and expensive vanities'.[15] Ludlow remarked that Ireton had instead 'erected for himself a more glorious monument, in the hearts of good men by his affection to his country, his abilities of mind, his impartial justice, his diligence in the public service and his other virtues, which were a far greater honour to his memory than a dormitory amongst the ashes of kings'.[16]

Nevertheless, the government commissioned stonemason William Wright to carve a 'superb' tomb for their dead hero at a cost of £120.[17] This not only featured an effigy of Ireton but a pre-emptive one of Bridget too, cementing her place at the centre of the Commonwealth's life story. While he lived, the abstemious Ireton had refused a grant of £2,000 from Parliament which Bridget's well-wishers now lobbied should be granted to her in recompense for her husband's service. Parliament agreed given that Ireton had 'wasted and ware out himself in their immediate service', and with this and income from Ireton's lands in Ireland, Bridget now had some means of support.[18] But with Ireton's death she had lost not only her husband but her social position. Parliament had granted Ireton's vacant position of Lord Deputy of Ireland to gallant, glamorous John Lambert, a commander of sufficient stature to fill his shoes. Lambert and his vivacious wife Frances had expensive tastes and reportedly spent much of their own money preparing to take up their new positions as the foremost couple of Ireland. In the midst of this, Lucy Hutchinson recounts that Frances Lambert snubbed Bridget while walking in St James's Park by insisting that she should walk ahead of her as the new Lord Deputy's wife.[19]

The park had become a treacherous place for Oliver's family as they experienced the dark side of wealth and fame. Henry Cromwell was jeered with cries of 'Way for the Prince!' as he walked there and rumours circulated that the Spring Garden in the north-east corner had been closed after Elizabeth Cromwell and her daughters were insulted by passers-by. Rivalries and petty quarrels also abounded. Lucy Hutchinson's own husband had taken offence at not being accorded a special invitation to Ireton's funeral, flouncing into the House of Lords in a scarlet cloak to make his point.[20] Sexual politics too played a part in the public reputations of the new Commonwealth's elite. Frances Lambert (and her husband) had for several years been dragged into the virulent anti-Cromwellian sexual libel pedalled by royalist writers. 'King Cromwell' was regularly attacked as a metaphorical adulterer who had cuckolded Charles I with 'Mistress Parliament', and then increasingly as a literal adulterer, satirised as the 'Bull of Ely' whose trademark large red nose he used to pleasure his conquests. In this role Oliver had indulged in every sexual misconduct from debauching local girls as a youth, begetting bastards and spreading sexual diseases, to pimping his own wife and children and conducting an affair with Frances Lambert – with whom he was well known to have a close friendship – feeding upon her 'sweet flesh'.[21]

Writers used the traditional link between lust and tyranny to undermine the Commonwealth's legitimacy through their attacks on Oliver. But they also used his family as a means to the same ends. Oliver's supposed sexual proclivities were traced backwards to corrupt his whole lineage with his 'great Grand Father' (presumably Richard Williams alias Cromwell) accused of committing incest with his own daughter and then murdering their child.[22] Meanwhile, Oliver's wife Elizabeth was presented as an inveterate adulteress. She, they said, slept with many of her husband's colleagues and one 'impoverished Cavalier' who practised the 'in and in' with Oliver's 'yeast and grains Lady'; Elizabeth's rustic homeliness was evidently no impediment to her attractions.[23] These dalliances not only rendered Oliver a cuckold but threw his children's legitimacy into doubt, questions which bubbled under the surface again when Richard became Lord Protector and flooded the popular press at the Restoration.

Elizabeth was also accused of lust for power and position, in appalling contrast to her and Oliver's popularly imagined background in trade. So several pamphlets dramatised her squabbling with Lady Fairfax over whose husband should be king. In one she asks 'And is not Noll Cromwell's wife as likely a woman to be Queen of England, as you? . . . my Noll has a head-piece, a face of brass, (full of majesty) and a nose will light the whole Kingdom to walk after him; I say he will grace a crown, being naturally adorned with diamonds and rubies already; And for myself (though I say it) I have a person as fit for a queen as another.'[24] Lucy Hutchinson captured the charges of gaucheness and hypocrisy commonly levelled at the Cromwell family, commenting that Oliver's 'wife and children were setting up for the principality, which suited no better with any of them than scarlet on the ape'.[25]

The drama of Frances Lambert's slight against Bridget Ireton in St James's Park would have delighted these satirists, seeming as it did to pit leading wives of the Commonwealth against each other. Yet the incident had a happy outcome for Bridget as it flushed out a new suitor for her hand. Also strolling in the park at the time was another protégé of Oliver's who had made his name rising through the ranks of Parliament's army, the youngest son of a Northamptonshire Royalist with fair curls, Lieutenant General Charles Fleetwood. Fleetwood had lost his own wife around the same time that Ireton died, leaving him with two children. Witnessing Bridget's distress, Fleetwood stepped in to salvage her dignity and escort her home, thereby beginning a rapid courtship which culminated in their marriage on 8 June 1652, blending together their two half-families.[26] Future years would show Fleetwood to be a loving father and stepfather to Ireton's children, though he preserved their patrilineal identity. 'Through mercy our dear children and servants are in a hopeful way of recovery,' he wrote to his brother-in-law Henry Cromwell during a worrying bout of household illness in 1656. 'Only poor Biddy Ireton hath still a dangerous, feverish distemper upon hir.'[27]

Charles Fleetwood was a sensible choice of second husband. He had long been a close friend and follower of Oliver's and of sufficient trust to the family that he was probably an overseer of the investment of Parliament's recompense payment to Bridget and her children on Ireton's death – a position he recused himself from later after their marriage.[28] It is likely, though, that Bridget continued to be haunted by the loss of Henry Ireton. Writing to Fleetwood the next year, Oliver asked him to urge Bridget to 'beware of a bondage spirit' and to avoid self-recrimination through 'her vain reasoning' along the lines that 'if I had done this, if I had avoided that how well it had been with mee'. If this was fear 'the antidote is love', he explained gently, the glorious love of God.[29] At least Fleetwood could have understood Bridget's grief, having known and revered her first husband, and spoken the same language of their common faith. But though he shared Ireton's godly principles, he did not match his talents. For Fleetwood's was a starkly contrasting character whose providentialism magnified an indecisive, pliable and highly strung temperament which would eventually prove fatal to the family he now joined.

In the short term, however, Bridget's second marriage led her in an unexpected direction. Only a few weeks before her wedding, Parliament abolished the two offices of Lord Lieutenant and Lord Deputy of Ireland. Lambert, smarting to be left with only the less prestigious role of commander of the Army and civil commissioner in Ireland, refused it and Fleetwood was appointed instead. Thus in September 1652, less than a year after Ireton's death, Bridget found herself and her children on the deck of the *Revenge* returning to Ireland once more as the wife of its ruler. Inevitably tongues wagged at the strange and sudden sequence of events with the caustic Lucy Hutchinson explaining it as contrived by Oliver to 'restore his daughter to the honour she had fallen from'.[30] Yet Oliver was sad to see them go, for 'Biddie' was 'a joy to my heart' and Fleetwood, as he wrote regretfully of his departure, was someone to 'whom I can unbowel myself'.[31]

Oliver had need of trusted confidants now he had exchanged 'adventurous war' for the 'inglorious arts of peace'. After returning to London from his triumphant conquests in 1651 with high expectations of the political progress his victories could now enable, he spent the next eighteen months as an ordinary MP growing increasingly frustrated with the Rump Parliament's failure to advance any meaningful reforms. These were clearly needed in the structure of government and elections, the reduction of wartime taxation, the outdated legal system and the confused Church. Some progress was made: a Toleration Act repealing compulsory church attendance and an Act of General Pardon and Oblivion for defeated Royalists. Yet the MPs stalled in every other direction, preferring instead to legislate harsh penalties for blasphemy and adultery and, to Oliver's despair, the persecution of the many Royalists exempted from the Act of Oblivion and brutal plans for Ireland. In the coming years he would do his best to mitigate these on behalf of individuals, as he had done at the end of the First Civil War for the royalist Launde and Hinchingbrooke Cromwells. For now, war against the Dutch over shipping rights contributed a further distraction for the embattled Parliament. Throughout, the press hailed Oliver as the champion of reform which must have made him feel its stagnation keenly.

Faced with all this, Oliver took up his former role of coalition-builder, trying to re-establish the broad base of support needed to push through reform and reduce the fluid gap between the Army and Parliament which had once again widened. He confided his desires and fears to Bulstrode Whitelocke in November 1652 while walking in St James's Park, the space so charged for his family. Above all, he wished 'to unite our counsels, and hands, and hearts, to make good what we have so dearly bought, with so much hazard, blood, and treasure, and that the Lord having given us an entire conquest over our enemies, we should not now hazard all again by our private jangling, and bring those mischiefs upon ourselves, which our enemies could never do'.[32]

By April 1653, Oliver's hopes of unified progressive action had foundered. The Rump, he now believed, had squandered its opportunities in the service of enriching and perpetuating itself. Over two days, he summoned likeminded MPs and Army officers to the family home at the Cockpit to discuss options for the Rump to dissolve itself and call fresh elections, presumably over Elizabeth's famed small beer and bread. But on the second day, 20 April, news reached them that the Rump had rejected Oliver's plan and was rushing through its own bill instead. Yet again, Oliver was caught between Parliament and the Army and, as before in moments of crisis, he chose the latter. Despite being dressed in only his casual home clothes of a black suit and grey stockings, Oliver seized his broad hat and hurried down King Street to Parliament with a party of musketeers. There he took his seat and listened to the debate for some time before rising to his feet for one of the most famous moments in English political history.

Oliver began pleasantly enough by praising the Rump's achievements, his hat in his hand, before his angry passion swept him down to pace the floor of the House, his hat now on his head, as he accused the outraged MPs of corruption and oppression. 'You are no Parliament; I will put an end to your sitting' he thundered. 'Go! get you out! make haste!', he went on in some variation of words which are most famously remembered as 'in the name of God, go!'[33] With this, he called to Thomas Harrison to bring in the soldiers to force the members from the chamber. Now arguing with individual MPs who railed at him as they left, Oliver picked up the mace which symbolised Parliament's authority and ordered the 'bauble' carried away, before seizing the draft bill which he hastily destroyed, further shrouding the events in mystery. The echoes of Charles I's attempted arrest of the five members were not lost on those present and, if anything,

Oliver's dissolution of the Rump Parliament was a more autocratic action and one that did lasting damage to his parliamentary reputation.

In ejecting Parliament, Oliver arrogated monarchical powers to himself, reinforcing recent rumours that he planned to make himself king; a theoretical step he had himself put to Whitelocke in their discussion in St James's Park. His imminent elevation, and that of his family, was widely predicted in the weeks that followed. Dorothy Osborne, who had jilted Henry Cromwell, wryly expressed her regret to the man she would marry that 'if I had been so wise as to have taken hold of the offer was made me by Henry Cromwell, I might have been in a fair way of preferment, for, sure, they will be greater now than ever'.[34] If she had accepted Henry, it might have been her wedding that took place a mere twenty days after Oliver dissolved the Rump when Henry married Elizabeth Russell, the daughter of Oliver's good friend and Cambridgeshire colleague Sir Francis Russell of Chippenham Park. The marriage was a devoted one, with Elizabeth once writing to tell her parents of Henry's 'love and kindness', prompting her mother to cry for joy and her father to laugh, though he later shared his wife's thanks with Henry for 'loving her daughter so well'.[35]

The timing of Henry Cromwell's wedding, so soon after his father's dismissal of the Rump, is in itself intriguing. It was seen as another sign of Oliver's commitment to the Army, with the Venetian ambassador noting the advantage to Oliver in acquiring 'the daughter of a colonel of scanty fortune but of great influence among the military'.[36] The occasion also offered Oliver a much needed opportunity to blow off steam by indulging in the high-jinks that weddings in particular seemed to rouse in him. A letter only lately discovered reveals a raucous affair, with Oliver all night 'throwing wine, water and custards upon the ladies, and cushions to boot', contrary to what the author reports would be expected from 'puritans'.[37] Here is the same Oliver who threw a cushion at Edmund Ludlow then ran away after their heated meeting in 1648 and reportedly flicked ink over Charles I's death warrant. Such behaviour seems to have been intrinsic to his nature, but what may have passed for rustic foolery in the obscurity of his youth now struck a more jarring note in his elevated state. As the guest at Henry and Elizabeth's wedding remarked, 'we see how inconsistent old goodness & new greatness are'.

Oliver may have acquired some aura of new greatness, but although he had undoubtedly mounted a military coup, he had not done so to take permanent power for himself. Many indeed were pleased to see the back of the Rump which had, after all, sat for an uninterrupted thirteen years, the last four of which it had ruled unilaterally and unchecked. It was not Oliver individually but the Army Council which now stepped into the power vacuum, choosing a new Council of State which opted for the solution suggested by the Fifth Monarchist Thomas Harrison to summon a small interim Nominated Assembly of 140 godly representatives modelled on the Jewish Sanhedrin. This body was to agree upon a workable constitution in time to hold full parliamentary elections the following autumn. 'The Barebones Parliament' as it came to be known after one of its most prominent members, the leather seller Praise-God Barebone, convened in July 1653, newlywed Henry Cromwell among its members to represent Ireland.

The Army Council surrendered their power to the Assembly, Oliver and other members declining their invitation to join its ranks. Instead, they watched from a distance as the Assembly carried their hopes high before it. 'Never was there a supreme authority consisting of such a body as you are, under such a notion, in such a way, owing God and being owned by him,' Oliver expounded excitedly at its opening during a two-hour oration explaining the extraordinary events that had brought them all together.[38] 'Have a care of the whole flock,' he urged them, yet over the next five months the Assembly could agree to nothing beyond tying itself in knots with its radical and moderate members at loggerheads. In December, the moderate members colluded with some of the Army leaders to dissolve themselves and surrender power back to Oliver and the Council of State.

John Lambert, fortunately not in Dublin as Lord Deputy but at his grand home in the former royal palace in Wimbledon, came forward with a plan: a new constitution, the *Instrument of Government*, which drew on the *Heads of Proposals* Lambert had worked on with Ireton and was inspired by the Levellers' constitutional workings. With this Lambert stepped into Ireton's shoes as the details-man who created the intellectual framework for Oliver's instinctive actions. His *Instrument* encompassed a new separation of powers, vesting government in a single person working with a strong council and regular Parliaments. The person's title was still unclear and it is possible that in the following days the title of 'King' was watered down to the more transient, less threatening 'Lord Protector' – a title taken from English history, borne a century earlier by Gregory Cromwell's brother-in-law Edward Seymour while he minded the throne for his nephew King Edward VI.

The person, though, was obvious: Oliver Cromwell. Wits were quick to joke that the Lord Protector's 'instrument' was 'found under my Lady Lambert's petticoat'.[39] Yet, though Oliver was the beneficiary, as with Pride's Purge he left no evidence behind that he orchestrated or even knew the details of Lambert's intentions. Indeed, it is highly unlikely Oliver set out to acquire supreme power as his detractors maintained. The collapse of the Nominated Assembly came as a crushing blow to him, forcing him from the dizzying heights of idealism back to the drawing board of pragmatic solutions to unstable and chaotic government. Moreover, becoming chief magistrate himself would divide not only the population as a whole but his friends and family. There was no denying that the scheme had its attractions, however. Perhaps a Protectorate was a way finally to reconcile the radical minority's desire for godly reform and the conservative majority's desire for traditional government?

Whatever his private feelings, after four days and 'with many tears' Oliver resigned himself to the path God – or at least Lambert – had laid out for him, seeing 'it was necessary at that time to keep the nation from falling into extreme disorder'.[40] Accordingly, at 1 pm on 16 December, dressed in a simple black suit and cloak with a gold band around his hat, Oliver set out from his Cockpit home for the last time as a private man. In a coach accompanied by his mounted Life Guard, led by Charles Howard of the illustrious house of Norfolk, and the chief officers of the Army on foot, he travelled the short distance to Westminster Hall. The streets were lined with soldiers and before him stretched a train of coaches containing government officials, judges, the City's Lord Mayor and scarlet-cloaked aldermen, and the incoming Council of State. Lambert led him into the Hall bearing the sword of state and Oliver stood bare-headed to hear the *Instrument of Government* read out before swearing to 'take upon mee the protection and government of these nations' and 'to the best of my understanding' to 'govern these nations according to the laws, statutes and customs, seeking their peace, and causing justice and law to be equally administered'.[41] He then sat down upon the throne, replacing his hat, while everyone else remained bare-headed as was customary only in the presence of a monarch. Henceforth, only the foreign ambassadors who swiftly flocked to pay their respects to him at Whitehall kept their hats on in his company as representatives of Oliver's only equals – other heads of state.

Oliver had surpassed even the formidable power of his forebear Thomas to arrive at a nearer status to his royal master. For where Thomas's fate had always rested in the hands of Henry VIII however high he rose, Oliver's future was in no-one's hands but his own. He himself was the owner of the Great Seal, not its custodian as Thomas, the Lord Privy Seal, had risen to become in 1536. Thus, when the City sword and recently minted Great Seal of the Commonwealth were presented to Oliver as symbols of his new office at his investiture, he returned them to their keepers. The new seal was updated to represent the Protectorate, depicting a mounted Oliver riding across London on one side with the rampant lion of the Cromwell family incorporated into the Commonwealth arms of England, Scotland and Ireland on the other. Oliver was now 'his Highness Oliver, Lord Protector of the Commonwealth of England, Scotland and Ireland, and the Dominions and Territories thereunto belonging'.

With the form 'Highness', the new Lord Protector turned the clock back to the early years of Henry VIII's reign before Henry had copied the Holy Roman Emperor Charles V by taking the grander title 'Majesty', a title thereafter preferred by the Stuarts. If the Welsh Tudors who had raised his own Welsh forebears were back in fashion, the Scottish House of Stuart, of course, lay in the dust: the rafters of Westminster Hall festooned with captured royalist standards; Rubens' King James I on the ceiling of the Banqueting House watching in silence as Oliver listened to his investiture sermon that followed the ceremony, the sounds of bells and bonfire smells drifting in from the streets. A page had turned and the mood was peaceful, so that 'The Protector began his Reign with seeming Serenity, insomuch that many expected Halcyon days . . .'[42] The nations of Britain and Ireland had their first written constitution and, ruling under it, the first of the Protectoral House of Cromwell. As a contemporary panegyric rhapsodised 'divine providence has allowed no monarch of any nation to rejoice in the name of Oliver, and in consequence he is Oliver the First in every respect'.[43]

Halcyon days

Oliver Cromwell and his ordinary wife and children were now the effective royal family of England, Scotland and Ireland. They may have been presiding over a republic, but the necessities of projecting political power and stability at home and abroad meant presenting the Cromwells in a reassuringly regal style. During the wars and the four kingless years since Charles I's execution, the Crown estates had either fallen into a dilapidated state of disrepair or in many cases been sold to pay the Commonwealth's vast war debts. Now the new Protectoral Council of State hastily set about re-acquiring what it could and placing the portfolio at the disposal of Oliver and his successors 'for the maintenance of his and their state and dignity'.[44] Though Oliver could have used all of the former royal residences for himself, he chose only two: the former homes of Cardinal Wolsey which Thomas Cromwell had known so well, Whitehall Palace and Hampton Court. The rest were put to other uses as barracks, stables, prisons, storage facilities and foreign ambassadors' accommodation. The government's surveyor of works immediately began frantic renovations to render the palaces habitable. His budget was large (he would go on to spend nearly £11,000 a year – about £1.1 million today – for the rest of Oliver's Protectorate) but necessary to rehouse squatters, revive the gardens and repair the fabric of the buildings so that they could be redecorated and refurnished.[45]

By March 1654, the two palaces were ready and the press reported that 'his Highness the Lord Protector, with his Lady and family, this day dined at Whitehall, whither his Highness and family are removed, and did this day lie there, and do there continue'.[46] There was much speculation about how the Cromwells adjusted to their move. Edmund Ludlow observed that Oliver's 'wife seemed at first unwilling to remove thither, though afterwards she became better satisfied with her grandeur; but his mother, who by reason of her great age was not so easily flattered with these temptations, very much mistrusted the issue of affairs, and would often be afraid, when she heard the noise of a musket, that her son was shot, being exceedingly dissatisfied unless she might see him once a day at least'.[47]

Ludlow's comment may contain some truth of a naturally shy,

middle-aged woman accustoming herself to a daunting new role, while a shrewd elderly woman balks at the upheaval and fears its consequences. But it also encapsulates the double criticism commonly laid at Elizabeth Cromwell, that she was at once too humble to adequately fill the role of *de facto* queen and also too greedy to bring to it any dignity. As the satirical royalist cookbook containing her recipes put it 'Much ado she had at first to raise her mind and deportment to this sovereign grandeur; and very difficult it was for her to lay aside those impertinent meanesses of her private fortune . . . till the fawning observances and reverences of her slaves had raised her to a confidence, not long after sublimed into an impudence'.[48] Certainly Oliver's family were now public property to be hounded and gawped at, as captured by a newsletter of May 1654 which recounted how Oliver's daughters riding in his State carriage were 'hunted' around the park by a 'great multitude' of other coaches and riders galloping after them 'with all reverent haste'.[49]

As the new first family, the Cromwells now lived at the centre of a restored court structure. Elizabeth Cromwell, now Lady Protectoress, sat at the apex of a huge household – a 'family' in the words of the Council. This was modelled on the former royal household, with three departments: the household above stairs, the household below stairs, and the stables. The scale of the household was notably smaller, however, costing around one-twentieth of the government's budget where 25 years earlier the royal household probably took up more than half the Crown's income.[50] As monarchs before them, Oliver and Elizabeth now spent their days surrounded by a retinue of hangers-on. One contemporary described Oliver bustling about with 'at least thirty young fellows, his sons and attendants' while Elizabeth was accompanied everywhere by 'twenty proud women'. The family had their own kitchen and cooks with seven separate tables for meals for their household, Oliver and Elizabeth each presiding over their own table where they entertained dignitaries.[51] A Dutch envoy recorded his meal with the Protectoral couple in April 1654 where Oliver had hosted them on one table, his councillors and other lords at another, while 'At the table of my Lady Protectrice dined my Lady Nieuport [the ambassador's wife], my wife, and my lady Lambert, my lord Protector's daughter, and mine. The music played all the while we were at dinner.'[52] The contrast with the Cromwells' previous life provided much to lampoon. Many satirised the outward pretensions of a man of plain tastes whose frugal wife they joked supplied home comforts from the dairy she established at Whitehall with cows grazing in that favourite spot for Cromwellian mockery, St James's Park.[53]

Oliver conducted his official state business during the week at Whitehall, receiving ambassadors in elaborate public receptions in the Banqueting House which had been decorated with 'extraordinary rich hangings'. These were ritualistic ceremonies designed to impress, with the ambassadors conveyed in the Protector's own liveried coach or barge and the room, galleries and surrounding courtyards packed with gentlemen and ladies watching the spectacle of Oliver progressing in to sit on a chair of state behind a railed-off area at the upper end. They were duly impressed, with the Dutch delegation noting the grandeur of the event, though at a subsequent reception the irony of the old European powers cosying up to farmer Cromwell in the holiest shrine to Stuart divine right prevented the Swedish ambassador Christer Bonde from looking on it 'without emotion and compassion for the mutabilities of this world'.[54]

The visiting Royalist John Evelyn must have mused on the same when he found Whitehall now 'glorious and well-furnished', hung with rich tapestries and paintings by Titian, Gentileschi and Raphael.[55] Most furnishings had come from the former royal collection, of which up to a possible £48,000 worth had been saved from sale to the lasting benefit of posterity, many items marked in the inventories as 'reserved for his Highness'.[56] Some may have been specifically chosen by Oliver, while Elizabeth too may have taken a hand in the selections as it was reported that the family's lodgings were furnished 'according to instructions from her Highness the Lady Cromwell'. Decorating the royal palaces in 1654 offers an inverted image to the bustle at Thomas Cromwell's Austin Friars in 1538. Where then the Cromwells were finding space at home to store away sacred images rounded up from the dissolved religious houses, now they were bringing works of art out of storage for display: so it was goodbye to 'Our Lady of Ipswich', hello to the 'Madonna and Child with St Elizabeth'.[57]

On Fridays, Oliver's family travelled out to their country retreat of Hampton Court either by road or river, returning to London on Mondays when Oliver usually feasted his officers at Whitehall to keep his finger on the Army's pulse. Dividing the week this way was a new routine for a reigning family and an early example of the modern concept of the 'week-end' (an unexpected legacy for Britain's most famous Puritans). At Hampton Court, Oliver chose to live not in the dead King's former rooms but in the Queen's apartments in the east wing, built originally by Henry VIII for Anne Boleyn and remodelled in the French style by Henrietta Maria. Perhaps this reflected a troubled conscience, perhaps a taste for the latest mod cons, but it most likely arose from Oliver's desire to remain a family man. For Henrietta Maria's rooms conformed to the French style of having a large, formal bedroom for receiving visitors and a smaller private bedroom in which to sleep. This enabled Oliver to share his bed with his wife, as he had done for the last 34 years, breaking with royal tradition to set a new precedent which the later Stuart monarchs would follow.[58]

The couple also kept their children close by, preserving a sense of their former family life amid the extraordinary opulence. There were no separate establishments for these new *de facto* princes and princesses, as was the custom with previous royal families, but cheek by jowl domesticity. Bridget was still in Ireland with Charles Fleetwood, but the other three Cromwell daughters now lived permanently in the royal palaces. At Hampton Court, 17-year-old Mary occupied the former lodgings of the Duke of Richmond while 16-year-old Frances slept in Charles I's former study. With Betty's husband John Claypole given the exulted role of Master of Horse overseeing the Protectoral stables, the Claypoles took the fine suite of rooms which accompanied the post. Part of the archbishop of Canterbury's former lodgings was given over to a nursery for their children – conveniently close for Oliver who often took one of his grandchildren with him to sit on his lap in Council meetings.[59] There Oliver found loving respite from his workload, as Marvell recorded: 'With her [Betty] each day the passing hour he shares / And at her aspects calms his growing cares; / or with a grandsire's joy her children sees / Hanging about her neck or at his knees.'[60]

The Cromwell sons also spent time at court, though they continued to live part of the time at their in-laws' country estates at Hursley and Chippenham. At Whitehall, the admiralty commissioners were evicted so that Richard could occupy their rooms which were probably those in which the late King himself had lived. Henry was also allocated central lodgings at Whitehall from which he often accompanied his father to events, sitting next to him for instance at the 'sumptuous banquet' thrown to welcome the new

Lord Protector by the City of London in February 1654 at which Oliver used his sovereign prerogative to knight the Lord Mayor. The whole family drew together multiple times a day for meals, public and private functions and services in the pared-back royal chapels where Oliver occupied the monarch's seat. As a newspaper reported to readers greedy for any detail of the Cromwells' new lives: 'There is every day of the week twice, viz. at ten o'clock in the morning, and at six at night, a meeting of the Lord Protector's family at the chapel of Whitehall where his Highness's chaplain, Mr Lockyer, expounds to them.'[61]

❦ ❦ ❦

Where Oliver's public apartments were splendidly furnished for the benefit of high-ranking visitors, the private rooms he shared with his wife were more sparse: his dressing room merely contained two carpets, a table and stools, an old cupboard and tools for the fire. Oliver's tastes were reflected throughout, however, most notably his love of tapestries which hung in most rooms, including several of the famous sets which had been commissioned by Henry VIII and Cardinal Wolsey. Despite their contrasting religious outlook, Oliver shared Henry VIII's preference for Biblical subjects in public rooms and classical or mythological stories in private. Thus he chose the sordid story of Vulcan and Venus – a tale of adultery among the classical gods – for the tapestries in his private study and marital bedroom. Perhaps only a man completely secure in his and his wife's fidelity to each other could decorate his bedroom with the patron of cuckolds. Oliver's other clearest choice was to display Andrea Mantegna's huge sequence of paintings, the 'Triumphs of Caesar', down the long gallery which linked the Cromwells' public and private rooms. These he prized, commissioning tapestry copies to be made. Maybe, like some of his contemporaries, he too saw parallels between himself and the most famous conquering general turned ruler of antiquity.

Oliver's refined tastes extended into the palace's gardens and grounds. These he not only restored but upgraded to match those of other foreign courts in the 1650s, with the ponds in what is now Bushy Park dug to improve water supply, Charles I's bowling green brought back, and the privy gardens re-laid and embellished. Classical statues were returned and placed around a huge fountain summoned from Somerset House to be the centrepiece of the garden, echoing the regal iconography of the palace tapestries. Today known as the 'Diana Fountain', this magnificent edifice with the goddess surrounded by scallops, scrolls and sea-monsters, semi-naked nymphs, dolphins and boys testifies to the Protector's catholic, broad-minded tastes and love of artistry – traits Puritans of his ilk did not see as incompatible with life as a godly Protestant.

More radical Puritans, however, could neither accept the cultural tastes of a gentleman of Oliver's background nor the aesthetic requirements of projecting his new power in the international language of monarchical display. One wrote to Cromwell requesting he 'demolish those monsters which are set up as ornaments in the Privy Garden' as, 'though you see no evil in them', they might provoke God into striking him down at any moment.[62] A Quaker cook later broke into the garden at Hampton Court and smashed its statues with a hammer. It may have been in part to avoid these judgements that Oliver kept his weekend life at Hampton Court relatively private. There he liked to relax and live more informally, indulging his personal passions with his nearest and dearest. From his youth spent in the environs of Hinchingbrooke, Oliver shared the Jacobean elite's customary enthusiasm for outdoor sports and activities, particularly hunting and hawking. Now he regularly hunted in Hampton Court's deer park, his hounds chasing the descendants of the herds pursued so vigorously by his Tudor and Stuart forebears, and newer animals like the young deer gifted by the President of the Providence Plantation in New England. Indeed, this was a lifestyle Thomas Cromwell would have recognised with the large retinue that always accompanied him on his travels around southern England in the 1530s including greyhounds, spaniels, hawks, falcons and the grooms, and 'spaniel keepers' and falconers to keep them.[63]

Falconry was an interest in Oliver's early life as shown by his letter about the missing hawk in 1631. In this he was a man of his generation as hawking had peaked during his adolescence under James I but subsequently fallen out of fashion. Oliver's love of this quintessentially old-fashioned, pastoral activity spawned its revival during the Protectorate. Hawks were sourced from the far corners of the Commonwealth, leading figures including Henry Cromwell, Charles Fleetwood and John Lambert importing them from Ireland and Scotland, while in 1654 the Prince of East Friesland sent Oliver some hawks as a present.[64] In judging these specimens, Oliver would have benefited from Gregory's granddaughter Catherine Tollemache's *Book of Secrets* from Helmingham Hall with its guidance on what made a 'fair hawk'.[65] Falconry also provided a cultural meeting point between the Protectorate regime and its opponents. When Oliver was hawking at Hounslow Heath near Hampton Court, he came upon a cavalier and 'great falconer' and 'discoursing with him, fell in love with his company, and commanded him to wear his sword, and to meet him a Hawking'.[66]

Horse-breeding was another great passion of Oliver's, and the current vogue for this provided a similarly useful cultural melting pot, as Oliver explored all available expert networks in his ambitions for the Protectoral stud to outshine the other courts of Europe. He spent huge amounts sourcing exotic breeds including 'Neapolitan coursers', Barbary and Arabian horses. Most came second hand from Europe, but Oliver went to great lengths to try and obtain them first hand from North Africa, although Syria proved too difficult an export market for his agents to penetrate.[67] In this the Lord Protector harnessed networks as extensive as those that had kept Thomas supplied with rare animals for his menagerie: cages of birds, beavers from Danzig and an unnamed 'strange beast', perhaps a leopard, he gave to Henry VIII.[68] Horse-racing too was a diversion Oliver and his children enjoyed. Oliver raced his own horse, the 'Dun Arabian', at Epsom Downs in March 1654 while Richard gifted £30 to the corporation of Winchester near his estate of Hursley for a race cup three years later. In her later married life, Mary bet on the races at Newmarket.[69] Henry meanwhile enjoyed a race held in his honour at Youghal in County Cork in 1658.

In England in the 1650s, such occasions had to be fitted in around the sporadic bans on horse-racing brought in by the government at moments of heightened security risk to prevent Royalists using meets to assemble cavalry for uprisings. 'I do not think these are unlawful,' Oliver explained of races and other sports to a complaining Parliament in 1656, 'but to make them recreations, that they will not endure to be abridged of them' was the mistake.[70] In other words, such sports should be enjoyed in moderation, not used as an excuse for drunken gambling and rabble-rousing vice. Oliver, as much as anyone, enjoyed sports as community entertainment, happily watching a hurling match between two teams of fifty Cornishmen and a display of Cornish wrestling in Hyde Park on May Day 1654.[71]

Indoors, the pre-eminent pastime at the Protectoral court was music. Now moved from a religious to a domestic context, music was for all to enjoy, and none more so than Oliver who himself took lessons in the virginal and enjoyed playing duets with his wife. He was 'a great lover of music, and entertained the most skilful in that science in his pay and family', admiring 'all ingenious and eximious persons in any arts, whom he arranged to be sent or brought to him', even Oliver's scathing biographer James Heath admitted. Oliver had two organs installed in the great hall at Hampton Court, including the one he requisitioned from Magdalen College Oxford. At Whitehall, meanwhile, he made use of the Cockpit theatre for musical entertainments. These were coordinated by the organist John Hingston, employed as Master of Music on an annual salary of £100, who also trained boy choristers to sing Latin motets which 'Oliver was most taken with', and gave singing lessons to Mary and Frances. One of the seven other musicians retained was the virtuoso violinist David Mell as solo violin playing was the latest fashion. Oliver, 'who loved a good voice and instrumental music well', enjoyed the performance of the bass singer James Quin so much he got him drunk and offered him any favour. Quin, who had been expelled from his student place at Christ Church Oxford for particular views, asked the Lord Protector to restore his place which Oliver duly did.[72]

Sponsoring musicians and poets like Andrew Marvell and Payne Fisher, and with many devotees of the arts such as John Lambert, Bulstrode Whitelocke and John Milton among the Protectoral elite, Oliver's court soon developed a reputation for its fine musical entertainments. In 1658 the government newspaper *Mercurius Politicus* described how Oliver feasted the Speaker and members of Parliament in the Banqueting House with 'a most princely entertainment'. 'After dinner his Highness withdrew to the Cockpit and there entertained them with rare music, both of instruments and voices, till the evening.'[73] Informal, spontaneous concerts also occurred at Whitehall. In 1654, Oliver stopped to listen to the Royalist Roger L'Estrange play his viol with a group of court musicians. L'Estrange, previously sentenced to death for spying, had recently returned from exile and had his sentence annulled by Oliver, whose appreciation of his playing earned L'Estrange the nickname of 'Noll's Fiddler' for the rest of his life.[74] All of this patronage contributed to a boom in private recitals and concurrent fashion for songs, instrumentals and dance tunes to be performed at home. The London music publisher John Playford sold instruction manuals for dancing, singing and violin playing and even a list of recognised music teachers, while musical clubs sprang up in homes and taverns in London and Oxford alongside the first coffee houses.

A new Committee for the Advancement of Music further pushed the dial though it could not raise enough funds to found the official college of music the 'Gentlemen of his Highness Music' petitioned for. This expansion of court music echoed that which Thomas Cromwell had presided over in 1539–40 when he directed the English resident in Venice to oversee the recruitment of musical families from Italy.[75] English chamber music and songs flourished and the vogue for musical entertainment in the domestic setting was firmly established, as vividly captured in Samuel Pepys' *Diary* a few short years later. The leading composers of the day used this musical renaissance to circumvent the closure of theatres which was motivated by the same social and security concerns as the ban on horse-racing. William Davenant, the pug-faced self-professed son of Shakespeare, smuggled plays past the censors by setting them to music, thus inventing English opera. He presented lavish productions with virtuous, bellicose themes that appealed to the government, including *The Siege of Rhodes*, featuring the first English actress to appear on the public stage, and *The Cruelty of the Spaniards in Peru* at the Cockpit itself. Thespians found other ways to continue their art under the unconcerned noses of the government, staging shorter circus-style plays known as 'drolls' at the surviving Red Bull Theatre, producing private performances at grand houses and freely publishing satires on the regime to be read rather than acted.

In all this Oliver was at pains to keep the Army at arm's length. His was to be a cultured court not a martial headquarters. Few courtiers were soldiers, and Oliver dispensed court jobs to distant relatives.[76] The most visible military presence at court – Oliver's Life Guard – was also stocked with some reliable family members including Oliver's son Henry Cromwell's brother-in-law and, as their captain after his lavish Whitehall wedding to Oliver's niece Lavinia Whetstone, Richard Beke.[77] Oliver's daughters were at the centre of the family atmosphere at his cultivated court, as we learn in the Swedish ambassador Christer Bonde's account of his visit to Hampton Court. Oliver generally avoided hosting foreign dignitaries at his retreat, but Bonde was a favourite and so allowed to glimpse the more informal Cromwells at work and play. Bonde describes his reception by Oliver with a small group of friends, including his sons-in-law, where they dined on oysters and listened to music. Then they hunted in the park and brought down a stag before moving on to a game of bowls. Lastly, Bonde was taken to the Lady Protectoress's apartments where he 'kissed the hand of Cromwell's wife, and his daughter's cheek' and enjoyed some Spanish wine with them before bidding them farewell.[78] This could have been Mary or Frances – effectively in finishing school before they entered the Protectoral marriage market as the greatest prizes of all – or the vivacious Betty Claypole, seemingly Oliver's favourite, who was now the greatest ornament of his court.

Unleashed upon the royal palaces, Betty took to her new life like a duck to water, impressing with her regality, having 'the elevation of mind, and dignity of deportment, of one born of a royal stem, and all the affability and goodness of the most humble'.[79] She was politically astute and skilled at managing egos, soothing Whitelocke's ruffled feathers after a quarrel with Oliver by playing on his high opinion of himself.[80] She deployed her 'princely qualities' to intercede on behalf of the marginalised with the father who adored her.[81] This earned Betty the derision of satirist Samuel Butler, who labelled her 'her Grace Maid-Marion Claypole', but others sought her help.[82] Thus the philosopher James Harrington, having copies of his new treatise *The Oceana* seized by the censors, bent his steps to Whitehall having 'remembered that Oliver's favorite daughter, the lady Claypole, acted the part of a princess very naturally, obliging all persons with her civility, and frequently interceding for the unhappy'. Some repartee over games with Betty's three-year-old daughter led Betty to promise to procure her father's consent for publication so long as the work did not prejudice him. Thus Harrington dedicated *The Oceana* to the Lord Protector, whom he flattered just sufficiently as the founder of the constitution for his essentially republican utopia.[83]

Betty also interceded with her father where it suited her own interests, notably her traditional Anglican faith and love of high fashion. The former caused her to plead for the conservative cleric John Hewett when he later conspired against the Protectorate. The latter prompted her to go to Oliver 'in a huff' on the arrest of her royalist friend Sir John Southcote who she had commissioned, when he was in Paris, to procure for her 'two damask beds, one with gold, the other with silver fringes, and also very many yards of the richest gold and silver stuffs for her own wearing'. Oliver immediately ordered Southcote's release, sending a 'complimentary excuse'.[84] A portrait of Betty from this time by the circle of Sir Peter Lely shows her in all her fashion-forwardness, with loose, informal hair tumbling over bare shoulders revealed by the low-set sleeves more commonly associated with the portraits of Charles II's mistresses.

The Cromwells may have lived splendidly and been treated as any of the other royal families that ambassador Bonde would encounter on his travels, but they remained subtly different as those who had not been apprenticed in regality but elevated to it, and not even from the nobility. Oliver was, in fact, the first commoner to rule, and as a contemporary saw it, now lived 'in the condition of a prince, with the moderation of a private man'.[85] He did not lose himself in the grandeur of his new status but held onto his family lineage as a way of coping with the confusing identity he now inhabited. Oliver kept a copy of his grandfather Sir Henry Cromwell's family pedigree and proudly displayed the Cromwell arms on his Protectoral heraldry; the Cromwellian lion holding Sir Richard Williams' diamond ring now signifiying his political marriage to the Crown of the three kingdoms. Once more, a personal, family escutcheon was the device of government; the addition of the Tudors' heraldic supporters of a crowned lion and a winged dragon presenting the Cromwells as their direct royal heirs. Many accepted this elevation as they believed Oliver to be 'of an honourable extraction', while others made still more of his heritage, emphasising its princely bloodline of Powys, particularly as the Protectorate went on.[86]

Visually Oliver preserved his past self by retaining a simpler style of clothes than the other members of his family: to one observer, being 'no friend to false shows, nor the prodigal vaingloriousnes of garbs, he went plain and grave in his habit, more like a senator than a soldier'. This did not mean the unending Mayflower black in which he is popularly portrayed – a 1649 full-length portrait shows him in a yellow and silver suit embroidered with gold thread and tassels with fashionable bucket-topped boots – but it did mean simpler clothes than his fellow sovereigns would have worn. Soon his very unfashionableness became fashionable as 'in Imitation of him, gaudy fashions & costly garbs were laid aside in England'.[87] Regality had been stripped of its showier aspects. Substance not style was what counted. Where Charles I's court had once cost 40 per cent of government expenditure, Oliver's cost 4 per cent and would eventually be financed through a separate, ring-fenced budget anticipating the later Civil List.

Yet there was also a power in simplicity when done with authenticity and intention. Elizabeth Cromwell commissioned portraits of her husband from Robert Walker, whose huge studio churned out endless repetitions of his warted and armoured Lord Protector which she then distributed around the courts of Europe to awe his 'brother monarchs'.[88] In Sir Philip Warwick's eyes, the ill-suited, shabby MP he had first encountered in 1640 had transformed 'by multiplied good successes, and by real, but usurped power (having a better tailor, and more converse among good company)' to now 'appear of a great and majestic deportment and comely presence' being 'extraordinarily designed for those extraordinary things'.[89] But Oliver's new status was not merely to be enjoyed. The government hoped its monarchical elements would convey continuity and familiarity to reassure a cautious public. This would enable not a conservative return to monarchy itself but rather provide a new platform for Oliver and his allies to pursue the hard-won reforms which had always eluded them. There were extraordinary things to do.

Doors of hope

In the 1650s John Wilkins, the Warden of Wadham College Oxford, built a spaceship in the college garden. It was only a model, based on the full-scale 'flying chariot' he proposed for 'sky voyagers' in his 1640 supplement *A Discourse Concerning a New Planet* to his bestseller of two years earlier *The Discovery of a World in the Moone* and developed further in his 1648 work *Mathematical Magick: Or The Wonders That May Be Performed By Mechanical Geometry*. Yet the ship-like machine 'by the help of Springs and Wings raised and sustained itself in the Air'.[90] Space travel might indeed be possible. Colleagues and visitors watching the test flight would have seen other wonders in Wilkins's garden: an 80-foot focal length telescope to observe the planets, rainbowed 'water-works of pleasure', transparent beehives and a speaking statue. Those like John Evelyn treated to 'magnificent entertainment', could stroll afterwards in the masters' lodgings, marvelling at the collection of scientific and mathematical instruments, dials, perspectives, thermometers and magnets collected by Wilkins and his assistant, 'that miracle of a youth' Christopher Wren.[91] There they may have met Wilkins's wife and step-children, the first to live in the Warden's Lodgings now that wardens were allowed to marry. She was an attraction in herself: the woman with the famous name – perhaps the famous family nose – whose coming had propelled Wilkins to the summit of Oxford's post-Civil War hierarchy as 'the rising sun' of the now blossoming city. For the mistress of the cultured and free-spirited Wadham was Robina Cromwell, the Lord Protector's youngest sister.[92]

Founded in 1612, Wadham was a young college, built with the proceeds of the Reformation upon the site of an Augustinian friary, its honey-coloured stone, hewn by masons from its founders' native Somerset, still gleaming. A statue of James I gazed across the quad at Robina Cromwell's rooms. James had seen a great deal of upheaval in the last 15 years as the Civil War ravaged the King's Royalist headquarters of Oxford, bringing the university grinding to a halt. But the years of violent disruption had given way to peaceful stability. Under the Commonwealth the university began to function once more, lectures and graduations resumed, college building works restarted.[93] In spring 1649, Oxford rolled out the red carpet for the conquering Parliamentarian leaders Oliver and Sir Thomas Fairfax, conferring honorary doctorates in Civil Law on them. The generals were welcomed with speeches (deemed 'bad, but good enough for soldiers' by the observing historian Anthony Wood), to which Oliver replied in his typically emollient fashion, explaining that no Commonwealth could flourish without learning and reassuring the assembly that the new government would encourage it whatever they might hear to the contrary.[94]

It was perhaps this visit, and these sentiments, that prompted the university to offer Oliver its Chancellorship the following year. As a commoner, regicide and Cambridge man, Oliver seems a surprising choice, yet he was known by then to be a conciliatory figure keen to promote 'piety and learning'.[95] It is questionable how much time he found to devote himself to this post while on campaign and then busy at Westminster (a point he made himself in his letter responding to the invitation).[96] Yet the appointment of the physician Jonathan Goddard (who would later be involved in the founding of the Royal Society) as his assistant and a five-member board to carry out some of his duties on the ground, must have helped. Still Oliver kept an eye on the city of dreaming spires, encouraging reform, making appointments and defending the university from more radical forces; a benign, limited level of interference Oxford seemed to welcome. In 1653, the elevation of its own Chancellor to the position of head of state had been welcomed warmly by the university which, though some opponents of the new regime remained in its ranks, was now wholly 'devoted' to Oliver.[97] Excitedly, they sent John Wilkins to him bearing a book of poems, thanks that 'we owe it to your favour that the university survives today', and flamboyant congratulations for taking 'the floundering world of letters' into his care.[98] This Oliver was delighted to do, firmly believing that the universities of Oxford and Cambridge were the breeding ground for the open-minded, intellectual and godly men who would lead the settled and reformed nation of the future.

Such men now sprouted as green shoots from the mortared rubble of Oxford. In its destruction of society's traditional structures, the Civil Wars had created space for fresh ideas and uprooted those who could develop them, circulating them in new intellectual networks across Europe just as William Harvey now claimed blood moved around the body. Oxford, having been purged of many of its old academics who had refused the Commonwealth's Engagement Oath, was now heaving with young scholars sharing their 'flying thoughts' at the weekly meetings of the Experimental Philosophical Club – the forerunner of the Restoration Royal Society – which met at Warden Wilkins's lodgings in Wadham, a short stroll from the conviviality of England's first coffeehouse.[99] At Wadham, the 'most obliging and universally-curious' Wilkins created an inclusive, intellectual haven which welcomed the sons of Royalists, Anglicans and Puritans alike. Around Wilkins orbited luminous celestial bodies from eclectic backgrounds: the young Christopher Wren, Robert Hooke, Seth Ward, John Wallis, Robert Boyle and William Petty among others. They believed practical, methodical experimentation, not the study of ancient tomes, to be the route to discovery; and achievements in medicine, astronomy, chemistry, physics and mathematics were winning Cromwellian Oxford international renown.[100]

Catherine Tollemache had anticipated this scientific golden age several decades earlier perfecting her 'culinary chemistry' in her study at Helmingham Hall. Indeed, when twenty-first-century biochemists examined her recipes, they concluded that her methodical, precise and clearly communicated research marked her out as an early empirical scientist.

The experimental scientific circles in Oxford had been closely aligned with its Chancellor Oliver for some years. Both Robina's first husband, the 'excellent preacher' Peter French of Christ Church, and her second husband Wilkins had been on his university board.[101] Wilkins indeed had been protected by Oliver like many others when he had refused the Engagement Oath. French had preached to the Protectoral Council, sharing lodgings with Robina in Whitehall, and now Robina enjoyed similar visits to her brother at Whitehall with Wilkins as he advised Oliver's government. Like her niece Bridget, Robina had married the nearest possible replacement to her first husband, keeping Oliver's family circle tight. When in town, Wilkins called in on his friends at the London scientific circle which met at Gresham College. Oliver was a patron here too, giving Wren his first appointment as the college's Chair of Astronomy. Wren's colleague, the renowned German-born, Polish-English intellectual, scientist and educational reformer Samuel Hartlib, was another favourite of the Lord Protector who employed him as an unofficial patent surveyor and paid him a retainer of £300 a year to support his work. Wren collaborated on Hartlib's 1655 book, *The Reformed Commonwealth of Bees*, which promoted new bee-keeping techniques and included Wren's drawing of the design for the transparent, three-storey, hexagonal hives Wilkins kept at Wadham.[102] Seeing these on his visit to Wadham, John Evelyn had likened them to 'castles and palaces'. He was delighted to take one home, which both Hartlib's London neighbour Samuel Pepys and King Charles II would later admire.[103]

The new technology behind these beehives, Hartlib hoped, could swell yields sufficiently for honey to replace the expensive cane sugar now being cultivated in the West Indies. But bees represented more than efficient food supply to Hartlib and his philosophical circle of 'ingenious friends' which met regularly at the fashionable London salon of the Puritan luminary Katherine Viscountess Ranelagh.[104] To them, the organisation of a bee colony was a model for contemporary human society: not a hierarchical monarchy as previous generations had seen it, but an industrious, well-ordered, egalitarian community of free workers engaged in public service and loyal to their natural, benevolent leader. Talent could come from anywhere, as Wilkins's Wadham student, inventor and future cartographer of Ireland, William Petty explained in his published advice to Hartlib on education reform, which advised 'That all children of above seven years old may be presented to this kind of education, none being to be excluded by reason of the poverty and inability of their parents, for hereby it hath come to passe, that many are now holding the plough, which might have been made fit to steer the state'.[105]

An early copy of Hartlib's book on bee-keeping was presented to Oliver, the Commonwealth's own queen bee. As Lord Protector, Oliver was himself the living embodiment of Petty's calls for equality of opportunity, having laid down his plough to serve the State. This was, in fact, how Oliver liked to see himself and have others describe him, his ambiguous social status useful in portraying him as a Biblical figure like the shepherd David or farmer Gideon called out of rural obscurity by God to rule; not a power-hungry potentate but 'a good constable to keep the peace of the parish'. Fond of such reassuringly rustic language and imagery, Oliver no doubt appreciated Hartlib's apian metaphor for his own regime as he and his councillors now buzzed about their own programme of reform.[106]

❦ ❦ ❦

The Protectoral Council was considerably more powerful than previous royal privy councils had been. While the new constitution, *The Instrument of Government*, granted Oliver the Crown's traditional prerogative powers of veto over parliamentary legislation, it constrained him as no monarch had been before. His veto could be overridden by Parliament after twenty days and he had to always 'govern . . . by the advice of the Council', acting on key matters, such as going to war, only with the consent of the majority of his Council. The Council were a varied selection pragmatically chosen, comprising not only the expected army grandees like the *Instrument*'s author John Lambert but also conservative, civilian politicians like Anthony Ashley Cooper, the future Earl of Shaftesbury, who had once supported the King. Most of its original 15 members appointed by the *Instrument* for life shared a personal connection or loyalty to Oliver, however, and several were family members: his brother-in-law John Desborough, son-in-law Charles Fleetwood, and Richard Cromwell's father-in-law Richard Major. Nonetheless, the Council was no mere rubber-stamp of Oliver's wishes and frequently disagreed with him and among themselves, the divisions between its civilian and military members in particular hardening as the Protectorate progressed. The fact that Oliver could not dismiss or appoint councillors at will as previous monarchs had done also strengthened the Council's independence.

The *Instrument* continued its emphasis on checks and balances by constraining Parliament in a sign that its author Lambert had learned to mistrust both over-mighty monarchs and over-mighty Parliaments through his experience of Charles I and the Rump. Most notably, it provided for Oliver and his beefed-up Council to govern in between parliamentary sessions by issuing ordinances similar to modern executive orders in the United States, though these would eventually need to be confirmed by the next Parliament. They produced 82 of these in the first eight months of the regime, advancing broadly the same agenda that Oliver and his allies had been promoting since Ireton's *Heads of Proposals* in 1647. This programme, which Oliver would largely adhere to throughout his Protectorate, boiled down to two central and sometimes conflicting ambitions: settlement and reformation. To help the former, the oath of engagement all men had been forced to swear to the new Commonwealth was scrapped and Presbyterian exiles were allowed home. Oliver removed judges hostile to former Royalists, instructing the remainder to show them clemency, and often intervened in personal cases to restore their fortunes and estates. Those previously cast out of public life for past allegiances swiftly learned that personal appeals to him were the surest route to leniency. Edward Hyde at the exiled court praised Oliver's magnanimity and the dexterity with which he promoted men regardless of their past allegiance, explaining that 'He was not a man of blood, and totally declines Machiavell's method, which prescribes upon any alteration of a government, as a thing absolutely necessary, to cut off the heads of those, and extirpate their families, who are friends to the old [one] . . .'[107]

The permanent settlement of Scotland and Ireland was a continuing headache for the Protectorate, grappling as it was with the novelty of ruling both former kingdoms for the first time from London. The first step in foreign policy, meanwhile, was to live up to Oliver's personal motto *Pax Quaeritur Bello* ('Peace is sought through war') and settle the Commonwealth's glorious but ruinously expensive naval war with their Dutch mercantile rivals. Oliver himself had long been keen to secure peace with England's likeminded Protestant, republican neighbour, telling the Dutch commissioners in July 1653 that 'The world was wide enough for both; and if the two peoples could only thoroughly well understand each other, the two countries could overrule all others and control the markets and dictate the conditions and that therefore in this regard good order should be established.'[108] Peace was finally achieved in April 1654 with a favourable treaty which preserved England's Navigation Act curtailing Dutch shipping, prevented the Dutch from any longer hosting the exiled House of Stuart and excluded the Stuarts' relatives the House of Orange from the office of Stadtholder. Oliver went on to use his naval strength and new Dutch alliance to secure peace in the Baltic, mediating between warring Sweden and Denmark and imposing a peace agreement on them. Peace was a shrewd policy, despite Sir Philip Warwick's later aspersions that Oliver would never have agreed to it 'but as he saw it might contribute to his single-ship, or the settling him and his family in the throne'.[109] Trade deals with the newly pacified Sweden and Denmark, Portugal, Tunis and Algiers further boosted the new Protectorate's prosperity and prestige abroad while laying foundations for Britain's global trading empire.

Stability through settlement would have been enough for Oliver had he wished merely to keep his head down and consolidate his own power. But the radical soldier of the 1640s pulsed beneath the skin of the conservative statesman of the 1650s. A lasting settlement was the foundation for the reformation providence commanded him to build. These twin principles were expressed in 1655 when a national fast and prayer day was arranged to expedite 'a settlement and reformation as hath been so long contended for, as had the weight of the work of this generation'.[110] In their first months in office, Oliver and his council implemented long-awaited structural reform of the national church. The vexing issue of tithes continued unresolved, and the limits of toleration remained a flashpoint for argument, but the foundational work of a stable Cromwellian church settlement was done. This would be a pluralist but pragmatic church inclusive enough for the godly but not so ideological it alienated the mainstream majority. A central commission, broad enough to contain religious Independents, Presbyterians and a few Baptists, chose candidates for parish ministry while those already in place were examined for suitability by local committees of 'Ejectors'. Those chosen would, it was hoped, steer their congregations towards the same spiritual awakening Oliver had himself experienced. No common liturgy was imposed on the church which would continue to exist as an umbrella sheltering the many Protestant sects that had sprung up in recent years so long as their members did not disturb the peace. As Oliver put it, 'who ever hath this faith, let his form be what it will, [if] he [is] walking peaceably without the prejudicing of others under another form'.[111] This unprecedented degree of toleration was not only Oliver's foremost desire as so often expressed, but was enshrined in the *Instrument* under which he operated. Church attendance was voluntary and no-one was to be forced by penalties into any particular faith but rather 'endeavours be used to win them by sound doctrine and the example of good conversation'.[112]

These generous terms precluded those who wished to worship under the hierarchical rule of bishops (Anglicans) and, as before, Catholics. Yet in reality, both groups found their experience softened by Oliver himself who not only had friends and relations among their number but was now convinced of the need for reconciliation with those of alternative opinions who nevertheless lived peaceably. It was better that too many enjoyed liberty of conscience than that a few should suffer unjustly or, as Oliver is recorded as saying once: 'he had rather that Mahumetanism [Islam] were permitted amongst us, then that one of God's Children should be persecuted'.[113] In 1647, he had responded to a request to help a relative of John Williams, the Royalist Archbishop of York, on the strength that he was a 'cousin' who claimed shared kinship through the Williams family. 'Your kinsman shall be very welcome to me,' Oliver wrote in reply. 'I shall study to serve him for kindred's sake, amongst whom let not be forgotten, my Lord, your cousin and servant.'[114] Now Oliver listened to the concerns of bishops about ejected Anglicans, particularly his friend James Ussher, Archbishop of Armagh and Primate of Ireland, for whom upon his death Oliver commanded a state-funded funeral in Westminster Abbey which he thoughtfully allowed to be conducted according to the defunct Book of Common Prayer. Oliver collaborated with his Catholic friend Sir Kenelm Digby, meanwhile, on an accommodation for Catholics which culminated in a bold, though ultimately unsuccessful, secret mission to the Vatican to strike an agreement with the Pope.

Witnessing Oliver's personal interventions to help individual Catholics recover their estates, and the permission granted for the Venetian ambassador to hold public masses, the French ambassador observed that England's Catholics found the Protectorate a more sympathetic regime than those which preceded it (and that which followed, we can add with hindsight).

As Lord Protector, Oliver opened the door to another religious group who were more accustomed to persecution. The Jews had been expelled from England in the thirteenth century and in 1655 a delegation led by the Portuguese rabbi Menasseh ben Israel arrived at Whitehall to petition Oliver to re-admit them. Oliver was keen on the idea and arranged for Menasseh to stay in rooms on the Strand nearby while a Council subcommittee and then a public conference considered the question. Oliver's personal eagerness stemmed in part from his capacious view of religious toleration but even more so from the millenarian view he shared with his circle of reformers that the 'Second Coming of Christ' would be hastened if the Jews were converted to Protestant Christianity. Both the English and the Jews were God's chosen people and the Jews, for their part, believed coming to England would help their messiah to appear among them as they in turn spread their own faith. The year 1656 was also considered auspicious for such a seismic event, reflecting the 1,656 years it was believed elapsed between the Creation and the Flood. There were more practical benefits too in admitting the Jews who would bring with them their commercial expertise and useful intelligence networks. The proposal met stiff opposition, however, particularly from City merchants who did not want the commercial competition. Menasseh prayed for God to strengthen the 'mind of the prince' and Oliver stepped up to break the deadlock. As the Jews had been expelled by royal prerogative, he argued, so he could re-admit them. He assured the small existing community of his protection and gave permission for a burial ground in Mile End and a synagogue near the Tower, on land which belonged to Magdalene College Cambridge where his former secretary, the lawyer and Hebraist John Sadler, was Master. For this, Oliver is still admired today by Jewish communities around the world.

Oliver's quest for godly reformation encompassed many of the same 'commonwealth' notions of social justice his great-great-great-uncle Thomas and his circle had pursued in the 1530s. Oliver's words after the battle of Dunbar – 'If there be any that makes many poor to make a few rich that suits not a Commonwealth' – have the distinctly Cromwellian ring of his forebear. Thus, beyond the realm of religion, government, law and education also needed reform if the Protectorate was to realise the idealised, just society Oliver and the New Model Army had fought for. An immediate reduction in troop numbers and the taxes to pay for them together with a streamlining of government bureaucracy were popular measures aiding both settlement and reformation. Transport and infrastructure too were tackled, with highways repaired, streets cleaned and the sometimes dangerous hansom cabs (forerunners to the taxi) regulated for the first time. More complex was the enduring need for legal reform, into the deep, murky waters of which Oliver and his council now waded. Reform of the arcane Chancery court was unwisely entrusted to eminent members of the legal profession whose vested interest hampered any practical progress. Yet the Protectorate made some small advances, bringing in William Sheppard, a reforming lawyer, to act as a government 'tsar', and issuing an ordinance which sped up court decisions, reduced corruption, widened and improved access to justice and made it cheaper. The aim, Oliver later explained, was to make laws 'plain and short, and less chargeable to the people'.[115]

Oliver had long been interested in education reform which was a pet subject for Puritans. During the 1640s, Hartlib had invited the famous Bohemian educationalist Comenius to England to establish a scientific college, and in 1644 Milton wrote an open letter to Hartlib advocating for a broad school curriculum. In 1649 the Rump began a pilot project through its Commission for the Propagation of the Gospel in Wales which opened a number of schools. The climate of the 1650s encouraged experimentation and Hartlib's circle saw education as the best means to build a peaceful world after the violence of war. With Hartlib, and his fellow educationalist John Drury's advice, the Protectorate busied itself particularly on the question of the character of educators, scrutinising school and university visitors and ejecting schoolmasters it deemed theologically unsound or of loose morality. But it also took the matter of financing education seriously, drawing up plans for the 'advancement of learning' in Ireland, buying soldiers' debentures to endow a 'foreign correspondency' and, in England, issuing grants for school upkeep and teachers' pay and exempting the salaries of all scholars and teachers from assessment for war taxation.[116]

Oliver also wished to broaden access to education, particularly through founding new institutions. Hartlib's group had opened an academy at Bethnal Green in 1649 which not only educated the sons of gentlemen but staged weekly public lectures open to all, though it only lasted a year before running out of funds. Oliver now drafted plans for a new college at Oxford to be called St Mary's Hall and financed by voluntary subscription. This was to be an inclusive institution, a Calvinist refuge explicitly designed to further the Protestant cause with 'poor Protestant ministers and scholars being foreigners and strangers born' to be maintained to study divinity, and money set aside for the production of 'a general synopsis of the true reformed Protestant christian religion proposed in this commonwealth'.[117] More radical still was the idea which had been gathering steam for some years of establishing a new college of learning in the north – originally conceived as a school. First suggested at Manchester in 1640, then in York, the project had finally coalesced around Durham with funding from the cathedral. Oliver had long supported the concept, writing a letter of endorsement to Parliament in March 1651. This was a scheme of which Thomas Cromwell would have approved: conducive to 'the promoting of learning and piety in those poor, rude, and ignorant parts' while benefiting from the 'pleasantness and aptness of situation, healthful air, and plenty of provisions' to be found in Durham, producing 'such happy and glorious fruit as are scarce thought on or foreseen'.[118]

As Lord Protector, Oliver threw his weight behind the scheme and letters patent were issued in May 1657, echoing Oliver's levelling-up arguments 'that the founding of a College at Durham will be of great advantage to those Counties and to all the Northern Parts of this Island'. Eminent Protectoral worthies were named to the committee to establish the college and the list of Visitors to supervise it. But as the project grew in ambition – conceived of now as a university more than a mere school – so it attracted enemies, from the Quakers who distrusted State-sponsored religious education, to Oxford University which, unsurprisingly, did not wish its duopoly with Cambridge broken. Oliver's letters patent for Durham envisaged a college founded by 'Us and our Successors' to last 'hereafter for ever'.[119] But with his death the dream of a third university at Durham shattered, a petition to Richard during his short rule insufficient to save it.[120] Had the Protectorate endured longer, it may well have established Durham University and perhaps even pursued the progressive ideas of Hartlib and Drury, who advocated a full state-school system with common schools for academic subjects to be followed by mechanical schools offering vocational training.

For now, in 1654, Oliver had reached the limits of what he and his administration could achieve without wider support and funds. The *Instrument* required him to summon a Parliament and Oliver himself was eager to do so as he continued his quest to find a legitimate legislative body he could work with productively. The first Protectorate Parliament (which included MPs from Scotland and Ireland for the first time, as well as Oliver's sons Richard and Henry and 21 other relations) duly convened in early September and, riding to Westminster in 'a very gorgeous coach' with his son Henry and John Lambert with him, Oliver looked upon 'the hopefullest day that ever mine eyes saw, as to considerations of this world'.[121] This hope rested on his expectation that Parliament would confirm and continue his programme of reform. As he explained in his lengthy and exuberant opening speech in the Painted Chamber, the government's actions so far were 'but entrances and doors of hope', the first miles out of Egypt towards the land of Canaan. If the MPs now discharged their duty 'you will be enabled to put the top-stone of this work', avoiding the Israelites' struggle in the Wilderness to 'enter into rest, and peace'.[122]

Such hopes were swiftly dashed. The *Instrument*'s redistribution of seats had produced a confident Parliament disinclined to toe the Protectoral line and implement its minority agenda. Immediately its members set about debating the new constitution itself, dismantling this 'arbitrary power' clause by clause, clawing back parliamentary power by vehemently attacking the principles Oliver had to remind them were the 'fundamentals' of the regime: government by a single person and Parliament who shared control of the Army; no perpetuating of Parliaments but regular elections; and his cherished liberty of conscience. Backed into a corner, Oliver and his Council played their constitutional card to exclude those MPs who failed to sign a 'Recognition' of these principles. Notably none of his kin rebelled against him.[123] Yet even this purge did not much improve matters and members continued to work on a substitute constitution, demand the reduction of the size and expense of the Army and legislate for the punishment of 'damnable heresies'. 'Where shall we have men of a universal spirit?' an exasperated Oliver asked. 'Everyone desires to have liberty but none will give it.'[124] Eventually Oliver's patience snapped and he dismissed Parliament, using the ambiguous drafting of the *Instrument* to close it after five lunar rather than calendar months. Not a single piece of legislation had been produced and Oliver would spend the rest of his Protectorate searching for those same doors of hope.

In these dark days of discord, Oliver would have benefited from emulating Thomas's techniques in managing Parliament. Yet, though he himself had scored previous successes as a political fixer during the 1640s, he and his Council were largely inexperienced in the delicate art of steering a new assembly and had not done nearly enough to prepare for the session. As a peacekeeping 'constable', Oliver saw his role as keeping above the fray rather than fighting down in the melee, and he had emphasised to the House that he had not sought his own elevation but 'hoped to have had leave to have retired to a private life'.[125] This might have seemed particularly appealing as the autumn nights drew in, in Milton's mind shattering the leaves before the mellowing year.[126] But, like Milton and Shakespeare, the ejected minister and poet Robert Herrick living close by in London saw the presage of death in the change of season. 'Die ere long, I'm sure, I shall; After leaves, the tree must fall,' he wrote in 'After Autumn, Winter'.[127]

Sure enough, before the leaves fell, Oliver cheated death when trying out his newest toy, six grey Frieslands gifted him by the Count of Oldenburg. Driving them himself in Hyde Park, he fell from the coach and was carried along by the runaway team with his foot stuck in their reins. The fall then set off a pistol which narrowly missed him – the whole incident a black farce which frightened his allies and delighted his enemies. Once the trees were bare, death came again to Whitehall to try its luck. In November 1654, 65 years after losing her first husband and baby, 37 years since the death of her second husband, Oliver's redoubtable mother Elizabeth, so recently transplanted into the royal palace, died aged 89. She kept close to the beloved son who had transformed her life until the last. Nearing the end, she blessed him: 'The Lord cause his face to shine upon you, and comfort you in all your adversities, and enable you to do great things for the glory of your most high God, and to be a relief unto his people; my dear son, I leave my heart with thee, a good night.'

Oliver was bereft of the woman with whom he had shared his eventful life. Even as Lord Protector he had sought her out regularly. 'Never a week passed but he went to see her, treating her with filial affection and great respect,' the Venetian ambassador reported in December 1654.[128] It may have been around this time too that he commissioned Robert Walker to paint the portrait reputed to be of her which now hangs in the London Museum. In its frame an old woman exquisitely dressed in a modest black gown and head dress with white sleeves and pearls peeking out from a lace cape fixes a confident gaze down her long nose.[129] If the portrait does not depict Oliver's mother another, only recently acquired by the Cromwell Museum, may yet do, though seemingly younger and more luxuriously dressed in pale blue satin. Whichever – if either – captures Oliver's mother's likeness, Oliver himself would see her real face no more. With solemn grandeur the Lord Protector arranged a funeral for his mother at Westminster Abbey where, 'amongst others needless ceremonies', his detractors sniffed, he 'caused many hundred torches to be carried with the hearse, though she was buried by daylight'.[130] The great Puritan matriarch Elizabeth Cromwell had not earned her eternal resting place alongside the former kings and queens of England by championing Parliament like John Pym or leading its army to revolution as Henry Ireton had done. She was celebrated as the 'noble Root that didst afford Great Britain's Weal's Affector', for her achievement was of a simpler, yet no less vital task: to birth and nurture a new ruling dynasty.[131]

Nine

Dynasty

The longer the Protector sits in the saddle, the securer his seat in it; so that there is every likelihood that his government may last for the remainder of his life . . . [I] believe . . . that he will very shortly assume the title of king. There are indeed reasons which might seem to hinder such a step . . . The struggle between the nation on the one hand and the royal family of Stuart on the other would thereby be transformed into a private quarrel between the House of Cromwell and Stuart . . .

Ambassador Coyet in London to Charles X, King of Sweden, 1 June 1655

Weeds and nettles

In August 1655, an elderly man was caught out in a summer storm. At 94 years old – reputedly the oldest knight in England – Sir Oliver Cromwell knew to take care not to catch cold.[1] His advanced age and declining health had confined the old cavalier to his home at Ramsey in recent years, as he explained in his appeal to the compounding committee in the late 1640s. This was a welcome step to his Parliamentarian sister Elizabeth Hampden who sighed 'I wish he had taken the same course 30 years ago, so would it have been happy for all his.'[2] For Sir Oliver, of course, had been the near ruin of his family; his conniving marriage to the Palavacino heiress insufficient to save Hinchingbrooke from the debts accrued through his playboy lifestyle and endless entertainment of visiting royals. His support for the King's cause in the Civil War had almost cost him Ramsey but for the intervention of his influential nephew. Now, alone with his thoughts as he dried himself by the fire, perhaps his mind turned to that nephew, the Lord Protector, his own flesh and blood and namesake godson, in gratitude for his hearth and home. Perhaps not. The warm flames would stave off a dangerous chill and Sir Oliver leaned closer. But suddenly 'some weakness or swoon' overcame him and he fell into the fire, burning himself so badly he was dead within two days. Sir Oliver was buried in the Cromwell family vault beneath the tower of St Thomas à Becket's Church in Ramsey that night, it was said, so his creditors could not seize his body.[3] On his last earthly journey he would have passed the parliamentary colours his sons had captured in the wars which reportedly hung in the church until 1687.

While Sir Oliver died unreconciled to the Protectorate, other Royalists navigated it differently. Some withdrew from public life into rural nostalgia, consoling themselves with gentler pursuits like poetry and angling. Many actively befriended the regime, either genuinely persuaded of its merits or to give themselves cover as they quietly kept their options open. One such was Elizabeth 'Bess' Murray – daughter of Charles I's whipping boy William Murray, Earl of Dysart (at whose death in 1655 she became Countess of Dysart in her own right) and also mistress of Helmingham Hall as the bride of the current Lionel Tollemache. Like her predecessor, Gregory's granddaughter Catherine Tollemache, Bess was a 'a great student', quick in mind with considerable learning in mathematics, philosophy, divinity and history.[4] A 'pretty, witty lass', Bess was also courageous, resourceful and an engaging conversationalist; just the kind of young woman to entrance London society and captivate the Lord Protector himself. It was perhaps Oliver's daughter Betty Claypole who introduced her friend Bess to the Cromwell family when they were at Hampton Court only a few miles downriver from Bess's own Ham House.[5] Rumours soon circulated that Bess was Oliver's mistress: 'She is Bess of my heart, she was Bess of Old Noll,' went the rhyme.[6] This was highly unlikely for the uxorious Oliver, who undoubtedly valued in Bess the same sparkling, female company he enjoyed with other young women including his own daughters, daughters-in-law and Frances Lambert. He eventually paid heed to the gossip and distanced himself, though not soon enough to prevent the tale spreading that he had fathered her second child, Thomas Tollemache, a slim legend in which Tollemache himself basked in later life.[7] If this had been true, Tollemache would have been a Cromwell twice over: great-great-grandson to both Gregory and Richard.

Bess had other reasons for soliciting the Lord Protector's friendship, and he for treating her with caution. Though they had ostensibly kept their powder dry, the Tollemaches were part of a royalist circle which included the network known to its members as the 'Sealed Knot', named for the supposedly unbreakable security device of a knot sealed with hot wax. Its participants – mostly younger sons with little to lose – formed a sleeper cell, living quietly under the Protectorate as they waited for opportune moments to raise an uprising to restore the exiled Charles II. Helmingham Hall was one location for their clandestine meetings and Bess herself may have acted as a messenger for the group when she travelled to the continent, her passage smoothed by Oliver's protection. Two letters survive at the Hall written by Charles II from Paris around 1654 to an unnamed woman, almost certainly Bess, in which he professes his friendship to her family and looks forward to a future where he and not Oliver Cromwell rules. 'I have sufficient evidence of the continuance of your good wishes for me,' he writes, 'of which I have a very just sense, and doubt not but that I shall live to give you thanks for it at Whitehall.'[8]

In early 1655, that future seemed within tantalising reach. Opposition to the Protectorate spiked as a minority of diehard Royalists stepped up their plans for insurrection and Oliver's government caught word that 'some great plot is intended'.[9] In this darkening atmosphere it was useful to remind a complacent public of these threats and when Oliver dismissed his first Parliament in January 1655, he likened its members to trees under whose shadow 'Weeds and Nettles, Briars and Thorns, have thriven'.[10] Gone were the 'doors of hope' from his opening of Parliament mere months earlier to be replaced by unwelcome plants lurking underfoot to threaten the Protectorate's Garden of Eden. These not only included the most ardent Royalists, but also many of Oliver's former allies: republican MPs who could not forgive his dismissal of their cherished Rump Parliament; Levellers who damned an ambitious Oliver for betraying their cause; and Fifth Monarchists like Thomas Harrison who believed the nation should prepare for the reign of Christ and had placed all their hopes in the failed Nominated Assembly. Most concerningly, some of these enemies had begun to work together, meeting around the back of the Protectorate to form previously unthinkable unholy alliances.

Where opposition existed in daylight, Oliver tried to counter it with the *Instrument*'s preferred weapon of 'good conversation'. Meeting the Fifth Monarchists, including Henry Ireton's younger brother Clement, he listened as they railed against him and refused his request to keep the peace. Nevertheless, Oliver offered them immunity from prosecution if they withdrew to their country estates. Thomas Harrison required further personal warning before he was eventually placed under arrest. Oliver also tried to find accord with George Fox, leader of the radical Quakers who were at the time treated with widespread suspicion. 'Come again to my house,' he told Fox at Whitehall, taking his hand and inviting him to dine with him that evening in the Banqueting House, 'for if thou and I were but an hour in a day together we should be nearer one to the other.'[11]

Where subversion occurred in the shadows, Oliver had the astonishingly capable John Thurloe and his intelligence network to cut off the hydra's heads. In Thurloe, a shrewd lawyer who had risen in Cromwellian circles, Oliver had his own Thomas Cromwell: a chief minister to serve him and help keep him safe. As Secretary to the Council, Thurloe became the gatekeeper for all Protectoral business just as Thomas had been as Henry VIII's Principal Secretary. Just as Thomas's friends looked to him to see the nub of their problems, Thurloe was renowned for being adept at picking the lock that led to the hearts of men. More practically, his ability to open anyone's post from his hub at the centre of a new state postal system, and to deploy civil servants like John Milton to translate languages and Felsted alumnus and Oxford mathematician John Wallis to crack ciphers, also helped his masterful statecraft and spycraft. Thus, when in March 1655 the rumoured royalist uprising led by Colonel John Penruddock bubbled to the surface in Wiltshire, Thurloe's agents ensured it was swiftly put down, its scattered, limp efforts fizzling out almost as soon as it started.

Oliver's personal security, meanwhile, was a full-time job in itself, as regular attempts were made on his life. At a distance some of these appear hapless attempts of dark, comic brilliance such as when Oliver thwarted a would-be sniper in Hyde Park by going over to him to compliment him on his horse. However, at the time they were deeply frightening – it was no wonder Oliver's mother had jumped every time she heard a musket shot fearing for her son's life. The Cromwells' security was closely monitored with barricades built around Hampton Court's perimeter and the route and mode of travel for their weekly journeys there only ever decided at the last minute. Oliver's bedroom door at Hampton Court was secured by a specially commissioned elaborate lock now in the Cromwell Museum's collections. Yet the Lord Protector himself remained unperturbed as even his enemies admitted. 'By these unsuccessful plots they were only the obstructors of what they sought to advance,' Lucy Hutchinson sneered at the fumbling plotters, 'while, to speak truth, Cromwell's personal courage and magnanimity upheld him against all enemies and malcontents.'[12]

If these were the threats at home, Oliver also had to spar with other states, many of whom viewed his kingless regime with open hostility. For, like all monarchs before him (and prime ministers since), he found his day-to-day work dominated by foreign affairs. He too faced the perennial dilemma of early modern English sovereigns: whether to ally with one of Europe's strongest powers, France or Spain, against the risks that, if he allied with neither, the two warring powers might make peace and together invade England (and now to restore the House of Stuart). This was quite a challenge for an ordinary man who had not been educated in preparation for the leading role he now assumed on the international stage and lacked the travel experience or fluency in other languages upon which to draw for first-hand knowledge of continental Europe. Oliver was upfront about his shortcomings, telling ambassador Bonde 'it was a matter of grief to him that he had been so ill-educated that he scarcely ventured to speak any language other than English'.[13] The fact that Bonde spoke English was a key reason they got on so well, as other ambassadors had to rely on translators or the Protector's halting, schoolboy Latin.

Oliver approached the steep learning curve before him with humility, freely admitting his ignorance to ambassadors and envoys.'[14] In these circumstances, it was only sensible for him to solicit advice on international statecraft, and he freely acknowledged to the Dutch ambassador that 'he himself without the Council did not dispose of such affairs'.[15] Nevertheless, Oliver's personal limitations did not prevent him going toe to toe with foreign leaders – he signed off his missives to the Grand Duke of Tuscany as 'Bonus Amicus Oliver P', described himself as the friend of King Louis XIV of France and Cardinal Mazarin, the leader of his regency government, who was so awed by His Highness Oliver he 'would change countenance whenever he heard him named'. Neither was he afraid to challenge other rulers as he pursued a bolder, more interventionist foreign policy than the Stuarts before or indeed after him. 'God has not brought us hither,' Oliver told the Council of State, 'but to consider the work that we may do in the world as well as at home.'[16] This work rested on Oliver's 'fundamenta' – the principles of security, free trade and the Protestant cause – which he tried but did not always manage to align.[17]

The Treaty of Westphalia in 1648, which largely ended the Thirty Years War, had redrawn the map of Europe and enshrined the principle of state sovereignty. It also signalled the ebb of Habsburg Spain's historic dominance and the rise of Bourbon France to take its place, though the two powers continued to tussle while France also struggled with its own civil wars. In spring 1654, both France and Spain were wooing England for an alliance against the other, their governments prostrating themselves offering substantial sums and territories to the Lord Protector as they sought to outbid each other.[18] England had now 'made itself the third power in Europe', the Spanish chief minister observed and, with its mighty navy now freed up from fighting the Dutch, Oliver and his Council debated which great power to sail against.[19] At first, France was the more tempting target, particularly as Oliver felt a strong personal desire to help its Protestant Huguenot community which had been abandoned by Charles I and the Duke of Buckingham after their botched intervention at La Rochelle in the late 1620s. Oliver dispatched agents to sound out the appetite for revolt, declaring 'with passion . . . that England had ruined that party and it fell to England to re-establish them'.[20] This, after all, would only be fair retaliation for the unofficial help the French had given to Charles II's Scottish expedition. However, Mazarin was, by then, in command of the domestic situation with the ongoing Fronde rebellion finally quashed. Yet Oliver did not forget the Huguenots and, in his continuing talks with Mazarin, insisted on guarantees for their protection as a condition for any alliance.

It was becoming clearer, meanwhile, that the Spanish could not afford the payment Oliver demanded (nor, equally, to finance an invasion by Charles II). With France stronger, more popular and closer to the Stuarts than Spain, it was now the greater threat and Oliver sided with the councillors urging war against the great Elizabethan enemy of Catholic Spain. A colonial attack was deemed a less risky option than conflict in Europe itself, and so in December 1654 an English army was dispatched to fight the Spanish in the Caribbean. The result was a disaster. Crippled by disease and poor supplies, the English failed to take the island of Hispaniola (in the West Indies) in a humiliating defeat.[21] Though they accidentally captured the smaller but strategically important island of Jamaica and the expedition paved the way for an eventual fruitful alliance with France, in the short term the failure of this 'Western Design' was a bitter blow to Oliver and his regime and the Lord Protector was soon stricken with self-doubt and its characteristic accompanying illness.

God had seemingly abandoned Oliver and the godly cause abroad. This was apparent not only on the far side of the world but also closer to home. In May 1655, shocking news reached the court that the Catholic Duke of Savoy, under the influence of his mother, Henrietta Maria's sister, had massacred hundreds of Vaudois or Waldensian Protestants in western Piedmont in the north of Italy. There was widespread outrage, likening the atrocity to that of the Irish rebellion in 1641. 'Avenge O Lord thy slaughtered saints / whose bones Lie scattered on the Alpine mountains cold,' Milton cried in the sonnet he poured out in his distress. Oliver, meanwhile, lost no time in organising a national relief fund to which he contributed £2,000 of his own money and leading an international coalition to pressurise the Duke into a settlement. This 'lightning' intervention, as it was praised by the later Prime Minister William Gladstone who advanced his own godly foreign policy, not only saved lives, set a precedent and impressed European leaders, but further strengthened Oliver's hand in his negotiations with Mazarin, with whom he agreed an alliance in November 1655 cemented by toleration for the Huguenots.[22] A full treaty would not take effect until March 1656 and Oliver had to wait until the following winter to go into military action with his new ally.

Before then, beset by enemies at home and abroad, in the face of the aborted Parliament, Penruddock's uprising, the Piedmont massacre and, above all, the bruising failure of the Western Design, Oliver and his Council doubled down. Provoked into something of a 'siege mentality', they reached for a revolutionary, authoritarian response:

an experiment in direct local government by military leaders tasked to improve security and impose the 'reformation of manners' that God so evidently demanded.[23] 'It is not to be denied,' Oliver wrote in October 1655, 'but the Lord hath greatly humbled us, in that sad loss sustained at Hispaniola, no doubt but we have provoked the Lord, and it is good for us to know so, and to be abased for the same.'[24] England was parcelled up into 10 (later 11) regions and 19 major-generals from the Army were assigned to rule them following the example of John Desborough's mopping-up operation in the West Country following Penruddock's uprising.

As a cohort, the major-generals were young – mostly under 40 – and of middling social status, though several of them had bought substantial sequestered royalist estates. They certainly needed energy for the ambitious task handed to them, which caused many to complain of their workload and tiredness and, in the case of the zealous Major-General Charles Worsley, hastened him like Henry Ireton to an early death through overwork. The government brought in a hasty and ill-thought-through 'decimation' tax upon Royalists to fund the scheme, though, confusingly, Oliver continued his penchant for intervening to help particular royalist families avoid stringent penalties. The tax was both insufficient and also deleterious to Oliver's formerly expressed quest for 'healing and settling' which, in his current bullish mood, he accused royalist delinquents of endangering. Newly appointed commissioners and locally raised militia assisted the major-generals who, in their early months, chalked up some success in securing the country from further unrest, disarming Royalists and Catholics, imposing bonds for good behaviour and checking their movements while collecting the decimation tax. Royalist networks were unnerved and minority Puritan communities reassured.

The major-generals' secondary objective of imposing morality at the point of a musket was a much greater challenge, however, and their attempts to regulate ale-houses, close down country sports and entertainments, deal with beggars, purge unacceptable clergy and clamp down on drunkenness, swearing and sexual misconduct were of limited effectiveness. Morality simply could not be policed in the early modern state in such a way as to fundamentally alter it. Thus they struggled to enforce the Long Parliament's 1647 ban on celebrating Christmas (as well as other holy days and festivals) which had emerged initially as a goodwill gesture towards the Presbyterian Scots when

Parliament first allied with them in 1643. Though Oliver was not much interested in the subject, as Lord Protector he did not reverse the Christmas ban he inherited, and the major-generals were empowered to break up festive parties and issue fines. Yet Christmas was simply irrepressible. When MPs attended Parliament on Christmas Day in 1656, they complained they had been kept up all night by their neighbours' Christmas parties. The most notable impact of the major-generals' rule was the opprobrium they incurred from the general population who resented rule by the sword and hated officious prudes. As an MP in a later Protectorate Parliament memorably complained, 'the little finger of the Major-Generals have I found heavier than the loins of the greatest tyrant kings that went before'.[25]

Consequently, these figures of fear, and later of fun, have gone down in national memory as synonymous with a repressive, military Cromwellian Protectorate. Yet the reality of the experimental regime was that the major-generals' remit was too broad and their time and support too insufficient for them to have been the tinpot dictators of our imaginations.[26] Nevertheless, their impact upon Protectoral politics would be profound as the major-generals' vision for a revolutionary, muscular and militarised Protectorate clashed with that of a traditional, inclusive and monarchical government increasingly advocated by a civilian, Parliamentarian faction at court. The competing worldviews of these coalescing 'military' and 'civilian' groups pulled the innovated Protectorate in opposite directions, towards an armed republic or a constitutional monarchy. Oliver himself straddled the divide, consciously keeping the two forces around him in balance – just as Henry VIII had done – but his children were drawn into the tug of war as they struggled to place themselves in his brave new world.

Heirs and spares

In September 1655, Oliver summoned his son-in-law and veteran colleague Charles Fleetwood home from Ireland to take up a place on the Council of State and among the ruling major-generals. Fleetwood's tenure as Ireland's Lord Deputy had not been a success by any measure. Sent to assess his brother-in-law's administration the previous year, Henry Cromwell had penned an unflinching report to his father.[27] The military conquest of Ireland had long been completed – by Henry Ireton and his successor, the republican Edmund Ludlow – since which Fleetwood had continued the unpleasant work of transplanting the native Irish west to Connaught with as much vigour as he could, given Oliver's constant willingness to make exceptions. Yet the soldier Fleetwood had not successfully moved government onto a peaceful, administrative footing but remained in hock to powerful voices in the Army, particularly the radical and violent Baptists who had come to dominate the forces and the country they had conquered. Fleetwood, Henry said, was eager to come home and the whole administration should be overhauled. Ireland, broken and bleeding, now needed to be healed and settled. But by whom? With his Irish experience, Oliver's son Henry himself was an obvious choice but one fraught with political and familial implications given the intractable issue at the centre of the Cromwellian project: the succession.[28]

The first Protectorate Parliament had decided future Protectors should be elected and not hereditary. This suited Oliver well for, as he was at pains to explain and true to his actions, he had never sought to promote his own family. If the *Instrument* had placed the Protectorate 'in my Family Hereditary,' Oliver expounded, he would have rejected it for 'who knoweth whether he may begat a fool or a wise.'[29] Nevertheless, it was widely assumed Oliver would have a say in nominating a successor and so the issue remained politically charged. Distasteful rumours that he would become king also persisted. Conscious of this, Oliver was highly sensitive to charges of nepotism and dynasticism. 'But if any man shall object, It is an easy thing to talk of necessities when men create necessities,' he quoted his critics rhetorically when he had closed Parliament, 'would not the Lord Protector make himself great, and his family great? doth not he make these necessities?'[30]

Oliver was loath to prove these voices right by advancing his sons Richard and Henry. He had become comfortable handing out jobs to wider family members, as was the custom for monarchs wielding patronage. Accusations of cronyism were a price he deemed worth paying to be surrounded and served by men he knew well and trusted in such uncertain times. But promoting his sons carried implications for the contested question of the succession, and the charge of greedy personal enrichment and aggrandisement which offended his

Puritan sensibilities but seemed unavoidable for a private man trying to operate as head of state; always walking the tightrope between being too monarchical and not monarchical enough. Yet with the doors of hope closing and his enemies gathering around him, Oliver had need of loyal men, and perhaps there was some sense in preparing his sons for the vicissitudes of the future. 'The Lord knows, my desire was for him [Henry] and his brother [Richard] to have lived private lives in the country,' Oliver wrote to Fleetwood in June 1655, 'and Harry knows this very well, and how difficultly I was persuaded to give him his commission for his present place. This I say from a simple and sincere heart. The noise of my being crown'd etc. are like malicious figments.'[31]

Slowly, Oliver edged Richard and Henry onto a more public stage. In August 1655, both deputised for their father in inspecting the London militia.[32] When at home in Hampshire, Richard moved up from serving on local commissions to being warden of the New Forest and supporting the local major-general William Goffe. While in London, he chaired several government committees, including that which organised the fundraising for the massacred Piedmontese. Richard's profile was certainly rising, with the Swedish ambassador hearing rumours he was to be appointed Lord Deputy to govern Scotland or as Lord High Admiral.[33] But in the end neither job materialised. Richard, while put to work in the family business, was kept closer to home in relative quiet. Yet, while Oliver held his older son in reserve for a rainy day, in June 1655 he moved his younger son as a chess piece across the Irish Sea.

The implicit replacement of Fleetwood with Henry was enormously awkward for the Cromwell family. With his customary fear of being branded nepotistic, Oliver did not officially appoint Henry Lord Deputy of Ireland in Fleetwood's stead, but rather made him head of the Army in Ireland and added him to the Irish council. This left Henry exposed in an almost impossible job of immense responsibility in which he was never fully supported. Neither had Oliver managed Fleetwood's expectations, assuring him he was not being replaced and recalled to London which he seemed in fact not to want. The result was an excruciating, extended limbo where the chain of command was opaque and Oliver juggled the hurt feelings and increasingly divergent views of his son and son-in-law. 'I desire thee to know, I most dearly love thee . . . It's reported, that you are to be sent for, and Harry to be deputy, which truly never entered into my heart,' Oliver wrote to Fleetwood even as Henry's ship crossed the sea. 'The wretched jalousies that are amongst us, and the spirit of calumny turns all into gall and wormwood.'[34] The parlous state of the country Henry and Fleetwood both governed, meanwhile, contrasted starkly with their own exalted roles. As a newspaper reported of Henry's arrival with his wife Elizabeth and baby daughter: 'On Monday morning the Lord Henry Cromwell arrived at the Bay of Dublin, and was met on the sands by the Lord Deputy [Fleetwood] and Council, most of the officers and gentry of Ireland, nigh 500 horses, with ten coaches of six and four horses apiece, and a very magnificent entertainment, more than could be expected from so poor and ruined a country.'[35]

The Fleetwoods hosted the Cromwells for three months before returning to London. If this felt like a demotion, their splendid new home of Wallingford House near Whitehall must have eased the transition with its 54 rooms including a long gallery, great drawing room and a chapel.[36] Close to but not inside Whitehall Palace itself, Wallingford offered Fleetwood an independent base of operations which would become its own political centre as divisions grew within the Cromwell family in the coming years. Though now in London, Fleetwood officially retained the title of Lord Deputy of Ireland which he had in the end been granted, continuing a power struggle with Henry from Whitehall as he influenced the Council and briefed against his brother-in-law. The ensuing ill-feeling between the two is captured in Bridget's one surviving letter, written to her brother Henry and examining their decaying relationship. Bridget, revealing the self-flagellating personality Oliver fretted over, alludes to their dwindling sibling affection for which 'I blame none but myself'. This was essential indeed, as too often lately she had blamed or judged others 'wherein my corrupt heart hath taken advantage'. Bridget desires to be 'humbled' for it and, whatever other people's 'unkindnesses' may be, not to 'weaken that love and affection' which she ought to feel for Henry and wants to 'find and nourish' towards him though it might not be 'much cared for'.[37] Far from the easy breeziness of many of the other letters between the Cromwell siblings which shimmer with humour and affection, every word here feels as if it has been squeezed from a stone.

Henry meanwhile lost no time in changing direction in Dublin. While he sought to strengthen the Protectorate in all he did, it was his father's impulse towards a broad-based settlement that Henry emulated, not his desire for religious reformation. He moved against the 'stark mad' Baptists at once, removing them from key positions and amplifying more moderate voices, wooing the local traditionalist Protestant elite whatever their past allegiances and conciliating the Presbyterian Scots in Ulster.[38] The Baptists would keep their 'liberty and countenance,' he explained to Thurloe, but 'to rule me, or to rule with me, I should not approve of.'[39] The Baptists would not forget or forgive him for this and in Fleetwood they had a sympathetic ear for their complaints. Yet for Henry, with radicalism dampened, reprisals could give way to rebuilding: re-organising the Protestant church, restarting trade, restoring local government in the towns, establishing more schools and perhaps a second college at Dublin to aid the 'advancement of ingenious learning'.[40] In some areas Henry softened anti-Catholic policies but it was out of his power to reverse the juggernaut of transplantation, and his occasional callous references to the native Irish Catholics show that the Cromwellian apple had not fallen entirely out of sight of the tree.

In many ways Henry was well suited to the Sisyphean task before him: he was hard working and analytical, open-minded and fair, pragmatic and courageous. A believer in moderation not violence. 'I like gradual proceedings best,' he once said, and with enough support and enough time, real progress could be made in reconstructing a shattered Ireland which Henry, more than any other governor of the period, believed deserved a bright future for its own sake. Indeed, to him, Ireland could even be a laboratory to test new policies before they were introduced in England.[41] But in reality the Protectoral government in London often made his job more, not less, difficult. Unhelpful decisions were made over his head, his advice on military reorganisation was ignored and the budget for Ireland slashed. This, in turn, plunged him into self-doubt of the kind his father ought to have recognised. 'Your highness cannot but be sensible, that by reason of my youth and inability, that my trials and temptations are too great for me, as well as my employment,' he wrote to Oliver a few months into his posting.[42] At a low ebb the following year, he confessed to Thurloe 'the apprehension I have hade of my own unfitness for so great and difficult a work'.[43]

Oliver's responses to Henry were inconsistent, some written in reassurance, others in rebuke. Always there was affectionate love for

'Son Harry' and his young family. Early on Oliver was 'glad to hear, what I have heard, of your carriage' and thought 'the Anabaptists are to blame in not being pleased with you'. Others too conveyed Oliver's love and pride for his son. 'He hath, I do perceive, a love for you, and mentions you with a kind of delight and satisfaction,' Henry's father-in-law wrote, while another friend Vincent Gookin reported how Oliver had spoken of Henry to Richard, Thurloe and councillor Sir Gilbert Pickering, giving him 'the highest and well grounded applauses imaginable, with tears of joy on his cheeks'. Yet the dark shadow of Fleetwood and his allies always lurked under the surface. Gookin's letter continued: 'I cannot but smile to think what a simple owlish game your enemies have played, to make lies to such a father, upon a son.'

Oliver himself was fully aware of the problem between the two men he both considered his sons. 'Pray take notice,' Gookin went on, 'that these words were spoken before Sir Gilbert, who, his highness well knows, tells all to the L[ord] D[eputy] [i.e. Fleetwood]; and therefore be assured it was spoken that it might be noted.' But Oliver, closely bonded to Fleetwood, was defensive of his son-in-law who he refused to believe harboured malicious intentions towards his son. 'H[is] H[ighness] deals with me as a son indeed,' Henry complained to Thurloe, 'that is, as one in whom filial obedience must make all things swallow easily well.'[44] Fleetwood himself insincerely professed his innocence of any conniving in letters to his 'Dear brother' Henry, and Oliver chided his son for 'being over jealous'. 'I am sorry you wrote me some sad apprehensions of some enemies of yours to be about me,' he wrote, 'truly none dare appear so and I am persuaded if you think your B[rother] Fleetwood to be so, you are mistaken, it were dangerous for you to think soe, and he not be so, and safer for you to be mistaken, for indeed none (I hope) can wrong you with me.'[45]

Oliver's own phobia of hubris continued to play a political role in his parenting. Around him, many of the Protectoral elite were using their pole positions to buy up sequestered land and build great estates just as the Cromwells and their contemporaries had done with the monastic spoils of the Reformation, inviting accusations of corruption. Henry himself was living grandly in Ireland. He spent his working days living with his family in Cork House in Dublin, using the state rooms in Dublin Castle for formal events. Each summer, while on his annual tour of inspection around Ireland, he visited the various properties he had acquired, including the large Portumna Estate in Galway. Leisure was chiefly to be had at the family's country home of Phoenix Park on the edge of Dublin which, in true Cromwellian fashion, Henry extended and filled with hawks and beagles. But Oliver remained wary of any overt aggrandisement of his family, advising Henry not 'to lay for yourself the foundation of a great estate. It will be a snare to you, they will watch you, bad men will be confirmed in covetousness, the thing is an evil which God abhors, I pray you think of me in this'.[46] It was perhaps with this advice in mind that Henry refused Parliament's grant of £1,500 worth of Irish lands in 1657 citing Ireland's poverty and England's debts.[47]

Yet such gestures could not outweigh the Cromwells' growing status, nor their swelling numbers. Oliver saw at least 19 grandchildren born – of whom perhaps 12 survived childhood – with many more coming after his death.[48] Henry Cromwell's son Oliver, born with noted ease to his wife Elizabeth at Cork House in Dublin on 18 April 1656, was met as a prince with bonfires and celebrations in the streets and banquets in the castle. Even his baptism was political, as a rejoinder to Henry's enemies the Baptists who believed only adults should be baptised. All this was reported in the London press and the news was received with great happiness by the Protectoral family.[49] Grandfather Oliver rejoiced while Richard wrote to his brother: 'Now the crowds of the congratulations are over for the joy of your welcome son, I shall as one truly and sincerely obliged give you mine, and with the scripture joy I tender it, desiring that God will make it a blessing to our family.'[50] It is a charming, affectionate letter from Richard who, in another missive to Henry, ran himself down admitting that 'though I much love and honour you, yet writing to my unskilful hand is very irksome'.[51] Perhaps this is why he took some weeks to congratulate Henry, though such a silence hardly signified between 'the near relations of brothers . . . especially betwixt yourself and me. Our loves are not to begin acquaintance'.[52] That their love overcame the many miles between them was a common refrain, 'there being a belief in me of community with you, and that foreign distances cannot hinder the operation of love in good dispositions, nor the many waters betwixt England and Ireland squench that beat which admits of no winter of snow or frost in that breast where it dwelleth'.[53] In all their correspondence in these years, Richard's attitude to his younger yet more powerful and successful brother was never resentful but entirely guileless. He conceded his own 'private condition' and Henry's contrasting 'weighty undertaking' but never complained of this, instead recommending friends and servants to Henry's service and 'with very great cheerfulness' sending him a care package of 'eight couple of beagles' with his customary self-deprecation, 'though poor, it being in dogs, companions they have been for princes'.[54]

Along with his congratulations on Henry's new son, Richard sent his love to his 'sister', Henry's 'deare consort' Elizabeth, hoping she 'quickly forgot her pain for joy' and joking that he imagined 'her delight in being surveyor-general of the nursery'. Love came too from his whole household who were awaiting their own near arrival: 'I rejoice with you and my sister, soe do my wife and Hursley friends. We are daily expecting the fruit of my wife's womb, and what God pleases to send will be acceptable.'[55] In early July, God sent Richard and Dorothy their own healthy baby boy (also named Oliver). Henry's jocular father-in-law, writing to Henry from Whitehall, was quick to joke about the reassertion of the family succession now the older son had his heir: 'There is another young Oliver come into this troublesome world, so that yours is to be called but plain Noll.'[56] An Oliver born to Richard trumped an Oliver born to Henry in family precedence. The same might have been said of the Protector's third grandson named Oliver, 'a very lusty boy', who was born to Betty Claypole in July the following year.[57]

❦ ❦ ❦

The significance of male heirs for Oliver's male heirs was not lost on anyone. Rule by the fruitful and secure Cromwell dynasty seemed more and more the answer to civilian politicians appalled at the major-generals' revolutionary rule by the sword which they considered ruinously expensive, unpopular, unconstitutional and undermining of the Protectorate. Coalesced around Oliver's artful chief secretary John Thurloe, this civilian faction contained distinguished old parliamentary colleagues like Bulstrode Whitelocke and Oliver's cousin Oliver St John but also younger men of diverse political backgrounds. Men like the Anglo-Irish Protestant peer Roger Boyle, Lord Broghill, who aligned with Oliver during his campaigns in Ireland and later represented the Protectorate as lord president of the council in Scotland. What united these politicians was a desire for a more traditional, monarchical government liberated from the

Army's influence, and strong personal loyalty to Oliver himself – fealty extended to the whole Cromwell family, particularly for those younger men like Broghill and the naval commander Edward Montagu who were closer in age to Richard and Henry Cromwell and saw the future in them.

The civilian faction disliked the Army's constitution, *The Instrument of Government*, which Major-General John Lambert had drafted to establish the Protectorate, and now explored two obvious ways to vest political power more permanently in the Cromwell dynasty: either to make the Protectorate hereditary or to convert the Protectorate into a monarchy.[58] Both ideas now fed into popular speculation. It was likely 'the succession to this high dignity will be given to his eldest son', the Venetial ambassador Francesco Giavarina wrote of Oliver, 'rendering the government of the three kingdoms and all this most powerful nation perpetual in the house of Cromwell.'[59] The long-awaited capture of the Spanish treasure fleet, Crowning a successful summer naval campaign, also seemed to herald a new regality. Some of the hoard was re-minted as coins bearing a classical profile of Oliver crowned by a laurel wreath on one side, his family arms and motto *Pax Quaeritur Bello* on the reverse. Edmund Waller, meanwhile, hoped more treasure-funded regalia would follow:

> *Let the rich ore forthwith be melted down*
> *And the state fixed by making him a crown*
> *With ermine clad and purple, let him hold*
> *A royal sceptre, made of Spanish gold.*[60]

Yet nothing would come of these rumours unless the civilian faction neutralised the major-generals' opposition and – crucially – persuaded Oliver himself.

The prospect of a new Parliament in September 1656 promised the opportunity to thrash out these differences once and for all and perhaps forge a new constitutional settlement. The elections themselves showcased the major-generals' unpopularity with many of their supporters defeated. Unnerved, the Council sought to mitigate opposition to the regime by using its powers under the *Instrument* to exclude about a hundred of the new MPs. The resulting Parliament was altogether more amenable and productive than the last and set about answering the rising threats of a feared Spanish invasion and assassination plots against Oliver with two security Acts: one to bar any member of the house of Stuart from the throne, and the other in mirror image to secure the Lord Protector's person by treating attempts on his life as acts of treason.

These were pressing issues, for the regime's entire dependence on Oliver's personal safety left it fragile; a reality brought home by the shocking discovery in January 1657 of a new Gunpowder Plot by the strange bedfellows of Levellers and Royalists, financed by Spain. A basket of primed explosives was discovered in the chapel at Whitehall, beneath Oliver's apartments. Just as Guy Fawkes and Robert Catesby – who had been Edward Cromwell's near companion in prison in 1601 – had smuggled gunpowder beneath Parliament from a rented house in Westminster in 1605, so Miles Sindercombe and his cabal based themselves nearby carrying weapons around in an instrument case like Ealing Studios' *Ladykillers* or Frederick Forsyth's *Jackal.* This was just the latest in five or six assassination attempts on the Lord Protector, the conspirators confessed, all arranged with inside information from one of Oliver's own Life Guard. It was clear to all that Oliver and the peaceful stability he guaranteed could be snatched away in an instant; a point only emphasised when, at a service of thanksgiving for the Cromwell family's safe deliverance from the Sindercombe plot, a staircase in the Banqueting House collapsed injuring several people including Richard Cromwell himself.

The security crisis faced by the Protector and his second Parliament over the winter of 1656–7 prompted both the civilian and military factions to propose rival strategies. Broghill and his civilian allies pressed on with their ideas for evolving the Protectorate in a monarchical direction by making the succession 'hereditary in the house of his Highness'.[61] But Oliver 'shut his ears to them', repeatedly declining 'the honour' until it was put aside by his Highness who compelled them 'not to go any further'.[62] Oliver's well-known objection to the Protectorate becoming hereditary remained an insurmountable obstacle. It was, for him, a question of principle. Yet so surprisingly selfless was his resistance to those around him, Giavarina could only speculate either that it was 'mere artifice' or that 'in his innermost self he knows that none of his sons after his death would be capable of directing this great machine', being 'none too strong and capable . . . to bear so heavy a burden'.[63]

The military faction, meanwhile, argued that the Protectorate's best guarantee of security was to upgrade the major-generals' regime. In this they were led by John Desborough, 'the grim giant' to the satirists, who had good reason to be glum as his wife Jane – Oliver's younger sister – had just died in October and received the now customary Cromwellian funeral at Westminster Abbey.[64] The grieving Desborough now proposed a Militia Bill levying a decimation tax on Royalists to fund the extension of the major-generals. Desborough's fellow major-generals Charles Fleetwood and John Lambert supported him, as the plan would keep the Protectorate dependent on the Army, and its leaders on the Council in pole position to steer the succession under the *Instrument* should anything happen to Oliver.

The fault lines in the bitter argument that ensued ran right through the Cromwell family itself. Desborough and Fleetwood on the military side found other younger members of their own family leading the civilian charge against them. Betty Cromwell's husband, Oliver's Master of Horse John Claypole, opened the speeches in opposition to the Militia Bill, an unusual occurrence according to Ludlow who reports him saying 'he could but start the game, and must leave those who had more experience to follow the chase'; an attitude which chimes with Giavarina's verdict that Claypole 'seems to prefer other matters to affairs of state'. Betty herself was open in her support for her husband's civilian faction, earning the typically classist sneer from one Royalist observer that she and Frances Lambert so hated each other they did now 'grow within one degree of fishwives of Billingsgate'.[65] Sharp dynamics divided her too from her own sister, Fleetwood's wife Bridget, who remained an Army loyalist alongside her husband.

Further family opposition to the major-generals came in the somewhat surprising person of Oliver's cousin from the Hinchingbrooke Cromwells, Sir Oliver Cromwell's grandson Harry Cromwell. With his Royalist grandfather dead, the Ramsey coffers bare, and the rest of his family now broadly behind the Lord Protector, Harry had accommodated himself to the Protectorate, serving as a colonel in the local militia and representing Huntingdon in Parliament. Yet he kept his options open, persisting as 'Williams alias Cromwell' in the local records throughout the 1650s. Meanwhile his home remained a space for Royalist reflection under the auspices of his literary wife Anna – his own Hinchingbrooke cousin he had married in straitened circumstances so his father, her guardian, could avoid paying her dowry. This year, 1656, Anna 'the poetess Cromwell' had begun a 200-page commonplace book including her own prayers, meditations, personal insights and poems by her and her Hinchingbrooke relations.[66] Here she not only preserved her fervent faith and touching domestic concerns, but also her devotion to the memory of Charles I. Harry too is captured in its pages, saying his morning prayer and navigating the delicate culture wars of the 1650s by preserving the local maypole festival while moving it from a Sunday.[67]

Now at Westminster Harry waded in against the maypole-hating major-generals arguing, no doubt with feeling given his own Royalist pedigree, that given many people thought it just 'that because some of the cavaliers had done amiss, therefore all should be punished; by the same argument . . . because some of the major-generals have done amiss, which I offer to prove, therefore all of them deserve to be punished'. For this he was dubbed 'honest' by those who agreed, while his opponents warned that he would displease the Lord Protector by going against the major-generals. But Harry probably felt he knew his relative better. Relying on their kinship, he went to see Oliver to make his case in person, and rather than a reprimand received a reward for his pains. 'His highness answered him in raillery, and took a rich scarlet cloak from his back, and gloves from his hands, and gave them to Harry, who strutted with his new cloak and gloves in the house this day.'[68] Oliver's diplomatic use of clothing and gestures to smooth family feathers recalls his visit to Harry's grandfather Sir Oliver Cromwell at Ramsey at the outset of the war when Oliver removed his hat and asked his uncle's blessing even while his troops loomed outside.[69] Now young Harry Cromwell left his cousin's court committed to his service.

While Oliver's official position remained one of support for his government's major-generals' regime, his family's actions reveal how his stance had privately shifted. Surely, the affable John Claypole – husband of Oliver's cherished Betty and one of his chief courtiers – would only have made his uncharacteristically bold attack on the major-generals with his father-in-law's tacit encouragement? Likewise, Harry Cromwell's hostility to the military scheme could be more readily forgiven by a Lord Protector who had already moved on from it. Oliver had fallen out of love with the divisive rule of his old comrades the major-generals and was now listening to the counsel of his newer friends in the civilian faction who envisioned a softer future for the Protectorate. They now had Oliver's ear, but could they convince him to aggrandise himself and his family further to secure the stable and lasting settlement they wanted?

Kingship and courtship

At the end of January 1657, the civilian faction succeeded in defeating the major-generals' Militia Bill, effectively spelling the end for the experimental military regime. Seizing their moment, Broghill, Thurloe and their parliamentary allies broke cover to move the agenda on decisively with a proposal to replace the Protectorate with a monarchy and re-establish a House of Lords to be known as the 'Other House'. Eventually presented to Oliver by Parliament as a draft constitution, the *Humble Petition and Advice*, this was a return to the ancient rule by king, lords and commons but set on a new footing. In a pre-emptive compromise, the title would not be inherited by Oliver's children, but he had the new right to nominate his successor which could, of course, still be his eldest son. The idea of a hereditary Protectorate had been abandoned for a non-hereditary monarchy in the hope that the supernatural endurance of kingship beyond the mortal lives of individual kings would safeguard a smooth succession in any event.

Predictably, the Army leaders were immediately opposed. Their power would be greatly diminished under the *Humble Petition* and so Desborough and Fleetwood joined Lambert in his consternation that his *Instrument* should be replaced. The objections were heartfelt for men who had personally fought against the Stuarts, hardening themselves to the institution of monarchy itself as Charles I had caused the first civil war to give way to a second and his son had then instigated a third. The thought of monarchy alone was enough to reduce Fleetwood to tears during the 'pitched battle' debate which followed, while Desborough predicted that if Oliver took the crown 'he then gave the cause and Cromwell's family also for lost'.[70] The generation below Oliver, Fleetwood and Lambert may also have been put out by the prospect of Richard Cromwell's possible succession at their own expense.[71] Lambert, the second most powerful man in the nation, had long been talked of as a potential successor to an elective

Protectorate. Fleetwood meanwhile was a contender with both a meritocratic and familial claim and one he could pass down to his own son, Oliver's grandson, Cromwell Fleetwood. 'I thought, if there be any of my Lord Protectors posterity that the Lord would make use of, its likeliest to be his daughter [Bridget] and his good son [Fleetwood],' a close observer remarked.[72] Such an eventuality could have dire consequences for the rest of the Cromwell family, as Henry Cromwell realised: 'I only hope, that things will be so ordered, as that there shall be no necessity one his highness's successors to crush and undo his friends and relations causelessly,' he wrote to Thurloe.[73] Suspicion of vested interest remained on both sides, meanwhile, as Henry heard from his father-in-law: 'I was told the other day by Colonel Pride that I was for a king because I hoped the next would [be] Henry's turn.'[74]

With the exception of Fleetwood and Desborough, all of Oliver's relations supported the *Humble Petition and Advice*, including the 27 family members in Parliament.[75] Yet they remained conflicted over whether he should accept the title of king – the one sticking point for Oliver himself who asked Parliament for time to give his answer. There were compelling reasons for Oliver now to accept the crown, as his new brother-in-law, the polymath John Wilkins of Wadham advised and the parliamentary committee of Broghill, Whitelocke, Oliver St John, Edward Montagu and their civilian faction pressed upon him in impassioned speeches in five lengthy meetings, earning them the label of 'kinglings'.[76] The office of king was hard-wired into England's laws and customs, not least those on treason which would automatically apply to the frequent assassination attempts on Oliver's life were he to become king – something Penruddock himself had argued in reverse in his defence after the uprising of 1655. A return to such laws would also enable ordinary people to understand both their rights and responsibilities and what they could expect from their sovereign: 'people do love what they know' as Oliver himself conceded.[77] Furthermore, by nominating his own successor, Oliver could future-proof the regime from an unsuitable candidate exploiting the unavoidable power vacuum that would follow his death. Pragmatically too, assuming the throne would protect Oliver's supporters from any future vengeance by the house of Stuart as they could prove they served a legitimate king. For the kinglings, King Oliver I offered the best chance of securing a stable and lasting settlement under their preferred form of government by limited monarchy, but with the Crown now vested in a person they trusted and revered. What was more, theirs was the official advice of his Parliament, the representative of the sovereign people, which Oliver was bound to accept as he did not share Charles I's belief in his own divine right.

There was another, religious argument for Oliver to take the crown, one which had been highlighted in the recent dramatic case of the Quaker James Nayler which had inflamed the already tense parliamentary session. Nayler was accused of blasphemy for processing into Bristol on horseback in emulation of Christ entering Jerusalem on Palm Sunday. Eventually, after long nights of debates lit by extra candles, the MPs had voted for Nayler to be put in the pillory, have his tongue bored with a red-hot iron and the letter 'B' for blasphemer branded on his forehead. Oliver and his fellow proponents of liberty of conscience were horrified, not only at the brutality of the sentence, but also at its wider implications for religious freedom. 'The case of James Naylor might happen to be your own case,' he reminded a meeting of the Army officers in February.[78] The whole affair reminded Oliver that it was only as king that he could protect future individuals from Parliament's own religious intolerance. Conversely, it may have strengthened his resolve not to accept a hereditary succession, for the more religiously conventional Richard Cromwell had reportedly said over dinner that he thought Nayler should be hanged.[79]

Oliver had demonstrated throughout his career his belief that a constitutionally limited monarchy was the best government where circumstances allowed. This had proved unachievable under the Stuarts but was now within reach if only he could accept the sin of pride involved in taking it upon himself. Furthermore, this would be kingship made by Parliament itself, which promised to confer at last the legitimacy he craved. 'It is time to come to a settlement, and lay aside arbitrary proceedings, so unacceptable to the nation,' he explained to the audience most hostile to the change, the officers of the Army.[80] These were spiky exchanges, with Oliver exasperated at his brothers-in-arms' complaints that a resumption of monarchy would betray the Good Old Cause and open the door to Charles Stuart. It was the major-generals, he reminded them, who had urged him to call a Parliament to finance their regime and war with Spain and who had a hand in selecting its members. It was they who had meddled in it, not he, and yet now they complained to him? As to the title of king, had they not previously pressed it upon him in the first iteration of the *Instrument*? For himself, he railed, 'he loved not the title, a feather in a hat, as little as they did' but the nation had to be settled somehow, and this was the will of Parliament. More than the title of king, it was in his eyes the new Other House that would be essential in checking the power of an intolerant House of Commons.[81]

Oliver had personal, family considerations to weigh alongside the political as he agonised in these long weeks. For years now, while he had done the work of a monarch his nearest and dearest had suffered the accusations of living like royalty without the protection it afforded. Richard and Henry had to live under constant suspicions of their ambition, their public careers unstable and ambiguous, while uncertainty about Oliver's coming kingship had halted young Mary and Frances's marriage negotiations. Frances's love life was in a particular tangle. She had fallen in love with 23-year-old Robert Rich, grandson and heir of the parliamentary grandee the Earl of Warwick and descendant of the slippery Richard Rich, Thomas Cromwell's protégé. Robert had lost his venerated mother young and was a somewhat wayward dandy, described by Richard Cromwell as 'my lady Frances's gallant, flying his plumes in Whitehall'.[82] Although he would one day inherit the earldom of Warwick and the beautiful Leez Priory in Essex, Oliver was unimpressed, taking 'a dislike to the young person' who he had heard was 'a vicious man, given to play, and such like things'.[83] Consequently, he played hardball negotiating a marriage settlement with Robert's grandparents. But Frances fought her corner to force the issue: 'truly I must tell you privately', Mary confided to Henry, 'that they are so far engaged, as the match cannot be broke off. She acquainted none of her friends with her resolution, when she did it'. Whether 'it' was an anticipation of her wedding night, Mary certainly believed Frances 'ought to beg of God to pardon her in her doing of this thing'.[84] And she was not alone in her suspicions, for Andrew Marvell later alluded to Frances and Robert's pre-marital intimacy in his composition for Mary's wedding.

Remarkably, at the height of this kingship crisis in April 1657 when Oliver was wracked by the weightiest concerns of state, Henry's father-in-law reported to him that there 'hath bin some troubles about the business of Mr Rich and my lady Frances; they seem to me yet to continue and to trouble the minds of both your father and mother more than anything else'.[85] Now an observer reported to a contact in Paris that the match would be abandoned for 'this new dignity had altered it' and instead 'a match may be found in your parts'.[86] Perhaps with Oliver rumoured to become king, Frances would be married off to a foreign noble or prince. There was even a story that Broghill had proposed a marriage between the exiled Charles II and Frances: a new union of houses, like that between the Lancastrian Henry VII and Elizabeth of York which had healed the Wars of the Roses. Thus would Oliver secure his family's future safety by restoring Charles Stuart as his son-in-law and perhaps grandfathering future monarchs. If this was ever proposed, Oliver reportedly closed the idea down quickly, not only because he did not believe the young king over the water would ever forgive him for his part in executing his father, but because he had heard he was 'so damnably debauched, he cannot be trusted'. Personal qualities still trumped inherited position when it came to the future happiness of Oliver's children.[87]

Yet Oliver could not have failed to reflect that it was his children who would be in the greatest danger of all were he to die suddenly and Charles Stuart find a way to return, however unlikely this outcome seemed for the present. Perhaps accepting the Crown and thereby reducing the Civil Wars to a 'private quarrel between the House of Cromwell and Stuart' would take the wind from the sails of the exiled king, as the Swedish ambassador thought and Charles's chief adviser Edward Hyde himself feared.[88] Henry Cromwell agreed that the new constitution meant 'much greater security is taken against the reviving of Charles Stewart's interest then was heretofore'. Henry also urged his father to listen to his friend Broghill, otherwise he 'must expose these nations and his family to much calamity'.[89] But Henry was careful not to broadcast strong views on the question of kingship itself, about which 'I dare say nothing', he said, as his opinion would be considered 'tainted'. Instead he expressed his 'desire (and I hope all others of his highness's relations do so too) to be prepared with a spirit of self-denial and submission to every future dispensation of providence herein'.[90] Henry did, however, advise his father that 'titles and names are of little moment', and that he could 'not apprehend the necessity' of Oliver taking 'the name of king' which he thought Parliament was too much focused on.[91]

Meanwhile Richard, who sat in Parliament now as MP for Cambridge University having taken the seat over from Henry, was 'shut out' of the debate 'for a wrangler'. Though he was spotted with a copy of the new constitution, he told Henry, 'there is a bar to my pen in state affairs, yet I know no law against brotherly affection'. This did not shield him from 'the spattering dirt which is thrown about here', however, which he thought Henry was well off out of.[92] A veiled remark to Henry criticising those ambitious men standing in the way of national settlement as it would hinder them 'getting into the saddle' suggests his opposition to the Army leaders. He did not need to name them to his brother, he explained continuing his hunting metaphor, 'you having knowledge of the fox by his smell'.[93]

Spring passed in collective anxiety. Oliver paced the palace and played for time, smoking heavily and wrestling with the inner voices that spoke to him loudest of all: the 'councel of God, and of my own heart'.[94] He asked whether he could accept part of the new constitution but not the whole and was told no. Meanwhile, those around the Lord Protector watched him closely, reporting his every mood swing. 'His highness keeps everybody in suspense as to his acceptance of the Advice,' Thurloe told Henry. 'Certainly H[is] H[ighness] hath great difficulties in his own mind, although he hath had the clearest call that ever man had.'[95] Though Oliver tried to listen to his own thoughts, those of others constantly intruded upon them. Some he solicited – on many nights he put 'aside his greatness' to invite the kinglings Thurloe, Whitelocke and Broghill to discuss the issue with him privately over a pipe and sometimes a pen when they soothed themselves by composing poetry together.[96] Others found their way to him. An old Army colleague who had 'gone along with you from Edge-hill to Dunbar' wrote to warn him against the Crown, reminding him of the tears Oliver had shed on the battlefields which were 'bottled by God himself' and urging him to 'not provoke the vials of God's wrath to break the glasses where your tears yet are'.[97] The Quaker George Fox, coming upon him brooding on a walk in St James's Park, added his two penn'orth, counselling that 'they that would put him on a crown would take away his life' and that Oliver should 'mind the crown that was immortal'.[98]

These questions spoke to Oliver's own doubts that God had rejected monarchy and would think him sinful and ambitious for taking it up again. By becoming king, Oliver risked repeating the sin of the Bible's Achan whose greed at taking 'the accursed thing' after the siege of Jericho had angered God, bringing destruction not only upon himself but his whole family.[99] It was Fleetwood and Desborough who could work this angle most powerfully, as they did at a private dinner party recounted by Ludlow and, fatefully, 'in the very nick of time' on 6 May – the day before Oliver was due to meet with Parliament's committee to give his answer – when they ambushed the Lord Protector with Lambert walking in St James's Park and threatened to resign their commissions if he became king.[100] They probably acted on intelligence that Oliver was about to accept the crown: this was what the French ambassador reported.[101] Whitelocke too noted that Oliver had told members of his family as much, which may have informed Francis Russell to write to Henry on 27 April with less caution than his circumspect son-in-law would have desired: 'I do in this (I think so) desire to take leave of your lordship, for my next is likely to be to the Duke of York. Your father begins to come out of the clouds, and it appears to us that he will take the kingly power upon him.'[102]

Yet when Russell next wrote on 25 May it was not to a prince, and indeed a chastened postscript hoped his new letter would overtake the last. For on 8 May 1657, after two months' anguished deliberation, Oliver had astonished everyone by refusing the crown – his own 'accursed thing'. 'I cannot undertake this government, with the title of a king,' he told the flabbergasted Parliament gathered under the gaze of James I from the Banqueting House ceiling.[103] Oliver could see the legal convenience of kingship but not its spiritual necessity. Indeed, kingship was rooted in the past, not the future, and would not give him the flexible means to the ends he craved: leading an uncertain England into the Promised Land. To take the crown would be an ignoble, prideful step, unsanctioned by God and contrary to all he had laboured for. Ultimately Oliver had listened to the emotional appeals of his Army brethren which echoed those of his own conscience, choosing the will of God over that of the people expressed in Parliament: his own version of the divine right doctrine. 'I will not seek to set up that which providence hath destroyed, and laid in the dust,' he declared. 'I would not build Jericho again.'[104]

Parliament had gambled by telling Oliver he could accept all the new constitution or none of it and he had called their bluff. Beaten down, they agreed to pass the whole *Humble Petition* without the title of king. Knitted to the Protectorate by family ties, Fleetwood and Desborough accepted the compromise, but an offended Lambert resigned from the Council and withdrew in state to Wimbledon to nurse the rejection of his beloved *Instrument*. Oliver stripped Lambert of his regiments, gifting one to Richard, but he made sure the man who had been his most important Army deputy and influential councillor received a generous pension. The military interest on the council was weakened, yet this was no clear victory for the civilian faction, nor the rest of the Cromwell family. Richard thought 'the public peace is tumbled and tossed . . . poor nation, what is it we would have?' Henry worried about the 'drowsiness' come over his allies while his father-in-law complained to him 'The truth is your father hath of late made more wise men fools than ever; he laughs and is merry, but they hang down their heads and are pitifully out of countenance.'[105] They were left with neither a monarchy nor a safely hereditary Protectorate while Oliver had what he wanted: the Other House but not the crown.

'He lacked nothing but the crown to appear a veritable king,' Giavarina observed after Oliver's lavish second investiture as Lord Protector on 26 June, though the subject was not closed, as he continued 'and no doubt, if he lives, it will be placed on his head'.[106] Welsh prophecies hailed Oliver as the conquering heir to Arthurian legend who had appeared following 'many tribulations and miseries' to connect England back to its Tudor past after the aberration of the Scottish Stuarts. These used Sir Henry Cromwell's pedigree to claim 'his Highness's lineal descent from the antient princes of Britain, clearly manifesting that he is the conqueror they so long prophesied of', predicting that 'he will be Protector in England, shall be crowned King in London, with great solemnity amongst his Peers, and he shall raign over England 55 years'.[107] But Oliver did not need the title of king to outdo his hero Elizabeth I, declaring himself that there had been 'more proceeds of justice and freedom' under his Protectorate than in 'double the years of either in Queen Elizabeth, King James or the late king', which were to his mind 'Halcyon days of peace'. His newly polished Protectorate, meanwhile, was perhaps the Elizabethan 'monarchical republic' just in reverse – a republic dressed up in the rich garments of monarchy. The similarities did not end there though, for beneath the glittering veneer, Oliver's Protectorate retained the canker at the heart of the childless Elizabeth's golden reign: an undeclared succession in the hands of a sovereign unwilling to face their own end.

If the future remained constitutionally uncertain, a series of 'domestic triumphs' showed that the younger generation of the Cromwell family would be central to it and the direction it took. Oliver's son Richard helped to organise his investiture and rode with him in his carriage, while his sons-in-law Charles Fleetwood and John Claypole were also prominent in the ceremony. Richard himself now took over his father's chancellorship of Oxford University, with his own grand installation at Whitehall on 29 July, and was later added to the Council of State. He undertook his chancellorship with great conscientiousness, applying himself to the day-to-day affairs of the university, ably assisted by his Aunt Robina's husband John Wilkins of Wadham who who advised him regularly, sending him previous Chancellors' letters to imitate and liaising with his private secretary.[108] Henry was finally promoted to Lord Deputy of Ireland (the role he had been effectively occupying since Fleetwood's departure two years earlier) and also elevated *in absentia* as a 'lord' to the new Other House alongside Richard.

Frances, meanwhile, was finally allowed to engage herself to Robert Rich while negotiations for a match for Mary which had been in limbo during the kingship crisis now resumed.[109] Her intended was a 29-year-old widower from the upper echelons of the Yorkshire gentry, Thomas Belasyse, Viscount Fauconberg. Though from a Catholic and largely Royalist family, Fauconberg himself was neither, and Oliver's intermediary – his nephew-in-law William Lockhart – found him 'a person of great merit with all the qualities to fit him for the service of his Highness and the country, for which he professes great zeal'.[110] Though an arranged match to bring another noble family in behind the Protectorate, Mary was delighted with Fauconberg, who was 'a person that hath a greater kindness to me than ever I could and have expected', and relieved that God 'has been pleased to despose of my heart so as that I have ben obedient to my parents'.[111] Oliver, meanwhile, lost no time in co-opting Fauconberg into the family business, nominating him to the Other House and gifting him one of John Lambert's regiments.

The engagements created a great stir when they were announced, such was the superior pedigree of the younger two sisters' husbands to the olders' of a decade earlier, and the Fauconberg match in particular caused universal amazement given the Viscount's notorious Royalist relations. 'Then the Earl of Warwick's grandchild and the Lord Falconbridge [Fauconberg] married his [Oliver's] two daughters; such pitiful slaves were the nobles of those days,' Lucy Hutchinson commented caustically. Oliver may have refused the crown, but it was clear to her these matches showed 'that Cromwell now intended to confirm the government in his own family' and was building the broad power base among the old nobility and former Royalists to support his heirs.[112]

A softening culture and hopeful outlook abounded in wider society with maypole festivities restarting and women wearing make-up again. London buzzed with entertainment opportunities from flirting in the Spring Gardens and shopping at the New Exchange to swimming, playing archery and tennis at Lisle's and Gibbons' Tennis Court, watching wrestling, rope-dancers or dancing horses, socialising in the new coffee houses and going to concerts and the opera. Newly translated French romances were all the rage while the handbook *The Arts of Wooing and Complimenting* caused a stir. The artist John Michael Wright used a deeply romantic style to paint Frances Cromwell, probably for her engagement. She sits in an ethereal landscape swathed in bluebell and lavender satin and draped in pearls, a white dove soft in her hands and fashionable black silk bracelet calling attention to her slim arms, her unstructured dress even lower cut and more cutting edge than Lely's sensuous portrait of Betty.[113]

The weddings themselves in November 1657 heralded this new atmosphere.[114] 'There seems to be a different spirit, dances having been held again during these past days, and the preachers of the older times are withdrawing from it,' the French ambassador observed after the wedding festivities, even if 'The subalterns of the army grumble at it.'[115] It was rumoured that Oliver indulged his daughters and sons-in-law by allowing them traditional Anglican marriage services after their official civil unions.[116] If so, the spirit of healing and settling was abroad indeed. Though technically private functions, theirs were effectively royal weddings, held a week apart at Whitehall and Hampton Court and celebrated, commented a sneering Hyde, 'with all imaginable pomp and lustre'.[117] 'The discourse of the town has been much filled up with the great marriage at Whitehall,' a contemporary noted, 'which was solemnized there three or four days last week, with music, dancing and great feasting, and now it begins two or three days at the Earl of Warwick's.'[118] The details of both were grandly reported in *Mercurius Politicus* to an eager public.[119] An orchestra of 48 violins and 50 trumpets played for the guests to engage in 'mixt dancing' until 5am, causing considerable comment, not least about the former Royalist courtiers who took part.[120] One of these danced with sword and cloak in the Jacobean style before drawing a knife on a prankster who attempted to ink the formerly famous stiletto beard he had shaved off to conform with Protectoral fashion back on his chin. Oliver too engaged in the pranks that family weddings seemed to inspire in him, throwing sack posset among the ladies and snatching off Robert Rich's fashionable periwig before sitting on it.[121] Thus the Stuart and Cromwellian cultures duelled and danced as they forged a new future.

At no moment was this clearer than in the new wedding masques commissioned from Waller, Marvell and Davenant as the Cromwells appropriated the ultimate royal art form.[122] Frances likely danced the part of the goddess Venus at her wedding ('Fair Venus from the Ocean sprang, she from the Prince that rules the sea') while Oliver himself may have acted the non-speaking part of the God Jove at Mary's. The older Royalist courtiers in the audience may have remembered watching Henrietta Maria descend from a heavenly cloud bursting through rays of light to be enthroned at Charles I's side and bring harmony to his fractious kingdom in 1640. Further back still, a masque had been the vehicle to bring Anne Boleyn before Henry VIII's eyes for the first time when she danced the part of Perseverance in 1522. But now it was the Cromwells, not the Tudors or Stuarts, who ruled both the real and allegorical worlds and whose future was assured. In allusion to the rampant lion of the Cromwell family coat of arms, Oliver was depicted as the Biblical lion slayed by Samson whose strong carcass gave way to sweetness made by the bees nesting inside it. Frances herself was the honey and 'So Honey from the Lion came, And sweetness from the strong.' Thus were the military and civilian factions so long at odds urged now to unite by the reassuring vision that their hero Oliver's warlike life would be followed by a peaceful future under a new generation of Cromwells.

Part Four: Infamy

You've both got Cromwell on the brain.

Lyrics to popular Edwardian music hall song 'It's A Bit Of A Ruin' by Harry Bedford and Terry Sullivan

Ten

Endings

And Richard yet, where his great parent led,
Beats on the rugged track: he, virtue dead,
Revives, and by his milder beams assures;
And yet how much of them his grief obscures?
He, as his father, long was kept from sight
In private, to be viewed by better light;
But opened once, what splendour does he throw?
A Cromwell in an hour a prince will grow.

Andrew Marvell, 'Ode Upon the Death of O.C.' (1658)

Annus horribilis

It was to a London baking in summer heat that the government shared the news of a miraculous 'deliverance' on the sand dunes around the Channel port of Dunkirk. The allied British-French forces had stalled the surging enemy, speeches were made and a grateful nation gave thanks.[1] The second time this happened, in 1940, Winston Churchill may have thought back to the first, in 1658. He was, after all, a student of Oliver Cromwell, whose surname was even now the codeword for the threatened German invasion and the planned defence against it. Back then it was a Spanish-Stuart armada which loomed over the narrow English Channel. 'Twas ever thus for our Island nation, as Churchill explained. But Oliver's New Model veterans and Cardinal Mazarin's troops had fought on the beaches to rout the Spanish and put their Royalist allies to flight, including the Duke of York, the future James II. Spanish-held Dunkirk surrendered and was handed over by the French to the ecstatic English who had waited a century to wipe clean the shame of Queen Mary I losing her father's treasured Calais in 1558. Oliver Cromwell had redeemed the Tudors' honour. 'Since him away the dismal tempest rent / Who once more joined us to the continent; Who planted England on the Flandric shore / And stretched out frontier to the Indian ore,' as Marvell enthused, while Hyde marvelled that Oliver's 'greatness at home was but a shadow of the glory he had abroad'.[2]

The 19-year-old future 'sun king' of France, Louis XIV, presented the town keys of Dunkirk himself to Oliver's representative, the key figure behind the alliance who now took over government of the English town, his nephew by marriage William Lockhart.[3] Lockhart symbolised much of what distinguished Oliver's Protectorate: its open-minded inclusivity, veneration of character and talent, and the centrality of the Cromwell family. A Scot, Lockhart had acted as an emissary for Charles I at the end of the First Civil War, fought in the Scottish-Royalist army which invaded England in 1648 and been taken prisoner by John Lambert at the battle of Preston. Yet Lockhart was tall and strong, a 'gallant and sober person' who had spent an adventurous youth in the Dutch and French armies. Impressing Oliver as a Scottish delegate in the 1652 Commonwealth negotiations over England's union with Scotland, Lockhart served in the brief Nominated Assembly and in 1654 was taken fully into the Protectoral bosom when he married Robina Sewster, the daughter of Oliver's long-dead sister Anna. With a firstborn son 'Cromwell' in the cradle, the loyal Lockhart was rewarded with the vital post of ambassador in Paris to negotiate Oliver's alliance with Mazarin which the failure of the Western Design had reinvigorated. His instructions were to persuade the French to fund a joint campaign to take and carve up Spanish-held Flanders and to secure the protection of the Huguenots.

Oliver and Mazarin's partnership was a delicate one, navigating the mutual mistrust of Protestant and Catholic powers. Much of French Catholic opinion was against the alliance and Lockhart had needed to keep his head down, shutting himself up in his house to avoid the hostile Parisian public.[4] Yet Lockhart was an adroit diplomat and well-liked at the court; Robina too who presided over their ambassadorial residence lavishly furnished from the former royal collection, and who was honoured by the Queen of France when she took leave of her before returning to England at the onset of the fighting season.[5] The French government had turned decisively from the exiled Stuart to the empowered Cromwellian interest, forcing Charles II to relocate to the Spanish Netherlands. On his own way out of France, Charles's brother James, Duke of York, happened to stop at the same post-house where Lockhart was staying. Snatching up his arms, Lockhart and the Duke stared daggers at each other as local people gathered to watch the showdown. James later claimed the French people would have fallen upon Lockhart had James given them 'the least word or intimation'.[6] Yet it was the Stuart prince who was ridden out of town and the Cromwellian ambassador who was feted at court after a quick visit back to London to be knighted by his delighted uncle Oliver – his second knighthood, having received one already from Charles I in 1646.

With the deal struck and the campaign underway, the veteran soldier Sir William Lockhart took to the field himself, commanding the English Army at the victorious battle of the Dunes around Dunkirk, leading them in a courageous charge up a sandbank. With Dunkirk his, Lockhart watched the reward of his hard work as the Allied forces advanced triumphantly through Flanders. England had its prized continental port, cleared of the pirates who had harried English shipping in the channel, and all Europe paid attention. 'Proud Rome, with dread, the fate of Dunkirk heard,' the Protectorate poets wrote in praise of Oliver, the 'English Lion' who 'made us Freemen of the Continent'.[7] Lockhart then governed with scrupulous care, protecting the Catholic inhabitants from the Puritan zealotry of the English soldiers and building a Fort Oliver a mile south of the town. Managing troops and civilians – the wounded, dying and irate – organising supplies and defence, liaising with the French army and government, his was no easy task but 'a work of so excessive fatigue, as I am not able to do what every minute requires from me', as Lockhart told Thurloe in one of his many long and meticulous updates.[8]

Lockhart was not the only member of the Cromwell family who could take credit for the Anglo-French success. In May, Oliver sent his new son-in-law, Mary's husband Viscount Fauconberg, across the Channel to sweeten the accord and 'kiss the royal hand'. As Gregory Cromwell had done in 1540, Fauconberg sailed over to Calais 'with great pomp' accompanied by a retinue of 100 men in two ships and gifts of hunting dogs and 'fine horses'. Oliver sent him with an effusive letter of recommendation, writing to Louis that though his son-in-law 'be a person who, unless we deceive ourselves, carries his own recommendations about him, where soever he goes; yet if he shall find himself somewhat the more favoured by your Majesty for our sake, we shall think ourselves honoured and obliged by the same kindness'.[9] Fauconberg certainly received princely treatment during his five-day visit. He was greeted by noble emissaries from the King and Queen at the quayside, the royal couple themselves watching his arrival from the town walls. Louis and Mazarin talked with him for many hours both in public and private – the King without a hat as a sign of respect to Oliver – while two feast tables were provided for his retinue. Fauconberg would have been pleased too to hear the court's praise for Lockhart. 'As to the siege of Dunkirk,' he reported, 'I find they infinitely esteem my lord Lockhart for his courage, care, and enduring the fatigue beyond all men they ever saw. These were their own words.' He knew Lockhart well himself as the friend and agent who had arranged his marriage to Mary. When Fauconberg left, Louis gave him a gold box inlaid with diamonds decorated with the arms of France and containing the King's miniature, while Mazarin gifted him twelve pieces of Genoese velvet and a set of Gobelin tapestry, and gold medals and money were spread about his companions.[10]

Fauconberg's visit was well-received by both sides. Mazarin proclaimed him a 'fort honnete seigneur' (very honest lord).[11] 'Your personal appearance in this negotiation did, without doubt, make it succeed the better,' Henry Cromwell wrote to his brother-in-law. 'I am glad his highness made so happy choice; I hope it is a good omen: and I hope good things will always attend your lordship like the French victory, which it seems trod upon your heels.'[12] Oliver, meanwhile, lost no time in returning the favour, receiving a high-status French delegation in the form of Mazarin's nephew and the King's Chief Gentleman of the Bedchamber in June. Fauconberg was again in the front line of court ceremonies, entertaining 'the Monsieurs' 'even nights as well as days', taking them to see Oliver at Whitehall and hunting near Hampton Court, so much so he took to his bed after they left, delaying his planned honeymoon north to show Mary his Yorkshire estates.[13]

This journey, when it finally took place in July, was less a honeymoon than a royal progress as the newlyweds of dual Royalist and Cromwellian heritage were ceremonially welcomed by fawning local dignitaries and huge crowds at every stop. Outside York they were received by the Lord Mayor, aldermen and 1,000 local worthies on horseback and, over the many feasts and entertainments, Fauconberg had much to tell his northern countrymen of the Lord Protector, his bride's father, of his allies Louis XIV and Cardinal Mazarin, and of Cromwell's Ironsides' triumph at Dunkirk.[14] When they eventually reached the Fauconbergs' house, the former Augustinian Priory of Newburgh, Mary found a home befitting her station: a grand house with a long gallery set in a large park with a great fishpond at the foot of the Hambleton hills. The West Country was similarly honoured that summer with a stately progress by Richard Cromwell and his wife Dorothy, dispatched by Oliver to spread the project of Cromwellian healing and settling to the former Royalist heartlands. Outside Bristol they were met by the local dignitaries with 600 mounted citizens and gentry, the city's cannons fired as they entered and the mayor hosted them at a banquet in the evening.[15] Richard enjoyed himself, wishing only that when at Bath he could have been at liberty to continue across the sea to see Henry, telling him 'I can assure [you] my affections often employs there sails for Ireland, but our bodies are too heavy for our souls.'[16]

The young ambassadors must have been relieved at an incident-free journey after Richard's recent run of terrible luck. Only weeks earlier he was injured when his coach crashed after he and his father had launched a new warship called the *Richard*. The previous year he had not only been hurt by the Banqueting House staircase collapse in February, but in September had taken a terrible fall while out hunting in the New Forest, dislocating his knee and smashing his thigh bone. This incident was 'a very great affliction to his highness and his family', not only for their personal fears for Richard's recovery but for what portent the accident to the Protector's eldest son could mean coming so soon after Oliver's kingly investiture. As an anxious Thurloe explained to Henry, 'If a sparrow falls not to the ground without the providence of God, much less doe such things fall upon a person of his quality by chance.'[17] Commentators also made the link between Richard's accident and his father's status, noting the significance that 'Prince Richard' had been hurt in the New Forest, 'that fatal place to the sons of our princes' where William the Conqueror's son and successor William Rufus had been killed.[18]

❦ ❦ ❦

The family were right to worry about their future. For where 1658 brought summer jaunts for two of the young Cromwell couples, the year had begun in tragedy for two others. The atmosphere at court was already tense with the abject failure of the second parliamentary session in the bitter January cold as MPs attacked the new Other House, leading to the familiar cycle of an angry Oliver dissolving a Parliament he had opened in great hope. The Other House was vulnerable to challenge by republicans who resented its check on the Commons' powers and conservatives who objected to its diverse membership of new life peers they considered upstarts in place of the old hereditary nobility. Accusations of nepotism did not help, with the second chamber denied as no more than Cromwell's 'sons and kindred, flattering courtiers, corrupt lawyers, degenerated swordmen, and . . . most of them self-interested salary-men.'[19] There was something in this. Though Oliver had invited some of the old nobility to join – including his former allies Lord Saye and Sele and Lord Wharton – they refused. Moreover, at least 15 out of the 70 nominees were Oliver's relations, including his two sons, Fleetwood, Desborough and Lockhart.[20] Parliament's dissolution and the triumph in Flanders turned up the volume of the stubborn rumours that Oliver would take the title of king which continued to play in the background as unsettling mood music. It was said two velvet caps 'worn only by princes' were commissioned by the Master of the Wardrobe.[21]

Meanwhile the Protectorate's enemies kept up their plots, the revelation of each heaping more pressure on Oliver to name his successor under the new constitution. The conspiracy uncovered in 1658 was particularly upsetting for the family as it involved Fauconberg's uncle by marriage and the Anglican Reverend John Hewett, who was a favourite cleric of Oliver's daughters and had likely performed the religious service at Mary and Fauconberg's wedding. The Fauconbergs and Betty reportedly pleaded with Oliver for the conspirators' lives, Mary even possibly enlisting the help of Mazarin, but this time to no avail and the plotters were executed.[22] Betty's ultimate loyalty was to the father she adored, however, as she wrote to her sister-in-law Henry's wife thanking God for 'delivering my father out of the hands of his enemies . . . for certainly not only his family would have been ruined, but in all probability the whole nation would have been involved in blood'.[23] The shock sent Betty into a reflective mood, contemplating 'the muttableness of these things', just as the Swedish ambassador Christer Bonde had wondered as he watched the Cromwells receive ambassadors in the Banqueting House, the shrine to Stuart divine right. So much change could only cause such musings.

As for death, the winter chill claimed its first victim in Oliver's niece Lavinia, the new wife of Richard Beke, captain of his Life Guard.[24] Lavinia was close to her uncle, aunt and cousins who had housed her for a time at the Cockpit and hosted her recent wedding at Whitehall. But her distressing death was only the beginning. Robert Rich fell ill soon after his triumphant wedding to his dancing Venus Frances Cromwell. He may have been suffering from 'scrofula' (then known as the King's Evil but now as an infection of the lymph nodes) for some time. When he and Frances had been courting, Robert's grandmother the Countess of Devonshire urged him to look after his health now more than ever given their 'romance'.[25] Now Robert deteriorated into 'languishing sickness' and he summoned his former tutor John Gauden to sit with him, comfort and advise him on which books to read to live a better life. Before his illness he had often told Gauden he thought he would die younger than his mother, who had died at 27. Now aged 23, there was no escape from what was coming. On the day Rich died, Gauden said, 'he deplored . . . the vain hopes of living which he had had, and that it was so late'. It was 16 February, the same day Lavinia died, and soon Rich 'calmly and suddenly expired without any great contest with death'.[26] Thurloe caught the moment in the two-sentence postscript of his latest letter to Henry, writing 'Mr. Rich is very weak, and like to dye. Since my writing, Mr. Rich is dead.'[27]

Nineteen-year-old Frances was beside herself with grief: 'nothing in the world can repair my loss,' she wrote to Henry in anguish. 'I hope it is my earnest desire to get him for my husband that will never die.'[28] Gauden spoke of the couple's devotion in the funeral sermon he delivered, which Frances subsequently asked him to publish as a 'monument' to her husband.[29] This he was well-qualified to do as the likely compiler of Charles I's spiritual autobiography *Eikon Basilike*. Gauden dedicated the publication to Frances in recognition of her devotion to Robert, for if the 'experience of virtuous love, conjugal respect, extraordinary tenderness, and passionate prudence . . . had not preserved his life, nothing could'.[30] The 'sudden eclipse and fall of this great star, which was but lately risen to its lustre and conspicuity', was marked by three days of formal mourning at court where

Oliver himself wore the traditional purple of a grieving king.[31] 'You have all contributed (what you can) to clothe this skeleton with a robe of state,' Gauden observed, as Rich's body lay 'in great state' in Warwick House, in the same rooms in which he had so lately celebrated his wedding.[32] It was done 'as they used to do for the great in the old days,' a witness said, 'so that at least he died as a prince.'[33]

The Earl of Warwick, though he showed great love and consideration to Frances, could not recover from the death of his only grandson, who he had indulged as his 'small cur', and compounded the Cromwell family's distress by dying a few months later, followed within a year by his son, Robert's father.[34] All were interred in the magnificent Rich family chapel at Felsted Church, yards from where the young Robert Cromwell had been buried 20 years earlier when he had died at school. Richard Cromwell must have thought of his long-lost older brother – the boy who should have been his father's heir – as he sat with Fauconberg representing the Cromwell family at Rich's funeral. Perhaps they visited his grave.[35]

❦ ❦ ❦

When Lockhart wrote to Thurloe on 15 June to tell him he was 'now master of Dunkirk' he had prayed 'the Lord continue his protection to his highness . . . and his family prosper'.[36] But the Lord had not listened. Two of Oliver and Elizabeth's baby grandchildren died: Bridget and Charles Fleetwood's daughter Anne, and Betty and John Claypole's son Oliver. Grief at the loss of the second of these weakened Betty in the face of the illness, probably cancer, which she had suffered from for some years. She had been seriously ill in December 1655, prompting the doctor to observe of Oliver and Elizabeth, 'I never saw two parents so affected (or more) than my lord protector and her highness.'[37] 'My lady Elizabeth continues very ill,' Fleetwood now informed Henry on the same day Lockhart wrote to Thurloe in June 1658, 'and as I fear, unless the Lord supports her, will be much worse, by the death of her youngest son Oliver: the Lord sanctify those sore dispensations!'[38] The Claypoles had hoped to visit Henry that summer but that was now impossible.[39] 'My sister Elizabeth is yet under heavy afflictings,' Richard told him on 2 June, and it was 11 days later that Betty herself had written to Henry's wife with her gratitude for Oliver's escape from assassination – her one surviving letter – opening 'I must beg your pardon, that I do not write to you so oft as I would do; but in earnest, I have been so extreme sickly of late, that it has made mee unfit for anything.'[40]

Betty's illness prevented Frances similarly writing to her sister-in-law, as she explained in a postscript to the same letter that she sent Henry expressing her terrible grief at losing her husband: 'my sister Elizabeth's going into the country tomorrow I had no time. She hath been very ill, but blessed be God we hope she is in the mending hand'.[41] Perhaps Frances placed her hopes in the remedy her former grandmother-in-law the Countess of Devonshire sent to her, perhaps in the healing waters summoned from Tunbridge, or the country air at Hampton Court.[42] But Betty's agonies continued. The Fauconbergs hurried back from Yorkshire to be by her side and Oliver sat up with her all night, eventually bringing all government to a standstill while he kept his vigil: 'the sickness of the Lady Elizabeth, which hath been and is a great affliction to him, hath hindered the consideration of these matters which my former letters mentioned, that very little or nothing hath been done therein for these fourteen days; which makes all men to stand at a gaze, and to doubt very much what will be the issue,' Thurloe wrote on 27 July.[43] Two days later Betty was shaken with fits and seemed to die before reviving again to great 'wonderment', prompting Richard to hope 'our dark and disconsolate family may once again revive and live', and that his father too would recover from his own illness accompanying his pre-emptive grief.[44]

It was a cruel false hope. We glimpse the paralysed family a few days later in the report of the Dutch ambassador Nieuport who, 'understanding that the lord protector and the whole court was in great sadness for the mortal distemper of the lady Claypole', waited to see Oliver at Whitehall before being summoned out to Hampton Court for a few snatched words with him on the State General's concerns. Oliver heard the headlines, but Nieuport wisely decided he 'did not think fit to trouble him with a large discourse', enabling Oliver to hurry away with promises to pick up the conversation once he was back in London the next week.[45]

Betty died at 3 am on 6 August, her final hours with her agonised father immortalised by Andrew Marvell who saw it for himself.

She lest He grieve hides what She can her pains,
And He to lessen hers his Sorrow feigns:
Yet both perceiv'd, yet both conceal'd their Skills,

And so diminishing increast their ills:
That whether by each others grief they fell,
Or on their own redoubled, none can tell.[46]

Mercurius Politicus reported her loss with reverence, remarking on 'her virtue, being a lady of an excellent spirit and judgment, and of a most noble disposition', while Oliver's contemporary biographer Samuel Carrington wrote of the 'majesty of her comportment' and 'Amazonian-like death, despising the pomps of the earth, and without any grief, save to leave an afflicted father perplexed at her so sudden being taken away' so that 'her death stuck more to his heart than all the heavy burdens of his affairs'.[47] Carrington contrasted the glorious victory at Dunkirk with the dark despair of Betty's death, even claiming the next success of the Flanders campaign – the capture of Gravelines – was won in retribution for her loss.

The leading princess of the Protectoral court was given an Arthurian funeral. A torchlit flotilla of barges floated her downstream to Westminster at twilight, silent crowds lining the riverbanks. Arriving around 11 pm she lay in the Painted Chamber in a 'stately hearse' before being carried over the road to the Abbey and lowered into the vault of the Henry VII Chapel beside her grandmother, aunt and niece, and her namesake queen, Oliver's idol Elizabeth I.[48] A magnificent posthumous portrait was commissioned from John Michael Wright which depicts Betty as Minerva, the Roman goddess of wisdom and daughter of Jupiter, wearing brightly coloured silks under a warrior's breastplate. Her father and their relationship are referenced everywhere in the portrait: in the olive trees, the crowns for his military victories and the cameo portrait – likely her mother's, of her father – in her hand. She leans on a plinth with a carving showing Minerva born from Jupiter's head and the inscription: *Ab Jove Principium* ('From Jove is my beginning'). Oliver had acted the part of Jove at one daughter's wedding only months before, and now he was Jove again to another daughter at her death.[49]

'We have been a family of much sorrow all this summer, and therefore we deserve not the envy of the word,' Richard wrote mournfully to Henry, as *Mercurius Politicus* reported the 'great grief' of Betty's husband John Claypole, her parents and the whole court.[50] Betty's loss was a 'great stroke,' Richard said, but almost worse was to have their sorrows visited 'with greater fears, for it is one thing to have the greatest bough lopped off, but when the axe is laid to the root, then there is no hopes remaining'.[51] The whole Cromwell family was in despair and danger for Oliver, the root of all their fortunes who had been too stricken to attend Betty's funeral, was now himself dying from his grief. As Marvell described it 'And now his Life, suspended by her breath / Ran out impetuously to hasting Death.'[52] Oliver had been ill since her funeral, with pains in his back and stomach, having trouble sleeping and slipping into regular fits.[53] This was a recurrence of the malaria, the 'tertian ague', which Oliver had suffered throughout his life and saw as God testing him, perhaps provoked by a blood infection following a kidney stone. He had always shaken the ague off before, and even now, when he rallied between fits, Oliver took hope of God's favour and his own recovery, reassuring those gathered anxiously around him. 'His highness hath hade very great discoveries of the Lord to him in his sickness,' a breathless Fleetwood reported to Henry, 'and hath had some assurances of his being restored, and made further serviceable in this work.'[54] Yet in reality, Oliver was too weak to fight. As one of his doctors explained to Henry 'The violent sickness of his highness fills me with sad apprehensions . . . His disease is a double tertian ague, which at this season, in a person of his age and constitution of body (being much distempered by his late grief and melancholy, besides his other infirmities) is a very violent companion.'[55] When the Quaker George Fox came upon Oliver riding in the gardens at Hampton Court on one of his better days, he thought he 'looked like a dead man'.[56]

At times, Oliver apprehended the danger he was in – or at least acknowledged his family's concerns. Richard told Henry how 'upon her Highness and his children's coming after dinner to him, he broke out his most secret thoughts . . . that he intended to settle his broken private fortune, having sent for his stewards and officers, desiring us to withdraw and be in readiness to be called in as he should have occasion in our particular concerns'.[57] But if Oliver ever for a moment contemplated the future beyond himself, he did not act upon it and formally choose his successor. Those around him throbbed with anxiety. His valet was sent up to Whitehall to search Oliver's desk for a sealed document in which he had apparently named his heir, but this could not be found despite being 'very narrowly looked for'. Oliver himself was moved up to Whitehall in the vain hope the change would fortify him. From there, on 30 August, Thurloe wrote to Henry, 'I fear our own divisions, which may be great enough, if his highness should not settle and fix his successor before he dies, which truly I believe he hath not yet done.'[58] Increasingly desperate, Thurloe pressed his master to name his heir while Oliver's sons-in-law acted contrasting parts. Writing to Henry the next day, the godly Fleetwood still spoke his belief in Oliver's own assurances of his miraculous recovery, while the pragmatic Fauconberg wrote that Oliver was too ill to name a successor for all Thurloe's attempts, that 'he has not done it, nor do I believe will'.[59]

Perhaps earthly concerns stayed Oliver's hand: he could not bring himself to nominate Richard publicly, endorsing the hereditary succession he had rejected for so long and confirming popular assumptions about his ambition for himself and his sons, but neither could he choose another and risk political fallout and a fractured family. Perhaps it was the heavenly reaction Oliver feared if he appeared to interfere with providence, hastening his own end by choosing his heir.[60] Lying in his grand bed, Oliver rambled and questioned, talking to himself and summoning his fierce faith in this, his final adversity. He had ministers read the Bible aloud to him, returning again and again to the passage from Philippians, 'I can do things through Christ which strengthened me', and recounting how this passage had saved his life when his eldest son Robert died. A tempest raged outside during his last hours while, inside the hush of the royal rooms at Whitehall, Oliver held his wife Elizabeth's hand and searched harder and harder, with fearful humility and loving joy, for the Lord who would gather him up.

At last, on 3 September, the anniversary of his great victories at Dunbar and Worcester, he found him. Oliver's thoughts turned to those he would leave behind, and he spoke to God of them. 'Thou hast made me, though very unworthy, a mean instrument to do them some good, and thee service; and many of them have set too high a value upon me, though others wish and would be glad of my death; Lord, however thou do dispose of me, continue and do good for them.' Offered a drink he declined, saying: 'It is not my design to drink or to sleep, but my design is to make what haste I can to be gone.' A few hours later he was.[61]

Oliver slipped at once out of life and into legend. The great storm stirred up superstitions 'as if the elements, as well as men, had waited for this day'.[62] Edmund Waller used his pen to urge 'We must resigne; Heaven His great Soul do's claime / In stormes as loud, as His

Immortall Fame.'[63] Enemies and admirers alike simply could not believe the giant who had 'kept such a bustle in the world, should not now be able to keep himself from crumbling into dust'. That he who 'shook all Europe by his name and forces' could not 'keep an ague from shaking him . . . even in the midst of victories and successes, that had raised both great fears and great expectations of him in both his enemies and allies'. That death had 'confined all his vast ambitions, all his cruel designs into the narrow compass of the grave'.[64] Never had there been such a reminder of man's mortality. As Oliver's servant John Maidstone reflected, 'A larger soul, I think, hath seldom dwelt in a house of clay.'[65] The news reverberated across Europe while for most ordinary people, of course, life continued as normal. 'Cromwell died, people not much minding it,' as one observer put it.[66]

'Moses my servant is dead,' Hugh Peter took as the text for his sermon in Whitehall Chapel the next Sunday.[67] Like Moses, Oliver had gone before he and his people had reached the Promised Land. He may have looked at the faces of his family gathered around his canopied bed with love, but he had left them possibly – certainly publicly – without naming his successor and securing their future. But for himself, at least, Oliver had confounded his enemies, inconveniently departing life peacefully on his promised day, dying a sovereign in his kingly bed, untouched by their hands. He was, 'the whole world knows . . . a man of war, yet he died in peace'.[68] Yet family was his beginning and his end. For all the stately pomp of his final days, Oliver's life had come full circle, so his ordinary past caught up with him. Many times death had come for him before: in the bullet that grazed his neck at Marston Moor, in the crippling illness in Scotland brought on by a hard campaign, in the carriage accident in St James's Park, in the guns and bombs of his would-be assassins. But it was the malaria he had caught as a boy in the fens that claimed him, and only as it found him weakened by grief for the beloved daughter born to him while an undistinguished Huntingdon gentleman. Only love could kill the great soldier and statesman who was otherwise indestructible. This was clear to all: to the poet Samuel Slater who eulogised Oliver 'Thy Daughter (know) / Toll'd thy Great Bell; the Prim-rose fading young / The old Stock-Gilly-flower could not last long'; to Hyde in exile who believed 'that which broke his peace was the death of his daughter Claypole, who had always been his greatest joy'; and to Marvell, who saw their closeness 'Doubling that knot which Destiny had ty'd' until 'The Parent-Tree unto the grief succeeds':

For he no duty by his height excus'd,
Nor though a Prince to be a Man refus'd:
But rather then in his Eliza's pain.
Not love, not grieve, would neither live nor reign.
And in himself so oft immortal try'd,
Yet in compassion of another dy'd.[69]

Richard IV

In the evening of 3 September 1658, a delegation of privy councillors informed 31-year-old Richard Cromwell that he had succeeded his father Oliver as Lord Protector. The news was proclaimed in London the next day, with cries of 'God save His Highness Richard Lord Protector!'. 'Moses, it is true, is dead, but we have a Joshua succeeding him,' Slater wrote, capturing the hopes of many.[70] There was no immediate disturbance, no violence or bloodshed beyond a barrage of carrot and turnip tops thrown by Oxford students at the announcement that the second of their Chancellors had been elevated to the highest office.[71] Rather, as the news spread across the nations, it was met with the customary bells and bonfires, salutes, trumpets, free flowing wine and beer.[72] 'It hath pleased God hitherto to give his highness your brother a very easy and peaceable entrance upon his government,' Thurloe reported to Henry with relief, 'There is not a dog that wags his tongue, so great a calm are we in.'[73] Yet the public calm masked a private turmoil. Several hours had elapsed between Oliver's death in the afternoon and the Council declaring Richard's succession, hours when the fate of the nation and the Cromwell family rested in the hands of 11 men.

Oliver had left no written evidence of Richard's nomination, but various councillors claimed that he had verbally confirmed his choice to them before he died. This was sufficiently uncertain to necessitate a long discussion, with witnesses summoned to give evidence, and a vote, but not so uncertain as to prevent the politically diverse Council emerging with a unanimous decision. The confused timeline Thurloe and others later gave for Oliver's supposed deathbed nomination has fuelled theories of a cover-up: that they either invented Oliver's declaration or substituted Richard's name for another's such as Charles Fleetwood or John Lambert.[74] Richard perhaps emerged as a compromise candidate both the military and civilian politicians could accept. Alternatively, the discrepancies may simply reflect the anguish of the men handling this crisis even as they processed their grief. 'I am not able to speak or write; this stroke is so sore, so unexpected,' Thurloe wrote to Henry on 4 September, 'the providence of God in it so stupendous, considering the person that is fallen, the time and season wherein God took him away, with other circumstances, I can do nothing but put my mouth in the dust'.[75] Certainly, the 'Chaos of Confusion' Oliver had been warned would follow his death if he did not declare his heir did not come to pass.[76] Even Fleetwood and Desborough fell into line behind Richard, bringing the Army with them, as the Council closed ranks to secure the nations from unrest.

History has famously written off Richard as 'Tumbledown Dick', a country bumpkin ill-suited to his new responsibility. 'A person well-skilled in hawking, hunting, horse-racing, with other sports and pastimes,' a savage critique of the Other House had commented, 'one whose undertakings, hazards, and services for the cause cannot well be numbered or set forth.'[77] Oliver's own anxieties about his son enhanced this popular image; comments like that on hearing the young Richard had overspent his allowance 'I cannot think I do well to feed a voluptuous humour in my son, if he should make pleasure the business of his life, in a time when some precious saints are bleeding, and breathing out their last, for the good and safety of the rest.'[78] But Richard was not the first Cromwell son and heir to cause his father sleepless nights for preferring sports to study, as Gregory had for Thomas. It is partly in consequence of this – the timeless complaints of parents about their youthful offspring – that both men have been dismissed by historians as pale copies of their overachieving fathers, following the anti-Cromwellian James Heath's jeer that, 'The vulture died and out of his ashes arose a titmouse.'[79]

In the last years of his life, Oliver trusted Richard with enough public responsibilities to put the notion that Dick was an inept wastrel firmly to bed. Indeed, promoting Richard to committee chairs, seats in the Commons and the Other House, the Chancellorship of Oxford and a place on the Privy Council, may indicate that Oliver was at least considering choosing his son to succeed him as many contemporaries assumed. He would have seen too the energy, conscientiousness and considerable charm with which Richard applied himself to his positions, which collectively involved sufficient work for Richard to keep a private secretary.[80] These experiences would have helped Richard now as he took the throne, but they hardly amounted to sufficient preparation for assuming stewardship of three nations still recovering from the traumas of civil war. Yet Richard's ill-preparedness did not doom him to fail as has traditionally been assumed. In fact, far from being a hindrance, Richard's inexperience may indeed have been an asset. He could pleasantly surprise with his graceful competence, as Whitelocke found watching his audience with the French ambassador where Richard 'did carry himself discreetly and better than was expected'.[81] Richard was surprisingly good too at public speaking. 'My Lord Protector spoke with such a grace and presence,' a newsletter reported, 'and with such oratory and steadiness, without the least interruption, and soe pertinently to the present occasion, as it was beyond all expectation.'[82]

Richard also made a virtue of his shortcomings by presenting these with winning humility, inviting the advice of others. 'I am not moulded to make speeches, I have infirmity, I want experience, and I want understanding; but I desire that I may learn to do my duty,' he told a church conference in October in the self-deprecating language recognisable from his private letters to Henry, even as he proved his self-criticism wrong by deploying the same successful rhetorical devices as his father. He rejoiced at the discourse he had listened to: 'I might say it is my place to hear what shall come from the mouths of my teachers; and had I such discourse often poured into me, and upon me, I should hope that it might have an impression, and that my short memory might be helped by a continual dropping.'[83]

Most of all, if Richard did not have his father's friends, neither did he have his enemies. He was no regicide, hammer of the Scots and Irish, or dissolver of parliaments. An untainted moderate, Richard attracted Presbyterians and other exiles back into the political fold who could never have countenanced a return under his father, against whom they held a personal animus. The Puritan spiritual writer Richard Baxter told him delightedly that 'many are persuaded that you have been strangely kept from participating in any of our late bloody contentions, that God might make you an healer of our breeches'.[84] Such sentiments likely inspired the loyal declarations that poured into Whitehall from the provinces at Richard's accession. By the end of the year, Richard had received the congratulations of the City of London, 28 counties, 24 towns and 5 contrasting groups of ministers, paeans of praise that eulogised his father, spoke of his throne and called him 'their lawful sovereign and Protector'.[85] The unassuming, inoffensive Richard was thus well-placed to continue the inclusive trajectory of his father's Protectorate, building a wider coalition of support than Oliver had managed, and so securing for it a lasting future.

This promising start did not go unnoticed, as Royalists who had rejoiced at the likely fall of the Protectorate upon Oliver's death gave way to despair. Looking back on this moment, Edward Hyde described how 'Never monarch, after he had inherited a crown by many descents, died with more silence, nor with less alteration; the same or a greater calm in the kingdom than had been before.' He noted Oliver's interment in the 'sepulchre of the kings, and with the obsequies due to such' and how Richard 'inherits all his greatness and all his glory, without that public hate that visibly attended the other'. With foreign princes sending condolences and renewing their alliances, and the English public joyfully praising 'their new Protector', 'the King's condition never appeared so hopeless, so desperate'.[86]

The greatest threat to the new Protector's regime in fact lay closer to home, indeed within his own family. Richard found natural supporters in the talented civilian politicians who had pressed the crown upon his father and, above all, in Thurloe who threw all his political skills at shoring up his prince. Richard could be sure too of the unwavering support of his brother-in-law Fauconberg who continued to negotiate for the regime with the French court, which had itself gone into formal mourning, as the English had done, out of respect for Oliver's death. Gifts of Barbary horses and jewels for Mary Fauconberg continued to oil the relationship between France and the Protectorate. Richard could also count on Henry in Ireland, whom he swiftly promoted to Lord Lieutenant, and loyalty from those Cromwellians governing other outposts: Lockhart in Dunkirk, George Monck in Scotland, and Edward Montagu with the fleet. All, like Montagu, were 'Wholly devoted to old Noll . . . and for his sake a great lover of all his family.'[87]

But Richard did not enjoy similar standing with the English Army. Many of its leaders mistrusted Richard's civilian political advisers while Desborough had a fractious relationship with his nephew despite their kinship. Meanwhile, for the soldiers, Richard was an unknown quantity with Presbyterian leanings who had not shared their intense comradeship forged on the battlefield doing God's work. They did not trust him to tolerate religious radicalism as Oliver had done, nor to refrain from meddling in their affairs. As Richard himself acknowledged to them, 'It is my disadvantage, that I have been so little amongst you, and am no better known to you.'[88] Within weeks, the Army was agitating for political concessions, and Richard went to meet the officers in person to reason with them as his father had done many times before. With considerable bravery and no little dexterity, Richard gave some ground in a well-judged speech, raising pay and appointing his brother-in-law Fleetwood commander though he retained ultimate control for himself. He wooed the officers as 'my father's companions in all his dangers and difficulties' in whom he had 'entire confidence', explaining that 'God hath raised me up in my father's stead, and put me in the same relation towards this nation and you, as he stood in. If now I may have the affections and prayers of my father's old friends . . . I shall esteem it a better portion then any thing else my father hath left me.'[89]

Rumours persisted that Fleetwood and Desborough harboured their own ambitions, however, and Fauconberg and Henry certainly did not trust them. 'I thought those, whom my father had raised from nothing, would not so soon have forgot him, and endeavour to destroy his family, before he is in his grave,' Henry wrote to Richard angrily, also enclosing a copy of his concurrent letter to his 'brother Fleetwood . . . that your highness may see, whether I am mistaken in my apprehension of things'.[90] In this, Henry posed a politely damning series of questions to Fleetwood about how the Army agitation had occurred and complained that the soldiers who revived the 'good old cause' disrespected his father's memory.[91] But Fleetwood at least urged the Army to unity and wrote to Henry that Richard 'hath hitherto much exceeded expectation, and did speak heartily to old friends', though, tellingly, he saw the Army's duty to support him 'that he may be kept up to walk in his father's paths'.[92]

His father, meanwhile, had one more earthly path to take. While government sailed on smoothly, a graceful swan above the surface and urgently paddling feet below, the household grieved their latest and ultimate loss and prepared for Oliver's funeral. 'Here is a sad family on all hands: the Lord support them!' Thurloe had written to Henry on 7 September, speaking of the shellshocked Richard that 'his highness's death is so sore a stroke unto him, and he is so sensible of it, that he is in no condition to write or do yet'.[93] Fauconberg gave Henry a further snapshot of the poleaxed family reeling from 'your incomparable father's death'. 'All the time his late highness was drawing on to his end, the consternation and astonishment of people is inexpressible: their hearts seemed as sunk within them. And if this [was] abroad in the family, your lordship may imagine, what it was in her highness and other near relations. My poor wife, I know not what in the earth to do with her; when seemingly quieted, she bursts out again into passion, that tears her very heart in pieces; nor can I blame her, considering what she has lost. It fares little better with others.'[94]

Mary was still inconsolable a month later, as Fauconberg opened his letter to Henry, 'Your sister is weeping so extremely by me, that I can scarce tell you in plain English', while Marvell recounted Frances's sorrow.[95] The family also had to cope with the loss of a third grandchild in one year, Richard and his pregnant wife Dorothy's baby daughter who died not long after Oliver's death. The loss of this 'illustrious Infant Lady' was 'entertained by their Highnesses with much sorrow of mind', *Mercurius Politicus* reported, and clergy correspondents of the devout new Lady Protectoress sent her spiritual comfort. As always, the death was God's will, and Dorothy's lot 'to bear children for heaven'. Their chief consolation indeed was that God had given 'his late Highness opportunity to see it before his death and to bless it which he did with very remarkable affections again, and again, even several times before he took his leave of it. Surely the child is gone to its grandfather.'[96]

Oliver's mortal remains also had to be dealt with. Faced with the delicate task of burying a sovereign who was not a king, the Council turned to the funeral of the last monarch who had died in his bed as a model: 'it was decided to follow the forms observed at the burial of King James,' Giavarina reported, 'but this will be much greater.' Like James and, more recently, his sons-in-law Henry Ireton and Robert Rich, the Lord Protector lay in state at Somerset House 'in extraordinary pomp'.[97] Members of the public flocked to see him in a candle-lit State bedchamber. Four giant pillars with carved, crowned

English lions and Welsh dragons referencing the Cromwell family's heritage stood at each corner of a State bed, Oliver's arms on great banners between them. Out of sight beneath the bed lay Oliver himself, embalmed, wrapped in lead, and encased in an elegant coffin with gold-hatched ironwork, filled with sweet spices and covered with purple velvet. Lying on the bed was an astonishing lifelike wooden effigy, carved and dressed as the Lord Protector himself in his best clothes, the new suit of uncut grey velvet 'of the Spanish fashion' he had made for Frances's wedding.[98] Over this it wore two purple velvet Robes of Estate edged with gold lace and tassels and trimmed in ermine, an embroidered belt and gilt sword hanging from its waist.

If anyone was in any further doubt as to Oliver's kingly status, the effigy held a sceptre and globe with a crown above its head 'after the antient and most becoming ceremony of the preceding princes of this nation . . . which point of honour is the more due to his memory, by how much he advanced the honour of our country by his incomparable actions, beyond the example of any that swayed the sceptre of his land before him.'[99] Thus old ideas of monarchy blended with new meritocratic notions: Oliver was given the honour due a hereditary king, but he had earned this by his own actions. Only to other monarchs was he now comparable, being for Marvell braver than King Arthur and holier than Edward the Confessor.[100] At some point during the lying in State, the spectacle grew stranger and more awesome still when the effigy was moved into the hall, stood up and its eyes opened and the imperial crown was placed on its head. Lit by hundreds of candles, the soul passed from Purgatory into heaven as the crown Oliver had rejected in life was finally given him in death.[101] 'We are all in a whist,' one observer wrote to a friend with feverish excitement, 'no news stirring but that the old Protector is now got upon his legs again at Somerset House, but when he shall be translated to the rest of the Gods at Westminster I cannot tell. Pray, do you come and see.'[102]

The Protector was transferred to Westminster Abbey in a great funeral procession a few weeks later but, like James I, it was not his own body that received these obsequies but the effigy. 'He is but a man,' Sir Francis Russell had realised during the kingship crisis, and the man had started to decay.[103] This may have been why Oliver's body was secretly buried in the Henry VII chapel of Westminster Abbey a fortnight earlier. Or perhaps his family wanted the simple

Puritan to miss the ritualistic theatre that followed and to say their own private goodbyes. The funeral procession took seven hours, as ambassadors, grandees and the whole Protectoral household down to the lowliest servant, marched to mournful drums with an open chariot bearing the crowned effigy through the soldier-lined streets of London. In their ranks walked the creative lights of the court: the musicians David Fell, John Hingston and his choir boys and the literary luminaries John Milton, Andrew Marvell and John Dryden. Inevitably, the solemnity was punctured by squabbles over precedence, raucous soldiers drinking and smoking, and even a pig reportedly snuffling around the mourners, so Evelyn could call it 'the joyfullest funeral that I ever saw; for there was none that cried but dogs'.[104] Others watched with mixed feelings. Quakers decried the idolatry and hypocrisy while the republican Ludlow reported that 'This folly and profusion so far provoked the people that they threw dirt in the night on Cromwell's escutcheon that was placed over the great gate of Somerset house.'[105] 'The hearse was magnificent, the idol crowned,' the poet Abraham Cowley declared, 'briefly, a great show, and yet, after all this, an ill sight.'[106]

By the time the pageant reached Westminster Abbey, it was cold and dark and the hearse was left abruptly in the Chapel with no prayers, rites or sermons. In the absence of these, the poet Samuel Slater wrote his own which mused on Oliver's last journey with the refrain 'Go CROMWELL then, Down to the Abbey go'.[107] Slater shows the Cromwell family colonising the Abbey – Henry VII's chapel the 'dormitory of kings' now 'Cromwell's Chapel' – as Oliver's mother and Betty welcome him home. Here Oliver is the hero of the Reformation, who the dust of Edward VI and Elizabeth I will rise to celebrate on the Resurrection Day. Thomas Cromwell too lurks in this chronicle of the Cromwellian Reformation and the irony of this final resting place for its chief iconoclast: 'But soft, Must Cromwell to an Abbey goe? / The name of Abbeys is to Cromwell's Foe.'[108] Thomas had been present at Oliver's funeral in other ways too. The procession's banner rolls not only celebrated the Hinchingbrooke Cromwells with the Williams family arms and those of the Cromwells' various in-laws, but also Thomas's descendants the Launde Cromwells with the arms of the Royalist Earls of Ardglass. Thus did the branches of Thomas's boys Gregory and Richard join hands for this greatest ceremony of their family.[109] Thomas was there too between the biographical lines at the foot of Oliver's effigy which summarised his life, revealing what mattered to his legend: his Williams–Cromwell inheritance, humble birth and peaceful death, education, military career and victories, culminating in Dunkirk. Over a third of these detailed his family – his ancestors and his children – now as central to Oliver's afterlife as they had been to his life. Oliver Cromwell may not have been born the head of a great dynasty, but he had died as one.

Oliver's funeral marked a brief moment of family unity. Most of Oliver's male relations had walked in his procession, with John Claypole leading the customary riderless 'Horse of Honour' that followed the hearse.[110] With Oliver's sons Henry in Ireland and Richard absent (as traditionally the new monarch should be), the role of chief mourner fell to Charles Fleetwood. Fleetwood's grief for his father-in-law, his great spiritual friend and mentor, was genuine but his role in his brother-in-law's new regime was far from straightforward. For Fleetwood now found himself, as Oliver had once been, an intermediary between the Army and the civilians in government. The tensions between the representatives of both sides on the Council erupted only a few weeks later when an angry Fleetwood accused Fauconberg, the Cromwells' cousin Richard Ingoldsby and Edward Montagu of plotting against him and Desborough. So vicious was the ensuing argument that Desborough became 'so angry as to say he would never set foot in the Council again, if Lord Faulconbridge [Fauconberg] . . . were not excluded'.[111]

Until now the Army's rumblings had been 'skinned over' by Richard's charming cajoling, but the Council's decision to call a Parliament would test their acquiescence.[112] Yet it was convention to summon a Parliament 'at the beginning of every prince's reign', Thurloe told Henry, and it was the only way to raise the money the government desperately needed.[113] The return to the franchise and seat distribution of 1640 and the freest elections in almost two decades resulted in a large and unpredictable Parliament: 'so great a mixture . . . that no man knows which way the major part will incline'.[114] Hopes were high and Richard rose to the occasion, opening the January 1659 session in a spirit of warm conciliation, promising to govern 'by the advice of my two Houses of Parliament', to 'be ready to spend my life' to defend peace, laws and liberties and urging that everyone worked together to make this 'an happy Parliament'.[115] He was received with matching warmth, his words accompanied by 'general hummings' of approval.[116] Though some ambiguity hung over Richard's nomination as the House debated recognising the new Lord Protector, members of all political backgrounds rushed to praise him personally. John Lambert announced that 'we are all for this honourable person that is now in power', while others praised his 'good disposition, free from guile' and lack of personal ambition or intention to 'grasp at greatness'. Even the Commonwealthsmen, alienated since Oliver's dissolution of the Rump Parliament in 1653, confessed their 'love' for his person and pledged to protect him with their lives even as they questioned rule by a single person. One MP even addressed him as 'Richard the Fourth', linking the second Lord Protector Cromwell back even before the Tudors to the mighty Plantagenet kings.[117]

For all the civility, progress was gradual as grandstanding MPs poured over the *Humble Petition and Advice*, re-litigating the balance between executive and legislative authority. The absence of most of Richard's closest civilian advisers from the Commons as they now sat in the Other House deprived him of able parliamentary managers to advance the government's agenda. Debates were so crowded and hot that two successive Speakers collapsed and died. Yet the fact that the *Humble Petition* was accepted as the working constitution this Parliament would refine was a promising start, and by mid- March Giavarina was predicting 'everything will in the end turn out in favour of the Protector' as Thurloe relaxed and Fauconberg shared his 'hopes of a settlement' with Henry in a letter kept short by his 'bad eyes'.[118] The Commons recognised the legitimacy of both Richard as Lord Protector and the Other House, while Richard and his Council got on with government, dispatching the fleet under Montagu to watch developing hostilities in the Baltic as Oliver would have done. But for every two steps forward there was one step back. The more cooperative and constructive Parliament appeared, the more the Army feared it would work with Richard to dismantle its own power. Tensions mounted between the civilian and military factions of the Council once more as an increasingly confident Richard made some tactless missteps such as supporting his relatives in the Army, Richard Ingoldsby and Edward Whalley, when they quarrelled with fellow soldiers.

Matters might have rested there if Richard had not given way to Fleetwood and Desborough's request to convene a Council of the

Officers which met at Fleetwood and Bridget's large home, Wallingford House on the Strand. At the behest of the radical junior officers, the 'Wallingford House group', as Fleetwood, Desborough and their allies would come to be known, drafted a petition, the *Humble Representation*, to the Lord Protector demanding Parliament vote to pay their soldiers. The demand may have been reasonable but the tone was threatening, speaking of 'plucking the wicked out of their places, wheresoever they may be discovered, either amongst ourselves, or any other places of trust'.[119] Richard, the ground beginning to shift beneath his feet, accepted it publicly but may have privately ordered Fleetwood to suppress it before caving in and sending the petition on to Parliament.[120] In a pattern which should have sounded warning bells for all those who remembered the arguments between Parliament and the Army in 1647, the House of Commons reacted with hostility, delaying even debating the *Representation* before passing two resolutions 'distasteful to the army', designed to strengthen parliamentary control over its political activity.[121] Henceforth, Parliament would say when the Council of Officers could meet and no soldier was to disturb Parliament's freedoms. Then they would set about finding money to pay their arrears.

Parliament and the Army seemed set on a collision course yet again, but what would the new Lord Protector do? At past moments like this, Oliver had wielded his powerful influence to prevent conflict or, when it became unavoidable, sided with the Army. He had never managed to prise the sword from the Army's hand and integrate it fully into the peacetime state. Bequeathed this fundamental instability, Richard decided to try the opposite tack to his father: to side with Parliament and confront the Army. Perhaps his emotional distance from the Army would enable him to achieve what his father had not. Fatefully buoyed up by what Broghill's sister Lady Ranelagh called 'his own hopes and his young Councillors', on 18 April 1659 Richard ordered the Council of Officers to follow the Commons' resolutions and disband. The officers ignored him and when Richard summoned Fleetwood 'the messenger returned without an answer'.[122]

The temperature rose, 'those officers, that are of the protector's party, were with him, and have promised him to live and die with him', an informant told the watching Hyde, while the 'same night they were in some fear at Whitehall to have the protector's person ceased [seized] on by the other party; and accordingly were vigilant, had strong guards, and new provision of ammunition'.[123] The brothers-in-law were on the brink of the abyss, but even now the Cromwell family could have avoided the fall. Late at night on 20 April, Fleetwood, Desborough and a few other senior officers met Richard privately in the tense rooms of Whitehall.[124] Richard promised them he would not let Parliament push him into asserting control over the Army but, the very next day, this was exactly what the Commons began to debate, even suggesting the forces be settled as a militia under Parliament. Richard and Fleetwood both found a new decisiveness at the same moment. Fleetwood ordered the Army to gather at St James's Palace as Richard counter-ordered the soldiers to come to him at Whitehall. A few colonels loyal to Richard hastened to his side but their regiments hurried off to Fleetwood and Richard's power vanished with them as 'a general without an army'.[125]

Thousands of soldiers clogged the streets of London, and at midday Desborough marched into the room where Richard and his advisers huddled in confusion and demanded he dissolve Parliament. If he did so 'the officers would take care of him', but if he refused, 'they would do it without him, and leave him to shift for himself'.[126] Richard turned to his civilian advisers Thurloe, Whitelocke, Broghill, Nathaniel Fiennes and Charles Wolsley. While he believed a dissolution 'would be both his ruin and theirs', most of the others recommended he capitulate to the Army's demands.[127] Messengers went back and forth all day, before Desborough stormed back in the evening. By 3 am all niceties were dropped and uncle bullied nephew into submission.[128] Diminished, Richard had little choice but to agree to dissolve Parliament, and in the morning, the Army locked the doors to the Commons. Desborough assured Richard the Protectorate would be safe, but the house of Cromwell which had seemed so unassailable just a few months earlier, now began to tremble.

Richard was down but not out. In the following days, Fleetwood and Desborough met with him regularly, discussing a reduced supremacy where he remained Protector but relinquished control of the Army. Had he galvanised the considerable forces still loyal to him then – Henry's regiments in Ireland, Monck's in Scotland, Lockhart's in Dunkirk and Montagu's fleet – the Protectorate could have survived. But Richard sent out no letters, no distress flares or smoke signals. News of Parliament's dissolution took weeks to reach his allies who received no clear instructions on how to respond. In the absence of these, Monck declined to intervene as, to his mind, Richard's inaction had released him from his 'promise to his Father, or regard to his memory'.[129] Henry was paralysed in a 'waiting frame', with only one consolation, that 'I am glad, at least, that our dear father went off in that glory, which was due to his actings.'[130] When Henry finally heard from Richard it was a letter of mixed messages. On the one hand he spoke vaguely of how the tide could be turned with a mere '500 horse' if he had the assistance of distant forces helped by 'friends and strong places here' and the cooperation of Monck. On the other he urged Henry to 'do nothing that may be for your ruin'. 'Though your provocation is very great and you have a great sense of the honour of my deceased father and the perishing condition of the family,' he warned, 'yet you will be wary what you do for your own sake and the sake of those that shall have an affection with you.' Either way, he did not see that any call to arms had to come from him, complaining: 'I have heard nothing from Scotland, nor Dunkirk, nor fleet.'[131]

If Henry had been allowed to return from Ireland to support Richard during the last eight months, as he had repeatedly asked to do, things might have been very different. Still more so perhaps if Oliver had nominated the able Henry himself as his successor. But Henry's enemies thought him better off out of the way and his friends thought he could do more good from his Irish powerbase. And so Richard was alone and abandoned, holed up at Whitehall a virtual prisoner. 'I am not able to advise,' he wrote again to Henry, 'my friends, my council and my relations having all forsaken me.'[132] He was criticised from all sides: Parliament saw him as a sell-out while the Army still thought he had betrayed them. Meanwhile, at Wallingford House, Fleetwood and Desborough formed a Committee of Safety with the republican MPs who, with the agitated junior officers of the Army, called for the return of the Rump Parliament which Oliver had dissolved in 1653. Fleetwood, perhaps now realising the Pandora's box he had opened, tried to bargain to keep Richard as Lord Protector, but he was voted down. Yet Monck pressed for Richard and his mother to be generously pensioned off, writing from Scotland with the demand 'That seeing his late highness hath been pleased to manifest so much self-denial and love to his country . . . you will use your endeavours . . . that himself and family (together with her highness dowager) may have so honourable a provision settled upon them, and such other dignities, as are suitable to the former great services of that family to these nations.'[133]

Fleetwood and the Committee of Safety requested the now re-assembled Rump Parliament pay Richard's debts of £29,000, grant him an income of £20,000 and £10,000 for his heirs forever, and grant Elizabeth, 'Her Highness Dowager', £8,000 and a suitable residence such as Somerset House.[134] Richard was still in Whitehall waiting for the money to materialise when the Rump smashed the Protectoral seal, pulled down his arms and ordered the palace cleared out so it could be put up for sale. On 25 May, Richard resigned with grace, explaining 'I love and value the peace of this Common-Wealth much above my own concernments.'[135] He blamed himself, 'my sins have brought what is come to pass upon us', while friends and enemies alike uncharitably compared the careless son with his courageous father.[136] Richard had shown 'simplicity . . . in his losing all that his father had left him', Montagu later told Samuel Pepys, while Hyde blamed his 'extreme pusillanimity' for suffering 'himself to be stripped in one moment of all the greatness and power which the father had acquired in many years with wonderful courage, industry and resolution'.[137] Oliver's own loss of status was immediately visible when his elaborate monument in Westminster Abbey was demolished and his crown, sceptre and other royal ornaments sold off. A Royalist reportedly erected a sign above the tomb's remains which read 'Great in policy but matchless in Tyranny'. It was hastily pulled down by a soldier. The battle over the Cromwellian legacy had begun.[138]

Thurloe captured the catastrophe of Richard's downfall in a letter to Lockhart. 'How this change doth afflict all of us here who had the honour to be related both to his father and himself I need not trouble your excellency with. I am in so much confusion that I can scarce constrain myself to write about it.'[139] Thurloe was not alone in his astonishment. No-one could believe this 'late great sudden and bloodless change' for none of this was inevitable.[140] It was Richard's misfortune, like Henry VIII, to be heir to a charismatic conqueror who founded a dynasty out of chaotic civil war, inheriting all the difficulties of shoring it up for future generations that this brings. Worse still, his father had ruled for only five years and had failed to prepare his son adequately to succeed him.

Richard had begun his reign well and in every moment of those crucial weeks in April 1659, men could have made different choices and avoided this outcome. The MPs could have avoided repeating the mistakes of the past by 'picking at the knot' of the constitution and needlessly antagonising the Army and instead voting through their pay.[141] The government could have managed the session properly or bought itself more time. Richard could have asserted his authority over the Army earlier by replacing Fleetwood and Desborough or taken a slow and soft approach to gradually reform and reduce the Army under their noses. He had the genial character and moderate instincts to have led a broad coalition to his father's Promised Land of lasting settlement.

But instead, the Army removed Richard before he had the chance. The Protectorate fell in a Shakespearian-style coup that would be the first of several acts of political suicide by which the Parliamentarian cause destroyed itself with no help from the Royalists. Richard's plight was now as his namesake king Richard II's: 'I have no name, no title . . . and know not now what name to call myself.'[142] It was Richard's own relatives who drew knives from their sleeves to slay the Cromwellian Protectorate in the ultimate dynastic act, and what would turn out to be perhaps the biggest own goal in British history. 'These men intend nothing less than ruin to us both,' Richard had warned Henry and so it had come to pass.[143] Oliver's true sons were left in the dust with nothing but bitterness for their in-laws. 'And for myself, those that were my father's friends, pretended ones only, were mine,' Richard wrote to Henry. 'It required time to acquaint myself with them, and they tripped up my heels before I knew them, for though they were relations yet they forsook me. I know Fleetwood and Desborough regard not ruin so that they may have their ends, they are pitiful creatures. God will avenge innocency.'[144] And so he did, though not in the way Richard hoped.

Indemnity and oblivion

Almost 50 years before his death as a grand Elizabethan statesman, in the panicked days after Thomas Cromwell's arrest in June 1540, the young Ralph Sadler slipped into Austin Friars. He moved quickly and left quietly, retreating to his home at Hackney with no-one the wiser.

Many came and went at Austin Friars that summer, asset-stripping the fallen minister's pride and joy, before the excavated house was handed over in the autumn to the man who had betrayed him: his amanuensis Thomas Wriothesley.[145] Wriothesley had spent so much time in his master's house he would have known each object missing from its rightful place. But what he did not know was that a few precious items were not now spoils in the King's treasury but relics stashed away and guarded by the Cromwellian faithful. Ralph had taken Holbein's portrait of Thomas Cromwell and hidden it, undoubtedly saving it from the flames so that we can see his master's face today. He had taken too some of Thomas's favourite books, including the 1527 jewelled *Book of Hours* which sits at his elbow in the portrait, its gilt edges shimmering against the green cloth. These, he may have taken in secret or legitimately under the terms of Thomas's will which had left his library to Ralph. Certainly, five years later, Ralph was at pains to assure the Privy Council when questioned that 'Except certain treaties delivered into the treasury of the Exchequer and a few books had into the King's library, all remain in the late lord Crumwell's library in the Augustynes.'[146]

The Sadlers preserved Thomas Cromwell's memory even as they remained loyal to the Crown. Ralph's son later entertained James I at the Standon mansion and, by 1623, the Holbein portrait had come out of hiding to be proudly displayed in the long gallery there. In 1607, Michael Drayton dedicated his admiring poem 'The Legend of Great Cromwell' to his patron, Ralph's granddaughter's husband Sir Walter Aston. Thomas's *Book of Hours* also enjoyed new appreciation by the wife of Ralph's grandson, Anne.[147] While her husband was a devotee of country sports who appeared with his 'pack of Otter dogs' in the gently Royalist publishing sensation of the 1650s, Izaak Walton's fishing treatise *The Compleat Angler,* Anne was a scholar and literary patron.[148] A committed Royalist, the destruction of the Civil Wars prompted her in 1649 to plan to give the *Book of Hours* and another of Thomas's books to her father's Alma Mater, Trinity College Cambridge, whenever 'the vulger people' restored Charles II.[149] In 1660 she did just that, though without mentioning the connection to Thomas himself. There the *Book of Hours* lived happily for another 350 years, its Cromwellian past dimming almost from sight before a new generation of scholars brought it blinking back into the light.[150]

In the same year as Anne Sadler's gift, Harry Cromwell of Ramsey's wife, the poet Anna Cromwell, picked up her pen and opened the front leaf of her commonplace book of poetry and prayers. At the top of this page, she read the words she had inscribed four years earlier: 'Anna Cromwell'. Now underneath she wrote her name once more: 'Anna Williams'. The house of Cromwell had fallen a second time, a tottering Thomas replaced by a tumbling Richard, and once more the name of Williams conveniently re-surfaced. The Tudor Cromwells had survived their collapse, even thrived. Could their descendants, fallen from an even greater height a century later, do the same?

The prompt for both Anne Sadler and Anna Cromwell's actions in 1660 was the return of the exiled Charles Stuart to the throne a year after Richard's abdication. This was the very last outcome that Fleetwood and Desborough had wanted when they sabotaged the Protectorate in spring 1659; indeed, it had scarcely been conceivable then for most people. The 12 months in between were not a steady slope down to an inevitable restoration of the Stuart monarchy but an accelerated re-run of the 1649–53 republican experiments and, for the Cromwells and their allies, an ever shifting landscape of competing loyalties and high stakes. This time, the family's descent happened in stages. Options would appear and then fade away again as so many false dawns throughout the year. Cardinal Mazarin pledged troops to restore Richard, with the French ambassador negotiating with Thurloe and the privy councillor Nathaniel Fiennes in May and June. But Thurloe was cautious, being 'not a man to enter into any warlike designs', and believing 'that it would be an undertaking which would lead to his [Richard's] total ruin and to the ruin of his friends, and which might also be prejudicial to France, were it not successful'.[151]

Meanwhile, William Lockhart fended off Mazarin's bribes to hand over Dunkirk, purportedly in exchange for the title of Marshal of France. Lockhart refused similar bribes from the exiled Stuart court to pass Dunkirk to Charles Stuart; a particularly brazen demand given that both Charles and James Duke of York had fought with the Spanish against Lockhart's English troops.[152] Yet Charles's chief adviser Edward Hyde, who had been in such despair at Richard's seamless accession, now harboured high hopes of reaching a deal with Lockhart and the other Cromwellians who had supported Richard. As soon as it had been wounded when Richard's Protectorate first wobbled in the spring, the Cromwell family had become an attractive potential ally who could perhaps help restore the king in exchange for his protection. The return of monarchical rule – even by the Stuarts – was perhaps more palatable to some of those who had supported Cromwellian kingship than the alternative of radical republicanism. Perhaps, having failed to do one thing his father could or would not – disempower the Army – Richard could achieve another outcome Oliver would not countenance, the restoration of the Stuart monarchy. As early as March 1659, Hyde asked his agent 'whether Henry Cromwell hath Ireland at his devotion, and be like to look on tamely whilst his Brother and Family are sacrificed, for it is madness to think when they have lost their power they can preserve any fortune'.[153] Hyde wrote to another agent, John Mordaunt, on 4 April that 'the way is the more open to treat with Cromwell' to agree a deal where Richard and his allies were protected if they helped to restore the king.[154]

A week later, Mordaunt replied to Charles himself claiming he had struck a deal with Richard who promised to rally Montagu, Lockhart and Henry in Ireland. In return, Richard was to have 'twenty thousand pounds a year, and an honour considerable' and Mordaunt assumed Henry, Lockhart and others would 'expect good terms too'. The plan, Mordaunt explained, was masterminded 'by Colonel Harry Cromwell, Grandchild to Sir. Oliver, who to serve his family has brought R[ichard] Cromwell to this'.[155] An intriguing possibility emerges here: that the formerly Royalist elder branch of the Cromwell family would now help the fallen younger branch to save itself, just as the triumphant Oliver had once helped his uncle and cousin escape their fines. Harry Cromwell of Ramsey's involvement is plausible given his and Anna's Royalist leanings and his staunch support for his cousin's Protectorate. It would also explain his later acceptance by the restored king who nominated him as a knight of the Royal Oak, then a gentleman of the privy chamber and captain in his Grenadier Guards.[156] The plan came to nothing, reportedly through a combination of Thurloe's delay and Richard's cold feet, and Harry went on to change his name to Williams with his wife, though neither this nor his later preferment could undo the ruinous financial legacy bequeathed to him by his father and grandfather. Ramsey was sold off at his childless death in 1673 which brought to an end the glorious line of Sir Richard Cromwell of Hinchingbrooke and the grandest family of Huntingdonshire.[157]

Another family member now threw in his lot with the Royalist cause. Oliver's nephew – his sister Katherine's son Thomas Whetstone – whom he had promoted and shielded in the Navy now turned Royalist agent. Claiming to have served the two Protectors 'by blood and need of subsistence', he now set to work for Hyde to persuade Montagu to join the king, as for him, as well as Monck and Henry Cromwell, 'their best game lies that way'.[158] Montagu, though, remained loyal to Richard, who himself urged caution, recommending Montagu retire to the country and that they remain friends 'without plottings against the powers over us', hoping that 'poor tossed England might at last find a quiet harbour!'.[159] Richard's desire for his own quiet ensured nothing came of the visit two Royalist agents paid him at Hursley.[160] Meanwhile, Hyde kept pressing Henry Cromwell for his support, instructing his agent 'that he may likewise undertake to H[enry] Cromwell, that he shall be gratified in all that he will propose, and it will be in the King's power, as soon as his declaration shall be known, to send over men, money and arms'.[161] But Henry remained firmly against the restoration of the Stuarts: 'My opinion is, that any extreme is more tolerable then returning to Ch[arles] St[uart],' he had written to Thurloe in March. 'Other disasters are temporary, and may be mended; those not.'[162] Instead, Henry sailed back to England with his family to make a formal report to Parliament which allowed him to retire to his father-in-law's estate of Chippenham.[163]

The Cromwell family were now dispersed in dejection. 'R[ichard]. Cromwell is retired into Hampshire having no money within his purse, nor without it, a friend,' Hyde's agent scoffed. 'Harry to his Father-in-law in Cambridgeshire; Claypole lurks for debt (being really very poor) and pretends himself in France. The old woman's wealth falls short of expectation, nor is Falconbridge [Fauconberg] any whit proud of the alliance.'[164] It was a fair, though brutal, assessment. Fauconberg had indeed been dismissed as a colonel, with his regiment returned to John Lambert, and had taken Mary back to his estate in Yorkshire. From there, he may have approached Monck in an attempt to raise support for Richard, and rumours circulated to that effect. His Royalist credentials also opened him up to danger under the restored Commonwealth, and in August 1659 he was sent to the Tower in the rounding-up of suspicious persons that followed a Royalist uprising in Cheshire, and only released after posting £10,000 bail.[165] It was perhaps this treatment that prompted him to hedge his bets by sending £1,000 to Charles Stuart's cause. Meanwhile, throughout the summer Oliver's widow Elizabeth had been living in St James's Palace with her widowed youngest daughter Frances, her finances uncertain as she waited for the promised pension. Though disempowered, Elizabeth maintained her dignity and did not merely resign herself to events but used what influence she still had in defence of her family. This she directed at the powerful couple who had taken themselves outside their circle of trust to hold the fate of all in their hands: her daughter Bridget and son-in-law Charles Fleetwood.

The Fleetwoods were at the centre of a gathering storm. The alliance between the Army and the Commonwealthsmen which had pulled down the Protectorate was only skin-deep. Now reinstalled, the Rump Parliament began to challenge the Army even as the soldiers received a morale boost from defeating the Royalist uprising. In October, 50 officers of Lambert's Northern Brigade drafted a petition at Derby demanding the Rump bring in the reforms it had promised, secure civil and religious liberty, and settle Fleetwood permanently as commander-in-chief with Lambert his deputy. Fleetwood dithered over what to do with this troublesome document before unwisely sharing it with the fiery Commonwealthsman Arthur Haselrig, who promptly accused Lambert of high treason in Parliament. In the uncertainty, there was talk again of restoring Richard's Protectorate and he himself may have been brought to Hampton Court to be on hand if need be. Instead, Desborough presented another petition while Fleetwood tried to keep the peace, but the MPs voted to dismiss Lambert and Desborough and demote Fleetwood, handing the Army over to a parliamentary commission which included Haselrig, Edmund Ludlow and Oliver's brother-in-law Valentine Walton. In a repeat of the events of April, three of the new commissioners summoned troops to defend Parliament. In response, Lambert – fired up by his northern victory and now seeing red – channelled the spirits of Charles I and Oliver Cromwell by marching his troops on Westminster. The Rump WAS ejected and the Council of State dismissed early in the morning on 13 October, just as they had been in April 1653, and the Commonwealth ship of state foundered on the rocks.

It seemed to many that Lambert now aimed at his own power and was using Fleetwood as his stooge – as they thought Oliver had done with Sir Thomas Fairfax. The grandiosity of both men's houses at

Wimbledon and Wallingford House on Whitehall only added to the impression of unalloyed ambition. Together, Fleetwood, Desborough and Lambert hastily created a Committee of Safety to run government, but a letter from Monck in Scotland demanded the resumption of Parliament on pain of bloodshed. Once more the dreadful prospect of civil war appeared in the form of an army marching south from Scotland. The Committee sent Lambert north with 12,000 men to meet it in early November. Left behind to hold the fort, Fleetwood was hopelessly out of his depth. For all his sniping and backroom antics against Henry Cromwell, Fleetwood – who Oliver had once branded a 'milksop' – was constitutionally ill-suited to conflict or decisive action; even more so since Oliver's death had left him exposed. Instead, his thoughts lingered on providence while his manners were characterised to Milton's mind by 'civility, gentleness and courtesy'. The Cromwell women of his family were not so reticent, however, showing every sign of the shrewd political understanding he lacked. On 5 December, Fleetwood heard from his mother-in-law:

'The Lady Dowager sent one of her gentlemen to my Lord Fleetwood yesterday before he was up, and told him he came from her Highness, who wished him to call to mind the saying of her husband to him before his death, that he would never leave his whimsies till he had put the Nation in blood, and wished him seriously to consider of it, and call it to mind, and how near he was in effecting it, and bid him consider what wrong he had done to her son R[ichard], whether as affairs stood they had any better way to preserve themselves and the nation then to restore him. He lay in bed all the time like a stock, and answered not a word.'[166]

It is hard to imagine Bridget's first husband Henry Ireton acting so passively. A week later we glimpse her own efforts to shield her second husband from the consequences of his actions when Ludlow visited them at Wallingford House. Ludlow implored Fleetwood to restore Parliament otherwise he would return to Ireland and, overhearing this, Bridget came in and 'with tears began to lament the present condition of her husband', who had never acted against Parliament, with which she had 'always solicited him to comply'. Indeed, Bridget revealed how, recognising the danger of the Army's Derby petition, she 'had taken the original, and locked it up in her cabinet, where it still was'. Ludlow was 'moved with the discourse of the lady' but resolved to leave nonetheless as he thought reconciliation impossible, at which Fleetwood and Bridget 'seemed much troubled'.[167] They were right to worry. Monck had succeeded in rallying others to his cause, not least the great Sir Thomas Fairfax, coaxed out of his stately retirement. Fauconberg too answered his call, linking up with Monck as he passed through Yorkshire. Lambert could only look on in despair. Meanwhile, Haselrig persuaded the Portsmouth garrison to declare for Parliament, Fleetwood's own troops mutinying in the process, and Broghill's soldiers seized Dublin Castle for Parliament, ousting the radical officers who had resumed power when Henry Cromwell had left.

Back in London, Bulstrode Whitelocke persuaded Fleetwood that the time had come to act decisively – either to declare for a free Parliament or negotiate with Charles Stuart for a conditional restoration – but the intransigent Desborough talked him out of it again. Fleetwood, reduced to tears, refused to act without Lambert's consent. 'I cannot do it', 'I cannot help it' he said in despair even as Whitelocke predicted 'you will ruin yourself and your friends'.[168] Breaking under the pressure, at Christmas he resigned, wailing that 'the Lord had blasted them and spit in their faces'.[169] Once the most powerful man in the country, Fleetwood left Wallingford House with Bridget for Norfolk, the last Cromwells of influence reduced to the uncertain status of the rest of their family. Dramatists were soon savouring the family fall-out, showing Oliver's widow castigating Fleetwood for having ruined them all. 'Call me not Mother' Mrs Cromwell snarls at Fleetwood, while sighing over the sainted Ireton 'my best of sons', in the 1660 play *The Rump* which Pepys deemed 'very silly'.[170]

Fleetwood was out but, now that Richard's enemies in the Army leadership had been removed, there was still a slim chance that his Protectorate could return. With the Rump now restored, a triumphant Monck in London, a rejected Lambert in the Tower, and civilian Cromwellians like Thurloe, Broghill, Montagu and Ingoldsby reinstated in the government and the Army, Pepys observed that 'Great is the talk of a single person, and that it would now be Charles [Stuart], George [Monck], or Richard [Cromwell] again' and Montagu later confided in him that there were at that moment 'great endeavours to bring in the Protector again.'[171] Hyde also received word of plans 'to reinvest Richard Cromwell' though his agents were quick to inform him that this had come to nothing with the 'design proving too weak'.[172] The house of Cromwell had fallen too far to provide the return to traditional order that so many now craved. Instead, it was the cry for a full and free Parliament that now animated the citizens of London, crazed after so much chaos. The Rump ignored this, but Monck did not, adding his own voice to the demand to restore the MPs excluded at Pride's Purge, prompting wild celebrations and the roasting of rumps of meat in the streets. On 21 February 1660, Monck took matters into his own hands. Just as Oliver and Lambert had done before him, Monck launched a coup against Parliament. Yet this time, soldiers escorted MPs back into the House rather than marching them out of it.

In the middle of April, the republic made one last, valiant stand when the ever-resourceful Lambert escaped from the Tower down a rope into a boat on the river and rode north calling his men to him in defence of the republic. Not enough came. Lambert made for the hallowed ground of Edgehill where Monck's forces destroyed his nascent army and the great general and architect of the Protectorate was once more captured, this time by the Cromwells' cousin Richard Ingoldsby, who had already begun his metamorphosis from regicide to Royalist.[173] Lambert reportedly offered now to support Richard Cromwell, but Ingoldsby refused. It was as Richard Ingoldsby's brother Henry escorted their old colleague Lambert into Northampton, that Lambert reminded him of Oliver's prophetic warning in 1650 that the crowds who now cheered them would cheer as loudly to see them hang.[174]

The restored Long Parliament had by now dissolved itself and on 25 April 1660 a newly elected Parliament – later known as the Convention Parliament – met both in the Commons and the Lords. It was widely assumed that this Parliament would do what had been unthinkable only weeks before: recall Charles Stuart. It was not a long-held and widespread desire for the return of the King that achieved the Restoration, but the failure of all other options which left the King the last seat available for a weary public suffering an exhausting game of musical chairs. Many people had held the Stuart cause in their hearts over the previous 11 years, but still more had reconciled themselves to the Commonwealth and Protectoral regimes. It was only once the Army, the republican Commonwealthsmen and the Cromwellians had knocked out each other's first-choice

Oliver Cromwell's wife Elizabeth, painted in 1657 as Her Highness the Protectoress presiding over her husband's court

Oliver Cromwell's oldest surviving son Richard Cromwell who became Lord Protector on his father's death in 1658

Oliver Cromwell's second surviving son Henry Cromwell painted while he was governing Ireland

Oliver Cromwell's eldest daughter Bridget who married two Parliamentarian commanders

Bridget Cromwell's husbands, Henry Ireton and Charles Fleetwood. Both were leading generals, close colleagues of Oliver Cromwell and successive rulers of Ireland, though they had contrasting characters. Had Ireton not died unexpectedly in 1651, the future of the Cromwell family and of Britain might have been very different

Oliver Cromwell's second daughter Elizabeth (Betty) who married John Claypole. In this portrait, probably painted posthumously after her shocking death in August 1658, she is depicted as the goddess Minerva surrounded by symbols of her father's rule

Oliver Cromwell's youngest daughter Frances was also painted in a romantic style, either during her engagement to Robert Rich who she married at Whitehall in 1657, or soon after his early death the following year

Whitehall Palace where Oliver Cromwell and his family lived, first in the Cockpit and then in the State apartments, viewed from St James's Park where the family exercised and socialised. The Banqueting House where Oliver received ambassadors and hosted musical entertainments is at the back on the left side

Oliver Cromwell as Lord Protector riding in front of London wearing his best suit of uncut grey velvet bought for his daughter Frances's wedding and which clothed his funeral effigy

A contemporary image of Oliver Cromwell's effigy lying in State at Somerset House surrounded by all the trappings of monarchy and Cromwell family heraldry

The posthumous execution of Oliver Cromwell, Henry Ireton and John Bradshaw by the restored Stuart regime in 1661. The corpses were hanged, dismembered and their heads displayed on pikes above Westminster Hall

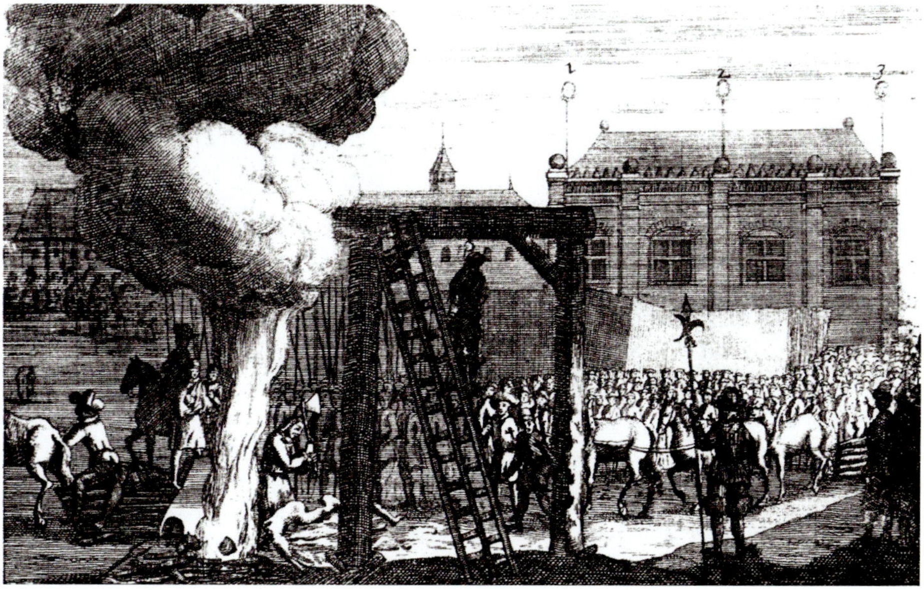

Oliver Cromwell's third daughter Mary lived grandly with her husband Viscount Fauconberg under the restored Stuarts, becoming a great curiosity in her old age for her resemblance to her father

The controversy over erecting a statute to Oliver Cromwell in Parliament provoked a national debate, with editorials and cartoons appearing in publications including *The Times*, *The Spectator*, *Punch* and this in *Vanity Fair*

(Opposite) Eventually in 1899 Sir Hamo Thorneycroft's statue was erected outside Parliament where it stands today. It faces the east end of Westminster Abbey where Oliver's beloved daughter Betty is still buried

OLIVER
CROMWELL
1599
1658

For most people today, Oliver Cromwell has been reduced to a Puritan caricature, though often the stereotype has continued political relevance as in this cartoon from *Private Eye* in May 2026

Thomas Cromwell, meanwhile, lives on in the books, stage and TV adaptations of Hilary Mantel's prize-winning *Wolf Hall* trilogy, portrayed here by Ben Miles for the RSC

regimes that Charles II emerged as the most viable runner-up. Thus the 'mad suicide' of Puritanism after Oliver's death restored the monarchy to Britain.[175]

The consummate Cromwellian pragmatists grasped this most easily and, in the weeks before the Long Parliament reassembled, Monck, Montagu and their allies finally responded to Hyde's communications to explore a controlled restoration. It was Montagu who left his retirement at the old Cromwell home of Hinchingbrooke to resume his parliamentary seat and, restored as general-at-sea, to sail across the Channel with his relative and protégé Samuel Pepys to collect the new King once the agreement had been made in May. The fleet was refitted en route, covering up the symbols of the Commonwealth and Protectorate as if they had never been. Carpenters removed the laurel-crowned, mounted figurehead of Montagu's old master Oliver Cromwell trampling conquered nations from the prow of the Protectoral flagship the *Naseby*, which his new master King Charles II renamed the *Royal Charles* when he stepped aboard. The process of state-sponsored amnesia had begun.

With the King's return, the Cromwell family faced a new and horrifying reality. Not only was the Stuart monarchy restored, but it returned with few conditions and without their help. The family that Edward Hyde had been wooing with solicitous promises of wealth and pardons mere months before was now in grave danger. 'Our fames are now brought to the slaughter houses, and the very names of the Cromwells will become far more odious', a satirised Elizabeth Cromwell wailed on the stage. The real Elizabeth had only just left St James's Palace with Frances when the crowds celebrating Charles II's arrival burned lifelike figures of her and Oliver on top of a huge bonfire and hung Oliver's funeral effigy from a window at Westminster.[176] Vitriol poured off the presses too as emboldened Royalists and republicans vied to reshape the posthumous narrative of the Protectorate. Tracts mixed violent revenge fantasy and coarse pantomime humour. Typically, the dead victors Oliver and sometimes Ireton attracted the former, with writers imagining them enduring the tortures of hell. *Hells Higher Court of Justice* featured the usurper Oliver tied to a red-hot throne with a burning crown and robes.[177] The living failures Richard and Fleetwood meanwhile were ridiculed and derided. 'Sir,

Your son Richard is a simple fool, your son Harry, a stupid asse; Fleetwood a sordid base fellow; Disborow, a perfidious Renegado,' Hugh Peters informed Oliver's ghost in one satirical pamphlet.[178] Richard was 'Queen Dick', one writer even asking 'Whether Richard was Oliver's son or no?'[179] Elizabeth herself appeared in these slanders, telling her husband that Richard 'knew no more how to govern than did a dog'. Fleetwood meanwhile was mocked for his weakness and propensity to cry, the playwright Aphra Behn later characterising him as 'that son of a custard, always quaking'.[180]

There was much to quake at now. Where in 1540 the Cromwells' fates had been in the hands of the murderous Henry VIII, they now lay in the hands of the vengeful Charles II. While the new king was careful to speak of reconciliation and forgiveness before his return, Oliver's belief that he would never forgive his father's killers was not so wide of the mark. Worse still the King was now supported by a Parliament even keener to settle scores, its MPs hotly debating the names of those to be excluded from the blanket pardon under the new Act of Indemnity and Oblivion. Parliamentarians of all kinds rushed to appeal to the King's mercy, to the disgust of Ludlow who saw 'everyone striving who should offer up the greatest sacrifice to this rising sun'.[181] Those like him who had signed Charles I's death warrant were in the greatest danger and many hurried into exile to be hunted for years to come by the King's agents. After public show trials, ten regicides were hanged, drawn and quartered in October 1660, three more in April 1662 having been captured in the Low Countries, and in June the only non-regicide to be exempted from pardon – the republican Sir Henry Vane – was executed. While the new government considered their deaths a necessary public cleanse, many observers like Pepys were horrified by the gruesome spectacle and impressed by the condemned men's bravery and commitment to their lost cause to the end.

Violent retribution was not only meted out against the living but also the dead. Executing the regicides was not enough to exorcise the ghosts of the revolutionary past. The new regime needed a greater ritual, an act of high theatre to expunge the scapegoats who had hijacked history. So Parliament issued a retrospective Act of Attainder for treason against Oliver just as it had once done to Thomas Cromwell. This condemned the long-buried bodies of Oliver, alongside those of Henry Ireton and the president of the court which tried

Charles I, John Bradshaw, to public execution. The heroes of the Commonwealth could not be allowed to slumber eternally in Henry VII's Chapel of Kings. This extended to the women and children of the Protector's family and so Oliver's mother, sister and Bridget's baby were disinterred and thrown into a common pit in the adjacent churchyard of St Margaret's. Charles the fortunate would replace Oliver the conqueror as the great Henry VII's heir. And just like Henry VII, he would sponsor a smear campaign to traduce his dead foe which was every bit as vigorous as the one the triumphant Tudors waged against Richard III.

It took three days for the grave robbers to hack Oliver, Ireton and Bradshaw out of the Abbey's layers of marble, wood and lead. Fortunately, there was money to be made in the sacrilegious spectacle. The men were paid well, their sergeant further lining his pocket by stealing the inscribed golden plate from Oliver's coffin only to find later it was of gilt copper not gold.[182] Meanwhile spectators paid sixpence for a glimpse of the Protector in very different circumstances to his previous lying in State.[183] Eventually, the three coffins were taken at night to the unlikely venue of the Red Lion pub in Holborn to await their grisly fate. A few days later, on the 12th anniversary of Charles I's execution, 30 January 1661, Oliver and his dead companions suffered a ceremony designed not only to reverse the symbolism of the regicide but also the pomp of Oliver's State funeral. The three open coffins were dragged from Holborn to the 'Triple Tree' gallows at Tyburn on sledges. As Oliver had once predicted, the crowds did indeed turn out to see him hang, with thousands of people crowding around the gallows.

The corruption of the 'odious carcases' – particularly Bradshaw who had died most recently but not been embalmed – contributed to a gruesome scene as the three men swung on the huge gibbet from morning until 4 pm, 'Cromwell in a green-seare cloth, very fresh, embalmed; Ireton having been buried long, hung like a dried rat, yet corrupted about the fundament. Bradshaw, in his winding-sheet, the fingers of his right hand and his nose perished, having wet the sheet through.'[184] At dusk, the men were cut down and beheaded. Oliver's head took eight blows to separate from his body, his nose damaged in the process, while spectators clambered to pocket severed body parts, for some reason particularly prizing Bradshaw's toes. Then the trunks were discarded into a pit below the gallows, the heads borne off in triumph for one further spectacle. Impaled on spiked 20-foot poles, Oliver, Ireton and Bradshaw's heads were fixed on the roof of Westminster Hall, the venue not only of Charles I's trial but of Oliver's regal investiture as Lord Protector a mere four years earlier. So Oliver shared the fate of his forebear Thomas whose own decapitated head had watched over London Bridge more than a century before.

For Royalists, it was a celebratory scene and 'marvellous act of justice'.[185] But the horrific act designed to obliterate Oliver's body had other, unintended consequences. Some observers baulked at the desecration: 'it doth trouble me that a man of so great courage as he was should have that dishonour, though otherwise he might deserve it enough,' Pepys thought.[186] What is more, at the axe stroke Oliver was re-animated in public consciousness, corrupted versions of his famous portrait by Robert Walker festooned with hangman's nooses, devils and crowns papering the presses of London; an act of oblivion instead cementing his lasting legend. The ghastly goings-on inspired immediate ghost stories and enduring myths about the whereabouts of his body. This had been swapped for another's, either before its first burial in the Abbey or while it lay so unnecessarily and lightly guarded in the Red Lion. Oliver had been buried instead in Red Lion Square where an obelisk now stands, or ploughed into the field at Naseby, or rescued by his daughters and taken to their mother at Northborough or to Mary's secluded home of Newburgh in Yorkshire where a sealed attic vault claims to house him to this day. Not even a king can force it to be opened as the future Edward VII reportedly tried to do.

The other living members of the Cromwell family who had been regicides suffered a variety of fates. Valentine Walton, who had been married to Oliver's late sister Margaret, fled to Germany and Flanders where he disguised himself as a gardener before dying in 1661, leaving his second wife to die in obscure penury in Oxford, and his daughters adrift.[187] Oliver's cousin Edward Whalley fled to the American colonies with his son-in-law William Goffe, never to be seen again.[188] John Jones, Oliver's sister Katherine's second husband, took no such precautions and was arrested while walking in Finsbury. He was executed on 17 October and showed such courage and faith that stories circulated immediately of men seen in the sky in Hertfordshire and a crab tree blossoming on his estate.[189] Richard Ingoldsby of the Hinchingbrooke Cromwells, meanwhile, was the only regicide to escape punishment on account of his fighting against Lambert's last stand in the spring, and his spurious tale that his cousin Oliver had held his hand forcing him to sign Charles I's death warrant. Not merely pardoned, Ingoldsby was made a knight of the Bath at the King's coronation and served as gentleman of the privy chamber.

Lambert – so unwittingly helpful to Ingoldsby's case – was far less fortunate. At first sentenced to death, Charles II reprieved him. Yet the architect of the Protectorate and brilliant general was too famous and charismatic to be allowed to live freely. So Lambert spent the rest of his life in prison, first on Guernsey and then Drake Island off Plymouth. Although, after an appeal by Facounberg and others, he was able to have his wife and children close by and enjoyed landscaping the prison gardens, these were long and distressing years for the great man who had offered the last resistance to the Restoration. His fellow triumvirs Desborough and Fleetwood fared better. Both were barred from holding office for life, though Desborough roused suspicions by moving abroad and so suffered spells in prison when he eventually returned home. In 1667, Pepys passed him on the street and declared he looked well 'and just as he used to do heretofore'.[190] Fleetwood may have been helped by Monck and Montagu, to both of whom he wrote appeals for friendship and protection. After leaving Wallingford House, he had taken Bridget and their children into 'great retirement' in the country – probably to his house at Feltwell in Norfolk – where he emphasised 'I carry myself inoffensively to the public.'[191] The fact that the new regime did not feel the need to imprison Fleetwood, as they did Lambert, reveals what a failure he was now considered.

Pledges of peacefulness and the intercession of influential friends also helped Henry Cromwell who chose to face the music head on, petitioning the King for pardon. Henry presented himself as a conciliatory and conservative administrator of Ireland who bore no personal animus towards the Stuarts but rather had acted 'only out of natural duty to his late father'. As to the present, Henry wished to serve Charles 'without fear' and begged the King to show the same clemency God had shown to him and 'not suffer your petitioner, his wife and children to perish from the face of the Earth, but rather to live and expiate what hath been done amiss with their future services and prayers for your Majesty'. For the future, Henry focused on his descendants and their troublesome inheritance, asking 'that no distinction between himself and other your Majesty's good subjects may be branded on him to posterity'.[192] Friends and foes alike spoke up for the popular Henry, notably Edward Hyde – now created the Earl of Clarendon as Charles II's Lord Chancellor – who Henry wrote to in gratitude two years later.[193] A brief note from Monck on 9 June 1660 shows how delicately Henry's case had to be handled. In four lines he advised Henry not to come up to London as it was not yet 'convenient', but assured him that 'when it is seasonable I shall acquaint you with it'.[194]

The King chose not to prosecute Henry and the rest of the immediate Cromwell family. Much as Oliver had always done, Charles appreciated the pragmatic need to overlook past allegiances in the service of building present stability. Yet, though the Cromwells 'scaped in the crowd', as Henry put it, they suffered in many other lasting ways.[195] Henry was subjected to travel restrictions. Moving to the nearby house of Spinney Abbey he bought from his in-laws, on 12 October 1665 Henry was bound by a bond of £3,000 to the King not to travel more than five miles from it, though he had leave sometimes to visit relations at Chippenham and Newmarket.[196] In material terms, having lived public lives as the first family of the nation, the Cromwells now found their financial positions precarious. In his petition, Henry cited losses of £2,000 a year on his English and £6,000 on his Irish property at the Restoration.[197] Things could have been worse, however, had the King not allowed him to keep his Irish lands in Meath and Connaught – as part of his wider confirmation of the Cromwellian land settlement – the income from which kept him in reasonable comfort.[198]

Richard, meanwhile, was much deeper in debt. His parliamentary pension had never been paid and, even before Charles's return, Richard wrote to Monck that his 'present exigencies' had caused him 'for some time of late to retire into hiding-places to avoid arrest for debts contracted upon the public account'. He hoped Monck would out of affection help him avoid 'utter ruin'.[199] Richard wrote to Oxford too, resigning his Chancellorship, telling the university 'it is no small trouble to my thoughts when I consider how little serviceable I have been to you'. He would 'always retain my affection and esteem for you', he wrote with his hopes that Oxford would 'still abide flourishing and fruitful' to prosper 'amidst the many examples of the instability and revolutions of human affairs'.[200] In July 1660, financial desperation drove Richard into exile leaving his three children Oliver,

Elizabeth and Anne and his pregnant wife Dorothy behind. None had any idea when – or if – they would ever see each other again.

Financial and legal troubles also plagued the Cromwell couple living at Northborough near Peterborough. This was Betty's widower John Claypole's house, to which he retired with his bereft children. It was probably their needs, as her only grandchildren who had lost a mother, which prompted Oliver's widow Elizabeth to move in with Claypole; mother-in-law and son-in-law a curious mirror in life of the pairing of the lost Oliver and Betty in death. Claypole had secured a pardon from the King, but his circumstances were greatly reduced, and indeed would never recover. Pepys recorded that in August 1660 Claypole toyed with buying Pepys' modest house in Axe Yard which was a 'very great change'.[201] Creditors hounded Claypole and his mother-in-law at Northborough, even breaking into the house to search for jewels Elizabeth had supposedly stolen from the royal treasury as Lady Protectoress – accusations which fitted perfectly with the slanderous characterisation soon to be circulating in the satirical cookbook *The Court and Kitchen of Elizabeth, Commonly called Joan Cromwell, the Wife of the Late Usurper*.[202] This persecution forced Elizabeth to petition the King directly, as Henry had done, not only refuting the charge of jewellery theft among 'her many sorrows', but swearing that she 'never intermeddled with any of those public transactions which have been prejudicial to his late or present Majesty, and is ready to yield humble and faithful obedience to his government; prays therefore for a protection, without which she cannot expect in her old age, a safe retirement in any place of His Majesty's dominions'.[203]

Elizabeth received an answer to her petition from the Secretary of State in equal parts reassurance and rebuke. The King, she learned, was 'pleased to distinguish between the concernment of your petitioner, and those of her relatives who have been obnoxious'.[204] Elizabeth may have kept only her own jewellery, but even this was not safe. Several creditors sued Claypole in Chancery proceedings for the repayment of expenses incurred by him for his family while he was the Protectoral Master of Horse. Elizabeth tried to pay one of them off with money and jewels worth £300. Poignantly, these contained a diamond ring – the potent symbol of the Cromwell family's ascendancy clasped in their rampant lion's hand ever since Henry VIII gave Richard Cromwell his own diamond ring at the 1540 May Day tournament. More poignant still is the list of disbursements held over Claypole's head which contained black coach decorations for Oliver's funeral, bow and arrows, pouches, gloves and girdles for Claypole's young son Cromwell Claypole and his nephew little Henry Ireton, and medicines for Betty in her final illness.[205] Claypole argued these were public not personal debts but it was a hard case to make for a once ruling family now denounced as usurpers.

All this was perhaps too much for some of the Cromwells to take. Bridget suffered particularly cruelly, seeing her baby, her first husband and her father exhumed and desecrated. She died the next year, in June 1662, aged 38, leaving Fleetwood to raise both Henry Ireton's children and his own alone. Her mother Elizabeth did not long outlive her. The death of Betty's daughter Martha Claypole in 1664 perhaps hastened Elizabeth's end just as Betty's own had hastened Oliver's. Henry and Mary visited their mother at Northborough as she ailed, likely Frances too. Mary lamented her condition with Cromwellian anguished acceptance, writing to Henry:

'My poor mother is so affecting a spectacle as I scarce know what to write; she continuing much the same as she was when you were here. The Lord knows best what is best for us to suffer, and therefore I desire we may willingly submit to his will; but the condition she is in is very sad: the Lord help her and us to bear it. I am now able to say no more, my heart being so oppressed.'[206]

Elizabeth, the former Lady Protectoress, died aged 67 on 19 November 1665 and was buried in the Northborough village church of St Andrew's, her long and extraordinary earthly journey complete. Both church and ancient manor house still stand today, their stalwart stones suffused with Cromwellian folklore: Oliver, once a regular visitor to the Claypoles' home, used to sleep in the tiny room above the porch – ever since known as 'Cromwell's Closet' – so he could make a speedy getaway on his horse. He garrisoned his troops in the gatehouse during local campaigns, stopping them from ransacking local churches. The walls in Elizabeth's bedroom where she died weep blood when England is in danger. The nineteenth-century poet John Clare, who lived in Northborough, saw the house this way, as a custodian of a lost Cromwellian past:

Absorbing time that all things overwhelms
Will round the castle ancient thoughts recall

The fragment of a moat the tripple elms
The cannon holes that pierce the massy wall
The ancient arching gateway striding high
Where cromwells stubborn army entered through
The castle barn the stranger passes bye
& the old house which many a pencil drew
Some dim seen paintings triump[h] on the walls
& travellers still the antique rooms admire
Where my lords parlour still the past recalls
Where Cromwell doubtless would from strife retire
The locked up room where superstition sleeps
& cromwells memory in dread mystery keeps.[207]

Eleven

Afterlives

But here we may well see, and truly this may say, that England once had a Cromwell.

John Foxe, Acts and Monuments *(1570 edition)*

So now get up

The Hinchingbrooke Cromwells may have reverted to Williams, but a few years into the Restoration, the Cromwell name began to sound differently to those with buyer's remorse. The gilt had rubbed off the so-called 'merry monarch' Charles II quickly, as Pepys noted in 1667, 'it is strange how . . . everybody doth nowadays reflect upon Oliver and commend him, so brave things he did and made all the neighbour princes fear him; while here a prince, come in with all the love and prayers and good liking of his people, and have given greater signs of loyalty and willingness to serve him with their estates than ever was done by any people, hath lost all so soon.'[1] A series of catastrophes had rocked Restoration England and helped topple Clarendon: the plague in 1665, the Great Fire of London in 1666, and the humiliating Dutch raid on the Medway in 1667, when the Dutch sailed up the Thames and towed away the *Royal Charles*, formerly Oliver's great warship the *Naseby* which had once borne his triumphant figure on its prow. With the break-up of the Cromwellian union with Scotland and Ireland, the British polity had re-fractured, while Charles had squandered much of Oliver's legacy in foreign affairs, acting as a supplicant to France to whom he resold Dunkirk and later secretly pledged to personally convert to Catholicism.[2]

This, together with his government's repressive religious policy and the lascivious lifestyle of his court, measured poorly against the memory of the uxorious, plain-speaking Protector who was fearsome abroad and tolerant at home. One member of the wider Cromwell family illustrated the changed climate. Abigail, the wife of Sir Oliver Cromwell of Hinchingbrooke's younger son, left her husband to live openly with one of Pepys' friends. Described by a disapproving Pepys as 'some painted lady', 'Madam Williams' made the most of the loosened social rules of Restoration London. She was much in Pepys' company, appearing in his *Diary* 65 times, including one particularly ironic occasion in 1668 when Pepys went to the King's playhouse 'and there sat to avoid seeing Knepp in a box above where Mrs. Williams happened to be, and there saw "The Usurper"; a pretty good play, in all but what is designed to resemble Cromwell and Hugh Peters, which is mighty silly.'[3]

Even in its contrast, Restoration culture was a product of the upheaval of the Civil Wars and Commonwealth. The unpleasant public dissection of Charles I, Henrietta Maria and Oliver Cromwell's sex lives paved the way for Charles II to embrace his libidinous reputation.[4] Yet this was a high-risk strategy. The execution of Charles I and Oliver's Protectorate had changed kingship forever, transforming it from a divine right into a job conditional on the character and performance of its occupant. The Cromwellian Edward Montagu had seen this even amidst the temporary hysteria of the Restoration, commenting that he did not believe the King would last long 'unless he carry himself very soberly and well'.[5] His protégé Pepys bemoaned the 'ill condition' of the court, its 'vices of swearing, drinking and whoring', reflecting on the 'bad management of things now compared with what it was in the late rebellious times, when men, some for fear and some for religion, minded their business; which none do now, by being void of both'. He and his dining companions now 'talked much of Cromwell; all saying he was a brave fellow, and did owe his crown he got to himself as much as any man that ever got one'.[6] The government's public cancellation of the past 11 years could not prevent such reflections in private. Nonetheless, it persevered in its mandated oblivion, outlawing speaking of the

'Interregnum', repealing all laws created during that time, and backdating Charles II's reign to the moment his father's head was struck from his body.

The Cromwell family contravened these policies simply by existing and serving as living reminders to those around them. Many shared Pepys' lively interest in what he called 'the old matters of the Protector and his family' who now lived a strange, liminal life in Restoration England.[7] Of these, Mary was the most visible, the exalted marriage Oliver had arranged for her to Viscount Fauconberg safeguarding her future just as the match Thomas had organised for Gregory with Elizabeth Seymour had done. The pair lived grandly in the fine house of Sutton Court in the village of Chiswick near London with gardens, a game enclosure and bowling green large enough to occupy 40 gardeners.[8] In 1665, they even hosted the Duke of York and his wife for an extended stay at Newburgh, and four years later Fauconberg was appointed Ambassador Extraordinary to Venice. So the son-in-law who Oliver Cromwell had sent in embassy to Louis XIV once more sampled the delights of the courts of Europe, now representing Charles II. Yet Mary's Cromwellian pedigree was not entirely forgotten. Seeing Fauconberg and 'his Lady, my Lady Mary Cromwell' at the theatre in 1663, Pepys noted she 'looks as well as I have known her and well-clad; but when the House begun to fill, she put on her vizard and so kept it on all the play – which is of late become a great fashion among the ladies, which hides their whole face'.[9]

Frances also benefited from her brief marriage, with her late husband Robert Rich's Royalist relations steering her through the treacherous times, promoting a petition on her behalf.[10] Afterwards, while living with her sister-in-law Dorothy at Richard's abandoned home of Hursley, Frances found a measure of happiness in a second marriage to Henry Cromwell's brother-in-law John Russell, who soon inherited the baronetcy of Chippenham. The trauma of recent years combined with Frances's natural vivacity to sculpt a wry approach to this new relationship worthy of Elizabeth Bennet. Assured in a series of love letters of the fluctuating 'ecstasies' and 'torments' Russell suffered lest his love be unrequited, Frances commiserated with his affliction, explaining 'you will not wonder if I take care to preserve myself from the passion which has done you so much mischief . . . and . . . must needs be very dangerous to a poor silly woman'. Her humour held out but not her heart, as Frances later wrote to Russell: 'I will not now complain of you or chide you, otherwise I could take it ill you should, after all that has passed between yourself and me, say you are in a doubt whether I love you.'[11] Yet she did not forget her former life and love, naming her second son Rich; 'a brave boy' according to his father.[12]

Like Mary, Frances retained some residue of real status as Oliver's daughter, attracting attention and a degree of discreet deference, if always just outside court society. So in 1669, Cosimo III de' Medici, heir to the Grand Duke of Tuscany, took a detour from his visit to Charles II at his palace at Newmarket to call on the Russells at Chippenham. After touring the magnificent villa and climbing the roof to look at Ely Cathedral through a telescope, Cosimo conversed in French and 'with the greatest politeness' with Frances, 'giving her the place of honour' and receiving her children 'with great affability and kindness'.[13] His attitude no doubt reflected the friendship that had existed between his father, Grand Duke Ferdinando II, and Oliver, to whom Ferdinando had once sent the expensive gift of a walnut and ebony medicine chest containing 50 glass pomade jars.[14] Cosimo understood too the fluctuating fortunes of ruling houses; his own family the Medici had been suffering one of their several expulsions from Florence when Thomas Cromwell had called the city his home. The Russells were often at the Fauconbergs' London house, rubbing shoulders with other rehabilitated figures from their past lives like George Monck and Sir Thomas Fairfax. Memories of former times were shared more happily among this set. Frances flirted with the new Venetian ambassador, while the old Jacobean courtier who had danced and been pranked at her first wedding was reported to her as being 'as much yours as formerly . . . As for his apparel, from head to foot they are the same you remember in your father's time, not so much as a pair of new shoes, or a hair altered in his periwig'.[15] But Frances's gaiety was short-lived. In cruel answer to her wish at Robert Rich's death to have a second husband who never died, Frances was bereaved again after only six years of marriage. Widowed twice by the age of 30, she would not marry again and spent much of the rest of her long life with the devoted, childless Fauconbergs who doted on her children as their own.

It was perhaps easier for female Cromwells shorn of their infamous name to pass unnoticed through society – or, if noticed, to be forgiven where their husbands' talents were reusable. This was also the case with Oliver's niece Robina and her husband, the diplomat William Lockhart. After a quiet decade in Scotland and Huntingdonshire after his return from Dunkirk in 1660, Lockhart was recruited as a 'secret councillor for Scotland' and then sent on various foreign embassies, culminating in a return to his former role as ambassador to France. There he met and personally financed the now exiled Clarendon, who had once tried so hard to persuade him to help the Restoration as governor of Dunkirk. The family remained in touch with their Cromwell relations, the young Lockharts later cavorting with Richard Cromwell's son, taking him 'horse racing . . . drinking, gaming, swearing', to trouble their parents as all young male Cromwells were wont to do.[16]

❦ ❦ ❦

At an individual level there was far greater continuity from the Protectorate to the Restoration regimes than usually assumed. Some of Oliver's closest adherents like Monck, his former councillors Montagu and Anthony Ashley Cooper, and diplomats George Downing, Lockhart and Fauconberg all prospered at the new Stuart court. So too in wider culture and society. Oliver's brother-in-law John Wilkins played a leading role in inaugurating the new Royal Society, to which his scientific circle now belonged; its Restoration foundation obscuring its true origins during the Civil Wars and under Oliver's Protectorate. Though Wilkins lost the mastership of Trinity College, Cambridge Richard had bestowed on him, the fact that his wife Robina was Oliver's sister did not prevent him accumulating church positions, culminating in his appointment as a royal chaplain and Bishop of Chester, all while the pair supported their less acceptable Cromwell relations – probably taking in Valentine Walton's parentless daughters and advising the exiled Richard, for whom Wilkins had spoken to Clarendon.[17] Wilkins, when challenged over having married 'too near unto you know who', claimed he had married Robina under duress, though this seems uncharacteristically unchivalrous for the genial man. Robina's daughter Elizabeth French, meanwhile, married Wilkins' amenuensis John Tillotson, and spent her time making medicines and sharing her recipes with a grateful Robert Hooke.[18]

Yet if the Fauconbergs, Lockharts and Wilkins were the family success stories, many other Cromwells remained unpalatable, even suspicious to the new regime, particularly those who had been the most conspicuously political. Clusters of Cromwellians and Commonwealthsmen formed to create safe spaces for shared memories – groups which the government kept under close watch and harassed at moments of State insecurity. One such circle gathered at Charles Fleetwood's new home at Stoke Newington which he acquired with his third marriage, two years after Bridget's death.[19] Here he raised his children with Bridget, as well as his two children by his first wife, and Bridget's four children from her marriage to Henry Ireton. Fleetwood House, as it came to be known, was a 60-room mansion and so there was plenty of space not only for the many half siblings but also for old friends.[20] The independent preacher John Owen, and perhaps others, lived there, forming a conventicle church which attracted large numbers of New Model veterans including Desborough who moved close by.[21] Thus these grandchildren of Oliver Cromwell spent their late childhood and adolescence in a radical enclave hearing the stories of their famous parents and grandparents from those who counted them heroes.

Richard Cromwell's family at Hursley also formed a space outside Restoration society which supported non-conformist religion. Dorothy Cromwell – so briefly *de facto* queen as Lady Protectoress – achieved a degree of fame in the locality for helping dissenting clergy now ejected from the church under the government's Uniformity Act of 1662.[22] One clergyman even celebrated her in poetry:

All things here supernatural seem to me;
I think God made them purposefully for thee,
Who hath all joys to your fair self consin'd,
Whose humble head a golden crown resign'd/
Th'ill judging world's mistaken; you're a Queen,
In spite of fate till now, your pow'r is seen
In your own little world, where you control
Th'unruly passions which disturb the soul.[23]

At least in this little corner of Hampshire, Dorothy reigned still. Yet it was a poor consolation for the perpetual absence of her husband and the lot of single motherhood, made yet worse when her father, mother, sister and brother-in-law died, leaving her alone by the late

1660s to raise her three orphaned nieces as well as her own fatherless children.

Richard meanwhile languished in lonely, impoverished exile, moving around Europe under assumed names always beginning with 'C' – an anonymous Mr Clarke or Mr Cranberry. Accounts reached London that he was in France before his uncle John Wilkins reportedly recommended he move to Spain or Italy.[24] A story recorded by Clarendon places him at Pezenas en route to Geneva in the late 1660s where he met the Prince of Conti. Conti, not knowing the identity of the unknown Englishman, opined that Richard Cromwell was 'the basest fellow alive', a 'coxcomb, coquin, poltroon', to which the embittered Richard replied that the young Protector had 'been betrayed by those he most trusted' before changing the subject.[25] Even absent, Richard was a focal point for resistance and repression, just as Charles Stuart had been in the 1650s. In 1665, there were reports that Colonel Ingoldsby and others were trying to reinstate him, while the following year, the government published his name among those wanted for questioning and sent soldiers to Hursley to search for him.[26] They even frisked the family, finding a letter hidden down Richard's daughter's 'bosom' which outlined the route by which the family smuggled money to him in Paris, and questioned his servant who testified to his master's innocence of any plotting. Far from scheming in exile, he said, Richard was being tutored in the sciences, 'drawing landscapes and reading books'.[27]

Richard's chief comfort, as Oliver's had been when away on campaign, was news from home. 'My hopes are in thee,' he wrote to his eldest daughter Elizabeth who became his chief correspondent, 'and in my greatest troubles deprivements of dearest and nearest relations, in my solitary life, when I have looked about and cast my thoughts upon my children . . . my whole soul hath been refreshed.'[28] But letters from home could also bring fresh torment. In 1675, by which time Richard had been away for 15 years missing the whole of his children's childhoods, he learned from them that Dorothy was gravely ill. He replied with 'great grief and sorrow', begging that God 'would look upon a poor afflicted family'. 'Pray embrace thy mother for me,' he wrote, 'I do love her . . . A good mother and a loving wife – her name is a sweet ointment, her soul is precious.'[29] Dorothy died soon afterwards having never seen Richard again. Providence had dealt a terrible life sentence for the convivial, sociable Richard in punishment for the nine months in power he had never sought. Not only Dorothy, his mother and sister Bridget had died before he could return, but also the brother he adored who, more than anyone else, had shared the extraordinary and devastating course of his life. Henry Cromwell was only 46 when he died in 1674 after 14 years of supervised seclusion at Spinney Abbey; the dynamic ruler of Ireland and Protectoral prince reduced to obsolescence and obscurity. Gone too were all of the happy Claypoles who had lived in the nurseries of the royal palaces. The last of Betty and John's children had died in 1678. While Claypole himself, who had kept in touch with his brothers and sisters-in-law, now cut a sad figure, estranged from his second wife (a merchant's widow) and living out his last years with a laundress in chambers in London's Middle Temple, his beloved Northborough sold to ward off bankruptcy.[30]

It was a poor homecoming for Richard when he finally returned in 1680–1. Though he felt it was now possible to live again in his own country, he did not deem it safe enough to live under his own name nor return openly to his family at Hursley – now managed by his only surviving son and heir Oliver, the baby who had been born to so much rejoicing at the height of his grandfather's Protectorate. It was still a 'very sharp, and a solitary time' made worse when his youngest daughter Dorothy, whom he had never met, herself died in 1681.[31] 'The weight is heavy, our way is rugged, and the night is very dark,' he wrote. Yet life improved in 1683 when Richard was introduced to the Pengellys – perhaps through their links to Fleetwood's family – with whom he lodged first in East Finchley and then Cheshunt for the rest of his life.[32] They became a surrogate family to 'our gentleman', as they always referred to him, and Richard supported their son Tom in his education and later legal career.

Their accounts reveal a material life which was at least pleasant for the purposeless Richard. The former Lord Protector cultivated an interest in home remedies and enjoyed tea, wine, sherry, brandy and preserves, with a particular fondness for potted meats. A true Cromwell, he smoked and kept dogs, eventually splashing out on a horse and manservant, the swarthy 'Black Robert'. He must have been a debonair figure as he gradually journeyed further to Peckham and London, sporting silver buttons, doeskin gloves, periwigs, an expensive sword and glasses.[33] One visit took him to a dinner party in

Westminster with his old family chaplain from where he may have chosen to visit his father's head still perched above Westminster Hall. His complicated feelings on his loss – what Bishop Burnet called 'the instability of human greatness' – emerge from the anecdotes of those who knew him.[34] Contemporaries spoke of his gravity, piety and modesty, reporting that he 'was not very free to speak of his former elevation'. When he did, wry humour and bitterness mingled. Several accounts record his careful preservation of a small green trunk within which he kept many loyal addresses he had received as Lord Protector. There, he joked, he kept 'the lives and fortunes of all the good people of England.'[35]

Richard was right to keep his head down, for these were stormy years for English politics. Charles II's rule had become increasingly autocratic and there was widespread concern when it was revealed that his heir, his brother James Duke of York, was a Catholic. New political parties emerged from the Exclusion Crisis of 1678–81 when the 'Whigs' sought to prevent James from succeeding his brother and urged new constraints on the powers of the Crown against the opposition of the 'Tories'. The ghosts of the Parliamentarians and regicides came alive in the press once more as people said that '[sixteen-]forty-one is come again'.[36] Whigs used the Civil Wars as a rallying cry now that Stuart absolutism and 'popery' again threatened England's constitutional and religious liberties. The government, meanwhile, abandoned its explicit policy of forgetting the conflict to remind the public of the anarchy it had brought. This included casting around for conspirators in Cromwellian and Commonwealth circles. Inevitably Richard's name resurfaced and, when the Rye House Plot to assassinate Charles and James on their return from Newmarket races was uncovered in 1683, Charles II ordered 'Mr. Richard Cromwell, the late pretended Protector, brought before him in order to be examined', although he could not be found.[37] Treason was surely hereditary and the commission investigating the plot was told that 'Mr Cromwell, son of Richard Cromwell, who usually goes by the name of Mr. Cranbourne, was so vain as to endeavour to make a party for himself or his father in the city'. Young Oliver had a famous accomplice, moreover, as it was 'believed the said Mr. Cromwell and Mr. Ireton, the son of the Lieutenant-General Ireton, would assist in the intended assassination of the King and the Duke of York'.[38] Once more the unstoppable alliance of an Oliver Cromwell and a Henry Ireton threatened revolution against Stuart autocracy.

If the cautious Richard and his son's involvement was unlikely, that is not true of Oliver's grandson Henry Ireton, son of the regicide Henry Ireton and Bridget Cromwell who had been raised in the radical enclave of Fleetwood House in Stoke Newington. Henry Ireton junior was a chip off the old block, remembered by his wife for his 'great probity and equality of mind, together with the love of his country' and his father's austerity, having 'an unusual command of his appetites and passions, from the natural force of his reason, and the motives of the Christian religion'.[39] He associated with known plotters, including his father's old sparring partner from the Putney Debates, the Leveller John Wildman. Henry avoided arrest after the Rye House plot in 1684, travelling to the continent where it was rumoured he was received by William of Orange, the Protestant stadholder of the United Provinces of the Netherlands and Stuart cousin who had become a figurehead for Whig opposition.[40] Henry returned in April 1685, two months after Charles II's death and James II's accession, with instructions for a planned uprising by Charles's illegitimate son, the Duke of Monmouth, known as the Monmouth Rebellion.[41]

Henry's sister Bridget Ireton, meanwhile, had also inherited their parents' godliness, radicalism and courage. Married to the lawyer Thomas Bendish, son of Oliver Cromwell's former ambassador to the Ottoman Empire, she lived close to her half-sister Mary Fleetwood and her husband in the bustling port town of Great Yarmouth which had a strong Independent congregation and radical community fond of celebrating Oliver Cromwell's memory.[42] Here Bridget helped her husband run salt marshes and a saltworks on Cobholm Island, dabbling in the occasional bout of smuggling.[43] She was also well-placed to aid her brother when he was arrested on his arrival back in England in 1685. Bridget later claimed she helped him escape, yet Henry was soon re-arrested and charged with high treason after appearing before King James II himself.[44] Though committed to Newgate prison in November, Henry was treated well, with the King personally permitting Bridget to visit.[45] April saw him pardoned and released, perhaps on account of illness as a well-disposed James assigned him a nurse on his release order.[46]

Such magnanimity did not extend to Henry's stepfather Charles Fleetwood, however. Fleetwood's stepson had argued for James's exclusion from the succession and in 1686 both men were fined £7,000 when informers infiltrated Fleetwood House's non-conformist conventicles.[47] Fleetwood was also officially named a disaffected person and likely Whig supporter who should provide security for good behaviour.[48] It is likely too that Henry Cromwell's son and namesake sympathised with the Monmouth Rebellion, for two of his wife Hannah's brothers took part. A spirited non-conformist, she courageously pleaded with James II himself on their behalf, raising £2,000 to pay the infamous Judge Jeffreys, who presided over the 'Bloody Assizes' which tried the rebels, reportedly even clinging to his coach until she was whipped away. The blood money could not spare them execution, but it saved Hannah's brothers from being disembowelled first.[49]

With more heads joining Oliver's above Westminster Hall, the Monmouth Rebellion brutally crushed and the Tories in the ascendancy, it seemed that absolute monarchy was again the order of the day. As one poet saw it, 'Whilst the brave Tudors wore th'Imperial crown, / But since the race of Stewarts came / It has recoil'd to Popery and shame . . . Let Cromwell's Ghost smile with Contempt to see / old England struggling under Slavery.'[50] Yet change was in the wind. Sometime towards the end of James's short reign, a violent storm snapped the pole bearing Oliver's head and it blew down to land at the feet of a sentry who secreted it in the chimney of his house. Oliver was on his travels again while his family considered once more how to free themselves from the Stuarts.

Protestant wind

Around this time, in November 1688, a fleet of over 400 Dutch ships crossed the Channel to invade England. The 'Protestant Wind' which blew the Dutch fleet towards England's shores had blown before, exactly a century earlier, only then to scatter England's enemies. The Spanish Armada of 130 ships which approached the English coast in July 1588 had posed an existential threat as the Catholic King Philip II sought to conquer the heretical country of his former sister-in-law Elizabeth I. Thomas Cromwell's Reformation stood in grave peril, but a new generation of Cromwells then rose to its defence. Edward Cromwell, Thomas's great-grandson and heir to Gregory's barony, was already a professional soldier and ready to serve his Queen. So too was the head of the Hinchingbrooke branch of the family. Mustering the men of Huntingdon, Sir Henry Cromwell urged his neighbours that they must all 'provide to the uttermost of our powers this larger proportion which her majesty doth require at our hands for the defence of our own lives liberties wives wealth children and country and especially the true gospel of christ'. 'Lay aside all malice and privy grudges,' he exhorted them, and 'join hands and hearts together in the united bands of amity and unity.'[51] This they did, and leaving his son in charge of the town of Ramsey, Sir Henry marched his horse troop and 400 infantry to join the Army at Tilbury where Edward Cromwell's brother-in-law, Catherine's husband Sir Lionel Tollemache of Helmingham Hall, also stood ready to do his duty.[52] Both men may have been close enough to the mounted, armour-clad Elizabeth to hear her famous declaration that she had 'the heart and stomach of a king, and of a king of England too, and think foul scorn that Parma or Spain, or any prince of Europe should dare to invade the borders of my realm'.

Now in 1688, Thomas's Reformation was in danger once more. So too was Oliver's legacy of the Civil Wars, and the latest generation of Cromwells stepped up to defend both. The recent birth of a son to the Catholic James II had forced his opponents to take action and Mary Cromwell's husband Viscount Fauconberg joined with other nobles to invite James's daughter Princess Mary and her Protestant husband William, Prince of Orange, to take the throne.[53] Bridget Cromwell's daughter, Bridget Bendish, played a part too, being privy to 'the Secret of the Revolution', distributing William's publicity materials from her coach when ostensibly out shopping.[54] Once William landed, James's position collapsed and he fled into exile. The Stuart dynasty had been overthrown for a second time. It was William now who was perceived to take up Oliver's mantle 'to deliver our miserable and distressed kingdoms from popery and slavery'.[55] This time there would be no uncertainty and no way back. Although its constitutional status was ambiguous, the Bill of Rights, with which Parliament settled the crown jointly on William and Mary and their Protestant heirs, reaffirmed the parliamentary and personal freedoms for which the parliamentary Good Old Cause of the Civil Wars had been fought. This 'Glorious Revolution' made the monarchy accountable to the law and to the people as represented in Parliament, renouncing Stuart attitudes to return England to the *de facto* monarchical republic (or republican monarchy) of Elizabeth I and the Cromwells.[56]

The surviving members of the Cromwell family embraced the change. Although they had shown outward support for the returned Stuart kings, their loyalty was only ever skin deep. Oliver's heirs were natural Whigs. As Richard wrote when looking for a wife for his son, 'a little Whig' would be preferable to 'a great Tory'.[57] Fauconberg was rewarded by the new King with an earldom and he and Mary entertained the new Queen at Sutton Court.[58] There they also welcomed John Tillotson – John and Robina Wilkins' son-in-law – who became a favourite of Queen Mary and was made Archbishop of Canterbury despite his Cromwell wife.[59] Tillotson also introduced Bridget Bendish to Queen Mary who supposedly promised her a pension for supporting the Glorious Revolution.[60] Bridget's brother Henry Ireton was also rehabilitated, appointed an equerry to King William and gentleman of horse, and rising high in the Army before becoming a Whig-supporting MP.[61] Henry Cromwell's son and namesake enjoyed a similar career, though he relied on his relations for help: financial support, recommendation from the favoured Fauconbergs, and even a spell living with his uncle Charles Fleetwood – all bitterness over Fleetwood's role in bringing down his father Henry and uncle Richard's Protectorate evidently forgiven with the passage of time.[62] It was there that Henry's last child was born in 1691, a final baby for the experienced father and stepfather Fleetwood to dote on before his death the following year and fitting amends to the long-dead brother-in-law he had done so much to frustrate.[63] 'I have sufficient cause from experience to trust the Lord with children whom I shall leave behind me. His blessing with a little is great riches,' Fleetwood had once said – a belief which must have strengthened the infamous milksop at the end.[64]

If the political context had somewhat softened after 1688, the Cromwell name continued to carry stigma, for Oliver Cromwell had not been entirely rehabilitated by the Glorious Revolution even if many of his principles were. Though more people now began to talk of Oliver's greatness and achievements, and balanced – if not positive – biographies started to appear, both high Tories and radical

Whigs and republicans continued to curse his name. Richard's family still suffered from this stigma, with his son Oliver prevented from raising a regiment of horse to fight for William against James II in Ireland and then barred from taking up a parliamentary seat. Consequently, Richard refused to come out of hiding in spite of his daughter's hopes that 'the turns made of late by the Wheel of providence may lead you from your cell and hermit's life that your family may be made happy by your presence', after God had 'so wonderfully preserved us these 28 years wandering apart'. Instead, Richard bemoaned his son's rashness in drawing attention upon them, while despairing of public life: 'Pray do not call me a fanatic why all our world are mad . . . And is it not a strange sight to see a sober man in a mad world.' 'I have born alone thirty years banished and under silence; and my strength and safety is to be retired, quiet, and silent,' he explained, 'our world is to be lamented, the day is only happy or rather favourable to them that have least to do in it.' At last Richard consented to see his family in person, but his son Oliver – unable to take up employment – frittered away money and mismanaged the Hursley estate before his early death in 1705. Richard and his daughters fell out over who should inherit the estate that had originally belonged to Richard's wife Dorothy; a distressing argument, drawing in the wider family, which was not resolved until it ended up in court.[65]

Dynamics were complex in a family that had experienced such vacillating fortunes. Talk of the past continued to inflame the tempers of Bridget Bendish and her aunts Mary and Frances, with Bridget once reprimanding Mary for disparaging Oliver, saying 'If I did not believe my grandmother to have been one of the most virtuous women in the world, I should consider your ladyship a bastard. I wonder how it could be possible that the daughter of the greatest and best man that ever lived could be so degenerate as not only to sit with patience to hear his memory so ill-treated, but to seem to assent to it.'[66] Members of the public were also in line for a sharp reprimand from Bridget if they spoke out of turn about her grandfather. Hearing a fellow passenger denigrate Oliver on a public coach to London, Bridget railed against him for the rest of the journey and, on their arrival, snatched another passenger's sword and challenged the man to a duel.[67] The complex Bridget spent her days 'stumping about' among her labourers at the salt pans, before dressing up for evenings in Great Yarmouth society which afforded her the utmost deference 'as a lady, who once expected, at this time, to have been one of the finest persons in Europe'.[68] That former life of Bridget's exalted childhood under her grandfather's rule certainly exerted a powerful pull on her mind. 'She looked upon him as at the first and greatest of mankind' and, if complimented on any of her own qualities, 'would say she learned it of her grandfather,' a friend wrote. One of these was the 'art of secret-keeping' which she claimed to have learned aged six sitting between Oliver's knees at Council meetings.[69]

'It is impossible to say what figure she might not have made in the world had she been placed in an elevated station,' an acquaintance wrote of Bridget, while her friend Samuel Say certainly saw her as Oliver's heir, having 'inherited more of his constitution of body, and complexion of mind, than any of his other descendants and relations', many of whom he had met.[70] 'Richard's son Oliver,' he conceded, 'had something indeed of the spirit of his grandfather, but all his other distinguishing qualifications seemed vastly inferior to the lady.'[71] The superiority of Bridget Cromwell's offspring by the dynamic Henry Ireton over the children of the lacklustre Richard struck another family member, who claimed Richard's daughters carried 'a consciousness of high rank, accompanied with a secret dread that those with whom they conversed should not observe and acknowledge it . . . as the daughter of Ireton had dignity without pride, the daughters of Richard Cromwell had pride without much dignity'.[72] Bishop Burnet joined the chorus of admirers for the bloodstock of Oliver's daughters, believing that Oliver had bequeathed them his best qualities and that they, given the chance, could have wielded political power better than his sons. Mary Fauconberg, he wrote, 'was a wise and worthy woman, more likely to have maintained the post (of Protector) than either of her brothers'.[73]

❦ ❦ ❦

The 1680s also saw the line of Thomas Cromwell's direct descendants – the Launde Cromwells who became the Royalist Irish Earls of Ardglass – emerge in a formidable woman, the inevitably named Elizabeth Cromwell. Thomas Cromwell's male line had ended with the death of Elizabeth's father, Baron Vere Essex Cromwell, in 1687. But that was not how his four times great-granddaughter saw it.[74] Elizabeth assumed the title of Baron Cromwell for herself and, despite much debate about the legality of this, she was listed as such years later at Queen Mary's funeral and her sister Queen Anne's coronation.[75] Beautiful, wilful and a substantial heiress, Elizabeth, 'Baroness Cromwell', cut a dash through English and Irish society at the turn of the eighteenth century, making friends and breaking hearts as she travelled from house party to house party.[76] In unrequited love letters from a young Virginian-born admirer in 1703, Baroness Cromwell dazzles with the charm, witty conversation and magnetic presence of the best of her family, 'glittering' in Dublin society. Soon after she married Edward Southwell, a precociously talented MP, academic and administrator with Tory views and evangelical leanings who had just been made chief secretary to the new Lord Lieutenant of Ireland.[77] While dying of consumption just six years later, Baroness Cromwell's correspondence was 'all the talk' of London, with speculation: 'Her eldest son will be Lord Crumwell, but some say he will not.'[78] In the event he opted not to use his mother's disputed title and thus the Cromwell name and the barony Henry VIII had granted to Gregory after Thomas's fall in 1540 were lost. But Thomas's genes continued to flow through the illustrious line of Southwells who maintained a key place in the Anglo-Irish elite and seats in Parliament for several generations.

By then the Stuart dynasty's days were numbered. Three of Oliver Cromwell's children – Richard, Mary and Frances – lived to see the Stuarts replaced in the line of succession to the throne. Between them the monarchs William, Mary and Anne had no living children, and in 1701 Parliament passed an Act of Succession leapfrogging over many nearer Catholic Stuart relatives to divert the crown to the Protestant Hanoverians, descendants of James I's daughter Elizabeth, Queen of Bohemia. Left out in the cold once more, the Stuart line of James II continued its quest to regain the throne from exile, his son the 'Old Pretender' James Stuart and grandson the 'Young Pretender' Bonnie Prince Charlie raising doomed Jacobite rebellions over the coming decades. There was no doubt for the last Cromwell siblings – or anyone else – that this was elective, parliamentary monarchy, not monarchy by divine right or strict inheritance; the achievement of their parents' Civil Wars was complete. Moreover, this was a British monarchy, the Stuart-sympathising Scots bound into the project through a formal union with England into a new Great Britain in 1707: the ultimate act of Cromwellian state-building in the manner of

Thomas's 1536 Act of Union with Wales. A union which James I and Charles I had longed for and which Oliver had briefly achieved under different terms in the 1650s. It was this strong, confident Britain which built on Oliver's achievements abroad to forge its global empire, which lasted into the twentieth century.

In 1712, two years before Queen Anne, the last of the Stuarts, died, another former head of state met his maker. Richard Cromwell died peacefully aged 85, after several years of ailing health, his final words a hopeful end to a traumatic life: 'Live in love, I am going to the God of love.'[79] It was not until 2015 that Queen Elizabeth II surpassed his record as the longest-lived head of state. Six years later, Richard's daughters sold Hursley for £35,000 and moved to Bedford Row in London. The new owner soon demolished the house, either because it was in a parlous state or, one story went, because he could not bear to live in a house of the Cromwells. Yet the memory of the Cromwells could not be so easily expunged. During the demolition, the die of Richard's Great Seal of the Commonwealth was found hidden in a wall.[80] When Richard's last daughter died unmarried at a great age in 1731, she requested her executors, Henry Cromwell's grandsons, erect a monument to the family in Hursley Church: the tablet bears the Cromwell name and coat of arms but no mention of Richard or Oliver's positions as Lord Protectors.[81] Hursley Park itself is now a research laboratory belonging to the company IBM.

Richard's daughters died without children, bringing to an end Oliver's eldest male line. Richard's sister Mary Fauconberg also died childless, and only a few months after her brother. Mary had been widowed since New Year's Eve 1700, her husband entombed in the parish church near Newburgh with a magnificent monument attributed to the great Grinling Gibbons. Mary reportedly wished the inscription to record Fauconberg's marriage to the daughter of his Highness, the then Lord Protector of England, and when the inscriber objected, she replied that no-one could dispute matters of fact. In compromise, as at Hursley, the name Cromwell does appear but not the title Lord Protector.[82] Newburgh passed to Fauconberg's nephew (neatly married to Frances's daughter), but Mary kept Sutton Court and its contents where she and Frances spent much of their dotage together, the last survivors of their shipwrecked family. Here a visitor in the early eighteenth century recorded seeing Mary, who he viewed as 'that curious piece of antiquity, the daughter of Oliver Cromwell, still fresh and gay though of great age'. Frances inherited much of Mary's estate at her death. Outlasting Queen Anne, she lived a further seven years into the reign of the first Hanoverian, George I, dying at 83 in 1721, 63 years after she lost her first husband Robert Rich who had been mourned as a prince. Frances was buried with Mary in St Nicholas's Church in Chiswick: Oliver's 'little wenches' together in death as they had been so much in life.

But the Cromwells' story did not end. Frances, together with two of her siblings – the long-dead Henry and Bridget – left descendants scattered across the English-speaking world who genealogists have made a sport of tracing (reckoned to number over 1,000 by the late nineteenth century and now more than 5,000).[83] None now carries the name Cromwell itself. The kaleidoscope of descent produces a dizzying array of soldiers, scholars, reformers, poets, peers, and, curiously often, first-class cricketers.[84] It did not take long for the Protector's blood to re-enter the establishment it had once overthrown, and by the Victorian era the family tree was thick with grand names – Pelham, Frankland, Harcourt, Clarendon, Salisbury, Bulwer-Lytton, Worsley and de Grey – and none more prolific than the extraordinarily fecund Villiers, descended also from Charles II's mistress Barbara Villiers. The lines of Thomas and Oliver Cromwell themselves also rejoined in the Irish aristocracy through the Wingfields. Among English peers today, a startling number trace descent from the Protector, including the Earl of St Andrews, son of the late Duchess of Kent (a Worsley), who was tenth in line to the throne at his birth – a Cromwell within touching distance of the crown.

In politics, each of the great offices of state has been occupied by a genetic Cromwell at least once, with the prime minister Viscount Goderich at the vanguard. Dozens more served as MPs, ministers and cabinet members. Secretaries of State for War in both World Wars I and II were descendants of Cromwell, as was the latter conflict's Director of Military Intelligence, Major-General Frederick Beaumont-Nesbitt. In previous generations, many others channelled their Cromwellian energy into empire and exploration, becoming governors of Bombay and Madras, or governors-general of India, Canada and South Africa. Franklands and Gardiners especially fought and fell in the service of war, science and evangelism – from Waterloo, Lucknow and Vera Cruz to Tierra del Fuego, Sierra Leone and Persia. Dozens died in World War I, among them the poet Julian

Grenfell. A scholarly strain ran through Oxford and Cambridge dons, antiquarians, composers, pioneering engineers, naturalists, scientists and mathematicians and historians, including two historians of the seventeenth century itself, Samuel Rawson Gardiner and Maria Theresa Lewis. Following the story of the Cromwells since 1660 is like reading a miniature history of England itself, from colonial governors, archdeacons and suffragettes to business leaders, BBC presenters and Olympic medallists. Taken together they form a kind of national pageant: the afterlives of the Cromwells whose blood still moves quietly through England's veins. For all those of notable achievements, still more Cromwells were modest individuals, often minor professionals of non-conformist faith and liberal politics.[85] Like so many George Eliot's Dorothea Brookes, they had no earthly titles 'but a vein of sincere piety' was 'their most distinguished ornament in the silent and retired paths of private life.'[86]

The Cromwells' famous name and ancestry was of passing interest to the public. In 1792, the *Gentleman's Magazine* carried the death notice of 'Mrs. Elizabeth Cromwell, eldest daughter and last surviving child of Mr. Richard Cromwell, grandson of Henry Lord-Lieutenant of Ireland. She has left the bulk of her fortune to Mr. Oliver Cromwell, attorney, clerk of the Million-Bank.'[87] But their heritage meant more to themselves, kept alive through heirlooms and the constant use of family names. Oliver's great-grandson Richard Cromwell, a keen family genealogist and collector, chose to get married in the chapel of the Banqueting House on the Protectorate's holy day, 3 September 1723. His three unmarried daughters – the Miss Cromwells of Hampstead – guarded their family treasures inherited from the Hursley branch, including Protector Richard Cromwell's trunk of papers. One reportedly told the family's first chronicler that she disliked giving way to the royal family as it was 'disagreeable to give place to those who are in that elevated state which I ought to possess', though her sisters later denied this: even in the 1780s, Cromwells had to be careful what they said of those in power.[88]

But the nature of power had changed, thanks in part to the Cromwells, even if it had been over a century since they held it themselves. Two months after Frances died in 1721, the Whig Robert Walpole became the first British prime minister. From then on, it was not monarchs but increasingly prime ministers who wielded political power, and so it is fitting that they are surrounded by reminders of the Cromwell family to this day. The Cockpit in Whitehall where the family once lived is now 10 Downing Street, and, by his second marriage in 1715, Frances's son John, who had been the East India Company's Governor of Bengal, acquired Chequers Court in Buckinghamshire which later became the prime minister's country retreat. There, family heirlooms are favourite curios that prime ministers like to show visiting dignitaries, while portraits of Oliver and his wife Elizabeth, Bridget, Betty and Frances hang alongside monarchs and nobles, watching over the glittering receptions and anxious summits that had once been their domain. Harold Wilson used to love showing guests around Chequers while Tony Blair enjoyed living in a house 'stuffed with Cromwell memorabilia'. At a negotiation for the 1998 Good Friday Agreement, he showed Oliver's death mask to Sinn Féin's chief negotiator Martin McGuinness, saying: 'So you see, he really is dead.'

'I wouldn't bet on it,' McGuinness replied.[89]

Proper attention

Thomas Cromwell once said 'that there was nothing he desired so much in this world as to leave a good name behind him'. This he conspicuously failed to do, for all that his descendants nursed a quiet pride in their lineage. His name, and that he bequeathed his family, has been lauded and loathed, eulogised and demonised, the subject of almost five hundred years of unresolved argument. The name Cromwell has been everything else, but never simply 'good'. The two most famous men who bore it have seen their reputations fluctuate wildly down the centuries, often in inverse directions. Both Thomas and Oliver were villainised in the immediate years after their deaths when those who had triumphed over them in death gleefully and somewhat desperately assassinated their characters or airbrushed them out of the story entirely. But for each, a significant minority of the population ignored the Tudor and Stuart publicity machines and remembered the Cromwells' unarguable talent. Elizabeth I's principal secretary bemoaned a generation after Thomas's death, 'Would God England had a Cromwell: I will say no more', and similar sentiments bubbled to the surface frequently in the years following Oliver's death once disillusionment with the Restoration set in.[90]

But then Thomas and Oliver's paths diverged. The Protestant writers of the later sixteenth century rescued Thomas from the reputational exile into which the spiteful Henry VIII had thrown him, raising him up as a hero: the 'valiant soldier and captain of Christ' who laid the foundations for England's Reformation.[91] Bishop Burnet, who wrote sympathetically of Oliver and his children in their own time, judged Thomas 'a man of mean birth but noble qualities'.[92] This favourable judgement lasted into the nineteenth century, though Whig historians concerned with parliamentary progress preferred to emphasise Thomas's political and administrative reforms over his religious drive, and to ignore his ruthless streak. Oliver too was secularised, his volcanic faith neutered, but in the service of a contrasting, overwhelmingly negative reputation fuelled by the propaganda of the restored Stuarts that endured until the Victorian age. Under the Restoration's long shadow, he was demonised as a hellish bogeyman wheeled out to frighten children; a canting hypocrite and unscrupulous Machiavellian whose faith, where it wasn't criticised as fanatical, was a smokescreen for ruthless ambition. Alexander Pope – himself a close friend and published correspondent of Sir Henry Cromwell of Hinchingbrooke's great grandson – considered Oliver 'damned to everlasting fame', exemplifying how 'all that raised the hero, sunk the man'.[93] Oliver was, to his old enemy Edward Hyde, the Earl of Clarendon, a 'brave bad man'.[94]

No views were dispassionate. In 1773, James Boswell fled from the room when his father and the diarist Samuel Johnson engaged in an 'altercation' over Oliver which was 'exceedingly warm and violent'.[95] Then, both Oliver and Thomas were household names, occupying secure spots in the national imagination. Though the travel writer Thomas Byng showed how the two Cromwells were often confused with each other in their desecration of churches and castles, he used both as commonly understood historical references in his 1788 poem about his own family history. In this he gives his four-year-old son the positive examples of 'Noll' (Oliver), 'the glory of this land', and 'Cromwell' (Thomas), taught by Wolsey 'How to find the way / Out of his fall to rise in.'[96] Byron's Childe Harold looked to Oliver's example as 'the sagest of usurpers'. Meanwhile, people paid to see the gruesome spectacle of Oliver's head which had been retrieved from its hiding place in the sentry's chimney and sold on as a commercial curiosity. The popularity of Shakespeare's *Henry VIII* from the eighteenth into the nineteenth century kept Thomas in public consciousness; it was this play that Fanny Price was reading aloud in Jane Austen's 1814 *Mansfield Park* when the untrustworthy Henry Crawford took it off her to play all the parts, including 'Cromwell's'.[97] Victorian theatregoers flocked to watch the play performed, with the villainous Cardinal Wolsey, undone by his ambition before the eyes of his protégé Cromwell, a coveted role for leading actors.

It was the Victorians who changed the conversation, as they so often did, broadly reversing the two Cromwells' fortunes. Campaigns for Catholic freedoms and nostalgia for the pre-Reformation England challenged Thomas's formerly heroic status, recasting him as an unprincipled, greedy and 'brutal blacksmith'.[98] Members of the reactionary Oxford Movement, reluctant to criticise a monarch, blamed Thomas rather than Henry VIII for the destructive Reformation, and carried their hostility forward to the later generations of Puritan Cromwells too. High Tory, high Anglican John Keble was vicar of Richard Cromwell's village of Hursley from 1836 to 1866 during which time he made the small Hampshire village a model Oxford Movement community. Keble was so uncomfortable sharing the village with the long-dead Cromwells, he removed the monument to Richard Cromwell in the church, concealed the precise location of his tomb, and sealed off the crypt under the chancel where he and his family members were buried. The monument had to wait for Keble's death to be reinstated in a less high-profile position beneath the tower at the west end, and it remains in a poor state today.[99]

As the nineteenth century progressed, Thomas Cromwell moved into the nation's Machiavellian top spot as Oliver vacated it. Proponents of electoral reform revisited Oliver, with one wit advertising for a political champion concluding 'Any person of the name of Cromwell would be preferred'. In 1843, while at Oxford the poet Matthew Arnold won the university's prestigious Newdigate Prize for his adulatory poem on a heroic Oliver Cromwell. Two years later, the publishing phenomenon of Thomas Carlyle's *Letters and Speeches of Oliver Cromwell* rescued the Lord Protector from ignominy, enabling the public to hear his own voice for the first time. Carlyle himself believed he had performed this miracle just in time before Oliver became unreachable, stretching back over two centuries of vitriol 'across the death-chasms, and howling figures of decay'.[100] Reading Oliver's own words, working-class radicals found a self-made, anti-establishment warrior while mainstream Victorians discovered virtues that chimed with their own: godliness, toleration and virtuous morality. Many saw Oliver as the ultimate Englishman, 'the greatest because the most typical Englishman of all time' as the consummate Civil War historian and Oliver's descendant Samuel Rawson Gardiner described him. Assumed narratives were overturned left, right and centre. Only a nation 'ashamed' of Oliver, one popular lecturer said in 1849, could have overblown the 'small affair of 1688' at the expense of 'the mighty business of 1642'.[101]

This high age of non-conformity claimed Oliver for its own. Experts examined the relic of Oliver's head for its authenticity and people debated whether it should be displayed in a museum or given a Christian burial. For the first time, there were campaigns for statues and memorials to the hitherto disavowed giant of British history. These exposed Oliver's contested reputation and the hostility to him still entrenched in the establishment. Suggestions in 1845 to include Oliver in the newly commissioned statuary inside Parliament, as partial redress for the shame of his body's public desecration in 1661, were hotly debated in the press before being refused. Campaigners eventually achieved statues in Manchester (1875), two in Warrington (1899) and Oliver's one-time hometown of St Ives (1901), while several non-conformist churches commissioned stained-glass depictions. Only the dedication of the Liberal Party leader Lord Rosebery, amid the nationwide celebrations of the tricentenary of Oliver's birth in 1899, secured the magnificent bronze figure by Sir Hamo Thornycroft which still stands guard outside Parliament. Even then, opponents prevented the statue's unveiling on 'Cromwell Day', 3 September, and when it was revealed by a workman weeks later, it was at 7.30 am with no ceremony to avoid protests.[102] The unusual combination of English monarchists and Irish nationalists still protest the statue today, especially on 3 September.

By the early twentieth century, both the famed Cromwells were firmly part of popular culture, with the fragile connection between them preserved. The Edwardian music hall sensation Marie Lloyd delighted fans with a wry song that blended drunken violence with popular history, for which the chorus ran:

It's one of the ruins that Cromwell knocked about a bit
One that Oliver Cromwell knocked about a bit

In the gay old days there used to be some doings
No wonder that the poor old Abbey went to ruins
Those who've studied history sing and shout of it
And you can bet your life that isn't a doubt of it
Outside the Oliver Cromwell last Saturday night
I was one of the ruins Cromwell knocked about a bit.

It was, in fact, the last song she ever sang, for Marie collapsed while performing it at the Edmonton Empire in November 1922, dying later that night. Hundreds of people, from stage stars to flower boys, taxi drivers and trade unions, sent wreaths to mark Marie's death. T. S. Eliot called her funeral 'a significant moment in English history'. For Marie had 'represented and expressed that part of the English nation which has perhaps the greatest vitality and interest': a working-class culture in which the historic muddle between Thomas and Oliver Cromwell as the amalgamated despoiler of abbeys was an instantly recognisable throwaway reference, and the Cromwell name adorned pubs and street signs across the land.[103]

❧ ❧ ❧

Down the centuries, Oliver's complex reputation has travelled more internationally than Thomas's, though the latter's largely unsung impact on the development of the British Empire and formation of the United States is incontestable. The name of Cromwell had particular resonance in the late eighteenth-century period of revolution. Oliver was a figure of fascination in France and the revolutionary Maximilien Robespierre's opponents regularly branded him a Cromwellian tyrant during the Terror of the 1790s. Edward Sexby's 1657 pamphlet *Killing No Murder* which had justified assassinating Oliver was even published in translation in Paris to call for Robespierre's death.[104] In the next century, Alexander Dumas's sequel to *The Three Musketeers* featured Oliver manipulating the musketeers' plot to save Charles I on the scaffold; while Victor Hugo wrote *Oliver Cromwell*, a wildly imagined and monumental play of 7,000 verses dramatising the fascinating 'vast historical scene' of Oliver's rejection of the Crown. Napoleon's rule revived memories of Oliver again on both sides of the Channel. This worked both ways, fanning perceptions of Oliver's tyranny, but also reminding the English now celebrating the victories of Wellington and Nelson that they had an older, perhaps even greater, martial hero to revere, and one who had inspired awe in the French of his day.

Oliver's afterlife in America was even more complex. Soaked in its seventeenth-century Puritan heritage, the new country drew inspiration from the old. Patriots seeking independence from Britain venerated the early leaders of the Good Old Cause. When future presidents John Adams and Thomas Jefferson toured England's Civil War battlefields in 1786, Adams deplored the ignorance and carelessness the native English displayed towards the 'holy ground' of Worcester. 'Do Englishmen so soon forget the ground where liberty was fought for?' he wondered, prescribing that 'All England should come in pilgrimage to this hill, once a year.'[105] Yet Oliver's personal reputation was more disputed, as some patriots considered him the grand betrayer of the English republic. Loyalists demonised the regicide of 1649 and Oliver's perceived tyranny so effectively in their efforts to prevent independence, that patriots referenced both with care. Some leaned into Oliver's example nevertheless, with the Boston committee of correspondence issuing orders during the Tea Party signed 'O. C.' and one group of patriots punishing an Anglican clergyman by shutting him in a pub room to stare at a picture of Oliver.[106] George Washington, whose own career so closely resembled Oliver's, was often addressed as 'Great Cromwell' and 'Lord Protector'.[107] South Americans too used Oliver as a historical analogue in their wars for independence from Spain in the early nineteenth century. Both the Venezuelan General Simón Bolívar and Argentine General José de San Martin referenced Oliver positively in their campaigns.[108]

Oliver was resurrected too during the American Civil War of the 1860s, his popular reputation endlessly malleable in the hands of both sides keen both to appropriate and weaponise his legacy. Generally, the war was framed as a struggle between Southern confederate 'cavaliers' and Northern unionist 'roundheads'. Many southerners associated Abraham Lincoln with Oliver in what they considered his fanatical anti-slavery campaign and likened the invasion of the South to Oliver's invasion of Ireland; while Northern abolitionists claimed their Puritan heritage, with black soldiers enlisted to the unionist army encouraged to think of themselves as Cromwellians in their quest for liberty. John Brown, the radical anti-slavery campaigner whose body still famously lies 'a-mouldering in the grave', was seen as 'a regular Cromwellian, dug up from two centuries' and 'the Oliver

Cromwell of America'.[109] Yet, with southerners as much as northerners devouring Carlyle's recent literary version of Cromwell as the devout and sturdy hero, the confederates sought their own Cromwellian to deliver victory, alighting on General Thomas 'Stonewall' Jackson. 'General Jackson is the exact counterpart of Oliver as Carlyle draws him,' the confederate general William Pendleton wrote in his diary, while others called him a 'Cromwell in grey'.[110] The fascination with Oliver continued with Theodore Roosevelt penning an admiring biography of Oliver in 1900, shortly before he became president.

Irish emigrants brought more hostile views of Oliver across the Atlantic to add to the ongoing debate. Popular Irish lecturers spoke vividly of Oliver's crimes alongside those of Henry VIII who was also vilified, and folklore continued to travel well.[111] Migrated memories took on a new character in the American context and helped to bind Irish Americans together and connect them to the country they had left behind. In their homeland, meanwhile, Oliver's reputation as a bloody usurper shape-shifted through politics, society and myth, his name more powerful and emotive even than in England. Drogheda and Wexford remained bywords for brutality while 'Cromwell' or 'Cromwellian' swelled to become curse, insult, slander, shorthand, scar and scapegoat. Oliver was a harbinger of doom, a master of the dark arts whose army brought flocks of scavenging 'Cromwell's crows'. 'Cromwell's tracks in Ireland may be followed over ruins which yet seem fresh,' a Unitarian minister wrote in 1846. 'We can trace him as we do a ravenous animal by the blotches where he lay to rest or by the bloody fragments where he tore his prey.'[112] William Makepeace Thackeray recorded how he had 'heard the name many times from the Irish peasant, who still has an awe of the grim resolute Protector'.[113]

Ireland saw the only significant bloodshed of the Glorious Revolution of 1688 and, for many Irish, William III joined Oliver Cromwell in the national rogues' gallery. Jacobites paired the two conquerors often, imagining them sharing a cell in hell, with one popular song suggesting 'Disloyal' Whigs 'visit Noll and Will below'.[114] William's supporters, the Orangemen, meanwhile, went on their own journey, which took them from arguing over Oliver's reputation and relationship to 'King Billy', to embracing him, despite their avowed monarchism. Down to the modern era, Oliver has been re-animated at times of political change and sectarian conflict and been treated with particular caution in Anglo-Irish diplomacy. At one negotiation in 1998, David Trimble of the Ulster Unionist Party deliberately leafed through a biography of Oliver and flourished it under the nose of the Irish republican president of Sinn Féin, Gerry Adams.

The Cromwell name had continued to evolve over the twentieth century, often in ways shaped by world affairs. Oliver suffered from unfavourable comparisons with the century's dictators, and Hitler himself evidently admired him. Criticising the British politician Oswald Mosley's decision to call his followers fascists and black-shirts, Hitler suggested 'something typically English' instead, for 'if he had been starting a party in England he would have gone back to Cromwell & perhaps called his SA [Sturmabteilung] "Ironsides"' – a notion Unity Mitford deemed 'a sweet idea'.[115] At the other end of the political spectrum, some social revolutionaries saw Oliver as a positive example, although the growing interest among the public and left-wing historians in Oliver's old frenemies the Levellers generally damaged his standing. To the Russian communist Leon Trotsky, 'Cromwell was a great revolutionary of his time . . . the dead lion of the seventeenth century is in this sense immeasurably greater than many living dogs.' Despite Charles II's best efforts, he wrote, 'pre-Cromwellian society could not be re-established by any restoration . . . what has been written with the sword cannot be wiped out by the pen.' Instead, to Trotsky, the revolutionary changes of the sixteenth-century Reformation and the eighteenth-century Enlightenment met in the person of Oliver: 'In Cromwell Luther joins hands with Robespierre.'[116]

Thomas meanwhile continued his journey as the corrupt and faithless Machiavel, cemented in the public's imagination as the thuggish villain of the play and 1966 film *A Man For All Seasons* which took Thomas Stateside when it swept the Oscars. The 1970 film *Cromwell* briefly brought Oliver back to a wider audience, including the Presbyterian leader of the Democratic Unionist Party Iain Paisley, who claimed it to be the first film that tempted him into the cinema aged 44.[117] Oliver's head, meanwhile, had finally finished its long and bizarre journey to find eternal rest in a secret location in the chapel of his old Cambridge college Sidney Sussex. In these decades, academic historical opinion shifted more favourably for both Cromwells. From the 1950s, the historian Geoffrey Elton performed a similar rescue mission for Thomas that Carlyle had done for Oliver, championing a political and social reformer whose 'revolution in government' rendered him 'England's first parliamentary statesman'.[118] Since then, the sincerity of Thomas's faith has been largely restored to him, just as in recent decades the centrality of Oliver's Puritanism has been acknowledged in the mostly favourable accounts of his life.

❦ ❦ ❦

If Thomas's reputation had been broadly good and then bad, and Oliver's broadly bad and then good, both have been challenged by modern attitudes, not the least of which is apathy. Hilary Mantel shifted popular perceptions of Thomas Cromwell through her *Wolf Hall* trilogy, revitalising Thomas in public consciousness and rehabilitating his reputation. Her influence was such that Oliver felt a knock-on effect. Mantel recounted how, when she first told people decades earlier that she was working on Thomas Cromwell, they would ask in bewildered tones 'Don't you mean *Oliver*?' Yet, after *Wolf Hall*, the eminent Civil War historian Blair Worden found his editor asking him to specify that he meant Oliver and *not Thomas* in the title of one his own publications.[119] Since the millennium, when Oliver Cromwell was voted the 10th greatest Briton, he has dwindled further from public consciousness to languish largely in a Restoration landscape as if his Victorian revival never happened. Where he is remembered, it is usually in the popular caricature of the king-killing, Christmas-cancelling, Puritan killjoy: the pantomime villain of a *Horrible Histories* play singing 'we're the Puritans and we hate fun!' to the delighted shrieks of children.[120] The stubborn conviction that a Grinch-like Oliver personally stole Christmas is a far juicier story than the reality of his renowned charm and conviviality. Royalist narratives predominate in popular culture, particularly in novels and screen drama where 'the King wins the fictional argument'.[121] In these imaginings Parliamentarians are joyless thugs, and life under Oliver's repressive rule dark, fearful, and often characterised by superstition and stories of witch-hunting. A 2025 YouGov poll of Britons' attitudes to 43 monarchs since 1066 placed him second to last in popularity – losing out only (and ironically) to Henry VIII – but, like Henry, he made it into the top five for name recognition.[122]

Semi-official narratives meanwhile prefer to ignore him completely. The curious visitor struggles to find any mention, let alone any detail, of Oliver and his Protectorate on the information boards at Historic Royal Palaces' Hampton Court and the Banqueting House, or in Westminster Hall. His family, meanwhile, are hardly known at all despite their once prominent positions. Thus, if today's limited public view of Oliver Cromwell is subconscious, it derives in large part from the conscious views disseminated by those in political power. For them, Thomas and Oliver have each been convenient historical scapegoats and stunt doubles for the monarchy. From the start, Thomas drew direct flak away from Henry VIII in the traditional role of 'evil counsellor' who could be blamed as a stand-in for an unimpeachable monarch. Thomas not Henry was culpable for the destruction of the Reformation: 'an agent of Satan sent by the devil to lure King Henry to damnation,' in the influential words of Reginald Pole. It was Thomas not Henry who was attacked in the Pilgrimage of Grace. Even when Henry was allowed agency, Thomas's heir Oliver became the instrument of retribution for the crimes of the Reformation. So Henry Spelman, framing a national story at the Restoration, argued 'The King [Henry VIII] makes use of a Crumwell [Thomas] to dissolve the monasteries, and [G]od of a Crumwell [Oliver] borne in a dissolved monastery to punish the King [Charles I] . . . Thus our punishment sprang from our sins.'[123] Elsewhere Oliver too took punches for Henry VIII (and Elizabeth I) by standing in for their violent imperialist expansions in Ireland as the single, representative villain for the whole Tudor and Stuart period, thereby letting generations of politicians off the hook. He performs similar whipping boy services for the reputations of the 'martyr' Charles I and 'merry monarch' Charles II as the aggressor in the Civil Wars and the ambitious villain who single-handedly diverted England from its monarchical destiny. Since the moment Charles II stepped ashore in 1660, it has been far easier to blame one dead man as an aberration than to confront the deeper reasons why a generation of naturally inclined monarchists resorted to violence against the house of Stuart.

Later monarchs inherited these techniques, subverting or removing Oliver from the picture, keeping him permanently on the naughty step. Queen Victoria objected to Oliver's statue in Manchester (which at that point stood proudly in the city centre close to the cathedral). George V refused Winston Churchill's repeated requests to name a battleship *Oliver Cromwell*, despite Churchill's arguments – supported by Prime Minister Asquith – that Oliver was a founder and champion of the Navy, his name made England's enemies tremble, and that 'nothing in history will justify the view that the adoption of such a name would constitute any reflection, however vague, upon His Majesty's Royal House'.[124] Two generations on, Elizabeth II blocked Oliver's inclusion in a set of stamps commemorating all heads of state since James I, causing the whole project to be abandoned. Until only recently, Oliver's portrait at his old Cambridge college Sidney Sussex had its own curtains to cover his warty face from the serene gaze of any visiting royal. The monarchy has shown hostility even against ordinary members of the Cromwell family. Stories survive from the late eighteenth and early nineteenth century of Oliver's last direct male descendant, despairing that at least seven times heirs named Oliver Cromwell had died prematurely, seeking royal permission for his son-in-law to adopt the Cromwell surname and arms to prevent their loss. Accounts differ as to whether it was George III, George IV or William IV who refused, but the reaction was the same: 'No, no – no more Cromwells.'[125]

The unstable power of the Cromwell name – a word which alone could make the fearsome Cardinal Mazarin change colour – attests to the family's importance. No other non-royal family has had the same impact on British history, yet the Cromwells languish in categorised limbo. As the only non-royal heads of state, they are excluded from our monarchical pantheon; but the very endurance of that monarchy overshadows interest in other elite dynasties that in the US characterises the prominence of presidential families like the Kennedys or Bushes or in Europe maintains the importance of families like the Medici who ruled over republican city states. Even where the Cromwells are included in lists of British heads of state it is rarely on the same terms. A recent Penguin 'monarchs' series of biographies includes Oliver Cromwell, but where all other sovereigns' books have white dust jackets, Oliver's is black. Thus the Cromwells slip unseen between the cracks, leaving our understanding of the evolution of the British church and state impoverished as a result. Re-inserting the Cromwell dynasty alongside that of the Tudors and Stuarts does not undermine the monarchical and parliamentary foundations of Britain's identity but reinforces them. As Churchill saw it in 1912, 'the great movement in politics and in religion of which [Oliver] Cromwell was the instrument, was intimately connected with all of those forces which, through a long succession of Princes, have brought His Majesty to the Throne of a Constitutional and a Protestant country . . . His Majesty is the heir of all the glories of the nation, and there is no chapter of English history from which he should feel himself divided.'[126]

For themselves, Thomas and Oliver's lives, and even their fates, were shaped by family forces. In building his great house, Thomas overreached himself to anger the nobles at court and, eventually, the King himself; flying like Icarus too close to the sun, so that his 'dynastic ambitions' were 'one leading cause of his fall'.[127] Oliver too might have avoided the subsequent fall of his son Richard's Protectorate if he had taken a different attitude to his family during his lifetime. Perhaps if he had accepted the Crown or fully empowered and supported his sons or, alternatively, categorically rejected hereditary succession in his own family entirely and nominated another more capable successor, the Protectorate might have endured longer than nine months after his death, and he would now enjoy the reputation of a founding father figure in the mould of George Washington. Counterfactuals carpet the 1650s like corpses along the side of the road. Instead, the conflicted family Oliver left behind weakened rather than strengthened Richard's position and it was his own uncle and brother-in-law who misguidedly torpedoed his regime.

But if the Cromwell family contributed to its own double downfall, it was also its own saviour. In 1540 Gregory's wife, Jane Seymour's sister Elizabeth, rescued her husband's family through her place in the royal family and perfectly pitched appeal to her brother-in-law Henry VIII. In 1660, Oliver's widow, children and grandchildren helped each other navigate and survive the perilous waters of the Restoration. Down the decades, shrewd, industrious Cromwells like Sir Richard and his son Sir Henry of Hinchingbrooke built up the family's name and fortune, while greedy and reckless Cromwells like their heir Sir Oliver and Gregory's grandson Baron Edward Cromwell of Launde dissipated it. Launde, Oakham, Hinchingbrooke, Ramsey, Hursley and other estates all slipped through the family's hands and a twin inheritance of conservatism and radicalism split the family into entrenched Royalist and Parliamentarian camps. Yet Cromwellian characteristics endured financial fluctuations and divisive politics, often in the women of the family: in the brilliant mind of Thomas's polymath great-granddaughter Catherine Tollemache of

Helmingham Hall; in the insistent nobility of Elizabeth Southwell, the last Baron Cromwell; and in the staunchness of the idiosyncratic Bridget Bendish who defended her grandfather Oliver Cromwell's memory at the point of a sword.

The twin peaks of their power were enough for Thomas and Oliver to secure the grand and peaceful resting places for their children that they themselves were denied. Gregory still slumbers in splendour at Launde, Richard in his longed-for quiet at Hursley and, most extraordinarily of all, Betty Claypole remains a princess in Westminster Abbey, her grave alone among the Commonwealth heroes and Cromwell family members undisturbed at the Restoration. From his vantage point standing in stone guard across the road outside Parliament, Oliver can still watch over the precious daughter whose tragic fate was entwined with his own. But with central roles in the two seismic transformations of the Reformation and Civil Wars, Thomas and Oliver left grander lasting legacies, their fingerprints all over the early modern England and global Britain they moulded whose Protestant church, constitutional monarchy and ideas of liberty reached into every corner of the world.

Though men of often devastating action, it is perhaps through words that they have endured longest. In the almost five hundred years of baptism, wedding and burial entries that Thomas ordered recorded for the first time in England's parish registers, Oliver's mutilated baptism entry just one among them. In the English words of the Great Bible Thomas, above all others, brought into being at so much hazard to himself, so that it could justly be known as 'Cromwell's Bible'.[128] This Bible was the foundational text for all subsequent translations, including the Geneva Bible of 1560 whose words Oliver Cromwell lived his life by, and which infused his own speeches and sayings. The impact of this lineage is hard to overstate. Indeed, it has been well said that from the middle of the reign of Elizabeth I to the meeting of the Long Parliament in 1640, the English became the people of a book, the Bible, and that 'No greater moral change ever passed over a nation.'[129] Heir to both Thomas's words and Henry VIII's power, it was Oliver as Lord Protector who in 1656 granted a new monopoly in printing an English Bible, corrected by his handpicked expert, at the affordable price of two shillings.[130] This would have meant something to the man who had never been short of the Bible's comfort even on the battlefield, as Parliament had issued a 'Pocket

Bible' with 150 verse quotations from the Geneva Bible to every soldier in 1643. Thus Oliver always carried the legacy of his great-great-great uncle with him in his pocket, his mind and heart. Oliver's own multitudinous, compelling and oft-quoted words enjoyed a parallel fate three hundred years later when a pocket anthology of excerpts from his letters and speeches was issued to the armed services during World War II to 'strengthen our fortitude'.[131] *Cromwell Speaks!* was an apt title for the morale-boosting booklet, for indeed his is a voice that has never quieted.

At the turn of the eighteenth century, an old man who had avoided attention for 40 years shuffled into a courtroom, dapperly dressed in spite of his age. Vengeful kings and their ministers, spies and soldiers, loan-sharks and revolutionaries had never prised him from his hiding places. Only a family squabble over an estate and the meddling of lawyers had finally forced him out of anonymity. Many in the courtroom did not know who he was: they knew him merely as Mr Cranberry, perhaps Mr Cranbourne. But the judge knew him to be the one-time Lord Protector Richard Cromwell and demanded the usher find him a chair. Queen Anne, the last of the Stuart monarchs, later commended the justice for showing proper attention to a former head of state.[132] John Donne, writing in the middle of the two Cromwell centuries, deemed attention the essential demand of the human condition.[133] Proper attention is what the house of Cromwell now deserves.

ACKNOWLEDGEMENTS

This book is the product of many years' thought, research and discussion. Numerous fellow authors and academic colleagues have inspired and contributed to it in different ways, and I am grateful to them all. I would particularly like to thank my former supervisors Dr David Smith, Dr Gabriel Glickman and Professor John Morrill of Cambridge University for their continued support and advice. I have been fortunate too to be one of the first authors to benefit from John Morrill's new edition of Oliver Cromwell's *Writings, Letters and Speeches* which has been an inestimable resource. In addition, I am enormously grateful to Professor Diarmaid MacCulloch of Oxford University for his generous guidance throughout the course of writing this book, and for his own magisterial biography of Thomas Cromwell. My co-trustees of the Cromwell Association are another rich source of expertise and fellowship, as are my colleagues Dr Jonathan Healey, Dr Patrick Little and Professor Ronald Hutton, all of whom provided invaluable input into the book.

I would also like to thank all the people who helped me on research trips to Cromwell locations and archives, including: Stuart Orme of the Cromwell Museum for numerous instances of help and advice; Edward and Sophie Tollemache and Louise Kennedy at Helmingham Hall for their generous hospitality and research assistance on many occasions; Elaine Wyspianski and the team at Launde Abbey for making me so welcome and providing access to their archive; Bradley, Charlie (and Bertie) for a sublime afternoon at Northborough and the kind loan of their framed Cromwell family tree; Tom Wheeley for showing me around Hinchingbrooke School and sharing his knowledge of the house's history; Rakesh Pathak and his colleagues for hosting me at Felsted School and Christopher Dawkins for showing me the archive; the Revd Colin Taylor of Holy Cross, Felsted for helping with my enquiries; the Verger of St Mary's, Plympton for opening the church for me to look around; Joanne Walker for her help at Oakham Castle; Beckie Egan for photographing Catherine Tollemache's portrait; and the very helpful staff at the Bodleain Library, British Library, Cambridge University Library, Cambridgeshire Archives in Huntingdon, Sheffield City Archives, Trinity College Dublin and the Wren Library, Trinity College Cambridge, for their assistance.

Writing is a solitary business, but much less so thanks to the sociable networks facilitated by the incomparable Aspects of History, the lovely Historical Writers Association, the elite sportspersons of the Authors XI cricket team, the inspiring Wolf Hall Weekend, and the convivial Urban Writers Retreat where I love to hibernate with my fabulous friend and fellow writer Isabelle Fox. Indeed it was a conversation with Tom Holland at the last book launch before lockdown which sparked my idea for the book. These forums have gifted me many new and wonderful friends and opportunities, but particular thanks for their unstinting friendship and encouragement go to Richard Foreman, Oliver Webb-Carter, Antonia Senior, Jessie Childs, Roger Moorhouse, Saul David and Rob Lyman. Podcasting has become a passion in recent years and I am grateful to all those who have hosted me on their own shows, and to my wonderful co-host Paul Lay and our super producer Hugh Costello for creating our podcast *1666 And All That* which I promise to have more time for now this book is done.

My fantastic agents Emma Bal and Phoebe Fawcett of MMA have championed this book, as has my editor, Arabella Pike, Publishing Director of William Collins, whose wisdom, vision and editorial skill have done so much to sculpt and enhance it. I am grateful as well to the wider team at MMA and to Freya Alsop, Sam Harding, Nicola Webb, Jack Mascall, Liv Marsden and the rest of the team at William Collins for their hard work, help and resourcefulness at every stage. I have also had the immense pleasure of working with my US editor,

Michael Flamini of St Martin's Press, and thank him, Sara Beth Haring and the team for so enthusiastically taking the Cromwells stateside.

Final thanks go to my friends and family for their loving support over the last few years of toil. My brilliant husband Charlie Corn is such fit help as Milton dreamed of, the perfect companion through Marvell's long love's day. He and our wonderful sons Theodore and Orlando have shared me with the Cromwells with nothing but open-hearted kindness and patience - now we will have world enough and time. *The House of Cromwell* should be dedicated to them, but I know they understand that it is in fact dedicated to my adored and lamented mother Joanna, who never saw this book which would have meant so much to her, but who always believed I would write it. My greatest thanks are, and always will be, to her.

ABBREVIATIONS

CHC:	*The Correspondence of Henry Cromwell* ed. P. Gaunt
CSP:	*Clarendon State Papers* ed. W. Dunn Macray
CSPD:	*Calendar of State Papers, Domestic*
CSPS:	*Calendar of State Papers, Spain*
CSPV:	*Calendar of State Papers Relating To English Affairs in the Archives of Venice*
HP:	*History of Parliament*: House of Commons volumes
HMC:	Historical Manuscripts Commission
JHC:	*Journal of the House of Commons*
JHL:	*Journal of the House of Lords*
LP:	*Letters and Papers of the reign of Henry VIII* ed. J. S. Brewer
LWS:	*Letters, Writings and Speeches of Oliver Cromwell* ed. J. Morrill
ODNB:	*Oxford Dictionary of National Biography*
TAMO:	John Foxe, *The Unabridged Acts and Monuments Online*
TSP:	*Thurloe State Papers* ed. T. Birch

NOTES

INTRODUCTION

1. Rare exceptions can be found in *The Cromwell Family* by J. Cooper and S. Morris (1987); and J. Schofield, *Cromwell to Cromwell* (2009).
2. J. Byng, *The Torrington diaries containing the tour through England and Wales of the Hon. John Byng (later fifth Viscount Torrington) between the years 1781 and 1794*, ed. C. Bruyn Andrews, (4 vols, 1970), Vol 2, p. 199.
3. G. R. Elton, *The Tudor Revolution in Government: administrative changes in the reign of Henry VIII* (1953); and H. Trevor-Roper, *Historical Essays* (1957), p. 74.

1. ORIGINS

1. J. Fraser, *Triennial Travels*, Aberdeen University Library, MS 2538, discussed in L. L. Knoppers, *Constructing Cromwell: Ceremony, Portrait and Print* (2000), p. 126.
2. Mr John Maidston to John Winthrop, esq, governor of the colony of Connecticut in New England, *TSP*, Vol 1, Letters from Mr Corker 5:5.
3. *The English Revolution III, Newsbooks 5, Volume 15, Mercurius Politicus 1657* (1971), pp. 297–300; and R. Sherwood, *Oliver Cromwell King in All But Name 1653-1658* (1997), pp. 95-101.
4. E. Waller, *A panegyric to my Lord Protector, by a gentleman that loves the peace, union, and prosperity of the English nation* (1655), p. 6.
5. W. Rye, *Two Cromwellian Myths* (1925).
6. T. Pugh, *British and Outlandish Prophesies* (1658).
7. T. Davyes, *The tenth worthy. Or, Several anagrams in Latine, Welsh, and English, upon the name of that most highly renowned worthy of worthies, Oliver late Lord Protector. Together with some elegeical verses upon his*

much lamented death, who dyed in body Sept. 3. 1658. And also more anagrams on his now Highness, and others of that most noble and puissant family (1658).

8. *Calendar of Ancient Records of Dublin*, ed. J. T. Gilbert (19 vols, 1889), Vol 1, p. 314 as cited in P. Slattery, *Social Life in Pre-Reformation Dublin, 1450–1540* (2019), p. 47. I am grateful to Professor Diarmaid MacCulloch for directing me to this source; *LP*, Vol 13(1), no. 471[4], 'Scandals reported in Ireland'; C. L. Kingsford ed. 'Two London Chronicles from the Collections of John Stow . . .', *Camden Miscellany 12* (Camden 3rd series 18, 1910), pp. 1-57, at p. 15; and see D. MacCulloch, *Thomas Cromwell* (2018), pp. 16–17 for analysis of these sources.
9. R. B. Merriman, *Life and Letters of Thomas Cromwell* (2 vols, 1902), Vol 1, p. 2.
10. J. Phillips, 'The Cromwell family', *Antiquary 2* (1880), p. 166.
11. J. Foxe, *TAMO* (The Digital Humanities Institute, Sheffield, 2011) (1570 edition), Book 8, p. 1385.
12. D. Gerhold, *Thomas Cromwell and his Family in Putney and Wandsworth* (Wandsworth Historical Society Papers 31, 2017), pp. 11–14.
13. S. C. Hall, 'Throwley Hall' in *The Baronial Halls of England* (1858), Vol 1.
14. Thomas, Baron Cromwell, Viscount Lecale and later 1st Earl of Ardglass married Elizabeth Meverell.
15. *Extracts from the Court Rolls of the Manor of Wimbledon* (1866), pp. 73–5.
16. Gerhold, op. cit., pp. 16–17.
17. Eustace Chapuys to [Granvelle], 21 November 1535, *LP*, Vol 9, no. 862; Gerhold, op. cit., pp. 6, 18.
18. Anthony St Leger to Thomas Cromwell, 17 October 1536, *LP*, Vol 11, no. 746.
19. Richard Jones to [Cromwell], December 1532, *LP*, Vol 5, no. 1680.
20. G. R. Elton, *Studies in Tudor and Stuart Politics and Government*, (4 vols, 1974–92), Vol 4, p. 90.
21. CRO/H, Accession 4880 (Oliver's sale of land in Huntingdon to Arthur Ashton in 1627); and M. Noble, *Memoirs of the Protectoral House of Cromwell* (2 vols, 1784), Vol 1, p. 124.
22. Sherwood, *King in All But Name*, p. 148.
23. *Llyfr Baglan (Book of Baglan)*, compiled by J. Williams (1600–1607); pedigree of Sir Henry Cromwell (1602), Cambridgeshire Archives KHAC5/5170.
24. C. V. Wedgwood, *Oliver Cromwell* (1939), p.16 cited in L. Bowen, 'Oliver Cromwell (alias Williams) and Wales', in P. Little, ed., *Oliver Cromwell New Perspectives* (2009), p. 169.
25. MacCulloch, op. cit., p. 5.
26. Confession of William Breyar, 22 October 1536, *LP*, Vol 11, no. 841.

27. Norfolk to Cromwell, 2 February 1537, *LP*, Vol 12(1), no. 318.
28. Chapuys to [Granvelle], 21 November 1535, *LP*, Vol 9, no. 862.
29. For more on this, see Knoppers, *Constructing Cromwell*.
30. *A curse against Parliament-ale. With a blessing to the juncto; a thanksgiving to the councel of state; and psalm to Oliver* (London, 1649).
31. 'The Protecting Brewer' in *Rump, or, An exact collection of the choycest poems and songs relating to the late times by the most eminent wits from anno 1639 to anno 1661* by Alexander Brome (1662), pp. 331–3.
32. Foxe, *TAMO* (1570 edition), Book 8, p. 1386.
33. Eustace Chapuys to the Emperor, 23 May 1535, *CSPS*, Vol 5(1), no. 165, p. 468.
34. *Writings and Speeches of Oliver Cromwell*, ed. W. C. Abbott (4 vols, 1937–47), Vol 2, p. 410.
35. G. E. Cokayne, V. Gibbs, et al, *The Complete Peerage of England, Scotland and Ireland, Great Britain and the United Kingdom, Extant, Extinct or Dormant* (14 vols, 1910), Vol 3, pp. 551–4; and Noble, op. cit., p. 13.
36. *Hall's chronicle: containing the history of England, during the reign of Henry the Fourth, and the succeeding monarchs, to the end of the reign of Henry the Eighth, in which are particularly described the manners and customs of those periods. Carefully collated with the editions of 1548 and 1550* (1809), p. 839; Foxe, *TAMO* (1563 edition), Book 3, p. 654.
37. Oliver Cromwell's Speech to Parliament, 12 September 1654, *LWS*, Vol 3, p. 85.
38. Oliver Cromwell's Speech to the committee of Parliament in Whitehall, 13 April 1657, Ibid., p. 373.
39. Foxe, *TAMO* (1570 edition), Book 8, p. 1385; and *The Third volume of Chronicles . . . first collected by Raphaell Holinshed, and by him extended to the yeare 1577; now newlie recognised, augmented and continued . . . to the year 1586* (1586), Vol 3, p. 952.
40. J. Aubrey, *Brief Lives*, ed. A. Clark (2 vols, 1898), Vol 1, p. 328.
41. Noble, op. cit., p. 92.
42. For example, the tradition of 'Cromwell's well' at Maldon, Essex, tells how Oliver nearly drowned there when watering his horse. Folklore from Bridgwater in Somerset claims Oliver and the commander of the New Model Army Sir Thomas Fairfax nearly drowned in a boat reconnoitring during their siege of the town in 1645. For commentary on these stories see J. Westwood and J. Simpson, *The Lore of the Land: A guide to England's Legends, From Spring-Heeled Jack to the Witches of Warboys* (2005), pp. 361–5.
43. A. Marvell, 'An Horatian Ode upon Cromwell's Return from Ireland' (1650).
44. J. Morrill, 'Oliver Cromwell' in *ODNB*.
45. S. R. Gardiner, *History of the Great Civil War 1642–1649* (4 vols, 1893), Vol 3, p. 316.

46. *The Diary of Samuel Pepys*, ed. R. C. Latham and W. Matthews (11 vols, 1970), Vol 1, p. 1.
47. D. Starkey, 'The Age of the Household: Politics, Society and the Arts c. 1350–1550' in S. Medcalf ed. *The Later Middle Ages* (1981), pp. 264–5.
48. MacCulloch, op. cit., p. 18.

2. INHERITANCE

1. Thomas Frisby to Cromwell, 14 January [1531?], *LP*, Vol 4, no. 6146; and *LP*, Vol 5, no. 718.
2. October 1539, Cromwell's Remembrances, *LP*, Vol 14(2), no. 427.
3. M. L. Robertson, 'Profit and Purpose in the Development of Thomas Cromwell's Landed Estates', *The Journal of British Studies*, Vol 29, no. 4 (1990), pp. 317–46, at p. 318.
4. T. Borman, *Thomas Cromwell* (2014), p. 180; and Robertson, Ibid.
5. Edward Herbert, Lord Chirbury, *The life and raigne of King Henry the Eighth* (1649), p. 456.
6. R. Horrox, 'Hinchingbrooke Priory c.1200–1536' in *New Perspectives on Hinchingbrooke 1200–1970*, eds. T. Wheeley, R. Mitchell and S. Bell (2022), p. 5.
7. *LP*, Vol 14(2), no. 782, 'Cromwell's Accounts from 1537', fos. 59 & 117, Sept 1539.
8. T. Wheeley, 'The Skeletons in the Closet: the Hinchingbrooke Bones' in *New Perspectives on Hinchingbrooke*. The two skeletons have been sweetly reinterred in the under-stairs cupboard of Hinchingbrooke – now a school – to delight or terrorise future generations of children.
9. Huntingdon Archive KR/R42/17/3 (Translation of Grant of Manor of Ramsey etc. to Richard Williams, otherwise Cromwell, 31 Hen VIII); and *New Perspectives on Hinchingbrooke*, p. 11.
10. Richard Cromwell to [Cromwell], 15 October 1538, *LP*, Vol 13(2), no. 612.
11. C. Wriothesley, *A Chronicle of England During the Reigns of the Tudors, From A.D.1485 to 1559*, ed. W. D. Hamilton (2 vols, 1875), Vol 1, pp. 116–18; *LP*, Vol 15, nos. 616 & 617; and J. Stow, 'The Citie of Westminster', in *A Survey of London. Reprinted From the Text of 1603*, ed. C. L. Kingsford (1908), p. 99.
12. Noble, op. cit., p. 11.
13. This can still be seen carved into the Great Bow Window at Hinchingbrooke.
14. Although largely hidden by later plaster, the damaged section still visible on one wall gives a sense of the murals' phenomenal scale and drama. This panel depicts a group jousting melee. It is reported that the wall at ninety degrees to this, facing the fireplace, depicted the hand-to-hand combat of the tournament. And, having visited the room, it seems possible to me that the third wall at a further ninety

degrees to the second (now occupied by a later window) completed the story, perhaps depicting the fairytale moment of Sir Richard's knighthood by the King. The Cromwells and their visitors could have thus relived the whole event in life-size cinematic panorama as they warmed themselves by the parlour fire.

15. Richard Hilles to Henry Bullinger, [February 1541?], *LP*, Vol 16, no. 578.
16. 'Grants in November 1538', *LP*, Vol 13(2), no. 967[54]; and G. A. Carthew, *The Hundred of Launditch and Deanery of Brisley* (1877), Vol 2, pp. 519–20.
17. Henry Ughtred married Elizabeth Paulet while Henry Cromwell married her sister Mary. Ughtred's alliance with the Paulets would be a fractious one for he spent much of his later life litigating against his step-brother over the execution of John Paulet's will.
18. Duke of Norfolk to Thomas Cromwell, 25 March [1538], *LP*, Vol 13(1), no. 593.
19. A. H. Smith, *County and Court. Government and Politics in Norfolk 1558–1603* (1974), pp. 27, 247–53.
20. [30] June 1572, *JHL*, Vol 1, pp. 726–7; and [House of Lords] Sir Nicholas Bacon's speech on Lord Cromwell's case, in *Proceedings in the Parliament of Elizabeth I*, ed. T. E. Hartley (3 vols, 1981), Vol 1, pp. 265–6. Though the Lords found for Baron Henry, they added a proviso that this decision should not prevent future lords being arrested if they deserved to be.
21. Carthew, op. cit., pp. 524–5. Henry left furniture and their late mother's jewellery to his younger son Gregory and daughter Catherine; a young colt to Catherine's husband Lionel Tollemache; the lease on a Westminster house to his MP brother Thomas; and the discharge of historic debts and income from his deer park to his cousin James Cromwell. He left gifts to his friends and servants, with an annual allowance of fabric to be used to make cloaks for six poor people of the parish every Christmas.
22. 12 July 1529, Thomas Cromwell's will, *LP*, Vol 4, no. 5772.
23. Catherine's first child John died soon after his birth and was buried at North Elmham not Helmingham.
24. Two of these can still be seen in the bedrooms at Helmingham Hall. For further analysis, see M. Coleman, *Fruitful Endeavours: The 16th-Century Household Secrets of Catherine Tollemache of Helmingham Hall* (2012), pp. 130, 143.
25. D. L. Smith, 'The Cromwells of Hinchingbrooke 1538–1627', in *New Perspectives on Hinchingbrooke*, p. 11.
26. J. Venn and J. A. Venn eds. *Alumni Cantabrigienses* (4 vols, 1922–7), Vol 1, p. 422; and *Lincoln's Inn Admissions* (7 March 1557), Vol 1, p. 64.
27. Noble, op. cit., p. 22.
28. Henry Cromwell alias Williams, in *HP 1558–1603*, ed. P. W. Hasler (1981).

29. A. R. DeWindt and E. B. DeWindt, *Ramsey: The Lives of an English Fenland Town, 1200–1600* (2006), pp. 131–2.
30. J. Nichols, *The Progresses and Public Processions of Queen Elizabeth I* (5 vols, 2014), Vol 1, p. 432; Smith, 'The Cromwells of Hinchingbrooke' in *New Perspectives on Hinchingbrooke*, p. 11.
31. G. Walker, 'Conscience and Satire in John Heywood's Play of Love' (2013) in *Yearbook of English Studies*, Vol 43, pp. 223–42, at p. 236.
32. Nichols, op. cit., Vol 2, p. 569.
33. For more on the Muchwood case, see Dewindt & Dewindt, *Ramsey.*
34. All quotes taken from the one account of the case which survives: *The most strange and admirable Discoverie of the three Witches of Warboys . . .* (1593). For more on the Warboys case, see P. Almond, *The Witches of Warboys: an extraordinary story of sorcery, sadism and satanic possession* (2008).
35. Remarkably, the sermons continued until 1812, though the message evolved as belief in witchcraft abated. By the time M. J. Naylor came to preach – which he did four times from 1792 to 1795 – it was the 'inantity [sic] and mischief of vulgar superstitions' which the good people of Huntingdon were warned against: see M. J. Naylor, *The inantity [sic] and mischief of vulgar superstitions. Four sermons, preached at All-Saint's church, Huntingdon, on the 25th day of March, in the years 1792, 1793, 1794, 1795. By M. J. Naylor, . . . To which is added, some account of the witches of Warboys* (1795).
36. Henry Cromwell alias Williams, in *HP*.
37. Pedigree of Sir Henry Cromwell 1602, Cambridgeshire Archives KHAC5/5170.
38. Venn, op. cit., p. 423.
39. A bundle of letters in Ely Diocesan Records (EDR H/2/6), two of which are reproduced in A. Gibbons ed. *Ely Episcopal Records: A Calendar and Concise View of the Episcopal Records preserved in the Muniment Room of the Palace of Ely* (1891); and A. Barclay, *Electing Cromwell: The Making of a Politician* (2011), p. 46.
40. Foxe, *TAMO* (1563 edition), Book 3, p. 645.
41. Bible, Book of Exodus 34:7.
42. *The two books of homilies appointed to be read in churches* (1547) ed. J. Griffiths (Oxford, 1859), p. 497.
43. K. Thomas, *Religion and the Decline of Magic: studies in popular beliefs in sixteenth and seventeenth century England* (1971), pp. 98, 95.
44. E. K. Chambers, *William Shakespeare: A Study of Facts and Problems* (2 vols, 1930), Vol 2, pp. 323–27; and *Essex: The cultural impact of an Elizabethan courtier*, eds. A. Connolly and L. Hopkins (2013), 'Introduction' and Chapter 3 'Essex and the practice of theatre' by G. Ioppolo, pp. 63–80.
45. Sir John Fortescue to Sir Robert Cecil, 9 February 1601, *Calendar of the Cecil Papers in Hatfield House*, Vol 11, p. 37.

46. Thomas Coningsby, John Gough Nichols eds. *Journal of the Siege of Rouen, 1591* (Camden Society, 1847) p. 10.
47. Nichols, op. cit., Vol 4, pp. 42–3.
48. W. B. Devereux, *Lives and Letters of the Devereux, Earls of Essex in the reigns of Elizabeth I, James I and Charles I 1540–1646* (2 vols, 1853), Vol 2, p. 9.
49. Carthew, op. cit., pp. 521, 578; Edward Cromwell to Robert Cecil, 3 November 1598 in *Cecil Papers,* Vol 8, p. 421.
50. Edward Cromwell to Sir Robert Cecil, 25 March 1599, Ibid., Vol 9 (1902), p. 116.
51. Edward served under Essex in campaigns throughout the 1590s and was among those special friends Essex arranged to receive honorary degrees at Cambridge after a three day knees-up in February 1595; see P. Hammer, *The Polarisation of Elizabethan Politics: The Political Career of Robert Devereux, 2nd Earl of Essex, 1585–1597* (1999), p. 304.
52. Robert Cecil to Sir George Carew, [4?] March 1601(2) in *Letters from Sir Robert Cecil to Sir George Carew*, ed. John Maclean (Camden Society, 1864), p. 74.
53. Edward Cromwell to Sir Edward Coke, 21 August 1601 in Carthew, op. cit., pp. 568–9.
54. Lord Cromwell to Sir Robert Cecil, 22 August 1601, *Cecil Papers,* Vol 11, p. 356.
55. Lord Cromwell to Sir Robert Cecil, 8 March 1602[3], Ibid., Vol 12, p. 665.
56. Nichols, op. cit., p. 244.
57. King James to [Viscount Cranborne] [?, 1604], *Cecil Papers,* Vol 16, p. 397.
58. Lord Cromwell to the Earl of Salisbury, [1605], Ibid., Vol 17, p. 585.
59. Letter from Roger Jones to Catherine Tollemache, 20 December 1605, Helmingham Hall Archive T/Hel/1/5.
60. Catalogue of the library at Helmingham Hall and *Catalogue of highly important manuscripts & printed books* (Sotheby & Co, 1961).
61. Helmingham Hall Library, *Book of Secrets MS* LJ/II/6.
62. Helmingham Hall Library, *Catherine Tollemache's Receipts of Pastery, Confectionary Etc.* LJ /I/15.
63. *Helmingham Hall. An inventorie taken there the 29 of September 1597* (Helmingham Hall Archive T/Hel/9/1/1); and M. Coleman ed. *Household inventories of Helmingham Hall, 1597–1741* (2018) and *Fruitful Endeavours.*
64. Helmingham Hall Archive, *16th century Miscellany* T/Hel/10/8.
65. Thomas Cromwell [c.1540–2013 c.1611] in *HP 1558–1603.*
66. G. Burnet, *Burnet's History of My Own Time: Part 1 The Reign of Charles the Second,* ed. O. Airy (2 vols, 1897–1900), Vol 1, p. 149.
67. *The History of the Worthies of England by Thomas Fuller*, ed. P. A. Nuttall (3 vols, 1840), Vol 2, p. 107.
68. A. Fraser, *Cromwell Our Chief of Men* (1973), p. 13.
69. L. Stone, *An Elizabethan: Horatio Palvacino* (1956), p. 299.

70. B. J. Harris, 'Women and Politics in Early Tudor England', *Historical Journal 33* (1990), pp. 259–81, at p. 261.
71. 1626[?] 'Case respecting the debt due from the Crown and the City of London to the representatives of Sir Horatio Pallavicino; and also respecting an arrangement, stated to have been founded on deceitful pretences, whereby lands of the value of 500l. per annum were granted to Sir Oliver Cromwell, who married Dame Anne, widow and executrix of Sir Horatio; with opinion of some legal person thereon', in *CSPD Charles I 1625–6* (1858), pp. 527–8.
72. Though Sir Henry Cromwell's son Sir Oliver had not yet been knighted at the point, I refer to him as Sir Oliver Cromwell throughout the book to distinguish him from his nephew Oliver.
73. J. Nichols, *The Progresses, Processions, and Magnificent Festivities of King James the First* (4 vols, 1828), Vol 1, pp. 98–102.
74. Noble, op. cit., p. 94.
75. D. L. Smith, 'The Cromwells of Hinchingbrooke 1538–1627,' in *New Perspectives on Hinchingbrooke*, pp. 10–15 at p. 14.
76. *CSPD, op. cit.,* p. 67, no. 91. 20 July 1625: 'Warrant to pay to Sir Oliver Cromwell 300l., impressed upon account for special service.'
77. Stone, op. cit., p. 316; and *Diary of John Manningham 1602–1603*, ed. J. Bruce (1868), p. 50.
78. Stone, op. cit., p. xvii.

3. HOME

1. *The Novels of Matteo Bandello*, trans. J. Payne (6 vols, 1890), Vol 4, pp. 106–16; Foxe, *TAMO* (1570 edition), Book 8, pp. 1396–7.
2. Harry Lord Morley to Thomas Cromwell, 13 February [1530?], *LP,* Vol 14(1), no. 285. For a discussion on the dating of this letter, see MacCulloch, *Cromwell*, p. 28, footnote 32.
3. Bandello, op. cit., pp. 106–7.
4. *The Italian Wars, 1494–1559: War, State and Society in Early Modern Europe*, eds. M. Mallett and C. Shaw (2012), pp. 68–9.
5. Bandello, op. cit., pp. 106–7; *TAMO* (1570 edition), Book 8, p. 1396; and Chapuys to [Granvelle], 21 November 1535, *LP*, Vol 9, no. 862.
6. Foxe, *TAMO* (1576 edition), Book 8, p. 1173[1172].
7. This discovery has been made by Antonio Pattori of the University of Oxford who will be setting out his findings in a forthcoming publication. I am grateful to Professor Diarmaid MacCulloch for alerting me to this research and to Antonio Pattori for sharing his work with me.
8. Bandello, op. cit., pp. 106–7.
9. George Elyot, mercer, to Cromwell, 28 June [1536], *LP,* Vol 10, no. 1218.
10. MacCulloch, op. cit., p. 23.
11. Chapuys to [Granvelle], 21 November 1535, *LP*, Vol 9, no. 862.

12. J. A. Muller (ed.), *The Letters of Stephen Gardiner* (1933), p. 399.
13. G. C. Moore-Smith ed. *Gabriel Harvey's Marginalia* (1913), pp. 141, 196.
14. [Starkey to Cromwell], February 1535[?], *LP,* Vol 8, nos. 215 and 216.
15. Thomas Bedyll to Cromwell, 15 January 1536, *LP,* Vol 10, no. 103.
16. MacCulloch, op. cit., p. 28.
17. Bonner to Cromwell, April 1530[?], *LP,* Vol 4, no. 6346.
18. The Doge and Senate to the Venetian Consul and his Successors in England, 22 March 1540, *CSPV*, Vol 5, p. 82, nos. 211 and 212.
19. T. Mayer, *The Correspondence of Reginald Pole: a calendar* (3 vols, 2000–04), Vol 1, pp. 212–3; and P. van Dyke, 'Reginald Pole and Thomas Cromwell: An Examination of the Apologia Ad Carolum' in *The American Historical Review,* Vol 9, No. 4 (Jul., 1904), pp. 696–724.
20. W. M. Popley to Thomas Cromwell, 15 January 1522, *LP,* Vol 3, no. 1963.
21. 'Broadstreete warde', in Stow's Survey.
22. Foxe, *TAMO* (1570 edition), Book 8, pp. 1385–6.
23. Elizabeth was by 1522 being greeted in her husband's correspondence. See William Popley to Thomas Cromwell, 15 January 1522, *LP,* Vol 3, no. 1963; and John Robinson to Thomas Cromwell, 10 May 1523, *LP*, Vol 3, no. 3015.
24. Henry Wyckes to Thomas Cromwell, 2 November 1523[?], *LP,* Vol 3, no. 3502.
25. Many past historians have named her as Elizabeth Williams, believing her to have been the widow of one Thomas Williams, a Welsh Yeoman of the Guard, but the source for this is slight, relying on a coincidence of names. See Gerhold, op. cit., p. 27.
26. See Harris, 'Women and Politics', p. 267 for more on this.
27. *The Love Letters of Henry VIII to Anne Boleyn With Notes* (1906), p. 6.
28. H. Ellis, *Original Letters illustrative of English History . . . from autographs in the British Museum and . . . other collections* (11 vols, 1827), Series 2, Vol 2 (1827), p. 125.
29. Will of Thomas Cromwell, 12 July 1529, *LP,* Vol 4, no. 5772; and Merriman, *Life and Letters,* Vol 1, pp. 56–63.
30. Raphael Holinshed, *Chronicles* (complied 1577, printed 1586), Vol 3, p. 952.
31. M. C. Erler, *Reading and Writing During the Dissolution* (2016), p. 105 & App 4.
32. MacCulloch, op. cit., p. 36.
33. John Chekyng to Cromwell, 27 July 1528, *LP,* Vol 4, no. 4560; and the same to the same, 8 November 1528, *LP*, Vol 4, no. 4916.
34. Stow's Survey, p. 179.
35. The boke of the wardemote, 21 December 1523, *LP,* Vol 3, no. 3657.
36. Stow's Survey, op. cit.
37. Inventory of Master Crumwell's goods in his house, 26 June 19 Hen. VIII, 26 June 1527, *LP* Vol 4, no. 3197; and see also N. Holder, *The Friaries of Medieval London: from foundation to dissolution* (2017).
38. Chapuys to [Granvelle], 21 November 1535, *LP*, Vol 9, no. 862.

39. [?] to [Cromwell], *LP*, Vol 13(2), no. 1223. The letter is likely from Dr John Oliver and, while dated here as 1538, MacCulloch thinks it was written in autumn 1536. See MacCulloch, op. cit., pp. 151–2 and Elton, *Reform and Renewal: Thomas Cromwell and the Common Weal* (1973), p. 28.
40. Thomas's will left to Gregory, among other prized items, 'my best joined bed of Flanders work, with the best syler and tester; my best press carven of Flanders work, and best cupboard of the same, 6 joint stools of Flanders work, and 6 cushions'. Will of Thomas Cromwell, 12 July 1529, *LP*, Vol 4, no. 5772; and Merriman, *Life and Letters*, Vol 1, pp. 56–63.
41. Inventory of Master Crumwell's goods in his house, 26 June 1527, *LP*, Vol 4, no, 3197.
42. Ibid.; and MacCulloch, op. cit., p. 35, footnote 62.
43. William Cowper to Cromwell, 5 June 1535, *LP*, Vol 4, no. 1385; Richard Morison to Cromwell, 1536, *LP*, Vol 11, no. 1481; and Stephen Vaughan to Cromwell, 15 December 1528, *LP*, Vol 4, no. 5034.
44. Thomas Alvard to Cromwell, 2 November 1532, *LP*, Vol 5, no. 1509.
45. John Chekyng to Cromwell, 8 November 1528, *LP*, Vol 4, no. 4916; and two letters from Margaret Vernon to Cromwell, undated [1531], *LP*, Vol 5, nos. 15 and 18.
46. MacCulloch, op. cit., p. 37; Phillips, op. cit., p. 168; and also https://www.british-history.ac.uk/fasti-ecclesiae/1300-1541/vol10/pp27-29.
47. William Wellyfed to Thomas Cromwell, 5 October 1536, *LP*, Vol 11, nos. 548–551.
48. Thomas Cromwell to John Checkyng, 5 July 1529, *LP*, Vol 4, no. 5757 ii.
49. After Rotherham's death Alice married Ralph Astry of Harlington Woodend in Bedfordshire. 'Cromwell Papers', 1533, *LP*, Vol 6, no. 1625(5); and *Genealogical memoirs of the families of Chester of Bristol, Barton Regis, London, and Almondsbury: descended from Henry Chester, sheriff of Bristol 1470; and also of the families of Astry of London, Kent, Beds, Hunts, Oxon, and Gloucestershire, descended from Sir Ralph Astry, kt., Lord Mayor of London, 1493 / attempted by Robt. Edmond Chester Waters* (1881).
50. Joan Williamson married Sir John Price of Herefordshire, MP, public notary, royal ecclesiastical registrar and secretary of the Council in Wales and the Marches and expert on Welsh history and stories. See Sir John Price (1502?–55) by E. D. Jones in *Dictionary of Welsh Biography.*
51. Will of Thomas Cromwell, 12 July 1529, *LP*, Vol 4, no. 5772.
52. *State-worthies: or, the statesmen and favourites of England from the reformation to the revolution . . . By David Lloyd. To this edition is added the characters of the Kings and Queens . . . By Charles Whitworth* (1766), Vol 1, p. 106.

53. Ralph Sadler [1507–87] in *HP 1509–1558*, ed. S.T. Bindoff (1982).
54. Beard's work was several times reissued and augmented and was a rich fund of material for subsequent preachers and moralists. An abridgement *The Thunderbolt of God's Wrath* was published in 1618 (Thomas, *Religion and the Decline of Magic*, p. 91).
55. *A retractiue from the Romish religion contayning thirteene forcible motiues, disswading from the communion with the Church of Rome: wherein is demonstratiuely proued, that the now Romish religion (so farre forth as it is Romish) is not the true Catholike religion of Christ, but the seduction of Antichrist: by Tho. Beard* . . . (1616).
56. J. Morrill, 'The Making of Oliver Cromwell' in Morrill ed. *Oliver Cromwell and the English Revolution* (1990), p. 27.
57. The Hinchingbrooke Cromwells traditionally favoured Queens' College with Oliver's grandfather Sir Henry, uncle Sir Oliver, and father Robert Cromwell all educated there as well as some of Oliver's cousins. See Venn, op. cit; and J. Morrill, 'Cromwell Day Address 2021 Cromwell and Friendship', *Cromwelliana* (2022), p. 7.
58. C. H. Cooper, *Annals of Cambridge* (5 vols, 1842–1908), Vol 3, p. 283.
59. Letter from Oliver Cromwell to Henry Downhall, 14 October 1626, *LWS*, Vol 1, pp. 3–4; and Morrill, 'Cromwell and Friendship'.
60. *The history of the life and death of His Most Serene Highness, Oliver, late Lord Protector wherein, from his cradle to his tomb, are impartially transmitted to posterity, the most weighty transactions forreign or domestique that have happened in his time, either in matters of law, proceedings in Parliaments, or other affairs in church or state / by S. Carrington* (1659), p. 244.
61. Fraser, op. cit., p. 18.
62. Speech of Oliver Cromwell to the committee of Parliament in Whitehall, 21 April 1657, *LWS*, Vol 3, pp. 390–412, at p. 411.
63. Letter from Christer Bonde to Charles X, 3 August 1655, in M. Roberts ed. *Swedish Diplomats at Cromwell's Court, 1655–1656* (Camden Society, Fourth Series, 36, 1988), p.114.
64. Burnet, op. cit., p. 116.
65. J. Heath, *Flagellum, or, The life and death, birth and burial of Oliver Cromwel faithfully described in an exact account of his policies and successes, not heretofore published or discovered* (1663), p. 8.
66. D. Masson, *The Life of John Milton* (7 vols, 1877), Vol 4, p. 603.
67. Oliver Cromwell to Richard Cromwell, 2 April 1650, *LWS*, Vol 2, pp. 238–40.
68. Letter from Oliver Cromwell to Richard Major, 17 July 1650, Ibid., Vol 2, pp. 289–90; Letter from Oliver Cromwell to Richard Major, 13 August 1649, Ibid., Vol 2, pp. 70–2.
69. Speech of Oliver Cromwell to Parliament in the Painted Chamber, 17 September 1656, Ibid., Vol 3, pp. 288–317.
70. Roberts, op. cit., pp. 83–4.

71. Letter from Oliver Cromwell to Richard Major, 28 April 1649, *LWS*, Vol 2, pp. 40–1.
72. Letter from Oliver Cromwell to Elizabeth Cromwell, 15 December 1651, Ibid., Vol 2, pp. 521–2.
73. Autograph letter from Katherine Whetstone, Ely, to Mrs. Wind, Bargen, 16 February 1648(9), Folger Shakespeare Library (formerly MS Add 974, now X.c.53); and J. Waylen, *The House of Cromwell and the Story of Dunkirk* (1880), p. 379.
74. Heath, op. cit., p. 111; and Fraser, op. cit., p. 379.
75. Heath, op. cit., pp. 12–13.
76. The first Mrs St John was Oliver's third cousin (granddaughter of his aunt Joan) and the second Mrs St John was Oliver's first cousin (daughter of his uncle Henry Cromwell of Upwood). See the analysis of the letter from Cromwell to Mrs St John in *LWS*, Vol 1, pp. 14–17.
77. D. Roberts, *Matrimoniall Honour* (1642); and K. Gillespie, 'Elizabeth Cromwell's Kitchen Court: Republicanism and the Consort', *Genders 1998-2013, Issue 33: First Ladies? Political Wives in Seventeenth-century England* (October 2001).
78. Letter from Oliver Cromwell to Elizabeth Cromwell, 3 May 1651, *LWS*, Vol 2, pp. 446–7; and letter from Elizabeth to Oliver Cromwell, 27 December 1650 in J. Nichols, *Original Letters and Papers of State Addressed to Oliver Cromwell* (1743), p. 40.
79. Fraser, op. cit., p. 428.
80. Nichols, op. cit.
81. Letter from Oliver to Elizabeth Cromwell, 12 April 1651, *LWS*, Vol 2, pp. 439–40.
82. Letter from Oliver Cromwell to Colonel Richard Norton, 3 April 1648, Ibid., Vol 1, pp. 502–4.
83. CRO/H, Accession 4880 (Oliver's two sales of land on 19 December 1627); and C. Clifford and A. Akeroyd, *Risen from Obscurity? Oliver Cromwell and Huntingdonshire* (2002), p. 30.
84. Morrill, 'Making of Oliver Cromwell', p. 33. Huntingdon Archive KHMR/17/1 has 'Jane Cromwell spinster' admitted to the Manor of Slepe on 21 April 1636 and later fined for not repairing her road.
85. Since 1679, a Puritan bequest has funded annual 'Bible dicing' where children compete at throwing dice to win a Bible each Whit Tuesday.
86. Letter from Oliver Cromwell to [John Newdigate], 1 April 1631, *LWS*, Vol 1, pp. 6–8.
87. St Ives Manor Court Book 1632–1661, Huntingdon Archive KHMR/17/1: An entry of 19 October 1633 states in Latin that 'the Homage present the shepherd of Mr Crumwell for keeping 10 beasts on the demesne and he is in mercy: 20d'.
88. CRO/H 3870/1; and Clifford and Akeroyd, op. cit., p. 23.

89. CRO/H 3734/8/1, now displayed in the Cromwell Museum; and Clifford and Akeroyd op. cit., p. 33.
90. Noble, op. cit., p. 105n.
91. Morrill, 'Making', in *Cromwell and the English Revolution*, p. 35; and H. Trevor Roper, *Europe's Physician: the Various Life of Sir Theodore de Mayerne* (2006), p. 8.
92. T. Becon, *The Sick Man's Salve Wherin the faithfull christians may learne both how to behaue them selues paciently and thankefully, in the tyme of sickenes, and also vertuously to dispose their temporall goodes, and finally to prepare them selues gladly and godly to die. Made and newly recognised by Maister Tho. Becon. 1561.*, (1561), p. 349; and R. Burton, *The Anatomy of Melancholy* (1621).
93. Letter from Oliver Cromwell to Elizabeth Cromwell, 4 September 1650, *LWS*, Vol 2, pp. 344–6; and the same to the same, 12 April 1651, Ibid., pp. 439–40.
94. Sir Philip Warwick, *Memoirs of the reign of King Charles I* (1813), pp. 275–6.
95. Oliver Cromwell to Elizabeth St John, 13 October 1638, *LWS*, Vol 1, pp. 14–17.
96. A. G. Rickford, *Garde de Foy: The Riche Heritage of Felsted School 1564–2014* (2013), p. 34; and *Sermons; now first printed from the original manuscripts of John Wallis, . . . To which are prefixed, memoirs of the author, . . . by the Rev. C. E. de Coetlogon, M.A.* (1791), pp. xiii–xv.
97. Rickford, Ibid., p. 35.
98. Register of Baptisms, Marriages and Burials of Holy Cross Felsted, Essex Record Office, D/P 99/1/2. James Waylen observed that Oliver is the only person in these records referred to in Latin as an 'honourable man' (see Waylen, *House of Cromwell*, pp. 6–7).
99. M. Craze, *A History of Felsted School 1564–1947* (1955), p. 54.
100. W. Shakespeare, *King John*, Act III, Scene 4.
101. *The Diary of John Evelyn*, ed. A Dobson (3 vols, 1906), Vol 2, pp. 127-30.
102 *An Account of the Last Houres of the late Renowned Oliver Lord Protector . . . Drawn up and published by one who was an Eye and Ear-Witness of the most part of it, 1659* (1659), pp. 10–11.
103. Will of Thomas Cromwell, 12 July 1529, *LP*, Vol 4, no. 5772; MacCulloch, op. cit., p. 1; and Merriman, *Life and Letters*, Vol 1, pp. 56–63.
104. Richard Cave to Thomas Cromwell, 18 June 1528, *LP*, Vol 4, no. 4388.
105. C. Angus, *The Private Life of Thomas Cromwell* (2022), pp. 54–5.
106. Edward Lewkenor to Cromwell, 13 April 1529, *LP*, Addenda Vol 1 Part 1 (1929), p. 214, no. 640.
107. Lady Elizabeth Ughtred to Thomas Cromwell, 18 March 1537, *LP*, Vol 12(1), no. 678.
108. Duke of Norfolk to Thomas Cromwell, 5 June 1537, *LP*, Vol 12(2), no. 35.
109. Cromwell's Accounts, from AD 1537, II. Payments by me, Thos. Avery, from 1 Jan. 28 Hen. VIII, May 1538, *LP*, Vol 14(2), no. 782.

110. Margaret Vernon to Thomas Cromwell, 24 January 1530, *LP*, Vol 14(1), no. 130.
111. Stephen Vaughan to Thomas Cromwell, 23 March 1529, *LP*, Vol 4, no. 5398.
112. John Williamson to Thomas Cromwell, 5 September 1528, *LP*, Vol 4, Appendix, no. 237.
113. Will of Thomas Cromwell, 12 July 1529, *LP*, Vol 4, no. 5772; and Merriman, *Life and Letters*, Vol 1, pp. 56–63.
114. Inventory of Master Crumwell's goods in his house, 26 June 1527, *LP*, Vol 4, no. 3197.
115. Letters between Thomas Cromwell and Cardinal Wolsey, *LP*, Vol 4, nos. 6076 and 6391.
116. MacCulloch, op. cit., p. 1.
117. Foxe, *TAMO* (1570 edition), Book 8, p. 1386.
118. Letter from Oliver Cromwell to Mrs St John, 13 October 1638, *LWS*, Vol 1, pp. 14–16.
119. BL Add Charters, 33159; and DeWindt, op. cit., p. 131.
120. Heath, op. cit., p. 14.
121. B. Worden, *Roundhead Reputations* (2001), p. 269.
122. C. Hill, 'Oliver Cromwell' in *The Collected Essays of Christopher Hill*, Vol 3, (1986), p. 75.
123. Thomas, *Religion and the Decline of Magic*, p. 80.
124. Edward, Earl of Clarendon, *The History of the Rebellion and Civil Wars in England*, ed. W. D. Macray (6 vols, 1888), Vol 1, pp. 419–20.
125. If so, Oliver's untaken journey to the New World adds to the tantalising counterfactuals of his life. Could the man who so fascinated the United States' Founding Fathers have made a name for himself as one of their own countrymen?
126. A. Barclay, *Electing Cromwell*, Chapter 5: 'The Nonconformists in the fens?'.
127. *Hall's chronicle: containing the history of England, during the reign of Henry the Fourth, and the succeeding monarchs, to the end of the reign of Henry the Eighth, in which are particularly described the manners and customs of those periods. Carefully collated with the editions of 1548 and 1550* (1809), pp. 838–9; and see quotations and discussion of these in *LWS*, Vol 2, p. 307 and in J. Morrill, 'The religious context of the Cromwellian conquest of Ireland', *Cromwelliana* (2014), pp. 33–4.
128. *An Account of the Last Houres*, op. cit.
129. Morrill, op. cit., p. 22; and S. Healey, 'The Unmaking of Oliver Cromwell?' in Little (ed.), *Oliver Cromwell New Perspectives* (2009).
130. Letter from Oliver Cromwell to Sir Henry Vane junior, Charles Fleetwood and Thomas Harrison, 10 July 1649, *LWS* Vol 2, pp. 63–4; and Letter from Oliver Cromwell to William Penn, 25 February 1653, Morrill, Ibid., Vol 2, pp. 594–5.

131. Richard Cromwell to Thomas Cromwell, 11 July 1537, *LP*, Vol 12(2), no. 241; and MacCulloch, op. cit., pp. 19–20.
132. Morrill, 'Cromwell and Friendship', op. cit., and 'Blood and Marriage: why kin mattered to Oliver Cromwell', *Cromwelliana* (2024).
133. Thomas Cromwell to Nicholas Shaxton, bishop of Salisbury, March 1538, Merriman, *Life and Letters*, Vol 2, pp. 128–31, at p. 129; and *An Account of the Last Houres*, op. cit., pp. 12–13. This is the deathbed prayer Abbott uses (*LWS*, Vol 4, p. 872) but Morrill provides an alternative version (*LWS*, Vol 3, p. 521).
134. Letter from Oliver Cromwell to Mrs St John, 13 October 1638, *LWS*, Vol 1, pp. 14–16.

4. EMERGENCE

1. Oliver Cromwell to Valentine Walton, 5 September 1644, *LWS*, Vol 1, pp. 202–4.
2. Thomas Cromwell to John Creke, 17 August 1523, Merriman, *Life and Letters*, Vol 1, pp. 313–4.
3. W. Shakespeare, *Henry VIII*, Act III, scene 2.
4. *The Life of Cardinal Wolsey* by G. Cavendish, ed. S. W. Singer (1827), pp. 258–61.
5. For further analysis of this see MacCulloch, op. cit., p. 89 and fn. 43.
6. Stephen Vaughan to Thomas Cromwell, 30 October 1529, *LP*, Vol 4, no. 6036.
7. Cardinal Wolsey to Thomas Cromwell, December 1529, *LP*, Vol 4, no. 6098.
8. Cavendish, op. cit., pp. 274–5.
9. Ibid., op. cit., pp. 292–3.
10. Foxe, *TAMO* (1570 edition), Book 8, pp. 1386–7.
11. For a full analysis of Pole's account, see MacCulloch, op. cit., pp. 108–110.
12. Cavendish, op. cit., p. 298.
13. Letters between Thomas Cromwell and Cardinal Wolsey, *LP*, Vol 4, no. 6076.
14. Letters between Thomas Cromwell and Cardinal Wolsey, *LP*, Vol 4, no. 6076; Cardinal Wolsey to Thomas Cromwell, *LP*, Vol 4, no. 6080; the same to the same, December 1529, *LP*, Vol 4, no. 6098; and the same to the same, *LP*, Vol 4, no. 6114.
15. Cardinal Wolsey to Thomas Cromwell, [10] August 1530, *LP*, Vol 4, no. 6554; and Thomas Cromwell to Cardinal Wolsey, 21 October 1530, *LP*, Vol 4, no. 6699.
16. Letter from Laurence Stubbs to Cardinal Wolsey [1527] in H. Ellis, *Original Letters illustrative of English History . . . from autographs in the British Museum and . . . other collections* (11 vols, 1824–1846), Series 3, Vol 2 (1846), pp. 62–6.

17. This is a translation of the French original of this letter given in MacCulloch, op. cit., p. 127.
18. W. Roper, *The Life of Sir Thomas Moore, Knt* (1905), p. 55.
19. Chapuys to the Emperor, 6 June 1636, *CSPS*, Vol 5(2), no. 61, p. 145.
20. BM Sloane MSS. 1523, fo. 29a.
21. J. Strype, *Ecclesiastical memorials; relating chiefly to religion, and the reformation of it, and the emergencies of the Church of England, under King Henry VIII. King Edward VI. and Queen Mary the First* (3 vols, 1721), Vol 1, p. 364.
22. M. L. Robertson, 'Thomas Cromwell's Servants: The Ministerial Household in Early Tudor Government and Society', Ph.D. diss., University of California, Los Angeles (1975).
23. 'Of orders and customes of the Citizens', Stow's Survey, p. 89.
24. Miscellaneous, 1531, *LP*, Vol 5, no. 628.
25. Sir George Throkmorton to [Henry VIII], 20 October 1537, *LP*, Vol 12(2), no. 952.
26. Thomas Winter to Cromwell, 20 October 1532, *LP*, Vol 5, no. 1452.
27. Grants in May 1532, *LP*, Vol 5, no. 1065(33).
28. For further analysis, see MacCulloch, op. cit., pp. 172–3.
29. This was almost certainly the same book recently identified in the collection of the Wren Library at Trinity College, Cambridge. See O. Emerson and K. McCaffrey, *Holbein's Hidden Gem: rediscovering Thomas Cromwell's lost book* (2023).
30. Sir George Throkmorton to [Henry VIII], 20 October 1537, *LP*, Vol 12(2), no. 952.
31. J. E. Neale, *Elizabeth and her Parliaments* (1953–7), Vol 1, p. 28.
32. The diary is listed as 'State Papers' in the Library of Trinity College Dublin (IE TCD MS 1045); excerpts are printed in *Proceedings in the Parliament of Elizabeth I*, ed. T. E. Hartley (3 vols, 1981); and see G. R. Elton, *The Parliament of England 1559–1581* (1986), pp. 13–14 for a detailed analysis of Cecil and Cromwell's relationship.
33. Neale, op. cit., Vol 2, pp. 437–8.
34. Barclay, *Electing Cromwell.*
35. Ibid.; and Patrick Little, 'Cromwell and Ireland before 1649' in Little ed. *New Perspectives*, p. 119.
36. Warwick, *Memoirs*, pp. 273–5.
37. J. S. A. Adamson, 'Oliver Cromwell and the Long Parliament' in Morrill ed. *Oliver Cromwell and the English Revolution*; and S. K. Roberts, 'One that Would Sit Well at the Mark: The Early Parliamentary Career of Oliver Cromwell, 1640–1642' in Little ed. *New Perspectives.*
38. S. J. Weyman, 'Oliver Cromwell's Kinsfolk', *English Historical Review 6* (1891), pp. 48–60, at p. 56; and Morrill, 'Blood and Marriage'.
39. Warwick, op. cit., p. 278.
40. Barry Coward, *Cromwell*, p. 17; and Roberts, op. cit.

41. J. C. Davis, *Oliver Cromwell* (2001); and D. Farr, *Oliver Cromwell's Kin, 1643–1726: The Private and Public Worlds of the English Revolution and Restoration* (2023).
42. Warwick, op. cit., pp. 273–4.
43. G. Skutt, *A letter from an ejected Member of the House of Commons, to Sir Jo: Evelyn* (1648), p. 6.
44. Little, 'Cromwell and Ireland', pp. 118–19.
45. J. Rushworth, 'Historical Collections: The impeachment of Edward Montagu', in *Historical Collections of Private Passages of State: Volume 4, 1640–42* (1721), p. 478.
46. For more on the build-up to this point, see J. Adamson, *The Noble Revolt: The Overthrow of Charles I* (2007); and J. Healey, *The Blood in Winter: A Nation Descends, 1642* (2025).
47. H. Parker, *Observations upon some of His Majesties late answers and expresses* (1642); and Q. Skinner 'Classical liberty, Renaissance translation and the English civil war' in Skinner, *Visions of Politics, Vol 2: Renaissance Virtues* (2002), pp. 308-43.
48. Cavendish, op. cit., pp. 491–501 and fn. 1 to pp. 341–2.
49. Ibid., p. 501.
50. Ibid., p. 494.
51. The historian Blair Worden has explored the role of conscience in this period in numerous works.
52. Thomas Lord Cromwell to Buckingham, 8 September 1625, *CSPD Charles I 1625–6*, p. 99, no. 30; and Thomas Lord Cromwell to [Algernon Earl of Northumberland?], 5 October 1634, *CSPD Charles I 1634–5* (1858), pp. 228–9, no. 23.
53. This is the portrait now in the National Portrait Gallery, number 1727. MacCulloch, op. cit., p. 175; for more information on the portrait belonging to the family of Thomas's descendants the Earls of Ardglass, see R. Strong, 'Holbein in England – I and II', *The Burlington Magazine*, Vol 109, no. 770 (May, 1967), pp. 276–81.
54. Lecale had seen military service in Ireland, at sea and was then appointed to command a regiment in the German mercenary commander Count Ernest von Mansfeld's abortive expedition to recover the Palatinate for James's son-in-law the Elector Palatine. See G. E. Cokayne, *The Complete Peerage of England, Scotland, Ireland, Great Britain and the United Kingdom*, eds. V. Gibbs et al, Vol 3, pp. 558–9. See also *CSPD Charles I 1631–3* (1858), p. 534; and *CSPD Charles I 1633–4* (1858), p. 64; and C. R. Mayes, 'The Early Stuarts and the Irish Peerage', in *The English Historical Review*, Vol 73, no. 287 (April 1958), pp. 227–51, at p. 237.
55. Lord Cromwell's coat of arms features four lions surmounted by a helmet surrounded by ermine and a gold pelican pecking its breast, and supported by red winged unicorns. Illuminated letters patent creating Thomas Cromwell the Viscount Lecale, Dublin, 12 November 22nd James I [1624], https://www.bonhams.com/auction/27374/lot/20/

ireland-james-i-illuminated-letters-patent-creating-thomas-cromwell-the-viscount-lecale-dublin-12-november-22nd-james-i-1624/

56. Mayes, op. cit., pp. 227–51, at p. 249.
57. Still today the splendid Norman Great Hall of Oakham displays hundreds of horseshoes. These include oversized, decorative horseshoes presented by illustrious visitors including the Duke of Wellington, the future Queen Victoria, George VI and Elizabeth II. Yet, the most poignant of the collection must be number 28: the ordinary horseshoe donated in 1631 by Thomas Cromwell, 4th Baron Cromwell and 1st Viscount Lecale. See T. H. McK. Clough, *The Horseshoes of Oakham Castle* (1978), identified horseshoe number 28.
58. Thomas Cromwell to Thomas Wentworth, 20 January 1635(6?), Sheffield City Archives WWM/StrP/15/303; copy of letter from Thomas Wentworth to Thomas Cromwell, Viscount Lecale, afterwards Earl of Ardglass, 3 April 1634, Sheffield City Archives WWM/StrP/8/100-101; and Account of payments for Household expenses paid out by a servant of Lord Conway from 7 July 1534 to today, 19 March 1634(5), *CSPD Charles I 1634–5* (1858), pp. 589–90.
59. Letter from 'Thomas Lord Cromwell to [Algernon Earl of Northumberland?], 5 October 1634, *CSPD Charles I 1634–5*, pp. 228–9, no. 23; and Henry Lord Moore to Edward Viscount Conway and Killultagh, 18 August 1634 in Ibid., p. 192, no. 53. This incident was a strange echo of the death of another servant a century earlier: Jerome Lyne, Thomas Cromwell's man, who died at Drogheda during the English campaign of 1538 when he was surprised in a bog and slain. See *LP*, Vol 13(1), no. 771, 15 April 1538.
60. Thomas Cromwell to Thomas Wentworth, 12 January 1635(6), Sheffield City Archives WWM/StrP/15/320; the same to the same, 20 January 1635(6), Sheffield City Archives WWM/StrP/15/303; and Thomas Cromwell to Thomas Wentworth, 19 March 1638(9), Sheffield City Archives WWM/StrP/18/186.
61. Sir John Borough to Sec. Windebank, 3 June 1639, *CSPD Charles I 1639* (1858), pp. 267–8. Lecale's complaint to Viscount Conway once back in Ireland may allude to this when he wrote 'I did hope I should have had charge of a regiment here or in England, but none I have, so must go as a private captain in my Lord-General's regiment, though I have had a regiment of horse and of foot and 300l a month pay.' Yet Lecale's commitment to the Crown was such as to outweigh this deprivation.
62. Thomas Lord Cromwell to Edward Viscount Conwy, 31 March 1640, *CSPD Charles I 1639–40* (1858), p. 608, no. 47.
63. Thomas Wiseman to Sir John Penington, 11 November 1641, *CSPD Charles I 1641–3* (1858), p. 163, no. 72.
64. *LWS*, Vol 1, p. 356, fn. 3.

65. K. Forkan, 'Army List of the Ulster British Forces, 1642–1646', *Archivium Hibernicum*, 2005, Vol 59 (2005), pp. 51–65, at p. 60.
66. When the garrison of Ashby-de-la-Zouch surrendered to Parliament in February 1646, they included various offices 'besides 16 gentlemen of quality not listed, amongst the latter being Mr. Vere Cromwell'. (List of officers and gentlemen in the garrison of Ashby-de-la-Zouch at its surrender, 24 February 1645(6), *CSPD Charles I 1645–7* (London, 1858), p. 352.) Wingfield Cromwell was later taken prisoner at Chester while fighting for the Royalist cause (see Cokayne, *Peerage*, Vol 1, p. 193).
67. John Morrill estimates this date and the number recruited.
68. These included the Hampdens, Whalleys and Ingoldsbys and Oliver's cousin Major Oliver Cromwell (son of Sir Oliver's younger brother Sir Philip Cromwell) who died at the siege of Waterford in Ireland in December 1649. Oliver wrote to his cousin Anne Cromwell to break the news of the death of his 'Kinsman' (*LWS*, Vol 2, pp. 167–8).
69. Weyman, 'Oliver Cromwell's Kinsfolk'.
70. A muster roll signed by him exists from September 1638 recruiting troops to the King's force to fight the Scots in the Bishops' Wars, though his recruiting rate was slower than his nephew's efforts four years later, HUTCM L85. I am grateful to Stuart Orme, Curator of the Cromwell Museum, for showing me this. See also 'Persons appointed for disarming Recusants in the several Counties, 30 August 1641', in *JHL*, Vol 4, 1629–42 (1767–1830).
71. Letter from John Merrill to Viscount Mandeville, 1642, Huntingdon Archive [3646/(503)]; Venn, *Alumni Cantabrigienses*, Vol 1, 1922, pp. 422–3; and S. Reid, *Officers and Regiments of the Royalist Army* (1988), Vol 1.
72. Letter from John Merrill to Viscount Mandeville, 1642, Huntingdon Archive [3646/(503)]; and R. Hutton, *The Making of Oliver Cromwell* (2021), p. 79.
73. Warwick, op. cit., p. 278.
74. Today the junction of the Great Whyte and the High Street.
75. Noble, op. cit., pp. 46–7.
76. Oliver Cromwell to Oliver St John, 11 September 1643, *LWS*, Vol 1, pp. 168–71.
77. Oliver Cromwell to Sir William Spring and Maurice Barrowe, 11 September 1643[?], Ibid., Vol 1, pp. 164–8.
78. Letter from Oliver Cromwell to Sir Thomas Barrington, 6 October 1643, Ibid., Vol 1, pp. 177–8.
79. Letter from Oliver Cromwell to Oliver St John, 11 September 1643, Ibid., Vol 1, pp. 168–71.
80. I am grateful to Stuart Orme, curator of the Cromwell Museum, for showing me this letter (HUTCM L18).

81. B. Whitelocke, *Memorials of the English affairs from the beginning of the reign of Charles the First to the happy restoration of King Charles the Second* (4 vols, 1853), Vol 1, p. 209.
82. Letter from Oliver Cromwell to Valentine Walton, 5 July 1644, *LWS*, Vol 1, pp. 196–9.
83. Ibid.
84. Waylen, *House of Cromwell*, p. 10.
85. Ibid., p. 9.
86. *LWS*, Vol 1, p. 192.
87. Abbott, *Writings and Speeches*, Vol 1, p. 299.
88. Ibid.
89. Warrant from Oliver Cromwell and others to Dr [Richard] Staine, treasurer for the Isle of Ely, *LWS*, Vol 1, p. 194.
90. J. Lilburne, *England's Birth-Right Justified* (1645), pp. 31–2.
91. A. Marvell, 'The First Anniversary of the Government under O.C.'

5. VICTORY

1. 'Alexander Alesius to Queen Elizabeth I, 1558', in E. Norton, *The Anne Boleyn Papers* (2013), p. 325.
2. *The Correspondence of Sir Thomas More*, ed. E. F. Rogers (1947) p. 554.
3. *The Papers of George Wyatt Esquire*, ed. D. M. Loades (Camden 4th series, Volume 5, 1968), p. 159.
4. Elton, *Reform and Renewal*, p. 29b.
5. G. Bray (ed.), *Documents of the English Reformation* (1994), p. 177.
6. *Documents Illustrative of Church History*, eds. H. Gee and W. J. Hardy (1896), p. 274.
7. S. E. Lehmberg, *The Later Parliaments of Henry VIII: 1536–1547* (1977), p. 67.
8. Thomas Legh to Cromwell, 30 October 1535, *LP*, Vol 9, no. 708.
9. Ellis, *Original Letters*, op. cit., Vol 3 (1846), pp. 31–7.
10. A. Walsham, *Generations: Age, Ancestry, and Memory in the English Reformations* (2023), Introduction.
11. Bodl., MS Eng. Hist. c. 485, fol. 100. The note is pasted into the back of John Speed's 'Catalogue of Religious Houses' thought to be from William Dugdale's collection.
12. *Memory and the English Reformation*, eds. A. Walsham, B. Wallace, C. Law and B. Cummings (2020), p. 13.
13. W. Dugdale, *The antiquities of Warwickshire illustrated : from records, leiger-books, manuscripts, charters, evidences, tombes, and armes : beautified with maps, prospects, and portraictures By William Dugdale. This edition is carefully copied, ... from the old one, published in the year 1656* (1765), Vol 2, pp. 492, 575.
14. *The history of the worthies of England who for parts and learning have been eminent in the several counties: together with an historical narrative*

of the native commodities and rarities in each county / endeavoured by Thomas Fuller (published posthumously in 1662); see also *Memory and the English Reformation*, op. cit., pp. 1–3.

15. A. Milton, *England's Second Reformation: The Battle for the Church of England 1625–1662* (2021); and P. Marshall ed., *The Impact of the English Reformation 1500–1640* (1997).
16. Two new editions of John Stow's *Annales* came out in 1615 and 1631, an extensively re-edited version of Foxe's *Acts and Monuments* was issued in 1632 and 1641, and Nicholas Harpsfield's 1560s–70s *Historia Anglicana ecclesiastica* was first published in 1622.
17. Edward Herbert, Lord Chirbury, *Life and Raigne of Henry VIII* (1649).
18. Edward Lord Herbert of Chirbury to Secretary Coke, 25 February 1635[6], *CSPD 1635–6*, p. 254, no. 80.
19. H. Lyon, 'Remembering the Dissolution of the Monasteries: Events, Chronology and Memory in Charles Wriothesley's Chronicle' and C. Highley, 'Henry VIII's Ghost in Cromwellian England' in *Memory and the English Reformation*; D. MacCulloch, 'The Myth of the English Reformation', *Journal of British Studies,* Vol 30, no. 1 (1991), pp. 1–19; Walsham, *Generations*, op. cit.; and Milton, *Second Reformation*, p. 53.
20. *The World Turned Upside-Down* (1646).
21. P. Collinson, *From Iconoclasm to Iconophobia: The Cultural Impact of the Second English Reformation*, 1985 Stenton Lecture (1986).
22. Abbott, *Writings and Speeches*, Vol 1, pp. 226–7.
23. Letter from Oliver Cromwell to William Hitch, 10 January 1644, *LWS*, Vol 1, pp. 181–2; see also Morrill, 'Cromwell and Friendship', op. cit., pp. 5–11, at p. 9; and G. Hart, 'Oliver Cromwell, Iconoclasm and Ely Cathedral', *Historical Research*, Vol 87, no. 236 (2014), pp. 270–6.
24. *Memory and the English Reformation*, 'Chapter 6: Converting the Cross: Monuments, Memory and Time in Post-Reformation England', p. 147; and A. Fox, *Oral and Literate Culture 1500–1700* (2000), pp. 255–7.
25. J. Byng, *Torrington diaries,* Vol 1, p. 6.
26. Byng, Ibid., Vol 1, p. 253 & Vol 3, p. 272.
27. For more examples of this conflation, see J. Westwood and J. Simpson, *The Lore of the Land: A Guide to England's Legends, from Spring-heeled Jack to the Witches of Warboys* (2005).
28. P. Hausted, *Ad Populum: or, a lecture to the people* (1644), pp. 7–8.
29. *A case for Nol Cromwells nose, and the cure of Tom Fairfax's gout. Both which rebells are dead, and their deaths kept close, by the policy of our new states* (1648), pp.4-5; and Masson, op. cit., pp. 602–3.
30. Christopher Highley, 'Henry VIII's Ghost in Cromwellian England' in *Memory and the English Reformation*; and Thomas, *Religion and the Decline of Magic*, p. 99.
31. Robertson, op. cit.
32. Erler, op. cit., p. 99; and *LP*, Vol 8, no. 108.
33. Chapuys to [Granvelle], 21 November 1535, *LP*, Vol 9, no. 862.

34. Chapuys to Charles V, 27 Sept 1533, *LP*, Vol 6, no. 1164.
35. D. Lysons, 'Stepney', in *The Environs of London: Volume 3, County of Middlesex* (1795).
36. Thomas Thacker to Thomas Cromwell, 11 August 1535, *LP*, Vol 9, no. 66; and no. 131.
37. Christopher Wellyfed to his Father and Mother, 23 January 1533, *LP*, Vol 6, no. 70.
38. John Ap Rice to Cromwell, 23 August 1535, *LP*, Vol 9, no.160.
39. Cromwell to Gardiner, January 1532, Merriman, *Life and Letters*, Vol I, pp. 343–4.
40. T. Derbye to Richard Cromwell, 30 Sept 1533, *LP*, Vol 6, no. 1177.
41. Rowland Lee to Thomas *Cromwell*, 1 January [1533], *LP*, Addenda Vol 1(1), p. 244, no. 724. MacCulloch dates this to 1533 (*Cromwell*, p. 204, fn. 79).
42. Henry Dowes to Thomas Cromwell, 6 September 1534, *LP*, Vol 7, no. 1135.
43. Henry Dowes to Thomas Cromwell, Ellis, *Original Letters*, 1, pp. 343–5.
44. Henry Dowes to Cromwell, 30 April 1535, *LP*, Vol 8, no. 618.
45. Gregory Cromwell to Thomas Cromwell, 25 October 1531, Ellis, *Original Letters*, p. 340.
46. Eustace Chapuys to Nicolas de Granvelle, 15 November 1535, *CSPS, Volume 5(2): Henry VIII, 1536–1538,* ed. P. de Gayangos (1888), no. 228, p. 569.
47. 'Cromwell's Accounts from 1537', *LP*, Vol 14(2), no. 782; Stow's Survey, p. 89; and Nick Holder, Ph.D. thesis, 'The Medieval Friaries of London, A topographic and archaeological history, before and after the Dissolution' (London, 2011), pp. 160–70.
48. Thomas Alvard to Cromwell, 2 November 1532, *LP*, Vol 5, no. 1509.
49. For more on this, see Morrill, 'Cromwell and Friendship', op. cit., pp. 5–11, at p. 9.
50. Though the eldest son of his family, Henry Ireton was not due to inherit the family estate in Attenborough as Nottinghamshire practised ultimogeniture where the youngest son inherited.
51. See Anthony Wood's verdict on him in his *Athenae Oxonienses*, ed. P. Bliss, (4 vols, 1813–1820), Vol 3 (1817), pp. 298–9.
52. Whitelocke, *Memorials*, Vol 3, p. 371; L. Hutchinson, *Memoirs of the Life of Colonel Hutchinson,* ed. N. H. Keeble (2000), p. 251.
53. Hutchinson, op. cit., pp. 256–7.
54. Oliver Cromwell to Bridget Ireton, 25 October 1646, Morrill, *LWS*, Vol 1, pp. 353–5; Oliver Cromwell to Elizabeth Cromwell, 12 April 1651, Ibid., Vol 2, pp. 439–40.
55. MS Harleian 2311, Item 38, fos. 48r–49v (Anna Cromwell Williams's commonplace book).
56. A. Guerdon, *A most learned, conscientious, and devout-exercise: held forth the last Lords-day, at Sir Peter Temples, in Lincolnes-Inne-Fields; / by Lieut.-General Crumwell. As it was faithfully taken in characters by Aaron Guerdon* (1649), p.13.

57. Oliver Cromwell to Bridget Ireton, 25 October 1646, *LWS*, Vol 1, pp. 353–5.
58. Farr, *Oliver Cromwell's Kin*, op. cit., p. 5.
59. *Lincoln's Inn Admissions, 1420–1799* (1896), Vol 1, p. 255.
60. *The Court and Kitchen of Elizabeth Cromwell, Commonly Called Joan Cromwell, the Wife of the Late Usurper* (1664), reprinted as *Mrs Cromwell's Cookbook*, ed. S. Orme (2020), pp. 28–9, 32–3.
61. 'Sir Oliver Cromwell, alias Williams, K.B., of Ramsey, and Col. Henry Cromwell, his Son, of Upwood, both Co. Hunts.' in 'Cases before the Committee: November 21st-30th, 1645', in *Calendar of Proceedings for the Committee for Compounding etc. With Delinquents*, Vol 2 Cases 1643–46, ed. M. A. E. Green (1890).
62. Cokayne, *Complete Peerage*, Vol 1, p. 192.
63. Lord Cromwell's petition, 7 November 1645, *JHL*, Vol 7, 1644 (1767–1830); and 'Thomas, 4th Lord Cromwell, Baron of Oakham, Co. Rutland, Throwley, Co. Stafford', 7 November 1645 in 'Cases before the Committee: November 1st–20th, 1645', in *Calendar, Committee For Compounding*, op. cit.
64. Cockayne, *Complete Peerage*, pp. 192–3.
65. Letter from Oliver Cromwell to Robert Jenner MP, 29 October 1646, *LWS*, Vol 1, pp. 356–7; and 'Thomas Lord Cromwell' entry in *Calendar, Committee For Compounding*, op. cit.
66. J. Berkley, *Memoirs of Sir John Berkley* (1699), p. 27.
67. Trinity College Wren Library, Munby.c.1 *Poems by Michael Drayton* (1607?), p. 371.
68. Phillips, *Antiquary*, op. cit., and Gerhold, *Cromwell and his Family*, op. cit.; and *Perfect Occurrences 35* (27 August–3 September 1647), p. 234.
69. Oliver Cromwell's contributions to the New Model Army Debate at Putney, 28 October 1647, Morrill, *LWS*, Vol 1, p. 437.
70. Berkley, op. cit., pp. 16, 40– 2; and *Calendar of the Clarendon State Papers preserved in the Bodleian Library*, ed. Rev. W. Dunn Macray et al. (5 vols, 1872–1970), Vol 2, Appendix, p. xl.
71. Berkley, op. cit., pp. 40–2. The story circulated in pamphlets and was repeated in the House of Commons' examination of John Lilburne in February 1648 (see R. Hutton, *Oliver Cromwell: Commander in Chief* (2024), p. 108); G. Masterton, *The Triumph Stain'd* (9 February 1648), p. 11; and J. Wildman, *Truths triumph, or Treachery anatomized* (1 February 1648), p. 7.
72. Oliver Cromwell's contributions to the New Model Army Debate at Putney, 28 October & 1 November 1647, *LWS*, Vol 1, pp. 452, 465.
73. For a detailed analysis of these statements, see J. Morrill and P. Baker, 'Oliver Cromwell, the Regicide and the Sons of Zeruiah', in J. Peacey ed. *The Regicides and the Execution of Charles I* (2001).
74. *The World Turned Upside-Down.*

75. Morrill and Baker, op. cit.
76. Speech by Oliver Cromwell at the opening of the nominated Assembly, 4 July 1653, *LWS*, Vol 2, p. 689.
77. E. Ludlow, *The Memoirs of Edmund Ludlow, 1625–1672*, ed. C. H. Firth (2 vols, 1894), Vol 1, pp. 183–6.

6. FALLOUT

1. Ralph Sadler to Thomas Cromwell, 11 January 1636, *LP*, Vol 10, no. 76.
2. M. A. S. Hume, *Chronicle of King Henry VIII of England* (1889), p. 62.
3. Sir Thomas Wyatt, 'Whoso List To Hunt'.
4. Chapuys to Charles V, 1 April 1536, *CSPS*, Vol 5(2), no. 43, p. 81.
5. Chapuys to Charles V, 6 June 1536, *LP*, Vol 10, no. 1069.
6. Chapuys to Charles V, 21 April 1536, *LP*, Vol 10, nos. 699 and 700.
7. Hume, *Chronicle*, op. cit., pp. 63–4.
8. 'Circa Regna tonat' by Sir Thomas Wyatt.
9. Cromwell to Gardiner and Wallop, 14 May 1536, Merriman, *Life and Letters*, Vol 2, pp. 11–13; and Chapuys to the Emperor, 6 June 1536, *CSPS*, Vol 5(2), no. 61, p. 137.
10. Chapuys to Granvelle, 2 May 1536, *LP*, Vol 10, no. 783.
11. Berkley, op. cit., p. 91.
12. 'A Remonstrance of his Excellency Sir Thomas Fairfax . . . and of the General Council of Officers' ([16 Nov.] 1648, E473/11), reprinted in *The Parliamentary or Constitutional History of England* (24 vols, 1761–3), Vol 18, pp. 161–238.
13. D. Farr, *Henry Ireton and the English Revolution* (2006).
14. *Letters between Colonel Robert Hammond governor of the Isle and the Committee of Lords and Commons at Derby House, General Fairfax, Lieutenant-General Cromwell, Commissary General Ireton etc. relating to King Charles I while he was confined in Carisbrooke castle in that Island*, ed. T. Birch (1764), p. 78.
15. Ibid., p. 87.
16. Ibid., p. 95.
17. J. Lilburne, *A discourse betwixt Lieutenant Colonel John Lilburn, close prisoner in the Tower of London, and Mr Hugh Peter: upon May 25. 1649* (1649), p. 8.
18. For further analysis of this sequence of letters, see M. Malins, 'Dear Robin: The Correspondence of Oliver Cromwell and Robert Hammond', *Cromwelliana* (2012), pp. 61–78.
19. For further discussion of this letter, see Morrill and Baker, op. cit.
20. For a detailed examination of these events, see D. Underdown, *Pride's Purge* (1971); and B. Worden, *The Rump Parliament 1648–1653* (1974).
21. Underdown, op. cit., p. 167.
22. Whitelocke, *Memorials*, Vol 2, p. 477 .

23. S. Kelsey, 'The death of Charles I', *The Historical Journal 45* (2002), pp. 727–54.
24. Hutchinson, op. cit., pp. 234, 279, 287; and Abbott, op. cit., Vol 1, p. 743.
25. R. Perrinchief, *Nuntius a mortuis: or, a messenger from the dead. That is, a stupendous and dreadfull colloquie, distinctly and alternately heard by divers, betwixt the ghosts of Henry the Eight, and Charles the First, both Kings of England, who lye entombed in the church of Windsor. Wherein, (as with a pencill from heaven) is liquidly (from head to foot) set forth, the whole series of the judgements of God, upon the sinnes of these unfortunate jslands. Translated out of the Latine copie, by G.T.* (1657), pp. 29–30.
26. Ibid., p. 6.
27. Morrill and Baker, op. cit.
28. Thomas Cromwell to Nicholas Shaxton, bishop of Salisbury, March 1538, Merriman, *Life and Letters,* Vol 2, pp. 128–31, at p. 129.
29. Princess Mary to Cromwell, 23 June 1536, *LP*, Vol 10, no. 1186.
30. Richard Tomyow to Cromwell, 18 August 1536, *LP*, Vol 11, no. 321; Thomas Thacker to Cromwell, 20 August 1536, *LP*, Vol 11, no. 335; and MacCulloch, *Cromwell*, p. 37.
31. For a detailed examination of these processes see D. MacCulloch, 'The consolidation of England 1485–1603', pp. 35–52 and S. G. Ellis, 'The Tudor Borderlands, 1485-1603', pp. 53–73, in J. Morrill ed. *The Oxford Illustrated History of Tudor & Stuart Britain* (1996).
32. MacCulloch, *Cromwell*, p. 323.
33. Thomas Cromwell to John Creke, 17 August 1523, Merriman, *Life and Letters,* Vol 1, pp. 313–4; and William Wellyfed to Thomas Cromwell, 5 October 1536, *LP*, Vol 11, no. 548.
34. Elton, *Reform and Renewal*, p. 103.
35. Cromwell to Henry VIII, January 1534, Merriman, *Life and Letters,* Vol 1, p. 373.
36. 'Index of Failed Bills' in Elton, op. cit., p. 169.
37. G. Burgess, ed. *The New British History: Founding a Modern State 1603–1715* (1999), Ch 6: 'Patterns of British Identity: 'Britain' and its Rivals in the Sixteenth and Seventeenth Centuries' by A. Williamson, p. 152.
38. MacCulloch, op. cit., p. 387.
39. Verses for the rebels in the Pilgrimage of Grace, 19 October 1536, *LP*, Vol 11, no. 786(3); and Confession of William Breyar, 22 October 1536, *LP*, Vol 11, no. 841.
40. 'The Northern Rebellion', 19 January 1537, *LP,* Vol 12(1), no. 163.
41. Thomas Cromwell to Sir Thomas Butler, 30 October 1536, in Merriman, *Life and Letters,* Vol 2, p. 35.
42. 'The Northern Rebellion', 24 April 1537, *LP*, Vol 12(1), no. 1018.
43. [Chapuys's Nephew] to the Queen of Hungary, 15 October 1536, *LP*, Vol 11, no. 714.

44. Richard Cotton to Thomas Cromwell, 21 October 1536, *LP*, Vol 11, no. 831; and Richard Cromwell to Thomas Cromwell, [8 October] 1536, *LP*, Vol 11, no. 607.
45. Sir Robert Constable, 10 April 1537, *LP*, Vol 12(1), no. 891.
46. Richard Cromwell to Thomas Cromwell, [11 October] 1536, *LP*, Vol 11, no. 658.
47. Fitzwilliam to Cromwell, *LP*, Vol 11, no. 865; and [Sir] J. Russell to Cromwell, 25 October 1536, *LP*, Vol 11, no. 866.
48. *The English Court: from the Wars of the Roses to the Civil War*, ed. D. Starkey (1987), p. 112.
49. MacCulloch, op. cit., p. 386 for his translation of the letter from Chapuys to Charles V, 7 October 1536, *CSPS*, Vol 5(2), no. 104, at p. 268.
50. Cromwell and Darcy, 19 April 1537, *LP*, Vol 12(1), no. 976.
51. Hume, *Chronicle*, op. cit., p. 34.
52. [Henry VIII], 'Answere made by the Kynges Hyghnes to the Petitions of the Rebelles in Yorkshire, sig A4v'. For further analysis of the sequence of these draft proclamations, see MacCulloch, op. cit., pp. 393–4.
53. Gervis Clyfton to Mr. Banks, 11 November 1536, *LP, Vol, 11*, no. 1042.
54. Hume, op. cit., p. 36.
55. Cromwell's Accounts, from A.D. 1537, II. Payments by me, Thos. Avery, from 1 Jan. 28 Hen. VIII, January 1537, *LP*, Vol 14(2), no. 782.
56. Ellis, *Original Letters*, Vol 2 (1846), pp. 225–6.
57. Cromwell's Accounts, from A.D. 1537, II. Payments by me, Thos. Avery, from 1 Jan. 28 Hen. VIII, January 1537, *LP*, Vol 14(2), no. 782.
58. Privy Council to Norfolk, 12 March 1537, *LP*, Vol 12(1), no. 636.
59. Ralph Sadler to Henry VIII, 23 March 1543, *LP*, Vol 18(1), no. 313; also *The state papers and letters of Sir Ralph Sadler, knight-banneret /edited by Arthur Clifford . . . ; to which is added a memoir of the life of Sir Ralph Sadler, with historical notes, by Walter Scott.* (2 vols, 1809), Vol 1, p. 88.
60. Ralph Sadler to Henry VIII, 13 July 1543, *LP*, Vol 18(1), no. 880, written in answer to Henry VIII to Ralph Sadler, 7 July 1543, Ibid., no. 834.
61. Ralph Sadler's speech on the succession in Parliament, Hartley (ed.), *Proceedings in the Parliaments*, Vol 1, pp. 87–9; also printed in *The state papers and letters of Sir Ralph Sadler*, op. cit., Vol 2, pp. 557–61.
62. A. J. Slavin, *Politics and Profit: A Study of Sir Ralph Sadler 1507–1547* (1966), p. 127.
63. Ralph Sadler to Suffolk and Tunstal, 5 September 1543, *LP*, Vol 18(2), no. 133.
64. *The state papers and letters of Sir Ralph Sadler*, op. cit., pp. 334–5, 380.
65. Ibid., p. 419.
66. Ibid., p. 380.
67. Neale, *Parliaments*, Vol 2, p. 109.
68. Ibid., p. 166.

69. Francis Bacon, 'A Letter to the Lord Chancellor, Touching the History of Britain' (1605), *Works of Francis Bacon*, ed. J. Spedding, R. L. Ellis and D. D. Heath (11 vols, 1857–1874), Vol 10 (1868), pp. 249–50.
70. P. Collinson, 'The Monarchical Republic of Queen Elizabeth I', in *Bulletin of the John Rylands University Library of Manchester* (1987); P. Collinson, *De Republica Anglorum: Or, History with the Politics Put Back* (1990), reprinted in P. Collinson, *Elizabethan Essays* (1994), pp. 1–29; S. Alford, *The Early Elizabethan Polity: William Cecil and the British Succession Crisis 1558–1569* (1998); and *The Monarchical Republic of Early Modern England: Essays in Response to Patrick Collinson*, ed. J. F. McDiarmid (2007).
71. T. Smith, *De Republica Anglorum* (1583).
72. G. R. Elton, 'The Political Creed of Thomas Cromwell', in Elton, *Studies in Tudor and Stuart Politics and Government* (4 vols, 1974–92), Vol 2, pp. 215–35.
73. For the latest research on James's succession, see S. Doran, *From Tudor to Stuart* (2024); C. Jackson, *The Mirror of Great Britain* (2025); and T. Borman, *The Stolen Crown* (2025).
74. Bacon, op. cit.
75. James VI & I, *Basilikon Doron* and *The True Law of Free Monarchies.*
76. *Tetrachordon* [1645], ed. Chilton Latham Powell, in J. Milton, *The Works* (23, vols 1931), Vol 4, p. 231, cited in J. F. McDiarmid, 'Common Consent, Latinas, and the Monarchical Republic in mid-Tudor Humanism', in *The Monarchical Republic of Early Modern England*, op. cit., pp. 55–74, at p. 74; J. Milton, *The Tenure of Kings and Magistrates* (1649).
77. *A Declaration of the Parliament of England, Expressing the Grounds of their late Proceedings, And of Setling the present Government in the way of A Free State* (1649).
78. *Eikon Basilike: the pourtraicture of His Sacred Majestie in his solitudes and sufferings* (1649).
79. J. Lilburne, *Englands New Chains Discovered; Or The Serious Apprehensions of a Part of the People, in Behalf of the Commonwealth; (being Presenters, Promoters, and Approvers of the Large Petition of September 11. 1648.) Presented to the Supreme Authority of England, the Representers of the People in Parliament Assembled* (1649).
80. Abbott, op. cit., pp. 41–2.
81. In May 1645 'Col. John Cromwell and other colonels and officers in the Low Countries' had requested permission from the Committee of Both Kingdoms to replenish their regiments with royalist prisoners which the Committee duly granted in June. In 1644 a set of accounts records a 'Colonel John Cromwell and Abigail his wife, daughter of Sir Henry Clere, Bart', though a Colonel John Cromwell was also reported to have been killed in a duel with Lord Craven in October 1645, *CSPD Charles I 1644–5*, pp. 516–7, 599; Ibid., *1645–7*, pp. 179–81; Ibid., *Addenda 1625–49*, p. 54.

82. Heath, op. cit., pp. 49–50, 69–71. Oliver's hostile biographer James Heath recounts the two meeting in 1647 when Oliver spoke warmly of the King to his relative and then again when John Cromwell arrived at his house in January 1649 to plead for the King's life.
83. Katherine Whetstone to Mrs Bargen Wind, 16 February 1648(9), Folger Shakespeare Library (formerly MS Add 974, now X.c.53).
84. Whitelocke, *Memorials*, Vol 2, p. 540.
85. Ibid.
86. Fraser, op. cit., p. 305.
87. *LWS*, Vol 2, p. 3; and *The History of Hursley Park*, ed. D. L. Peach (1974), p. 20. For details of Richard and Dorothy's courtship, see letter from Oliver Cromwell to Richard Major, 26 February 1649, *LWS*, Vol 2, pp. 14-15; and the same to the same, 6 April 1649, Ibid., pp. 36–7.
88. Letter from Oliver Cromwell to Richard Major, 14 March 1649, *LWS*, Vol 2, pp. 19–21; op. cit., 25 March 1649, pp. 30–2; Oliver Cromwell to Richard Major, 14 March 1649, *LWS*, Vol 2, pp. 19–21; and P. Little, 'Cromwell and daughters. Financing the marriage settlements of Mary and Frances Cromwell', *Cromwelliana* (2021).
89. Oliver Cromwell to Richard Major, 19 July 1649, *LWS*, Vol 2, pp. 64–6. See also Huntingdon Archive, KAcc731/D/26 (marriage settlement between Richard Cromwell and Dorothy Major).
90. Letter from Oliver Cromwell to Richard Major, 26 February 1649, *LWS*, Vol 2, pp. 14–15; and Oliver Cromwell to Dorothy Cromwell [nee Major], 13 August 1649, Ibid., Vol 2, pp. 73–5.
91. Letter from Oliver Cromwell to Richard Major, 19 July 1649, Ibid., Vol 2, pp. 64–6.
92. Letter from Oliver Cromwell to Dorothy Cromwell [nee Major], 13 August 1649, Ibid., Vol 2, pp. 73–5.
93. J. Morrill, 'The English Revolution in British and Irish Context', in *The Oxford Handbook of the English Revolution*, ed. M. J. Braddick (2015), pp. 555–76.
94. G. Burgess ed. *The New British History: Founding a Modern State 1603–1715* (1999).
95. Hutton, *Commander in Chief*, p. 193.
96. Data Structure Report: Geophysical Survey and Excavation at Dundrum Castle, County Down 2012 and 2013, Vol 1, by P. Macdonald, p. 18.
97. *A perfect diurnall of some passages*, Number 318, 27 August-3 September 1649.
98. Speech by Oliver Cromwell to the people of Dublin, 15 August 1649, *LWS*, Vol 2, pp. 75–6.
99. MacCulloch, op. cit., p. 328.
100. Letter from Oliver Cromwell to Sir Arthur Aston governor of Drogheda, 10 September 1649, *LWS*, Vol 2, pp. 87–8.
101. See Hutton, *Commander in Chief*, p. 198 for an examination of these figures.

102. Letter from Oliver Cromwell to William Lenthall, 17 September 1649, *LWS*, Vol 2, pp. 93–100.
103. Letter from Oliver Cromwell to William Lethal, Speaker of the House of Commons, 14 October 1649, Ibid., Vol 2, pp. 112–17.
104. Letter from Oliver Cromwell to William Lenthall, 17 September 1649, Ibid., Vol 2, pp. 93–100.
105. For more on the debate over Cromwell's actions in Ireland, see J. Morrill, 'The Religious Context of the Cromwellian Conquest of Ireland' and J. Cunningham, 'Cromwell and the Irish land Settlement' in *Cromwelliana* (2014); M. Ó Siochrú, *God's executioner: Oliver Cromwell and the conquest of Ireland* (2008); and T. Reilly, *Cromwell: An Honourable Enemy* (2008).
106. J. Nickolls (ed.), *Original Letters and Papers of State Addressed to Oliver Cromwell* (1743), pp. 6–7.
107. Sir Henry Ingoldsby was one of Sir Oliver's Parliamentarian grandsons. See Conversation between Oliver Cromwell and John Lambert and Sir Henry Ingoldsby, 31[?] July 1650, *LWS*, Vol 2, pp. 305–6; and Burnet, op. cit., Vol 1, p. 154., Vol 1, p. 154.
108. Letter from Oliver Cromwell to the General Assembly of the Kirk of Scotland, 3 August 1650, LWS, Vol 2, pp. 306–10; and Abbott, op. cit., p. 305.
109. Letter from Oliver Cromwell to Henry Ireton, 4 September 1650, Ibid., Vol 2, pp. 340–2.
110. Ibid.
111. Letter from Oliver Cromwell to Richard Major, 4 September 1650, Ibid., Vol 2, pp. 346–7.
112. Letter from Oliver Cromwell to Richard Major, 17 July 1650, Ibid., Vol 2, pp. 289–90.
113. Letter from Oliver to Elizabeth Cromwell, 12 April 1651, Ibid., Vol 2, pp. 439–40.
114. Letter from Oliver to Elizabeth Cromwell, 4 September 1650, Ibid., Vol 2, pp. 344–6.
115. Letter from Oliver to Elizabeth Cromwell, 12 April 1651, Ibid., Vol 2, pp. 439–40.
116. See Proclamation by Oliver Cromwell concerning the wounded at Dunbar, 4 September 1650, and subsequent correspondence on 4–5 September, *LWS*, Vol 2, pp. 335–49.
117. See *LWS*, Vol 2, p. 348, fn. 3 for more details.
118. A. Marvell, 'An Horatian Ode. upon Cromwell's Return from Ireland'.

7. SURVIVAL

1. Cromwell's Accounts, from A.D. 1537, II. Payments by me, Thos. Avery, from 1 Jan. 28 Hen. VIII, April 1538, *LP*, Vol 14(2), no. 782.

2. F. Madden (ed.), *Privy purse expenses of the Princess Mary afterwards Queen Mary: with a memoir of the princess*, (1831), pp. 66, 69.
3. Cromwell's Accounts, from A.D. 1537, II. Payments by me, Thos. Avery, from 1 Jan. 28 Hen. VIII, April 1538, *LP*, Vol 14(2), no. 782.
4. Sir Arthur Darcy to Elizabeth Ughtred, 15 June 1537?, *LP*, Vol 12(2), no. 97.
5. Strong, op. cit.; MacCulloch, op. cit., plate 27; and E. Norton, *Jane Seymour: Patronage, Material Culture and Image Crafting* (2026), p.13.
6. Helmingham Hall Library, *Catherine Tollemache's Receipts of Pastery, Confectionary Etc.* LJ /I/15.
7. Cromwell's Accounts, from A.D. 1537, II. Payments by me, Thos. Avery, from 1 Jan. 28 Hen. VIII, May–August 1537, *LP*, Vol 14(2), no. 782.
8. Gregory Cromwell to Elizabeth Cromwell, 9 December 1539, in Ellis, *Original Letters*, pp. 251–4.
9. Edward Beauchamp to Thomas Cromwell, 2 September 1537, *LP*, Vol 12(2), no. 629.
10. M. A. E. Wood, *Letters of Royal and Illustrious Ladies of Great Britain*, (3 vols, 1846), Vol 2, pp. 355–6.
11. For a full analysis of this heraldic statement, see MacCulloch, op. cit., pp. 427–8.
12. Hume, op. cit., p. 36.
13. For further analysis of this see Robertson, 'Profit and Purpose', pp. 317–46; and MacCulloch, op. cit., pp. 430–5.
14. Giovanni Portinari to Cromwell, 20 March 1538, *LP*, Vol 13(1), no. 554; and the same to the same, 24 March 1538, *LP*, Vol 13(1), no. 590.
15. Gregory Cromwell to Thomas Cromwell, 11 April 1538, in Ellis, *Original Letters*, pp. 192–4.
16. Richard Bishop of Chichester to Richard Cromwell, *LP*, Vol 13(1), no. 1200.
17. MacCulloch, op. cit., p. 483.
18. Wood, op. cit., Vol 2, pp. 355–6.
19. Gregory Cromwell to Elizabeth Cromwell, 9 December 1539, in Ellis, *Original Letters*, pp. 251–4.
20. John Williamson to Thomas Cromwell, 2 August 1539, *LP*, Vol 14(2), no. 12.
21. Ibid., May 1538, *LP*, Vol 14(2), no. 782.
22. Ibid.
23. Later described as the 'base daughter of Thomas Cromwell, Earl of Essex', Jane's eventual marriage to the Cheshire gentleman William Hough, son of one of her father's servants, took her – ironically – into a prominent Catholic household.
24. Richard Cromwell to Thomas Cromwell, [15 May] 1538, *LP*, Vol 13(1), no. 1006.
25. John Husee to Lord Lisle, 8 May [1539], M. St. Clare Byrne (ed.), *The Lisle Letters* (6 vols, 1981), Vol 5, no. 1406, pp. 466–7; and T. Lott,

'Account of the Muster of the Citizens of London in the 31st Year of the Reign of Henry VIII', *Archaeologica* 32 (1847), 30–37.
26. Borman, *Cromwell*, p. 292.
27. G. Bray (ed.), *Documents of the English Reformation* (1994), p. 222.
28. MacCulloch, op. cit., p. 443.
29. Gregory Cromwell to Thomas Cromwell, 1 & 3 December 1539, *LP*, Vol 14(2), nos. 622, 630.
30. 'Anne of Cleves', [January] 1540, *LP*, Vol 15, no. 14.
31. 'Anne of Cleves', 2 January 1540, *LP*, Vol 15, no. 10.
32. E. D. H. Tollemache, *The Tollemaches of Helmingham Hall* (1949), p. 37.
33. Hume, op. cit., pp. 90–1.
34. Cromwell to Henry VIII, [June 1540], *LP*, Vol 15, nos. 823, 824.
35. Merriman, *Life and Letters*, Vol 2, p. 270; and 'The Divorce from Anne of Cleves', [7 July] 1540, *LP*, Vol 15, no. 850(11).
36. Add. MS 48,028 (Yelverton MS 32), fos. 160–165 – Act of Attainder of Thomas Cromwell, Earl of Essex, 29 June 1540; and Merriman, *Life and Letters*, Vol 2, pp. 264–7.
37. Foxe, *TAMO* (1570 edition), Book 8, p. 1399.
38. Add. MS 48,028 (Yelverton MS 32), fos. 160–165 – Act of Attainder of Thomas Cromwell, Earl of Essex, 29 June 1540.
39. Marillac to Montmorency, 10 April 1540, *LP*, Vol 15, no. 486.
40. C. Wriothesley, *A Chronicle of England During the Reigns of the Tudors, From A.D.1485 to 1559*, ed. W. D. Hamilton (2 vols, Camden Society, 2nd set 1875), Vol 1, p. 117.
41. Chapuys to Charles V, 1 April 1536, *LP*, Vol 10, no. 601.
42. Marillac to Montmorency, 23 June 1540, *LP*, Vol 15, no. 804.
43. Cromwell's Accounts, from A.D. 1537, II. Payments by me, Thos. Avery, from 1 Jan. 28 Hen. VIII, April 1538, *LP*, Vol 14(2), no. 782.
44. Marillac to Montmorency, 23 June 1540, *LP*, Vol 15, no. 804.
45. Cromwell's Goods, 27 July 1540, *LP*, Vol 15, no. 917. This appropriation was neatly reversed in 1649 on Charles I's death when one set of his 'Rich Guilt Armor' was singled out from the collection which went to the Tower and sent to Oliver Cromwell. See *Henry VIII and His Afterlives: Literature, Politics and Art*, eds. M. Rankin, C. Highley and J. N. King (2009), Chapter 8, 'The Remains of Henry VIII' by C. Highley, p. 167.
46. Cromwell to Henry VIII, 5 February 1539, Merriman, *Life and Letters*, Vol 2, pp. 176–8, at p. 177.
47. Marillac to Montmorency, 23 June 1540, *LP*, Vol 15, no. 804.
48. Ibid.
49. Add. MS 48,028 (Yelverton MS 32), fos. 160–165 – Act of Attainder of Thomas Cromwell, Earl of Essex, 29 June 1540; and Hume, op. cit., p. 100.
50. Ibid.
51. *The Life of Cardinal Wolsey by George Cavendish and Metrical Visions*, ed., S. W. Singer, 2 vols (1825), Vol 2, pp. 52.

52. Add. MS 48,028 (Yelverton MS 32), fos. 160–165 – Act of Attainder of Thomas Cromwell, Earl of Essex, 29 June 1540.
53. Hume, op. cit., p. 36.
54. *The Novels of Matteo Bandello*, op. cit., pp. 114.
55. Chirbury, *Life and Raigne*, p. 456.
56. T. Fuller, *The Church-History of Britain, from the Birth of Jesus Christ, until the Year M.DC.XLVIII and The History of the University of Cambridge, since the Conquest* (1655), p. 231.
57. Borman, op. cit., p. 359.
58. Hume, op. cit., p. 99.
59. For an examination of this, see MacCulloch, op. cit., p. 526.
60. Foxe, *TAMO* (1570 edition), Book 8, p. 1400; *The life and death of Thomas, Lord Cromwell: By Mr. William Shakespear* (1734), p. 43.
61. Chirbury, op. cit., p. 457; and Cranmer to Henry VIII, [11?] June 1540, *LP*, Vol 15, no. 770.
62. 'Lux, My Fair Falcon' by Sir Thomas Wyatt, lines 4–5.
63. Thomas Wriothesley to Thomas Cromwell, 7 February 1549, *LP*, Vol 14(1), no. 247.
64. S. Brigden, *Thomas Wyatt: the heart's forest* (2012), p. 229.
65. Marillac to Montmorency, 23 June 1540, *LP*, Vol 15, no. 804.
66. Cromwell to Henry VIII, 12 June 1540, Merriman, *Life and Letters*, Vol 2, p. 264–7, at p. 265.
67. Cromwell to Henry VIII, 30 June 1540, *LP*, Vol 15, nos. 823–4; Merriman, *Life and Letters*, Vol 2, pp. 268–73; and Foxe, *TAMO* (1570 edition), Book 8, p. 1400.
68. Cromwell to Henry VIII, June 1540, *LP*, Vol 15, no. 824.
69. Hume, op. cit., p. 103.
70. *Hall's chronicle*, op. cit., pp. 838–9; and Foxe, *TAMO* (1563 edition), Book 3, p. 654.
71. Elton, op. cit., p, 61.
72. Hume, op. cit., p. 104.
73. W. Shakespeare, *Henry VIII*, Act III, Scene 2.
74. Letters from Thomas Cromwell to Thomas Wyatt in Merriman, Vol 2, pp. 94–5, 102–5; and Thomas Wyatt, No. CCXXXVI, in *Collected Poems of Sir Thomas Wyatt*, ed. K. Muir and P. Thomson (1969), p. 238.
75. Will of Thomas Cromwell, 12 July 1529, *LP*, Vol 4, no. 5772; and Merriman, *Life and Letters*, Vol 1, pp. 56–63.
76. 'Cromwell, Thomas (c. 1540–1610/11)' by D. Dean in *ODNB* (2004).
77. 'Stand Whoso List' by Sir Thomas Wyatt, line 1.
78. Interrogated in December 1539, Christopher Chaitour quoted the Latin motto 'Lubricus est primus locus apud reges', in *LP*, Vol 14(2), no. 750; and John Desborough to Oliver Cromwell, 30 September 1650, in J. Nickolls ed. *Original letters and papers of state* (1743), pp. 26–7.
79. *Hall's chronicle*, op. cit., pp. 838–9.

80. Hume, op. cit., p. 103.
81. MacCulloch, op. cit., p. 534.
82. 'Apparel', 21 July 1540, *LP*, Vol 15, no. 900.
83. 'Henry VIII. to the Duke of Suffolk, Earl of Southampton, and Sir Thos. Wriothesley' in Sadler's hand, 13 July 1540, *LP*, Vol 15, no. 883.
84. 'The King's Payments', *LP*, Vol 16, no. 380.
85. 'Grants in July 1540', *LP*, Vol 15, no. 942 [111]; 'Grants in December 1540', *LP*, Vol 16, no. 379 [26]; and 'Grants in November 1540: Sheriff Roll', *LP*, Vol 16, no. 305 [80].
86. Foxe, *TAMO* (1563 edition), p. 654.
87. Marillac to Constable Montmorency, 3 March 1541, *LP*, Vol 16, no. 590.
88. Elizabeth Cromwell to Henry VIII, [autumn] 1540, *LP*, Vol 15, no. 940; reprinted in Wood, *Letters*, pp. 159–60.
89. 'Grants in December 1540', *LP*, Vol 16, no. 379 [34].
90. See Chapuys to the Queen of Hungary, 17 January 1541, Ibid., no. 461; and Marillac to Francis I, 18 January 1541, Ibid., no. 466.
91. Marillac to Montmorency, 18 January 1541, Ibid., no. 467; and Marillac to Francis I, 18 January 1541, Ibid., no. 466.
92. K. Muir, *The Life and Letters of Sir Thomas Wyatt* (1963), p. 192.
93. Marillac to Francis I, 25 January 1541, Ibid., no. 482.
94. Marillac to Francis I, 3 March 1541, Ibid., no. 589.
95. Marillac to Francis I, 25 March 1541, Ibid., no. 650.
96. Sir Ralph Sadleyr to Cranmer and Others, [12] November 1541, Ibid., no. 1333.
97. Wallop to the Council, 28 August 1543, *LP*, Vol 18(2), no. 92.
98. Entries for Gregory Cromwell and Richard Cromwell alias Williams in *HP 1509–1558*, ed. S. T. Bindoff (1982).
99. See Slavin, *Politics and Profit*, pp. 213–18 for an analysis of the story's history.
100. Sir Ralph Sadler by G. Phillips, *ODNB* (2004).
101. 'Grants in November 1545', 29 November 1545, *LP*, Vol 20(2), no. 910(78).
102. 23 November 1545, *LP*, Vol 20(2), no. 850(19).
103. Slavin, op. cit., p. 138.
104. Foxe, *TAMO* (1563 edition), Book 4, p. 784[784].
105. Gregory Cromwell in *HP*.
106. D. MacCulloch, *Suffolk and the Tudors: Politics and Religion in an English County 1500–1600* (1986), p. 307.
107. BL Harleian MS 2194, ff. 20r–20v.
108. Rev. Hastings Robinson, *Original Letters Relative to the English Reformation*, I, The Parker Society LIII (1846–7), no. 165, p. 340.
109. Wood, *Letters*, Vol. 3 (London, 1846): Henry Colburn, pp. 260–2.
110. J. G. Nicholls ed. *The Diary of Henry Machyn* (London, 1848), p. 7.
111. N. Pevsner, *The Buildings of England: Leicestershire and Rutland* (1960), 2nd edition revised by E. Williamson with G. K. Brandwood (1984), p. 198.

112. Cokayne et al, op. cit., Vol 12, part 2, p. 764.
113. *The state papers and letters of Sir Ralph Sadler*, op. cit; W. Scott, *Kenilworth* (1821), Chapter VII.
114. D. Lloyd, *State-worthies: or, the statesmen and favourites of England from the reformation to the revolution . . . By David Lloyd. To this edition is added the characters of the Kings and Queens . . . with a translation of the Latin passages, and other additions. In two volumes. By Charles Whitworth* (1766), Vol 1, pp. 107–8.

8. SPLENDOUR

1. Works at Westminster & Building Stone, 27 [May?] 1530, *LP*, Vol 8, nos. 260, 261.
2. *JHC*, February 1650.
3. B. Capp., *England's Culture Wars: Puritan Reformation and its Enemies in the Interregnum, 1649-1660* (2012), p. 177.
4. Letter from Oliver Cromwell to Philip Wharton, Lord Wharton, 30 June 1652, *LWS*, Vol 2, p. 547.
5. *Letters from Dorothy Osborne to Sir William Temple 1652–54*, ed. E. A. Parry (1903), pp. 65, 90, 166.
6. M. Cary, *The Little Horn's Doom and Downfall, Or a Scripture-Prophesie of King James, and King Charles, and of this present Parliament unfolded. Wherein it appears that the late Tragedies that have bin enacted upon the Scene of these three nation: and particularly, the late King's doom and death, was so long ago, as by Daniel predeclared. And what the issue of it all will be, is also discovered; which follows in the second Part* (1651).
7. Ludlow, *Memoirs*, Vol 1, pp. 259–60.
8. 19 April 1650(1), Thomas Patient to Oliver Cromwell, in Nickolls, *Original Letters and Papers of State*, pp. 6–7.
9. Ludlow, op. cit., pp. 278-9.
10. Ibid., pp. 292–4.
11. J. Owen, *The labouring saints dismission to rest. A sermon / preached at the funeral of the Right Honourable Henry Ireton Lord Deputy of Ireland: in the Abbey Church at Westminster, the 6th. day of February 1651. By John Owen, minister of the Gospel. Licensed and entered according to order*, (1652), Dedication.
12. Letter from Oliver Cromwell to Elizabeth Cromwell, 15 December 1651, *LWS*, Vol 2, pp. 521–2.
13. Whitelocke, *Memorials*, Vol 3, p. 371.
14. Owen, *Labouring Saints.*
15. Ludlow, op. cit., Vol 1, p. 295.
16. Ibid.
17. Evelyn, *Diary*, Vol 2, p. 158; Farr, *Cromwell's Kin*, p. 38; and R. W. Ramsey, *Henry Ireton* (1949), p. 201.

18. Farr, op. cit., pp. 43, 47.
19. Hutchinson, op. cit., pp. 251–2; and Fraser, op. cit., pp. 429–30.
20. Hutchinson, op. cit., pp. 250–1.
21. *Pragmaticus (for King Charles II), no. 11, E.562[21]* (26 June–3 July 1649), sig. L3r; for further specific examples and analysis of this literature, see S. Fullerton, 'Fatal Adulteries: Sexual Politics in the English Revolution', *Journal of British Studies* 60 (October 2021), pp. 793–821.
22. *A new bull-bayting: or, A match play'd at the tovvn-bull of Ely.: By twelve mungrills. Viz. 4 English 4 Irish 4 Scotch doggs. Iohn Lilburn, Richard Overton, Thomas Prince, and William Walwyn, to stave and nose. With his last will and testament, and several legacies bequeathed to the Iuncto, the Councel of State, and army. Too him my dogge; ha-loe there; now hee's down: bayted to death, and forfeit to the Crown* (1649), pp. 6–7.
23. Fullerton, op. cit., p. 808.
24. *The cuckoo's-nest a [sic] Westminster, or the Parlement between two lady-birds, Quean Fairfax, and Lady Cromwell, concerning negotiations of estate, and their severall interests in the Kingdom; sadly bemoaning the fate of their deer and ab-hor'ed husbands. Who buyes a cuckoes-nest, hatch'd in an ayre . . . to springe her for her base disloyalty. by Mercurius Melancholicus* (1648), p. 8; *A tragi-comedy, called New-Market-Fayre, or A Parliament out-cry: of state-commodities, set to sale. The prologue sung by the cryer . . .* (1649); and Gillespie, 'Elizabeth Cromwell's Kitchen Court'.
25. Hutchinson, op. cit., pp. 256–7.
26. Ibid., pp. 251–2.
27. Charles Fleetwood to Henry Cromwell, 20 May 1656, *CHC*, pp. 128–9. Fortunately little Biddy Ireton did recover (Ibid., p. 133).
28. Farr, op. cit., p. 48.
29. Letter from Oliver Cromwell to Charles Fleetwood, 8[?] September 1652, *LWS*, Vol 2, pp. 564–6.
30. Hutchinson, op. cit., p. 252.
31. Letter from Oliver Cromwell to Charles Fleetwood, 22 June 1655, *LWS*, Vol 3, pp. 203–5; and Letter from Oliver Cromwell to an unnamed friend, 1 September 1652, in Ibid., Vol 2, pp. 562–3.
32. Conversation between Oliver Cromwell and Bulstrode Whitelocke, 30[?] November 1652, Ibid., Vol 2, pp. 573–81.
33. The various versions of this speech are recorded in Morrill, *LWS*, Vol 2, pp. 607–614.
34. Dorothy Osborne to William Temple, [24 April?] 1653, *The Letters of Dorothy Osborne to Sir William Temple 1652–54*, ed. E. A. Parry (London, 1903), pp. 78–9.
35. Huntingdon Archive, KAcc731/D/29 (marriage settlement between Henry Cromwell and Elizabeth Russell). Five years later, during a separation, Henry wrote to Elizabeth that until he returned 'my heart will not be perfectly at ease for thou art very Dear to me; thou

art indeed. And through grace there shall never be any thing wanting in me to express it to thee.' On her side, Elizabeth once wrote to Henry 'that you shall ever find me a loving, constant wife'. See Henry Cromwell to Elizabeth Cromwell, 14 August 1658, Huntingdon Archives 731/74 (Surviving Letters to and from Henry Cromwell, 1655–1660); and Elizabeth Cromwell to Henry Cromwell, undated, in *CHC*, p. 520.

36. Lorenzo Paulucci, Venetian Secretary in England, to Giovanni Sagredo, the Ambassador in France, 30 May 1653, *CSPV*, Vol 29, no. 112.
37. Northants RO, Montagu MS 191, 'Letters on public events' folder, no. 9, discovered by Dr David Scott of the History of Parliament. I am grateful to Dr Patrick Little for sharing this discovery with me and his analysis of it. See also P. Little, 'Custards and cushions: new evidence for Oliver Cromwell's sense of humour', *Cromwelliana* (2024).
38. Speech by Oliver Cromwell at the opening of the Nominated Assembly, 4 July 1653, *LWS*, Vol 2, pp. 664–86.
39. Heath, op. cit., p. 15.
40. Burnet, op. cit., Vol 1, p. 121.
41. *The government of the Common-wealth of England, Scotland, & Ireland, and the dominions thereto belonging; as it was publickly declared at Westminster the 16. Day of December 1653. In the presence of the Lords Commissioners of the Great Seal of England, the Lord Maior and aldermen of the City of London, divers of the judges of the land, the officers of state and army, and many other persons of quality, at which time and place His Highness, Oliver Lord Protector of the said Commonwealth, took a solemn oath for observing the same. Published by His Highness the Lord Protector's special commandment* (1653), pp. 45–6.
42. H. Fletcher, *The perfect politician, or, A full view of the life and action (military and civil) of O. Cromwel . . .* (1660).
43. L. de Gand, *Parallelum Olivae nec non Olivarii* (1656), p. 2; and Sherwood, *King in All But Name* (1997), p. 3.
44. *JHC*, Vol 7: 19 December 1654, p. 404.
45. P. Little, 'The Culture of the Cromwellian Court', *Cromwelliana* (2009), pp. 12–13.
46. R. Sherwood, *The Court of Oliver Cromwell* (1977), p. 21.
47. Ludlow, *op. cit.*, p. 379.
48. *Court and Kitchen*, pp. 40–1.
49. R. W. Ramsey, *Cromwell's Family Circle* (1930), p. 8.
50. A. Woolrych, *Britain in Revolution 1625–1660* (2002), p. 595.
51. Fraser, op. cit., p. 462 (citing the *Weekly Intelligencer*, 14– 21 March 1654).
52. Jongestall, to his excellency William Friderick, earl of Nassau, &c., 28 April 1654, *TSP*, Vol 2, p. 257.
53. *Court and Kitchen*, pp. 41–3.

54. Letter from Christer Bonde to Charles X, 23 August 1655, in Roberts, *Swedish Diplomats* p. 125.
55. Fraser, op. cit., 459; and Evelyn, *Diary*, Vol 2, p. 108.
56. '1659 Inventory of Hampton Court', *Cromwelliana* (2009); and Little, 'The Culture of the Cromwellian Court', p. 14.
57. MacCulloch, op. cit., p. 464; P. Hunneyball, 'Cromwellian Style: The Architectural Trappings of the Protectorate Regime' in P. Little ed. *The Cromwellian Protectorate* (2007), p. 72; and Fraser, op. cit., p. 458.
58. '1659 Inventory of Hampton Court'; and S. Thurley, 'Revolutionary State? Royal Palaces in Cromwell's England' (Gresham College lecture, 11 March 2015), https://www.gresham.ac.uk/
59. '1659 Inventory of Hampton Court'; Little, 'Culture of the Cromwellian Court'; L. Prosser, 'The Palace of the Republic', *Cromwelliana* (2009); and S. Thurley, *Hampton Court – A Social and Architectural History* (2003).
60. A. Marvell, 'A Poem Upon the Death of O.C.', lines 47–50.
61. Sherwood, *The Court* p. 106; and S. Thurley, 'The Stuart Kings, Oliver Cromwell and the Chapel Royal 1618-1685', *Architectural History*, Vol. 45 (2002), 238–274.
62. Nickolls, *Original Letters*, p. 115.
63. Cromwell's Accounts, from A.D. 1537, *LP*, Vol 14(2), no. 782.
64. Little, 'Culture of the Cromwellian Court' and 'Cromwell and Falconry', *Cromwelliana* (2008), pp. 67–74.
65. Helmingham Hall Library, *Book of Secrets* MS LJ/II/6.
66. Little, 'Falconry', p. 70.
67. Little, 'Culture of the Cromwellian Court', pp. 25–6; and Little, 'Uncovering a Protectoral stud: horses and horsebreeding at the court of Oliver Cromwell, 1653-8', *Historical Research*, vol. 82, no. 216 (May 2009).
68. Joannes a Werden to Thomas Cromwell, 24 July 1538, *LP*, Vol 13(1), no. 1450; Luteke Scepenstede to Thomas Cromwell, 25 August 1539, *LP*, Vol 14(2), no. 84; and Cromwell's Accounts, from A.D. 1537, *LP*, Vol 14(2), no. 782.
69. Ramsey, op. cit., p. 115.
70. Speech of Oliver Cromwell to Parliament in the Painted Chamber, 17 September 1656, *LWS*, Vol 3, p. 316.
71. Fraser, op. cit., p. 473.
72. Ibid., p. 464; and Sherwood, op. cit., p. 136.
73. *Mercurius Politicus*, 19–26 February 1658.
74. R. L'Estrange, *Truth and Loyalty Vindicated* (1662), p. 50; and A. Dunan-Page, B. Lynch, *Roger L'Estrange and the Making of Restoration Culture* (2008), pp. 4, 9.
75. *Henry the VIII and his Afterlives*, 'Chapter 9: Henry VIII: his musical contribution and posthumous reputation', M. Spring, p. 197.
76. Oliver gave places as gentlemen of the bedchamber to John Barrington from his Aunt Joan's family and to one of his mother's relations, Edward Rolt; Oliver's wife Elizabeth's cousin Nathaniel Waterhouse

was joint steward and then master of the household; and Oliver's cousin Sir Oliver Flemyng continued his pre-Protectorate role as master of ceremonies.

77. A. Barclay, 'The Lord Protector and his Court' in Little ed. *New Perspectives*, pp. 202–3; and Sherwood, op. cit., pp 81, 142.
78. Roberts, *Swedish Diplomats*, p. 120.
79. Noble, op. cit., Vol 1, p. 136.
80. Whitelocke, *Memorials*, Vol 3, pp. 474-75 .
81. *The English Revolution III, Newsbooks 5, Volume 17, Mercurius Politicus 1657–58* (1971), p. 427.
82. S. Butler, 'A ballad upon the Parliament which deliberated about making Oliver King', reproduced in *The Poetical Works of Samuel Butler* (1835), ed. W. Pickering.
83. *The Oceana and Other Works of James Harrington, with an Account of His Life* by J. Toland (1771), para 14.
84. HMC, *Appendix to the Second Report*, p. 148.
85. R. Fleckno, *The Idea of His Highness Oliver Lord Protector etc. With certain brief reflexions on his life* (1659), p. 66.
86. H. Fletcher, *The perfect politician, or, A full view of the life and action (military and civil) of O. Cromwel whereunto is added his character, and a compleat catalogue of all the honours conferr'd by him on several persons* (London, 1660), p. 1; and K. Sharpe, *Image Wars: Promoting Kings and Commonwealths in England, 1603-1660* (2010), Chapter 17: Painting Protectoral Power.
87. Knoppers, op. cit., p. 129.
88. *Autographed receipt for a painting of Oliver Cromwell by Robert Walker*, B59, The Cromwell Museum.
89. Warwick, *Memoirs*, p. 275.
90. A. Chapman, 'Fly me to the Moon', *Astronomy & Geophysics*, Vol 55(1), February 2014, pp. 1.26–1.31; and J. Wilkins, *The discovery of a world in the moone* (1638), *A discourse concerning a new world and anoth[er] planet. In 2 bookes [The first book. The discovery of a new world. Or, a discourse tending to prove, that 'tis probable there may be another habitable world in the moone. With a discourse concerning the possibility of a passage thither. The third impression. A discourse concerning a new planet. Tending to prove, that 'tis probable our earth is one of the planets. The second booke, now first published* (1640) and *Mathematical Magick; or, The Wonders that may be performed by Mechanical Geometry* (1648).
91. B. Worden, *God's Instruments: Political Conduct in the England of Oliver Cromwell* (2012), p. 120.
92. B. J. Shapiro, *John Wilkins 1614–1672, An Intellectual Biography* (1969), p. 112.
93. Many of the medieval colleges of Oxford were rebuilt in the seventeenth century; work which was halted during the war and re-started under the Commonwealth.

94. Abbott, op. cit., p. 74.
95. 'Politics, Piety, and Learning: Cromwellian Oxford', in Worden, *God's Instruments.*
96. Letter from Oliver Cromwell to Daniel Greenwood, the vice-chancellor, and the convocation of the University of Oxford, 4 February 1651, *LWS*, Vol 2, pp. 420–2.
97. Worden, op. cit., p. 115.
98. Ibid., p. 127.
99. W. Petty, *The advice of W.P. to Mr. Samuel Hartlib for the advancement of some particular parts of learning* (1647), Dedication.
100. Evelyn, *Diary*, Vol 2, p. 79; and Worden, op. cit.
101. Coleman, *Fruitful Endeavours*, p. 149; and Worden, op. cit., p. 118.
102. S. Hartlib, *The reformed common-wealth of bees* (1655).
103. Evelyn, op. cit.
104. Petty, op. cit.
105. Ibid., p. 4.
106. P. Little, 'Farmer Oliver? The cultivation of Cromwell's image during the Protectorate', *Cromwelliana* (2012).
107. Clarendon, *History*, Vol 6, p. 97; and B. Coward, *Cromwell* (1991), p. 101.
108. Speech by Oliver Cromwell to the Dutch commissioners, 14 July 1653, *LWS*, Vol 2, pp. 718–9.
109. Warwick, *Memoirs*, p. 411.
110. Coward, *Cromwell*, p. 137.
111. Speech of Oliver Cromwell to Parliament in the Painted Chamber, 17 September 1656, *LWS*, Vol 3, p. 307.
112. *Instrument of Government*, Clauses 36 and 37.
113. Two speeches by Oliver Cromwell in a Parliamentary committee, 28[?] February 1652, *LWS*, Vol 2, pp. 530–2.
114. Letter from Oliver Cromwell to John Williams, Archbishop of York, 1 September 1647, Ibid., Vol 1, pp. 426–7.
115. Speech of Oliver Cromwell to the first Protectorate Parliament in the Painted Chamber, 4 September 1654, Ibid., Vol 3, pp. 66–82.
116. Letter from Oliver Cromwell to the Lord Deputy and Council of Ireland, 30 December 1657, Ibid., Vol 3, pp. 457–8.
117. Fraser, op. cit., p. 622; and Worden, op. cit., p. 158.
118. Letter from Oliver Cromwell to William Lenthall, Speaker of the House of Commons, 11 March 1651, *LWS*, Vol 2, pp. 427–8.
119. J. A. Mills, 'Durham, County Durham', *Cromwelliana* (2003), p. 46.
120. Yet the university which was eventually founded in 1832 remembered its first champion: in 1950 a motion was put forward to name a new college at Durham Cromwell College, though this was rejected in the face of 'astonishingly fierce opposition'.
121. Morrill, 'Blood and Marriage', p. 49; Speech of Oliver Cromwell to the first Protectorate Parliament in the Painted Chamber, 22 January 1655, *LWS*, Vol 3, pp.129–151; and Fraser, op. cit., p. 506.

122. Speech of Oliver Cromwell to the first Protectorate Parliament in the Painted Chamber, 4 September 1654, *LWS,* Vol 3, pp. 66–82. He was the first ruler since Henry VIII to use the Painted Chamber and not the House of Lords to deliver an opening speech.
123. Morrill, 'Blood and Marriage', p. 49.
124. *The Clarke Papers: selections from the papers of W. Clarke, Secretary to the Council of the army, 1647–9, and to General Monck and the commanders of the army in Scotland, 1651–62,* ed. C. H. Firth (4 vols, 1891–4), Vol 2, pp. xxxiv–xxxvii.
125. Speech of Oliver Cromwell to the first Protectorate Parliament in the Painted Chamber, 12 September 1654, *LWS,* Vol 3, pp. 82–99.
126. J. Milton, 'Lycidas' (1638), line 5.
127. R. Herrick, 'After Autumn, Winter'.
128. Lorenzo Paulucci, Venetian Secretary in England, to Giovanni Sagredo, the Ambassador in France, 6 December 1654, *CSPV, Volume 29, 1653–1654,* ed. A. B. Hinds (1929), no. 346.
129. L. Nunn, '"An hundred times fitter for a Barn than a Palace": A gendered analysis of the Protectoral portraits of Elizabeth Cromwell and her daughters Cromwelliana' (2021).
130. Ludlow, op. cit., Vol 1, p. 379.
131. *An epitaph on the late deceased, that truely-noble and renowned lady Elizabeth Cromwel (mother to His Highness the Lo. Protector of Great Britain and Ireland, &c.) who lived to the age of 89. and died Nov. 16. 1654. and lieth buried in Westminster-Abbey* (1655).

9. DYNASTY

1. *The History of the Worthies of England by Thomas Fuller*, ed. P. A. Nuttall, 3 vols (1840), Vol 2, p. 107.
2. *Barrington Letters*, ed. A. Searle (Camden Society, ser 4. xxviii), pp. 156–7 (cited in 'Sir Oliver Cromwelll', in *HP 1604–1629*).
3. Ibid.
4. S. Meakins, 'Elizabeth Murray, Countess of Dysart and Duchess of Lauderdale (1626–1698)', *Cromwelliana* (2017), p. 42; and Burnet, op. cit., Vol 1, pp. 437-8.
5. Ibid.; and A. Fraser, 'Bess and Old Noll', *Horizon Magazine*, Vol xiii (1971), pp. 106-111.
6. Fraser, *Chief of Men*, pp. 478-80.
7. Burnet, op. cit.
8. The letters are in the collection at Helmingham Hall.
9. P. Lay, *Providence Lost: The Rise and Fall of Cromwell's Protectorate* (2020), p. 87.
10. Speech of Oliver Cromwell to the first Protectorate Parliament in the Painted Chamber, 22 January 1655, *LWS*, Vol 3, p. 135.
11. Lay, op. cit., p. 82.

12. Hutchinson, op. cit., p. 258.
13. Roberts, *Swedish Diplomats*, p. 114.
14. M. Roberts, *Essays in Swedish History* (1967), p. 178, fn. 48.
15. H. Dunthorne, 'Cromwell and Europe' in Mills, *Cromwell's Legacy*, p. 220.
16. Debate between Oliver Cromwell and the Protectoral Council, 20 July 1654, *LWS*, Vol 3, pp. 58–60.
17. For a further exploration of this, see Dunthorne, 'Cromwell and Europe'.
18. *The embassador and his functions. By Monsieur de Wicquefort. To which is added, an historical discourse, concerning the election of the emperor and the electors. By the same author. Translated into English by Mr. Digby* (1716), pp. 17-18; and Clarendon, *History*, Vol 5, p. 309 & Vol 6, p. 94.
19. Dunthorne, 'Cromwell and Europe'.
20. T. Venning, 'Cromwell and the Huguenots: Ethical Foreign Policy or Strategic Realpolitik?', *Cromwelliana* (2000), pp. 36–44.
21. T. Venning, 'Cromwell's Foreign Policy and the "Western Design"', *Cromwelliana* (1994), pp. 41–52.
22. Thurloe described Huguenot toleration as the 'cement of this union'. See Venning, 'Cromwell and the Huguenots', p. 42.
23. Coward, *Cromwell*, and Lay, *Providence Lost*, explore Cromwell's siege mentality at this moment of crisis.
24. Letter from Oliver Cromwell to Vice Admiral William Goodsonn, 30[?] October 1655, *LWS*, Vol 3, pp. 229–31.
25. C. Durston, 'Godly Governors: the Rule of Cromwell's Major-Generals', *Cromwelliana* (2004), p. 61.
26. For further analysis of the Rule of the Major-Generals see C. Durston, *Cromwell's Major-Generals: Godly Government during the English Revolution* (2001).
27. Ludlow, op. cit., pp. 380–2.
28. For further analysis of this see J. Peacey 'Fit for Public Services: The Upbringing of Richard Cromwell' in Little ed. *New Perspectives*; and P. Little, 'Cromwell and Sons', in Mills, *Cromwell's Legacy*.
29. Speech of Oliver Cromwell to the first Protectorate Parliament in the Painted Chamber, 22 January 1655, *LWS*, Vol 3, pp. 129–51.
30. Ibid.
31. Letter from Oliver Cromwell to Charles Fleetwood, Lord Deputy of Ireland, 22 June 1655, Ibid., Vol 3, pp. 203–5.
32. *Weekly Intelligencer*, no. 2 (21–28 August 1655), pp. 6–7.
33. Roberts, *Swedish Ambassadors*, pp. 72, 80.
34. Letter from Oliver Cromwell to Charles Fleetwood, Lord Deputy of Ireland, 22 June 1655, *LWS*, Vol 3, pp. 203–5.
35. P. B. Ellis, *Hell to Connaught: The Cromwellian Colonisation of Ireland 1652–1660* (1975), p. 141.
36. Farr, *Kinship*, p. 137.

37. Bridget Fleetwood to Henry Cromwell, [undated, sometime between November 1657 and November 1658], *CHC*, p. 521.
38. Henry Cromwell to John Thurloe, 28 November 1655, *TSP*, Vol 4, pp. 254–5.
39. Henry Cromwell to John Thurloe, 18 January 1655, *TSP*, Vol 4, p. 433.
40. Robert Wood to Samuel Hartlib, 23 Novemebr 1656, *The Hartlib Papers*, 33/1/7A-8B.
41. Henry Cromwell to John Thurloe, 3 June 1657, *TSP*, Vol 6, p. 330; and Burgess, *New British History*, Ch 8: 'British and Irish History' by T. C. Barnard, p. 207.
42. Henry Cromwell to Oliver Cromwell, 9 October 1655, *TSP*, Vol 4, pp. 73–4.
43. Henry Cromwell to John Thurloe, 24 December 1656, *TSP*, Vol 5, pp. 729–30.
44. Henry Cromwell to John Thurloe, [August 1657?], *TSP*, Vol 6, pp. 446–7.
45. For the full text of these letters and detailed analysis, see J. Halcomb and P. Little, 'Writings and Sources XVI: "Your Loving Father", Letters from Oliver to Henry Cromwell, 1656–1658', *Cromwelliana* (2014), pp. 64–83.
46. Letter from Oliver Cromwell to Henry Cromwell, 21 April 1656, *LWS*, Vol 3, pp. 253–5.
47. Fraser, op. cit., pp. 579–80.
48. P. Gaunt, *The Cromwellian Gazetteer* (1987), pp. 238–9 as applied by P. Little, 'Cromwell and sons', p. 19.
49. *The English Revolution III, Newsbooks 5, Volume 13, Mercurius Politicus 1656* (London, 1971), p.142.
50. Richard Cromwell to Henry Cromwell, 14 June 1656, *CHC*, pp. 138–9.
51. Richard Cromwell to Henry Cromwell, 27 November 1655, in *Ibid.*, pp. 75–6.
52. Richard Cromwell to Henry Cromwell, 14 June 1656, in *Ibid.*, pp. 138–9.
53. Richard Cromwell to Henry Cromwell, 27 November 1655, in *Ibid.*, pp. 75–6.
54. Richard Cromwell to Henry Cromwell, 27 November 1655, in *Ibid.*, pp. 75–6; and Richard Cromwell to Henry Cromwell, 27 March 1656, in *Ibid.*, p. 116.
55. Richard Cromwell to Henry Cromwell, 14 June 1656, in *Ibid.*, pp. 138–9.
56. Francis Russell to Henry Cromwell, 11 July 1656, in *Ibid.*, pp. 158–9.
57. Richard Cromwell to Henry Cromwell, 8 July 1657, in *Ibid.*, pp. 300–1.
58. For more on this group and its actions, see P. Little, 'Thurloe and the Offer of the Crown', in *New Perspectives*; J. Fitzgibbons, 'Hereditary Succession and the Cromwellian Protectorate: The Offer of the Crown Reconsidered', *The English Historical Review*, Vol 128, No. 534 (October 2013), pp. 1095–1128; and M. Malins, 'Conservative Cromwellians and the Restoration c. 1657–c.1677' (PhD thesis, University

of Cambridge) and 'Monarchical Cromwellians and the Restoration', *Cromwelliana* (2016).

59. Francesco Giavarina, Venetian Resident in England, to the Doge and Senate, 14 July 1656, *CSPV, Vol 30, 1655–1656*, ed. A. B. Hinds (1930), no. 343.
60. E. Waller, 'Of A War With Spain and Fight At Sea', in *Poetical Works of Edmund Waller and Sir John Denham*, ed. G. Gilfillan (1862).
61. Francesco Giavarina, Venetian Resident in England, to the Doge and Senate, 24 November 1656, *CSPV, Vol 30*, no. 389.
62. Francesco Giavarina, Venetian Resident in England, to the Doge and Senate, 12 January 1657, in Ibid., *Vol 31, 1657–1659*, ed. A. B. Hinds (1931), no.1; and the same to the same, 8 December 1656, in Ibid., *Vol 30*, no. 393.
63. Francesco Giavarina, Venetian Resident in England, to the Doge and Senate, 8 December 1656, in Ibid., no. 393; and the same to the same, 24 November 1656, in Ibid., no. 389.
64. T. Flatman, *Don Juan Lamberto: or, a comical history of the late times. The first part. By Montelion Knight of the Oracle, &c.* (1661).
65. Ludlow, *Memoirs*, Vol 2, p. 20; Francesco Giavarina to the Doge and Senate, 14 December 1657, *CSPV, Vol 31*, no 114; and *Calendar of the Clarendon State Papers*, Vol 3, p. 239.
66. BL Harley MS 2311, Anna Cromwell Williams, 'A Booke of severall devotional collected by good men from the worst of sinners'; M. J. M. Ezell, 'The Exemplary Wife: Anna Cromwell Williams's Book of Secrets', in *In the Prayse of Writing, Early Modern Manuscript Studies Essays in Honour of Peter Beal*, ed. S. P. Cerasano and S. W. May (British Library, 2012), pp. 281–99; https://perdita.warwick.ac.uk/ms_BLH2311.htm; and Noble, *Memoirs*, Vol 1, pp. 250–1.
67. BL Harley MS 2311, fols. 18v–19r.
68. Noble, Vol 1, pp. 67–8.
69. Morrill, 'Blood and Marriage.'
70. John Reynolds to Henry Cromwell, 24 Match 1657, *CHC*, pp. 235–6.
71. For more analysis on this see Little, 'Cromwell and Sons'.
72. *Diary of Sir Archibald Johnston of Wariston*, ed. J. D. Ogilvie (1940), Vol 3, 1655-1660, p. 85.
73. Henry Cromwell to John Thurloe, 4 March 1656[7], *TSP*, Vol 6, p. 94. For more discussion of these tensions, see Little, 'Cromwell and Sons'.
74. Francis Russell to Henry Cromwell, 27 April 1657, *CHC*, p. 264.
75. Morrill, 'Blood and Marriage', p. 49.
76. *Monarchy asserted to be the best, most ancient, and legall form of government in a conference had at Whitehall with Oliver, late Lord Protector, & a committee of Parliament* . . . (1660); and Malins, 'Conservative Cromwellians'.
77. Speech of Oliver Cromwell to the committee of Parliament in Whitehall, 13 April 1657, *LWS*, Vol 3, pp. 366–83.

78. Speech of Oliver Cromwell to the army officers, 27 February 1657, Ibid., Vol 3, pp. 339–45.
79. *The Diary of Thomas Burton*, ed. J. T. Rutt (1828), Vol 1, 12 December 1656, p. 126.
80. Speech of Oliver Cromwell to the army officers, 27 February 1657, *LWS*, Vol 3, p. 341.
81. Ibid., pp. 339–45.
82. Richard Cromwell to Henry Cromwell, 7 March 1657, *CHC*, pp. 220–1.
83. Mary Cromwell to Henry Cromwell, 23 June 1656, *TSP*, Vol 5, p. 146.
84. Ibid.
85. Francis Russell to Henry Cromwell, 27 April 1657, *CHC*, p. 264; see also P. Little, 'Cromwell and Daughters: Financing the Marriage Settlements of Mary and Frances Cromwell', *Cromwelliana* (2021), pp. 22–9.
86. 28 March 1657, *CSPD: Interregnum, 1656-7*, ed. M. A. E. Green (1883), no. 46, p. 322.
87. *A Collection of State Letters of the Right Honourable Roger Boyle, the first Earl of Orrery*, ed. T. Morrice (1742), pp. 21–2; Noble, op. cit., Vol 1, pp. 149–51; and Pepys, *Diary*, Vol 5, pp. 296–7.
88. Ambassador Coyet in London to Charles X, King of Sweden, 1 June 1655, *Swedish Diplomats*, pp. 75–6; and Clarendon, *History*, Vol 6, p. 21.
89. Draft of a letter from Henry Cromwell to Lord Broghill, January 1657, *CHC*, pp. 194–5; and J. Fitzgibbons, 'Hereditary Succession and the Cromwellian Protectorate: The Offer of the Crown Reconsidered', *The English Historical Review*, Vol. 128, No. 534 (October 2013), pp. 1095–1128, at p. 1114.
90. Henry Cromwell to John Thurloe, 4 March 1657, *TSP*, Vol 6, pp. 93–4; Henry Cromwell to John Thurloe, 8 April 1657, Ibid, pp. 182–3; and Henry Cromwell to Oliver Cromwell, 22 April 1657, Ibid, pp. 222–3.
91. Henry Cromwell to Oliver Cromwell, 22 April 1657, Ibid, pp. 222.
92. C. H. Firth, *The Last Years of the Protectorate 1656–1658* (1909), Vol 1, p. 129; and Richard Cromwell to Henry Cromwell, 7 March 1657, *CHC*, pp. 220–1.
93. Richard Cromwell to Henry Cromwell, 18 June 1657, Ibid., pp. 286–7.
94. Speech of Oliver Cromwell to the House of Commons in the Banqueting House, 31 March 1657, *LWS*, Vol 3, pp. 345–9.
95. John Thurloe to Henry Cromwell, *TSP*, Vol 6, p. 219.
96. Whitelocke, op. cit., Vol 4, pp. 289–90.
97. Fraser, op. cit., p. 605.
98. Conversation of Oliver Cromwell with George Fox, 31 March 1657, *LWS*, Vol 3, p. 350.
99. See B. Worden, 'Oliver Cromwell and the Sin of Achan' in D. L. Smith ed. *Cromwell and the Interregnum* (2003); and Little, 'Cromwell and Sons'.
100. Ludlow, *Memoirs*, Vol 2, pp. 24–5; and *TSP*, op. cit., p. 287.

101. D. L. Smith, 'The Monarchical Republic of Oliver Cromwell', *Cromwelliana* (2016), p. 8.
102. Francis Russell to Henry Cromwell, 27 April 1657, *CHC*, p. 264.
103. Speech of Oliver Cromwell to the second Protectorate Parliament in the Banqueting House, 8 May 1657, *LWS*, Vol 3, pp. 418–23.
104. Speech of Oliver Cromwell to the committee of Parliament in Whitehall, 13 April 1657, Ibid., Vol 3, pp. 366–83. For one of the best examinations of Oliver's motives in refusing the Crown, see J. Morrill, 'King Oliver?', in *Cromwell Four Centuries On* (2013), pp. 93–7.
105. Richard Cromwell to Henry Cromwell, 18 June 1657, *CHC*, pp. 286–7; draft of a letter by Henry Cromwell to John Thurloe, [May 1657], Ibid., p. 275; and Francis Russell to Henry Cromwell, 25 May 1657, Ibid., pp. 272–3.
106. Francesco Giavarina, Venetian Resident in England, to the Doge and Senate, 13 July 1657, *CSPV, Vol 31*, no. 63.
107. Pugh, *British and Outlandish Prophesies.*
108. Dr. John Wilkins to M. Rosine, his Highness's secretary, 21 May 1658, *CSPD: Interregnum, 1658–9*, no. 11; J. Butler, 'Richard Cromwell and Oxford 1657–1660', *Cromwelliana* (1982), pp. 21–32; Clarendon, *History*, Vol 6, pp. 33–4; and Shapiro, op. cit., p. 111.
109. Ambassador Lockhart to John Thurloe, 26 May/7 June, *CSPD: Interregnum, 1656–7*, no. 46.
110. Ambassador Lockhart to John Thurloe, March 21/31 1657, Ibid., no. 36.
111. Mary Belasyse, Viscountess Fauconberg to Henry Cromwell, 1 December 1657, *CHC*, pp. 353–4.
112. Hutchinson, op. cit., p. 295.
113. Nunn, 'An Hundred Times Fitter for a Barn than a Palace', p. 58.
114. For further analysis of this, see M. Malins, '"All Imaginable Pomp and Lustre": Family Occasions at Cromwell's Court', *Cromwelliana* (2021), pp. 5–21.
115. Abbott, op. cit., Vol 4, p. 670.
116. Clarendon, *History*, Vol 6, p. 34.
117. Ibid.
118. HMC Fifth Report Appendix, pp. 145, 183.
119. *The English Revolution III, Newsbooks 5, Volume 16, Mercurius Politicus 1657* (1971), pp. 212, 233.
120. HMC Fifth Report Appendix, p. 177.
121. British Library, Harleian MS 991, p. 23.
122. E. Waller, 'On the Marriage of Mts. Frances Cromwell with Mr. Rich Grandchild to the Earle of Warwicke'; A. Marvell, 'Two Songs at the Marriage of the Lord Fauconberg and the Lady Mary Cromwell'. For a detailed analysis of these, see Chapter 6, 'Soe Honny from the Lyon came', in E. Holberton, *Poetry and the Cromwellian Protectorate* (2008).

10. ENDINGS

1. June 1940 Speech; *A Declaration of His Highnesse the Lord Protector for a Day of Publick Thanksgiving* (London, [3] July 1658).
2. A. Marvell, 'A Poem Upon the Death of O.C.' (1658); and Clarendon, *History*, Vol 6, p. 94.
3. Waylen, *House of Cromwell*, p. 214.
4. *CSPD, Vol 31: 1657–1659*, p. 150; and D. L. Smith, 'Diplomacy and the religious question: Mazarin, Cromwell and the treaties of 1655 and 1657', https://doi.org/10.17863/CAM.27549.
5. Council. Day's Proceedings, 3 February 1657, *CSPD: Interregnum, 1656–7*, no. 78; and Waylen, op. cit., p. 198.
6. Rev. J. S. Clarke ed. *The Life of James the Second King of England* (2 vols, 1816), Vol 1, pp. 277–8.
7. *Three poems upon the death of the late usurper Oliver Cromwel written by Mr Jo. Drydon, Mr Sprat of Oxford, Mr Edm. Waller* (1659).
8. Colonel Lockhart to Secretary Thurloe, June 17/27 1658, *TSP*, Vol 7, pp. 166–79.
9. Abbott, op. cit., Vol 4, p. 807.
10. Viscount Fauconberg to Henry Cromwell, 8 June 1658, *TSP*, Vol 7, p. 158; Viscount Fauconberg to Secretary Thurloe, 29 May 1658, Ibid., pp. 141–53; and Waylen, op. cit., pp. 200–2.
11. Letter from Cardinal Mazarin to M. de Bordeaux, Public Record Office: Transcripts from French Archives, PRO 31/3/102, 13–14 June 1658.
12. Henry Cromwell to Viscount Fauconberg, 16 June 1568, *TSP*, Vol 7, pp. 166–79.
13. Lord Fauconberg to Henry Cromwell, 22 June 1658, Ibid., pp. 190–203.
14. Waylen, op. cit., p. 219.
15. R. W. Ramsey, *Richard Cromwell Protector of England* (1935), p. 32.
16. Richard Cromwell to Henry Cromwell, 29 July 1658, *CHC*, pp. 395–6.
17. John Thurloe to Henry Cromwell, 11 September 1657, *TSP*, Vol 6, pp. 492–502.
18. Peacey, 'Upbringing of Richard Cromwell', *Cromwelliana* (2010).
19. *A Second Narrative of the Late Parliament (so-called)* (1658), pp. 23–4.
20. Burton, *Diary*, Vol 2, pp. 513, 515; and Morrill, 'Blood and Marriage', p. 49.
21. *Clarke Papers*, op. cit., Vol 3, p. 150.
22. Ludlow, op. cit., Vol 2, p. 41; and Firth, *Last Years*, pp. 81–2.
23. Lady Eliz. Claypole to the lady of H. Cromwell, 12 June [1658], *TSP*, Vol 7, pp. 166–79.
24. *Clarke Papers*, op. cit., pp. 141, 142.
25. HMC, *Report on the Manuscripts of Mrs Frankland Russell-Astley of Chequers Court, Bucks* (1900), p. 22.
26. J. Gauden, *Funerals made cordials: in a sermon prepared and (in part) preached at the solemn interment of the corps of the Right Honorable*

Robert Rich, heire apparent to the Earldom of Warwick . . . (1658), pp. 103, 109–10.

27. John Thurloe to Henry Cromwell, 16 February 1658, *TSP*, Vol 6, p. 807.
28. Frances Rich to Henry Cromwell, 19 June 1658, *CHC*, pp. 386–7.
29. John and Elizabeth Gauden to Henry Cromwell, 24 May 1658, *CHC*, pp. 371–2.
30. Gauden, *Funerals*, Dedication and p. 104.
31. Firth, *Last Years*, Vol 2, p. 297 quoting a contemporary newsletter.
32. Gauden, *Funerals*, Dedication and p. 1.
33. *Clarke Papers*, op. cit., Vol 3, pp. 141–2; Fraser, op. cit., p. 641.
34. HMC, *Report on the Manuscripts of Mrs Frankland Russell-Astley of Chequers Court, Bucks* (1900), pp. 23–4.
35. 'Thomas Belasyse' in *HP 1640–1660*.
36. Colonel Lockhart to Secretary Thurloe, 15/25 June 1658, *TSP*, Vol 7, pp. 166–79.
37. *CHC*, p. 85.
38. General Fleetwood to H. Cromwell, lord deputy of Ireland, 15 June 1658, *TSP*, Vol 7, pp. 166–79.
39. John Claypole to Henry Cromwell, lord deputy of Ireland, 26 April 1658, Ibid., pp. 88–100.
40. Richard Cromwell to Henry Cromwell, 2 June 1658, *CHC*, pp. 376–7; and Lady Eliz. Claypole to the lady of H. Cromwell, 12 June [1658], *TSP*, Vol 7, pp. 166–79.
41. Frances Rich to Henry Cromwell, 19 June 1658, *CHC*, pp. 386–7.
42. HMC, *Report on Mrs. Frankland-Russell-Astley's MSS*, p. 23.
43. John Thurloe to Henry Cromwell, 27 July 1658, *TSP*, Vol 7, pp. 294–5.
44. Richard Cromwell to Henry Cromwell, 29 July 1658, *CHC*, pp. 395–6.
45. Nieuport, the Dutch ambassador in England, to the states general, *TSP*, Vol 7, pp. 297–307.
46. Marvell, 'A Poem Upon the Death of O.C.'
47. *The English Revolution III, Newsbooks 5, Volume 17, Mercurius Politicus 1657–58* (1971), p. 427; and S. Carrington, *The History of the Life and Death of His Most Serene Highness, Oliver, Late Lord Protector* (1659), pp. 218–20, 263–4.
48. *The English Revolution III*, op. cit., p. 436. For more analysis see Malins, 'All Imaginable Pomp and Lustre'.
49. Nunn, 'An hundred times fitter for a barn than a palace', pp. 60–1.
50. *The English Revolution III*, op. cit., p. 427.
51. Richard Cromwell to Henry Cromwell, 24 August 1658, *CHC*, pp. 400–1.
52. Marvell, op. cit.
53. General Fleetwood to H. Cromwell, lord deputy of Ireland, 17 August 1658, *TSP*, Vol 7, pp. 339–52.
54. Charles Fleetwood to Henry Cromwell, 24 Aug. 1658, Ibid., pp. 352–69.

55. Thomas Clarges to Henry Cromwell, 1 September 1658, Ibid., p. 369.
56. Conversation of Oliver Cromwell with George Fox, 1[?] August 1658, *LWS,* Vol 3, p. 520.
57. Richard Cromwell to Henry Cromwell, 24 August 1658, *CHC,* pp. 400–1.
58. Secretary Thurloe to H. Cromwell, lord deputy of Ireland, 30 August 1658, *TSP*, Vol 7, pp. 352–69.
59. J. Fitzgibbons, '"Not in any doubtfull dispute"? Reassessing the nomination of Richard Cromwell', *Historical Research*, vol. 83, no. 220 (May 2010), p. 283.
60. Ibid., p. 285.
61. *An Account of the Last Houres*, op. cit., pp. 10–13; and Dr George Bate, *Elenchus motuum nuperorum in Anglia* (1685), pp. 234–6.
62. Warwick, op. cit., p. 389.
63. E. Waller, *Upon the Late Storm and of the Death of H. H. Ensuing the Same* (1658).
64. The Countess of Ranelagh to the Lord Broghill, her brother, 17 September 1658, *TSP,* Vol 7, p. 395; and Hutchinson, op. cit., p. 345.
65. Mr John Maidston to John Winthrop, esq; governor of the colony of Connecticut in New England, *TSP,* Vol 1, Letters from Mr Corker 5:5.
66. R. Josselin, *The diary of Ralph Josselin 1616–1683*, ed. A. MacFarlane (1976), p. 430.
67. Sherwood, *King In All But Name*, p. 136.
68. *The Speech of the Right Honourable Nathaniel, Lord Fiennes, One of the Lord Keepers of the Great Seale of England, Made before his Highnesse and both Houses of Parliament, 27 January 1658* (1659), p. 6.
69. S. Slater, *A rhetorical rapture as composed into a funeral oration at the mournfull moving of His Highnes stately effigies from Somerset-House* (1658); Clarendon, *History*, Vol 6, p. 90; and Andrew Marvell, 'Ode Upon the Death of O.C.' (1658).
70. S. Slater, *The Protectors Protection: Or, The Pious Prince guarded by a Praying People* (1659), p. 58.
71. Peacey, 'Upbringing', p. 23.
72. Sherwood, op. cit., p. 140.
73. John Thurloe to Henry Cromwell, 7 September 1658, *TSP*, Vol 7, pp. 369–80.
74. See Fitzgibbons, 'Not in any doubtfull dispute?'
75. John Thurloe to Henry Cromwell, 4 September 1658, *TSP*, Vol 7, pp. 369–80.
76. 'Two letters addressed to Cromwell', ed. C. H. Firth, *English Historical Review*, xxii (1907), p. 313.
77. Sir G. Wharton, *A Second Narrative of the late Parliament* (1658), p. 11.
78. Letter from Oliver Cromwell to Richard Major, 28 June 1651, Morrill, *Letters, Writings and Speeches*, Vol 2, p. 463.
79. J. Heath, *A Brief Chronicle of the late Intestine War* (1663), p. 737.

80. Sherwood, *Court*, p. 59.
81. Whitelocke, *Memorials*, Vol 4, p. 337.
82. *Clarke Papers*, op. cit., p. 176.
83. C. H. Firth 'A Speech of Richard Cromwell, 18 October 1658', *English Historical Review*, 23 (1908), pp. 734–5.
84. R. Baxter, *Five Disputations of Church-Government, and Worship* (1659), Epistle Dedicatory.
85. Statistics from R. Hutton, *The Restoration* (1986), pp. 21–2; Sherwood, *King in All But Name*, p. 142.
86. Clarendon, *History*, Vol 6, pp. 98–9.
87. Mr Herbert to Charles II, 15 June 1659, *CSP*, Vol 3, p. 488.
88. The speech of the protector Richard to the officers of the army: in the handwriting of secretary Thurloe, and corrected by him, *TSP*, Vol 7, pp. 447–9.
89. Ibid.
90. Henry Cromwell to Richard Cromwell, 20 October 1658, Ibid.,, pp. 447–61.
91. Ibid.
92. Charles Fleetwood to Henry Cromwell, 21 September 1658, Ibid., pp. 405–17.
93. John Thurloe to Henry Cromwell, 7 September 1658, Ibid, pp. 369–80.
94. Lord Fauconberg to Henry Cromwell, 7 September 1658, Ibid., pp. 369–80.
95. Lord Fauconberg to Henry Cromwell, 12 October 1658, Ibid., pp. 429–47; and Marvell, 'A Poem Upon the Death of O.C.'
96. Ramsey, *Richard Cromwell*, p. 69; and Huntingdon Archive, KHAC2/2828 (Letters from Puritan divines to Richard Cromwell's wife), Samuel Tomlyns to Dorothy Cromwell, 15 December 1658 & Walter Marshall to [Dorothy Cromwell], [1658].
97. Francesco Giavarina, Venetian Resident in England, to the Doge and Senate, 20 September 1658, *CSPV, Volume 31*, no. 217; and Francesco Giavarina, Venetian Resident in England, to the Doge and Senate, 4 October 1658, Ibid., no. 225.
98. Sherwood, op. cit., pp. 144–5; and *The English Revolution III, Newsbooks 5, Volume 18, Mercurius Politicus 1658–59* (1971), pp. 163–4.
99. Knoppers, op. cit., p. 140.
100. Marvell, op. cit.
101. For more analysis see Knoppers, op. cit. and Sherwood, op. cit., p. 180. Marvell talks of Oliver anticipating 'a better Crown' in echo of 'a corruptible to an incorruptible Crown' in *Eikon Basilike*.
102. Knoppers, op. cit., p. 141.
103. Francis Russell to Henry Cromwell, 25 May 1657, *CHC*, pp. 272–3.
104. Knoppers, op. cit., p. 145.
105. Ibid.
106. Fraser, op. cit., pp. 684–5.

107. Slater, *A rhetorical rapture.*
108. For further analysis, see Holberton, op. cit., pp. 173–6.
109. Prestwitch, op. cit., pp. 182–7.
110. Morrill, 'Blood and Marriage', p. 51.
111. F. Guizot, *History of Richard Cromwell,* trans. A. R. Scobie (2 vols, 1856), Vol 1, pp. 271, 273–4.
112. Secretary Thurloe to H. Cromwell, lord lieutenant of Ireland, 28 December 1658, *TSP*, Vol 7, pp. 578–86.
113. Secretary Thurloe to Henry Cromwell, lord lieutenant of Ireland, 30 November 1658, Ibid., p. 541.
114. Secretary Thurloe to Henry Cromwell, lord lieutenant of Ireland, 18 January 1658, Ibid., p. 594.
115. Richard Cromwell, *The Speech of His Highness the Lord Protector, made to both Houses of Parliament at their first meeting on Thursday the 17th of January 1658[/9],* (1658/9), pp. 4–5, 9.
116. *Clarke Papers*, op. cit., p. 176.
117. Diary of Thomas Burton, Vol 3, pp. 65, 87–104, 132, 146 & 262; Fitzgibbons, 'Not in any doubtfull dispute?', pp. 281–2; and D. L. Smith, 'Richard Cromwell's Parliament', *Cromwelliana,* (2010), pp. 46–60.
118. Francesco Giavarina to the Doge and Senate, 14 March 1659, *CSPV, Volume 31,* no, 270; and; Viscount Fauconberg to Henry Cromwell, 29 March 1659, *CHC*, p. 486.
119. H. Reece, *The Fall: Last Days of the English Republic* (2024), p, 84.
120. *The English Revolution III, Newsbooks 5, Volume 19, Mercurius Politicus 1659* (London, 1971), p. 84; Mr Mordaunt to Edward Hyde, 14 April 1659, *Clarendon State Papers,* Vol 3, pp. 451–2.
121. Whitelocke, *Diary,* p. 512; and Whitelocke, *Memorials,* Vol 4, p. 342.
122. Ludlow, op. cit., pp. 68–9. See also *CSPD, 1659–61,* pp. 10–12.
123. Mr John Barwick to Sir Edward Hyde, 20 April 1659, *TSP*, Vol 7, pp. 654–5.
124. Burton, *Diary,* Vol 4, pp. 464–9; and *Clarke Papers,* Vol 3, pp. 192, 212.
125. Ludlow, op. cit., p. 69 (see also *Clarke Papers,* Vol 3, pp. 193–4).
126. Ludlow, op. cit., p. 69; and Guizot, *Richard Cromwell,* Vol 1, p. 366.
127. Reece, *The Fall,* p. 102.
128. Guizot, op. cit., Vol 1, pp. 370–1.
129. Mr Hancock (Broderick) to Edward Hyde, 16 December 1659, *CSPD, Vol 3,* pp. 638–9.
130. Henry Cromwell to Richard Cromwell, 23 May 1659, *TSP*, Vol 7, p. 674.
131. Richard Cromwell to Henry Cromwell, 12 May 1659, *CHC,* pp. 515-16.
132. Richard Cromwell to Henry Cromwell, 17 May 1658, Ibid., pp. 516–17.
133. General Monck, &c. to general Fleetwood, to be communicated to the generall council of officers, at Wallingford house, 12 May 1657, *TSP*, Vol 7.
134. Ramsey, op. cit., p. 149.

135. A. Hunt, *Republic: Britain's Revolutionary Decade 1649–1660* (2024), p. 349.
136. Richard Cromwell to Henry Cromwell, 12 May 1659, *CHC*, pp. 515–16.
137. Pepys, *Diary*, Vol 1, p. 180; and Clarendon, *History*, Vol 6, pp. 103–4.
138. *Weekly Post*, 31 May–7 June 1659.
139. John Thurloe to William Lockhart, 5 May 1659, *CSP*, Vol 3, p. 461.
140. Reece, *The Fall*, p. 80.
141. *The Speech of the Right Honourable Nathaniel, Lord Fiennes, One of the Lord Keepers of the Great Seale of England, Made before his Highnesse and both Houses of Parliament, 27 January 1658* (1659), p. 621.
142. W. Shakespeare, *Richard II*, Act IV, Scene I.
143. Richard Cromwell to Henry Cromwell, 17 May 1658, *CHC*, pp. 516–17. He also refers here to 'our case' knitting the two brothers together in their adversity.
144. Ibid.
145. Hume, op. cit., p. 105; Holder, op. cit., p. 169.
146. Sadler to the Council, 11 April 1545, *LP*, Vol 20(1), no. 506.
147. Anne was the daughter of the famous lawyer and Lord Chief Justice Sir Edward Coke.
148. I. Walton, *Complete Angler* (1653), Chapter 1.
149. A. Hunt, 'The Books, Manuscripts and Literary Patronage of Mrs Anne Sadleir (1585-1670)', in V. Burke, J. Gibson eds. *Early Modern Women's Manuscript Writing, 1st ed.* (Routledge, 2017); and *Holbein's Hidden Gem.*
150. *Holbein's Hidden Gem.*
151. Guizot, *History of Richard Cromwell,* Vol 1, pp. 389–93, 402–5.
152. William Lockhart by T. Venning, *ODNB.*
153. Edward Hyde to Mr Broderick, 10 March 1659, *CSP*, Vol 2, pp. 434–5.
154. Edward Hyde to Mordaunt, 4 April 1659, *CSP*, Vol 3, pp. 448–9.
155. Mordaunt to Charles Stuart, 11 May 1659, Ibid., p. 469.
156. Burke, *Viscissitudes*; and 'Henry Cromwell' in *HP 1660–1690,* Vol 4, pp. 463–7.
157. Burke, *Viscissitudes.*
158. T. W[hetstone] to Adm. [Montague], [June] 1659, in *CSP*, Vol 4, p. 255; see also *LWS*, Vol 3, pp. 115–16 & pp. 124–5; and Edward Hyde to ?, 17 June 1659, Bodl., MS Clarendon 61, f. 228.
159. Edward Montagu to Richard Cromwell, 20 September 1659, MS Carte 73, f. 312; and Richard Cromwell to Edward Montagu, 25 September 1659, MS Carte 73, f. 314.
160. Richard Ollard, *Cromwell's Earl* (1994), p. 268.
161. Edward Hyde to Ned Villiers, 20 June 1659, *CSP*, Vol 3, pp. 500–2.
162. Henry Cromwell to John Thurloe, 21 March 1658[9], *TSP*, Vol 7, p. 635.
163. *CSPD, 1659–60*, p. 26; *JHC*, Vol 7, p. 705a.
164. Mr Broderick to Edward Hyde, 16 July 1659, *CSP*, Vol 3, pp. 526–8.

165. 'Thomas Belasyse' in *HP 1640-1660*; and; Whitelocke, *Diary*, p. 532.
166. Letter to Mr William Clarke, 6 December 1659, *Clarke Papers*, Vol 4, xxxii. f. 159.
167. Ludlow, op. cit., Vol 2, pp. 179–80.
168. Whitelocke, *Diary*, pp. 551–3.
169. Newsletter, 24 December 1659, *Clarke Papers*, Vol 4, p. 220.
170. J. Tatham, *The Rump* (1660), pp. 21 & 57; and Pepys, *Diary*, Vol 1, p. 289.
171. Pepys, *Diary*, Vol 1, pp. 74, 79.
172. Mr Hancock (Broderick) to Edward Hyde, 2 March 1660, *CSP*, Vol 3, p. 693; and 'An informer to Edward Hyde, 9 March 1660', Bodl., MS Clarendon 70, f. 132.
173. Warwick, op. cit., p. 469.
174. Conversation between Oliver Cromwell and John Lambert and Sir Henry Ingoldsby, 31[?] July 1650, *LWS*, Vol 2, pp. 305–6; see above p.
175. Carlyle quoted in Worden, op. cit., p. 277.
176. Tatham, *The Rump*, p. 17; Butler, *A Biography of Richard Cromwell, 1626–1712, The Second Protector* (1994), p. 142; and *The Diurnal of Thomas Rugg 1659–61*, ed. W. L. Sachse (1961), p. 90.
177. *Hells Higher Court of Justice* (1661).
178. *A Conference held between the Old Lord Protector and the New Lord General truly reported by Hugh Peters* (1660), p. 2.
179. E986(18), *Fourty Four Queries to the Life of Queen Dick* (1659); and Knoppers, *Constructing Cromwell*, p. 178.
180. A. Behn, *The Roundheads, of The Good Old Cause a comedy* (1682), p. 3.
181. E. Ludlow, *A Voyce from the Watch Tower*, Part Five: 1660–1662, ed., A. B. Worden (Camden fourth series, Volume 21, 1978), p. 126.
182. Noble, op. cit., pp. 288–91.
183. *Diurnal of Thomas Rugg*, p. 143.
184. T. R. Nash ed. *Notes on Hudibras* (London, 1793), Part 3, pp. 379–80.
185. Knoppers, op. cit., p. 184.
186. Pepys, *Diary*, Vol 1, p. 309.
187. Noble, op. cit., Vol 2, p. 308.
188. These are the two protagonists of Robert Harris's 2022 novel *Act of Oblivion*.
189. 'John Jones', by S K. Roberts in *ODNB*.
190. Pepys, *Diary*, Vol 8, p. 169.
191. Reece, *The Fall*, p. 336.
192. Huntingdon Archive, 731/146, 'The Humble Petition of Henry Cromwell'; and petition by Henry Cromwell to Charles II, date unknown, in Waylen, *House of Cromwell*, pp. 25–6.
193. Letter from Henry Cromwell to the Earl of Clarendon, 9 April 1662, in BL Add MS 4159, f. 74; see also letters and papers in Huntingdon Archive, 731/76-7 & 731/148.
194. Huntingdon Archive 731/75, Letter from George Monck to Henry Cromwell, 9 June 1660.

195. Letter from Henry Cromwell to the Earl of Clarendon, 9 April 1662, in BL Add MS 4159, f. 74
196. Huntingdon Archive, 731/152.
197. Huntingdon Archive, 731/146; and Waylen, op. cit., pp. 25–6.
198. Henry Cromwell in *HP* 1640–1660.
199. Butler, *Richard Cromwell*, p. 142.
200. J. Butler, 'Richard Cromwell and Oxford 1657–1660', *Cromwelliana* (1982), pp. 21–32.
201. Pepys, *Diary*, Vol 1, p. 218.
202. *Court and Kitchen* (1664).
203. *CSPD 1660*, pp. 392–3, no. 144.
204. D. Nicholas, *Mr Secretary Nicholas (1593–1669) His Life and Letters* (1955), p. 301.
205. Ramsey, *Studies in Cromwell's Family Circle*, Chapter 2, 'The Lord Protector's Master of Horse', pp. 20–34; and Farr, *Oliver Cromwell's Kin*, pp. 228–32.
206. Mary Fauconberg to Henry Cromwell (1665?) in Waylen, *House of Cromwell*, p. 102.
207. John Clare, 'Absorbing time that all things overwhelms', *Northborough Sonnets* (1832–1837).

11. AFTERLIVES

1. Pepys, *Diary*, Vol 8, p. 332.
2. Burgess, *New British History*, Ch 10: 'Critical Perspectives: The Autonomy of English History' by T. Harris, p. 269.
3. Pepys, *Diary*, Vol 6, p. 204 and Vol 9, p. 381.
4. Fullerton, 'Fatal Adulteries'.
5. Pepys, *Diary*, Vol 1, p. 79.
6. Ibid., Vol 8, p. 50.
7. Ibid., Vol 7, p. 94.
8. HMC, *Report on the Manuscripts of Mrs Frankland-Russell-Astley, of Chequers Court, Bucks* (1900), p. 50.
9. Pepys, *Diary*, Vol 4, p. 181.
10. HMC, *Frankland-Russell*, pp. 24–5.
11. Ibid., pp. 25–7.
12. Ibid., p. 35
13. *Travels of Cosmo the third, Grand Duke of Tuscany, through England during the reign of King Charles the second (1669). Tr. from the Italian manuscript in the Laurentian library at Florence. To which is prefixed, a memoir of his life* (London, 1821), pp. 212–4.
14. This 'Pietra Dure' can still be seen on display in the Cromwell Museum, Huntingdon.
15. HMC, *Frankland-Russell*, Sir John Russell to his wife, [July? 1667], p. 32 and Frances Russell to Sir John Russell, 10 February 1669, p. 37.

16. A. S. Burn ed. 'Correspondence of Richard Cromwell', *English Historical Review*, Vol 13 (1898), p. 105.
17. C. S. L. Davies, 'The family and connections of John Wilkins, 1614–72', *Oxoniensia*, 69 (2003), pp. 93–107; and Ramsey, *Richard Cromwell*, p. 124.
18. Davies, op. cit., pp. 103–4; and J. G. Crowther, *Founders of British Science* (1960), p. 219.
19. A. J. Shirren, *The Chronicles of Fleetwood House* (1951), pp. 76–7.
20. Ibid., pp. 1, 152–66. The house later became Newington Academy for Girls, a Quaker school famed for the world's first school bus.
21. For more on the circle at Fleetwood House, see Farr, *Kinship*.
22. Butler, op. cit., p. 145.
23. Huntingdon Library, Cromwell Museum MSS, Cromwell-Bush MS, cited in J. A. Butler, *Richard Cromwell* (1994), p. 144.
24. Pepys, *Diary*, Vol 5 1664, p. 296 & Vol 7 1666, p. 94; and *CSPD, 1665–6*, p. 299. For more detail on Richard's life in exile, see M. Malins, 'My Solitary Life: Richard Cromwell 1659–1712', C*romwelliana* (2010).
25. Clarendon, *History*, Vol 6, pp. 107–8.
26. Col Rogers to Williamson, 25 June 1671, *CSPD: Charles II, 1671*, ed. F H Blackburne Daniell (1895), p. 340; and Examination of Wm. Mumford, 15 March 1666, *CSPD: Charles II, 1665-6*, ed. M. A. E. Green (1864), p. 299, no. 17.
27. Ibid., p. 131; and *CSPD, 1665–6*, p. 299.
28. Burn, *Correspondence*, p. 95.
29. Ibid., p. 94; and see Cambridge Archives, Huntingdon, KAcc731/81-122: Bush Collection of Cromwell documents for more of Richard's letters.
30. HMC, *Frankland-Russell*, p. 31; 'John Claypole' in *HP*, 1640–1660.
31. Burn, *Correspondence*, p. 95.
32. Ibid., p. 96; Butler, *Richard Cromwell*, p. 155; and Farr, *Networks*, pp. 265–6.
33. BL Add MSS 32456; Burn, *Correspondence*, p. 96; Ramsey, *Richard Cromwell*, pp. 142–5; and Butler, *Richard Cromwell*, p. 156.
34. Burnet, *History*, Vol 1, p. 418.
35. Noble, *Memoirs*, Vol 1, p. 180; Butler, *Richard Cromwell*, pp. 82, 170.
36. J. Healey, *The Blazing World: A New History of Revolutionary England* (2023), p. 384.
37. *CSPD, July 1 to September 30 1683*, p. 33.
38. Butler, op. cit., p. 159.
39. 'Henry Ireton', *HP*, 1640–1660.
40. R. L. Greaves, *Secrets of the Kingdom: British Radicals from the Popish Plot to the Revolution of 1688–1689* (1992), p. 259.
41. Ibid., p. 275; and *CSPD*, 22 April 1685, p. 136, no. 576.
42. For more detail of the Yarmouth community, see Farr, *Kinship*.
43. Bridget Bendish by S. Lee revised by S. Handley, *ODNB*.

44. Greaves, op. cit., p. 275; Farr, *Oliver Cromwell's Kin*, p. 287; and *CSPD, 26 September 1685*, p. 337, nos. 1669, 1671.
45. *CSPD, 25 November 1685*, p. 394, no. 1951; and *CSPD, 21 December 1685*, p. 417, no. 2086.
46. *CSPD, 19 April 1686*, p. 104, no. 422; and Greaves, op. cit., p. 293.
47. Shirren, *Fleetwood House*, p. 85.
48. Greaves, op. cit., p. 207.
49. Dorset History Centre Archive, Ph/681 'Account by Hannah Hewling of the last days of her brothers, Benjamin and William, executed at Taunton and Lyme for their part in the Monmouth Rebellion. 1685'; J. A. Mills, 'Cromwellian Britain XVII: Lyme Regis, Dorset', *Cromwelliana* (2004); and Waylen, op. cit., pp. 31–2.
50. T. Harris, *Restoration: Charles II and his Kingdoms, 1660–1685* (2005), pp. 80–1.
51. W. Mackreth Noble, *Huntingdonshire and the Spanish Armada* (1896), pp. 18–19, 20–1.
52. Ibid.; and *Tollemaches of Helmingham Hall*, p. 43.
53. HMC, *Frankland-Russell*, pp. 60–1; and 'Thomas Belasyse', *HP*, 1640–60.
54. Waylen, op. cit., pp. 106–7.
55. Healey, *Blazing* World, p. 414.
56. Q. Skinner, 'The Monarchical Republic Enthroned', in McDiarmid ed. *Monarchical Republic*, op. cit., pp. 233–244.
57. Burn, *Correspondence*, p. 113.
58. Ramsey, *Cromwell's Family Circle*, p. 55.
59. John Tillotson by I. Rivers, in *ODNB*.
60. M. Zook, *Protestantism, Politics and Women in Britain, 1660–1714* (2013), p. 197. Tillotson was buried in the chancel of St Lawrence Jewry in London beside his father-in-law John Wilkins where Oliver's sister, nephew and three nieces also rest to this day: Davies, 'The Family and Connections of John Wilkins', p. 104.
61. 'Henry Ireton' (1652–1711), *HP, 1690–1715.*
62. Henry Cromwell became a gentleman of the privy chamber and captain in a dragoon regiment, recommissioned in 1702 by William and Mary's successor, Mary's sister Anne 'reposing especial trust and confidence in your loyalty courage and good conduct'. In 1699, Henry Cromwell was arrested for debt owed to his regiment and his formidable female relations rallied round, Richard wryly observing how they were 'arm'd, how sharpe their weapons were & how they clattered I cannot tell'. Eventually glory and much needed earnings came with service abroad as major of a foot regiment, but death too in the form of a fever in Lisbon in 1711. See Ramsey, *Circle*, pp. 55, 59; Cambridgeshire Archives, Huntingdon KAcc731/731/154-5; and Burn, *Correspondence*, p.117.
63. Waylen, op. cit., p. 68.

64. Fleetwood to Thurloe, *TSP,* Vol 7, p. 595.
65. Burn, *Correspondence*, pp. 96, 104–6, 110, 114.
66. Noble, *Memoirs*, Vol 2, pp. 317–18.
67. Ibid., pp. 316-17; and Shirren, *Fleetwood House*, p. 105.
68. Waylen, *House of Cromwell*, p. 104; S. Say, *Character of Mrs B[ridget] B[endish], Grand-daughter of Oliver Cromwell*... (1780), pp. 29–30; and Farr, *Kinship*.
69. Shirren, *Fleetwood House*, p. 105.
70. Waylen, op. cit., p. 80.
71. *The Character of Mrs B*, p. 31.
72. Waylen, op. cit., p. 20.
73. Burnet, *History,* Vol 1, p. 149.
74. This branch of the family had continued their Anglo-Irish life since the first Earl Thomas, Viscount Lecale, had died in 1653. They had been fortunate in finance since, steadily rebuilding the family's estates from their lowest point under their forebear, Edward Cromwell of the Essex Rebellion, and his son, the rakish first Earl. Producing children, however, had been less straightforward. Thomas's son Wingfield, the second Earl, died in 1668 leaving an only son from two marriages who he named after his father. This Thomas Cromwell, the third Earl, married well but left no children behind when he died in 1682. The title of Earl of Ardglass therefore passed to Thomas's uncle, Vere Essex Cromwell. The former Royalist now supported James II, with Vere commanding his own Regiment of Horse. It was perhaps through time on military service in Ireland, that he found himself drawn back to the land that had become his family's home when they were forced from England at the beginning of the century. When Vere died in his home of Booncastle, County Down, in 1687, he was buried in Downpatrick Cathedral beside his grandfather Edward Cromwell in a joint tomb the family could finally afford. See *CSPD June 1687–Feb 1689,* p. 41, no. 198 and p. 77, no. 384.
75. Burnet, *History,* op. cit.
76. When she married, Elizabeth Baroness Cromwell brought some £35,000 of un-encumbered property to the marriage. See 'Edward Southwell', *HP,* 1690–1715.
77. *The Correspondence of the Three William Byrds of Westover, Virginia 1684–1776,* ed. M. Tinling (1977), Vol 1, pp. 195, 216–17, 226, 229, 236–7, 241.
78. *The Wentworth Papers, 1705–1739,* ed. J. J. Cartwright (1883), p. 70.
79. Ramsey, *Richard Cromwell,* p. 224; Butler, op. cit., p. 180.
80. Waylen, op. cit., p. 20; D. L. Peach, *The History of Hursley Park* (1974), p. 22.
81. Huntingdon Archive, KAcc731/D/41, Will of Elizabeth Cromwell.
82. Ramsey, *Circle*, p. 58.
83. Waylen, op. cit., p. 172; Burke, *Vicissitudes*; Noble, op. cit.; and www.thepeerage.com

84. Among them Ivo Bligh, the English captain in the first Ashes series.
85. A group of family members and friends were buried together in the non-conformist cemetery of Bunhill Fields including Charles Fleetwood, three of Oliver's grandsons and the poet Isaac Watts who worked for and was inspired by the family.
86. A writer in the *Gentleman's Magazine* for June 1777 quoted in Waylen, op. cit., p. 43.
87. Waylen, op. cit., p. 37.
88. J. Goldsmith, 'Does Cromwelliana exist?', in Mills, *Cromwell's Legacy*, pp. 42–4.
89. T. Blair, *A Journey: My Political Life* (New York, 2010), pp. 154–5.
90. T. Wilson, *A Discourse Upon Usury* (1572), ed. R. H. Tawney (1925), p. 182.
91. Foxe, *TAMO* (1563 edition), p. 654.
92. G. Burnet, *The History of the Reformation of the Church of England. The first part, of the progress made in it during the Reign of K. Henry the VIII By Gilbert Burnet* (2 vols, 1679), pp. 281–5 & 454.
93. A. Pope, *Essay on Man* (1734), Epistle IV, Line 284.
94. Clarendon, *History*, Vol 6, p. 97.
95. J. Boswell, *The Journals of James Boswell, 1762–1795*, ed. J. Wain (1991), p. 273.
96. Byng, *Torrington diaries*, Vol 1, pp. 344–6.
97. Lord Byron, *Childe Harold's Pilgrimage* (1812–18); and J. Austen, *Mansfield Park* (1814), Chapter 3.
98. W. Cobbett, *History of the Protestant Reformation in England and Ireland*, (1824–7), Vol 1, pp. 157, 189.
99. R. C. Richardson, 'A Most Uncomfortable Pairing: Richard Cromwell and John Keble at Hursley, Hampshire', *Southern History*, Vol 42 (2020), pp. 73–93. Currently the church and the Cromwell Association are raising funds for the monument's repair.
100. Worden, *Roundhead Reputations*, Chapter 10, 'Carlyle's Cromwell'; J. Fitgibbons, *Cromwell's Head* (2008), p. 189; and M. Arnold, 'Cromwell: a prize poem, recited in the theatre, Oxford, June 28 1843' (1863).
101. Worden, op. cit., p. 249.
102. For the detailed story of this, see Ibid.; and 'Oliver's Statue is Unveiled by a Workman', *Evening Herald*, 15 November 1899, p. 2.
103. 'MISS MARIE LLOYD: HER LAST APPEARANCE.' *The Times of India* (1861-) November 7 1922: 10-. Print; T. S. Eliot, 'London Letter', *The Dial magazine* New York, Vol 73.6 (December 1922), pp. 659–63; and Midge Gillies, *Marie Lloyd The One and Only* (1999), pp. 274–5.
104. C. Jones, *The Fall of Robespierre*, p. 213.
105. John Adams diary 44, 27 March–21 July 1786 [electronic edition], Adams Family Papers: An Electronic Archive, Massachusetts Historical Society.

106. T. Ingersoll, *The Loyalist Problem in Revolutionary New England* (2016), pp. 501, 123; and S. Covington, *The Devil from Over the Sea* (2022), p. 290.
107. Mills, op. cit., p. 251.
108. K. Racine, '"Puritans, patriots and porotectors": The relevance of Oliver Cromwell and his regime for Spanish Americans during the Independence Era, 1808–1826', in Mills, *Legacy*.
109. T. A. Smith, *Weird John Brown: Divine Violence and the Limits of Ethics* (2015), p. 42.
110. E. G. Manger, *Cavalier South vs Puritan North? Hypocrisy and Identity in the American Civil War*, (2004); Covington, *The Devil From Over the Sea*, p. 302.
111. Ibid., p. 316.
112. Ibid., p. 217.
113. W. M. Thackeray, *The Irish Sketchbook of 1842* (1911), p. 271.
114. Covington, op. cit., p. 120.
115. Letter from Unity Mitford to her sister Diana Mosley, 8 April 1937, in *The Mitfords: Letters Between Six Sisters*, ed. C. Mosley (2008), p. 89.
116. *Trotsky's Writings on Britain*, ed. A. Clinton (1975), online edition - https://www.marxists.org/
117. Covington, op. cit., p. 334.
118. Elton, 'Political Creed', in *Studies*, Vol 2, pp. 225, 234.
119. Hilary Mantel interviewed for 'Hilary Mantel: Return to Wolf Hall', BBC2 (2020); and Blair Worden in his review of Anna Keay's *The Restless Republic*, in *TLS* (2022).
120. BBC poll, Great Britons – who is the Greatest of them all? (2002); and *Horrible Histories – Horrible Christmas* (Symphony Hall, Birmingham, December 2023)
121. F. Mendlesohn, *Creating Memory: Historical Fiction and the English Civil Wars* (2020), p. 26.
122. YouGov poll, Who are the most and least popular kings and queens of England and Britain? (2025)
123. DUL, Special Collections, Cosin Letter Book, 1, 1B, p. 94 (cited in H. Lyon, *Memory and the dissolution of the monasteries in early modern England* (2022), p. 227).
124. Correspondence between Winston Churchill and King George V, Lord Stamfordham, Lord Morley, and Prince Louis of Battenberg, October–November 1912, *The Churchill Documents*, ed. Randolph S. Churchill (1969), Vol 5, pp. 1664–71. Churchill did get to see the Cromwell name bestowed on a new tank deployed in 1944. One of the fastest tanks of World War II, Cromwells led the six-day dash across Europe which freed Antwerp and Brussels at speeds which prevented the Germans from establishing strong defence lines. They remained in service for some years after the war and a few served with British forces in Korea. See https://tankmuseum.org/tank-nuts/tank-collection/cromwell

125. Waylen, op. cit., pp. 41–2.
126. *The Churchill Documents*, ed. R. S. Churchill, Vol 5, p. 1665.
127. MacCulloch, *Cromwell*, p. 4.
128. Diarmaid MacCulloch makes a compelling argument for seeing the Great Bible as 'Cromwell's Bible' in *Cromwell*, pp. 492–3.
129. Marshall, *Impact of the Reformation*, Chapter 11: 'From iconoclasm to iconophobia: the cultural impact of the Second English Reformation', P. Collinson, p. 282, citing J. R. Green's *History of the English People* (1876 edn. p. 447).
130. *The English Revolution III, Newsbooks 5, Volume 14, Mercurius Politicus 1656–57* (1971), p. 164.
131. *Cromwell speaks! Extracts from the letters and speeches of Oliver Cromwell . . . Prepared by the Cromwell Association, with a foreword by the Rt. Hon. Isaac Foot, P.C.* (1941).
132. Noble, Memoirs, Vol 1, pp. 226–7; and Peach, History of Hursley Park, op. cit., p. 22.
133. K. Rundell, *Super-Infinite: The Transformations of John Donne* (2022), p. 295.

BIBLIOGRAPHY

MANUSCRIPTS

Bodleian Library, Oxford

MS Carte 73: Montagu papers

MS Clarendon 61, 70: Clarendon correspondence

MS Eng.Hist.c.485: William Dugdale's copy of John Speed's 'Catalogue of Religious Houses'

MS Rawl.c.381: Thomas Whetstone's copybook

British Library, London

Additional MS 48,028 (Yelverton MS 32): Act of Attainder of Thomas Cromwell

Additional MS 4159: Clarendon correspondence

Harleian MS 69: 'The books of certaine Triumphes' detailing May 1540 joust

Harleian MS 991: notebook with Cromwell family details

Harleian MS 2194: Hayward, Life and Raigne of Edward VI

Harleian MS 2311: Anna Cromwell Williams' book of poems

Cambridgeshire Archives, Huntingdon

85: nine injunctions of Henry Cromwell as Sheriff of Huntingdonshire, 1593

3646/ (503): letter from John Merrill to Viscount Mandeville, 1642

B59: Autographed receipt for a painting of Oliver Cromwell by Robert Walker, the Cromwell Museum

CRO/H, 3870/1: St John's parish register

CRO/H, Accession 4880: Oliver Cromwell's two sales of land in 1627

CRO/H: St Ives Manor Court Book 1632–61

CRO/H 3734/8/1 Vestry Book 1626–1726 (currently displayed in the Cromwell Museum)

HUTCM L18: letter from Oliver Cromwell's mother Elizabeth to a cousin
HUTCM L85: Huntingdon muster roll, September 1638
KAcc731/1-217: Bush Collection of Cromwell documents, including family letters, deeds, wills, memoranda and commonplace books
KHAC2/2828: letters from Puritan divines to Dorothy Cromwell
KHAC5/5170: pedigree of Sir Henry Cromwell
KR/R1/1-2: two Cromwell family marriage deeds
KR/R42/17/3: Translation of Grant of Manor of Ramsey etc. to Richard Williams, otherwise Cromwell, 31 Hen,VIII

Cambridge University Library
GBR/0012/EDR H/2/1: Ely Diocesan Records, Correspondence of James Tabor, notary public, relating chiefly to diocesan affairs, 1591–1660, Beck Correspondence

Dorset History Centre Archive
Ph/681: 'Account by Hannah Hewling of the last days of her brothers, Benjamin and William, executed at Taunton and Lyme for their part in the Monmouth Rebellion. 1685'

Essex Record Office
D/P 99/1/2: Register of baptisms, marriages and burials at Holy Cross Felsted, 1630–1723

Folger Shakespeare Library
X.c. 53 (formerly MS Add 974): Autograph letter from Katherine Whetstone, Ely, to Mrs. Wind, Bargen, 16 February 1648(9)

Helmingham Hall
Archive T/Hel/1/5: Letter from Roger Jones to Catherine Tollemache
Archive T/Hel/9/1/1: *Helmingham Hall. An inventorie taken there the 29 of September 1597*
Archive T/Hel/10/8: *16th century Miscellany*
Letters from Charles II (on display)
Library LJ /I/15: *Catherine Tollemache's Receipts of Pastery, Confectionary Etc.*
Library MS LJ/II/6: *Book of Secrets*

Launde Abbey
Various papers, letters, archaeological reports and local histories of the Abbey and its owners

National Archives, Kew
Public Record Office: Transcripts from French Archives, PRO 31/3/102, 13–14 June 1658: Letter from Cardinal Mazarin to M. de Bordeaux

Sheffield City Archives

WWM/StrP: Wentworth Woodhouse Muniments Collection, Strafford Papers, letters between Thomas Cromwell, Viscount Lecale and Thomas Wentworth, Earl of Strafford, 1634–39 at 8/100–101; 14/166, 200, 273 & 324; 15/303 & 320; and 18/186

Trinity College, Dublin

IE TCD MS 1045: diary of Thomas Cromwell MP

IE TCD MS 11353: Cromwell family and estate papers

UNPUBLISHED DISSERTATIONS

Holder, N., 'The Medieval Friaries of London' (University of London PhD thesis, 2011)

Malins, M., 'Conservative Cromwellians and the Restoration c.1657–c.1677' (University of Cambridge, PhD thesis, 2010)

Robertson, M. L., 'Thomas Cromwell's Servants: The Ministerial Household in Early Tudor Government and Society' (University of California, Los Angeles PhD thesis, 1975)

NEWSPAPERS

A Perfect Diurnall

Evening Herald

Mercurius Elenticus

Mercurius Politicus

Mercurius Pragmaticus

Parliament Scout

Perfect Occurences

Times Literary Supplement

The Times of India

Weekly Intelligencer

Weekly Post

PRIMARY

A case for Nol Cromwells nose, and the cure of Tom Fairfax's gout. Both which rebells are dead, and their deaths kept close, by the policy of our new states (London, 1648)

An Account of the Last Houres of the late Renowned Oliver Lord Protector . . . Drawn up and published by one who was an Eye and Ear-Witness of the most part of it, 1659 (London, 1659)

Anon, *A Dialogue betwixt the ghosts of Charles I late king of England and Oliver, the last usurping protector* (London, June 1659)

Anon, *The life of Thomas Ld Cromwell, A Black-Smith's Son, born at Putney in Surry* (London, 1715)

Aubrey, J., *Brief Lives*, ed. A. Clark (2 vols, Oxford, 1898)

Aubrey, J., *The natural history and antiquities of the county of Surrey* (5 vols, London, 1718)

Bandello, M., *The Novels of Matteo Bandello Bishop of Ages now first done into English prose and verse, ed. And trans. J. Payne* (6 vols, London, 1890)

Bate, G., *Elenchus motuum nuperorum in Anglia or, A short historical account of the rise and progress of the late troubles in England In two parts . . .* (London, 1685)

Baxter, R., *Five Disputations of Church-Government, and Worship* (London, 1659)

Beard, T., *A retractiue from the Romish religion contayning thirteene forcible motiues, disswading from the communion with the Church of Rome: wherein is demonstratiuely proued, that the now Romish religion (so farre forth as it is Romish) is not the true Catholike religion of Christ, but the seduction of Antichrist* (London, 1616)

Becon, T., *The Sick Man's Salve Wherin the faithfull christians may learne both how to behaue them selues paciently and thankefully, in the tyme of sickenes, and also vertuously to dispose their temporall goodes, and finally to prepare them selues gladly and godly to die . . .* (London, 1561)

Behn, A., *The Roundheads, of The Good Old Cause a comedy* (London, 1682)

Berkley, J., *Memoirs of Sir John Berkley* (London, 1699)

Brome, A., *Rump, or, An exact collection of the choycest poems and songs relating to the late times by the most eminent wits from anno 1639 to anno 1661* (London, 1662)

Burnet, G., *Burnet's History of My Own Time: Part 1 The Reign of Charles the Second*, ed. O. Airy (2 vols, Oxford, 1897–1900)

Burnet, G., *The History of the Reformation of the Church of England. The first part, of the progress made in it during the Reign of K. Henry the VIII By Gilbert Burnet* (2 vols, London, 1679)

Burton, R., *The Anatomy of Melancholy* (Oxford, 1621)

Byng, John., *The Torrington diaries containing the tour through England and Wales of the Hon. John Byng (later fifth Viscount Torrington) between the years 1781 and 1794*, ed. C. Bruyn Andrews (4 vols, London, 1970)

Calendar of Ancient Records of Dublin, ed. J. T. Gilbert (19 vols, Dublin, 1889)

Calendar of the Cecil Papers in Hatfield House (24 vols, London, 1883–1976)

Calendar of the Clarendon State Papers preserved in the Bodleian Library, ed., Rev. W. Dunn Macray et al. (5 vols, Oxford, 1872–1970)

Calendar of the Close Rolls Preserved in the Public Record Office . . . Henry VII ed. K. H. Ledward and R. A. Latham (2 vols, London, 1955–63)

Calendar of Letters, Despatches and State Papers Relating to the Negotiations between England and Spain Preserved in the Archives at Simancas and Elsewhere ed. P. de Gayangos, G. Mattingly, M. A. S. Hume and R. Tyler (15 vols, London, 1862–1954)

Calendar of Proceedings for the Committee for Compounding etc. With Delinquents, Vol 2 Cases 1643-46, ed. M. A. E. Green (London, 1890)

Calendar of State Papers Domestic: Charles I, ed. J. Bruce (23 vols, London, 1858–97)

Calendar of State Papers Domestic: Charles II, ed. M. A. E. Green, F. H. Blackburne Daniell and F. Bickley (28 vols, London, 1860–1939)

Calendar of State Papers Domestic: Interregnum, ed. M. A. E. Green (13 vols, London, 1875–86)

Calendar of State Papers Domestic: James II, ed. E. K. Timings (3 vols, London, 1960–72)

Calendar of State Papers Relating To English Affairs in the Archives of Venice, ed. R. Brown, H. F. Brown and A. B. Hinds (38 vols, London, 1864–1947)

Carrington, S., *The History of the Life and Death of his Most Serene Highness, Oliver, late Lord Protector* (London, 1659).

Cary, M., *The Little Horn's Doom and Downfall, Or a Scripture-Prophesie of King James, and King Charles, and of this present Parliament unfolded . . .* (London, 1651)

The Case is altered. Or, Dreadful news from hell.: In a discourse between the ghost of this grand traytor and tyrant Oliver Croomwel, and sir reverence my Lady Joan his wife, at their late meeting neer the scaffold on Tower-hill . . . (London, 1660)

Cavendish, G., *The Life of Cardinal Wolsey by George Cavendish*, ed., S. W. Singer (London, 1827)

Cavendish, G., *The Life of Cardinal Wolsey by George Cavendish and Metrical Visions*, ed., S. W. Singer, 2 vols (Chiswick, 1825)

Carthew, G. A., *The Hundred of Launditch and Deanery of Brisley* (Brisley, 1877)

Chirbuy, Edward, Lord Herbert of, *The life and raigne of King Henry the Eighth* (London, 1649)

Clarendon, Edward Hyde, Earl of, *The History of the Rebellion and Civil Wars in England*, ed., W. D. Macray (6 vols, Oxford, 1888)

The Clarke Papers: selections from the papers of W. Clarke, Secretary to the Council of the army, 1647–9, and to General Monck and the commanders of the army in Scotland, 1651–62, ed. C. H. Firth (4 vols, 1891–1901)

Collected poems of Sir Thomas Wyatt edited by Kenneth Muir and Patricia Thomson (Liverpool, 1969)

A Collection of State Letters of the Right Honourable Roger Boyle, the first Earl of Orrery, ed. T. Morrice (London, 1742)

A Collection of the State Papers of John Thurloe, ed. T. Birch (7 vols, London, 1742)

A Conference held between the Old Lord Protector and the New Lord General truly reported by Hugh Peters (London, 1660)

Coningsby, Sir Thomas, *Journal of the Siege of Rouen 1591*, ed. J. G. Nichols (London, 1847)

The Correspondence of Henry Cromwell 1655–1659, ed., P. Gaunt, Camden 5th series, vol 31 (Cambridge, 2007)
The Correspondence of Reginald Pole: a calendar, ed. T Mayer (3 vols, Aldershot, 2000–2004)
The Correspondence of Sir Thomas More, ed. E. F. Rogers (Princeton, 1947)
The Correspondence of the Three William Byrds of Westover, Virginia 1684–1776, ed. M. Tinling (2 vols, Virginia, 1977)
The Court and Kitchen of Elizabeth Cromwell, Commonly called Joan Cromwell, the Wife of the Late Usurper (London, 1664), reissued as *Mrs Cromwell's Cookbook*, ed. S. Orme (King's Lynn, 2021)
The cuckoo's-nest a Westminster, or the Parlement between two lady-birds: Quean Fairfax, and Lady Cromwell . . . (London, 1648)
Danberry, H., The Portraiture of his Royal Highness, Oliver, Late Lord Protector &c. in His Life and Death (London, 1659)
A Declaration of His Highnesse the Lord Protector for a Day of Publick Thanksgiving (London, [3] July 1658)
A Declaration of the Parliament of England, Expressing the Grounds of their late Proceedings, And of Setling the present Government in the way of A Free State (London, 1649)
Diary of Thomas Burton Esq, ed. J. T. Rutt (4 vols, London, 1828)
The Diary of John Evelyn, ed. A. Dobson (3 vols, London, 1906)
Diary of Sir Archibald Johnston of Wariston, ed. J. D. Ogilvie (3 vols, Edinburgh, 1940)
The Diary of Ralph Josselin 1616–1683, ed. A. MacFarlane (London, 1976)
The Diary of Henry Machyn, ed. J. G. Nicholls (London, 1848)
Diary of John Manningham of the Middle Temple, and of Bradbourne, Kent, barrister-at-law, 1602–1603 ed. J. Bruce (London, 1868)
The Diary of Samuel Pepys, ed. R. C. Latham and W. Matthews (11 vols, London 1970)
The Diary of Bulstrode Whitelocke 1605–1675, ed. R. Spalding (Oxford, 1990)
The Diurnal of Thomas Rugg 1659–61, ed. W. L. Sachse (London, 1961)
Documents Illustrative of English Church History, ed. H. Gee and W. J. Hardy (London, 1914)
Drayton, M., *Poems by Michael Drayton* (London, 1607)
Dugdale, W., *The antiquities of Warwickshire illustrated: from records, leiger-books, manuscripts, charters, evidences, tombes, and armes: beautified with maps, prospects, and portraictures By William Dugdale. This edition is carefully copied, . . . from the old one, published in the year 1656* (2 vols, 2nd edition, London, 1973)
Eikon Basilike: the pourtraicture of His Sacred Majestie in his solitudes and sufferings (London, 1649)
Ellis, H., *Original Letters illustrative of English History . . . from autographs in the British Museum and . . . other collections* (11 vols, London, 1824–1846)
The embassador and his functions. By Monsieur de Wicquefort. To which is added, an historical discourse, concerning the election of the emperor and

the electors. By the same author. Translated into English by Mr. Digby (London, 1716)

The English Revolution III, Newsbooks 5: Mercurius Politicus, ed. R. Jeffs (19 vols, London, 1971)

Firth, C. H., 'A Speech of Richard Cromwell, 18 October 1658', *English Historical Review*, 23, 1908, 734–5.

Flatman, T., *Don Juan Lamberto: or, a comical history of the late times. The first part. By Montelion Knight of the Oracle, &c.* (London, 1661)

Fleckno, R., *The Idea of His Highness Oliver Lord Protector etc. With certain brief reflexions on his life* (London, 1659)

Fletcher, H., *The perfect politician, or, A full view of the life and action (military and civil) of O. Cromwel whereunto is added his character, and a compleat catalogue of all the honours conferr'd by him on several persons* (London, 1660)

Fourty four queries to the life of Queen Dick. By one who will at any time work a job of journey-work, to serve his country (London, 1659)

Foxe, J., *The Unabridged Acts and Monuments Online or TAMO* (The Digital Humanities Institute, Sheffield, 2011), http//www.dhi.ac.uk/foxe

Fuller, T., *The Church-History of Britain, from the Birth of Jesus Christ, until the Year M.DC.XLVIII* and *The History of the University of Cambridge, since the Conquest* (London, 1655)

Fuller, T., *The History of the Worthies of England* (London, 1662)

Fuller, T., *The History of the Worthies of England*, ed. P. A. Nuttall, 3 vols (London, 1840)

de Gand, L., *Parallelum Olivae nec non Olivarii* (London, 1656)

Gauden, J., *Funerals made cordials: in a sermon prepared and (in part) preached at the solemn interment of the corps of the Right Honorable Robert Rich, heire apparent to the Earldom of Warwick. (Who aged 23. died Febr. 16. at Whitehall, and was honorably buried March 5. 1657. At Felsted in Essex.)* (London, 1658)

Gibbons, A. ed., *Ely Episcopal Records: A Calendar and Concise View of the Episcopal Records preserved in the Muniment Room of the Palace of Ely* (Lincoln, 1891)

The government of the Common-wealth of England, Scotland, & Ireland, and the dominions thereto belonging; as it was publickly declared at Westminster the 16. day of December 1653. in the presence of the Lords Commissioners of the Great Seal of England, the Lord Maior and aldermen of the City of London, divers of the judges of the land, the officers of state and army, and many other persons of quality, at which time and place His Highness, Oliver Lord Protector of the said Commonwealth, took a solemn oath for observing the same. Published by His Highness the Lord Protector's special commandment (London, 1653)

Guerdon, A., *A most learned, conscientious, and devout- exercise: held forth the last Lords- day, at Sir Peter Temples, in Lincolnes- Inne- Fields; / by Lieut.- General Crumwell. As it was faithfully taken in characters by mAaron Guerdon* (1649)

Guizot, M., *History of Oliver Cromwell and the English Commonwealth, from the Execution of Charles the First to the Death of Cromwell*, trans. A. R. Scoble (2 vols, London, 1854)

Guizot, M., *History of Richard Cromwell and the restoration of Charles II*, trans. A. R. Scoble (2 vols, London, 1856)

Hall's chronicle: containing the history of England, during the reign of Henry the Fourth, and the succeeding monarchs, to the end of the reign of Henry the Eighth, in which are particularly described the manners and customs of those periods. Carefully collated with the editions of 1548 and 1550 (London, 1809)

Hartlib, S., *The reformed common- wealth of bees* (London, 1655)

The Hartlib Papers, ed. M. Greengrass, M. Leslie and M. Hannon (published by The Digital Humanities Institute, University of Sheffield 2013), http://www.dhi.ac.uk/hartlib

Hausted, P., *Ad Populum: or, a lecture to the people* (Oxford, 1644)

Heath, J., *Flagellum, or, The life and death, birth and burial of Oliver Cromwel faithfully described in an exact account of his policies and successes, not heretofore published or discovered* (London, 1663)

Heath, J., *A Brief Chronicle of the late Intestine War* (London, 1663)

Hells Higher Court of Justice (London, 1661)

Henfrey, Henry William, *Numismata Cromwelliana, Or, The Medallic History of Oliver Cromwell, Illustrated by His Coins, Medals, and Seals* (London, 1877)

HMC, Appendix to the Second Report (London, 1874)

HMC, Appendix to the Fifth Report (London, 1876)

HMC, Report on the Manuscripts of Mrs Frankland-Russell-Astley, of Chequers Court, Bucks (London, 1900)

Holinshed, R., *The Third volume of Chronicles . . . first collected by Raphaell Holinshed, and by him extended to the yeare 1577; now newlie recognised, augmented and continued . . . to the year 1586* (London, 1586)

Hume, M. A. S., *Chronicle of King Henry VIII of England* (London, 1889)

Hutchinson, L., *Memoirs of the Life of Colonel Hutchinson* ed. N. H. Keeble (London, 2000)

The Journal of Edward Mountagu, first Earl of Sandwich, admiral and general at sea, 1659–1665, ed. R. C. Anderson (London, 1929)

Kingsford, C. L., ed. 'Two London Chronicles from the Collections of John Stow . . .', *Camden Miscellany 12* (Camden 3rd series 18, London, 1910)

Lawrence, P. H., *Extracts from the court rolls of the manor of Wimbledon, extending from 1 Edward IV. to A.D. 1864* (London, 1866)

L'Estrange, R., *Truth and Loyalty Vindicated* (London, 1662)

Letters and Papers Foreign and Domestic of the reign of Henry VIII 1509–47, ed. J. S. Brewer et al, (21 vols and 2 appendix vols, London, 1862–1932)

Letters between Colonel Robert Hammond governor of the Isle and the Committee of Lords and Commons at Derby House, General Fairfax, Lieutenant-General Cromwell, Commissary General Ireton etc. relating to

King Charles I while he was confined in Carisbrooke castle in that Island . . . ed. T. Birch (London, 1764)

Letters from Sir Robert Cecil to Sir George Carew, ed. J. Maclean (Camden Society, 1864)

The Letters of Dorothy Osborne to Sir William Temple 1652–54, ed. E. A. Parry (London, 1903)

The Letters of Stephen Gardiner, ed. J. A. Muller (Cambridge, 1933)

The Letters, Writings and Speeches of Oliver Cromwell, ed. J. Morrill (3 vols, Oxford, 2022)

Life and Letters of Thomas Cromwell, ed. R. B. Merriman (2 vols, Oxford, 1902)

Life and Letters of Sir Thomas Wyatt, ed. K. Muir (Liverpool, 1963)

The life and death of Thomas, Lord Cromwell: By Mr. William Shakespear (London, 1734)

Lives and Letters of the Devereux, Earls of Essex in the reigns of Elizabeth I, James I and Charles I 1540–1646 ed. W. B. Devereux (2 vols, London, 1853)

Lilburne, J., *England's Birth-Right Justified* (London, 1645)

Lilburne, J., *A discourse betwixt Lieutenant Colonel John Lilburn, close prisoner in the Tower of London, and Mr Hugh Peter: upon May 25. 1649* (London, 1649)

Lilburne, J., *Englands New Chains Discovered; Or The Serious Apprehensions of a Part of the People, in Behalf of the Commonwealth;: (being Presenters, Promoters, and Approvers of the Large Petition of September 11. 1648.) Presented to the Supreme Authority of England, the Representers of the People in Parliament Assembled* (London, 1649)

Lincoln's Inn Admissions, Volume 1: 1420–1799 (London, 1896)

The Lisle Letters ed. M. St C. Byrne (6 vols, London and Chicago, 1981)

Llyfr Baglan (Book of Baglan), compiled by J. Williams (London, 1600–1607)

Long, J., *An epitaph on the late deceased, that truely-noble and renowned lady Elizabeth Cromwel (mother to His Highness the Lo. Protector of Great Britain and Ireland, &c.) who lived to the age of 89. and died Nov. 16. 1654. and lieth buried in Westminster-Abbey* (London, 1654)

Lott, T., 'Account of the Muster of the Citizens of London in the 31st Year of the Reign of Henry VIII', *Archaeologica* 32 (1847), 30–37

Ludlow, E., *A Voyce from the Watch Tower, Part Five: 1660–1662*, ed., A. B. Worden (Camden fourth series, Volume 21, London, 1978)

Andrew Marvell, ed. F. Kermode and K. Walker (Oxford, 1990)

Masterton, G., *The Triumph Stain'd* (London, 1648)

The Memoirs of Edmund Ludlow, 1625–1672, ed. C. H. Firth (2 vols, Oxford, 1894)

John Milton Complete Shorter Poems, 2nd edition, ed. John Carey (London, 1997)

Milton, J., *The Tenure of Kings and Magistrates* (1649)

Monarchy asserted to be the best, most ancient, and legall form of government in a conference had at Whitehall with Oliver, late Lord Protector, & a committee of Parliament . . . (London, 1660)

Newcourt, R., *Repertorium Ecclesiasticum Parochiale Londinense: An Acclesisatical Parochial History of the Diocese of London* (London, 1708)

Nicholas, D., *Mr Secretary Nicholas (1593–1669) His Life and Letters* (London, 1955)

John Nichols's The Progresses and Public Processions of Queen Elizabeth I, eds. E. Goldring, F. Eales, E. Clarke, J. E. Archer, et al (5 vols, Oxford, 2014)

Nichols, J., *The progresses, processions, and magnificent festivities, of King James the First: his royal consort, family, and court, collected from original manuscripts, scarce pamphlets, corporation records, parochial registers, &c., &c. . . . Illustrated with notes, historical, topographical, biographical and bibliographical.* (4 vols, London, 1828)

Original letters and papers of state, addressed to Oliver Cromwell; concerning the affairs of Great Britain. From the year MDCXLIX to MDCLVIII. Found among the political collections of Mr. John Milton. Now first published from the originals. ed. J. Nickolls (London, 1743)

Overton, R., *A new bull-bayting: or, A match play'd at the tovvn-bull of Ely . . .* (London, 1649)

Owen, J., *The labouring saints dismission to rest. A sermon / preached at the funeral of the Right Honourable Henry Ireton Lord Deputy of Ireland: in the Abbey Church at Westminster, the 6th. day of February 1651* (London, 1652)

The Papers of George Wyatt Esquire, ed. D. M. Loades (Camden 4th series, vol 5, London, 1968)

Parker, H., *Observations upon some of His Majesties late answers and expresses* (1642)

Perrinchief, R., *Nuntius a mortuis: or, a messenger from the dead. That is, a stupendous and dreadfull colloquie, distinctly and alternately heard by divers, betwixt the ghosts of Henry the Eight, and Charles the First, both Kings of England, who lye entombed in the church of Windsor . . .* (Paris, 1657)

Petty, W., *The advice of W.P. to Mr. Samuel Hartlib for the advancement of some particular parts of learning* (London, 1647)

Pope, A., *Essay on Man* (London, 1734)

'Prebendaries: Curborough', in *Fasti Ecclesiae Anglicanae 1300–1541: Volume 10, Coventry and Lichfield Diocese*, ed. B Jones (London, 1964), 27–29

Prestwich's Respublica, Or, A Display of the Honors, Ceremonies & Ensigns of the Common-wealth Under the Protectorship of Oliver Cromwell: Together with the Names, Armorial Bearings, Flags & Pennons of the Different Commanders of the English, Scotch, Irish Americans and French . . . . (London, 1787)

Privy purse expenses of the Princess Mary afterwards Queen Mary: with a memoir of the princess by F. Madden (London, 1831)

Proceedings in the Parliament of Elizabeth I, ed. T. E. Hartley (3 vols, Leicester, 1981)

Pugh, T., *Brittish and out-landish prophesies most of above a 1000 years antiquity, the rest very antient . . .* (London, 1658)

Roberts, D., *Matrimoniall Honour* (London, 1642)

Roper, W., *The Life of Sir Thomas Moore Knt* (London, 1905)

Rushworth, J., *Historical Collections of Private Passages of State* (8 vols, London, 1721)

Say, S., 'Character of Mrs B[ridget] B[endish], Grand-daughter of Oliver Cromwell written in 1719 on occasion of the closing Words of Lord Clarendon's character of her Grandfather', re-printed in *The Annual Register, or a view of the History, Politics and Literature for the Year 1773* (London, 1780), 77–80.

Sermons; now first printed from the original manuscripts of John Wallis . . . To which are prefixed, memoirs of the author . . . by the Rev. C. E. de Coetlogon, M.A. (London, 1791)

Skutt, G., *A letter from an ejected Member of the House of Commons, to Sir Jo: Evelyn* (London, 1648)

Slater, S., *The Protectors Protection: Or, The Pious Prince guarded by a Praying People (London, 1659)*

Slater, S., *A rhetorical rapture as composed into a funeral oration at the mournfull moving of His Highnes stately effigies from Somerset-House* (London, 1658)

The Speech of His Highness the Lord Protector, made to both Houses of Parliament at their first meeting on Thursday the 17th of January 1658[/9], (London, 1659)

The Speech of the Right Honourable Nathaniel, Lord Fiennes, One of the Lord Keepers of the Great Seale of England, Made before his Highnesse and both Houses of Parliament, 27 January 1658 (London, 1659)

State Papers Collected by Edward, Earl of Clarendon, commencing the year 1621., ed. R. Scrope and T. Monkhouse (3 vols, Oxford, 1767–86)

The state papers and letters of Sir Ralph Sadler, knight-banneret / edited by Arthur Clifford . . .; to which is added a memoir of the life of Sir Ralph Sadler, with historical notes, by Walter Scott. (2 vols, Edinburgh, 1809)

State-worthies: or, the statesmen and favourites of England from the reformation to the revolution.. By David Lloyd. To this edition is added the characters of the Kings and Queens . . . By Charles Whitworth (London, 1766)

Stow, J., *A Survey of London Written in the Year 1598*, ed. H. Morley (Stroud, 1994)

Strype, J., *Ecclesiastical Memorials, relating chiefly to Religion, and the reformation of it, and the emergencies of the Church of England, under King Henry VIII. King Edward VI. and Queen Mary the First . . .* 3 vols (London, 1721)

Tatham, J., *The Rump: or the mirror of the late times, a new comedy* (London, 1660)

Three poems upon the death of His late Highnesse Oliver Lord protector of England, Scotland, and Ireland written by Mr Edm. Waller, Mr Jo. Dryden, Mr Sprat of Oxford (London, 1659)

The Tollemache book of secrets: a descriptive index and complete facsimile with an introduction and transcriptions together with Catherine Tollemache's Receipts of pastery, confectionary etc., by J. Griffiths, completed by A. S. G. Edwards (The Roxburghe Club, 2001)

A tragi-comedy, called New-Market-Fayre, or A Parliament out-cry: of state-commodities, set to sale . . . (London, 1649)

Travels of Cosmo the third, Grand Duke of Tuscany, through England during the reign of King Charles the second (1669). Tr. from the Italian manuscript in the Laurentian library at Florence. To which is prefixed, a memoir of his life (London, 1821)

The two books of homilies appointed to be read in churches (1547), ed. J Griffiths (Oxford, 1859)

'Two letters addressed to Cromwell', ed. C. H. Firth, *English Historical Review*, xxii (1907)

Venn, J. & Venn, J. A. (eds.), A*lumni Cantabrigienses* (4 vols., Cambridge, 1922–7)

The Visitation of the County of Huntingdon, under the authority of William Camden . . . by his deputy Nicholas Charles Lancaster Herald, A.D. MDCXIII, ed. Sir H. Ellis (Camden Society Publications 43, 1849), 79–80

W. S., *The True Chronicle Historie of the Whole Life and Death of Thomas Lord Cromwell* (London, 1613)

Waller, E., *A panegyrick to my Lord Protector by a gentleman that loves peace, union, and prosperity of the English nation* (London, 1655)

Waller, E., *Upon the late storm and of the death of His Highnesse ensuing the same* (London, 1658)

Walton, I., *The Compleat Angler* (London, 1653)

Warwick, Sir Philip, *Memoirs of the Reign of King Charles I* (London, 1702)

Waters, R. E. C., *Genealogical memoirs of the families of Chester . . .* (London, 1881)

The Wentworth Papers, 1705–1739, ed. J. J. Cartwright (London, 1883)

Wharton, Sir G., *A Second Narrative of the late Parliament* (London, 1658)

Whitelocke, B., *Memorials of the English affairs from the beginning of the reign of Charles the First to the happy restoration of King Charles the* Second (4 vols, Oxford, 1853)

Wildman, J., *Truths triumph, or Treachery anatomized* (London, 1648)

Wilson, T., *A Discourse Upon Usury (1572)*, ed. R. H. Tawney (New York, 1925)

Wood, A., *Athenae Oxonienses : an exact history of all the writers and bishops who have had their education in the University of Oxford*, ed. P. Bliss (4 vols, London, 1813–1820)

Wood, M.A.E., *Letters of Royal and Illustrious Ladies of Great Britain* (3 vols, London, 1846)

Works of Francis Bacon, ed. J. Spedding, R. L. Ellis and D. D. Heath (11 vols, 1857–1874)

The World Turned Upside-Down, or, A briefe description of the ridiculous fashions of these distracted times by T.J., a well- willer to King, Parliament, and kingdom (London, 1647)

Wriothesley, C., *A Chronicle of England During the Reigns of the Tudors, From A.D.1485 to 1559*, ed. W. D. Hamilton (2 vols., Camden Society, 2nd set, London, 1875)

The Writings and Speeches of Oliver Cromwell, ed. W. C. Abbott (4 vols, Cambridge Massachusetts, 1937–47)

SECONDARY

John Adams diary 44, 27 March - 21 July 1786 (electronic edition), *Adams Family Papers: An Electronic Archive*, Massachusetts Historical Society, http://www.masshist.org/digitaladams/

Adamson, J., *The Noble Revolt: The Overthrow of Charles I* (London, 2007)

Angus, C., *The Private Life of Thomas Cromwell* (London, 2022)

Alford, S., *The Early Elizabethan Polity: William Cecil and the British Succession Crisis 1558–1569* (Cambridge, 1998)

Alford, S., *Burley: William Cecil at the court of Elizabeth I* (London, 2008)

Alford, S., *Kingship and Politics in the Reign of Edward VI* (Cambridge, 2002)

Almond, P., *The Witches of Warboys: an extraordinary story of sorcery, sadism and satanic possession* (London, 2008)

Arnold, M., *Cromwell: a prize poem, recited in the theatre, Oxford, June 28 1843* (Oxford, 2nd edition, 1863)

Austen, J., *Mansfield Park* (London, 1814)

Barclay, A., *Electing Cromwell: The Making of a Politician* (London, 2011)

Barker, N. ed., *Two East Anglian picture books: a facsimile of the Helmingham herbal and bestiary and Bodleian MS. Ashmole 1504* (London, 1988)

BBC poll, *Great Britons* (2002)

Bernard, G. W., 'The fall of Anne Boleyn', *English Historical Review* CVI (1991), 584–610

Bindoff, S. T., *The History of Parliament: The House of Commons 1509–1558* (London, 1982)

Blair, T., *A Journey: My Political Life* (New York, 2010)

Blatchly, John, *East Anglian Ex-Libris, Bookplates and labels made between 1700 and the present day (*The Bookplate Society, Dorchester, 2008)

Borman, T., *Thomas Cromwell* (London, 2014)

Borman, T., *The Stolen Crown* (London, 2025)

Boswell, J., *The Journals of James Boswell, 1762–1795*, ed. J. Wain (New Haven, 1991)

Braddick, M. J., *The Oxford Handbook of the English Revolution* (Oxford, 2015)

Bradshaw, B., 'Cromwellian Reform and the Origins of the Kildare Rebellion, 1533–34', *Transactions of the Royal Historical Society, 5th ser., 27* (1977)

Bradshaw, B., The Irish Constitutional Revolution of the Sixteenth Century (Cambridge, 1979)
Bray, G. ed., *Documents of the English Reformation* (Cambridge, 1994)
Brigden, S., *Thomas Wyatt: the heart's forest* (London, 2012)
Brigden, S., '"The Shadow That You Know": Sir Thomas Wyatt and Sir Francis Bryan at Court and in Embassy', *The Historical Journal*, Vol. 39, No. 1 (March 1996), 1–31
British History Online - www.british-history.ac.uk
Burgess, G., ed. *The New British History: Founding a Modern State 1603–1715* (London, 1999)
Burke, B., *Vicissitudes of Families* (Dublin, 1869)
Burke, V & Gibson, J (eds), *Early Modern Women's Manuscript Writing*, 1st ed. (Aldershot, 2004)
Burn, A. S., 'Correspondence of Richard Cromwell', *The English Historical Review*, Jan., 1898, Vol. 13, No. 49 (Jan., 1898), 93–124
Bush, M. L., 'The Lisle-Seymour land disputes: a study of power and influence in the 1530s', *Historical Journal IX* (1966), 255–74
Butler, J., 'Richard Cromwell and Oxford 1657–1660', in *Cromwelliana* (1982), 21–32.
Butler, J. A., *A Biography of Richard Cromwell, 1626–1712, The Second Protector* (New York, 1994)
Byron, Lord., *Childe Harold's Pilgrimage* (London, 1812–18)
Capp, B., *England's Culture Wars: Puritan Reformation and its Enemies in the Interregnum*, 1649-1660 (Oxford, 2012)
Carlson, E. J. ed. *Religion and the English People 1500–1640* (Kirksville 1998)
Catalogue of highly important manuscripts & printed books (London, 1961)
Cerasano, S. P., and May, S. W., ed. *In the Prayse of Writing, Early Modern Manuscript Studies Essays in Honour of Peter Beal* (London, 2012)
Chapman, A., *Thomas Cromwell a historical sourcebook* (2020)
Chambers, E. K., *William Shakespeare: A Study of Facts and Problems* (2 vols, Oxford, 1930)
Chapman, A., 'A World in the Moon - Wilkins and his Lunar Voyage of 1640', *Quarterly Journal of the Royal Astronomical Society* (1991), Vol. 32, no.2, 121–131
Chapman, A., 'Fly me to the Moon', *Astronomy & Geophysics*, Vol 55, Issue 1, February 2014, 1.26–1.31.
The Churchill Documents, ed. Randolph S. Churchill & Martin Gilbert (23 vols, Hillsdale, 2012)
'Cromwell's coffin plate' in *Westminster Abbey Chorister* (Summer 2015), 25–7
Clarke, Rev. J. S. (ed.), *The Life of James the Second King of England*, 2 volumes (London, 1816)
Clifford, C., and Akeroyd, A., *Risen from Obscurity? Oliver Cromwell and Huntingdonshire* (Huntingdon, 2002)
Clough, T. H. McK. *The Horseshoes of Oakham Castle* (Leicestershire, 1978)

Cobbett, W., *History of the Protestant Reformation in England and Ireland* (New York, 1824–7)

Cokayne, G. E., Gibbs, V., et al, *The Complete Peerage of England, Scotland and Ireland, Great Britain and the United Kingdom, Extant, Extinct or Dormant* (14 vols, London, 1910)

Coleman, M., *Fruitful Endeavours: The 16th-Century Household Secrets of Catherine Tollemache of Helmingham Hall* (Phillimore, 2012)

Coleman, M., ed. *Household inventories of Helmingham Hall, 1597–1741* (Suffolk, 2018)

Coleman, C., and Starkey, D., eds. *Revolution Reassessed: revisions in the history of Tudor government and administration* (Oxford, 1986)

Collinson, P., *From Iconoclasm to Iconophobia: The Cultural Impact of the Second English Reformation*, 1985 Stenton Lecture (Reading, 1986)

Collinson, P., 'The monarchical republic of Elizabeth I', *Bulletin of the John Rylands Library*, Vol 69, issue 2 (1987), 394–424

Collinson, P., *Elizabethan Eassys* (London, 1994)

Connolly, A., and Hopkins, L., ed. *Essex: The cultural impact of an Elizabethan courtier* (Manchester, 2013)

Cooper, C. H., *Annals of Cambridge* (5 vols, Cambridge, 1842–1908)

Cooper, J., *Oliver the First: Contemporary Images of Oliver Cromwell* (London, 1999)

Cooper, J. and Morris, S., *The Cromwell Family* (Cheltenham, 1987)

Covington, S., *The Devil From Over the Sea* (Oxford, 2022)

Coward, B., *Oliver Cromwell* (Harlow, 1991)

Coward, B., *The Cromwellian Protectorate* (Manchester, 2002)

Craze, Michael, *A History of Felsted School 1564–1947* (Ipswich, 1955)

Cressy, D., 'Remembrances of the Revolution: Histories and Historiographies of the 1640s', *Huntingdon Library Quarterly* 68, nos, 1–2 (2005), 257–68

Cromwell speaks! Extracts from the letters and speeches of Oliver Cromwell . . . Prepared by the Cromwell Association, with a foreword by the Rt. Hon. Isaac Foot, P.C. (1941)

Crowther, J. G., *Founders of British Science* (London, 1960)

Cunningham, J., 'Cromwell and the Irish land Settlement', *Cromwelliana* (2014), 50–63

Davidson, P. ed., *Poetry and Revolution An Anthology of British and Irish Verse 1625–1660* (Oxford, 1998)

Davies, C. S. L., 'The Cromwellian decade: authority and consent', *The Royal Historical Society 6th series 7* (1997), 177–95

Davies, C. S. L., 'The Family and Connections of John Wilkins, 1614–72', *Oxoniensia*, Vol. 68 (2003), 93–107

Davis, J. C., *Oliver Cromwell* (London, 2001)

DeWindt, A. R., & DeWindt, E. B., *Ramsey The Lives of an English Fenland Town 1200–1600* (Washington, 2006)

Dickens, A. G., *Thomas Cromwell and the English Reformation* (London, 1959)
Dictionary of Welsh Biography
Doran, S., *From Tudor to Stuart* (Oxford, 2024)
Duffy, E., *The Stripping of the Altars: Traditional Religion in England, c. 1400–c.1580* (London, 1992)
Dunan-Page, A. & Lynch, B., ed., *Roger L'Estrange and the Making of Restoration Culture* (Aldershot, 2008)
Durston, C., *Cromwell's Major-Generals: Godly Government during the English Revolution* (Manchester, 2001)
Durston, C., 'Godly Governors: the Rule of Cromwell's Major-Generals', *Cromwelliana* (2004), 52–64
Dyke, P., van, 'Reginald Pole and Thomas Cromwell: An Examination of the Apologia Ad Carolum Quintum', *The American Historical Review*, Vol. 9, No. 4 (July 1904), 696–724
Eliot, T.S. 'London Letter' *The Dial magazine*, Vol. 73.6 (New York, December 1922), 659–63
Ellis, P. B., *Hell or Connaught!: The Cromwellian Colonisation of Ireland, 1652–1660* (London, 1975)
Ellis, S. G., 'Thomas Cromwell and Ireland, 1532–1540', *Historical Journal 23* (1980), 497–519
Ellis, S. G., 'The Kildare Rebellion and the Early Henrician Reformation' *The Historical Journal*, Dec., 1976, Vol. 19, No. 4 (Dec., 1976), 807–830
Ellis, S. G., *Reform and Revival: English government in Ireland 1470–1534* (Royal Historical Society Studies in History 47, 1986)
Ellis, S. G., *Tudor Frontiers and Noble Power: the making of the British state* (Oxford, 1995)
Ellis, S. G,. *Ireland in the Age of the Tudors* (London, 1998)
Elton, G. R., *The Tudor Revolution in Government: administrative changes in the reign of Henry VIII* (Cambridge, 1953)
Elton, G. R., *England under the Tudors* (1955)
Elton, G. R., *Policy and Police: The Enforcement of the Reformation in the Age of Thomas Cromwell* (Cambridge, 1972)
Elton, G. R., *Reform and Renewal: Thomas Cromwell and the Common Weal* (Cambridge, 1973)
Elton, G. R., *Reform and Reformation: England 1509–1558* (London, 1977)
Elton, G. R., *Studies in Tudor and Stuart Politics and Government* (4 vols, Cambridge, 1974–92)
Elton, G. R., *The Parliament of England 1559–1581* (Cambridge, 1986)
Elton., G. R. 'A New Age of Reform?', *Historical Journal 30* (1987), 709–16
Elton, G. R., 'How corrupt was Thomas Cromwell?', *Historical Journal* 36 (1993), 905–8
Emerson, O., and McCaffrey, K., *Holbein's Hidden Gem: rediscovering Thomas Cromwell's lost book* (Exeter, 2023)
The Environs of London: Volume 3, County of Middlesex (1795)

Erler, M. C., *Reading and Writing during the Dissolution* (Cambridge, 2016)
Everett, M., *The Rise of Thomas Cromwell: power and politics in the reign of Henry VIII* (London, 2015)
Farr, D., *Brokerage and Networks in London's Global World* (Abingdon, 2022)
Farr, D., *Henry Ireton and the English Revolution* (Woodbridge, 2006)
Farr, D., *Oliver Cromwell's Kin, 1643–1726: The Private and Public Worlds of the English Revolution and Restoration* (London, 2023)
Firth, C. H., *The Last Years of the Protectorate 1656–1658* (2 vols, London, 1909)
Fitzgerald, T., and MacCulloch, D., 'Gregory Cromwell: two portrait miniatures by Hans Holbein the Younger', *Journal of Ecclesiastical History 67* (2016), 587–601
Fitzgibbons, J., *Cromwell's Head* (Richmond, 2008)
Fitzgibbons, J., 'Not in any doubtfull dispute'? Reassessing the nomination of Richard Cromwell, *Historical Research*, Vol. 83, no. 220 (May 2010), 281–300
Fitzgibbons, J., 'Hereditary Succession and the Cromwellian Protectorate: The Offer of the Crown Reconsidered', *The English Historical Review*, Vol. 128, No. 534 (October 2013), 1095–1128
Forkan, K., 'Army List of the Ulster British Forces, 1642–1646', *Archivium Hibernicum*, 2005, Vol. 59 (2005), 51–65
Fox, A., *Oral and Literate Culture in England 1500–1700* (Oxford, 2000)
Fraser, A., 'Bess and Old Noll', *Horizon Magazine*, Vol xiii (1971), 106-111.
Fraser, A., *Cromwell Our Chief of Men* (London, 1973)
Fullerton, S., 'Fatal Adulteries: Sexual Politics in the English Revolution', *Journal of British Studies 60* (October 2021), 793–821
Gardiner, S. R., *History of the Great Civil War 1642–1649* (4 vols, London, 1893)
Gaunt, P., *The Cromwellian Gazetteer* (Stroud, 1987)
Gaunt, P., *Oliver Cromwell* (Oxford, 1996)
Gaunt, P., ed. *Cromwell Four Centuries On* (Brentwood, 2013)
Genealogical memoirs of the families of Chester of Bristol, Barton Regis, London, and Almondsbury: descended from Henry Chester, sheriff of Bristol 1470; and also of the families of Astry of London, Kent, Beds, Hunts, Oxon, and Gloucestershire, descended from Sir Ralph Astry, kt., Lord Mayor of London, 1493 / attempted by Robt. Edmond Chester Waters (London, 1881)
Gerhold, D., *Thomas Cromwell and his Family in Putney and Wandsworth*, Wandsworth Historical Society Papers 31 (2017)
Gillespie, K., 'Elizabeth Cromwell's Kitchen Court: Republicanism and the Consort', *Genders 1998–2013*, Issue 33: First Ladies? Political Wives in Seventeenth-century England (October 2001)
Gillespie, K., *Women Writing in the English Republic 1625–1681* (Cambridge, 2017)
Gillies, M., *Marie Lloyd The One and Only* (London, 1999)
Greaves, Richard L., *Secrets of the Kingdom: British Radicals from the Popish Plot to the Revolution of 1688–1689* (Stanford, 1992)

Gristwood, Sarah, *The Tudors in Love: The Courtly Code behind the Last Medieval Dynasty* (London, 2021)

Gunn, S., 'The Structures of Politics in Early Tudor England', *Transactions of the Royal Historical Society*, Sixth Series, 5 (1995)

Guy, J.A., 'The Tudor Commonwealth: Revising Thomas Cromwell', *Historical Journal,* Vol. 23/3 (1980), 681–7

Halcomb, J., and Little, P., 'Writings and Sources XVI: 'Your Loving Father', Letters from Oliver to Henry Cromwell, 1656–1658', *Cromwelliana* (2014), 64–83

Hall, S. C., *The Baronial Halls of England,* 2 vols (London 1858)

Ham House: Four Hundred Years of Collecting and Patronage, Paul Mellon Centre for Studies in British Art, The Association of Human Rights Institutes series (2013)

Hammer, P., *The polarisation of Elizabethan politics: the political career of Robert Devereux, second earl of Essex, 1585–1597* (Cambridge, 1999)

Harris, B. J., 'Women and Politics in Early Tudor England', *Historical Journal 33* (1990), 259–281

Harris, T., *Restoration: Charles II and his Kingdoms, 1660–1685* (London, 2005)

Hart, G., 'Oliver Cromwell, Iconoclasm and Ely Cathedral', *Historical Research 87 no. 236* (2014), 270–6

Hasler, P. W., *The History of Parliament: The House of Commons 1558–1603* (London, 1981)

Hastings Robinson, the Rev., *Original Letters Relative to the English Reformation*, I, The Parker Society LIII (Cambridge, 1846–7)

Healey, J., *The Blazing World: A New History of Revolutionary England* (London, 2023)

Healey, J., *The Blood in Winter: A Nation Descends, 1642* (London, 2025)

Hexter, J. H., *Reappraisals in History* (London, 1961)

Hilary Mantel: Return to Wolf Hall, BBC2 (2020)

Highley, C., and King, J. N. ed. *John Foxe and his World* (Aldershot, 2002)

Hill, C., *The collected essays of Christopher Hill* (3 vols (Amherst, 1985)

Holberton, E., *Poetry and the Cromwellian Protectorate: Culture, Politics and Institutions* (Oxford, 2008)

Holder, N., T*he Friaries of Medieval London: from foundation to dissolution* (London, 2017)

Horrible Histories Horrible Christmas (Symphony Hall, Birmingham, December 2023)

https://www.bonhams.com

https://perdita.warwick.ac.uk

https://tankmuseum.org/ tank-nuts/tank-collection/cromwell

Hugo, V., *Cromwell* (1827), trans. G. B. Ives (modern reprint)

Hunt, A., *Republic: Britain's Revolutionary Decade 1649–1660* (London, 2024)

Hunting, P., *A History of the Drapers Company* (London, 1989)

Hutchinson, R., *Thomas Cromwell: The Rise and Fall of Henry VIII's most Notorious Minister* (London, 2007)

Hutton, R., *The Restoration: A Political and Religious History of England and Wales 1658–1667* (Oxford, 1986)
Hutton, R., *The British Republic 1649–1660* (Basingstoke, 1990)
Hutton, R., *The Making of Oliver Cromwell* (London, 2021)
Hutton, R., *Oliver Cromwell: Commander in Chief* (London, 2024)
Ingersoll, T., *The Loyalist Problem in Revolutionary New England* (Cambridge, 2016)
Jackson, C., 'Lord Herbert of Cherbury and the Presentation of the Henrician Reformation in his Life and Raigne of King Henry the Eighth', *The Seventeenth Century*, 28:2 (2013), 139–161
Jackson, C., *Devil-Land: England Under Siege, 1588–1688* (London, 2022)
Jackson, C., *The Mirror of Great Britain:* A Life of James VI & I (London, 2025)
Johnson, A. H., *The History of the Worshipful Company of the Drapers of London* (5 vols, Oxford, 1914–22)
Jones, C., *The Fall of Robespierre* (Oxford, 2023)
Keay, A., *The Restless Republic: Britain Without a Crown* (London, 2022)
Knoppers, L. L., 'Opening the Queen's Closet: Henrietta Maria, Elizabeth Cromwell, and the Politics of Cookery', *Renaissance Quarterly*, Vol. 60, No. 2 (Summer 2007), 464–499
Knoppers, L. L., *Constructing Cromwell: Ceremony, Portrait, and Print, 1645–1661* (Cambridge, 2000)
Laroche, R., 'Catherine Tollemache's Library', *Notes & Queries*, 251:2 (June, 2006) 251–2
Lay, P., *Providence Lost: The Rise and Fall of Cromwell's Protectorate* (London, 2020)
Lehmberg, S. E., *The Later Parliaments of Henry VIII: 1536–1547* (Cambridge, 1977)
Little, P., ed., *The Cromwellian Protectorate* (Woodbridge, 2007)
Little, P., ed., *Oliver Cromwell: New Perspectives* (Basingstoke, 2009)
Little, P., 'Cromwell and daughters: financing the marriage settlements of Mary and Frances Cromwell', *Cromwelliana* (2021)
Little, P., 'Uncovering a Protectoral stud: horses and horsebreeding at the court of Oliver Cromwell, 1653–8' *Historical Research* (2008), 252–267
Little, P., *Cromwell and Falconry* (2008), 667–74
Little, P., 'The Culture of the Cromwellian Court', Cromwelliana (2009), 11–29
Little, P., 'Farmer Oliver? The cultivation of Cromwell's image during the Protectorate', *Cromwelliana* (2012)
Little, P., '"High places are slippering": Charles Fleetwood, John Disbrowe and the fall of the House of Cromwell', *Cromwelliana* (2024), 28–47
Little, P., 'Custards and cushions: new evidence for Oliver Cromwell's sense of humour', *Cromwelliana* (2024), 57–61
Little, P., and Smith, D. L., *Parliaments and Politics during the Cromwellian Protectorate* (Cambridge, 2009)

Loades, D., *The Cecils: privilege and power behind the throne* (London, 2009)

Loades, D., *Thomas Cromwell* (Stroud, 2013)

Loades, D., *The Seymours of Wolf Hall* (Amberley, 2015)

Loades, D., ed. *John Foxe and the English Reformation* (Aldershot, 1997)

Lowenstein, D., *Milton and the Drama of History* (Cambridge, 1990)

Lowenstein, D., 'Scriptural Exegesis, Female Prophecy, and Radical Politics in Mary Cary' *Studies in English Literature, 1500–1900, Vol. 46, No. 1, The English Renaissance* (Winter, 2006), 133–153

Lyon, H., *Memory and the dissolution of the monasteries in early modern England* (Cambridge, 2022)

Macdonald, P., *Data Structure Report: Geophysical Survey and Excavation at Dundrum Castle, County Down 2012 and 2013, Volume 1* (with contributions by L. McQuillan and T. Young) (Licence Nos. AE/12/71 and AE/13/101) (SMR No. DOW 044:006)

Mackay, L., *Wolf Hall Companion* (London, 2020)

Mackreth Noble, W., *Huntingdonshire and the Spanish Armada* (London, 1896)

Malins, M., 'My Solitary Life: Richard Cromwell 1659–1712', *Cromwelliana* (2010)

Malins, M., 'Dear Robin: The Correspondence of Oliver Cromwell and Robert Hammond', *Cromwelliana* (2012), 61–78

Malins, M., 'Monarchical Cromwellians and the Restoration', *Cromwelliana* (2016), 60–79.

Malins, M., '"All Imaginable Pomp and Lustre": Family Occasions at Cromwell's Court', *Cromwelliana* (2021), 5–21

Mallett, M., & Shaw, C., eds. *The Italian Wars, 1494–1559: War, State and Society in Early Modern Europe* (Edinburgh, 2012)

MacCulloch, D., Suffolk and the Tudors: politics and religion in an English county 1500–1600 (1986)

MacCulloch, D., 'The Myth of the English Reformation', *Journal of British Studies*, 30 (1991), 1–19

MacCulloch, D., *Thomas Cromwell* (London 2018)

MacCulloch, D., *The Reformation: A History* (London, 2005)

Manger, E. G., *Cavalier South vs Puritan North? Hypocrisy and Identity in the American Civil War*, (Cambridge, 2004)

Mantel, H., Miles, B., and G., *The Wolf Hall Picture Book* (London, 2022)

Mantel, H., *Wolf Hall trilogy* (London, 2009–2020)

Marshall, P. ed. *The Impact of the English Reformation 1500–1640* (London, 1997)

Masson, D., *The Life of John Milton* (7 vols, London, 1877)

Mayes, C. R., *'The Early Stuarts and the Irish Peerage', The English Historical Review*, Apr., 1958, Vol. 73, No. 287 (Apr., 1958), 227–251

McDiarmid, J. F., *The monarchical republic of early Modern England essays in response to Patrick Collinson* (Burlington, 2007)

McElroy, A., *Educating the Tudors* (London, 2023)

Meakins, S., Elizabeth Murray, Countess of Dysart and Duchess of Lauderdale (1626–1698) *Cromwelliana* (2017), 41–8
Mears, N., 'Courts, Courtiers and Culture in Tudor England', *Historical Journal 46* (2003) 703–722
Medcalf, S., ed. *The Later Middle Ages* (London, 1981)
Mendlesohn, F., *Creating Memory: Historical Fiction and the English Civil Wars* (London, 2020)
Mills, J. A., 'Durham, County Durham', *Cromwelliana* (2003), 93–101
Mills, J. A., ed. *Cromwell's Legacy* (Manchester, 2012)
Milton, A., *England's Second Reformation: The Battle for the Church of England 1625–1662* (Cambridge, 2021).
Molekamp, F., *Women and the Bible in Early Modern England* (Oxford, 2013)
Mosley, C., ed. *The Mitfords: Letters Between Six Sisters* (London, 2008)
Morrill, J., ed. *Oliver Cromwell and the English Revolution* (Harlow, 1990)
Morrill, J., ed. *The Oxford Illustrated History of Tudor & Stuart Britain* (Oxford, 1996)
Morrill, J., "Cromwell, Parliament, Ireland and a Commonwealth in Crisis: 1652 Revisited." *Parliamentary history 30.2* (2011): 193–214
Morrill, J., 'The Religious Context of the Cromwellian Conquest of Ireland', *Cromwelliana* (2014), 29–35
Morrill, 'Cromwell Day Address 2021 Cromwell and Friendship', *Cromwelliana* (2022), 5–11
Morrill, J., 'Blood and Marriage: why kin mattered to Oliver Cromwell', *Cromwelliana* (2024), 48–56
Nash, T. R. ed., *Notes on Hudibras* (London, 1793)
Naylor, M. J., *The inantity [sic] and mischief of vulgar superstitions. Four sermons, preached at All-Saint's church, Huntingdon, on the 25th day of March, in the years 1792, 1793, 1794, 1795. By M. J. Naylor, . . . To which is added, some account of the witches of Warboys* (London, 1795)
Neale, J. E., *Elizabeth I and Her Parliaments 1559–1581* (London, 1953)
Neale, J. E., *Elizabeth I and Her Parliaments 1584–1601* (London, 1957)
Nichols, J., *History and Antiquities of the County of Leicester* (London, 1800)
Noble, M., *Memoirs of the Protectoral House of Cromwell* (2 vols, Birmingham, 1784)
Norton, E., *Jane Seymour: Patronage, Material Culture and Image Crafting* (London, 2026)
Norton, E., *The Anne Boleyn Papers* (Amberley, 2013)
Notes on the Helmingham Library (privately printed, 1957)
Nunn, L., '"An hundred times fitter for a Barn that a Palace": A gendered analysis of the Protectoral portraits of Elizabeth Cromwell and her daughters, *Cromwelliana* (2012), 45–68
Ollard, R., *Cromwell's Earl* (London, 1994)
Orgel, S., and Goldberg, J., *John Milton* (Oxford, 1991)
O'Siochru, M., *God's Executioner: Oliver Cromwell and the Conquest of Ireland* (London, 2008)

Oxford Dictionary of National Biography

Palmer, J. F., 'The Celt in Power: Tudor and Cromwell', *Transactions of the Royal Historical Society*, 1886, Vol. 3 (1886), 343–370

The Parliamentary or Constitutional History of England (24 vols, London, 1761– 3)

Patterson, W. B., *Thomas Fuller: Discovering England's Religious Past* (Oxford, 2018)

Pattori, A., and Brigden, S., 'The Sacrifice of Thomas Cromwell', *The Historical Journal* (2026), 69, 1–20

Peacey, J., ed., *The Regicides and the Execution of Charles I* (Basingstoke, 2001)

Peacey, J., 'The Upbringing of Richard Cromwell', *Cromwelliana* (2010), 13–27

Peach, D. L., *The History of Hursley Park* (IBM UK Laboratories Ltd., Hursley, 1974)

Penn, T., *Winter King: Henry VII and the Dawn of Tudor England* (London, 2011)

Peters, E., 'Trauma Narratives of the English Civil War', *Journal for Early Modern Cultural Studies, Vol. 16, No. 1* (Winter 2016)

Pevsner, N., *The Buildings of England: Leicestershire and Rutland* (1960), 2nd edition revised by E. Williamson with G. K. Brandwood (1984)

Phillips, J., 'The Cromwell family', *The Antiquary*, ed. E. Walford, Vol 2 (London, 1880), 164–8

Phillips, J., 'The Cromwells of Putney,' *Antiquarian Magazine and Bibliographer 2* (London, 1882), 56–62 & 178–186

Phillips, J., Wandsworth Notes and Queries (1898), part 3, 42–3

Poetical Works of Edmund Waller and Sir John Denham, ed. G. Gilfillan (Edinburgh, 1862)

Prosser, L., 'Hampton Court Palace: the Palace of the Republic' and 'Inventory of 1659', *Cromwelliana* (2009), 49–94

Quintrell, B., 'Oliver Cromwell and the Distraint of Knighthood', *Bulletin of the Institute of Historical Research 57* (1984), 224–30

Ramsey, R. W., 'Elizabeth Claypole', *The English Historical Review*, Vol. 7, No. 25 (Jan., 1892), 37–47

Ramsey, R. W., *Cromwell's Family Circle and other papers* (London, 1930)

Ramsey, *Henry Cromwell* (London, 1933)

Ramsey, R. W., *Richard Cromwell Protector of England* (London, 1935)

Ramsey, R. W., *Henry Ireton (London, 1949)*

Rankin, M., Highley, C., and King, J. N. ed., *Henry VIII and His Afterlives: Literature, Politics and Art* (Cambridge, 2009)

Reece, H., *The Fall: Last Days of the English Republic* (London, 2024)

Rees, J, *The Leveller Revolution: Radical Political Organisation in England, 1640–1650* (London, 2017)

Reid, S., *Officers and Regiments of the Royalist Army* (1988)

Reilly, T., *Cromwell: An Honourable Enemy, the Untold Story of the Cromwellian Invasion of Ireland* (Brandon, 1999)

Richardson, R. C., *Images of Oliver Cromwell* (Manchester, 1993)
Richardson, R. C., 'A Most Uncomfortable Pairing: Richard Cromwell and John Keble at Hursley, Hampshire', *Southern History, 42* (2020), 73–93
Ridsdill Smith, G., *In well beware: The Story of Newburgh Priory and the Belasyse Family 1145–1977* (Kineton, 1978)
Rundell, K., *Super-Infinite: The Transformations of John Donne* (London, 2022)
Russell, F. W., *Kett's Rebellion in Norfolk: being a history of the great civil commotion that occurred at the time of the Reformation, in the reign of Edward VI . . .* (London, 1859)
Rickford, A. G., *Garde de Foy: The Riche Heritage of Felsted School 1564–2014* (London, 2013)
Roberts, S. K., *The History of Parliament: The House of Commons 1640–1660* (9 vols, London, 2023)
Roberts, M., *Essays in Swedish History* (Minneapolis, 1967)
Robertson, M. L. 'Profit and Purpose in the Development of Thomas Cromwell's Landed Estates', *The Journal of British Studies*, Vol 29, no 4 (Cambridge, 1990), 317–346.
Robertson, M. L., 'The Art of the Possible': Thomas Cromwell's Management of West Country Government, *The Historical Journal*, Dec., 1989, Vol. 32, No. 4 (Dec., 1989), 793–816
Rose, K., *George V* (London, 1983)
Roth, F., *The English Austin Friars, 1249–1538* (Augustinian Historical Institute, New York 1966)
Rowell, C. ed., *Ham House: Four Hundred Years of Collecting and Patronage*, Paul Mellon Centre for Studies in British Art, The Association of Human Rights Institutes series (London, 2013)
Russell, C., 'Thomas Cromwell's Doctrine of Parliamentary Sovereignty', *Transactions of the Royal Historical Society* Vol. 7 (1997), 235–246
Russell, G, *The Palace: from the Tudors to the Windsors, 500 years of history at Hampton Court* (London, 2023)
Rye, W., *Two Cromwellian Myths* (Norwich, 1925)
Sadleir Stoney, F., *A Memoir of the Life and Times of the Right Honourable Sir Ralph Sadleir* (London, 1877)
Schofield, J., *The Rise and Fall of Thomas Cromwell, Henry VIII's Most Faithful Servant* (Stroud, 2008)
Schofield, J., *Cromwell to Cromwell; Reformation to Civil War (*Stroud, 2009)
Scott, W., *Kenilworth* (London, 1856)
Shapiro, B. J., *John Wilkins 1614–1672, An Intellectual Biography* (Berkley, 1969)
Sharpe, K., *Image Wars: Promoting Kings and Commonwealths in England, 1603–1660* (New Haven, 2010)
Shaw, W. A., Burtchaell, G. D., ed., *The Knights of England: A Complete Record from the Earliest Times to the Present Day of the Knights of All the Orders of Chivalry in England, Scotland and Ireland, and of Knights Bachelors (*London, 1906)

Sherwood, R., *The Court of Oliver Cromwell* (London, 1977)
Sherwood, R., *Oliver Cromwell King in All But Name 1653–1658* (Stroud, 1997)
Shirren, A. J., *The Chronicles of Fleetwood House* (London, 1951)
Skinner, Q., *Visions of Politics Volume 2: Renaissance Virtues* (Cambridge, 2002)
Slattery, P., *Social Life in Pre-Reformation Dublin, 1450–1540* (Four Courts Press: Dublin, 2019)
Slavin, A. J., *Politics and Profit: A Study of Sir Ralph Sadler 1507–1547* (Cambridge, 1966)
Smith, A., 'The image of Cromwell in folklore and tradition', *Folklore*, Vol 79 (1968), 17–39
Smith, A. H., *County and Court. Government and Politics in Norfolk 1558–1603* (1974)
Smith, D. L., (ed.), *Cromwell and the Interregnum* (Oxford, 2003)
Smith, D. L., 'Richard Cromwell's Parliament', *Cromwelliana* (2010), 46–60.
Smith, D. L., 'Diplomacy and the religious question: Mazarin, Cromwell and the treaties of 1655 and 1657' (2014) https://doi.org/10.17863/CAM.27549
Smith, D. L., 'Cromwell Day Address (September 2015) The Monarchical Republic of Oliver Cromwell', *Cromwelliana* (2016), 5–13
Smith, T. A., *Weird John Brown: Divine Violence and the Limits of Ethics* (Stanford, 2015)
Souden, S. and Worsley, L., *The Story of Hampton Court Palace* (London, 2015)
Speight, H. M., 'The Politics of Good Governance': Thomas Cromwell and the Government of the Southwest of England, *The Historical Journal*, Sep., 1994, Vol. 37, No. 3 (Sep., 1994), 623–638
Spraggon, J., *Puritan Iconoclasm during the English Civil War* (Woodbridge, 2003)
Starkey, D., *The English Court: from the Wars of the Roses to the Civil War* (London, 1987)
Stone, L., *An Elizabethan: Sir Horatio Palavicino* (Oxford, 1956)
Strong, R., 'Holbein in England - I and II', *The Burlington Magazine*, Vol. 109, No. 770 (May, 1967), 276–281
Swedish Diplomats at Cromwell's Court, 1655–1656: the missions of Peter Julius Coyet and Christer Bonde, ed. M. Roberts (Camden Fourth Series, Vol 36, July 1988)
Tatem, M., *The Witches of Warboys* (Cambridge, 1993)
Thackeray, W. M., *The Irish Sketchbook of 1842* (New York, 1911)
Thurley, S., *Whitehall Palace: an architectural history of the royal apartments, 1240–1698* (London, 1999)
Thurley, S., *Hampton Court: A Social and Architectural History* (London, 2003)
Thurley, S., 'The Stuart Kings, Oliver Cromwell and the Chapel Royal 1618–1685', *Architectural History*, Vol. 45 (2002), 238–274

Thurley, S., 'Revolutionary State? Royal Palaces in Cromwell's England' (Gresham College lecture, 11 March 2015), https://www.gresham.ac.uk/

Thomas, K., *The Perception of the Past in Early Modern England*, Creighton Trust Lecture (London, 1984)

Thomas, K., *Religion and the Decline of Magic* (first published 1971, Folio Society edition, 2 vols, London 2012)

Thrush, A., & Ferris, J. P, ed. *The History of Parliament: The House of Commons 1604–1629* (Cambridge, 2010)

Toland, J., *The Oceana and Other Works of James Harrington, with an Account of His Life* (London, 1771)

Tollemache, E. D. H., *The Tollemaches of Helmingham Hall* (Ipswich, 1949)

Trevor Roper, H., *Historical Essays* (London, 1957)

Trevor Roper, H., *Europe's Physician: the Various Life of Sir Theodore de Mayerne* (New Haven, 2006)

Trotsky's Writings on Britain, ed. A. Clinton (London, 1975), online edition - https://www.marxists.org/

Underdown, D., *Pride's Purge* (Oxford, 1971)

Van Dyke, P., 'Reginald Pole and Thomas Cromwell: An Examination of the Apologia Ad Carolum Quintum', *American Historical Review, 9* (1904), 696–724

Venning, T., 'Cromwell's Foreign Policy and the "Western Design"', *Cromwelliana* (1994), 41–52

Venning, T., 'Cromwell and the Huguenots: Ethical Foreign Policy or Strategic Realpolitik?', *Cromwelliana* (2000), 36–44

Wabuda, S., 'Cardinal Wolsey and Cambridge', *British Catholic History 32* (2015), 280–92

Walker, G., 'Conscience and Satire in John Heywood's Play of Love', *Yearbook of English Studies* (2013), no. 43, 223–42

Walsham, A., *Providence in Early Modern England* (Oxford, 1999)

Walsham, A., *The Reformation of the Landscape: Religion, Identity, and Memory in Early Modern Britain and Ireland* (Oxford, 2011)

Walsham, A., *Toleration, Pluralism and Coexistence: The Ambivalent Legacies of the Reformation* (London, 2017)

Walsham, A., 'History, Memory and the English Reformation', *Historical Journal*, Vol. 55, No. 4 (December 2012), 899–938

Walsham A., Wallace, B., Law, C., & Cummings, B., ed. *Memory and the English Reformation* (Cambridge, 2020)

Walsham, A., *Generations: age, ancestry, and memory in the English reformations* (Oxford, 2023)

Waters, R. E. C., *Genealogical memoirs of the families of Chester and Astry . . .* (London, 1881)

Waugh, E., *Scoop* (London, 1938)

Waylen, J., *The House of Cromwell and the Story of Dunkirk* (London, 1880)

Weave, F. W. and Herbert, C., *Notes & Queries for Somerset and Dorset* (Sherborne, 1903)

Westfall, S. R., *Patrons and Performance: early Tudor household revels* (Oxford, 1990)

Westwood, J., and Simpson, J., *The lore of the land : a guide to England's legends, from spring-heeled Jack to the Witches of Warboys* (London, 2005)

Weyman, S. J., 'Oliver Cromwell's Kinfolk', *The English Historical Review*, Vol 6, No. 21 (January 1891), 48–60

Wheeley, T., Mitchell, R. and Bell, S. ed., *New Perspectives on Hinchingbrooke 1200–1970* (Cambridge, 2022)

Wheeley, T., *Hinchingbrooke House* (Huntingdon, 2011)

Wilcher, R., *Andrew Marvell* (Cambridge, 1985)

Willie, R., *Staging the Revolution: Drama, reinvention and history, 1647–72* (Manchester, 2015)

Woolrych, A., *Britain in Revolution 1625–1660* (Oxford, 2002)

Worden, B., *The Rump Parliament 1648–1653* (Cambridge, 1977)

Worden, B., ed. *Stuart England* (Oxford, 1986)

Worden, B., *Roundhead Reputations: The English Civil Wars and the Passions of Posterity* (London, 2001)

Worden, B., *God's Instruments: Political Conduct in the England of Oliver Cromwell* (Oxford, 2012)

www.the peerage.com

YouGov poll, *Most and least popular kings and queens* (2025)

Zook, M., *Protestantism, Politics and Women in Britain, 1660–1714* (2013)

ILLUSTRATION CREDITS

FIRST PLATE SECTION

St Mary's Church, Putney (© David Purchase, Wikimedia commons)

Thomas Cromwell, portrait by Hans Holbein the Younger 1532-3 (The Frick Collection, public domain)

Gregory Cromwell, miniature by Hans Holbein the Younger, c. 1537 (Royal collection of the Netherlands, public domain)

Title page to the Apocrypha in Thomas Cromwell's parchment copy of the Great Bible, 1539 (St John's College, Cambridge, Bb.8.30. By permission of the Master and Fellows of St John's College, Cambridge)

Portrait of a lady, probably of the Cromwell Family formerly known as Catherine Howard, c. 1535-40, Hans Holbein the Younger (Toledo Museum of Art, public domain)

Launde Abbey, Leicestershire (© Author's own photograph)

Gregory Cromwell's monument in the Chapel of Launde Abbey (© Author's own photograph)

Portrait of Catherine Tollemache by Robert Peake the Elder (© Beckie Egan, by kind permission of the Tollemache family of Helmingham Hall)

Helmingham Hall, Suffolk (© Author's own photograph)

Hinchingbrooke House, Huntingdon (© Author's own photograph)

Detail from the Bow Window of Hinchingbrooke House (© Author's own photograph)

Panel detail, Hinchingbrooke House (© Author's own photograph)

Sir Henry Cromwell's pedigree (© Cambridgeshire Archives, Huntingdon)

Coat of arms of Thomas Cromwell, 1st Baron Cromwell (© FDRMRZUSA, Wikimedia Commons)

Coat of Arms of the Protectorate (1653–1659) (© Sodacan, Wikimedia Commons)

Portrait of Sir Oliver Cromwell, circle of Hieronimo Custodis, c.1580 (reproduced courtesy of the Cromwell Museum, Huntingdon, UK)
Portrait of Thomas Cromwell, 1st Earl of Ardglass, unknown English school (Private Collection/Bridgeman Images)
Cromwell's House in Ely (© G Laird, Wikimedia Commons)
Church of the Holy Cross and Felsted School, Essex (© Author's own photograph)
Portrait of Oliver Cromwell by Robert Walker c. 1649 (National Portrait Gallery, London, public domain)

SECOND PLATE SECTION

Portrait of Elizabeth Cromwell, the Protectoress by Robert Walker, c. 1655 (reproduced courtesy of the Cromwell Museum, Huntingdon, UK)
Portrait of Richard Cromwell, 2nd Lord Protector of England, Scotland and Wales by Gerard Soest (The Picture Art Collection/Alamy)
Portrait of Henry Cromwell by Christian Dusart, 1655 (reproduced courtesy of the Cromwell Museum, Huntingdon, UK)
Portrait of Bridget Cromwell by Cornelis Janssens van Ceulen (Pictorial Press Ltd/Alamy)
General Henry Ireton by Jacobus Houbraken (Yale Center for British Art, public domain)
Lieutenant-General Charles Fleetwood by Jacobus Houbraken (The History Collection/Alamy)
Portrait of Elizabeth Cromwell by John Michael Wright, 1658 (Private Collection/Bridgeman Images)
Frances Cromwell, portrait by John Michael Wright, c.1658 (© CSG CIC Glasgow Museums and Libraries Collection)
Palace of Whitehall from St James's Park by Hendrik Danckerts, c. 1674-5 (Government Art Collection, public domain)
Equestrian Portrait of Oliver Cromwell, English School, c.1655 (reproduced courtesy of the Cromwell Museum, Huntingdon, UK)
Oliver Cromwell lying in State at Somerset House, etching copy by James Caldwell late 18th century of an original image in the 1659 pamphlet *Some farther intelligence* (© National Portrait Gallery, London)
Execution of Cromwell, Bradshaw and Ireton, c. 1661 (© PeterSymonds, Wikimedia Commons)
Portrait of Mary, Lady Fauconberg (Cromwell), circle of Thomas Murray, c.1670 (reproduced courtesy of the Cromwell Museum, Huntingdon, UK)
'The Lord Protect Us!' by Harry Furniss chromolithograph, published in *Vanity Fair*, 1 December 1898 (© National Portrait Gallery, London)
Statue of Oliver Cromwell outside the Palace of Westminster by Sir Hamo Thorneycroft, 1899 (© Prioryman, Wikimedia Commons)
Apparently by Mike Barfield, 'Oliver Cromwell v. Keir Starmer: A Startling Comparison', *Private Eye*, May 2026 (reproduced by kind permission of PRIVATE EYE magazine)
Production photograph from 'The Mirror and the Light', directed by Jeremy Herrin, 2021, by Marc Brenner (© RSC)

INDEX

Oliver Cromwell is 'OC' throughout, while Thomas Cromwell is 'TC'.